# Walks
## through Britain's
## History

W · W · NORTON

NEW YORK · LONDON

Produced by AA Publishing

© Automobile Association Developments Limited 2001

Illustrations © Automobile Association Developments Limited 2001

This edition published by W.W. Norton & Company, Inc., 500 5th Avenue,
New York, New York 10110.
http://www.wwnorton.com

Ordnance Survey®  This product includes mapping data licensed from
Ordnance Survey® with the permission of the Controller of Her Majesty's
Stationery Office.
© Crown copyright 2001. All rights reserved. Licence number 399221

ISBN 0-393-32350-1

A CIP catalogue record for this book is available from the British Library.

With thanks to The Estate Office, Sandringham for their permission to use
mapping data, belonging to The Estate Office, Sandringham, to compile walk map
84, page 201.

Page layout: Andrew Milne Design
Map illustrations: Raymond Turvey
Illustrations: Ann Winterbotham

The contents of this book are believed to be correct at the time of printing.
Nevertheless, the publishers cannot be held responsible for any errors or
omissions or for any changes in the details given in this book or for any
consequences of any reliance on the information it provides. We have tried
to ensure accuracy in this book, but things do change and we would be
grateful if readers advise us of any inaccuracies they may encounter.

We have taken all reasonable steps to ensure that these walks are safe and
achievable by walkers with a realistic level of fitness. However, all outdoor
activities involve a degree of risk and the publishers accept no responsibility
for any injuries caused to readers while following these walks. For more advice
on walking see pages 12–13.

Visit the AA Publishing website at www.theAA.com

Colour reproduction Chromagraphics, Singapore
Printed and bound in Italy by Amilcare Pizzi Spa

**Front Cover:**
F/C (a)  AA Photo Library (Richard Elliott)
F/C (b)  The Art Archive/British Museum/Eileen Tweedy
F/C (c)  AA Photo Library (Jim Henderson)
F/C (d)  Edmund Nägele F.R.P.S.
F/C (e)  Kingston Brooch 6/7 C AD (City of Liverpool Museum, Merseyside/Bridgeman Art Library)

**Back Cover Montage:**
Bridgeman Art Library: Ms. 18 f.109v Edward IV of England landing in Calais, school of Rouen,
16th-century (manuscript) Memoirs of Philippe of Commines (1445-1509),
(Musee Thomas Dobree-Musee Archeologique, Nantes, France/Giraudon); Harl 4379 f.23v
Tournament, Vol.IV (vellum) Froissart's Chronicle, (late 15th century),
(British Library, London) English Heritage Photographic Library

# Walk's

## through Britain's History

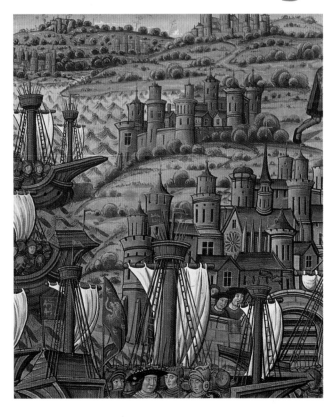

# Contents

4

Walk Locator Map 6

Introduction 8

## AGE OF MYSTERY
### 4500 BC–AD 43

**Early Britain** **14**

1 Cissbury: a tale of flint 16
2 The Cumbrian Druids' circle 18
3 Welsh mountain mysteries 20
4 Avebury and its wonders of the prehistoric world 22
5 *Feature Walk:* Bronze Age life on Dartmoor 24
6 Uffington's enduring enigma 26
7 Iron Age life in and around Pilsdon Pen 28
8 Shropshire's ancient defences 30
9 Scotland's towers of mystery 32

## IMPERIAL OUTPOST
### AD 43–410

**Roman** **34**

10 Striking gold in the Welsh hills 36
11 Silchester: a Roman wasteland 38
12 A Roman highway through the Mendips 40
13 The Romans at Ardoch 42
14 *Feature Walk:* The Antonine Wall 44
15 A Roman city in Britain 46
16 Home from Rome in Gloucestershire 48
17 From Rome to Hardknott 50
18 Imperial style in the South Downs 52

## INVASIONS & SAINTS
### 1485–1603

**Saxons and Vikings 410–1066** **54**

19 Celtic mysteries at Tintagel 56
20 Island of saints and kings 58
21 Urien's Palace in beautiful Llwyfenydd 60
22 Offa's impressive frontier 62
23 *Feature Walk:* Through Viking York 64
24 Saxon worship at Earls Barton 66
25 Llangorse – seat of kings 68
26 Winchester – King Alfred's capital 70
27 King Alfred's defence of Wessex 72

## ERA OF CONQUEST
### 1066–1300

**The Normans** **74**

28 The prince-bishops' Durham stronghold 76
29 The castle and priory-builder of Lewes 78
30 The Conqueror's New Forest 80
31 A little bit of old England 82
32 *Feature Walk:* Sarum's cathedrals old and new 84
33 The monks of Fountains Abbey 86
34 Echoes of Dundrennan's past glories 88
35 Restormel Castle – symbol of wealth and power 90
36 Conwy: a conqueror's town 92

## PLAGUE & CONFLICT
### 1300–1485

**Medieval** **94**

37 Clash of nations at Glen Trool 96
38 The battle of the Pass of Brander 98
39 Dunstanburgh – castle of legends 100
40 Abbottsbury and its Benedictine monks 102
41 *Feature Walk:* Warwick's medieval castle 104
42 Canterbury – centre of Christianity and pilgrimage 106
43 The desertion of Wharram Percy 108
44 Harlech and the Wars of the Roses 110
45 The Marcher Lords of Ludlow 112

## BUILDING A DYNASTY
### 1485–1603

**The Tudors** **114**

46 Lavenham: a Tudor wool town 116
47 St Catherine's Castle and the Saints' Way 118
48 Llyn Brianne and the Welsh Robin Hood 120
49 Furness Abbey and the dissolution of monasteries 122
50 *Feature Walk:* Shakespeare's Globe – the Glory of the Banke 124
51 The barons of Kendal 126
52 Sherborne Castle: Sir Walter Raleigh's refuge 128
53 The royal palace of Falkland 130
54 Around the majesty of Hardwick Hall 132

**1603-1714**

## GUNPOWDER TO WIG POWDER

**The Stuarts** — 134

| | | |
|---|---|---|
| 55 | Nordelph: at the heart of the Fens | 136 |
| 56 | Proud northern lady | 138 |
| 57 | Royal refuge at Boscobel | 140 |
| 58 | Dolgellau's Quaker trail | 142 |
| 59 | *Feature Walk:* Carisbrooke's royal prisoner | 144 |
| 60 | Wren's London – a city of churches | 146 |
| 61 | Bloodshed in the Pentland Hills | 148 |
| 62 | Monmouth's Rebellion and the Bloody Assize | 150 |
| 63 | The Jacobites' Highland Charge | 152 |

**1714-1837**

## BIRTH OF INDUSTRY

**Georgian** — 154

| | | |
|---|---|---|
| 64 | Arkengarthdale's mining legacy | 156 |
| 65 | The Prince in the heather | 158 |
| 66 | Shipwrecks and smugglers at Hartland Quay | 160 |
| 67 | Bristol and the slaving triangle | 162 |
| 68 | *Feature Walk:* The age of canals | 164 |
| 69 | The utopian village of New Lanark | 166 |
| 70 | One man went to Mow | 168 |
| 71 | The dispossessed of Strathnaver | 170 |
| 72 | Anglesey's masterpiece of engineering | 172 |

**1837-1901**

## AGE OF OPTIMISM

**Victorian** — 174

| | | |
|---|---|---|
| 73 | Climbing Neptune's Staircase | 176 |
| 74 | The wool mills of Marsden | 178 |
| 75 | The darker side of Cornwall | 180 |
| 76 | A poet's Lincolnshire garden | 182 |
| 77 | *Feature Walk:* The tracks of industry | 184 |
| 78 | On Darwin at Down House | 186 |
| 79 | A Victorian spa town | 188 |
| 80 | The peaceful waters of Lake Vyrnwy | 190 |
| 81 | Scarborough, queen of watering places | 192 |

**1901-1918**

## A NEW CENTURY

**Edwardian** — 194

| | | |
|---|---|---|
| 82 | Beatrix Potter's Sawrey | 196 |
| 83 | The first Garden City | 198 |
| 84 | Sandringham: a stretch of royal estate in Norfolk | 200 |
| 85 | A walk through Elgar country | 202 |
| 86 | *Feature Walk:* Port Sunlight: model industrial village | 204 |
| 87 | Casualties of war | 206 |
| 88 | Castle Drogo – Lutyens' masterpiece | 208 |
| 89 | Criccieth: the road to power | 210 |
| 90 | Steep: in the steps of Edward Thomas | 212 |

**1918-1945**

## JAZZ INTO THE ATOMIC AGE

**Depression and War** — 214

| | | |
|---|---|---|
| 91 | Wigan Pier: testament to poverty | 216 |
| 92 | The artists of St Ives | 218 |
| 93 | Dover: World War II frontline town | 220 |
| 94 | The Dambusters' dry run | 222 |
| 95 | *Feature Walk:* Portmeirion: one man's fantasy | 224 |
| 96 | The secrets of Slapton Sands | 226 |
| 97 | Scotland's wartime legacy | 228 |
| 98 | The war cemeteries of Cannock Chase | 230 |
| 99 | Dylan Thomas: master of words, slave to drink | 232 |

**1945-present**

## TO THE NEXT MILLENNIUM

**Modern Britain** — 234

| | | |
|---|---|---|
| 100 | Trespassers in the Peak | 236 |
| 101 | Still waters run deep | 238 |
| 102 | Spanning the Severn, gateway to Wales | 240 |
| 103 | The Beatles' Liverpool | 242 |
| 104 | *Feature Walk:* The Millennium Forest | 244 |
| 105 | The black gold of the North Sea | 246 |
| 106 | Past meets present in the heart of Wales | 248 |
| 107 | The Cuckoo Trail of Sussex | 250 |
| 108 | A visit to Eden | 252 |

| | |
|---|---|
| Index | 254 |
| Acknowledgements | 256 |

# Walking Through History

*WALKS THROUGH BRITAIN'S HISTORY brings you the opportunity to combine two wonderful aspects of living on this lovely island. You can follow carefully planned routes through beautiful and varied countryside, changing in character from mellow farmland to sweeping panoramas, from wild moorland to dramatic seascapes, from small villages to historic cities – often within just a few miles of each other, and each aspect itself changing with the seasons. But these are not simply scenic walks through town and country – instead, they tread some of the lesser-known paths of Britain's long, rich and fascinating history, with each period layered upon the one before not only chronologically but, often, quite literally, as a new age buries evidence of the preceding era below ground. You will soon discover that wherever you go in Britain, something exciting and memorable happened, perhaps only a hundred years ago, perhaps over a thousand.*

## Unearthing the Past

Some elements of history remain hidden – sometimes to be unearthed briefly by archaeologists, pored over with awe and wonder, and then covered up again; others are visible as small fragments or as reconstructions – a portion of a Roman city wall, for example, or a Viking trading centre where archaeological finds are displayed in a realistic setting. But there is still so much to be seen throughout Britain that tells a tale, often things that we take for granted as part of the landscape – hill forts and henges; castles and religious buildings, both intact and ruined; railways and canals; country houses and gardens; fortifications guarding the vulnerable coastlines. All these things are evidence of Britain's social and economic progress – of 'civilisation'.

## Creating a Landscape

Even the landscape itself is not completely natural, as we might expect it to be, but is more often than not man-made – forests were once cleared to make room for agriculture, then new forests were planted as hunting grounds; vast open areas were enclosed by hedges (and then opened up again, bringing about a shift in the balance of wildlife); whole tracts of land, such as the fenland in East Anglia, were drained and 'reclaimed' for farming; mineral-rich areas were mined, leaving the landscape ravaged and spent; even the remote, rugged Highlands of Scotland were made accessible by the building of roads and bridges.

## Bringing the Landscape to Life

It's not only the physical signs of history that make walking in Britain exciting, however – it's all the wonderful characters and legends, some very real and others, if not totally imaginary, at least moulded and romanticised into something more than they really were. The solid – but nonetheless often flamboyant and intriguing – figures of kings and queens, churchmen and aristocrats, inventors, philanthropists and rogues, as well as the common man going about his everyday life, sit alongside the more mysterious King Arthur, Celtic kings and characters such as the Welsh highwayman, Twm Sion Catti.

It is little wonder that, over many centuries, countless writers, poets, artists, and even musicians have been moved to record for posterity the history, landscape and legend of the land. Take a walk through Britain's history yourself, and you will begin to appreciate what inspired them.

PREVIOUS PAGE: *Eilean Donan Castle, Highland, Scotland.*

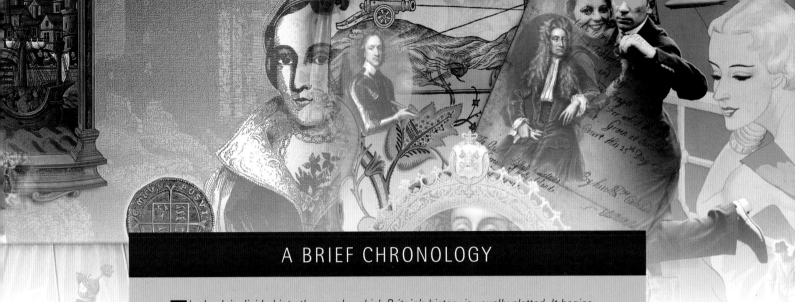

# A BRIEF CHRONOLOGY

T he book is divided into the eras by which Britain's history is usually plotted. It begins towards the end of a period that lasted for many thousands of years, and is known loosely as 'prehistoric'. This era has been divided by archaeologists into 'ages', and the period covered here (4500 BC to AD 43) is identified by the material being used at that time for making tools – hence, the Stone Age, the Bronze Age and the Iron Age. During this time, the Celts arrived from Europe and settled in southern Britain and in Ireland.

### Prehistory gives way to History

Then came the Romans, who created an imperial outpost and for almost four hundred years inhabited much of the island, imposing their culture upon the earlier settlers, and driving the Celts westwards into Wales and Cornwall. Their departure in AD 410 left the country open to further invasion, which came in the form of tribes from northern Europe – Angles (from which the name 'England' is derived), Saxons and Jutes – and later from the Scandinavian countries of Denmark and Norway – the Vikings. During this time also, Celts from Ireland – 'Scots' – settled in northern Britain, absorbing the native Pictish tribes into their culture and giving birth to Scotland.

### An Historical Landmark

Early in the second millennium after the birth of Christ came the last of the invasions, that of the Normans in 1066, led by one of the most famous figures in British history – William the Conqueror. The Conquest marks the opening of the medieval period. From this point to the present day, plenty of blood has been shed in wars fought against other countries, and sometimes within Britain, usually over rights to the throne. There have been many threats of invasion, from the Spanish, from the Dutch, from the French, from the Germans; but invaders have been held at bay.

The medieval age ended in 1485 with the conclusion of one of the most bitter and complex civil confrontations, the Wars of the Roses. Periods of history now began to be measured according to the name of the royal house in power – Tudor (1485–1603) and Stuart (1603–1714) – or by the names of the kings or queens – Georgian (1714–1836), Victorian (1837–1901), Edwardian (1901–1910). The 20th century is largely marked by the two world wars and their aftermath, and by rapid technological advance, as well as positive steps towards an environmentally aware new millennium.

### Setting the Scene

The walks included in the book represent a cross-section of historical events, although there are of course many more that have had to be left out. The places around which the walks are based have been put into the era in which they have a special significance, even though the cities in particular may have historical connections with several other eras. Both Winchester and Canterbury, for example, were originally Roman cities, but are respectively more well-known for being King Alfred's capital of Wessex, and a centre of pilgrimage following the martyrdom of St Thomas Becket and the tales of Geoffrey Chaucer, so they are placed in the 'Saxons and Vikings' and 'Medieval' sections.

# The Impact of History

*Discover Britain's fascinating history through the ages from the Stone Age to present day. Then walk the ancient trackways, explore mysterious landscapes and discover the people and events that made Britain's history.*

## New Stone Age

During the period beginning with the New Stone Age (from about 4500 BC), much of the British landscape was recovering from the ravages of the last Ice Age, and the hunter–gatherer lifestyle was slowly giving way to a more settled existence. Evidence of this new way of life is found in the prehistoric monuments dating from this period, which, incredibly, are still visible today – stone circles, hill forts, burial mounds, and even the mysterious figures cut into chalk hills.

## Romans

The Romans, whose arrival heralded a completely different civilisation, made use of some of the Iron Age hill forts, as well as establishing many settlements of their own. They brought with them new methods of building, engineering, administration and farming, new foods and wine, a new language and a new religion – Christianity. Although much of their building has long since disappeared below ground, Britain is rich in evidence of the Roman occupation – their characteristic long, straight roads; fragments of walls in cities; orderly military defences; excavated remains of sumptuous villas with their wonderful mosaic floors and sophisticated central heating systems; and the complex baths, in the city named 'Bath' after them.

The Romans' departure saw the disintegration of much of what they had established – cities fell into ruin, villas and temples were abandoned, and the country was overrun with pagan invaders. Gradually order was restored, and a new civilisation began. Christianity was re-established, via missionaries in the south and Celtic missionaries in the west and north. Christian churches and Benedictine monasteries were built, and the first magnificent illuminated manuscripts were created. Anglo-Saxon 'kingdoms' were formed and laws were established. The landscape was dotted about with Saxon villages consisting of dwellings of wood or wattle and daub, topped with thatched roofs. Forest was cleared and the land ploughed into long, narrow strips ('ridge and furrow') for cultivation. Remains excavated from Saxon burial sites, such as the burial

ABOVE: *Roman soldiers in a military camp.*

ship Raedwald of East Anglia at Sutton Hoo, Suffolk, indicates the great wealth of the chiefs.

## Vikings

The violent Viking invasions interrupted the Saxons' ordered lives; but eventually the Vikings, too, settled into an ordered existence, and the cultural similarities they shared with the Saxons enabled them to live relatively peacefully, side by side. The Saxons by now lived under a united kingdom; and it was a crack in the strength of the crown that allowed renewed Viking attacks towards the end of the 10th century, resulting in the reign of the Danish king, Canute. The line of succession became more complicated, and the death of King Edward 'the Confessor' in 1066 opened England up to invasion from a new quarter – Normandy, in northern France.

## Normans

With the Norman Conquest, led by a triumphant William of Normandy, came a period of rapid change. One of William's first tasks was to make his presence felt by erecting numerous castles. These were often built on the sites of Roman defences, and the first castles were usually of the wooden 'motte and bailey' type, later replaced by much sturdier stone castles, the remains of which can be seen throughout the country. The other architectural legacy of the Norman period lies in the religious buildings – from small country churches to the great monastic foundations with their magnificent cathedrals. Although many of these were largely rebuilt throughout the medieval period, becoming ever more elaborate, the distinctive rounded arches and heavy decoration that typify Norman, or Romanesque, architecture are still visible in most cathedrals.

The French language was introduced; however, the sound Anglo-Saxon system of law and administration was not abolished, but retained and built upon. Medieval new towns were laid out to a geometric plan, and vast areas of forest were planted as hunting grounds. The age of chivalry was born, a time when brave knights fought each other with colourful ceremony while their fair ladies looked on, and huge feasts were consumed in great halls. Centres of learning were founded, including the universities of Oxford and Cambridge and some of the famous public schools. This was also a time of constant wars, and of terrible plagues that were mortal to rich and poor alike.

In Scotland began the bitter fight for independence which was to last many centuries, while Wales provided the first Tudor king, ending the Wars of the Roses and restoring peace to England.

The reign of the notorious Henry VIII saw the birth of the navy and building of defences around the southern coastline; as well as the founding of new colleges and schools. The King's desperate bid to provide a male heir to the throne, resulted in a break with the Church in Rome and the introduction of the English Protestant Church. The consequences were far reaching as the dissolution of the monasteries also meant the destruction of countless medieval treasures and to religious persecution.

## Queen Elizabeth I

In spite of all Henry's efforts, it was a female heir who was to become the other great Tudor – Queen Elizabeth I. During the age of 'the Virgin Queen', exploration to far lands began in earnest, literature, painting and music flourished, and the distinctive black-and-white timbered buildings appeared. But there was no heir to carry on the Tudor name, and ironically it was the Stuart King of Scotland – son of Mary Queen of Scots, executed by Elizabeth – who succeeded her.

In the mid 17th century a new internal conflict erupted, as Crown and Parliament battled for political power, involving much of the population of Britain. For a short while, Parliament triumphed; but the death of the parliamentarian leader, Oliver Cromwell, led to the restoration of the monarchy. This century also saw yet another destructive plague, while the Great Fire of London enabled the architect Sir Christopher Wren to make his elegant mark in the rebuilding of the city.

## Industrial Revolution

Everyday life had for many centuries revolved around farming the land, both for providing crops and for breeding sheep – the wool trade brought great

prosperity, and many of the rich medieval towns were built by wealthy wool merchants. But a revolution was waiting in the wings that was to change the face of much of Britain – the industrial revolution. Great leaps in technological advancement during the Georgian and Victorian eras lured people into the towns, where huge factories provided employment. Towns developed rapidly with new homes to accommodate this labour, while some philanthropic factory owners built whole villages for the purpose.

Gradually, the whole of Britain was opened up with networks of new roads, bridges spanning rivers, shipping canals for transporting the produce of underground mines. Even the impenetrable highlands of Scotland could now be reached by road.

The introduction of train travel completed the new-found freedom. Ordinary working people, who had always stayed close to home, began to take trips to the seaside, or into the country. Towards the end of the 19th century, the wealthy could enjoy another revolutionary form of transport – the motor car.

## World War

The early years of the 20th century – the Edwardian era – are portrayed as a golden age. Modern civilisation was in place, but life still proceeded at a relatively gentle pace. Then came the World War I, followed by a strange mix of shock and grief and an almost unnatural jollity in the 'Roaring Twenties'; then years of depression, and before the world could barely draw breath, came World War II.
Air-raids over England left gaping holes and smouldering rubble where once buildings had stood; families were separated as children were sent away to the country for safety, and in some cases were never reunited; women worked the land and assembled munitions in the factories while their menfolk were scattered around the world.

As the second millennium drew to close, among the chief causes for celebration were advances in technology, great social and economic improvement and a greater understanding of ecological priorities. But for many people it also brought a nostalgic longing to slow down and tread the paths of history, perhaps to get a taste of a different existence, or perhaps to understand thoroughly the centuries of change that have brought us to where we are today.

ABOVE: *The Bishop's Palace in Wells, Somerset.*

BELOW: *Soldiers prepare to defend Dover against a German air attack in World War II.*

# How to Use the Book

*Each of the 12 sections in the book contains eight mapped, circular walks, ranging from one and a half to ten miles in length. Each map has a panel of useful information including the overall distance, the total distance of ascent, the quality of the paths, the nature of the terrain and of any gradients, where to park – and the all-important places to find refreshments.*

*The directions for the walks are clearly numbered and annotated. They not only guide you through the walk, but include useful tips such as where a track might become muddy, or what to look out for if the footpath has temporarily disappeared because, for example, a field has been ploughed. The maps are also illustrated with some of the landmarks you will pass on the route.*

*Each map is accompanied by the story behind the walk, as well as, where possible, a 'Don't Miss' panel giving information on other points of historical interest, either at the site or in the area.*

*In addition, each section also has an unmapped feature walk that gives you the opportunity to experience history at first hand – for instance, life in an Iron Age settlement, or a Viking city, or a Welsh fantasy-village. Many of these feature walks will appeal to readers with children, as there is plenty to enjoy here even for reluctant young walkers.*

## What to Wear

The walks are designed to be an informative ramble, not a physical challenge, but even so there are some simple and sensible rules to follow. The most important item for your comfort and safety is a good pair of walking boots, as these will support your ankles, especially in rough or hill country, and keep your feet warm and dry in all conditions. The vagaries of the British climate also make warm and waterproof clothing essential. A breathable waterproof jacket, waterproof trousers or gaiters and a warm hat may prove unexpectedly welcome whatever the season, and are a must for winter walking.

For the longer walks that may take a few hours, a rucksack is useful for carrying extra clothing, some energy food and a drink (a handful of dried fruit and a bottle of water is ideal), your map, and any other items such as binoculars and a camera.

## Emergencies

If anything should go wrong on your walk, send someone to alert the emergency services (phone 999), armed with a careful note of your exact location. If possible, someone should stay with an injured person,

keeping him or her warm and dry until help arrives. Mobile phones are an invaluable tool for such emergencies.

## Follow the Rules

The walks in this book follow only public rights of way or well-established, legal paths. You have a right to clear any blockage you may come across, although we recommend that, if possible, you report any problems to the responsible authority (usually the county council or the unitary authority highways department). If you stray from the right of way on to private property, you will technically be trespassing, although you cannot be prosecuted unless you do damage.

The main thing to remember is to be considerate and respect the life of the people who live and work along the route you are taking, whether it is in the town or in the country.

## Dogs

Many of the walks in this book are suitable for dogs but, again, observing your responsibility to other people is essential. Keep your dog on a lead and under control at all times.

BELOW: *The Taff Trail in South Wales.*

## Maps

Each of the walk maps has been carefully checked and can be used to guide you around the walk. However, some of the detail is inevitably lost because of the restrictions imposed by scale, and there is always a possibility that some of the landmarks indicated may change or disappear, if only with the seasons, in both town and country. For this reason, we strongly recommend that the walk maps are used in conjunction with a more detailed map designed for walkers, such as those produced by the Ordnance Survey or Harvey Map Services.

## Parking

All the walks are numbered starting from a suggested parking place. Where there is not an authorised car park, the suggested parking places have been chosen to minimise disruption to other road users. However, this does not guarantee that you have a right to park there. When you park your vehicle, please consider other traffic, and in the country, bear in mind the need for agricultural access. Where relevant, details of restricted access or access/entrance fees are included in the information panel alongside each map.

## Refreshments

The places mentioned in the text as serving refreshments have been suggested by field researchers because of their convenience to the route. Listing does not imply that they are AA inspected or recognised, although some may coincidentally carry an AA classification.

## Grading

The walks have been graded to give an indication of their difficulty. Easier walks, such as those around towns, over shorter distances, or with little total ascent, show one fleur-de-lys. The hardest walks – over greater distances, or including a lot of ascent, perhaps in hilly or otherwise difficult terrain – show three fleur-de-lys. Moderate walks show two fleur-de-lys. These gradings are relative to each other, and are for guidance only.

## Access

All the walks are on rights of way, permissive paths or on routes where de facto access for walkers is accepted. On routes in England and Wales which are not on legal rights of way, but where access for walkers is allowed by local agreements, no implication of a right of way is intended.

## Safety

Although each walk has been researched with a view to minimising risk to walkers, it is also good common sense to follow these guidelines:

❶ Be particularly careful on cliff paths and in hilly terrain, where the consequences of any slip can be very serious.

❷ Remember to check tidal conditions before walking on the seashore.

❸ Some sections of route are by busy roads, or cross them. Take care here, and remember that traffic is a danger even on minor country lanes.

❹ Be careful around farm machinery and livestock, especially if you have children with you.

❺ Find out what the weather forecast is for the day of your walk, and make sure you are equipped for changes.

BELOW: *Stonehenge in Wiltshire*

*For hundreds of thousands of years before recorded history began, people were living in Britain and shaping its landscape. Their world remains, on the whole, a mystery – though its monuments can still be found, scattered across 3rd-millennium Britain.*

## EARLY BRITAIN

4500 BC – AD 43

# Age of Mystery

Life for Britain's inhabitants hardly changed over hundreds of centuries: the most dramatic upheavals were caused by the weather. During several successive Ice Ages, glaciers provided a land bridge with Europe; in between, when the ice melted, Britain was an island again. Meanwhile, people wandered back and forth, adapting to the world around them. The first humans to reach Britain – about 450,000 years ago – were nomads, hunters and gatherers, who made tools of flint, and shelters of animal-hide and wood. In about 25,000 BC another Ice Age hit, and settlement was interrupted. When it resumed, about 10,000 years later, the settlers were 'modern' humans, of a different kind: *Homo sapiens*. They lived in and decorated cave shelters; they wore furs and elaborate bone jewellery; they hunted with spears and knives, and they communicated with sophisticated language.

By the 3rd millennium BC, Britain's neolithic communities were felling the trees that covered most of the country, creating clearings for crops and grazing. They shifted materials across land on sledges, or along the coasts and rivers by boat – little hide-covered coracles, common among Stone Age fishermen, are still used in Wales and Ireland today. During this era plain pottery was produced; tomb chambers and monuments built for the dead; and by 2800 BC, work had begun on Stonehenge.

### THE METAL AGE
An old way of life seemed to be changing from about 2750 BC – as well as old ways of death. Collective burial in chamber tombs gave way to cremation in henges or individual burial in round barrows. Here, skeletons were surrounded by decorated pottery beakers, tools, and ornaments made of gold and the new alloy – bronze. Some of the grave goods suggest considerable wealth and status: a beautifully embossed, leather-lined gold cape, excavated in Wales, is one spectacular example.

The Bronze Age revolved around farming, but other industries flourished, too. Any reasonably sized settlement had its own weaver, potter, carpenter, leatherworker and, of course, metalworker. By 1000 BC these settlements were being fortified with circular walls and palisades and earth ramparts, as migrating groups from the north competed for resources and threatened the security of herds and flocks.

After 600 BC a new group of tribes from Central Europe began settling in Ireland and Britain. The Celts had enjoyed trading links with the British for many years, but now they were taking centre stage. Using bronze and iron, the Celts produced weaponry and ornaments embellished with brilliant, swirling designs – such as the exquisite Battersea Shield, dredged from the Thames. They also made ploughs, enabling the most difficult soils to be worked. In the hierarchical Celtic society, slaves were at the bottom; freemen paid rent and produce to the tribal leaders, and the upper echelons of society included spiky-haired painted warriors, and druids. Religion permeated every part of life: gods and spirits inhabited trees, rocks and pools; sorcery and magic, woven through songs and stories, were passed down verbally and recited at court or round the central hearths of their circular houses.

The Celts lost their predominance after the Roman invasion, but they have never really gone away. Their language survives in Gaelic and Welsh, and in English words and place-names; and their fantastic tales live on in folk legends.

### HISTORIC SITES

**Stonehenge, Wiltshire:** developed in several stages over 1,700 years. Stones are aligned with the midsummer sunrise and midwinter sunset.

**Grimes's Graves, Norfolk:** network of flint mines worked between 2300 BC and 1600 BC.

**Skara Brae, Orkney:** well-preserved late neolithic village of eight single-room stone huts, complete with stone furniture.

**Bryn-Celli-Ddu, Anglesey:** passage grave built under a circular mound.

**Maiden Castle, Dorset:** earth ramparts of an Iron Age hill fort.

**Rollright Stones, Oxfordshire:** late neolithic stone circle.

**500,000 BC**

**500,000 BC** Earliest human remains, discovered so far in Britain, found at Boxsgrove (West Sussex), from the Palaeolithic (Old Stone) Age.

**225,000–200,000 BC** Neanderthal man uses caves as seasonal shelters.

**25,000 BC**

**25,000 BC** Ice covers the world as the last Ice Age begins, interrupting settlement but allowing people to move between continents.

**24,000–16,500 BC** The earliest burials in Britain are believed to have occurred during this time

**24,000 BC**

(human remains were discovered buried in a shallow grave in a Welsh cave).

**16,000 BC** Ice still covers most of Britain and Europe, as the Ice Age reaches its height.

**EARLY BRITAIN**

**AGE OF MYSTERY**

# Cissbury: a Tale of Flint

*Tracing the flint-workers of Cissbury Ring in West Sussex*

From around 1000 BC to the Roman invasion in AD 43, tribes and communities constructed the massive hilltop enclosures we call hill forts. Sussex claims 27 of them, the vast majority along the chalky heights of the South Downs. The earliest were probably not forts, but places for meeting, trading and conducting rituals.

However, Cissbury Ring, which dates from about 350 BC, seems admirably suited for defence, commanding a tremendous view along the coast from Beachy Head to the Isle of Wight. Its formidable ramparts were probably built up even higher than they are today, using timber: an enormous undertaking.

The size of Cissbury hints at the former presence of a substantial Iron Age community, living in large thatched round houses. Around the houses would have been pits and granaries for storing food, and areas for cooking and for such crafts as spinning, weaving, carpentry, flint-knapping, leather- and metal-working. There would also have been places for ritual and religious activities, enclosures for animals and fields with crops.

As you turn right along the ramparts you reach a disturbed area that far predates the hill fort. Here in neolithic times, between about 4500 BC and 2300 BC, people mined for flint, the hard greyish-black nodules of quartz that occur within chalk. Of the ten known prehistoric flint mine sites in England, Cissbury is one of the largest. The bushy hollows are filled-in remains of the shafts that were sunk, using picks made from antlers, to give access to the buried flint seams.

But why bother to mine flint when there was plenty on the surface? Archaeologists think the very act of mining may have had a ritual significance: tools made from mined flint may have been particularly valuable because it was so difficult to obtain – though we shall never know for certain. Excavations in these shafts have revealed graffiti scratched on the walls and several skeletons, including one of a woman, buried with tools and partly worked flint axes.

Before and after the introduction of metal, flint was used for all manner of implements, including scrapers, knives, arrowheads and axes for felling trees. Around the hollows there are large quantities of worked flint, mostly in the form of waste flakes that flew off when the flintworker was making a tool. It takes an experienced eye to distinguish such flakes from natural debris, but there are a few useful guidelines. First, consider the colour. Over the centuries a piece of broken-off flint will acquire a white patina. Next, look at the shape: a worked flake will tend to be a thin slice rather than a chunk, and with a slightly bulbous-edged platform where the flint was struck, at right angles to the smooth (originally inside) face. This face will have a series of ripples that appeared like shock waves when the flint was struck. Sometimes you may even find evidence that the flint was retouched along one edge to make it usable as a tool – for example, as a scraper for removing bark from a branch or flesh from a hide.

Cissbury is a Scheduled Ancient Monument and you may neither dig nor remove any worked flints. Content yourself with perusing the specimens brought to the surface by rabbits.

ABOVE: *Pottery and axe heads (c. 6000–4000 BC) from a New Stone Age camp.*

BELOW: *An aerial view of Cissbury Ring shows the huge fortifications that were built in 350 BC to protect the resident community.*

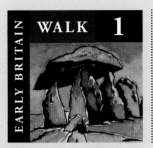
**ABOUT · CISSBURY RING**

*This walk in the South Downs offers superb views and a feast of ancient sites. These include the flint mines at Cissbury Ring, a scheduled ancient monument, mined between 4500–2300 BC, and an Iron Age hill fort, home to a large community in about 350 BC.*

**West Sussex · SE ENGLAND**

**DISTANCE ·** 8 miles (13km)

**TOTAL ASCENT ·** 700ft (213m)

**PATHS ·** clearly waymarked and defined tracks; some muddy sections

**TERRAIN ·** woodland and downland

**GRADIENTS ·** some steep sections

**REFRESHMENTS ·** none, but Cissbury Ring is a wonderful spot for picnics

**PARK ·** Chanctonbury car park and picnic site (signed Chanctonbury Ring), off A283 west of Steyning and east of the junction with A24

**OS MAP ·** Explorer 121 Arundel & Pulborough

# The flint mines at Cissbury Ring

**DIFFICULTY ✽✽**

❶ Turn left out of the car park and continue to the end of the surfaced road. Keep forward on a bridleway by 'unsuitable for motors' sign. Follow the bridleway as it bends right along the bottom edge of the woodland until a blue waymarker points left, uphill; 70yds (64m) later fork right.

❷ Emerge into the open at the four-way junction of tracks at the top of the slope, with trees marking Chanctonbury Ring prominent away to your right. Turn left on the South Downs Way, and avoid side turnings.

❸ At a four-way crossing before a gate (with a stone memorial beyond), turn right to leave the South Downs Way on a cinder track signed 'public right of way' with a green waymarker.

❹ In ½ mile (800m), turn left at the bottom of a deep valley and take the path along the valley floor, following blue waymarkers, first between intermittent hedgerows, later alongside a fence on the right.

❺ At the end of the valley, turn right at a T-junction of tracks and, ignoring a left path just after barn on the left, continue to the car park at the end of the road.

❻ Detour left to Cissbury Ring by the National Trust sign; go through the gate and follow the yellow waymarker. Carry on to the next gate and take the steps up to the top. Turn right and walk around the ramparts, looking for the hummocky flint mine site. Return via the steps; take the track opposite through the car park.

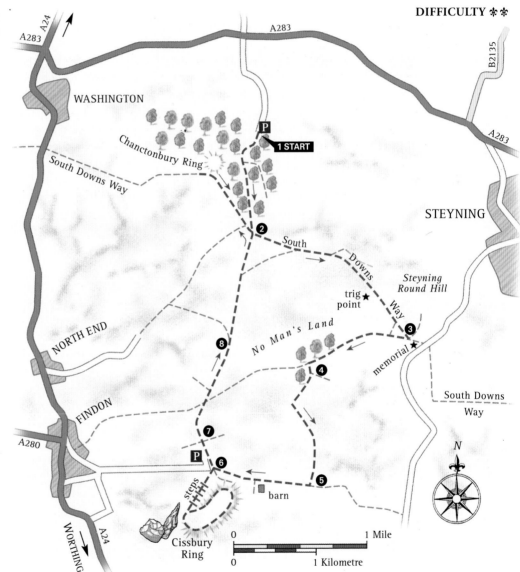

❼ Keep forward at the next major junction of tracks, following a green waymarker, and fork right 40yds (37m) further on. (Left is private property and is fenced off.) At the fork of tracks with a grass triangle in middle, keep forward following the green waymarker and avoid the immediate next right fork. Follow the green waymarker straight ahead, ignoring the path to the left.

❽ After passing trees on your right, continue straight ahead following the green waymarker. Pass trees on your left, ignoring a left turning. Continue to a junction passed earlier on the walk. Before descending ahead through woods, detour left along the South Downs Way to visit Chanctonbury Ring. Return to the junction of paths and follow the blue waymarked route to return to the car park.

**· DON'T MISS ·**

*Chanctonbury Ring, the famous clump of beech trees, is a sad shadow of its former self since the devastation caused by the 1987 storm. But the site still offers commanding views over Sussex and the Iron Age ramparts enclose the site of a Romano-British temple.*

**10,000 BC**

**10,000 BC** Last glaciers disappear from Britain; the Upper Palaeolithic (Early Stone) Age begins.

**10,000 BC** Early inhabitants use harpoons for fishing, and simple bone and stone tools and implements.

**10,000 BC**

**10,000 BC** Inhabitants begin to describe their world using drawings in caves (early drawings of a horse and a man discovered in the caves of Creswell Crags, Derbyshire, are believed to date from this period).

**9000 BC**

**9000 BC** Native people of the Americas make the first arrowheads for hunting.

**8500 BC** The Mesolithic (Middle Stone) Age begins; hunters and fishers spread across Britain.

# The Cumbrian Druids' Circle

*Experience the magical setting of Castlerigg, one of Britain's earliest stone circles*

EARLY BRITAIN

AGE OF MYSTERY

Go to the Druid's Circle at Castlerigg when the clouds cling low and the mist mingles with its megaliths and you will experience the true mystery of this ancient site. Perched high on a windswept field, the huge monument is ringed by brooding mountains. Thirty-eight stones, eight over 5ft (1.5m) high, form a rough circle some 100ft (30m) in diameter. Inside the circle there is an unusual inner rectangle of ten stones. Though it is probable that the stones are part of a ceremonial centre, archaeologists can only guess at their true purpose. It's likely to have been a temple, but the stones could also have been aligned to the sun's rays to determine the cycle of the farming year.

So who were these ancient builders who dragged the 48 mighty stones into place and hoisted them upright? They must have developed a sophisticated social order to co-ordinate such efforts. They were, in fact, from southern Europe and moved north during the late neolithic period. The Cumbria that greeted them would not have been the pretty countryside you'll see on this walk. Those green fields of the valley floor would have been swamp-like and thick with clumpy sedges and alders. Higher up the slopes there would have been a cover of oak, pine and birch. Only the rocky tops above 2000ft (610m) would be free of these trees.

Unlike earlier tribes, who were nomadic and left little trace of their lives on the planet, these new settlers were Britain's first farmers. They worked the land; they built temples, some huge like Stonehenge, and they buried their dead in tombs. What enabled them to do all this was their ability to fashion tools out of stone. They learned to recognise the hard volcanic rock that would make good axes, and they set up large-scale on-site factories. The rough-hewn axes were ground down to the required trapezoidal shape and mounted on wooden shafts.

Experiments suggest that using one of these flint axes one man could fell a tree the diameter of a telegraph pole within 30 minutes and clear 2.4 acres (1ha) of forest in about five weeks. Neolithic men built houses from the trunks and large branches, and used the brushwood to burn the tree stumps from the rough clearings. The ash fertilised the land for the crops. They had set the pattern for rural life.

This a challenging walk, which begins in Great Close Wood, a forest that has survived the clearings, though now its native trees have been supplemented with conifers. Climbing away from the shores of Derwent Water, you have to work for your view of Castlerigg, but it's pleasant walking, especially in Springs Wood, where Brockle Beck cascades down a rocky gorge. The stone circle is the high point of the walk and you may feel reluctant to leave, but the descent takes you back to the lapping shores of Derwent Water.

It is a view that inspired not only the likes of John Ruskin, Lord Alfred Tennyson and William Wordsworth, but also those neolithic farmers who lived on the hill.

ABOVE: *The ability of early settlers to make simple stone tools, such as flint knives, led to the more sophisticated skills required for working metals, such as bronze and iron.*

BELOW: *Castlerigg stone circle in Cumbria.*

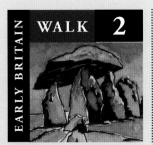
### ABOUT · CASTLERIGG STONE CIRCLE

*Castlerigg is one of Britain's earliest stone circles and is made up of 48 stones. Called the Druid's Circle, it was probably used as a type of ancient planting calendar. This is a challenging walk but the views on show have inspired poets and painters.*

## Cumbria · N ENGLAND

**DISTANCE** · 5½ miles (8.8km)

**TOTAL ASCENT** · 590ft (180m)

**PATHS** · some of the field paths to the circle can be muddy in winter

**TERRAIN** · woodland and pasture

**GRADIENTS** · short, steep climb from the car park, then easy gradients

**REFRESHMENTS** · none on the route. Many inns and cafés in nearby Keswick

**PARK** · Great Wood car park (NT), Borrowdale Road, by Derwent Water

**OS MAP** · Outdoor Leisure 4 The English Lakes – Northwestern Area

# Castlerigg's ancient stone circle

❶ From the back of the car park, go through a gate by a ticket machine and climb along the woodland path. Ignore the first left turn; at the next major junction of paths turn left to climb, steeply at first, beneath Walla Crag. Take the waymarked right fork, signed to the forest's edge, before following an enclosed path across fields.

❷ Turn right on meeting a path by a stream. Cross the footbridge over the stream and climb to the lane north of Rakefoot Farm. Go left for a few paces, then right on a sunken path signed Castlerigg Stone Circle. Follow a wall on the left, across fields, before it swings left beyond a ladder stile.

❸ Turn right along the A591 (ignore sign for Castlerigg Stone Circle). After 200yds (183m) turn left down the drive of The High Nest. A well-defined field path continues north across several fields.

❹ Turn left on meeting a lane, then left again through the next gate to reach the stone circle. Beyond the stile at the top right-hand corner of the field, follow Castle Lane back to the A591 and Point ❸ of the walk. Retrace the outward route to Point ❷. Now stay with the riverside path, bearing left at the junction of two paths, to enter Springs Wood, before descending further past Springs Farm.

❺ Follow the road beyond the farm and turn left along the enclosed path to Castlehead Wood, signed Castlehead and Lake Road. Take the widest path ahead, then the second right fork by the field

boundary, to emerge on the Borrowdale Road. Turn left along the path across the road, then go right towards Cockshot Wood.

❻ Once in the wood, turn left. Beyond a gate at the southern edge, the path cuts across a field to Strandshag Bay, on the shore of Derwent Water.

❼ Turn left along the path into the woods, then right along a stony lane passing Stable Hills (NT), back to the lake shore.

❽ After following the shore past Broomhill Point to Calfclose Bay the path goes inland through the wood. Pass an NT collection box to reach Borrowdale Road opposite the pedestrian access to the Great Wood car park.

### · DON'T MISS ·

*Near Broomhill Point you'll pass close to the **Centenary Sculpture**. Known as the Hundred Year Stone, it was sculpted by Peter Randall Page from a split glacial Borrowdale boulder. The sculpture is dedicated to the first 100 years of the National Trust, from the early pioneers like Canon Hardwicke Rawnsley to the 20th-century trust members.*

**DIFFICULTY** ✿ ✿ ✿

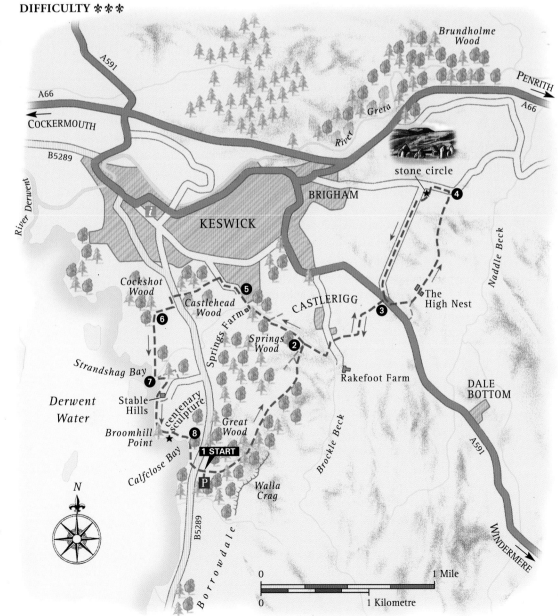

| 6000 BC | 4500 BC | 3500 BC |
|---|---|---|
| **6000 BC** Settlers arrive in Crete, in the Greek Islands. | **4500–4,000 BC** Neolithic farmers and craftsmen arrive in Britain from Western Asia. The new settlers clear forest, colonise the land and build stone and timber houses. | **3500 BC** The plough, developed in Asia and spread from there, is introduced to Britain and Europe. |
| **6000 BC** Neolithic farming communities develop in southeast Europe. | **4300 BC** In Brittany and Ireland the first megaliths are built. | **3500 BC** Chambered long barrows, made from earth and wood and used for burials, come into widespread use. |

# Welsh Mountain Mysteries

*A journey of discovery in the Preseli Hills, where humans have lived and worked for thousands of years*

Although small in geographical terms – the length of the main Preseli ridge is less than that of the Malverns – the Preseli Hills are a true wilderness, buffeted by seemingly relentless westerlies. The ridge is covered in its upper parts by coarse, ankle-rolling tussocks of grass and bog-loving flora, and grazed by Welsh Mountain sheep. Here and there miserly, inward-growing gorse bushes illustrate the dominance of the Atlantic winds. At first sight the description 'bleak and God-forsaken' does not seem misplaced – in the summer, it can seem incongruous that just a few miles away the beaches of Pembrokeshire are teeming with tourists. But, when patches of plum-purple heather and custard-yellow gorse adorn these largely barren hills, they are beautiful – you might even have the good fortune of a balmy, windless day.

Today you will see more sheep than people, but the scene was altogether different in prehistoric times. The ridge is littered with remnants of earlier human activity. Close to the start of our walk is Croes Fihangel ('Michael's Cross'), a Bronze Age burial chamber. Here archaeologists found the ashes of 3,000-year-old cremated bodies. At the highest point of the walk is Foel Feddau ('bare hill of the graves') topped by a Bronze Age tomb or 'barrow', but archaeologically more impressive is Foel Trigarn, the 'bare hill of three cairns'. These three Bronze Age cairns are substantial, but are encircled by a later, much larger earthwork: a magnificent Iron Age hill fort, which gave protection to perhaps 200 dwellings.

The greatest interest focuses on the 'bluestones' of Carn Alw and Carn Meini, although to the untrained eye these sites appear to be no more than quarry-like outcrops of massive stone slabs. The Preseli Hills were covered by 1,000ft (304m) of ice by the Irish Sea glacier about 120,000 years ago, and less thickly about 20,000 years ago. The glaciation produced these frost-shattered slabs. 'Bluestone' appears as a dark, bluish-grey rhyolite, peppered with distinctive white and pink spots. In 1923 a scientist

at the Geological Survey, Dr Thomas, demonstrated that the so-called 'foreign stones' of Stonehenge had come from these sites, most probably during the third millennium BC.

The route by which the stones were transported to Stonehenge – at least 150 miles (241km) – has been much debated. Were they hauled northwestwards overland, thence by sea on rafts around St David's Head, Land's End, and up the Hampshire Avon? Or were they hauled southwestwards, to Milford Haven, then taken by sea to the Bristol Avon, hauled overland again, and along the River Wylye and the Hampshire Avon? The former route is much longer overall, but the latter route entails a greater distance overland.

Since Dr Thomas's correlation, some geologists have argued against the 'human transport' theory, saying that the slabs came to be in the vicinity of Stonehenge via ice-sheet carriage in the Anglian glaciation. In 1994 this theory was put to the test when, by measuring the amount of the isotope chlorine-36 in a piece of bluestone, it was inferred that the stones of Stonehenge could only have been exposed to the air for about 14,000 years – well after any possible ice transport.

Towards the end of the walk there is a very noticeable change, superficial and, in the scale of things, very temporary: there has been a degree of afforestation, seen to the south of Foel Trigarn.

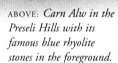

ABOVE: *Carn Alw in the Preseli Hills with its famous blue rhyolite stones in the foreground.*

ABOVE: *The ritual importance of Stonehenge still draws hundreds of Druids, tourists and solstice-worshippers to see in the summer solstice.*

**ABOUT • PRESELI HILLS**

*Hillwalkers know the delights of tramping this prehistoric highway. Dotted among the Bronze and Iron Age sites are blue rhyolite stones, relics of the Ice Age, believed to have been transported to and used to build Stonehenge, 150 miles (241km) away.*

**Pembrokeshire • WALES**

| | |
|---|---|
| **DISTANCE •** 10 miles (16km) | **GRADIENTS •** moderate |
| **TOTAL ASCENT •** 1,607ft (490m) | **REFRESHMENTS •** limited in Crymych |
| **PATHS •** some tracks; indistinct or pathless | **PARK •** in lay-by on the Mynachlog-ddu road, approximately 1 mile (1.6km) off the A478 at Crymych |
| **TERRAIN •** grassy; also rough (tussocky and boggy); occasionally rocky. **Note: this route is for experienced hillwalkers. It should not be attempted in poor weather conditions. Keep dogs on lead at all times on this walk** | **OS MAP •** Outdoor Leisure 35 North Pembrokeshire |

# A prehistoric puzzle in the Preseli Hills

❶ Take the track opposite the lay-by. When in open countryside, resist the temptation to climb the fine summit of Foel Trigarn; instead take a virtually level line, just above the boundary with the pasture below. Continue following the clear track ahead for 1 mile (1.6km).

❷ When the field boundary – a broad drystone wall topped with hedgerow – drops away to the right for the second time, you must follow it. (This avoids some extremely boggy ground designated a Site of Special Scientific Interest.)

❸ Follow the wall closely when it goes right then left. Descend gently, avoiding prickly gorse, to join a track from an untidy farmyard. Keep ahead on the main track, ignoring the fork to a farm on the right after 250yds (229m). Pass the elaborate post-box for Geulan Goch, and eventually reach a minor road and telephone box after ¾ mile (1.2km).

❹ Turn left, and left again within 100yds (91m); shortly take the left fork, which leads to Mirianog, a house; do not take the right-hand fork signed Tŷ Coch. Pass to the left of Mirianog, out into open country. (The hostile notice to dog owners echoes the difficulty of farming life here.)

❺ When the path forks take the left-hand option to visit the clustered slabs of Carn Alw. (Apart from its Stonehenge bluestones, this historic site was once a very small fort; aerial photographs reveal some evidence of field systems around it.)

❻ Aim right of another outcrop, Carn Breseb, on an indistinct path, eventually rejoining the path from Mirianog. On the ridge turn right, following this prehistoric highway, waymarked for some of its length by wooden posts, to the cairn and Bronze Age barrow atop Foel Feddau.

❼ (If time and energy permit, the Preseli's summit, Foel Cwm-cerwyn, is a good mile/1.6km ahead and to the left.) Retrace your steps, then go further east along the ridge, over Carn Pica to Bwlch Ungwr.

❽ Veer right of the obvious path to visit the frost-shattered rocks of Carn Meini. Continue eastwards, picking up a farm track to the far end of a block of planted conifers.

❾ Turn left on a sinuous but clear path to Foel Trigarn. After viewing this impressive earthwork take a path which soon sweeps to the right, rejoining the outward route some distance before it enters the lane to return to the lay-by.

**• DON'T MISS •**

*Pentre Ifan (off the A487, east of Newport) is a splendid burial chamber believed to be associated with Irish colonists, and dates from 3000 BC. The huge upright stones carry a massive, 17-ton capstone.*

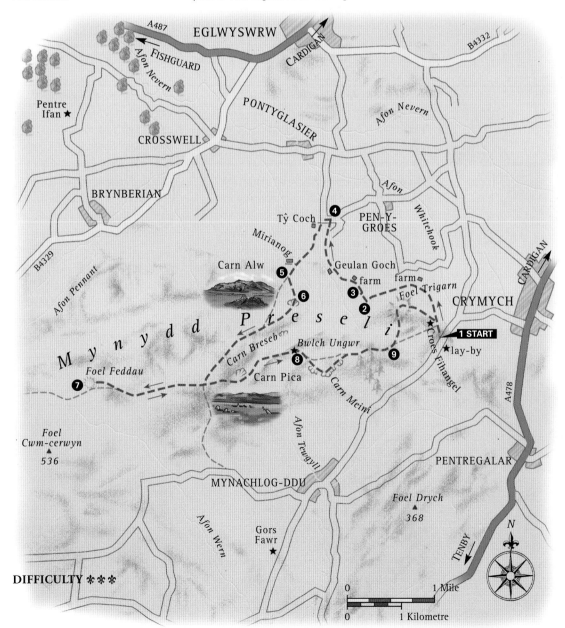

**DIFFICULTY** ✷ ✷ ✷

**3300 BC**

**3300 BC** Town settlements begin to appear along the Nile Valley, and hieroglyphics come into use.

**3200 BC** Sumerians develop a writing system on clay tablets. In Britain, stone circle building begins, for example at Castlerigg, Cumbria.

**3000 BC**

**3000 BC** Neolithic communities fell trees to create clearings for crops and grazing for cattle. Production of pottery begins. Desertification in the Sahara begins as a result of clearing of forests by early farmers.

**3000 BC**

**3000 BC** First urban civilisation in Crete develops with Knossos marking the centre of the Minoan civilisation. By 1450 BC this empire is giving way to the Myceneans.

**2920 BC** In Egypt, the reign of the Pharaohs begins.

# Avebury and its Wonders of the Prehistoric World

*The scale and complexity of some of Europe's most spectacular ceremonial monuments are revealed on this splendid Ridgeway walk*

ABOVE: *Silbury Hill with the Sanctuary in the distance.*

BACKGROUND: *Avebury Circle at sunrise, believed to date from 2600–2100 BC.*

Archaeological evidence from Windmill Hill, near Avebury, suggests that by the early neolithic period, around 3700 BC, there was a flourishing community here. Early farmers had started to clear forest for agriculture, and, in addition to hunting wild animals, they reared cattle, sheep and pigs for meat. They made tools from flints, animal bones and antlers; and clothes, tents and thongs from animal skins. They made, and in time decorated, pots, and they ground flour on quern stones. And they seem to have held seasonal gatherings on top of Windmill Hill – evidence has been found in the ditches of ritual feasting and human burials.

At the same time, the first chambered tombs were constructed for burials. Contemporary with Windmill Hill is West Kennet Long Barrow, in use for 1,500 years. Huge and well-preserved, it consists of passages and chambers constructed from local sarsen stones. As the skeletons found here were incomplete, it is thought the dead may first have been laid to rest – and rot – in the Sanctuary, a temple on nearby Overton Hill. Perhaps some bones were later removed for the Windmill Hill rituals.

The exact purpose of the Sanctuary remains one of Avebury's many enigmas. There is nothing to see but a mass of little posts representing a series of buildings dating from *c.*3000 BC. The Sanctuary being linked to the Avebury Circle by an avenue of standing stones suggests a cere-monial function. Even more of a mystery is the reason for the construction of Silbury Hill, that neat, conical mound that stands on the side of the A4. In total it must have taken some 80 million man-hours to construct this, the largest man-made mound in Europe – remember, there were only antlers for picks, and animal shoulder-blades for shovels. In 1776, archaeologists sank a shaft 100ft (31m) down from the top, looking for evidence of burials. When none was found, they plugged only the top of the shaft, leaving a void which collapsed dramatically during the heavy rains of December 2000. You are not allowed to climb the hill.

Avebury Circle dates from 2600–2100 BC and, unlike Stonehenge, is constructed from local sarsen stones. A detour takes you to an area of downland dotted with amazing numbers of these 25-million-year-old stones, deposited during the Ice Ages. The Circle is another part of the vast ceremonial complex. The scale of it is staggering – the area of the circle is 28.5 acres (11.5ha), divided into four sectors by roadways and encompassing part of the village that has stood here since Saxon times. When constructed, the ditch was up to 30ft (9m) deep; the bank 18ft (5.5m) high. Inside was a circle of 98 standing stones, between 9 and 19ft (3–6m) tall and weighing up to 20 tonnes each. Smaller circles stood within it.

The walk starts at the excellent Alexander Keiller Museum, goes through the Circle and up to an ancient track, the Ridgeway, with a magnificent view of Avebury's setting. You then pass the Sanctuary, West Kennet Long Barrow, and Silbury Hill. Leave time to explore the southern half of the Circle, which has been restored and is most impressive. The Stone Avenue is the 1.5 mile (2.4km) ceremonial route, lined with standing stones, that ran from the southern entrance to the Sanctuary. Some of the original stones in the first section have been exca-vated and restored; some were reused as building material in the village; and some, like many of Avebury's stones, remain underground, where they were buried in medieval times.

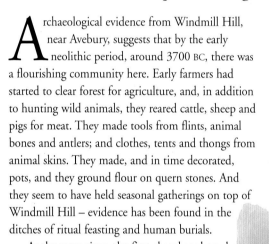

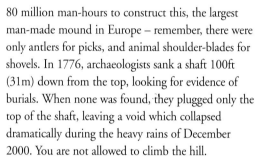

LEFT: *Aerial view of the Stone Avenue, Avebury, at dawn.*

## ABOUT • AVEBURY

*Avebury is the largest stone circle in the British Isles and part of the village is located in this mysterious henge, built between 2600–2100 BC. Starting at the Alexander Keiller Museum, the walk takes you to the Sanctuary, West Kennet Long Barrow, and Silbury Hill.*

## Wiltshire • SW ENGLAND

**DISTANCE** • 6½ miles (10.4km)

**TOTAL ASCENT** • 250ft (76m)

**PATHS** • well-marked; low-lying sections (especially path between Silbury Hill and car park) may be muddy after prolonged rain; otherwise firm

**TERRAIN** • downland tracks, field paths, stiles, woods.

**GRADIENTS** • gradual climbs to the Ridgeway and to West Kennet Long Barrow

**REFRESHMENTS** • in village

**PARK** • designated car and coach park, well signed on north side of A4361

**OS MAP** • Explorer 157 Marlborough & Savernake Forest

# Avebury's ancient monuments

**DIFFICULTY ✽✽**

❶ With the entrance to the car park behind you, take the path in the right-hand corner, passing information boards. The bank, ditch and standing stones of the south-western corner of the henge are ahead of you. At the road (High Street), turn left and cross into the churchyard. Visit the museum beyond the church. Continue past the Great Barn and the National Trust tea-shop.

❷ Climb steps ahead, just beyond the National Trust shop, and enter the henge. Walk around the perimeter of the henge with the bank on your left. Turn right on to the fenced footpath beside the road, by one of the largest stones in Avebury – the Swindon Stone. Cross the road to see the two impressive stones of the Cove, then continue to the gap in the bank in the right-hand corner.

❸ Through a gate and turn left on to a track (Green Street). Passing farm buildings the track becomes wider and climbs gradually.

❹ Meet the Ridgeway. Before turning right along this track, detour ahead to see the 25,000 sarsen stones on Fyfield Down (some are visible from The Ridgeway). Return to the Ridgeway and continue south for 1¾ miles (2.8km) to meet the A4.

❺ Cross this fast, busy road with extreme care. Before continuing down the track opposite, visit the Sanctuary. The route continues down the right-hand edge of a field. In the bottom corner, turn right through a blue waymarked gate, along the edge of fields with the River Kennet on your left.

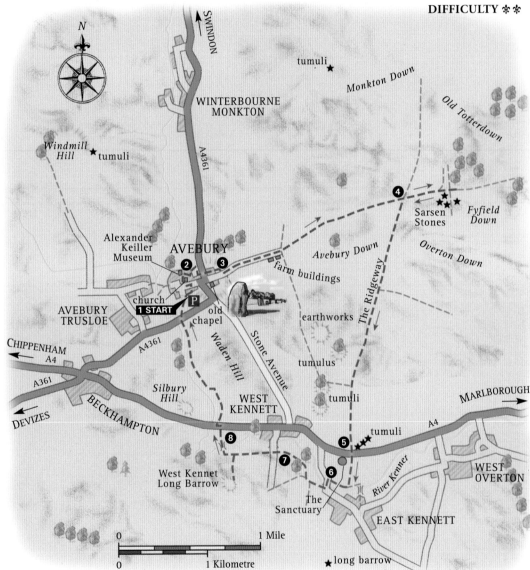

❻ Meet a road and turn left on to it, crossing a bridge. Turn right on to a signed byway on the the far side of a pumping station. When you reach a junction of paths, continue ahead following the footpath sign and almost immediately turn right (yellow waymark on tree) into a narrow tunnel of trees. Cross a stile and keep left round the edge of a field to meet a lane.

❼ Cross the lane and continue ahead. At the end of the second field, detour left to visit West Kennet Long Barrow. Return to the route and continue westwards and over the river to the A4.

❽ Cross the road, go through the gate almost opposite. Follow the sign for Avebury, passing close to Silbury Hill. Continue on the river bank to the A4361 and car park.

### • DON'T MISS •

*Windmill Hill is an early neolithic causeway enclosure thought to have been in use between 3700 and 2500 BC. It lies 1½ miles (2.4km) north of Avebury and can be reached on footpaths from Avebury High Street (or roadside parking at Avebury Trusloe).*

# Bronze Age Life on Dartmoor

*An easy linear walk across the open moor to the ancient settlement at Grimspound, and a visit to the third-highest pub in England*

## The Ground

It's hard to imagine what life on Dartmoor must have been like 3,500 years ago, during the Bronze Age, but you can get a glimpse of those times during this walk to the ancient settlement of Grimspound, by the Grimslake stream on the gentle slopes above the Challacombe valley. The climate was more equable then than now, and much of the moor was forested. It is thought that neolithic peoples, although not living on the actual moor, began to clear areas for pasturage.

That process was intensified during the Bronze Age, when it is estimated that there could have been over 5,000 people living here in small, stone-built settlements, following a peaceful agricultural existence. Dartmoor is peppered with evidence of their presence in the form of stone circles and rows, cairns, standing stones, hut circles and pounds.

## Legacy of a Community

Thought by many to be the moor's finest prehis-

toric monument, Grimspound is an impressive 4-acre (2ha) stone-walled enclosure, containing the remains of 24 hut circles, which could have housed up to 50 people and their livestock – sheep, goats, cattle and pigs – around 1300 BC.

The settlement was extensively examined and partly rebuilt by the Dartmoor Exploration Committee in 1894, when it was selected as its first site for archaeological investigation. The huts at Grimspound are characterised by their solid granite door frames and porches, and would have been thatched originally. The site has survived so well on account of its granite construction; its remoteness has also protected it from later raiding of the stone for the building of walls and roads. At one time the enclosure wall (or possibly double wall) was around 6ft (2m) high and 10ft (3m) wide.

Situated in a dip between Hookney and Hameldown tors, Grimspound has a lovely, open aspect, and would probably have been a pleasant place to live; its non-defensible position backs up the belief that those were peaceful times, and that such walled enclosures on the moor – around 150 have been located were built simply to contain livestock.

The route passes Warren House Inn, and from here you can see the Four Aces, four stone enclosures. Legend has it that Jan Reynolds made a deal with the devil that would ensure him success for seven years, at which time the devil could claim repayment. Jan made his fortune playing cards and forgot the agreement; when the devil caught up with him he cast the cards aside and the aces turned to stone. Interestingly the name 'Grimspound' also has demonic connotations: some think that the enclosure was named during Saxon times as 'Grim' (the devil's) pound' – the place where the devil kept his livestock.

FAR LEFT: *Hut circles at Grimspound built 3500 years ago and home to 5000 people.*

BELOW: *Ponies graze near Hounds Tor.*

BACKGROUND: *Life in an Iron Age settlement.*

# WALK 5 — A WALK THROUGH PREHISTORY

❶ Go through the gate where you park and walk straight on, following the signs for a public bridlepath to a road near Firth Bridge. Follow the path slightly uphill; about 100yds (91m) after leaving the wall and wood on your right the broad, grassy path forks; keep left, then left again about 50yds (46m) later to gain the hilltop near the memorial stone (left), commemorating the crew of an RAF bomber that crashed here in March 1941.

❷ Keep straight on; the path drops down gradually to reach the north entrance to Grimspound, with wonderful views ahead. In the centre of the enclosure you pass a large, restored hut circle. Walk on and out of the south entrance, and have a look at the ruins of the enclosure wall.

❸ Turn right and follow the restored walkway downhill to cross the Grimslake to meet the lane. Turn right again; after about 100yds (91m), just past a deep gully on the left, turn left and pick your way downhill to the footpath signpost to the right of Headland Warren farm. Go straight on (signed Warren House), keeping the wall left. Follow the path over the hill and down to meet a track leading through the old tin workings; bear right. Very soon the track meets a stream (left); turn left to cross this, then follow the track uphill to meet the road just east of the Warren House Inn.

❹ After your break, retrace your steps to the signpost by Headland Warren farm. For a variation on the route turn right (signed bridlepath for Challacombe farm) and walk through the gate and past the farmhouse. Stay on the farm drive to meet the lane, then turn left to reach the road just below Grimspound. Turn right and retrace your steps over the moor to Natsworthy Gate and your car.

**Distance:** 3¼ miles (5km)

**Total ascent:** 328ft (100m)

**Paths:** heathery moorland tracks and grassy paths

**Terrain:** open, rolling moorland

**Gradients:** one long steady climb from Natsworthy Gate, and a short steep ascent towards the Warren House

**Refreshments:** Warren House Inn on the B3212, the third-highest pub in England at 1,400ft (427m)

**Park:** by the lane at Natsworthy Gate; follow signs for Manaton and then Natsworthy (right at Heatree Cross) from the B3212 Moretonhampstead to Postbridge road, or signs for Natsworthy from the B3387 (from Bovey Tracey) just past the village green in the centre of Widecombe

**OS Map:** Outdoor Leisure 28 Dartmoor

**Difficulty:** ✳✳

BELOW: *The Bronze Age saw the development of a new skilled trade – metalworking.*

**2800 BC**

**2800 BC** Building of early henges intensifies, including Stonehenge. The henges are important features of community life.

**2700 BC** Pyramids are built in Egypt, and by 2550 BC the Great Pyramid is complete.

**2400 BC**

**2400 BC** In Western Europe, copper comes into widespread use.

**2000 BC** The Bronze Age marks the final building phase of Stonehenge; the blue rhyolite stones were probably transported there from the Preseli Hills in Wales.

**2000 BC**

**2000 BC** Decorated pottery is produced in Britain and stone chamber tombs are built. Complex village settlements, such as Jarlshof in Shetland and Chysauster in Cornwall, date from this time.

# Uffington's Enduring Enigma

*Follow ancient paths and tracks and discover some of Britain's greatest antiquities on this spectacular walk in remote downland country*

**EARLY BRITAIN**

**AGE OF MYSTERY**

High above the Oxfordshire countryside stands the chalk figure of a galloping horse. Shrouded in the mists of the past, this noted 856ft (260m) high landmark, 365ft (111m) long and 130ft (39m) tall, represents one of Britain's most famous antiquities.

The best time to see the horse is early on a summer's day or during the week in the middle of winter, when the crowds and the cars are scarce. It is then that the Uffington White Horse exudes its own peculiar air of mystery.

Regarded as far and away the most beautiful of all the British chalk hill figures, the horse is formed from a chalk-filled trench and, contrary to popular belief, not etched into the natural chalk. Its design is stylised, with an elegant, slender body and a distinctive beaked jaw similar to those displayed on early Iron Age coins. There have been countless theories over the years as to its age and exact purpose. A medieval document records it as one of the wonders of Britain, along with Stonehenge, while some sources suggest it was cut some time during the 1st century AD. Others claim it was established to celebrate King Alfred's victory over the Danes at the Battle of Ashdown in AD 871. In more recent times, the age of the horse has been scientifically pinpointed by a series of archaeological digs and analysis of soil samples, indicating that it dates back almost 3,000 years, to the late Bronze Age or early Iron Age.

The horse is not clearly appreciated other than from the air or from some distance away – which gives some credence to the theory that the White Horse may have acted as a tribal banner or badge for the inhabitants of the Vale of the White Horse,

ABOVE: *The mysterious White Horse at Uffington was recorded as 'a wonder' in medieval records.*

below. What does it symbolise, and why was this particular site chosen? There are no conclusive answers. Certainly the White Horse is closely associated with mythology. One legend claims that the figure is St George's steed and that the flat-topped chalk outcrop below, known as Dragon Hill, is where St George slew the beast. A bare patch on the summit is supposed to mark where the dragon's blood was spilt.

The Uffington White Horse has also attracted its fair share of literary figures. G K Chesterton wrote about it in his *Ballad of the White Horse*, and Thomas Hughes described the custom of scouring the horse, clearing it of grass and weeds, in *The Scouring of the White Horse*. It was Hughes who helped revive the tradition, which at one time attracted as many as 30,000 volunteers.

This walk to the White Horse Hill reveals more than a chalk figure. After exploring the lowland country of the Vale of the White Horse and visiting a couple of sleepy, picturesque villages, the walk climbs to the Ridgeway, Britain's oldest road, before making for Wayland's Smithy. This impressive 5,000-year-old long barrow occupies a remote, ghostly setting seemingly miles from civilisation. The walk ends with a visit to Uffington Castle, a prehistoric hill fort covering about 8 acres (3ha) and enclosed by a rampart and a deep, outer ditch.

ABOVE: *Aerial view of Uffington Castle, an Iron Age hill fort, situated high on the Ridgeway, England's oldest road.*

ABOVE: *Legend has it that Wayland's Smithy got its name from the Norse god, Wayland the Smith, who made shoes for the White Horse.*

**ABOUT • UFFINGTON WHITE HORSE**

*The White Horse was recorded in medieval records as 'a wonder', but its purpose remains a mystery. The walk also takes you to Wayland's Smithy, a 5000-year-old long barrow, along the Ridgeway, Britain's oldest road, and to Uffington Castle, an Iron Age hill fort.*

## Oxfordshire • SE ENGLAND

**DISTANCE •** 7 miles (11.3km)

**TOTAL ASCENT •** 415ft (126m)

**PATHS •** mixture of downland tracks, field paths and tarmac roads

**TERRAIN •** exposed downland and gentle farmland. Keep dogs on leads across the farmland of the Vale of the White Horse. Parts of the Ridgeway are suitable for dogs

**GRADIENTS •** one long, quite steep climb to the Ridgeway

**REFRESHMENTS •** The White Horse Inn at Woolstone

**PARK •** large free car park off B4507 signed Uffington White Horse & Waylands Smithy

**OS MAP •** Explorer 170 Abingdon, Wantage & Vale of White Horse

# The galloping white horse at Uffington

**❶** From the car park go through the gate and follow the outline of the grassy path along the lower slopes towards the hill. Make for a gate and cross the lane to join a bridleway. Keep left at the fork, by a bridleway waymark, and walk along to the head of Uffington White Horse.

**❷** Descend steeply on the path to the tarmac access road, keeping the chalk figure of the White Horse on your immediate left, or, if you wish to avoid the steep, grassy down slope, retrace your steps to the lane. Bear right and continue down to the junction with the B4507.

**❸** Cross over and follow the road towards Uffington. Pass Sower Hill Farm and continue to a path on the left for Woolstone. Cross the stile and keep the hedge on your right. Make for two stiles in the field corner. Continue across the next field to a stile, cut through trees to the next stile. Keep ahead with the hedgerow on your left.

**❹** Cross the stile, turn left at the road and walk through the picturesque village of Woolstone. Bear left by The White Horse Inn and follow the road left to All

Saints Church. As you approach it, veer right across the churchyard to a stile and a gate. Cross a paddock to a further gate and stile.

**❺** Turn left up the road and take the first right at the footpath sign. Follow the field edge, keeping the hedge on your left, to eventually reach a stile.

**❻** Turn right and walk through the trees to a footbridge. Cross it to a field, head diagonally left to a stile and turn right. Follow the field edge to a stile within sight of a thatched cottage. Cross and go ahead to a stile, the cottage is now level with you on the left.

**❼** Cross the road and follow the D'Arcy Dalton Way. Make for a stile, cross a paddock and head for the road by the village sign for Compton Beauchamp. Cross over and take the drive to the church, next to the manor. Retrace your steps to the sign and walk up to the junction with the B4507.

**❽** Cross over and climb quite steeply up to The Ridgeway. Turn right to visit Wayland's Smithy. Bear left to continue the walk. Follow the track to a crossroads signed Woolstone and continue on the Ridgeway uphill to reach the grassy ramparts of Uffington Castle on your left. Leave the track here, cut through the remains of the fort to the access road and return to the car park.

**DIFFICULTY** ✤ ✤

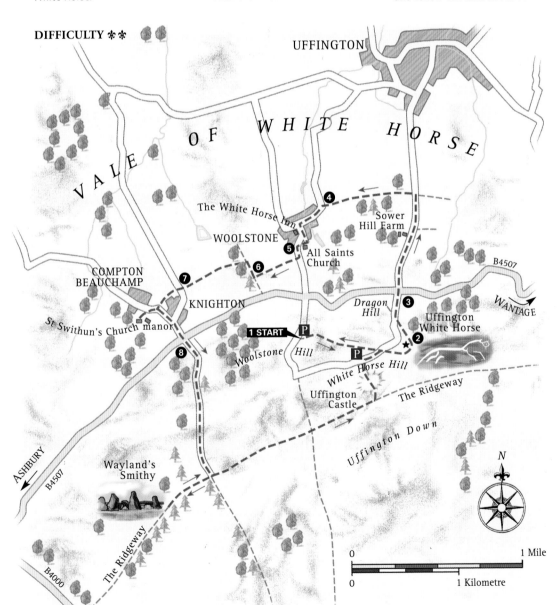

**• DON'T MISS •**

*All Saints Church at Woolstone is a lovely small, chalk-built church. Inside you will find a Norman lead font and some striking 20th-century Stations of the Cross. During World War II a German bomb blew out all the windows. Close by is the tiny village of Compton Beauchamp, with its Tudor and Georgian manor house.*

EARLY BRITAIN

AGE OF MYSTERY

| 1700 BC | 1500 BC | 1100 BC |
|---|---|---|
| **1700 BC** Copper and gold mining begin to develop in Britain. The settlers use these new materials to make sophisticated tools, weapons and jewellery. | **1500 BC** Foundation of Judaism. | **1100 BC** The earliest hilltop settlements start to appear in places such as Cissbury and Herefordshire Beacon; they remain in use for the next 300 years, often built upon and extended by successive generations. |
| **1500 BC** Egypt is at its largest and most powerful. | **1450 BC** The Mycenaean Empire conquers Crete and establishes colonies in the neighbouring Greek islands. | |

# Iron Age Life in and around Pilsdon Pen

*Spectacular views are with you all the way on this challenging and varied walk between two of Dorset's highest hills*

The vista from the lay-by where you park sets the tone for the whole of this walk. To left, right and ahead, the far-reaching views over Marshwood Vale to the ridge of coastal hills and the English Channel are nothing short of spectacular. However, make the short climb to the summit of Pilsdon Pen behind you (at 909ft [280m], Dorset's highest hill), and you have a 360-degree panorama, taking in the valley of the River Axe to the north.

The hill fort at the southern end of Pilsdon Pen, in which you will now be standing, is one of a concentration in Wessex that includes Hambledon, Eggardon, Hod and the text-book Maiden Castle. Maiden Castle may be bigger, but for scenic position it is far outstripped by Pilsdon. For our Iron Age ancestors, the views from Pilsdon made it an ideal site for a defensive camp.

There is evidence of the fortification of a few hill tops in the neolithic period, about 3000 BC, and again in the Bronze Age some 2,000 years later, when farmers began to protect their livestock. The 8th century BC heralded the start of the Iron Age, when Celtic settlers arrived from the Continent – bringing with them their iron-working skills and the Celtic language – and between the 8th and 6th centuries BC there was a rapid increase in the number of hill top enclosures in southern England. Some were constructed for the seasonal gathering of livestock; others appear to have been fortified homesteads. The peak period for the construction of hill forts was between the 6th and early 4th centuries BC. In many cases, a timber-faced or stone rampart and V-shaped ditch followed the natural contours of the hill. The forts provided safe, communal storage for grain, but the people lived mainly in satellite farmsteads and probably occupied the hill forts only in the short term, in times of danger. By the 4th century BC, however, there were a number of highly developed, well-defended hill forts in the south that were thriving villages and had grown into trading centres for grain, livestock, pottery and metalwork. Some, including Maiden Castle, were local tribal capitals.

Pilsdon Pen lay within the territory of the Durotriges, a tribe that lived in modern-day Dorset and parts of Wiltshire and Somerset. The Durotriges were subdued by the Romans in about AD 45, and Roman weapons found on Pilsdon suggest that this may have been one of the hill forts attacked by Vespasian. If it was destroyed then, however, it was evidently in use again in medieval times when, it is thought, the rectangle near the centre was used for rabbit breeding.

The walk follows the waymarked Wessex Ridgeway for much of its route, taking you down from the scrub of Pilsdon Pen, across farmland familiar to generations of Iron Age farmers. A narrow track, edged with high banks of trees and spring flowers, is crossed by a stream once used by farmers to wash their sheep. From here you climb between banks of windblown beech trees to the glorious beechwoods of Lewesdon Hill. This is an exhilarating walk of contrasting scenery – but the quality of the views remains a constant.

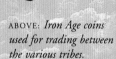

ABOVE: *Iron Age coins used for trading between the various tribes.*

BACKGROUND: *Pilsdon's hilltop position offered superb defence against possible attacks from enemy tribes.*

LEFT: *The scrubland of Pilsdon was used by Iron Age farmers to graze their livestock.*

**ABOUT • PILSDON PEN**

*Pilsdon Pen, territory of the Durotriges tribe, commands a superb defensive position. By 600–400 BC the hill fort was a busy trading centre and the farmland you cross on this walk would have been familiar to generations of Iron Age farmers.*

## Dorset • SW ENGLAND

**DISTANCE** • 6 miles (9.6km)

**TOTAL ASCENT** • 450ft (137m)

**PATHS** • well-marked; tracks may be muddy and difficult after prolonged rain (boots essential); otherwise firm; some road walking

**TERRAIN** • grassland, fields, scrub, woodland

**GRADIENTS** • one short, steep climb and descent; otherwise gradual

**REFRESHMENTS** • pub at Birdsmoorgate

**PARK** • lay-by on south side of B3164 at junction with minor road to Pilsdon village, 2 miles (3.2km) west of Broadwindsor

**OS MAP** • Explorer 116 Lyme Regis & Bridport

# The Iron Age farmers of Pilsdon Pen

❶ Cross the road and climb for 437yds (400m) to the top of Pilsdon Pen. Take the path in the far right corner, through three ramparts. At the fence, turn right to the National Trust notice board.

❷ Go through a gate, turn right with a plantation of young, broad-leaved trees on the left. Where the planting ends, turn downhill, diagonally right to a gateway. Follow the track to a lane. Cross and continue for ¼ mile (400m) to Lower Newnham Farm.

❸ At the farm, turn right, then left between barns. Keep ahead on the permissive path around the edge of field (can be muddy) to a bridge in a gap in the hedge. Cross the bridge and follow the track uphill. Before the track ends turn right over a stile and go along the field edge for 273yds (250m). Cross stiles and head diagonally right up the field to go through a gate.

❹ Turn right, down lane between high hedges. At a farm drive, keep ahead to the B3164. Turn left on to the road for 273yds (250m).

❺ Leave the road at the sign for Wall Farm. Immediately turn left uphill on a narrow track between banks with trees on top. As you enter woodland, keep ahead on a ridge, to the right of waymarked tree. Continue close to the ridge following the line of low-spreading beech trees to right.

❻ As the beech bank curves right before a clearing, walk straight ahead to the brow of the hill. Here, turn left on a crossing path and

head up to the line of trees on the horizon. Aim for the National Trust Lewesdon Hill sign, a third of the way along from the right.

❼ Enter beech woods and follow a

broad path. Over the rise, keep ahead on the grass, soon curving right, with steep beech hangers either side. At the end of the flat top, take the obvious, narrow path ahead, passing the NT sign. Beech trees crown the banks on either side. Keep near to the right bank and follow path into a gulley. Meet a track and turn right.

❽ Go through a gate and turn right on to a lane. Pass Higher

Brimley Coombe Farm and Lower Brimley Coombe Cottages. Keep straight ahead on the track. Drop down round a wooded gulley, and climb to a gate. Don't go through the gate, but follow the track uphill to the right, along the side of the hill. Where the main track swings right, turn left on to a narrow path between hedges. Go through a gate, then follow the blue waymarker uphill. Meet the B3164 and turn left to return to your car.

**DIFFICULTY ✿ ✿**

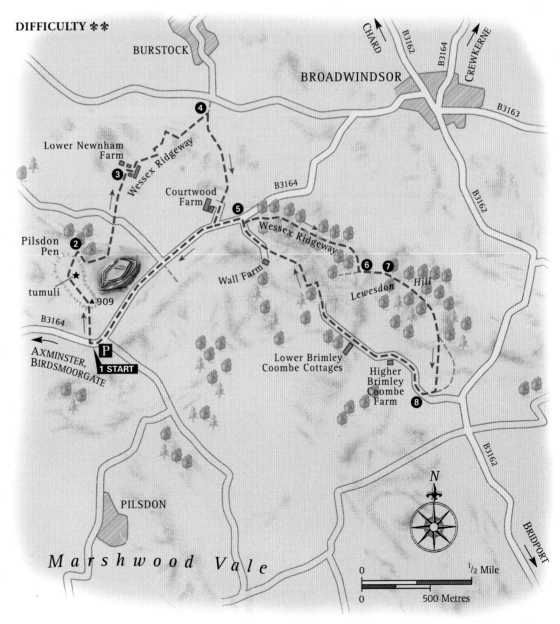

**1000 BC**

**1000 BC** Phoenicians develop the first alphabet.

**800 BC** Homer completes the *Iliad* and the *Odyssey*.

**776 BC** The first Olympic Games are held in Olympia, Greece.

**753 BC**

**753 BC** The Roman Empire is founded.

**700 BC** Britain enters the Iron Age. Iron revolutionalises weapon- and tool-making and enables intensive farming and building of hill forts.

**605 BC**

**605 BC** King Nebuchadnezzar comes to power in Babylon, and his conquests include the enslavement of the Jewish populace. He initiates the building of the Hanging Gardens of Babylon.

## Shropshire's Ancient Defences

*Exploring the Old Oswestry Iron Age site and hill fort
with a long history as a place of refuge*

EARLY BRITAIN

AGE OF MYSTERY

In contemporary Britain developers seem to favour green-field over brown-field sites, but in ancient Britain the reverse was true. With no JCBs to make short work of earth-moving – just the crudest of hand-tools – many hill forts were repeatedly enlarged and improved. Likewise, every advantage was taken of topography. In the case of Old Oswestry, where the ramparts enclose a very gently sloping 15-acre (6-ha) plateau, the steep eastern slope meant that less earth-moving was needed to build a substantial defence.

Old Oswestry saw at least three phases of fortress building, beginning at about 600–400 BC; this itself was pre-dated by a settlement, perhaps as long ago as 1000 BC, of circular wooden dwellings which had no fortifications. In the first phase the innermost ramparts were constructed, and inhabitants lived in circular stone dwellings. In each subsequent phase new, outer ramparts were added, enlarging the site. Despite the grand defences, the enclosed settlement probably accommodated only around 300 people.

You can read in detail about the phases of building when you visit the site; they are well-documented in a self-guided tour of five (somewhat weathered) information boards, erected by English Heritage. Allow yourself plenty of time to stroll around the hill fort. (It also has panoramic picnic opportunities.)

Old Oswestry hill fort was probably abandoned some time before the Roman invasion, an obsolescence presumably borne of the tribes in the region becoming less war-like than they had been when it was built. There is no evidence to suggest that the Romans attacked the Old Oswestry hill fort, nor to suggest that they had any interest in it. (Despite its formidable structure, this, and other hill forts like it, would have been less than insurmountable to a Roman force, equipped as it would have been with weaponry such as its long-range ballistas.) The Romans did have a significant presence locally: for example, they established what became their fourth largest town, *Viroconium* (now Wroxeter), beside the River Severn, just east of Shrewsbury. The Romans' attitude to hill-fort-dwellers, or those who sought refuge there, seems to have been characteristically pragmatic: rather than slaughter whole populations, they chose to enslave, exploit or simply 'Romanise' the people they had conquered.

There is some speculation that Old Oswestry was used in earnest in the 7th century, during and after the construction of the Wat's Dyke earthwork, believed to delineate the border between England and Celtic Wales.

The greatest visible change to Old Oswestry took place in the twentieth century, when a section of the A5 was built, by-passing modern-day Oswestry. The oak woodland was cleared in the early 1940s giving lovely views from the eastern ramparts and you may stumble upon the odd vestigial rotted tree-stump.

Whilst in the area the Llanymynech Hills are also worth a visit. Situated above the village of Pant, 5 miles (8km) south of Oswestry, there is a large, spectacularly sited hill fort. It was probably besieged by the Romans – it is a candidate for British leader Caractacus's last stand against the Roman forces.

ABOVE: *This bronze-handled dagger dates from 550–450 BC.*

LEFT: *A view from Old Oswestry hill fort towards the magnificent Malvern Hills.*

**ABOUT • OLD OSWESTRY HILL FORT**

*Old Oswestry hill fort probably underwent at least three phases of building, starting around 600–400 BC. Once you get to the site, information boards offer a self-guided tour and it is a good place, on a fine day, to stop and enjoy the panoramic views.*

## Shropshire • C ENGLAND

**DISTANCE •** 7 miles (11km)

**TOTAL ASCENT •** 450ft (137m)

**PATHS •** good ; some sticky mud possible

**TERRAIN •** tracks, field paths, stiles, tarmac roads

**GRADIENTS •** gentle

**REFRESHMENTS •** near by in Oswestry

**PARK •** Gatacre recreation ground. Take the B4580 from the town centre. Where the B4579 forks right, turn sharp right into Oak Street, then first left into York Street, left into Gittin Street and right into Gatacre Avenue. The car park is at the top.

**OS MAP •** Explorer 240 Oswestry, Chirk, Ellesmere & Pant

# Old Oswestry

❶ Go down Gatacre Road, passing to the right of some allotments. Turn right into Liverpool Road, which later becomes York Street. Turn right into Oak Street, left into Willow Street, then first right into Welsh Walls. At a sharp left-hand bend turn right into Brynhafod Road, later Brynhafod Lane.

❷ Take the hedged bridleway beside 'Everglades'. Follow this for ½ mile (800m), continuing straight ahead where the path crosses the road. At a gate, turn right over a stile (waymarked). After two fields cross a fence beside a tiny brook. Turn left. Within 55yds (50m), before a large oak, go left through a gate, then follow the fence on your right.

❸ Go across a very narrow field, keeping the cream cottage (High Fawr Cottage) and wooded strip one field to your right. Go diagonally left across the next field to the gate. Maintain this direction through several gates and across a track from High Fawr Farm, aiming for the white cottage with a red chimney (Oerley Cottage).

❹ In the corner of the field, by the cottage, turn sharp right to follow the plantation boundary. At the end of the trees, carry straight on across the field, crossing a fence by a big holly bush. Bear left to the far field corner; turn left through the gate and cross the field to another gate.

❺ Turn right on to the bridleway and continue for 400yds (366m). Cross the B4580. After 328yds (300m) take the Brogyntyn Estate driveway and continue for 1 mile (1.6km) to the gatehouse and the B4579. Cross diagonally left, on to a waymarked lane. Fork right of Pentre-Pant on a track. Waymarked fields, a hedged lane,

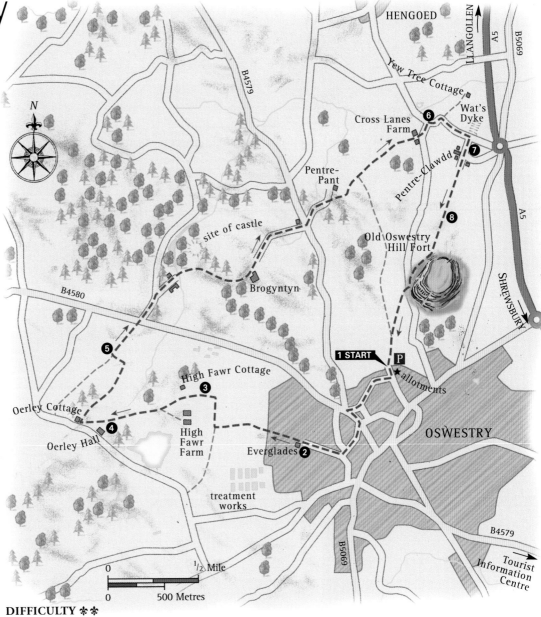

**DIFFICULTY** ✤ ✤

and several gates lead to Cross Lanes Farm. Go through the waymarked gate in the right-hand corner of the field and through the farmyard.

❻ Turn left on to the tarmac road. Soon turn right at a T-junction. Follow this winding lane (ignore Yew Tree Cottage driveway). At the first no through road sign turn

right, do not go ahead. Note Wat's Dyke on the left. Continue for 100yds (91m).

❼ At the second no through road sign keep straight ahead, not left. Shortly pass an enormous barn with traditional decorative brickwork. Go straight ahead to a waymarked stile, avoiding the farm.

❽ Follow a hedge aiming for Old Oswestry Hill Fort. At the fort turn right, and follow the boundary to reach a minor road. Turn left to the hill fort entrance. When you have finished exploring the site, go through the gate opposite and bear left across the field to the stile in the far corner and return to the car park.

**600 BC** Tribes of warlike people, known as the Celts, reach Britain and Ireland. They settle in hill forts and sow barley. Having spread in large numbers through Europe, Spain and Gaul, they have complex religious beliefs. They begin trading with other nations.

**509 BC** Roman Republic founded.

**500 BC** Mayan civilisation starts building pyramids.

**450–300 BC** The golden age of philosophy in Greece.

**431–401 BC** The Peloponnesian Wars between Athens and Sparta.

**350–200 BC** Taoism, Confucianism and Legalism develop in China.

**3 AD** The probable date of birth of Jesus of Nazareth, in Bethlehem.

**EARLY BRITAIN**

**AGE OF MYSTERY**

# Scotland's Towers of Mystery

*The Iron Age brochs of Glenelg give an intriguing glimpse of life over two millennia ago*

Brochs are unique to Scotland. These bell-shaped, dry-stone towers, consisting of thick inner and outer walls with tie stones and a staircase running between the two to provide stability, are found mainly in the West Highlands, the Hebrides, Caithness, Orkney and Shetland, where trees were in short supply but stone was plentiful. The best preserved broch is on the island of Mousa, Shetland, with intact walls standing to a height of 43ft (13m). Dun Telve at Glenelg survives to a height of 30ft (10m), but the walls are broken in places, allowing for closer examination – almost like a cross-section model, revealing the cells and galleries within the hollow walls. The only entrance to a broch was through a narrow passageway with a stout wooden door, which could be barred shut from inside. Behind this there was a small cell, which may have been a guard room.

Very little is known for certain about the origins and functions of the brochs, or, indeed, of the people who built them. The inhabitants would probably have lived in wooden structures inside the broch, rather than in the cramped and cold galleries between the two walls. Excavations at Glenelg, in 1920, revealed a set of ground holes in the interior, which could have contained stout wooden poles to support a raised wooden platform or floor. Their livestock could have been housed below, providing shelter for the beasts and extra warmth for the human inhabitants. A ledge high on the inner walls at Glenelg suggests that wooden roof beams were supported here. The roof was probably thatched with a central hole to let in the light and let out the smoke from the fire.

Brochs seem unlikely to be lookout towers, as they're not well located; lack of space for water supplies also makes them unlikely places of safety during invasion or siege, and the absence of arrow slits tends to rule out military uses in any case. One theory is that they were built by Iron Age farmers as communal dwellings and as a display of their wealth. However, we do know that Mousa Broch was used for romantic purposes at least twice by eloping lovers. *Egil's Saga* tells of a runaway Viking couple who found shelter at Mousa after being shipwrecked, and the Orkney *Inga Saga* recounts an incident in 1153 when a hero called Erland kidnapped the mother of an Orkney earl, holding her in Mousa long enough to obtain agreement to marry her.

The brochs were built over a period of six or seven hundred years, from the first Hebridean round houses (around 600 BC) to the more elaborate brochs of Orkney and Shetland (from 100 BC onwards). Whatever their origins, for over 2,000 years the brochs at Glenelg, Mousa and other sites across the north of Scotland stand as testimony to the enduring design and building skills of Scotland's early settlers.

ABOVE: *Dun Telve, shown here, is one of two brochs at Glenelg, which date back over 2000 years.*

BACKGROUND: *The Pictish Stone at Aberlemo.*

WALK 9

EARLY BRITAIN

ABOUT • GLENELG BROCHS

*Brochs, built from 100 BC, are found only in Scotland. On this scenic and remote walk you'll see two, Dun Telve and Dun Troddan. Their builders and purpose are a mystery, but these bell-shaped, dry-stone towers remain as a testimony to the skills of the engineers.*

## Highland • SCOTLAND

**DISTANCE** • 8 miles (13km)

**TOTAL ASCENT** • 148ft (45m)

**PATHS** • mostly good, but can be muddy after heavy rain

**TERRAIN** • metalled and forest roads; beach

**GRADIENTS** • mainly flat, one section with a gentle gradient

**REFRESHMENTS** • none on route. Five Sisters Restaurant, Sheil Bridge, 9 miles (14.5km) from Glenelg

**PARK** • at the war memorial near the end of Glenelg village

**OS MAP** • Pathfinder 220 Shiel Bridge

# The mysterious Iron Age brochs of Glenelg

❶ From the war memorial head south, following the signs for Glenelg Brochs. About a mile (1.6km) past the turning to Sandaig, the remains of a hill fort can be reached via a faint track leading up towards some rocky crags on the left.

❷ From the fort continue on the faint track to return to the road. Turn left and continue to the Dun Telve Broch on your right. Dun Troddan Broch is just a little further, on the left, a short distance up the hillside. Notice the proximity to good agricultural land which was essential to the Iron Age inhabitants and a notable feature of the location of many of the brochs in this part of Scotland.

Access is via the kissing gate and a path.

❸ Visible from Dun Troddan is a wooden house with a turf roof. Just beyond it, and before some caravans, is a turning on the right leading to a bridge over the river. Cross here and turn left on to a forest road.

❹ The road climbs gently from here, then forks. Go left, through a gate, then downhill towards a bridge over the river. Cross it, but take great care as it is in poor repair, then climb a gate on to a dirt track.

❺ Follow the track left, bear left where it joins the farm road and

continue past Balvraid farm. About 200yds (183m) past the farm look out for the chambered cairn on the right –a mound of stones covered in grass.

❻ From here continue on the road, cross a bridge by a modern bungalow and go left following this road for just over a mile (1.6km) back past the brochs to the outskirts of Glenelg. Leave the road here and walk along the beach back to the war memorial.

## • DON'T MISS •

*Nearby you can visit **Sandaig**, south of Glenelg, which featured as Camusfearna in* Ring of Bright Water *by naturalist Gavin Maxwell (1905–1962). The book became a best-seller and the subject of a film. Look for the memorial to his otter, Edal, which died in the fire that also destroyed his house in 1968. If you have some more time in the area it is worth travelling about 16 miles (25km) northeast of Glenelg Brochs to visit **Eilean Donan Castle**, an 18th-century Jacobite stronghold. It is one of the most picturesque castles in Scotland, built in the early 13th century by Alexander II of Scotland.*

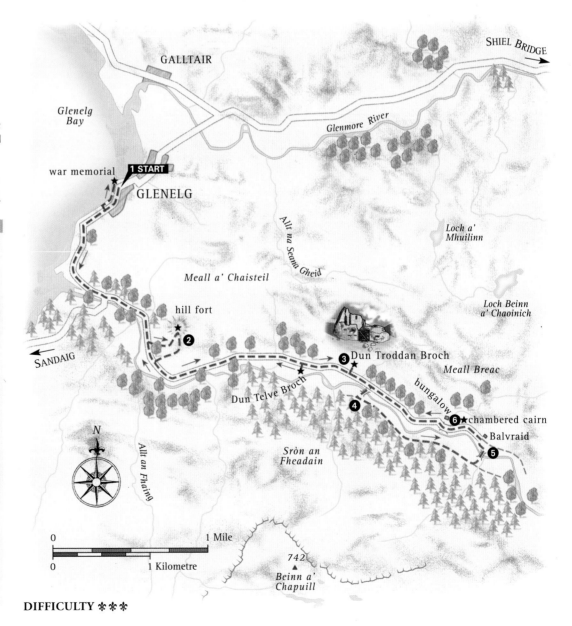

**DIFFICULTY** ❋❋❋

*When the Emperor Claudius sent troops to invade Britain in AD 43, he was tackling unfinished business. Ninety years earlier, Julius Caesar had led his warships on two raids against the 'barbarians' who lived on the northern edge of the Roman Empire.*

## ROMAN

## AD 43–410

# Imperial Outpost

Caesar's campaigns had yielded little more than a haul of prisoners and hostages and some good publicity in Rome; but they left us with the invaders' accounts of life among the Celtic tribes – and one particularly vivid glimpse of the druids of Anglesey, who faced their enemy across the Menai Strait, gesturing and praying, while wild-haired women waved flaming torches. The whole incident gave the Imperial legionnaires a severe fright!

A century later, Claudius, too, found that the British Celts were no walkover. Despite inter-tribal warfare and treachery, the Britons resisted the Romans for many years, notably under the determined leadership of Caractacus (Caradog), who, after his eventual capture, was rewarded for his valour with 'honourable exile' in Rome. Others kept up the struggle, even after they were deemed 'client kingdoms'. One such kingdom was the East Anglian Iceni people: in AD 60, their king's widow, Boudicca, took vengeance on the Romans for the rape of her daughters, massacring the citizens of *Camulodunum* (Colchester), London and *Verulamium* (St Albans). The Romans, in turn, slaughtered Boudicca's people and any others suspected of rebellion.

In the following years the Empire expanded its control of the new province, overrunning Wales, northern England and southern Scotland. Eventually troops were withdrawn to go and face other conflicts on the Danube – so northern Britain remained free of Roman rule, a division later marked by Emperor Hadrian's Wall, built from AD 122.

### ROMAN LIFE

Britain was part of the Roman Empire for four centuries and, after the terrible bloodletting of the 1st century AD, lived largely in peace with its masters (even Hadrian's Wall was as much a customs barrier as a military border). In the period of diplomacy that followed, self-governing tribal authorities were established, called civitates: each elected its own magistrate, and was centred on a large town. Towns of varying size and importance soon flourished, with aqueducts, amphitheatres and temples. Thousands of miles of long, straight roads were built to speed communications, armies and goods across country – many still function today. Roman religion mingled with British beliefs – in *Aquae Sulis* (Bath), the sacred springs of the Celtic water goddess, Sulis, were simply rebranded, and Sulis merged with the Roman goddess Minerva. Roman fashions and tastes were adopted by wealthy Britons, who Romanised their names, spoke Latin and built increasingly elaborate villas. The luxurious palace of Fishbourne, in Sussex, provided a perfect model – with its mosaics, underfloor heating and enclosed garden, it was more suggestive of the Mediterranean than of the damp Chichester coast. The demand grew for imports such as olive oil, wine, silk and glass, mainly for an elite minority; the daily drudge of most Britons carried on much as it always had.

It all began to crumble in the 4th and 5th centuries AD. The Roman Empire, vast and overstretched, was under attack on several fronts. In AD 408–9 Saxons began raiding the British coasts, and two years later the Emperor Honorius, struggling to contain troubles elsewhere, told the province to defend itself, without the aid of Imperial muscle. Rome maintained a hold on the northern isles for a few years – but its grasp was weakening. As the 5th century AD progressed, Britain entered another new phase of its history.

### HISTORIC SITES

**Fishbourne Palace, near Chichester:** Roman villa in the grand style.

**Caerleon, Gwent:** one of Europe's biggest Roman military sites.

**Hadrian's Wall:** the 73-mile (117km) border with the north.

**St Albans:** the walls of Roman Verulamium, and superb artefacts in the museum.

**Bath:** the Roman spa complex dedicated to Sulis Minerva.

**Cirencester:** everyday objects and mosaics in the Corinium Museum, and the Four Seasons mosaic at nearby Chedworth Roman Villa.

**AD 43**

**AD 43** Emperor Claudius, determined to capture Britain, dispatches 50,000 Roman troops to Britain, under the leadership of general Aulus Plautius. The army lands in Richborough, Kent, and heads for Colchester, the British tribal capital.

**AD 47**

**AD 47** The Fosse Way is established, running from Exeter to join Ermin Street Way at Lincoln.

**AD 48** Roman troops reach South Wales and, despite strong native resistance en route, successfully overrun native hill forts. Building of

**AD 48**

barracks commences at St Albans, Cirencester, Colchester and other strategic points.

**AD 48** Claudius visits Colchester, to see the city taken and accept the surrender of the Celts.

# Striking Gold in the Welsh Hills

*A walk in the Welsh uplands, focusing on the ancient gold mines of Dolaucothi*

Britain has fewer more restful places in which to soak up the landscape than the hills of mid-Wales, and those around Pumsaint are typical. The Afon Cothi valley is precious not only for its rare metal, concealed beneath its surface, but for its glorious wooded scenery – you will have to be cursed with particularly miserable weather to not enjoy a day here.

Gold mining sites in Wales include the Clwydian Hills (near Moel Fammau), in Pembrokeshire, and around the Rhinogs (the 'Dolgellau gold belt'), but it is quite likely that, in total, the greatest amount of gold to be mined has come from Dolaucothi.

One of the motives which probably led to the Roman invasion of Britain was the presence of scarce metals such as lead (used in the assaying of silver), copper and gold. It is known that lead was converted into 'pigs' before being exported. The export methodology for gold – conversion into ingots – is likely to have been similar; there is some archaeological evidence in London which supports the notion of gold-refining there.

The Dolaucothi mining area has been worked a total of four times. It is perhaps a testament to the Romans that a casual visitor may not readily be able to differentiate between a Roman adit (passage) and a 20th-century one. The so-called Ogafau Pit is Roman, as are several of the adits. The Romans reached a depth of almost 150ft (45m). To prevent flooding they built a series of wooden water wheels – a water wheel fragment has been unearthed here. Running water was made available by building the Cothi Leat, a narrow channel 7 miles (11km) long; they also excavated substantial water tanks – both these features may be traced today.

After abandonment by the Romans, the Dolaucothi mines were not worked again until 1844, and, it seems, only briefly then. A longer period of activity followed, from 1872 to 1912, when several of the Roman adits were extended. In 1931 extraction recommenced in earnest, when miners worked the so-called Roman Lode, a 'reef' of quartz. Although output peaked in 1938, when some 200 men were employed, the war took its toll by squeezing funds and conscripting men, closing the mine in 1940. (In fact this whole period of extraction failed to return any profit.)

Apart from the thriving museum, the mine area is also put to academic use by the University of Wales. There may yet be more gold to be hewn from these hills. A mining exploration company currently has a lease, running until 2012, which allows exploratory drilling.

Our walk is intentionally short, to allow for a visit to the extensive gold mine site. The site is part of the 2,500-acre (1,011ha) Dolaucothi Estate, given to The National Trust in 1943. The gift included the 17th-century Dolaucothi House, but it was structurally unsafe, and had to be demolished in 1955 – the route passes the site and the sad remains of its walled garden.

Note that the mines are open from April to September inclusive (underground tours from mid-May to mid-September), but if you come out of season you can pick up a comprehensive self-guided tour leaflet from the visitor centre.

LEFT: *A 3rd-century gold bracelet shows the intricate craftmanship of the Roman goldsmith.*

LEFT: *Dolaucothi gold mine, near Pumsaint – the promise of precious metals was probably one of the attractions of Britain that persuaded Rome that it was ripe for invasion.*

ROMAN

WALK 10

ABOUT • DOLAUCOTHI GOLD MINES

*Welsh gold is still highly prized today and it's probable that the promise of rare metals such as lead and gold was a factor in the Roman invasion in AD 43. The mines are open from April to September and out of season there is a self-guided tour leaflet available.*

· Carmarthenshire • **WALES**

DISTANCE • 4 miles (6.4km)

TOTAL ASCENT • 459ft (140m)

PATHS • good; slippery in places

TERRAIN • tracks, field paths, stiles and tarmac roads

GRADIENTS • some quite steep but not long

REFRESHMENTS • café at the gold mines, a pub in the village or take a picnic to have the trig point

PARK • National Trust Visitor Centre car park in Pumsaint village

OS MAP • Explorer 186 Llandeilo & Brechfa Forest, Llanybydder

# The Roman gold mines at Dolaucothi

❶ Turn left on to the main road for 44yds (40m); then left into a beech avenue. Just beyond a right turn, signed Dolaucothi Farm B&B, climb a stile (red waymarker).

❷ Ascend diagonally on a grassy sunken lane to enter a well-established conifer plantation through a gate. Go uphill (pasture on your left), soon bearing slightly right, deeper into the forest. In about 328yds (300m), after a gate, turn half-right, staying within the forest. Walk a further 164–219yds (150–200m).

❸ Here the path turns downhill, into thick dark forest. Within 109yds (100m) reach a clear T-junction. Turn left, uphill, through further dense woodland. Soon emerge from the woods on to a lovely curving track to reach a modern gate.

❹ Turn sharp left on to a new farm track; immediately go through a second gate. Soon, after 27yds (25m), turn sharply up to the right (no track) to a ridge and a hedge inside a new double fence.

❺ Follow this for 44yds (40m) beyond the Pen Lan-dolau trig point. Cross the fence and turn left. Follow red marker post over a stile through a felled area (hazardous tree stumps). Turn left to re-enter standing forest ahead. Soon reach a gravel track.

❻ Turn left. After about 328yds (300m) turn abruptly right (marker post) for a sharp descent on a forestry track. As soon as you see a gate 109yds (100m) ahead and, beyond it, a footbridge, stop.

❼ Turn right (marker post), on a narrow path into, initially, felled forestry. Soon this path forms a dark dense corridor and joins an old, narrow-gauge railway track. One field before the Dolaucothi Farm buildings, reach a corner with two gateways.

❽ Turn through the gate on the left. In 44yds (40m) turn right, and proceed through stiles to the dilapidated walled garden. Turn left on to a track; after 329yds (300m) cross a stone bridge. Just after the shady picnic site turn right over a stile, on to a delightful elevated riverside path, to a T-junction.

❾ Turn left here to visit the gold mine. Otherwise, turn right, go down steps, cross a stile into a meadow and follow the riverside to the road bridge. Turn right, soon passing the beech avenue taken earlier, to return to the start.

**DIFFICULTY ❀ ❀**

**• DON'T MISS •**

*The National Park visitor centre in Pumsaint is a 19th-century former coach house for visitors to the Dolaucothi Arms, and has a series of information panels on the village, the Dolaucothi Estate, and a Roman fort (no longer visible).*

**AD 50**

**AD 50–51** Roman soldiers destroy the druid stronghold of Anglesey, and the rebel chief Caractus (Caradog) surrenders.

**AD 60** Resistance to the Roman occupation remains strong. Imperial forces are concentrated in Wales,

**AD 60**

where the druids are stirring up trouble for the Roman soldiers.

**AD 60–61** Boudicca, Queen of the Iceni, leads a revolt against the Romans, rampaging through Colchester, St Albans and London. Suetonius Paulinus retaliates and

**AD 64**

his army cut down some 80,000 Iceni. Faced with total defeat, Boudicca takes her own life.

**AD 64** Persecution of Christians begins in Rome under Emperor Nero after a fire destroys Rome and the Christians are blamed.

ROMAN

IMPERIAL OUTPOST

# Silchester: a Roman wasteland

*A walk through the countryside and woodland surrounding the site of a major Roman settlement, where only the walls remain*

Finding the Roman site at Silchester is surprisingly difficult. The present settlement, a comfortable rural mix of pretty, older cottages and utilitarian modern housing, set some way off the main routes between Basingstoke and Reading, gives nothing away. In fact, the village grew up in medieval times to the west of the walled town, and the Roman site remains untouched, except for the 12th-century church of St Mary the Virgin on the far side.

Yet the aerial photographs in the site museum show that not quite 2,000 years ago Silchester was the hub of a bustling network of roads leading to London, Winchester, Chichester, Cirencester and Wales. The town was a regional administrative capital built to the traditional Roman grid pattern, complete with a basilica, baths, a forum, an amphitheatre to seat up to 7,000 citizens, a large inn, and a significant military base. Like modern Basingstoke, it was created artificially as a new urban centre, and its almost total disappearance is chilling.

The site had been occupied in neolithic times, and again in the Iron Age by the Atrebates tribe. The first part of this walk along ancient paths shows why: in an area of gently rolling countryside, this was the best defensive hilltop around. The Romans named it

Calleva Atrebatum. They began adding timber buildings around AD 45, and continued in stone, enclosing the whole site within a massive defensive wall around the end of the 3rd century. When the Romans pulled out of Britain in the early 5th century, their countrywide administration swiftly collapsed and Calleva (called Silchester by the Saxons) was abandoned. Unlike other major Roman centres, such as Bath, it never regained importance. However, it was hardly forgotten, either – the existence of its remarkable walls has been well documented over the centuries.

The amphitheatre is the clearest sign that this was a Roman town. A neat oval, it was built just outside the walls around AD 70. Excavations have failed to explain its precise purpose, but it was probably used for public events such as executions, as well as for gladiatorial contests. Shortly before the town was abandoned, the amphitheatre was given a stone retaining wall, and it was used on and off for the next hundred or so years. In the 12th century a house was built in the middle, and later it proved a convenient space for a chicken farm.

Silchester has no other big monuments to admire. The location of the actual town is marked in summer by the colourful tents of student archaeologists who sift through the level, grass-covered remains. Most of the site is private farmland, but a road runs across the middle and you can stand there to see the ring of the old walls all around you. This gives a good idea of the scale of the town – imagine timber-framed houses filling this vast circular space, one or two storeys high, with a central market square and shops, and a neat grid of paved streets, full of people and animals, carts, chickens and children. It's worth extending the walk and following the paths that go under and through the walls, and along the outer ditch. A loose-looking structure of flint and mortar, they tower up to 15 feet (4.5m) high, and clear gaps mark the ancient gateways.

LEFT: *An aerial view of the Roman site at Silchester shows clear evidence of an abandoned settlement.*

BACKGROUND: *The Roman walls in Silchester, one of the best-surviving examples in Britain.*

BELOW: *A Roman candlestick. The Museum of Reading has the main collection of artefacts excavated at Silchester on permanent display, including mosaics, coins and jewellery and other everyday artefacts.*

## ABOUT • SILCHESTER

*Calleva Atrebatum, or Silchester, was built shortly after AD 43. Once a bustling town complete with streets, temple and amphitheatre, it was inexplicably abandoned in AD 400–500. Uniquely, a complete circuit of walls remains at the site.*

## Hampshire • SE ENGLAND

**DISTANCE** • 5 miles (8km); optional circuit of walls, about 1 mile (1.6km)

**TOTAL ASCENT** • 98ft (30m)

**PATHS** • likely to be very muddy after rain

**TERRAIN** • fields, woodland, old lanes, some road walking

**GRADIENTS** • lots of stiles to negotiate, steep woodland paths

**REFRESHMENTS** • Calleva Arms pub, Silchester; Romans Hotel, Silchester

**PARK** • car park for Silchester Roman site on Wall Lane (free), on Mortimer side of modern Silchester

**OS MAP** • Explorer 159 Reading, Wokingham & Pangbourne

# Silchester Roman town

❶ Leave the car park via its entrance, cross the road, and take the old lane (fingerpost) directly opposite. Where the path rises, turn right at the fingerpost down a green tunnel of rhododendrons and holly. Cross a stile, keep left round the edge of the field and cross another stile. Cross a farm track and the stile opposite. Keep to the edge of the field, with the fence left, and cross the stile at the end.

❷ Ignore the track straight ahead, turn left along the old path at the field edge. Look right to see an ancient earthwork on the horizon. At the end, cross a stile and keep straight ahead along a line of oak trees. Continue downhill through the flinty field, following the hollow of an old field boundary, to a stream at the bottom.

❸ Cross a stile, footbridge and another stile, and keep straight up the hill. Half-way up, turn left and cross a stile into the woods. Cross the footbridge and continue up through birches (larch plantation on the left). At the top go through the gate and keep right along the field edge, to pass behind houses. After the last cottage (Rose Cottage), turn right over the stile and walk up the driveway.

❹ At the lane turn right, passing stables and an old farmhouse, right. Keep ahead down the old lane to the bottom of the hill. Where the track forks, keep right. After the bridge, turn left and go straight across the field towards a stile at the edge of the woods.

❺ Cross the stile and go ahead into trees. Cross a track, and a stile over a wire fence. Emerge from the woods and continue straight across the field towards a gate. Cross the stile and follow the path diagonally down to the right.

❻ At the bottom of the hollow, cross the bridge and stile and head diagonally left up the field. Before you reach the top corner, go through the squeeze gate on left, and turn right on to the gravel lane. This becomes a road by the thatched cottage (The Mount), and leads to a junction with a post-box. Turn right and through the squeeze gate for the Roman amphitheatre.

❼ Return to the road (Wall Lane) and turn right. Follow this past Manor Farm, into Church Lane. Stone walls can be seen on the right, and St Mary's Church. Keep heading downhill, and follow the path up on to the top of the wall.

❽ (Optional route: follow walls round for a complete circuit.) Retrace your route to this crossing point and stay inside the walls on a path along a fence. Turn right and go through the churchyard. Keep left, through a gate and along the path, with

farm buildings on your right. Keep on this path, and bear left on to a track which runs for ½ mile (800m) across the Roman town. Pass excavation site (closed).

❾ At the opposite side, go left, then right through the gate. Follow the path for ¾ mile (1.2km) to the museum. (To reach modern village, cross the road and bear left, to take footpath through the trees.) Retract your steps to point ❾ and go left. Turn right just before the wooden gate to the car park.

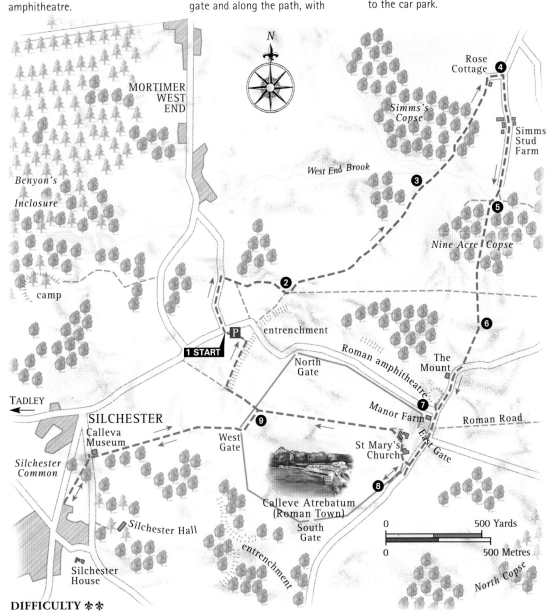

**DIFFICULTY** ✳ ✳

**AD 65**

**AD 65** Bath (*Aquae Sulis*) becomes an important Roman settlement. Today, Bath is one of the best-preserved Roman towns in Britain.

**AD 70–100** The writing of the Christian gospels.

**AD 71**

**AD 71–80** Fishbourne Palace in Sussex is built. The great Roman palace was probably built for Cogidnus, king of the Regni tribe, recognised by the Romans as a sub-ruler and created an honorary citizen of Rome.

**AD 75**

**AD 75–77** Roman forces, under the leadership of Agricola, establish a new frontier in Cambria (South Wales) and build a fort at Caerleon.

**AD 77** Agricola is made Governor of Wales and stamps out further resistance from the Welsh.

# A Roman Highway through the Mendips

*There is a long history behind a tiny stretch of ancient road near Radstock in north-east Somerset*

Standing on the Norton–Radstock Greenway, looking up the grassy field where the old railway-track bed crosses the Fosse Way, there seems to be little to see. Behind you, beyond the modern industrial units, a hedged-in path snakes its way up to Westfield. A line of green bollards signifies the crossing and a stile leads to the grassy field. Study the field harder and you will notice something unusual. Running up the left-hand side, to a gate in the top corner, is a grassy ridge, steep enough to cause the trodden footpath to steer around it to the right, before it, too, heads for the gate at the top. Here, in the old North Somerset Coalfield, there are many such bumps in many fields – old tramways and coal diggings – hidden beneath the top-soil. But the inquisitive may be drawn further; this is, after all, the line of the Fosse Way, a Roman highway that stretched from Lincoln to Exeter.

Through the gate at the top of the field you are enclosed by ancient hedgerows. The path seems to be raised above the field slightly, but the hedges crowd you to single file. Then, as the slope lessens and you reach the summit plateau, the hedges, too, drop away and you are on a raised bank above the fields. There are ditches to either side and the sense of elevation is heightened by the severe cropping of the hedgerows.

The path now seems to have the classic profile of a Roman road. It's raised; and the Romans built their roads on an agger, a raised platform above ditches on either side, the core created by the digging of the ditches. It's straight enough, and scuff the mud and dirt beneath your feet and you can feel its surface. Could it be a genuine piece of Roman highway?

For much of its route the Fosse Way is covered by modern tarmac. South of Bath it becomes the A367, but approaching Radstock, the old Bath Turnpike engineers who took over the road at the end of the 18th century diverted its course down a gentler slope into the centre of the mining town. The Clandown section was left to cattle-drovers and miners walking to work. When modern archaeologists investigated the site they found a road frozen in time, not 2,000 years old but just over 200. Digging deeper, they found the original Roman foundations, not on this raised agger but at field level. The ridge the path follows appears to have been created by two millennia of road repairs, adding new surface to old each time. The last repair seems to have been at the end of the 18th century – around the time the turnpike road was built.

The steep bank into Clandown Bottom is heavily rutted. A 21st-century tractor has replicated the action of centuries of carts and cattle. There is Roman debris on the surface here, and medieval fragments deep down where the ruts have been churned and re-churned. This is part of the changing historical landscape, a point worth reflection later in this walk, as you spy the conical spoil tip of Old Mills Colliery. It's no less impressive a remain than this section of ancient highway.

ABOVE: *Blackstone Edge, West Yorkshire, shows all the features of a Roman road although the experts are still debating its authenticity.*

FAR LEFT: *Statue of a Roman legionary in bronze, wearing a cuirass of overlapping metal bands, greaves on his legs and sandals. Soldiers would have also carried a short sword.*

BELOW: *View of Downside Abbey and School, Stratton-on-the-Fosse, near Radstock.*

**ABOUT • FOSSE WAY ROMAN ROAD**

*Shortly after the Roman invasion military roads were laid across Britain to enable speedy movement of troops. As well as being straight, you can often identify them by the agger, the raised platform between two ditches, which makes for their distinctive profile.*

**Somerset • SW ENGLAND**

**DISTANCE •** 5 miles (8km)

**TOTAL ASCENT •** 390ft (119m)

**PATHS •** field tracks, country lanes and a converted railway track bed

**TERRAIN •** pastureland and edge of town

**GRADIENTS •** steep ascent from Welton Hollow and Clandown Bottom

**REFRESHMENTS •** none on the route but several pubs in Radstock, Welton and Midsomer Norton

**PARK •** 100yds (91m) up Millards Hill or carefully down the lane towards Welton Manor Farm

**OS MAP •** Explorer 143 Shepton Mallet & Mendip Hills East

# The Exeter–Lincoln highway

**DIFFICULTY ✲✲**

**❶** Walk down the lane towards Welton Manor Farm, go through the left-hand gate and follow the right-hand field edge to a stile. Cross and continue for 300yds (274m) to another stile on the right. Walk diagonally across the field, heading for a railway bridge. Cross the stile and climb the steps to the Norton–Radstock Greenway. Turn left and follow the former railway for 500yds (457m) to some bollards across the track.

**❷** Turn left and cross the stile into the field. Keep the hedge on your left and follow the rising path to a gate into an enclosed lane. Follow this section of Roman road (the Fosse Way) between hedges and up on to the top of the hill. Continue as it dips back down between hedgerows to Clandown Bottom. Cross a stream and turn left as you emerge in housing.

**❸** Turn left at the T-junction along Springfield Place. Pass the old chapel (converted into housing) and go through an arch in the row of cottages ahead to a gate and field beyond. Follow the streamside path up the valley. At the end of the field cross the stile and continue on a better track with the stream on your left. Cross a stile by a gate and bear right to join a farm track coming down the hill. Turn immediately left and continue through a gate on to a road.

**❹** Cross, go through the gate opposite and walk up the track with the stream on your left. Near the head of the valley, aim for the top left-hand corner by a pond. Cross the stream, go through a gate and follow the left-hand field edge up to a stile in the corner. Stay with the hedge to the next stile. Cross, turn half-right aiming for a stile diagonally opposite.

**❺** Emerge on a road and take the lane directly opposite. After 100yds (91m), as the lane swings left, take the footpath on the right along the edge of a field. Cross a stile at the far corner and continue with the hedge on your right, then go across the opening to a side field. Turn left at the end on an enclosed lane; turn right. Cross the stile and turn left into a field. Follow the left-hand edge until it becomes an enclosed lane. Go through the gate and go down the hill to join a farm track. Turn left by Springfield Farm.

**❻** Turn right at the junction. In 200 yds (183m) turn left through a stile, then turn right beyond a gap in the hedge. Follow the hedge through two fields and, 50yds (46m) into a third field, turn left to join a crossing path over a stile on the far eastern side.

**❼** Follow the enclosed Binces Lodge Lane, past a white house on the left, until it becomes surfaced and joins a minor road on a bend. Go straight ahead to another junction on the right. Turn right past a row of houses. At the end of the road keep straight on down the snicket (narrow alley between houses) to emerge on the bend in Millards Hill, 100yds (91m) above the start.

**AD 79**

**AD 79** The Romans establish a major camp in Chester (Deva) to protect the surrounding fertile land from the Welsh tribesmen and establish the Roman northern front.

**AD 79** Vesuvius erupts, burying the Roman town of Pompeii.

**AD 82**

**AD 82** Agricola pushes the Roman frontier into Galloway and Ayrshire and defeats the Novantae tribe.

**AD 85** People living in the northern Pennines and the Scottish lowlands are finally subdued, and the northern tribes are defeated.

**AD 87**

**AD 87** Inchtuthill's fortress, still incomplete, is abandoned as Agricola returns to Rome and his conquests begin to diminish. Because of strong resistance by the Picts, Rome failed to conquer Scotland during their time in Britain.

ROMAN

IMPERIAL OUTPOST

# The Romans at Ardoch

*Huge earthworks in Perthshire recall a series of campaigns to conquer northern Britain*

Within four years of their invasion in AD 43, the Romans had occupied most of southern Britain and established a frontier between the Severn and the Humber. But the wilder country of the north and west took much longer to subdue and, despite a series of campaigns by several different emperors, the tribes of what was later to be Scotland were never truly conquered.

The first governor to attempt such a conquest was Julius Agricola. Having pacified Wales in AD 78, he advanced as far north as the River Tay and six years later was campaigning in the Highlands, where he won a victory over the Caledonians at *Mons Graupius*, near Inverness. This conquest was short-lived, however, for Agricola was soon recalled to Rome and the legions pulled back to the south. Then, in AD 138, the emperor Antoninus Pius launched a new campaign that pushed the frontier of the province back to the Firth of Forth and Firth of Clyde for a period of more than 20 years. Finally, in AD 208, Septimus Severus led a huge invasion into central Scotland that was abandoned only on account of the emperor's death in York in AD 211.

All three campaigns have left their mark at Ardoch, a river-crossing just below the foothills of the Highlands on the Romans' favoured route into the north. There is not another site throughout the empire that provides such dramatic evidence of Roman armies on the march or of the garrisons that they established when first occupying hostile territory. First, there is a series of enormous marching camps. These were overnight encampments for armies that might number up to 20,000 men, with banks and palisades that were constructed at the end of each day's march. The largest at Ardoch covers 130 acres (52ha) and was probably also a more permanent supply base during the campaign of Severus. The most dramatic feature of the site, however, is the fort that dates from the longer-lasting Antonine period of occupation. This formed part of a line of garrisons just below the Highlands that was linked by roads and signal stations to the main frontier between the Forth and the Clyde. Nearly 2,000 years after its abandonment, its massive ramparts still impart a sense of Rome's colossal military might.

The first part of this walk explores the Roman site, taking in the fort itself and some of the fainter earthworks to be seen around it. The route then follows the River Knaik through a gorge of woods and waterfalls that have scarcely changed over the millennia, before returning through the cultivated landscape of a great estate. There is a mansion at its heart rather than a villa, but this belongs to a world in which the Romans would have felt at home. They may have failed to conquer Scotland, but in the longer term it was their system and their culture that prevailed.

BELOW: *Roman soldiers building fortifications.*

ABOVE: *The ramparts of Ardoch Roman marching camps. Theses camps were often the temporary quarters for over 2000 foot soldiers at a time.*

BELOW: *Emperor Antonius (AD 86–161) launched an offensive on Scotland in AD 138.*

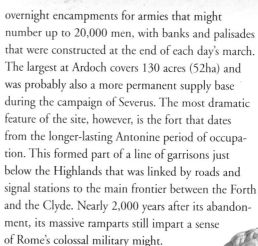

WALK 13

ROMAN

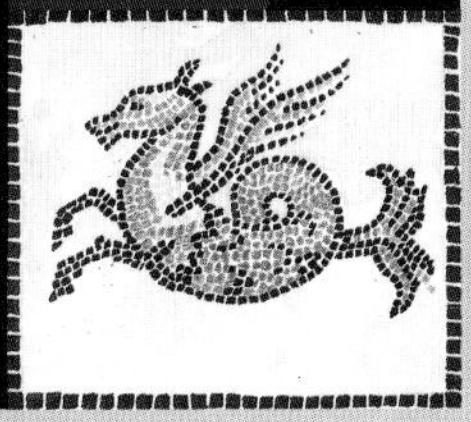

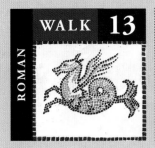

ABOUT • ARDOCH ROMAN FORT

*Unlike its more southerly neighbours, the hostile Scottish tribes proved no easy conquest for the Roman troops. Remains of the marching camps, forts and series of garrisons all point to Rome's might, 2000 years ago, and the strength of resistance they encountered.*

## Perth & Kinross • SCOTLAND

**DISTANCE** • 4 miles (6km)

**TOTAL ASCENT** • minimal

**PATHS** • firm, but there can be puddles after rain

**TERRAIN** • woodland and fields

**GRADIENTS** • minimal

**REFRESHMENTS** • Braco Hotel

**PARK** • on roadside in high street of Braco village

**OS MAP** • Explorer 369 Perth & Kinross

# The Roman campaign headquarters at Ardoch

❶ Park in the high street and walk through the village on the A822 Crieff road. Cross a bridge over the River Knaik, a stream which, under various names, flows from the foothills of the Highlands to the Allan Water and the Firth of Forth.

❷ Immediately beyond the bridge, turn right and enter Ardoch Fort through a small wooden gate. Following the forts' massive inner rampart, you can appreciate the complexity and strength of its defences. Walk in an anti-clockwise direction around the perimeter fence. (The land on the other side of the fence belongs to the Ardoch Estate.) Within the fence are a large number of impressive angular ditches built as a series of defence mechanisms. The great marching camps extend for more than ½ mile (800m) to the north, but are best seen from beside the road to Comrie. Once you have explored the site, return to the entrance and go back across the bridge.

❸ On the village side of the bridge, turn right through the stone-piered entrance of a private road. Follow the track through attractive woodland above the river's waterfalls and rapids, before veering to the left to reach a crossroads.

❹ Turn left, continuing on the track between two duck ponds. The hills on the south-east horizon are the Ochil Hills, which include the summit of Ben Cleuch at 721m. Behind you, to the north, you can glimpse the bracken-covered foothills of the Highlands. The Romans realised that if they were to conquer Scotland, they first had to control this broad and fertile valley through the hills now known as Strathallan.

❺ Turn left at a T-junction. Looking back across the fields from this point there is a good view of Braco Castle, an imposing mansion with medieval origins that, just like a Roman villa would be, is the focus of a large, well-run estate. The track skirts cultivated fields, grazing lands and managed woodland. Turn left at the juction with the B8033, opposite the remains of the tower of Braco Free Church (1845), and return to Braco high street and your car.

• DON'T MISS •

*Ardoch Old Bridge, just upstream from the present crossing, was built in the early 18th century to carry a military road from Stirling up into the Highlands. It formed part of a system involving roads and garrisons, intended to suppress the northern clans whose distant ancestors may have possibly battled with Agricola in Roman times.*

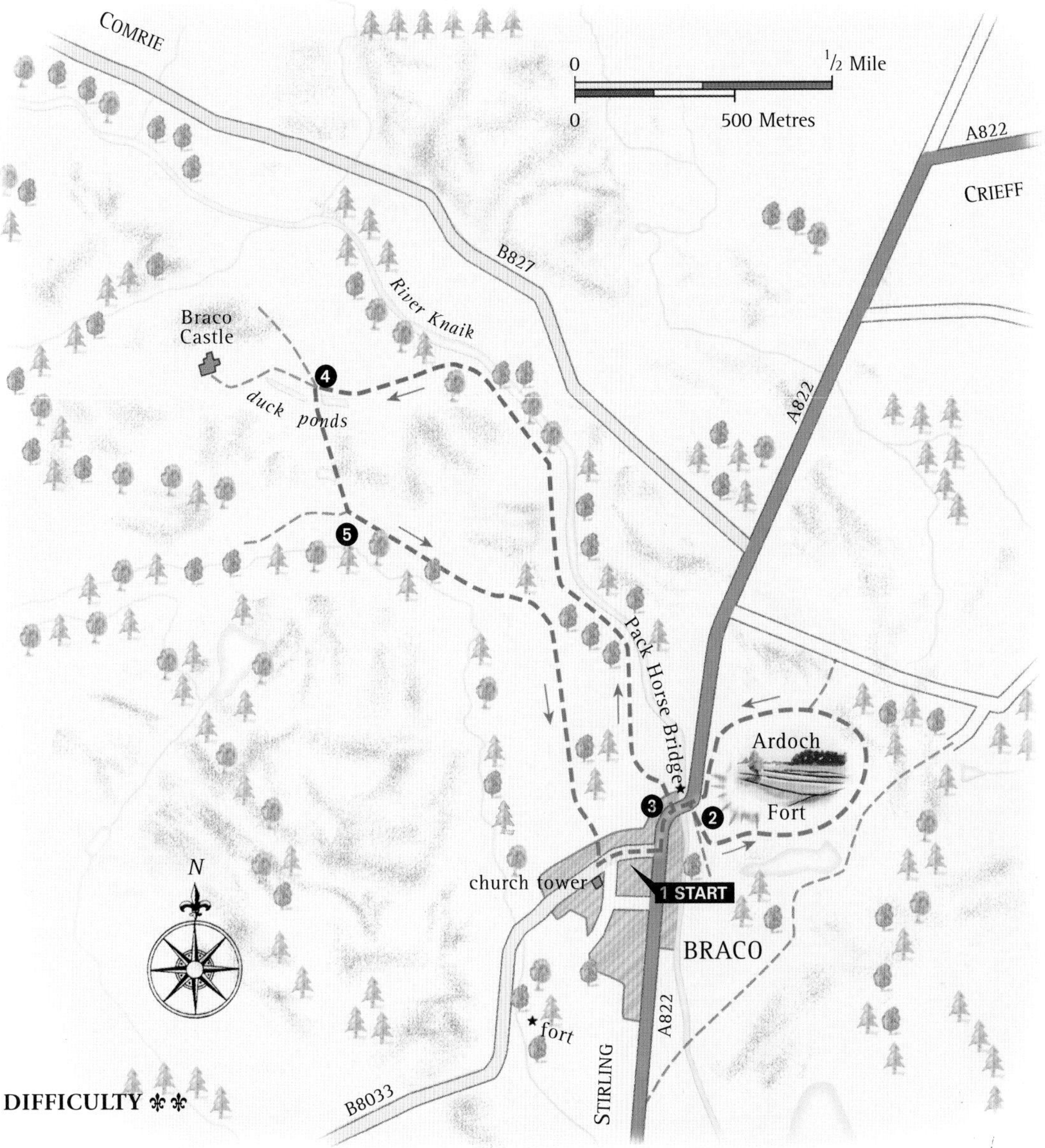


DIFFICULTY ✤✤

# The Antonine Wall

ABOVE: *Trees cover the mound of Antonine's Wall, which was built to deter incursions from the northern tribes.*

*The boundary that once marked the Roman Empire's northern limit, between the Forth and the Clyde*

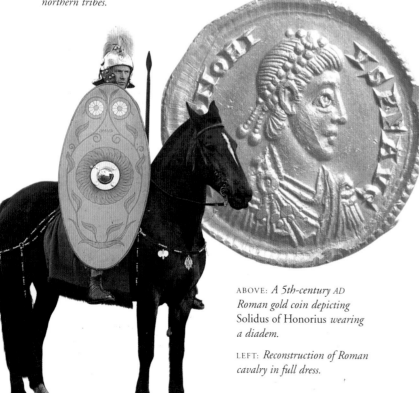

ABOVE: *A 5th-century AD Roman gold coin depicting* Solidus of Honorius *wearing a diadem.*

LEFT: *Reconstruction of Roman cavalry in full dress.*

## A Frontier for Brittania

Once the Romans had abandoned their ambition to include the whole of Britain in the empire, they had to decide on a northern frontier. In terms of controlling local tribes and protecting the rich province from invasion, they could rely on strategically positioned forts and military roads, but in times of peace a more formal frontier was required. There were taxes to be levied on imports; there were criminals and other undesirables whose movements needed to be checked. Most importantly, travellers should be suitably impressed when entering the greatest empire in the world.

The most substantial and long-lasting of these frontiers was the wall constructed on the orders of the Emperor Hadrian following his visit to Britain in AD 122. But within 15 years of completion a new emperor, Antoninus Pius, decided on a frontier 100 miles (160km) to the north, retaking lands in southern Scotland that the Romans had abandoned some 60 years before.

## A Wall of Turf

The Antonine Wall spans Britain's narrowest land-crossing, running 40 miles (64km) from the Firth of Forth to the Clyde. Unlike its predecessor, it was built of turf, but was nonetheless substantial, and 16 forts were built at regular intervals along its length. There were also signal stations, a military road and complex secondary defences to deter attack by cavalry or chariots. Manned, according to inscriptions, by auxiliaries from distant corners of the empire, the frontier served its purpose for some 20 years until about AD 158, when a further change in policy led to a withdrawal back south and the re-commissioning of Hadrian's Wall. One of the best-preserved sections of wall is at Rough Castle, near Bonnybridge, where its course may be followed to both west and east of the public car park.

ABOVE: *The turf ramparts over stone foundations mark the site of the Roman fort at Ardoch, constructed c. AD 140.*

BELOW: *Modern reconstruction of a line of Roman foot soldiers.*

## WALK 14

### A PATROL ALONG THE FRONTIER AT ROUGH CASTLE

❶ Having parked, return down the lane for about 300yds (274m) and turn right through a gate into a park-like field of trees and open grassland. The Roman frontier is still unmistakable: a deep, wide ditch, or vallum, overlooked by a substantial bank – all that remains of the turf wall.

❷ As you follow its course back to the car park and beyond, picture it when newly built. Set on stone foundations, it was a massive 15ft (4.5m) in width and stood at least 10ft (3m) high, with a timber palisade along the parapet. You may notice stones from the foundations half-buried in the turf, but your mind must recreate the watch-towers and beacon-platforms.

❸ Beyond a burn tumbling through a sheltered glen is Rough Castle fort: a four-square compound protected by ramparts. This was the base for a small garrison, together with administrative clerks and an officer elite. Enter through the west gate and imagine the barrack blocks and granaries on your route to the principia, or headquarters building.

❹ Turning left, exit through the north gate. Ahead of you is a serried grid of pits; each one contained a bunch of sharpened stakes, known as

lilia, or lilies, that could prove most effective in deterring an assault. Turning to the right and recrossing the frontier, you can explore the fort's 'annexe'. This contained the bath-house, potteries, blacksmiths and other workshops.

❺ Beyond the annexe, a stile leads on to a woodland path that follows the frontier for a further mile (1.6km) and, although the earthworks are overgrown, it is here that one can best imagine the landscape of 2,000 years ago. To the south lay an empire that stretched to Africa and Asia; to the north lay mountains and impenetrable forests haunted by barbarians. The wall was a boundary between two opposing worlds.

**Distance:** 2½ miles (4km)

**Total ascent:** 50ft (80m)

**Paths:** firm grass to west of Rough Castle; muddy stretches through woods to east of fort

**Terrain:** open grassland; woods

**Gradients:** easy

**Refreshments:** pubs and cafés in Bonnybridge and Falkirk

**Park:** car park at Rough Castle

**OS Map:** Explorer 349 Falkirk, Cumbernauld & Livingston

**Difficulty:** ✾✾

**AD 100**

**AD 100** The Roman Empire is at its height. Paper-making is developed in China; it is another 1,000 years before the skill spreads to Europe.

**AD 100–200** Cirencester is established as the administrative centre for the West Country.

**AD 122**

**AD 122** Emperor Hadrian visits Britain. The building of Hadrian's Wall, of stone and turf, is begun to mark the frontier from present-day Bowness in the west to Newcastle in the east. Fifteen garrison forts are built along it to control the movement of people on both sides.

**AD 142**

**AD 142** Antonine's Wall is built of turf, extending from the Clyde to the Firth of Forth, and marking Roman incursions into the Lowlands. Twenty years later the boundary reverts to Hadrian's Wall.

# A Roman City in Britain

*Walk through the ancient city of Chester and around its stone walls, first built by the Romans*

Chester was one of the most important Roman towns in Britain, and the Romans garrisoned their 20th Legion there. They knew the town, and the fortress, as Deva, the fort being built in AD 79 as a base for raids against the Welsh tribes. The city walls are a mix of Roman and medieval, with some modern reconstruction, but it is still possible to walk their entire 2-mile (3km) length around the city centre, as this walk indicates. There is also much else to see in this fascinating historical city, which boasts the largest Roman amphitheatre in Britain.

The walk begins by the cross, which has marked the centre of the city of Chester since the 1st century. That is when the Romans marked out the city's roughly rectangular street plan, though the first cross on the site was put up in 1407.

The present Watergate, at the end of Watergate Street, dates from 1788: the River Dee once flowed along here, between the walls and the Roodee Racecourse, England's oldest. A Roman stone harbour was found on the site of the racecourse.

The castle was begun by William the Conqueror, after Chester had fallen to the Normans in 1069 – the last British town to succumb to the invaders. By continuing along the walls you soon come to the most significant Roman remains in the city: the Roman Gardens and the Roman amphitheatre. The gardens bring together some of the Roman artefacts found in Chester, and the amphitheatre is the largest stone-built Roman example yet found in Britain. A wooden amphitheatre was first built on this site in the late 70s AD, but by the end of the 1st century it had been rebuilt in stone. It was finally abandoned in AD 350, 33 years before the Romans withdrew from Chester.

Continuing the circuit of the walls takes you past Northgate, with the North Wall being the most elevated and, in places, the narrowest section of the walls. After descending from the walls back at Watergate and going to Bridge Street, another major Roman remain is reached by the unlikely method of walking through the Spud-U-Like fast food shop. Behind it is the Roman bath and hypocaust, over 1,900 years old and yet still almost perfectly preserved.

On Bridge Street is the Rows, double-tiered and covered rows of shops thought to have been built up gradually between the 13th and 18th centuries. By including a look at the city's magnificent cathedral as well, this walk takes in many of Chester's historical highlights, including the lovely black and white half timbered buildings, while illustrating the particular signicance and influence of its Roman roots.

ABOVE: *Bronze Roman helmet, dating from 1st–2nd centuries AD and probably of a type worn by the soldiers garrisoned in Chester.*

LEFT: *The superb Roman remains in Chester.*

**ABOUT • CHESTER**

*The 20th legion of the Roman army was garrisoned in Chester onwards from AD 88 and a large civilian town grew up next to the fort. Apart from the Roman-Medieval walls, the city has a number of interesting Roman remains including an ampitheatre.*

**Cheshire • C ENGLAND**

| | |
|---|---|
| **DISTANCE** • 4 miles (6.4km) | **REFRESHMENTS** • many cafés and pubs in Chester |
| **TOTAL ASCENT** • 25ft (8m) | |
| **PATHS** • pavements | **PARK** • Little Roodee car park off Grosvenor Road; numerous other car parks; park-and-ride drops off in the city centre |
| **TERRAIN** • city streets | |
| **GRADIENTS** • one climb to the city walls | **OS MAP** • Explorer 266 Wirral & Chester |

# Roman drama in the heart of Chester

❶ Begin at The Cross in the city centre and walk west for 328yds (300m) along Watergate Street until you reach the junction with City Walls Road. Go right slightly to gain access to the red sandstone city walls and turn left to walk in an anti-clockwise direction along the walls, soon passing the Roodee Racecourse on your right.

❷ Cross over the A483 Wrexham road and follow the walls around for 437yds (400m), passing the early Norman Chester Castle, rebuilt from its ruinous state in the 19th century, on the left and following the course of the River Dee on the right. In 109yds (100m) cross Bridgegate. In 164yds (150m) the walls turn north, away from the river; the Roman Gardens are below on the right.

❸ Come down from the walls at New Gate and turn right into the Roman Gardens. After exploring the gardens, leave where you came in, turn right to see the Roman Amphitheatre in 55yds (50m), and the Chester Visitor Centre, which offers an excellent introduction to the city, further along on the far side of the road.

❹ Return to New Gate and continue the circuit of the walls. After 328yds (300m) swing west to cross Northgate and then St Martins Gate, then turn south to reach Watergate where you first ascended the walls.

❺ Descend the walls and turn left along Watergate Street, back to The Cross. Turn right down Bridge Street, with access to the Roman bath and hypocaust through the Spud-U-Like shop. (Not signed, but go in and down the stairs to the left of the counter.)

❻ Further down Bridge Street is the Chester Heritage Centre, well worth visiting before returning to The Cross. Here you turn right and immediately left up Northgate Street, until you reach Chester Cathedral which is set back slightly on your right.

❼ Spend some time exploring this fine 14th-century red sandstone cathedral with its fine Norman stonework and rich carvings. Once a Benedictine monastery until its dissolution in the 1540, unlike many Chester survived to become the cathedral for the Diocese of Chester just one year later. After visiting the cathedral, retrace your steps to The Cross to finish the walk.

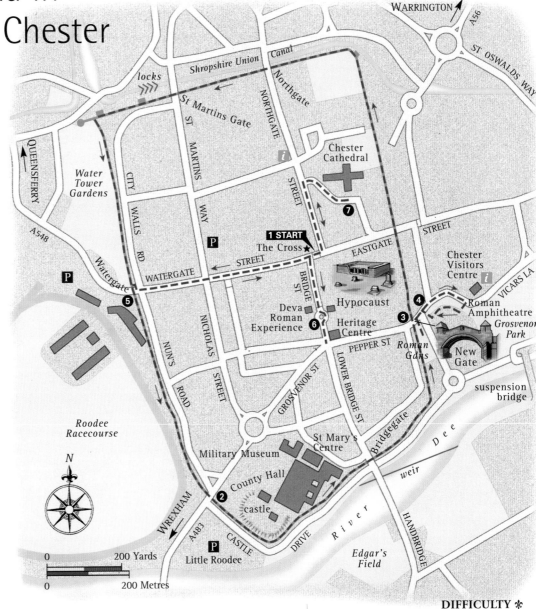

**DIFFICULTY ❊**

**DON'T MISS**

*Chester Zoo, to the north of the city, is one of the finest zoological parks in Europe, a pioneer in showing animals in their natural surroundings. At 110 acres (44ha), it is the second-largest in Britain after London Zoo.*

**AD 146**

AD 146 Rome invades Greece.

AD 160 In Rome, thousands die of the plague, causing a trading crisis which affects their economy.

AD 163 In Britain, the occupying Romans retreat once again to their

**AD 180**

original frontier at Hadrian's Wall, unable to withstand Pictish assaults.

AD 180 Early Christian Church institutions are founded.

AD 200 The road system is completed in Rome.

**AD 209**

AD 209 Septimus Severus is sent from Rome with reinforcements to meet attacks on Hadrian's Wall.

AD 250 Savage attacks by barbarians from northern Germany prompt the building of a series of forts on the south coast.

# Home from Rome in Gloucestershire

*The site of a Roman villa at Great Witcombe still keeps most of its secrets from the modern world*

The unearthing of several Roman antiquities during the construction of the Gloucestershire section of the M5 motorway invited speculation that there may be over 4,000 Romano-British sites in the Severn Vale, such as the one exposed at Great Witcombe in 1818, awaiting funds for excavation.

The Roman villa at Great Witcombe was constructed part-way up the Cotswold escarpment, in a position of particular strategic importance – its proximity to a water source suggests that the villa was surrounded by farmland. It is believed that this area was extensively farmed during this time and the discovery – among the finds when Great Witcombe was excavated – of a iron plough coulter and a bronze statuette of an ploughman with oxen team suggests that the villa's main source of income was farming the land surrounding the villa.

Unremarkable though the remains may be, the villa typifies what was affordable to perhaps a wealthy merchant of the Roman era – large but not unduly pretentious. But between the latter part of the 3rd and 4th centuries, Great Witcombe devel-

chose a scenically prime location, a fact this route exploits to the full. The beeches in Witcombe Wood are good companions in any season, and the view from Barrow Rake is more than just reward for the effort. Until the by-pass was built, the main east-west road through Birdlip was the Roman road known as Ermin Street (on some maps, Ermin Way). The gradient of the escarpment at Birdlip Hill obliged the Roman engineers to put in a couple of zigzags. This route crosses Ermin Street in Birdlip village, beside the school, and follows it very briefly down Birdlip Hill.

The exterior site is open at any reasonable time; this excludes the (covered) mosaic pavements. It is managed by English Heritage. In the summer season occasional guided tours of the Roman villa are given by the Cotswold Area of Outstanding Natural Beauty Partnership.

Other Roman attractions in Gloucestershire are the fabulous Chedworth Roman villa, boasting 32 identifiable rooms and several intact or at least discernible mosaic floors, and Nodens Roman Temple, overlooking the Severn Estuary, near Lydney (very limited opening).

BELOW: *Lovely woodland surrounds the Roman villa at Great Witcombe.*

ABOVE: *View over fields towards the site of the Roman villa at Great Witcombe.*

oped into an exquisite country house, built around three sides of a courtyard with several mosaic pavements, two bath suites, with hypocausts, and a colonnaded central gallery and portico.

Very little is known about the inhabitants of the villa except that it possibly belonged to the descendants of a veteran settled here when the area was established by the invading Roman army. Its creators

**ABOUT • GREAT WITCOMBE**

*The setting alone, reminiscent of a Mediterranean landscape, makes this walk worthwhile. The villa commands superb views across the valley and the remains, which show the original floor plan, leave you in no doubt that this was once a sumptuous country house.*

## Gloucestershire • SW ENGLAND

**DISTANCE** • 7½ miles (12km)

**TOTAL ASCENT** • 700ft (213m)

**PATHS** • good; slippery in places

**TERRAIN** • bridleways, tracks, field paths, stiles, tarmac roads

**GRADIENTS** • mostly gradual; climbs are steep but short

**REFRESHMENTS** • seasonal tea-shop near start; Air Balloon pub, Brockworth and Gloucester near by

**PARK** • Roman villa car park, 1½ miles (2.4km) from Brockworth turn-off A417

**OS MAP** • Explorer 179 Gloucester, Cheltenham & Stroud

# Great Witcombe's grand Roman villa

**❶** Take the path downhill from the car park for 33yds (30m). Follow waymarkers to a gate and the Cotswold Way; turn left. Soon pass The Haven Tea Garden on the left and continue to a big junction; here conifers have infiltrated the indigenous beeches. Turn left.

**❷** Soon pass a dilapidated ornamental gateway. After 437yds (400m) turn right at a T-junction (left is a private drive). Continue for 328yds (300m), to a clear fork of tracks. Go right, slightly uphill, for 186yds (170m).

**❸** Turn sharply right and back to leave the Cotswold Way and follow a bridleway signed Horse Trail to Brimpsfield, which goes uphill, then left to the B4070. Turn right and in 22yds (20m) cross the road and continue ahead signed Brimpsfield 1½ miles (2.4km). At a T-junction turn left. Keep the fence/wall on your right. The path, initially enclosed by tree-lined walls, opens on to a bend in the road. Continue ahead along the road to reach a T-junction of minor roads.

**❹** Cross the road and continue ahead on a bridleway. Join a farm track and in 22yds (20m) turn left over a stile to Birdlip. Turn left at the road. Take a path beside a school; walk on cricket field side of a football pitch fence. Beyond a flagpole turn half-left. At a B-road turn right, then take the old road, left, to Barrow Rake Viewpoint plaque.

**❺** Take the obvious path (Cotswold Way) on the escarpment. Later, in woodland, the track descends to a road. Go straight over and down through trees; soon turn right to rejoin the road. Just after a sharp bend take the public bridleway to the right.

**❻** Continue straight ahead, keeping the fence on your left. Go to end of barns being converted. Cross a stile, turn partially left, downslope, to another stile then a gap in trees. Follow right-hand edge of a field down to a house. Follow the path beside the house and down a long drive. Take the second footpath on left (shortly after footpath beside green-surfaced tennis court), climb stile and diagonally cross two small fields to another road. Go straight across into fields.

**❼** Take field paths, turning half-left across the third field towards houses. Follow a path between houses leading to a minor road. Turn left; in 44yds (40m) turn right (waymarked), and after 22yds (20m), at end of a garden, take the stile on the right to cross diagonally to the reservoir road. Cross the causeway.

**❽** Skirt Witcombe Reservoir on a good track (ignore a footpath on the right, beside buildings) which later rises with a stream on the left (ignore left turn signed Private). The track later deteriorates. Keep straight ahead uphill (do not cross the stream) through pastures. To enter the Roman villa proceed uphill and around it through farmyard. The car park is 328yds (300m) ahead.

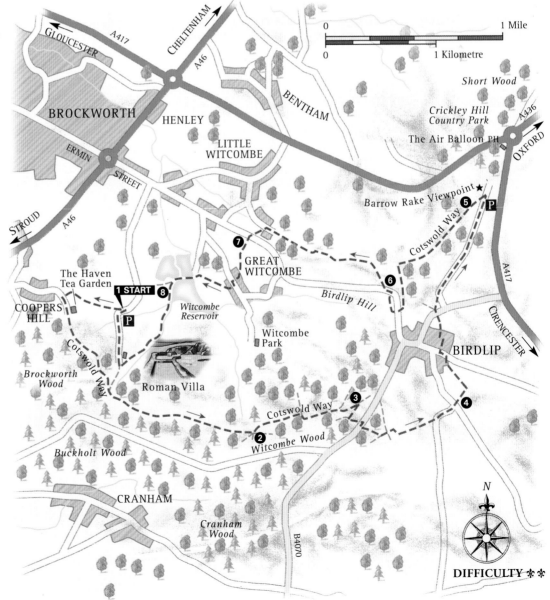

**DIFFICULTY ✿ ✿**

**AD 254**

**AD 254** Execution of St Alban, the first British Christian martyr.

**AD 270** The first use of a magnetic compass in China.

**AD 286–293** Rebellion of Carausius, who declares himself Emperor of Britain.

**AD 300**

**AD 300** Invention of the wheelbarrow in China, and the beginning of the classical period in Mayan civilisation.

**AD 306** Constantine is declared Emperor of York.

**AD 313**

**AD 313** Christianity is declared the official religion after Emperor Constantine recognises the Church and is baptised on his deathbed in AD 337. At this time, Christianity co-exists peaceably with other beliefs.

# From Rome to Hardknott

*The all-conquering Roman legions advanced from the south only to find a Cumbria of harsh winters, rugged mountains and defiant Celts*

ROMAN

IMPERIAL OUTPOST

High and exposed beneath the black rocks of Border End, this must have been one of the least hospitable sites in the whole of the Roman Empire. But here at Hardknott in the 2nd century AD, during the reign of Emperor Hadrian, the Romans built their fort, *Mediovogdum*.

In AD 78, 30 years after Aulius Plautius and Emperor Claudius had attacked southern England, the governor, Julius Agricola, marched his legion northwards to the Moray Firth. Inevitably, the advance brought increased resistance from the Celtic tribes. By AD 85 Agricola had been recalled and the Romans were forced to retreat to the Tyne–Solway Gap. For much of the time over the next four centuries, Cumbria would be the last outpost of the empire.

To establish their dominance over Britain the Romans built marching roads and forts. Three legions, each of about 5,000 highly trained troops from Rome, manned large forts at Caerleon, York and Chester. In the south the Romans brought sophistication to Britain, building towns such as Colchester and Bath, and setting up elaborate administrations. Though there were uprisings, life in southern Britain was good.

In the north, cohorts and auxiliaries, usually with 500 to 1,000 men recruited from non-Roman tribes, were left to man the frontier forts. Cumbria had been the territory of the Brigantes, who were led by Queen Cartimandua. She befriended the Romans by turning in the troublesome warrior chief, Caractacus. But Cartimandua was dethroned by her ex-husband Venutius, and the Brigantes would wreak havoc for four centuries.

Cumbria is criss-crossed by a series of Roman roads linking the forts of Hadrian's Wall with Penrith (*Brocavum*) and Ambleside (*Galava*). Perhaps the roughest of these ancient highways was the Ambleside to Ravenglass (*Glannaventa*) road, and on this one, huddled beneath the road's highest and wildest point, is Hardknott. The fort consisted of a large commandant's house, a granary, a bathhouse and barracks. Just above the main complex you'll notice a flattened area of the fell – the parade ground. The occupying Fourth Cohort came from Dalmatia, part of modern-day Croatia.

By the end of the 2nd century the fort was abandoned. Today the walls are just 6ft (10m) high, and only the foundations of the inner buildings remain. However, when you look over the crumbling walls, perched on the very edge of precipices, it's easy to imagine soldiers on the turrets watching out for invaders from across the seas. At the top of the Hardknott Pass the path looks down on Wrynose Bottom. While the modern tarmac road twists and turns tortuously down to the valley, you follow the line of the Roman road down to Black Hall. Though the shadowy spruce trees of the Dunnerdale Forest diminish the sense of remoteness, the views of the Duddon Valley and the Coniston Fells are magnificient.

ABOVE: *Detail from Trajan's Column (Italy) showing daily life in a Roman military camp.*

BELOW: *The magnificent setting of Hardknott fort set against the backdrop of the Cumbrian mountains.*

**ABOUT • HARDKNOTT FORT**

*From the Duddon Valley you see the fort as the high point of your journey. After rounding the craggy Harter Fell, you climb, in the invaders' footsteps, to reach the outer walls of the fort – against a backdrop of the mighty Cumbrian mountains.*

**Cumbria • N ENGLAND**

**DISTANCE •** 6 miles (10km)

**TOTAL ASCENT •** 1,509ft (460m)

**PATHS •** mountain paths, can be muddy and indistinct in places. Compass advised

**TERRAIN •** forest and rugged fellside

**GRADIENTS •** two steady climbs

**REFRESHMENTS •** none on the route. Newfield Arms, Seathwaite; Bower House Hotel, near Eskdale Green

**PARK •** Birks Bridge car park, near Birks

**OS MAP •** Outdoor Leisure 7 The English Lakes – South Eastern Area

# The Roman fort at Hardknott

❶ Cross the bridge over the River Duddon and immediately turn left along the waymarked bridleway which heads south before climbing through oak woods to Birks Farm. Once through the gate into the yard (caution – farm dogs), veer right on to a forestry road.

❷ Turn left at a T-junction of forestry roads, ignoring the bridleway signed to Harter Fell, the waymarked footpath to the right, and the two left forks. The track climbs steadily through the trees and rounds the southern flanks of Harter Fell before ending at a vehicle turning circle.

❸ Continue on a rocky bridleway traversing the west side of the fell for 500yds (457m) before leaving the forest through a gate. Stay close to Spothow Gill for ½ mile (800m) then swing right, cross a small gill and go through a gate to descend the bracken-clad slopes beneath Birker Fell's crags. Pass through another gate and cross Dodknott Gill to reach Jubilee Bridge, which spans Hardknott Gill.

❹ Climb out past a small car park to the Hardknott Pass road. Turn right here to climb paths that take short cuts between bends in the road. If you prefer, you can continue along the road but it can be very busy in summer.

❺ A footpath signpost (32in/81cm high) points the way left up the fellside to the fort at Hardknott. Continue on the faint path from the back of the fort towards the crags of Border End. Swing right short of the crags to emerge on the roadside just before the summit of Hardknott Pass.

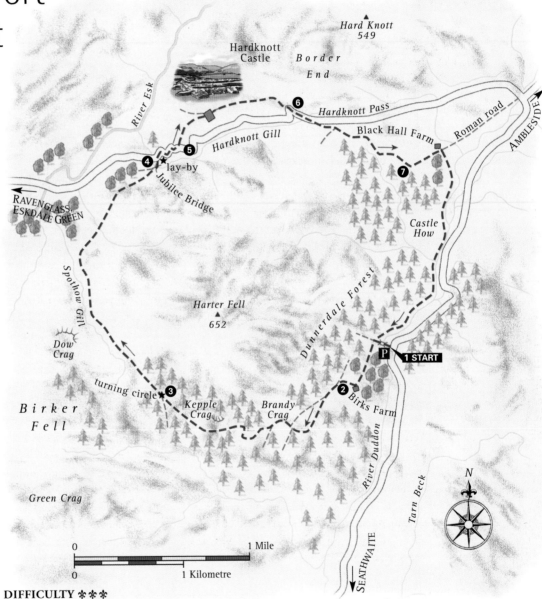

**DIFFICULTY ✤ ✤ ✤**

❻ Climb the short stretch of road before turning right on the bridleway, signed to Birks. At the highest point, the summit of Hardknott Pass, ignore the right turn, and descend south-eastwards down peaty slopes, keeping the spruce trees of Dunnerdale Forest on your right.

❼ At the foot of the slope go through a gate into a small enclosure, turn left over a step stile in the wall and through another gate, then continue on a grassy track towards Black Hall Farm. On reaching the farm, go over a stile, then turn right on a track heading towards the River Duddon. The well-defined track traverses rough pasture between the river bank and the forest to reach the bridge at the back of the car park.

**• DON'T MISS •**

*The Ravenglass and Eskdale steam-driven narrow-gauge railway, which runs from Ravenglass to Dalegarth, near Boot. Built as a 3ft (1m)-gauge line in 1875 to carry iron-ore, it was converted to the present 15in (38cm)-gauge in 1915, when the mine closed.*

**AD 324**

**AD 324** Constantinople is founded, the new imperial city of Rome.

**AD 325** Church doctrines are formalised.

**AD 367** Scots from Ireland, Picts from Scotland and Saxons and

**AD 367**

Franks from Nothern Europe attack Roman Britain, and the Emperor Valentinian dispatches Roman troops to restore order. However, the pressures of defending this far-flung northerly outpost of the empire become increasingly difficult.

**AD 410**

**AD 410** Rome, under attack itself by Alaric the Goth, is no longer able to afford to support its troops abroad, and they are rapidly withdrawn from Britain. The Roman Empire falls just 60 or so years later in AD 476.

# Imperial Style in the South Downs

*A glimpse of the high life of Roman Britain at the luxury villa of Bignor*

ROMAN

IMPERIAL OUTPOST

As you approach one of the greatest villa sites in England, you follow an evocative stretch of Stane Street, the Roman route between Chichester and London. This strikingly straight section runs along a pronounced man-made ridge, or agger. The road-builders surfaced this with flints, some of which can be seen protruding where rabbits have removed the turf.

You leave Stane Street for a breezy section along the South Downs Way, looking far north over the fertile lowlands of the Weald. It's an area scattered with Roman villa sites. Wealthy landowners chose sites as much for their views as for their good farmland, and both exist in abundance here.

At first sight Bignor Villa, lying just off the course of Stane Street, looks like a quaint group of thatched huts. These are the shelters erected over the Roman ruins in the early 19th century by John Hawkins, the farmer who turned the site into an early tourist attraction. The structures are period pieces in themselves, and are protected by listed building status.

In 1811 a ploughman called Joseph Tupper struck a chunk of masonry here – probably a Roman water-basin. Next to it, he uncovered a superb mosaic floor, depicting the legend of Ganymede's abduction by an eagle. Local landowner John Hawkins of Bignor Park called in the eminent antiquary Samuel Lysons, who spent the next eight years excavating the site.

Excavation proved that wealthy Roman-style country houses had existed in Britain. Previously, Roman Britain had been thought of as a barbaric frontier zone, where the only civilised life was in the cities. Not true – the owners of Bignor enjoyed the same luxuries, such as sauna-like baths and under-floor heating, as their counterparts did in Imperial Rome. Bignor's mosaic art, depicting scenes from the lives of gladiators and mythical subjects, would also have been familiar across the empire. Bignor is one of our largest villas, but there are many others with similar amenities across southern England.

The first known building at Bignor dates from about AD 190; the remains you see today are mainly 4th century, when successive extensions were added. These probably each housed a family, part of the extended family group of villa-owners. The residents would have shared the elaborate bath suite, meeting for baths and conversation every day. The room with the Medusa mosaic served as a heated changing room. After undressing, the bathers could have taken a cold plunge bath, or moved through the warm and hot rooms to the hot bath and then back again. Slaves would have kept a series of furnace rooms going from the outside.

Although they lived like Romans, Bignor's inhabitants are unlikely to have been Romans from Italy. The villa was the centre of a working farm, which would have prospered by supplying the nearby market at Chichester. Its owners were probably the descendants of Iron Age tribal leaders of Sussex, who had welcomed the Romans' arrival in AD 43.

It is easy to imagine the Romano-British people of Bignor appreciating a fine view and a hot bath, in much the same way as we do.

ABOVE: *Head of the Roman goddess of love, Venus, depicted in a floor-mosaic at Bignor.*

ABOVE: *A tour of Bignor reveals some intriguing Roman remains including a large bath suite – big enough for the whole family.*

LEFT: *View looking towards the South Downs high above Bignor Villa.*

## WALK 18 — ROMAN

**ABOUT • BIGNOR ROMAN VILLA**

*A stroll along a section of Roman road and the breezy South Downs leads you to Bignor Roman villa. The excavated remains at Bignor date from about the 4th century AD but suggest that the inhabitants enjoyed a lifestyle not so different from our own.*

## West Sussex • SE ENGLAND

**DISTANCE** • 8 miles (13km). Short walk omitting Stane Street 5½ miles (8.8km)

**TOTAL ASCENT** • 262ft (80m)

**PATHS** • clearly waymarked, defined tracks, quiet country lanes; some muddy sections

**TERRAIN** • woodland and downland

**GRADIENTS** • gentle to moderate, with one steady climb

**REFRESHMENTS** • White Horse pub, Sutton; tea room at Bignor Roman Villa. Picnic benches along Stane Street at Point 5 (in the woods) and Point 6 (in the open)

**PARK** • roadside parking near the White Horse pub, Sutton

**OS MAP** • Explorer 121 Arundel & Pulborough

# A slice of Roman life at Bignor

❶ Take the road left of the White Horse, signed Barlavington and Duncton. Beyond the edge of the village, bear left on to the road signed as a dead end, ignoring the right turn to Barlavington. After 250yds (229m), where the road bends left, bear right on to a bridleway. Continue and climb steadily up a wooded escarpment, ignoring a signed footpath, left.

❷ At staggered track junction at the top, continue ahead for 30yds (27m) then bear left following a blue waymark arrow up the hill and beyond the treeline towards two masts. At Bignor Hill NT sign fork left and in 50yds (46m) turn right. (For a shorter walk continue ahead, avoiding right turns, to the car park at Point ❼.)

❸ At a five-way junction (NT Slindon Estate sign, left), ignore South Downs Way (which crosses your path) and take next right turn on to a lesser path (fence on right, woodland on left). At next junction turn right towards forest.

❹ Soon after entering the forest, follow a blue waymark arrow left, downhill. The track is bordered on the left by an old boundary dyke. Follow the blue arrows.

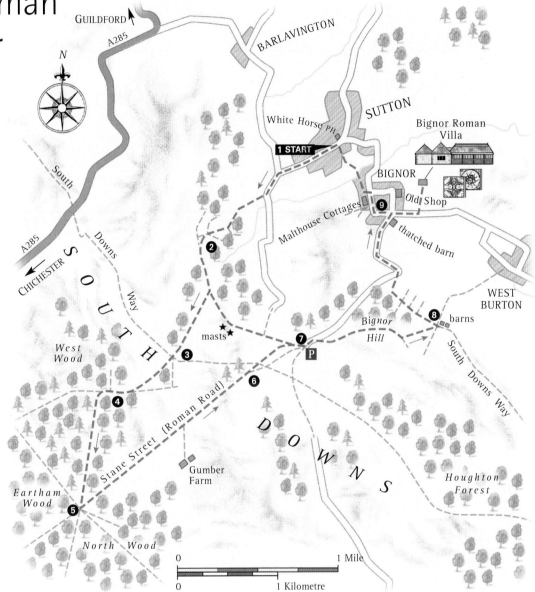

**DIFFICULTY** ✤ ✤

❺ At the bottom, at a seven-way junction by a bench, turn left, signed Bignor, along the ridge of Stane Street. Avoid side turns. Continue through a gate, across open land.

❻ By a bench, ½ mile (800m) after a NT sign on the right for Gumber Farm, avoid the gate ahead and take a stile up on your left behind a bench, cross the track and

continue along Stane Street. Keep forward at the junction on the South Downs Way (which joins from the left), turning right at the next signpost where the view opens out.

❼ At the car park (by a signpost with Roman names – *Londinium* etc), continue along the South Downs Way, which forks right on a track heading over the summit

of Bignor Hill. Continue on the South Downs Way, bearing left where signed.

❽ At a junction by barns, turn left on to a bridleway, heading slightly uphill through woods. Ignore side turns. The track levels, then descends. Turn right at a road T-junction, downhill. At T-junction by a thatched barn, turn left (go right for Bignor Roman Villa).

❾ After a right bend, take the second signed path on the left, just after Malthouse Cottages. Pass through the garden below the house, then alongside a stream on the left. Ignore the first footbridge. The path soon crosses footbridges and comes out into an open field. Continue up the field to a stile left of the nearest telegraph post. Cross the next field via an uncultivated strip to Sutton.

Post canis igitur magni caluda sed
constituta e. quá fabule poetarn intastra
mi          nerua que primu ea excogitasse
          muium fuerat hominib: pruu
          habet autem stellas
          mo mali in subcari

*The post-Roman era has been called the Dark Ages – though it was no intellectual desert. If there was a dark time, it was in the years of invasion, turbulence and change. The invaders themselves left no written records, but monks such as Gildas, Bede and Nennius chronicled the events of the period.*

## SAXONS AND VIKINGS

# Invasions & Saints

New masters replaced the Romans from 449, when German mercenaries – Saxons, Angles and Jutes – arrived at the invitation of a British leader, Vortigern. Their job was to help fend off foreign incursions, but instead they took the opportunity to establish their own rule in the south. Within 150 years much of the ex-Roman province was known as the Angles' Land – England. Meanwhile, the Britons continued to resist their invaders – commanded, according to legend, by King Arthur, who faced them in battle around the turn of the 6th century, culminating in the 12th and final battle on Mount Badon.

Religion was also about to undergo a profound change. In 565 a Celtic missionary monk, Columba, travelled to the Pictish lands in the north, and converted first their king, Bride, and then his people to Christianity. Pope Gregory, 30 years later, sent a missionary party to do the same for the English, and, under the protection of King Ethelbert, his man Augustine became the first Archbishop of Canterbury. In the 7th century churches sprang up across the country; landowners eager to secure their place in the afterlife provided land and funds for monasteries that soon accumulated huge wealth and influence. This was 'the age of saints'.

By now Britain was a patchwork of kingdoms, one of which, Mercia, set about swallowing up its neighbours by force and politics – particularly under its 8th-century king, Offa. His campaigns against the Welsh left an enduring legacy in Offa's Dyke, which still more or less marks the English-Welsh boundary.

Then, in 789, a lightning raid on the Dorset coast signalled the arrival of a new threat – the Vikings.

### THE NORSE CODE

For years the Vikings, or Norsemen, made sorties from Scandinavia to plunder the British coasts and their treasure-filled churches. After enduring several assaults, the monks on the Holy Island of Lindisfarne finally fled in 875, taking with them their beautifully illustrated Gospels. Gradually the Norsemen gained ground and established settlements – first in the north of Scotland, on Shetland and the Orkneys. But it didn't all go their way. Britain's inhabitants fought back, sometimes successfully – Viking leader Ragnor Lodbrook was captured and thrown into a snake-pit. His son, Ivar the Boneless, took his revenge by slaughtering the Northumbrians at York, and establishing Danish ascendancy in northern England.

Alfred, King of Wessex (the West Saxons), rallied his own people several times against the Danes. When not fighting the Danes, he bought their peace with gold – 'Danegeld'. In 886 Alfred's truce with the Danes divided England between Wessex, Mercia and the Danelaw – but this wasn't the end of the matter. Sporadic war continued between the Scandinavians and the Wessex kings, supported by the Welsh princes.

Danish attacks on the Picts wiped out their kingdom of Fortriu. In its place emerged Alba, kingdom of the Scots: their king, Constantine II, turned back the tide and held the Danes at bay for 50 years.

Life in Britain was unpredictable and sometimes violent. But that wasn't the whole picture. Scholarship, art and poetry flourished. New towns developed, law and administration regulated life, while the Saxons marked out an efficient system of shires and courts. Trade flourished and Britain was becoming affluent enough to attract the ambitious William of Normandy.

### HISTORIC SITES

**Glastonbury, Somerset:** 8th-century abbey and legendary resting-place of King Arthur.

**Wimborne Minster, Dorset:** founded in 705, looted by Vikings and refounded by Edward the Confessor in 1043.

**Burnsall, Yorkshire Dales:** Viking gravestones in St Wilfrid's churchyard.

**Ripon, North Yorkshire:** 7th-century cathedral crypt (England's oldest).

**Whitby Abbey, North Yorkshire:** setting of the Synod of Whitby in 664.

**St Laurence, Bradford-upon-Avon, Wiltshire:** rare intact Saxon church.

**449**

**449** Angles, Saxons and Jutes, led by Hengist and Horsa, land in Kent.

**500** Christianity starts to win converts throughout Ireland, Scotland and Wales as missionaries preach the gospels.

**563**

**563** St Columba lands on Iona and from here monks are sent out to establish missions on Lindisfarne and on the coast of Northumbria.

**570** The birth of Mohammed at Mecca brings the foundation of Islamic religion.

**597**

**597** St Augustine arrives in Britain from Rome, revives Christianity in the south, and founds a monastery on the site of Canterbury Cathedral.

SAXONS AND VIKINGS

# Celtic Mysteries at Tintagel

*A dramatic approach to the castle ruins, magnificently situated on the rugged north Cornish coast, where tales of King Arthur abound*

This route provides the best approach to Tintagel. The most popular way, which involves parking in the busy, commercialised village, is crowded; if you take the coast path from the south you fall upon the castle, missing out on stunning views of the island, which rises 250ft (76m) above sea level. The walk, starts in the deeply scored, craggily beautiful Rocky Valley (with St Nectan's Glen and waterfall a little upstream), before running along a particularly wild and lovely piece of the north Cornish coast, that instils a sense of drama, romance and mystery.

Most of the visible ruins date from the second quarter of the 13th century, there is evidence of Celtic occupation following a time of Roman military settlement. Small groups of Celts arrived in Cornwall during the 4th and 5th centuries from north-west Europe, and possibly from Ireland, and although it was once believed that there was a large 5th-century monastic community here, recent research suggests that it was more likely to have been the stronghold of a Celtic king in the 5th and 6th centuries. Its naturally defensive position was at

that time reinforced with a wall of stone, timber and earth across the neck of the island, which became known as Din Tagell. Cornwall was part of the kingdom of Dumnonia, and from the amount of pottery and glass fragments of Mediterranean origin discovered it is likely that someone of great importance lived at Tintagel. It was abandoned some time after the 8th century, and acquired in 1233 by Richard, Earl of Cornwall, who carried out a massive refortification, the substantial remnants of which are clearly seen as you approach the island.

There is also Celtic evidence at St Materiana's Church, set in splendid isolation on Glebe Cliff. Early slate-lined graves found here date from the 5th century, and indicate that this could have been a burial site for people of note – presumably from the castle. The 12th-century church is thought to have been built on the site of an oratory which had links with St Materiana's main shrine at Minster, a few miles east. She has been identified with St Madryn, a princess of Gwent, in South Wales, thought to have been active in this part of Cornwall around AD 500.

No visit to Tintagel is complete without a mention of King Arthur. Even The National Trust's plaque on Barras Nose has an evocative quote here by Alfred Lord Tennyson: 'Hard by was great Tintagel's table round, And there of old the flower of Arthur's knights, Made fair beginnings of a nobler time.'

This highly romanticised figure, most likely a warrior famed for his battles against Saxon invaders, became immortalised through the 12th-century works of Geoffrey of Monmouth. Everyone knows the stories of King Arthur and Guinevere, Merlin, Lancelot and the Knights of the Round Table. Tintagel has long been thought to be the birthplace of Arthur and, whether that's fact or fiction, it's not hard to believe when you stand on the cliffs overlooking Tintagel Haven and let yourself sink into the realms of fantasy – which, after all, is what Tintagel is all about.

ABOVE: *Generally associated with the legend of King Arthur, Tintagel was the more likely home of a Celtic King during the 5th–6th centuries. Not suprisingly modern Celts identify strongly with Tintagel as being an important part of their spiritual heritage*

LEFT: *An aerial view of Tintagel illustrates its superb position as a defensive settlement.*

BACKGROUND: *The legendary King Arthur and his knights, seated at the round table.*

**ABOUT • TINTAGEL**

*Steeped in Arthurian legend and lore, it's not surprising that Tintagel remains so popular. But this walk offers a different perpective on this famous landmark as it explores 'Din Tagell', part of the Dumnonia kingdom, the stronghold of a Celtic king.*

**Cornwall • SW ENGLAND**

**DISTANCE •** 4 miles (6.4km)

**TOTAL ASCENT •** 262ft (80m)

**PATHS •** undulating, sometimes rocky coast path; quiet lanes and fields, some muddy after wet weather

**TERRAIN •** rugged cliffs, coastal farmland

**GRADIENTS •** some steep ascents and descents on coast path

**REFRESHMENTS •** Castle Beach Café at the entrance to Tintagel (April to end October); pubs and cafés in Tintagel

**PARK •** lay-by on the right at the bottom of the hill on the B3263 Tintagel to Boscastle road, just past Willapark Manor Hotel

**OS MAP •** Explorer 111 Bude, Boscastle & Tintagel

# Tintagel's Celtic connection

❶ Cross the road and follow the sign to the coast path, which leads down a tarmac drive to pass Trout Leap restaurant and right over the stream on a railed footbridge. Follow the rocky path through the ruins of Trewethet Mill (Celtic Trust) and cross the stream to enter Rocky Valley (NT). By the next bridge keep straight on to join the coast path.

❷ The path veers left and continues up a long flight of steps to cross Bossiney Common above Benoath Cove, then drops steeply down concrete steps to a gritty track by Bossiney Haven.

❸ Walk straight on up concrete steps and over a stile, then down steps to cross the stream via a stile/wooden-railed footbridge and on to Willapark (NT). Follow the path up steps and through a wooden gate; keep straight ahead (herringbone wall, left) to reach the top. Turn right and walk to the end of the headland to enjoy the views ahead. Retrace your steps to the coast path.

❹ Continue right as the path undulates along Smith's Cliff, and through a kissing gate above Gullastem. The path leads on to Barras Nose (NT) via a stile and gate; follow the path to descend over craggy terrain to Tintagel Haven and the castle entrance via a footbridge over the stream.

❺ Turn left and walk inland past the English Heritage shop.

❻ Just past the toilets follow the coast path signs steeply right and uphill to pass another entrance to the castle, then left along Glebe

Cliff to reach St Materiana's Church. Turn left and follow the lane inland to Tintagel village.

❼ Turn left; follow the road to a sharp left bend, with Pendryn Guest House on the right. Go straight ahead on the track, signed to the coast path. Cross the stone stile and the next field, then cross a wooden stile and go straight on, keeping the wall on your right. Go

through the gate/stile and follow the wall round to the right to rejoin the coast path on Smith's Cliff. Retrace your steps to meet the gritty track by Bossiney Haven (Point 3).

❽ Turn right and walk inland to the edge of Bossiney via a kissing gate; toilets on the right. Cross the B3263; turn left and follow the pavement back to your car.

**DIFFICULTY** ✿ ✿

**• DON'T MISS •**

*The **cliffs south of Tintagel** were intensively quarried from the early 15th century for slate, leaving behind the remains of splitting-sheds and tramways. The sedimentary rock was used to build the slate stiles and herrringbone stone "hedges", seen along the coast path.*

0      ½ Mile

0      500 Metres

*Short Island*

*Long Island*

*The Sisters*

*Lye Rock*

*Willapark*

*Bossiney Haven*

*Benoath Cove*

*Rocky Valley*

*Trewethet Mill*

BOSCASTLE

B3263

**2**

*Barras Nose*

*Gullastem*

*Smith's Cliff*

**4**   **3**

**8**

*Bossiney Common*

**1 START**

*Tintagel Haven*

*Tintagel Head*

*chapel*

**5**

*shop*

**6**

*King Arthur's Castle*

*Willapark Manor Hotel*

P

TRETHEVEY

*St Nectan's Glen*

BOSSINEY

*Pendryn Guest House*

**7**

*Glebe Cliff*

*Dunderhole Point*

*St Materiana's Church*

TINTAGEL

TRENALE

*Penhallic Point*

*South West Coast Path*

*Trevillick Farm*

TREGATTA

N

*Hole Beach*

B3263

TREKNOW

*South West Coast Path*

**613**

**613** The Anglo Saxons, having driven away the Celts westwards, divide England into seven kingdoms: East Anglia, Kent, Sussex, Essex, Mercia, Wessex and Northumbria, which are known collectively as the Heptarchy.

**664**

**664** The Synod of Whitby opts to follow the doctrine of the Roman rather than the Celtic Church.

**731** The Venerable Bede, a monk at Jarrow monastery, writes his record of events, *An Ecclesiastical History of the English People*.

**757**

**757–96** Lead by Offa, Mercia extends its boundaries into North Wales and Bristol.

**779** Offa defeats the West Saxons and is recognised as the most powerful leader in England.

# Iona – Island of Saints and Kings

*History and myth combine to create a mystical atmosphere on the holy island of Iona*

The large, lug-sailed, Irish curragh approached landfall on the south coast of a small island off the west coast of Scotland. The year was 563 and in the boat were 13 men, banished from their native Ulster, seeking refuge on Iona. Their leader was an Irish prince, Columcille, or Columba, a warrior but also a holy man who had already founded a monastery at Durrow. For the remaining 34 years of his life he would devote himself to converting the heathen Picts to Christianity and establishing Iona as a leading European centre of learning and pilgrimage. When he died in 597 he had achieved his aims. Life continued peacefully for another two centuries until disaster struck in the shape of Viking raiders, marauding in their dragon-prowed longboats, sacking and pillaging their way throughout Britain and Ireland. The Norsemen knew that the religious houses provided rich pickings in gold and precious stones.

The Vikings first raided in 795 and the early monastery, constructed of wood, mud, wattle and thatch, was razed to the ground. The monks rebuilt the monastery but the Vikings came again in 798, 802 and 806 when, as well as burning the place, they murdered 68 monks at what is now Martyrs' Bay, just south of the ferry jetty.

The 986 annals of the monks record the murder of 15 monks and the abbot on the White Strand, in the north of the island. According to a 9th-century poem written by the German Benedictine monk, Walafrid Strabo, Dermait, the abbot of Iona, was abroad, leaving a monk called Blaithmac in temporary charge. He foresaw the raid and buried the treasures, including the shrine which contained St Columba's relics. As he was saying mass, the invaders arrived. They killed all the monks but offered to spare Blaithmac if he revealed where he had hidden the treasures. He refused and they hacked him to death before the altar. Whether this is a true story or not, it is documented that, after the raid of 825, the saint's relics and the illuminated manuscript now known as the Book of Kells were moved to Dunkeld in Scotland and Kells in Ireland.

It is hard to separate truth, legend and myth in Iona. The graveyard of Oran, Reilig Odhrain, is one of Scotland's most enduring myths. According to some 13th-century lists written in medieval Latin, the remains of 48 Scottish kings, including Macbeth and Duncan, lie buried in this tiny graveyard, along with four kings of Ireland and eight from Norway. Although widely believed, this has been dismissed by historians as a piece of propaganda by the monks of Iona. But the Reilig Odhrain does contain the grave of a man widely regarded in Scotland as a great leader. Politician John Smith was buried under a simple stone marker near the north-east corner of the enclosure in 1994.

ABOVE: *Saint Columba (521-597), a warrior, prince and later an abbot and missionary, who converted Scotland to Christianity.*

BELOW: *The sacred Iona Abbey and the graveyard of Oran, Reilig Odhrain, on Iona – according to legend, 48 Scottish kings are buried here.*

**ABOUT • IONA**

*Iona is still considered a sacred island and has long been associated with the spread of Christianity in Britain. In 563 St Columba landed on the island and founded a monastery. The monks deserted in 825 when the monastery suffered a series of savage Norse raids.*

**Strathclyde • SCOTLAND**

**DISTANCE** • 6 miles (9.6km)

**TOTAL ASCENT** • 140ft (43m)

**PATHS** • mostly good, even in bad weather

**TERRAIN** • made-up roads, farm tracks, hill paths, grass and beach

**GRADIENTS** • flat to moderate

**REFRESHMENTS** • in summer, restaurant and tea rooms in village

**PARK** • car park at the jetty on Fionnphort; ferry to Iona

**OS MAP** • Pathfinder 341 Iona & Bunessan

# The missionaries and myths of Iona

❶ After leaving the ferry, walk straight ahead, passing the Spar shop and the entrance to the nunnery. At the end of the road turn left, go through a gate and continue along a rough road until it reaches a collection of farm buildings.

❷ Turn left and follow a straight road until you reach a crossroads. Turn right and head west, along another straight road, towards the coast. Go through a metal gate, fork left and cross the machair (low lying land formed from sand and shell fragments) to the beach.

❸ Turn left and walk along the beach of a double bay then turn left and head across the machair until you reach a stony path. Turn right on to this and continue up hill until you reach a lochan.

❹ Take the left-hand path round the lochan. Follow it across a heather moor, past a series of mounds and downhill to the beach at St Columba's Bay, where Columba first landed in AD 563.

❺ Return by the same route but at the end of the stony path keep

**DIFFICULTY** ✿ ✿

**• DON'T MISS •**

*The neighbouring island of **Staffa** can be reached on a boat trip from Iona. From the landing spot you can walk along the top of the natural hexagonal basalt columns and enter Fingal's Cave, where the sound of the sea in the cave inspired Felix Mendelssohn to write Hebrides Overture.*

straight along the line of a fence and when it ends follow the faint track and a series of stone markers back to the road and the gate.

❻ Turn right through the gate and head east along the road. At the coast follow the road left to the village. Turn left at the jetty and right into the nunnery, exit by the far gate and follow the road to the

abbey. The abbey and nunnery, founded in 1203 by monks of the Benedictine order were only restored in the early twentieth century and the cell where St Columba slept excavated.

❼ Turn right through the gate into the graveyard. Note that only three of the tall crosses built here remain: the 9th-century St John's

Cross, 10th-century St Martin's Cross and 15th-century Maclean's Cross mark the remains of the eight Norwegian and many Scottish kings that were buried here, Follow the path anti-clockwise and exit by the far gate. Turn right into the abbey grounds. From here return to the road, turn left and follow it back to the village.

**780** The construction of Offa's Dyke begins to create a defensive border between Wales and England.

**789** The savage Viking raids, which were to continue for more than two centuries, begin along the English coast with a raid in Dorset.

**796** The death of the formidable Offa allows the overlord of Wessex to vie for supremacy with Mercia.

**800** The Christian community at Kells Monastery complete the superbly illustrated *Book of Kells*, now in Trinity College, Dublin.

**802–39** Ecgberht, King of Wessex, wins the allegiance of his neighbour kingdoms and in 825 defeats Mercia at the Battle of Ellandun. By 827 Ecgberht was considered the most powerful leader in England.

# Urien's Palace in Beautiful Llwyfenydd

*Chasing the shadows of a British warrior king in the Lyvennet Valley*

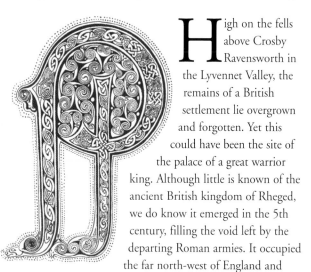

High on the fells above Crosby Ravensworth in the Lyvennet Valley, the remains of a British settlement lie overgrown and forgotten. Yet this could have been the site of the palace of a great warrior king. Although little is known of the ancient British kingdom of Rheged, we do know it emerged in the 5th century, filling the void left by the departing Roman armies. It occupied the far north-west of England and probably much of south-west Scotland too. Its inhabitants were Celts, speaking a language we know today as Welsh; and it is to the works of an ancient Welsh poet that we must look for documentary evidence of this so-called 'dark age'. The great poet Taliesin eulogised Rheged's greatest son, the mighty warrior King Urien:

*You are the best*
*for reason of your virtues,*
*Urien,*
*I praise your deeds.*

Taliesin's poetry tells of a golden age of British culture, when Gwyr y Gogledd, or 'The Men of the North', held off the advances from the Saxon kingdoms to the east. He was Urien's loyal bard and wove fine words around the King and his deeds. It is some of these that lead us to this remote village, at the head of the Lyvennet Valley. He wrote of the Urien's palace in 'Beautiful Llwyfenydd, by the fresh water'. It is quite feasible that 'Llwyfenydd' became modern Lyvennet and that the palace was one of the many British sites identified above Crosby Ravensworth. The largest site is Ewe Close, big enough in the 2nd century AD to warrant a deviation in the Roman road running north to the fort at Brougham. There isn't much to see today but a few bumps in a field to the left of the wall beyond Lane Head. Save your descent from High Haberwain for early evening and you'll see them better, brought out by the shadows, on the far side of the dale in front of you. The site at Ewe Locks is more tangible underfoot and was probably a farmstead. Here you can see the foundations of houses and barns, and appreciate the commanding position as the valley stretches away in front of you to the distant Pennines. Dipping back down to the Lyvennet Beck below Crosby Lodge, you'll pass other sites – up to your left on the promontory known as Cow Green, and up the bank from the ford at a site called Burwens. Perhaps these fit with Taliesin's description of Llwyfenydd, 'among the blossoms of Easter Time'.

Urien's reign coincided with a last flowering of Celtic culture in what was to become England. There seems little doubt that by the early 600s this golden age had passed. The warrior king was assassinated by one of his own lieutenants while laying siege to the Northumbrians at Lindisfarne, and the northern Britons were divided from their kinfolk in 'Wales' after the disastrous battle of Chester. Place-names point to an influx of English-speakers to Cumbria around this time. Some clues remain of the period of Celtic hegemony: Penrith, Penruddock, Blencathra, Glencoyne, Blencarn – the map still bears witness to a time when 'in the hall of the men of Rheged, there is every esteem and welcome'.

ABOVE: *Two actors from the Rheged Discovery Centre recreate the scene of Urien's time at Crosby Ravensworth.*

LEFT: *Anglo-Saxon illuminated letter from a 8th-century manuscript.*

RIGHT: *Footbridge over Lyvennet Beck, Crosby Ravensworth, Cumbria.*

### ABOUT • LYVENNET VALLEY

*This walk visits a series of sites including Ewe Close and Ewe Locks, part of the ancient kingdom of Urien, warrior king of Rheged. The Rheged Visitor Centre, on the edge of Penrith, celebrates the time of this old British kingdom and is well worth a visit.*

### Cumbria • N ENGLAND

**DISTANCE** • 6½ miles (10.4km)

**TOTAL ASCENT** • 720ft (219m)

**PATHS** • some unclear. Can be extremely muddy

**TERRAIN** • pastureland and open fell

**GRADIENTS** • some steep grassy slopes

**REFRESHMENTS** • The Butchers' Arms, Crosby Ravensworth

**PARK** • by the village hall in Crosby Ravensworth

**OS MAP** • Outdoor Leisure 19 Howgill Fells & Upper Eden Valley

# Valley of the kings

**DIFFICULTY ✳ ✳ ✳**

❶ Cross the bridge opposite village hall, turn right down left bank of beck. Turn left, signed Wickerslack, bear left between sheds, join track zigzagging up field beyond. At the top go ahead through a gate, cross field between telegraph poles. Over crown of the hill, aim for field corner nearest buildings. Cross stile and immediately another, walk diagonally across to a stile behind Crake Trees farm.

❷ Behind farm, turn left to a gate and a zigzag track up a field. The path is indistinct by remains of a stone enclosure. Follow its left-hand edge to a post and a thorn bush to your left. Cross ditch by the thorn and follow it to a wall. Turn right, wall on left, through two gates to a junction of tracks.

❸ Left through gate then right up road. In 100yds (91m) go left, pass a farm and down a lane, signed Haber. At the end, go through gate, bear right to a track. At the end, go through a gate into a field. Go half-left to bottom left-hand corner. Take right-hand gate, continue down the field; cut the corner at the bottom to go right, through gate. Bear left to Haber farm and go left of buildings. Turn left below cow sheds, go right through a gap in field boundary. Cross field and through a gap in wall. Turn left on to a muddy track, continue to the bottom.

❹ Turn right. Pass High Dalebanks. On grassy track follow signs to Oddendale (wall left). When track is enclosed by boulders, turn left to a bridge. Cross bridge and a stile, climb bank, bear right, between two humps. Walk to Slacks ruin. In farmyard bear right, through gate. Turn left to Lane Head. At top of farmyard (ruin) go through gate to open fell. Turn left, follow grassy track. In 100yds (91m) go right, to corner of wall on left. In 30yds (27m) beyond fence in field on left, the Roman road crosses your track. Beyond is Ewe Close.

❺ As track descends, carry on across fell (no footpath) for 200yds (183m) to Ewe Locks. Turn left downhill for ¾ mile (1.2km) on to track, Slack Randy. Turn right, by a boulder on to a good track.

❻ Right again through metal gate; double back across fellside. Follow path down to gate in left corner of field. Fence on right, pass through another gate. At crossroads of paths go left, to Lyvennet Beck.

❼ Ford beck (footbridge 200yds/ 183m upstream). Go through gate, turn left over a bridge to another gate. Ascend track to a gate. Turn left across field to a stile next to a gate, continue through three fields to Holme Bridge.

❽ Left over bridge then right over a footbridge into a field. At the far side, cross a stile and continue with beck on your right. Follow the path along the bottom of a steep bank, cross a stile and turn right over a ladder stile by a bridge. Turn left through a gate on to a lane, at the end turn left to village hall.

*Map labels: MAULDS MEABURN; Maulds Meaburn Moor; WICKERSLACK; Crake Trees ❷; Low Harberwain ❸; High Haberwain; stone circle; 1 START; village hall; The Butchers' Arms PH; CROSBY RAVENSWORTH; Haber ❹; Low Dalebanks; High Dalebanks; Ewe Close; ancient settlement; ODDENDALE; Lane Head (ruin); Slacks (ruin); stone circle; Ewe Locks ❺; ancient settlement; Slack Randy; Holme Bridge ❽; Lyvennet Beck ❻; ancient settlement; Cow Green ❼; Crosby Lodge; Bank Moor; Gaythorn Plain; Roman Road; Hazel Moor; Crosby Ravensworth Fell; JUNCTION 38, M6; APPLEBY-IN-WESTMORLAND; B6260; 0 1 Mile; 0 1 Kilometre; N*

**839**

**839** Aethelwulf accedes the throne on the death of Ecgberht.

**843** Kenneth McAlpin becomes king of all Scotland.

**865** The Danish army lands in East Anglia and begins its sweep

**865**

northwards, capturing York, before turning south and crushing every English kingdom except Wessex.

**871–99** Alfred's reign as king of Wessex. He embarks on a determined campaign to push back the invaders, ordering massive

**871**

warships, building fortresses and eventually driving the Danes from his territories.

**875** The monks of Lindisfarne, fleeing from the Danes, take the illuminated Lindisfarne Gospels, now in the British Museum.

# Offa's Impressive Frontier

*Follow part of Offa's Dyke, constructed by a Saxon king to define the boundary between England and Wales*

ABOVE: *Silver coin showing a portrait of King Offa (757–96), King of Mercia.*

Half of Llanymynech is in England and half in Wales – the Red Lion Hotel even has a bar in each country! This is an appropriate place, then, to begin exploring Offa's Dyke, the longest man-made border in medieval Europe. The foothills of the Welsh mountains have been a constant source of contention since pre-Roman times. Offa's Dyke was the first major attempt, by a powerful Saxon king, to define the border between England and Wales.

Offa (757–96) was king of Mercia, one of the seven original kingdoms of Anglo-Saxon England. However, by the end of Offa's reign, Mercia had effective control over four of the other kingdoms, so Offa may be considered the first king of a more or less united England. As such he was respected by the powerful rulers of Europe, including the Frankish king, Charlemagne. A number of innovations were introduced during Offa's reign, including the first widespread coin-based system of money in England since Roman times, facilitating trade both at home and abroad.

But Offa is mainly remembered for the dyke.

The Anglo-Saxon historian Asser, writing almost a century after its construction, states that King Offa ordered a dyke to be built between England and Wales, stretching 'from sea to sea'. The dyke takes the form of a ditch on the Welsh side and a rampart on the English side, and when built measured about 88ft (27m) wide and up to 26ft (8m) from the bottom of the ditch to the top of the bank. Although conceived as a whole, it is generally agreed that it would have been built in sections, with each local lord having responsibility for the completion of the section within his manor.

There has been much debate about its original purpose, but its lack of physical defences, and the fact that there are gaps along its length, makes it most likely that, unlike Hadrian's Wall, it was not defensive in intention. Rather, it served as a definition of the boundary between England and Wales, the result of negotiation with the Welsh princes.

Much of the dyke is still visible, and it more or less follows the line of the present-day border. The Offa's Dyke Path, one of a network of long-distance trails throughout Britain, was created in 1971. As you leave Llanymynech you join this path, and the walk later joins a stretch of the dyke in a magnificent, elevated position, with clear strategic advantages and wonderful views of the Tanat Valley in Wales. There are also panoramic views of the Shropshire plain from the path by the quarry at Llanymynech rocks.

Numerous sites of industrial archaeological interest along the route, although much later in date, give an indication of some of the mineral wealth of Wales which has made it of interest to the English over the centuries. The most spectacular of these is the former Llanymynech quarry, now a nature reserve. Another nature reserve you will pass through is Llynclys Common, a site of particular interest for its heath and grassland, and a haven of peace in the borderlands, which have seen their share of stormy times down the ages.

LEFT: *Offa's Dyke Path, near Chirk Castle, which still marks the rough boundary between England and Wales.*

ABOUT • OFFA'S DYKE

*In the 8th century Offa, King of Mercia ordered the construction of a dyke. It was to be both a physical border and emblematic of the division between Mercia and Welsh lands. This walk starts in Llanymynech, located in England and Wales.*

## Shropshire • C ENGLAND

**DISTANCE** • 6 miles (9.6km)

**TOTAL ASCENT** • 450ft (137m)

**PATHS** • clear paths, short section of road

**TERRAIN** • woodland, heathland, canal towpath

**GRADIENTS** • one steep ascent

**REFRESHMENTS** • tea rooms and pubs in Llanymynech

**PARK** • car park off B4398, behind Dolphin Inn and post office

**OS MAP** • Explorer 240 Oswestry, Chirk, Ellesmere & Pant

# From 'sea to sea' along Offa's Dyke

**DIFFICULTY ❀ ❀**

❶ At the far end of the car park, take the towpath east for 55yds (50m). Pass under the bridge, ascend steps to the A483, cross the road and walk north for 164yds (150m). Take the lane ahead signed Offa's Dyke Path (don't bear right).

❷ Just past The Coach House, take the right fork; 11yds (10m) beyond Peny Foel Cottages take the right fork. Go to the end of the tarmac (ignore Footpath 26 sign). Cross the stile that leads behind the end house, and in 109yds (100m) ascend steeply, left, signed Offa's Dyke Path. At the top turn left and cross the stile.

❸ At the quarry turn left and follow the Offa's Dyke Path signs carefully for 656yds (600m) round the foot of the rocks, until you reach a gate to the golf course. Follow the path to the left round the edge of the green.

❹ Follow Offa's Dyke Path in and out of the woods along the fourteenth hole. Beyond the green, at a waymarker, bear left and leave the golf course, without losing height, passing through scrub and woodland. In 437yds (400m) cross a stile into a coniferous plantation; 109yds (100m) beyond this, reach a redundant stile in a small gully. Do not follow Offa's Dyke Path left, but keep straight on ahead on a ridge to a stile beside a vegetable garden.

❺ Do not turn right to tarmac, but go straight ahead (waymarker in undergrowth), through woods. In 55yds (50m) keep left, hugging the escarpment edge. In 219yds (200m) take the kissing gate into

pasture. Continue, keeping the field boundary on your left, and ignore the second gate on the left in 11yds (10m).

❻ In 164yds (150m) pass through a bigger gate and go straight ahead along a track (fence rejoins in 98yds/90m). Go through another gate in 77yds (70m) and continue along a narrow muddy path, ignoring the left fork. In 273yds

(250m) reach a gravel track (building 33yds/30m ahead) and turn right.

❼ In 197yds (180m), where the track bends left to pass a dilapidated corrugated shed ahead, keep straight on up a muddy bridleway to a cream-painted stone-built cottage. Follow its access track for about 547yds (500m) to a T-junction at Green

Corner. Turn left and continue down the lane that becomes a road through a new estate, to the main road.

❽ Turn right on to the main road for about 200yds (183m); just after the 40mph sign turn left down Rhiw Revel Lane. Across the bridge turn left and left again on to the towpath. Follow the towpath back to Llanymynech.

# Through Viking York

*York's Jorvik Viking Centre recreates a 9th-century settlement whose winding streets are still walked today.*

BELOW: *Aerial view of the city of York and York Minster.*

INSET BELOW: *A Viking re-enactment group prepares for battle in York.*

## From Ivar the Boneless to Eric Bloodaxe

In 866 Danish invaders, led by Ivar the Boneless, sailed up the River Ouse and captured York. Since the Roman Legions had left in around 410, the city had been captured by the Anglians in 525, and become Christian when King Edwin was baptised in a new wooden church in 627. By the 9th century, York was a prominent centre of trade and learning – a rich prize for the Viking invaders. York became the capital of a Viking kingdom, with new streets, many more buildings – some several storeys high – and a thriving merchant class. Some of York's churches were founded, and the Minster rebuilt. The Jorvik Viking Centre, on the site of the major Coppergate archaeological excavation, vividly recreates life in Viking York. The Viking reign was brief, however. The last Viking king, Eric Bloodaxe, died at the Battle of Stainmore in 954, and the English King Athelstan ruled in York.

## In Viking footsteps

The Romans built a long, straight road from the

---

## WALK 23 — VIKING WAYS AND THE VITAL RIVER

❶ From the car park, turn right, then right again at the traffic-lights. Go through Micklegate Bar. Take the next right (Priory Street). At the end, turn left, pass the church, then turn right along Bishophill Senior. Opposite the Golden Ball pub, turn left down Carr's Lane. At the bottom, turn right along Skeldergate, keeping left at the fork. Go under Skeldergate Bridge. Continue along the river bank and cross the Millennium Bridge.

❷ Walk by the white gate and up Maple Grove to Fulford Road. Turn left towards city centre. Walk up Piccadilly between the Travelodge and medieval tower (Fishergate Postern). After the mini-roundabout, turn left along a glazed passage signed Castle Area, Jorvik Viking Centre. Go right, through glass doors, and into St Mary's Square. The Viking Centre is diagonally right.

❸ After your visit, continue from the square up the slope between the Viking Centre and Boots. At the top of the slope, turn right. At the traffic-lights, go straight on, and after the Marks and Spencer turn left up the Shambles. At the top, turn right. Go half-right across King's Square into Goodramgate. Where the road bends right, turn left and follow the road, between York Minster and St Michael-le-Belfrey Church. Continue ahead up High Petergate and through Bootham Bar.

❹ Cross at the lights and continue up Bootham. Turn left down Marygate by the circular tower. Just beyond the church, go left through the archway.

Continue ahead to leave the gardens by the lodge. Cross and continue ahead down Lendal, and straight on to the traffic-lights by St Michael's Church. Turn right, cross Ouse Bridge, go through two more sets of traffic-lights and up Micklegate. Pass through Micklegate Bar. Turn left back to the car park.

**Distance:** 5¼ miles (8.4km)

**Total ascent:** 75ft (23m)

**Paths:** city pavements

**Terrain:** historic city centre and riverside

**Gradients:** one climb, up Micklegate near the end of the walk

**Refreshments:** very wide selection in York city centre

**Park:** in pay-and-display car park in Nunnery Lane, off A1036

**OS Map:** Explorer 290 York, Selby & Tadcaster

**Difficulty:** ✱

south-west into the heart of York. Typically, the Vikings ignored it, forming their own, twisting path down to the river bank – Micklegate, the 'great street'. Irregular, diagonal routes served them best, linking their churches – such as Holy Trinity in Micklegate and St Mary Bishophill, both probably founded in late Viking times – and running alongside the River Ouse. It was the river that provided them with access to the sea, and along its banks and those of its tributary, the Foss, fish were landed, craftsmen made their wares and merchants set up their stalls.

The Coppergate excavations revealed the complex life of the densely packed Viking city. Nearby, the Danish kings had their palace; their quay beside Ouse Bridge, built out from the treacherous, muddy banks of the river, is still known as King's Staith. The bridge itself was originally a Viking structure of wood, and, except for ferries, was the only river crossing in the city

for a thousand years. Street names reflect their Viking origins: many end in 'gate' – *gata* is still the Scandinavian word for a street. Goodramgate was the street of Guthrum, one of the Viking kings, and Coney Street was the King's Street.

York's greatest church, the Minster, is near the site of the first wooden church. There was a 9th-century cemetery under the present south transept. A little way beyond the city walls, originally Roman and repaired and strengthened through the centuries, the northern Earls, who came to power at the end of the Viking period, built themselves a stronghold. Known as Earlsborough, it occupied a site between Bootham and Marygate. Linking Earlsborough to the heart of the city, the winding street, now successively Lendal, Coney Street and Spurriergate, brought the Viking inhabitants back to their wooden bridge and the foot of their new 'great street', Micklegate.

ABOVE: *Micklegate Bar leading to Micklegate built by the Vikings to be the 'great street' of the city of York.*

**878**

**878** Alfred defeats the Vikings. He is recognised as ruler of the south and overlord of the north.

**886** Alfred captures London and starts uniting the Anglo-Saxons under the Wessex dynasty, with the aim of becoming King of England.

**891**

**891–5** Monks complete the Anglo-Saxon chronicles and translate Bede's texts into Anglo-Saxon.

**899–925** Alfred's son, Edmund, wins other English lands, defeating the Danes and advancing into East Anglia, Essex and central England.

**925**

**925** The death of Edmund brings Aethelstan to power. He heads north and successfully beats back the fierce Viking leader Eric Bloodaxe, finally defeating him in 954.

ABOVE: *The Carpet Page of the Lichfield Gospels showing a highly illustrated cross.*

# Saxon Worship at Earls Barton

*A 10th-century church perched high above flood-meadows and abandoned gravel workings bordering the River Nene*

Christianity came to Britain with the Romans, but was soon displaced by pagan Germanic tribes, invading during the 5th century. However, the Church survived in Ireland and the west of Britain, and later, under the Northumbrian king, Oswald, Celtic Christianity began to spread through England. But another missionary force emerged, instigated by the monk Augustine. Sent by Pope Gregory to re-establish the Roman Church, he was equally successful in converting the pagan kingships of southern England. By the middle of the 7th century, the Roman traditions became accepted and the Church looked to the pope as its spiritual leader.

Monasteries and some churches were established during this early period, with distinct architectural styles reflecting the different traditions. In the south, the basilican plan was adopted, the nave separated from a small apsidal sanctuary by a high arch and often having transepts and a western porch. The Celtic style was much simpler, with only a narrow arch dividing the small chancel from the main body. Often of wood, few of these early buildings remain, but stability after 9th-century Viking raids encouraged a spate of church-building and a transition to stone. It is from this period that most Saxon survivals date.

At a time when most village buildings were of timber, wattle and daub, the builders brought faced stone blocks for the tower of Earls Barton's church along the River Nene from quarries at Barnack, near Peterborough. The use of stone emphasises the church's importance. But builders, inexperienced in working the new material, often translated the tried and tested techniques of carpentry. Door and window openings were narrow, usually capped with a lintel and, where arches were employed, they were round-headed, forming relatively narrow spans.

All Saints' Church, thought to date from around 970, has one of the finest and most complete Saxon towers still standing and bears many features characteristic of its period. (The church is open for services and on weekdays during the summer, and you are invited to look inside.) Rising in four stages, it probably also served as a look-out and defence and was apparently capped by a pyramid rather than the 15th-century battlements now evident. The dressed corner stones, quoins, alternately set on edge and laid laterally, are typical and known as 'long and short work', which with the vertical strips, pilasters, are reminiscent of timber frame construction. However, the pilasters here also serve a structural purpose, providing reinforcement to the rubble-built walls concealed beneath the rendering.

The upper arcading is particularly attractive, formed from semi-circular, solid lintels carried on rounded balusters. Other openings are capped by a simple two-stone abutment to form a triangular head – a primitive arch – and the small windows on the south face are splayed to maximise light entering the building.

Although the small high-roofed chancel, which originally extended east beneath the tower, has been lost in subsequent rebuilding and enlargement, each succeeding age has contributed to the evolution of the building and its place within the community.

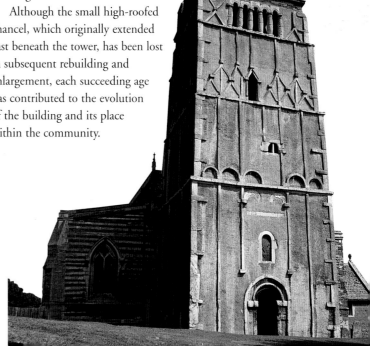

FAR LEFT: *St Guthlac being ordained by the Bishop Hedda.*

BELOW: *Earls Barton Church is one of the best examples of Saxon architecture.*

**ABOUT • EARLS BARTON**

*Earls Barton is one of the finest examples of Saxon architecture and building. Extensive church building in the 9th century marked the rise of Christianity in Britain and Earls Barton stands as testimony to the endurance of the church.*

## Northamptonshire • C ENGLAND

**DISTANCE** • 7½ miles (12km)

**TOTAL ASCENT** • 75m (246ft)

**PATHS** • outside the village the route follows good field paths (can be muddy) and well-surfaced tracks. Patches of nettles by the river

**TERRAIN** • open farmland

**REFRESHMENTS** • café in the village square, near the church

**PARK** • car park east of the village centre and street parking

**OS MAP** • Explorer 224 Corby, Kettering & Wellingborough

# The architects of Earls Barton

❶ Leave the churchyard by the western gate and walk out of the village along West Street to a main road. Turn left, continue for 100yds (91m) and pass through a kissing gate on the right.

❷ Walk down the field, passing a power line post to a stile at the bottom. Continue along the edge of the next field, leaving over a stream. Keep the same direction up the next field to a gap in the top hedge, and carry on along a path across two fields towards Ecton, which can eventually be seen ahead. In pasture, cross to a gate in the far right-hand corner and walk out on to the main street.

❸ Turn left, continue for ½ mile (800m) beyond Ecton and cross a road bridge. Immediately after, go left on to a track descending beside the main road and turn right on to a farm track across the fields. At the far end, continue ahead (on the right fork) along a fenced path. Ignore the crossing track ahead and continue over a branch of the Nene by a packhorse bridge into a flood meadow beyond. Another bridge by a sluice lock leads into a caravan site at Cogenhoe Mill.

❹ Carry on across more arteries of the river to pass the mill and then immediately turn left through a gate into a field, signed The Nene Way. A riverside path leads downstream, past Whiston Lock to a bridge, ¼ mile (400m) beyond. Cross the river and continue down to White Mills Lock, where the path emerges on to a lane.

❺ Walk right, cross the river by three bridges, then turn left into a picnic area. Follow a riverside track past a gravel works and then

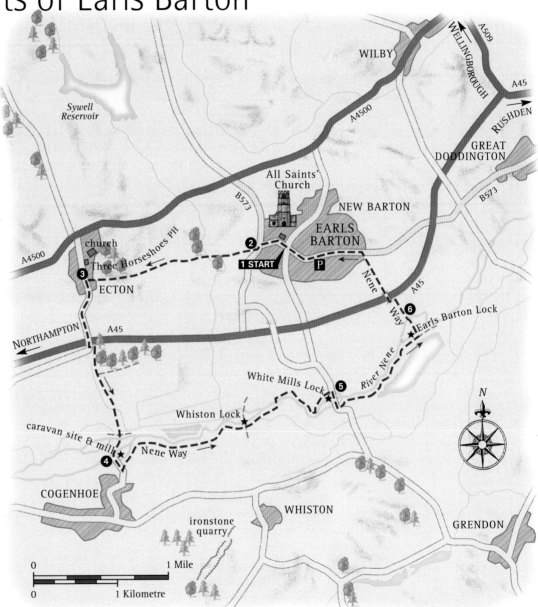

**DIFFICULTY ❀ ❀**

on beside a lake to reach Earls Barton Lock. Cross the river.

❻ Over the river, continue through a meadow, leaving by a stile by a mill cottage. From here a track climbs back up the hill and over the main road. Turn left at the top on to Doddington Road and return to Earls Barton.

**• DON'T MISS •**

*Ecton's church is another church worth a visit (keyholders are listed in the porch). As you walk through the village towards the church, note the the lovely mellow ironstone houses and the 18th-century village poor school, provided by John Palmer. Long before the Nene was improved by the installation of weirs and locks in the mid-18th century, it was an important transport route. Saxon builders brought the faced stone blocks for the tower of Earls Barton's church along it from quarries at Barnack located near Peterborough.*

**955**

**955** Eadred, great grandson of Alfred, reigns until his death in 959.

**959** Edgar becomes king. He is crowned in 973 by St Dunstan, Archbishop of Canterbury, undergoing the first 'coronation' style ceremony.

**975**

**975–78** The brief reign of Edward the Martyr ends in his murder on the orders of Aethelred, who succeeds him. In the same year, the Vikings begin another series of violent raids on English shores.

**979**

**979–1016** Aethelred II, the Unready, unable to defend England against the Vikings, attempts to bribe the invaders before ordering the massacre of all Danes in England. He is forced to flee to Normandy and is only restored briefly to the throne before his death in 1016.

# Llangorse – Seat of Kings

*The ancient base of the kings of Brycheiniog, surrounded by beautiful Llangorse Lake*

Nestling beneath the delightful Mynydd Llangorse (Llangorse mountain), and overlooked by the even shapelier Mynydd Troeg, is Llangorse Lake. This shallow, glacier-scoured expanse of water is a mini-mecca for watersports enthusiasts at midsummer weekends, and attracts its fair share of bird-watchers. Its shores are much-visited by migratory birds, and part of the Llangasty Nature Reserve, adjacent to the lake, is a protected area. Fishing is also a popular activity, as it always has been here – some of the oldest records pertaining to the lake commend its stock of fish.

Half a mile (800m) from the shore is the colourful village of Llangorse, consisting of little more than a sinuous road, a church, a chapel, a shop and sub-post office, and a couple of pubs. At its centre is the pretty church of Saint Paulinus, apparently standing on the site of a 6th-century building.

Aside from its natural charm, the most notable feature of Llangorse Lake is its crannog, or artificial island, the only known example in Wales. Its access causeway has long disappeared. Today it lies roughly 44 yds (40m) from the shore. There is precious little to see – to the uninformed and untrained eye its just a clump of reeds on a pile of stones, but it is rather more than that. The perimeter is made of pointed oak piles, hewn using a metal adze. It is thought to have supported several Iron Age dwellings on it: bones from many animals were found when it was excavated. In 1925 a dugout canoe, dated at around AD 800 was found close to the crannog; it is now kept in the Brecknock Museum in Brecon.

Brycheiniog was also raided by the Saxons from time to time but they did not settle in the region and when the Danes invaded parts of Wales from about AD 850, Brycheiniog did not escape their attentions. But the main significance of the crannog is that it is believed to have been the seat of the kings of Brycheiniog. King Brychan, probably of Irish descent, and father to 12 sons and 24 daughters, had a court at Talgarth, about 5 miles (8km) north of Llangorse. Brycheiniog means 'the land of Brychan'; its Anglicised forms are Brecknock and Brecon.

Several generations later, in 916, when the English king Edward's attention was focused on invading Danes, King Hwgan tried to expand his kingdom, but was defeated by forces directed by Ethelfleda, Edward's sister. Adding insult to injury, Ethelfleda pushed Hwgan further back, and is said to have stormed his castle at Llangorse, capturing his wife and several attendants. Given this, it is perhaps understandable that, according to local legend, the lake conceals an ancient city; its Welsh name, Llyn Syfaddan, means 'lake of the sunken island'.

The walk circumnavigates the lake, calling at Llangasty-Tal-y-llyn. Breaking up this name into its Welsh fragments, its translation is 'the church of St Gastyn at the end of the lake'. It then ascends the western side of Mynydd Llangorse; the rewards for this effort are higher meadows and woods with an almost Alpine look, memorable views of the lake and the striking profile of the central Brecon Beacons.

ABOVE: *The picturesque village church at Llangorse.*

BELOW: *Sunset from the summit of Mynydd Llangorse with views towards the lake, Pen-y-Fan and the Brecon Beacons National Park.*

### ABOUT • LLANGORSE LAKE

*The crannog (artificial island) in Llangorse Lake is thought to be the ancient seat of the kings of the kingdom of Brycheiniog. This walk circumnavigates the lake before an ascent offers stiking views of the lake and the Brecon Beacons.*

## Powys • WALES

**DISTANCE** • 8 miles (13km)

**TOTAL ASCENT** • 900ft (274m)

**PATHS** • good; slippery in places. Lakeside paths may be underwater after prolonged heavy rain in winter months

**TERRAIN** • tracks, field paths, stiles, tarmac roads; roots in forest

**GRADIENTS** • some steep sections

**REFRESHMENTS** • caravan park shop at start; pubs and a shop/post office in Llangorse village

**PARK** • car park beside public lavatories, between caravan park and sailing club

**OS MAP** • Outdoor Leisure 13 Brecon Beacons – Eastern Area

# Llangorse – 'lake of the sunken island'

**❶** Aim for a concrete footbridge, left of the caravan park on Llangorse Common. Go diagonally left, soon observe the crannog, cross more fields, circumnavigating the lake (partly fringed with woodland), to reach St Gastyn Church at Llangasty-Tal-y-llyn.

**❷** Turn right. After Llan (a house) take a waymarked footpath, left. Soon walk with the hedge on your right. Turn right, cross two fields diagonally, to a sunken lane, left of a farm. Turn right to a minor road.

**❸** Go left. Take the first left turn, signed Cathedine half a mile. Turn right, beside Rectory Cottage. Take stiles through three fields; cross the fourth field diagonally to the B4560 (fast road). Turn right for 55yds (50m). Take a rough track to the right of farm buildings.

**❹** Take a less distinct track (blue waymarker) before the ford, ascending along the left side of a lightly wooded stream. In an eroded gully find a gate up to the left. Follow this sunken lane until it peters out.

**❺** Turn left, above a fence and broken wall, then soon go through an old gate (blue waymarker) to pass a farmhouse ruin. Continue on a path, now through bracken, until 55yds (50m) before the track descends to a gate.

**❻** Turn sharp right, uphill, on a zigzagging green path. Turn left at a fence, then left again at fence corner. Descend to a converted barn. Continue to find a sheep track along field's left edge, go down to a gate among larches, beside overgrown, broken wall.

**❼** Walk through the forest, back into bracken. About 100yds (91m) beyond a stream crossing, descend beside a farm track. At the next gate cross the farm track, taking the line of greatest slope down the field to the riding and climbing centre below.

**❽** Turn right, then right again towards Cae-cottrel (farm). Take a stile on the left. Skirt this field to the left. Pass into the next field by a gap in the hedgerow (tiny stream), skirting left again, to farm buildings and a track.

**❾** Turn right, following the lanes to Llangorse village. At a blind corner, immediately before St Paulinus's churchyard, take a narrow signed footpath beside a house. Cross fields to return to the start of the walk.

### • DON'T MISS •

*St Gastyn Church at Llangasty-Tal-y-llyn is impressive for the simple beauty of its location and architecture (inside and out). The Brecknock Museum in Brecon is also worth a visit, as is Y Gaer (also called Brecon Gaer), about a mile (1.6km) from Brecon – a Roman fort, dated c. AD 80, and occupied well into the 4th century.*

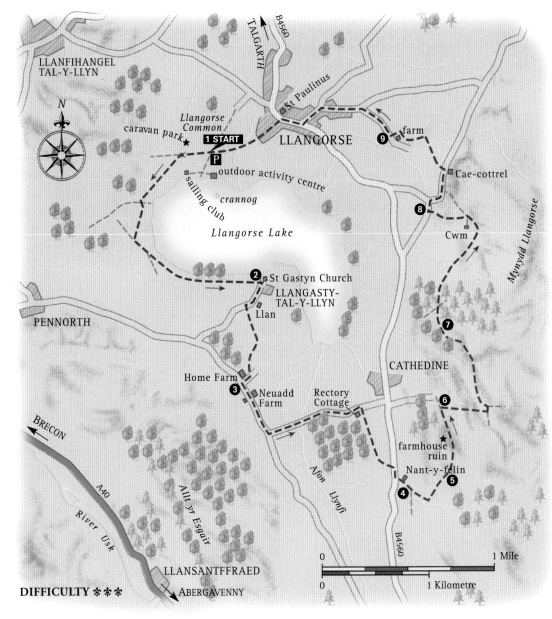

**DIFFICULTY ✱✱✱**

**1005**

**1005–34** Malcolm II of Scotland succeeds Kenneth III.

**1016** Ethelred dies. His son, Edmund Ironside, fights the Danish King Canute for the throne but is killed. Canute succeeds the throne as King of England.

**1016**

**1016–35** King Canute reigns. He modernises English laws and in 1017 divides England into four earldoms and marries Ethelred II's widow, Emma. He fulfils his promise 'to be a gracious lord'. England remains under Danish rule until 1066.

**1017**

**1031** Malcolm II of Scotland swears allegiance to King Canute.

**1034–1040** Duncan I rules Scotland.

**1040** Harthacanute accedes the English throne and declares himself King of Denmark and England.

SAXONS AND VIKINGS

INVASIONS & SAINTS

# Winchester – King Alfred's Capital

*Tranquil water meadows and a precious piece of chalk downland are just a short walk from the heart of Saxon Winchester*

The River Itchen makes for peaceful walking as it flows out of Winchester down towards Southampton. It was not so, however, in 860, when Norsemen sailed upriver to Winchester, capital of the Saxon kingdom of Wessex, and burned much of it to the ground. Norse raids had been going on for several decades and the Wessex that Alfred came to rule in 871 was in a desperate state.

By the time he died in 899, Alfred had restored peace, created a series of fortified towns, founded a navy, written a code of laws, established the exercise of justice and revived education. Winchester was an international centre of teaching and the arts.

Alfred was born in 849 with an appetite for learning. For a period he studied in Winchester with Bishop Swithun, later its patron saint. A few years after his coronation in Winchester in 871, Alfred secured the final defeat of the Norsemen, and in the period of peace that followed he returned to live in the capital. He reinforced the old Roman city walls, a small section of which you see on your walk. He laid out a grid system of streets around the old Roman High Street – the same system in use today. He founded a mint – some of its coins are in the City Museum. In Winchester, he wrote his *Laws*; with the help of scholars, he translated religious texts for his people; and he initiated the compilation of the *Anglo-Saxon Chronicles*.

There were three ecclesiastical communities in Saxon Winchester. Old Minster was built in the mid-7th century. Next to it, Alfred founded a new monastery, New Minster, but work was not complete when he died, and he was buried in Old Minster. It was his son, Edward the Elder, who saw the completion of New Minster, and Alfred was re-buried there. After Alfred's death, his wife, Ealswith, founded a Benedictine nunnery, Nunnaminster (later called St Mary's Abbey) on the site of the present-day Abbey Gardens. In about 980 Old Minster was rebuilt, only to be demolished a century later and replaced with the present cathedral. In 1109, the monks of New Minster, cramped by William the Conqueror's expansion of the adjacent royal palace, moved to a new, larger complex in Hyde, beyond the city walls, taking Alfred with them. In 1999, an excavation of the abbey church in the grounds of River Park Recreation Centre revealed three gravepits, believed to have held the remains of Alfred, his wife and their son. No part of the abbey complex survived the Dissolution in 1538.

Your route begins at Hamo Thornycroft's 1901 statue of Alfred, beside Abbey Gardens. From City Bridge, first built by St Swithun, follow the riverbank past a section of Roman wall and the high walls that surround the ruined medieval Wolvesey Palace, built on the site of the Saxon bishops' palace. Continue through the water meadows to St Catherine's Hill, renowned for its flora and fauna. On the summit, a mysterious miz-maze and views over the city will divert you before you drop back down to the water meadows. Return to the city past the Norman Hospital of St Cross. Back in town, visit the cathedral, whose treasures include the mortuary chests of Saxon kings and bishops. The foundations of Old Minster and New Minster can be seen next to the West Front. Nearby, the City Museum has excellent displays on Saxon Winchester.

ABOVE: *Statue of King Alfred (871–99) in the centre of Winchester.*

LEFT: *Aerial view of Winchester showing the ruins of Wolvesey Palace (also known as Wolvesey Castle) on the site of the Saxon Bishop's Palace.*

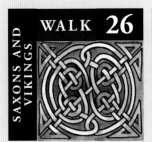
### ABOUT • WINCHESTER

*Even before the arrival of the Romans, Winchester was an important tribal centre, and under King Alfred's rule it became the capital of England. Winchester Cathedral was begun in 1079 and the library contains a 10th-century copy of Bede's history.*

## Hampshire • SE ENGLAND

**DISTANCE** • 6 miles (9.6km)

**TOTAL ASCENT** • 220ft (67m)

**PATHS** • well-marked throughout; some mud after rain on water meadow paths

**TERRAIN** • street pavements, downland, water meadows

**GRADIENTS** • flat, except for ascent and descent of St Catherine's Hill

**REFRESHMENTS** • wide choice in town

**PARK** • Chesil Street long-stay car park, or (Mon–Fri, 07.30–18.30, Sat 07.30–1800) Park-and-Ride from Bar End (signed from M3 Junctions 9 and 10) to King Alfred Statue, Broadway

**OS MAP** • Explorer 132 Winchester, New Alresford & East Meon

# Up the River Itchen to Saxon Winchester

**❶** At King Alfred's Statue look, as he does, up the High Street, with Abbey Gardens, site of the Nunnaminster, to the left. A few yards up the street, turn left into Abbey Passage to see the excavations of the abbey church. Return to the High Street and turn right. At City Bridge, opposite City Mill, turn right into The Weirs for the Riverside Walk (look out for the remains of a Roman wall). At a signpost, turn left over the River Itchen, then right to join a road for 100yds (91m). Cross at the corner into a private road.

**❷** In 50yds (46m), signed Itchen Way, turn right across the river. Continue through water meadows, with the river on your left, to a road bridge. Turn left over bridge, then right into a parking area.

**❸** With the river on your right, take the path for St Catherine's Hill under the railway bridge. Where the path divides, take the left fork. Follow the clear path to a crossing of paths at the summit. Turn right to the miz-maze.

**❹** Facing the maze at the point where you first reached it, turn right (the beech copse beyond the maze is now on your left). Walk to the edge of the hill for views of Winchester, right, and the Hospital of St Cross, left. Turn left and walk along the top of the hill, with the water meadows on your right. At a gap in the ramparts, take the long flight of wooden steps to the bottom of Plague Pits Valley.

**❺** Turn left on to the path by the Itchen Navigation. Go under the railway bridge and at a junction turn right, signed St Cross. Cross the Itchen, then turn right on to a farm road. The footpath continues ahead through a stile.

**❻** Continue straight ahead on the footpath past St Cross Hospital (detour left to visit). At the road, cross diagonally right and continue through the water meadows.

**❼** At Winchester College buildings, turn right, then left into College Walk. Turn left into College Street (keep ahead for Wolvesey Palace). At the end of College Street, turn right, go through Kingsgate, then right for the Close and cathedral.

**❽** With your back to the West Front and the site of Old and New Minsters, walk left of the war memorial, between trees, to the City Museum. Cross The Square for the High Street. Turn right for King Alfred's Statue.

---

### • DON'T MISS •

*Hyde Abbey Church*, King Alfred's final resting place. There is nothing to see, but the information panels in the 15th-century Hyde Gate (King Alfred Place) explain the abbey's layout. A self-guided walk is available from the Tourist Information Centre.

---

**Map labels:**

site of Hyde Abbey Church

FULLFLOOD

B3040

B3330

WINNALL

BASINGSTOKE

NEWBURY

M3

Winchester City Museum

**1 START** King Alfred Statue

City Mill

B3404

A31

❽ Winchester Cathedral

i

Wolvesey Castle

Abbey Gardens

P Chesil St

Winchester College ❼

❷

BAR END

water meadows

B3330

P park & ride

STANMORE

B3335

Junction 10

N

hospital

Itchen

❸ P

Itchen Navigation

ST CROSS

❻

water meadows

River

farm

❹ ★ Miz-maze

St Catherine's Hill

M3

A31

M3

❺ Plague Pits Valley

0          ½ Mile

0          500 Metres

A3090

Junction 11

A3090

SOUTHAMPTON

T w y f o r d    D o w n

**DIFFICULTY** ✳✳

**1042**

**1042** Edward 'the Confessor' reigns in England. He causes unrest by appointing lands and titles to Norman barons over their English counterparts.

**1052** Edward 'the Confessor' orders the construction of Westminster

**1057**

Abbey. Since 1066, all English monarchs except two have been crowned in the abbey.

**1057** Duncan's son, Malcolm, defeats and kills Macbeth in battle.

**1066**

**1066** The death of Edward 'the Confessor' leaves no heir and two ambitious men leap to claim the throne: William Duke of Normandy, who cites a long-standing promise of inheritance, and Harold Godwineson, who insists the dying king bequeathed the throne to him.

# King Alfred's Defence of Wessex

ABOVE: *Anglo-Saxon map, dated c. 950.*

*Exploring the Anglo-Saxon settlement of Burpham, from the age of the new towns*

Lying upstream from Arundel and placed just above the River Arun, Burpham at first sight looks like a typical, unspoilt Sussex village. But as you complete this walk you climb up on to an historical curio: a long, flat field, edged on all sides by a steeply dropping bank. It is obviously man-made, and the place-name, Burpham, gives a clue: 'burh' (or 'burgh'), meaning a fortified Anglo-Saxon settlement, and 'ham', denoting a homestead. 'Burh' occurs in dozens of other place-names, many now modified to 'bury' – Canterbury (the burh of the Cantware, or people of Kent), Malmesbury, Bury St Edmunds and Tewkesbury among them.

During the late Anglo-Saxon period, from the 9th to the 11th centuries, the first phase of town-building occurred since Roman times. The first Anglo-Saxon settlements to emerge as recognisable towns were trading and manufacturing centres on rivers and coast, such as Southampton. Archaeological digs at large burhs have revealed a great range of craft production: leather-working at Gloucester and Durham, wood-working at York, glass-making at Hereford and Lincoln, and pottery just about everywhere. By 1066 England had more than 100 towns, and a tenth of the population were town-dwellers.

In the 9th century King Alfred established 30 burhs along the boundaries of his kingdom of Wessex as a protection for his people against marauding Danes. He had probably got the idea from the similar defensive sites erected around the kingdom of Mercia – Hereford and Tamworth among them. The scheme was the largest programme of town-building in this era north of the Alps and,

conveniently for today's historians, Alfred's burhs were carefully listed in a document called the Burghal Hidage.

Some, including Winchester and Chichester, were re-occupied Roman walled towns, which had gone to seed after the last of the Roman militia departed in the 5th century. Others were planned new towns, surrounded by an earthen bank topped by a wooden palisade – among them Wareham and Oxford. Some new towns occupied promontories, such as Lewes, where you can still see the network of Anglo-Saxon twittens, or narrow lanes, leading at right angles downhill from the main street along the ridge. The central crossroads in such a town often doubled as the market place, and many of the larger burhs had their own mints for issuing coinage.

The Burghal Hidage also listed lesser settlements, including Burpham, which was more like a fortified village than a permanent administrative centre. Possibly already settled as far back as the Iron Age, it is a natural tongue of land which would have been surrounded on three sides by river marshes, easy to defend and in a good position to control access from the sea up the River Arun. Known locally as the Wall Field (or the War Field), the fort site looks across the valley to Arundel Castle.

Although Burpham ranked some way down in the list of burhs, its abandonment as nearby Arundel grew in importance has meant its survival as one of the most prominent earthworks of its kind. This walk gives you a feel for the rolling terrain over which the Anglo-Saxons kept watch.

ABOVE: *Looking back from the walk route towards Wedham Village.*

BELOW: *Arundel Castle, veiwed from above the River Arun.*

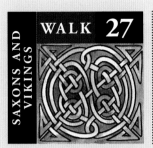

**ABOUT • BURPHAM**

*King Alfred established over 30 burhs, or settlements, along the boundary of the Kingdom of Wessex to protect his citizens from the plundering Danes. Set near the lovely Arundel Castle, this walk explores the fortified Anglo-Saxon settlement at Burpham.*

**West Sussex • SE ENGLAND**

**DISTANCE** • 5 miles (8km)

**TOTAL ASCENT** • 500ft (152m)

**PATHS** • clearly waymarked tracks and quiet lanes; some muddy sections

**TERRAIN** • chalk downland and forest; three stiles

**GRADIENTS** • gentle main ascent; shorter, steeper descent and ascent near end

**REFRESHMENTS** • George and Dragon, Burpham; picnic bench above River Arun

**PARK** • free car park by George and Dragon (not part of pub) at Burpham; plenty of roadside parking in village

**OS MAP** • Explorer 121 Arundel & Pulborough

# Burpham: Anglo-Saxon settlement

❶ Cross the road from the car park entrance and take the path into the churchyard. Keep right of the church, and by a signpost cross steps over the churchyard wall. Follow the right edge of the field. At a road, turn right, then keep forward downhill at the next road junction.

❷ Take the next left, Coombe Lane; this becomes unsurfaced by a house and a pumping station. On emerging into a field, fork right at a waymark post, on a rising path marked with a yellow arrow, and soon climb a stile. Turn left at a junction of tracks at the top.

❸ After the track curves round to the right, keep right at the first junction and turn left at the second. Take the next bridleway off to the right, through a gate and uphill. After passing through a belt of trees and a gate, the track veers slightly right, passing to the left of the trig point (summit pillar).

❹ Do not pass through the next gate just before a major track junction, but turn sharp right keeping in the field with the trig point, along the left edge of the field. Where the fence on your left reaches a corner, turn left along a row of trees as waymarked.

❺ Beyond the next gate enter a small field surrounded by trees and keep forward at a junction as signed, picking up a woodland track alongside a fence on your right. Avoid the next signed footpath on the right, and keep to the bridleway.

❻ Turn right at a five-way junction, then immediately fork right. Soon reach another signed junction of bridleways and keep forward downhill, on a sunken path. At the foot of the wooded slope turn left and left again.

❼ Where the main track is about to rise, fork right through a gate and follow the valley floor. Turn right at a signpost, up through a gate. Just after, keep forward to ascend steeply where main track bends left. The path leads along a wooded strip between fields.

❽ Emerge by a gate into a field, and keep forward to a gate into woodland. Follow the woodland path downhill and turn right along the road. In Wepham village, turn left at the road junction.

❾ Where the road bends right, take the signed path rising diagonally, on the left, up the bank of the Anglo-Saxon camp (or burh). Enter a recreation field via a stile, cross to the stile opposite (where a picnic bench just to the left gives a fine view of Arundel Castle and the river) and turn right to return to the car park.

**• DON'T MISS •**

*St Mary's Church in Burpham has two fine 12th-century Norman arches, one with a zig-zag decoration, the other with grotesque carvings of human and ape-like heads.*

**DIFFICULTY** ✤✤

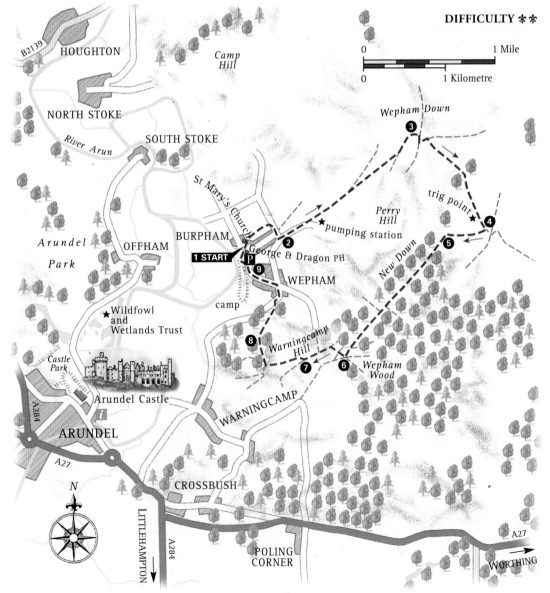

*Some time in the 1070s, Bishop Odo of Bayeux commissioned a tapestry to celebrate his half-brother William's victory at Hastings. The resulting medieval action adventure, with spies, chases and violence, is our most vivid account of the Norman Conquest.*

# THE NORMANS

## 1066–1300

# Era of Conquest

In the Bayeux Tapestry, the dying Edward the Confessor bequeaths his kingdom to William of Normandy; when Harold Godwineson takes the crown instead, William invades and kills his rival at the Battle of Hastings in 1066. Over subsequent years, William stamped out a succession of revolts, confiscating English lands and awarding them to his own men. The Normans were here to stay, and they brought with them new styles – the tapestry contrasts droopy-moustachioed Saxons with their shaven-headed enemies – and a new tongue, making Norman French the language of court and nobility. Among the most immediate effects of the invasion were the hundreds of stone castles that sprouted up across the country, and the massive cathedrals that were built in Durham, Chichester, Ely, Norwich and elsewhere, often on the sites of Anglo-Saxon cathedrals. The Scottish king, Malcolm III, had submitted to William at Abernethy in 1072, but continued to raid the Northumbrian territories; and the English-Welsh border or Marcher lands provided another flashpoint, where Norman lords were installed to make repeated inroads into Powys and Gwynedd. But by 1086 England, at least, was secure and William could survey his possessions in the Domesday Book.

## CRUSADES AND CONFLICT

The Norman dynasty held fast until another squabble over the crown turned into Civil War between William's grandson, Stephen, and cousin Matilda, wife of Geoffrey of Anjou. Matilda's son won the day, in 1154, for the Angevin cause, taking the crown as Henry II. His marriage to Eleanor of Aquitaine created a vast empire stretching from the Pyrenees to Scotland. Nevertheless, he is chiefly remembered for his long-running feud with Thomas Becket, Archbishop of Canterbury, whose insistence on clerical independence led to his brutal murder in the cathedral.

Richard the Lionheart, Henry's heir, spent most of his time fighting Turks in the Holy Land. Along with pilgrimages, crusades were the main mass events of the time: crowds flocked to answer the rallying calls of churchmen such as Giraldus Cambrensis, whose chronicles provide a colourful glimpse of 12th-century life. The crusaders brought back Oriental materials and fashions – women began wearing Mohammedan veils or wimples, hiding their faces, while still showing off their figures in tightly bodiced dresses.

Richard was succeeded by his brother John, whose bad press stems from the loss of his French lands and excessive cruelty to opponents. To keep the peace with his increasingly dissatisfied barons, John signed the Magna Carta in 1215, laying down the limitations of royal power and the rights of subjects.

By the 13th century Britain was an uneasy balancing act of feudal kingdoms and principalities, with the English king as overlord. This status was challenged in Wales by Llywelyn the Last, who refused to pay tribute to Edward I. Edward's response was rapid and devastating: his troops forged through Wales, leaving a ring of mighty fortresses. The principality was divided into English-style counties and the king's heir, Edward, was made their nominal prince.

In Scotland, Edward set about championing John Balliol, his candidate for the throne, in the face of opposition from Robert the Bruce. Although Edward's was successful in taking the Scottish 'stone of destiny' from Scone, the Scots were not beaten, and Britain entered the 14th century simmering with rebellions and resentments.

## HISTORIC SITES

**Oxford University, Oxon:** founded by French scholars in 1167.

**Cambridge University, Cambs:** founded by breakaway members of Oxford University in 1209.

**Lincoln, Lincs:** Norman-Gothic cathedral and the 12th-century Jew's House.

**Caernarfon, Gwynedd:** Edward I's imposing fortress.

**Windsor Castle, Berks:** built by William the Conqueror in 1070.

**Dunfermline:** ruins of 12th-century abbey founded by Malcolm III and palace where he married his queen, Margaret.

| 1066 | | 1067 | | 1072 | |
|---|---|---|---|---|---|

**1066** While William musters his troops, Harold Godwineson is pronounced king. Before long, hostile Norwegian forces land in Yorkshire but are defeated by Harold at Stamford Bridge. William lands in Pevensey and Harold hurries to resist invasion, but is

struck down in battle by an arrow through the eye, leaving William to be crowned king on Christmas day.

**1067–71** William spends the early years of his reign suppressing Saxon revolts in East Anglia, south-west and northern England.

**1072** William invades Scotland and demands that Malcolm III pay homage to him.

**1070** Building of Canterbury Cathedral begins after the original church is destroyed by fire.

# The Prince-Bishops' Durham Stronghold

*For more than 750 years the Bishops of Durham ruled as powerful overlords of the North from their stronghold above the River Wear*

For the Norman kings of England the very north of their country was for centuries troublesome and rebellious, harried by the Scots and full of intractable inhabitants. William I found this out when he sent the Earl of Northumberland to put down a rebellion in 1068. The Earl and 700 of his men were burned to death when the bishop's palace was torched by the rebels.

William came to wreak revenge, and appointed a new earl, Waltheof, as well as a new bishop, Walcher. Walcher paid the King the vast sum of £400 to succeed Waltheof, and became the first of the prince-bishops of Durham.

The bishops were already among the North's most powerful figures, as guardians of the relics of St Cuthbert. In AD 995 Cuthbert's bones came to rest in Durham after more than a century of being transported round the region by monks from Lindisfarne. As Cuthbert's spiritual successors, the new prince-bishops combined the two most powerful forces in the land – Church and State.

The prince-bishops acted as kings within their area – the Palatinate. They raised armies – the 13th-century Bishop Anthony Bek went into battle. They appointed judges, minted coins, imposed taxes, granted charters, created barons and claimed the rights over everything from coal mines to whales.

The bishops had 14 residences in the Palatinate. Durham Castle, set on the almost impregnable heights above the horseshoe loop of the River Wear, was the main base until 1832, when it was taken over by the new Durham University. Started by Waltheof in 1072, the castle retains its Norman core, including a Norman chapel and beautiful Norman gallery. The Black Staircase of 1662 leads from the medieval Great Hall to 18th-century state rooms. The massive keep was rebuilt in 1840.

From the castle the prince-bishops looked over to their other power-base, the cathedral. The present building was started in 1093, and its three solid

towers dominate the city. Inside, the huge columns of the nave support the earliest Gothic vaults in existence. St Cuthbert's grave is near the east end, and near by is the prince-bishop's throne – fittingly the most elevated in Britain. In the treasury, off the cloisters, are relics of St Cuthbert, including his cross and coffin, while the Galilee Chapel, at the cathedral's west end, holds the tomb of the first English historian, The Venerable Bede.

The prince-bishops built extensively for the city of Durham as well as for themselves. Framwelgate Bridge, on Silver Street, was built by Bishop Flambard at the beginning of the 12th century, and Elvet Bridge, leading to a new suburb of Elvet, by Bishop de Puiset about 1170.

The power of the prince-bishops survived throughout the Middle Ages. The Tudor monarchs managed to reduce their powers, and by the 17th century there were criticisms of their lordly lifestyle. It wasn't until 1836, however, on the death of Bishop Van Mildert, founder of the University, that their last rights went back to the Crown – after more than 750 years of regal power.

ABOVE: *St Cuthbert was finally laid to rest at Durham Cathedral, giving the prince-bishops power as the spiritual guardians of the bones.*

BELOW: *Durham Cathedral sited above the River Wear.*

**ABOUT •**

*Above the River Wear sit the imposing cathedral and castle – once the centre of power of the prince-bishops. In the 11th century William I conferred wide-ranging powers on the bishopric – effectively making them kings of the north.*

## Durham • N ENGLAND

**DISTANCE •** 1½ miles (2.4km)

**TOTAL ASCENT •** 300ft (91m)

**PATHS •** city pavements and riverside paths

**TERRAIN •** fortress rock with castle and cathedral, and ravine of the River Wear

**GRADIENTS •** moderate climbs from Market Place to Palace Green and from river bank to St Oswald's Church; otherwise easy

**REFRESHMENTS •** available throughout the centre of Durham, including on Palace Green and in the cathedral

**PARK •** city centre car parks in Durham, the Prince Bishop car park is the most convenient

**OS MAP •** Explorer 308 Durham & Sunderland, Chester-le-Street

# The mighty prince-bishops, overlords of the North

**❶** From the statue of Lord Londonderry in the Market Place, follow his horse's nose to pass the Nationwide building society and go up Saddler Street. Ascend the hill for 164yds (150m) and turn right up Owengate, signed Cathedral and Castle, and on to Palace Green.

**❷** At the top of the hill, turn right, to follow the wall for 55yds (50m) to the entrance of the castle. After visiting the castle return to the entrance and keep ahead to enter the cathedral by the north door.

**❸** After your visit, leave by the door opposite the one you entered by. Walk ahead down the cloisters. The treasury is to the right at the

*In the cathedral treasury is the 13th-century **Conyers Falchion**, a fearsome knife, that represents the defence of the bishopric. It is still presented, as for centuries past, to each new Bishop of Durham at the bridge over the River Tees at Croft, as he first enters the Palatinate officially.*

end. After visiting, continue around the cloisters and go right, signed Norman Undercroft Exhibition, into an irregular square, The College.

**❹** Follow the wall on your left until you reach the arch. Go through the arch and turn right on to South Bailey. Descend slightly for 273yds (250m) to Prebends Bridge. Do not cross, but turn right along the lower riverside path.

**❺** Follow the path for 328yds (300m) passing the Old Fulling Mill Museum of Archaeology. Continue ahead for another 328yds (300m) and ascend a slope then steps up on to Silver Street. Turn left and cross Framwellgate Bridge. Over the bridge, turn left down steps by the Coach and Eight pub to the banks of the River Wear.

**❻** Go straight ahead, passing behind the riverside buildings to reach the end of Prebends Bridge. Do not cross, but continue beside the river for 600yds (656m) until the path ascends into St Oswald's churchyard. Go through the churchyard on to Church Street and turn left.

**❼** At the traffic lights continue on the main road – New Elvet. At the next crossroads turn left over Elvet Bridge and ascend the slope at the end. Turn right, back to the Market Place.

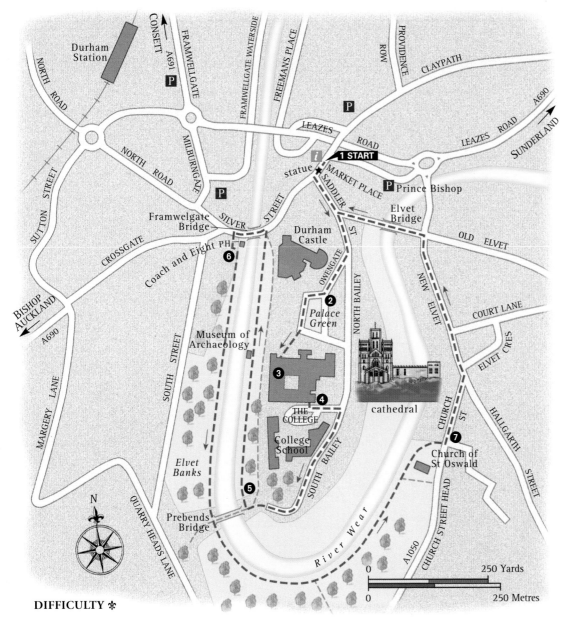

**DIFFICULTY ✱**

1066–1300

**1078**

**1078** Construction of the White Tower in London begins, and takes about 20 years to complete.

**1079** The foundations of Winchester Cathedral are laid, and the New Forest is designated a royal hunting area.

**1086**

**1086–87** William sets out to profit from his hard work and commissions the Domesday Book to survey all taxable lands and their owners.

**1087** William falls from his horse in France, and dies from his injuries. He is buried in Caen.

**1087**

**1087–1100** William II, a reputed tyrant and younger son of William I, takes the throne but is killed while hunting in the New Forest. There is speculation about whether his death was accidental or murder. The place where he fell is marked by the Rufus stone.

78

# The Castle and Priory-builder of Lewes

*A legacy of conquest and a symbol of Norman power on the Sussex coast*

**THE NORMANS**

**ERA OF CONQUEST**

Within two years of William the Conqueror's victory at the Battle of Hastings in 1066, his brother-in-law William de Warenne put Lewes firmly on the Norman map, constructing Lewes Castle at the highest point within the town. It perches dramatically on an artificial mound that, like the nearby Brack Mount, may well be of pre-Norman or even prehistoric origin.

From the top of the keep the view extends southwards to a notch in the coastline at Newhaven, and inland over the Weald; but the chalk hills block the view eastwards. Archaeologists now believe that the Normans established an outpost of the castle on Mount Caburn, high up on the South Downs: it is an obvious strategic lookout eastwards towards the coast around Eastbourne, and it would have been possible to signal from there to Lewes Castle to warn of impending trouble. What you see at Mount Caburn is earlier in date: the inner ramparts are Iron Age and the bolder outer ones Saxon, but excavations have revealed Norman pottery sherds.

Beyond the two castle arches over Castle Gate, the elaborate barbican is post-Norman, but the simpler second arch is original. At a viewpoint by the railings you look over a valley to chalk cliffs, to the left of which is the site of the Battle of Lewes, where in 1262 a group of barons led by Simon de Montfort defeated the inept Henry III. Their victory on the battlefield was a milestone on the road to parliamentary government, as Henry was forced by his defeat to sign a treaty limiting the powers of monarchy.

The Normans strengthened the town's Saxon fortifications. The quaint alley Pipe Passage leads along a section of the town wall, which you can see from below in adjacent Westgate, named after one of the now vanished town gateways. Another stretch of town wall is evident along Southover Road, near the bottom of Keere Street.

In the Southover district of Lewes William de Warenne and his wife Gundrada also founded a Cluniac priory (for French monks from Cluny) dedicated to St Pancras. It was blown up during Henry VIII's dissolution of the monasteries in 1538, leaving a picturesque ruin, and the construction of the Lewes–Brighton railway line in 1845 destroyed much that remained. Today the most prominent relic is the dormitory block, with 40 latrines – about one for each monk. Priory tours are given in summer from the nearby Anne of Cleves House, a museum of local history within a striking timber-frame house.

Much of the priory's Caen limestone, brought over from Normandy, was taken by the townsfolk, and chunks of columns and masonry are seen in the numerous and varied boundary walls. Most spectacular is Southover Grange, an Elizabethan house built entirely of priory stone; within the garden (now a public park) some masonry has been used to create fanciful arches. Southover's Church of St John the Baptist probably originated as a reception chapel for priory visitors and townsfolk. On its left side is the only surviving priory gateway. Inside the church, to the right of the organ, a side chapel displays the ornate tomb slab of William and Gundrada, and the lead caskets containing their bones.

**BACKGROUND:** *Built in 1070, Lewes Castle has two mottes, one at each end of the bailey.*

**LEFT:** *St Pancras Priory in the Southover District of Lewes, a Cluniac monastery founded by William de Warenne and his wife, Gundrada.*

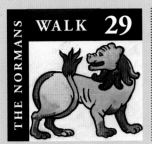

**ABOUT • LEWES**

*Lewes has a long and rich history. Shortly after the Battle of Hastings William de Warenne, brother to William I, built Lewes Castle. Close by is the Battle of Lewes site where Simon de Montfort's victory over Henry III eventually led to the first parliament.*

## East Sussex • SE ENGLAND

**DISTANCE** • 7½ miles (12km)

**TOTAL ASCENT** • 900ft (274m)

**PATHS** • waymarked paths and defined tracks; sheep runs can be muddy

**TERRAIN** • town and downland

**GRADIENTS** • an initial steep ascent, two gentler climbs later

**REFRESHMENTS** • plenty of pubs, cafés and restaurants in Lewes

**PARK** • Lewes rail station car park or pay-and-display car park on the other side of the rail line

**OS MAP** • Explorer 122 South Downs Way – Steyning to Newhaven

# Lewes – town of the conquerors

❶ Leave the station car park by the way you entered. Turn right at immediate junction by the White Star Inn, then left before All Saints Centre (former church), up Church Twitten. At the top, turn right, down the High Street. Go forward at the traffic-lights through the precinct to the far end of town.

❷ Go forward at the road junction, up Chapel Hill (width restriction sign). Climb steeply and after a stone seat on your left and before a golf course sign, turn left. Before a gate with Cuilfail Estate sign, turn right, up the path. Emerge on to the golf course, go forward to tallest post (yellow arrow and 'take care' sign), with a memorial obelisk on the left, and continue ascending gently following posts.

❸ At far end of golf course, avoid descending but take a stile into pasture, over another stile and continue to a stile on the skyline where the view opens out ahead. Go forward towards trees as waymarked, to go down a track with a fence and woods on left.

❹ At the bottom, by a large concrete-based pond (usually dry), do not go through the gate but turn right, uphill (licensed path to Mount Caburn, landowner allows public use). Avoid two forks to the right, to follow a wide grassy path to view Mount Caburn that is soon joined by a fence on the left and head towards to the mound.

❺ Reach the gate and sign for Mount Caburn National Nature Reserve. Walk around the ramparts or climb the mound for a magnificent view and return to the

**DIFFICULTY** ✿✿

gate. Retrace 200yds (183m), then left over the stile and follow path downhill. At the bottom, cross a stile and follow the valley floor.

❻ Pass to the left of the concrete-based pond, cross two waymarked stiles (may be muddy) and in 75yds (70m) go diagonally right, up past marker post. Continue uphill to the golf course car park and turn left on the road to descend into Lewes.

Follow main route back through town and up the High Street.

❼ Beyond the war memorial and traffic lights, turn right into Castle Gate, passing under two castle archways. Go left at the viewpoint by the railings, down Castle Lane. At New Road, take steps up on the left (Pipe Passage). Turn right on High Street, then left down cobbled Keere Street (quite steep).

❽ Go forward at the road junction at the bottom (pass Southover Grange and gardens on the left), and right along Southover High Street. Turn left after the church into Cockshut Road. Turn left after the rail bridge on the path past the priory ruins and Battle of Lewes Memorial, left around the sports field and left on the path past the mound to road. Turn left, then right to the station car park.

**1100**

**1100–35** The reign of Henry I. Before his death Henry I promises the Crown to his daughter Maltida. However, she and her husband, Geoffrey of Anjou, are disliked by the English barons and quarrel with the king, and on his deathbed Henry names Stephen de Blois as heir.

**1135**

**1135** To Matilda's fury, Stephen of Blois, her cousin, is crowned.

**1139** Matilda lands at Wareham to claim her inheritance. There is conflict for the next nine years as the two sovereigns claim rightful succession to the throne.

**1148**

**1148** Unable to rally support, Matilda at last leaves Britain.

**1154** Stephen dies and is buried at the Cluniac monastery in Faversham, Kent.

# The Conqueror's New Forest

*Discover the real magic of the New Forest, with its air of tranquillity and sense of timelessness*

ABOVE: *A penny coin depicting the portrait of William I, the Conqueror, of England 1066-87.*

**THE NORMANS**

**ERA OF CONQUEST**

Exploring the New Forest today, with its tourist attractions and regular influx of visitors, it seems hard to believe that it all began in the reign of William the Conqueror, when the King seized upon the idea of establishing a deer park here, as it was so close to his capital at Winchester. Associated with dark legends and romantic stories, the New Forest is the largest remaining medieval forest in western Europe, its vast, wooded landscape covering more than 90,000 acres (82,296ha).

It was over 900 years ago, in 1079, that William declared the wilderness of Ytene, named after the Jutes who settled here in the early part of the 5th century, to be his own exclusive hunting ground – his *Nova Foresta*. The name 'forest' means 'royal hunting ground', as opposed to a chase, which is a nobleman's hunting ground. At that time, this entire area consisted mainly of heath and woodland, extending from the coast to the Wiltshire border and from Southampton west to the Avon Valley and beyond.

William decreed that the land within these boundaries should be afforested and therefore subject to the tough Norman forest law. The red deer were to roam undisturbed to provide sport for a monarch who greatly enjoyed hunting, and no other man could hunt within the forest or enclose any part of the land. William ruled that any property standing in the path of the new park should be destroyed. Not surprisingly, his decision to create a royal preserve in this corner of southern England was not greeted warmly by all his subjects. The Saxons were left in no doubt that William was in control: his strict code of law showed that he meant business. The New Forest remains a royal property to this day.

If William the Conqueror rode his horse through the New Forest today, he would see many changes. Yet he would

probably conclude that, in essence, the place remains the same, its character, atmosphere and identity intact. He would be surprised to find herds of fallow deer instead of red, and he might be puzzled by the absence of wolves and wild boar. The pine trees would catch his eye, too, for they were introduced in large numbers around the middle of the 19th century. His journey on horseback would no longer

be unrestricted. Forest settlements have evolved and expanded over the years and farms have encroached upon the boundaries. However, the New Forest still offers more than 140 square miles (356sq km) of woodland and heath to enjoy, and its popularity as a vast recreational resource is confirmed by the hordes of visitors – between 7 and 8 million of them – who descend upon it every year.

The region is managed by the Forestry Commission, and benefits from an impressive network of paths and tracks. Beginning in the bustling village of Brockenhurst – the name means 'the badger's wood' – the walk heads for peaceful woodland glades, trickling streams and heathery expanses. Here, in this secret, silent world, the New Forest casts its spell.

ABOVE: *The wooded depths of the New Forest, near Brockenhurst, are home to a host of flora and fauna including herds of shy New Forest deer.*

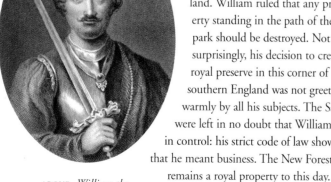

ABOVE: *William the Conqueror established the New Forest as a royal hunting ground in 1079.*

**ABOUT • THE NEW FOREST**

*From Brockenhurst explore the once-exclusive royal hunting preserve of William the Conqueror. Established by William in 1079, the New Forest is still a magical place and the natural habitat for a wide variety of flora and fauna.*

### Hampshire • SE ENGLAND

**DISTANCE** • 6 miles (9.6km)

**TOTAL ASCENT** • 33ft (10m)

**PATHS** • paths and tracks, well-defined in places. Can be wet in winter

**TERRAIN** • village streets, heath and woodland. Keep dogs on leads at all times

**GRADIENTS** • one very gentle climb

**REFRESHMENTS** • Brockenhurst has a choice of inns and hotels

**PARK** • free car park in Brookley Road, Brockenhurst

**OS MAP** • Outdoor Leisure 22 New Forest

# The New Forest: king among deer parks

❶ From the car park turn right and follow Brookley Road to the Watersplash, a local landmark. Bear right and pass railings. On the right are the entrances to Overbrook and Brocket Green, beyond them take a kissing gate by the entrance to Brookway and join a footpath alongside a stream.

❷ Pass a row of houses and gardens. Go through two kissing gates and turn left at the next road. Follow Butts Lawn and head for the next junction by a telephone box. Bear left for a few paces, then swing right on a track signed access to allotments.

❸ Approaching the allotments, veer a little to the right, continuing across heathland known as Black Knowl, keeping woodland to your right. Continue between gorse bushes and at a clear path, turn right towards trees. When the path ends, keep left to a wide track, turn right and head for Bolderford Bridge.

❹ Cross the bridge and swing left in front of the gate by the sign for Lyndhurst. Keep right at the fork and follow the path to cross a footbridge, keeping the fence close to your right-hand side.

❺ Turn left at the next junction, by a bridge. Follow the track across open heath to a gate by silver birch trees. Continue for several hundred yards, turn sharp left at the junction. Follow the grassy track by pine trees to a stile.

❻ Head diagonally right, following the clear path through the heather, towards an opening in the trees. Cross the river at the bridge with wooden handrails. Continue ahead using small footbridge (no handrails) then swing right towards Aldridgehill Cottage.

❼ Keep the cottage on your right and follow the drive for 50yds (46m). Take the left fork and follow the woodland path down to the footbridge over Ober Water. Continue ahead following the path up the gentle slope to a bend in the road. Go straight on alongside a car park to the next junction.

❽ Turn right, then left by Ober Lodge. Follow the track towards the Burley road. As you approach it, veer left to a parallel track which joins the road. Continue along the path parallel to the road. Make for Brookley Road on the right and return to the car park.

**• DON'T MISS •**

*Brockenhurst's **Church of St Saviours**, originally built as a private chapel for nearby Rhinefield House in 1905. Look out for **mink** – animal rights protesters released a number of these rarely seen animals from a New Forest mink farm in the late 1990s. Mink are most commonly seen by water, so keep a sharp eye out on the riverside sections.*

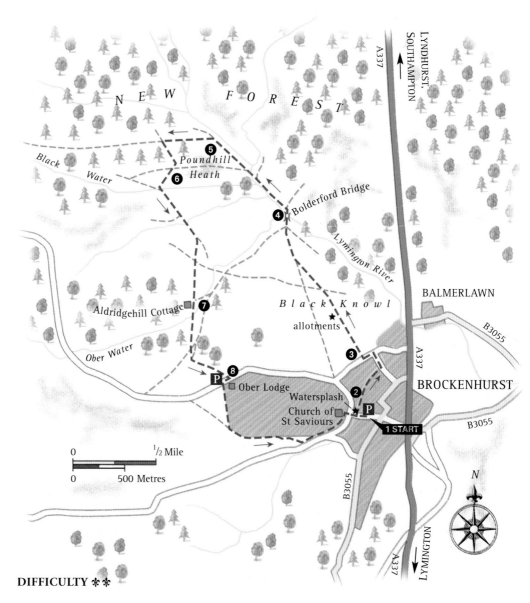

**DIFFICULTY** ❀ ❀

**1154**

**1154–89** The reign of Henry II. He appoints his adviser Thomas Becket as Chancellor of England and then to the powerful position of Archbishop of Canterbury, hoping for an ally within the Church. Becket proves unexpectedly to wish to serve only the Church.

**1164**

**1164** Henry limits the Church's power of jurisdiction over the clergy and causes a row between himself and the Archbishop.

**1167** Henry II invades Ireland, demanding the submission of the Irish kings.

**1170**

**1170** Thomas Becket is murdered by four of Henry's knights while he is at prayer in Canterbury Cathedral. A repentant Henry II creates the most famous and revered of English martyrs.

# A Little Bit of Old England

*The village of Laxton in Nottinghamshire is a rare survival of a medieval landscape based on the open-field farming system*

ABOVE: *'August' – detail from a harvesting calendar c.1030.*

Travelling through the tightly enclosed, hawthorn-hedged fields of north Nottinghamshire, it comes as a bit of a surprise to happen upon the broad, open fields of Laxton. It is as if the prairies of East Anglia have been transposed to the Midlands.

This amazing remnant of old England is thought to be due to the fact that the two major landowners, Earl Manvers and the Earl of Scarborough, could not reach agreement on enclosures in the early 19th century. Although some partial enclosure did take place, by the start of the 20th century Laxton's importance as a unique little bit of old England was recognised, and the emphasis moved to the preservation of the old system.

ABOVE: *Judges of the Court Leet meet at Laxton each year to mark out the field system for the coming year.*

Laxton (or Laxintune, or Lexington, as it has also been known) was already a well-established village at the time of the Norman Conquest. Roman remains have been found at Fiddler's Balk in West Field, and the name comes from the Anglo-Saxon and means 'the settlement of Leaxa's people'. Many of the field names still in use, such as toft, flatt, gate and syke, are of Danish origin, showing that Scandinavian invaders also left their mark on the landscape.

The well-preserved Norman motte and bailey castle on the northern edge of the village dates from the late 11th century, and has an unusual extra cone on the summit of the motte, the mound on which the original timber tower was built. Today, the fine views from the motte overlook the power stations of the Trent Valley, but originally the castle was a venue for the courts of the great royal hunting Forest of Sherwood, and was visited by a succession of monarchs from Henry I to Edward I.

In William the Conqueror's great land register, the Domesday Book of 1086, 'Laxintune' is shown to be a well-cultivated and populated village, consisting of around 35 villeins, bordars and serfs (including one female serf or ancilla), supporting a total population of perhaps 100–120 people. The Domesday entry shows that the people of Laxton were cultivating about 720 acres (291ha) of arable land, with about 40 acres (16ha) of pasture for mowing, and woodland providing pannage (acorns and beechmast) for pigs, and for fuel and building timber.

The village's open field system was probably partly already in place by the time of Domesday. Basically it relies on a three-field rotation system, where in any one year, one field is winter-sown wheat; the second is a spring-sown crop such as barley, and the third is left fallow. All village farmers have the right to use the land in strips or furlongs in the three great open fields of Laxton: West Field, Mill Field and South Field.

Uniquely, Laxton's open field system is still administered by the Court Leet, a form of manorial government which survives from medieval times. The court meets in the Dovecote Inn in late November or early December, appointing a jury to inspect the fallow field for the next annual cycle, and to judge disputes.

BELOW: *Sunset over Laxton – one of the last remaining open-field cultivation systems in England.*

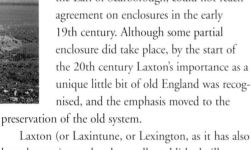

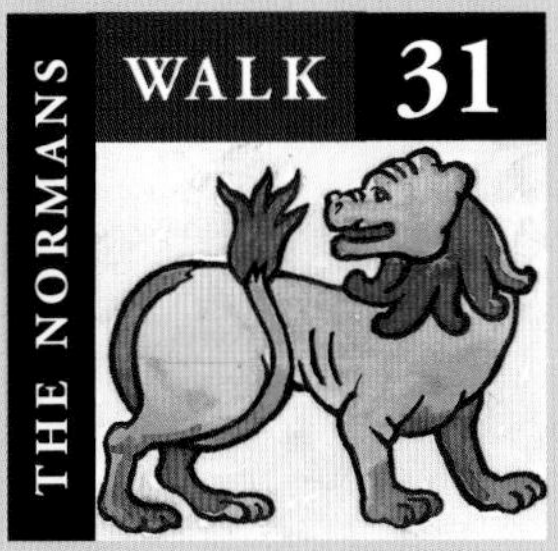


**ABOUT • LAXTON**

*Laxton, a tiny village east of Ollerton, is a survival of the open-field system of agriculture, common during the Middle Ages. All the village farmers can use the land and the system is still administered by the Court Leet, which meets annually at the Dovecote Inn.*

**Nottinghamshire • C ENGLAND**

**DISTANCE** • 2½ miles (4km)
**TOTAL ASCENT** • 33ft (10m)
**PATHS** • field paths and lanes
**TERRAIN** • the deep hollow ways can be very wet and muddy after rain
**GRADIENTS** • none of any note
**REFRESHMENTS** • the Dovecote Inn, Laxton
**PARK** • Laxton village car park, next to the Dovecote Inn and Laxton Visitor Centre
**OS MAP** • Explorer 271 Newark-on-Trent, Retford, Southwell & Saxilby

# Farming medieval-style in Laxton

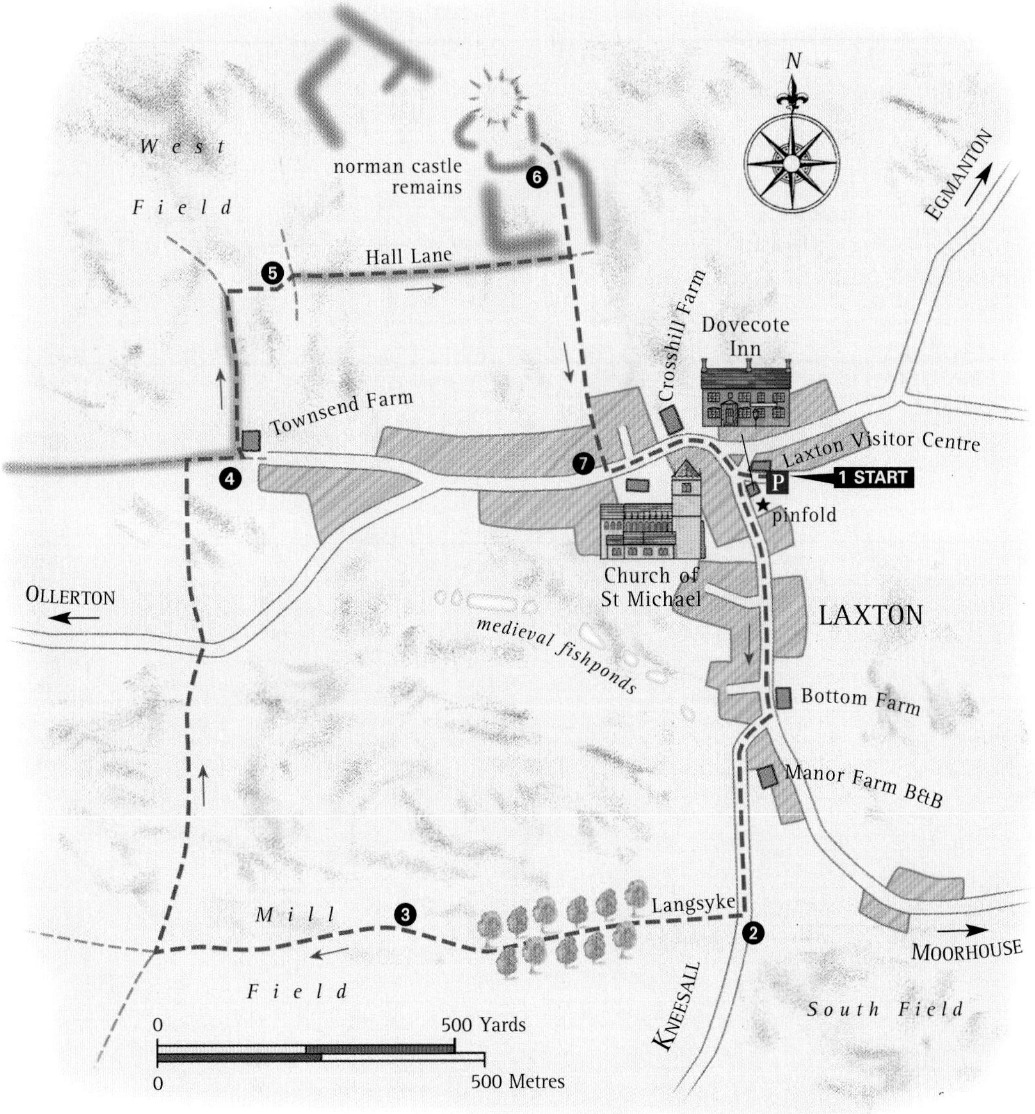


❶ From the village car park walk past the Dovecote Inn and turn left on the road, passing the site of the pinfold (for stray animals) down the Kneesall road for about ½ mile (800m), bearing right at the junction with the Moorhouse road.

❷ After about 200yds (183m), turn right by the second wooden footpath sign on to the broad, muddy trackway of the Langsyke. This leads up through a gate and an avenue of young beeches into a hollow way and out on to Mill Field, the largest of the three great open fields of Laxton. In summer, if the field is in arable use, you will be able to see different crops growing in the strips.

❸ Ascend the broad green headland for about 500yds (457m), turning sharp right at a prominent interpretative sign on to a metalled farm track which leads out to the Ollerton road. After crossing the road, follow a grassy, often wet hollow way, turning right at the junction with another towards the end of the main street of the village, with the church tower ahead.

❹ Just before reaching the street, turn left on to a farm track. After about 150yds (137m), leave the track, turning right over a stile by a notice board which is partly hidden by the hedge.

❺ Cross another stile which leads across the West Field via Hall, or Back, Lane, a muddy, deeply-hedged green track. Follow the lane for about 500yds (457m), where a gate and sign on your left leads across a field towards the motte and bailey castle, following the green arrows of the former MAFF (Ministry of Agriculture, Fisheries, and Food) conservation walk.

❻ Retrace your steps back to the lane, where you go straight ahead arriving back in the village almost opposite the church.

❼ Turn left to walk down the main street and back to the car park.

**DIFFICULTY** ⚜

**• DON'T MISS •**

*It is worth stopping at the visitor centre in **Laxton**, which offers lots of information on the open-field system of farming. And don't miss the beautiful, mainly 13th-century, decorated parish **Church of St Michael, the Archangel**. The church had fallen into disuse and 'impious neglect' until it was remodelled by Earl Manvers, the lord of the manor, in 1854. He dismantled and rebuilt the tower, and shortened the nave by one bay. You'll also find the well-preserved mound of a motte-and-bailey castle in the village.*

# Sarum's Cathedrals Old and New

*Follow the Avon from New Sarum's majestic cathedral to fortified Old Sarum, Salisbury's medieval forerunner*

RIGHT: *Fortified in the Iron Age, the hill fort at Old Sarum was chosen by William I in 1070 as a suitable payment for his conquering armies.*

FAR RIGHT: *The cathedral was moved to Salisbury in the 13th century when the old city outgrew its water supply and a new site was needed.*

BELOW: *An archer, wearing traditional dress reconstructs the scene.*

## Old Sarum – Iron Age Hill Fort to Medieval City

Set on a bleak hill overlooking Salisbury stands the massive, deserted ramparts and earthworks of the original settlement of Old Sarum. People lived on this windswept hilltop for some 5,000 years: the outer banks and ditches were part of an Iron Age hill fort, and several Roman roads converge on the site. The Saxons followed and developed a town within the prehistoric ramparts.

Normans built the inner earthworks and, within them, a royal castle and two palaces. In 1075 Bishop Osmund, William the Conqueror's nephew, constructed the first cathedral. Old Sarum rapidly developed and for 150 years it was a thriving medieval city, well placed at a major crossroads. Lack of space, shortage of water, tensions between clergy and royals and the exposed site led to a gradual decline during the late 12th century, and a new cathedral was built at New Sarum in 1220. Today you can roam across the 56 acres (23ha) of ramparts and ruins, but a fee is charged to view the inner bailey ruins.

## Old Sarum and the Rise of Christianity

Norman rule had a profound effect on English society, in particular upon the Church, remodelling its structure, giving a new impetus to the building or reconstruction of parish churches. This is nowhere more evident that at Old and New Sarum.

The Normans' policy towards religion differed radically from that of the Anglo-Saxons. Bishops were ordered to transfer their headquarters from Saxon rural minsters to more populous centres, part of a centralisation that enabled the Normans to control the population. The rapid growth of Old Sarum from 1070 led to the transference of the rural see of Sherborne to the emerging city in 1075. Old Sarum was closer to the geographical centre of the huge diocese and, more importantly, the new bishop was Osmund, William the

Conqueror's nephew and former chancellor.

Bishop Osmund built a fine cathedral close to the castle and palace, and endowed it with much land. The cathedral set new standards, which were widely adopted in cathedrals throughout England. Instead of being run on monastic lines, it was served by 36 canons living in separate lodgings under the direction of four officers. Architecture was Romanesque and characterised by its lavish scale and rich library. Following Osmund's death in 1099, Bishop Roger built elaborate palaces and was responsible for the ambitious rebuilding of the cathedral.

As the cathedral grew more powerful, friction developed between the clergy and the military governor of the castle at Old Sarum. The vitality and wealth of the Church, combined with the exposed site, lack of space to expand the cathedral, and the shortage of water at Old Sarum, led to the removal of the cathedral to a new city by the River Avon in the early 13th century. Building work began in 1220 and was largely completed by 1250. Set within a spacious close, this new and elegant building provided a model for parish churches throughout the area.

## WALK 32 — ALONG THE AVON TO OLD SARUM

❶ Enter the shopping area close to Sainsbury's and turn left to follow the Riverside Walk sign before the covered walkway. Walk beside the Avon, cross the car park access road and continue beneath two bridges. Cross a road and keep to the tarmac path beside a green. Ignore the footbridge on the right, cross a bridge over a side channel and bear right along the raised riverside path.

❷ Keep to the river bank along a boardwalk to a metal gate. Continue beside the river. Soon, bear half-left away from the river to a gate. Turn right between a hedge and fencing to reach a pitted tarmac path. Turn right, cross a footbridge over the Avon and soon bear right along a metalled track to the road in Stratford-sub-Castle.

❸ Turn right along the pavement, then just beyond Old Forge Cottage, cross the road to join a wide path beside Dairy Cottage, that gradually climbs to Old Sarum. At a T-junction of paths, keep left along the base of the hill fort; then, at a fork, bear right and ascend on to the outer rampart. Bear left around the fortifications, eventually descending to a stile by the access road. Follow the road right to tour the earth fortifications and to visit the inner bailey.

❹ Retrace your steps through the outer earthwork and turn right to pass through a gate. Go through a further gate and, just before the road, turn right, signed Stratford, alongside the hedge. Go through a gate and keep left, downhill to another gate by the Parliamentary Tree memorial stone. Turn right and enter Stratford-sub-Castle. Keep ahead and, shortly, cross by the right-hand bend to follow the path beside houses, signed City Centre.

❺ Reach a wide track and in a few paces cross the tiny footbridge on your right. Keep right along a gravel path through the grounds of the Sports Centre, the path bearing left alongside the river. Soon cross the footbridge to join the outward route back to the city centre and your car.

**Distance:** 5 miles (8km)

**Total ascent:** 230ft (70m)

**Paths:** mostly good; metalled close to the city centre; can be wet and muddy beside the Avon

**Terrain:** water meadow, city centre and farmland

**Gradients:** mainly flat; one gradual climb to Old Sarum

**Refreshments:** plenty of choice in Salisbury; The Old Castle opposite entrance to Old Sarum

**Parking:** main central car park close to Sainsbury's; signed off Ring Road, west of city centre

**OS Map:** Explorer 130 Salisbury & Stonehenge

**Difficulty:** ✿✿

**1189**

**1189–99** Richard I 'the Lionheart' spends most of his reign crusading in the Holy Land. His defeat of Saladin in the Third Crusade enables Richard to reach an agreement that guarantees safe passage to Christians on pilgrimage to the Holy Land.

**1189**

**1189** In return for money to help fund the crusades, Richard I recognises Scotland as an independent state.

**1194** Llywelyn the Great declares himself prince of all Wales.

**1199**

**1199** On Richard's death, the empire of the Plantagenets stretches from the Atlantic to the Mediterranean. Within five years of acceding the throne, John has lost all the French possessions and much of England is in the hands of opponents.

# The Monks of Fountains Abbey

*From modest foundations, this Yorkshire abbey became the greatest in England*

**THE NORMANS**

**ERA OF CONQUEST**

In 1207, a Fountains Abbey monk recalled his brethren's first sight of the valley of the River Skell in the winter of 1132: 'A place remote from the world, uninhabited, thickset with thorns – fit more, it seemed, for the dens of wild beasts than for the uses of mankind.'

The 13 monks who travelled from St Mary's Abbey in York to Ripon, and on up the Skell Valley, were members of the Benedictine Order. The group had become dissatisfied with the way their abbey was being run, and enlisted the help of Archbishop Thurstan. It was he who directed them here. Early in 1133 they joined the Cistercian Order.

When Hugh, Dean of York, retired to Fountains in 1135, bringing his riches with him as an endowment, its success was assured. It acquired property – it is said that in the 13th century you could travel more than 30 miles (48km) west from Fountains without leaving the abbey's estates – and ever-increasing wealth, as the extensive ruins of the abbey's buildings testify.

The massive surrounding wall you pass near the beginning of the walk survives surprisingly intact. The abbey church was 360ft (97m) long – larger than many cathedrals. The other buildings, laid out along

(and over) the river, give a vivid impression of life here in the Middle Ages. The monks rose at about 2am for the first service, Vigil. Two more services and a meeting followed before they dined at midday in the refectory, remains of which can be seen south of the cloisters. They spent the afternoon working, and after three more services retired to bed around 8.30pm.

Some of the manual work in the abbey and on its estate was done by the monks, but the Cistercians also had working lay brothers. They took simple vows and had their own church services. The impressive undercroft, with its rows of pillars, west of the cloisters, was below their dormitory. This tradition of lay brothers in English monasteries was ended by the Black Death in the 14th century.

The last of the builders, Abbot Marmaduke Huby, built his huge tower, a symbol of what he believed to be the enduring power of his abbey. Ironically, less than 20 years later, in 1539, all ended abruptly when Henry VIII closed the abbey. He confiscated its riches, dispersed the monks and left the buildings desolate.

The estate was eventually sold to Sir Stephen Proctor, who in 1611 used the stone from the abbey buildings to construct Fountains Hall. From the end of the 17th century onwards John Aislabie, disgraced Chancellor of the Exchequer after the financial scandal of the South Sea Bubble in 1720, laid out his stunning garden at Studley Royal. It was his son William, however, who finally purchased the ruins of Fountains Abbey to be the highlight of his estate in 1768.

ABOVE: *Looking through the stone undercroft at Fountains Abbey.*

BELOW: *Fountains Abbey offers some authentic reminders of what life must have been like for the monks, with its dormitories, lavatories and warming house.*

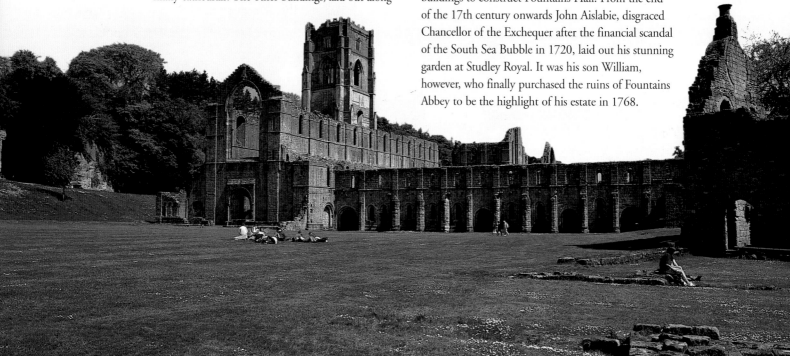

**ABOUT • FOUNTAINS ABBEY**

*Founded in 1132, Fountains Abbey rose to become the richest monastery in England. The substantial ruins offer one of the most complete pictures of the life of a Cistercian monk and the walk approaches the abbey ruins through the beautiful grounds of Studley Royal.*

**North Yorkshire • N ENGLAND**

**DISTANCE •** 7 miles (11.3km)

**TOTAL ASCENT •** 443ft (135m)

**PATHS •** field paths, tracks, metalled drives and garden paths

**TERRAIN •** estate grounds and gardens, with some farmland and woodland

**GRADIENTS •** moderate, but a stiff climb from and to the visitor centre. Alternative

parking for disabled people at west end of estate avoids this climb

**REFRESHMENTS •** Fountains Abbey visitor centre and in the Lakeside tea room

**PARK •** Fountains Abbey visitor centre, signed from the B6265

**OS MAP •** Explorer 299 Ripon & Boroughbridge, Easingwold

# Holy orders and riches at Fountains Abbey

❶ From the visitor centre pay desk go through the door and turn right. Follow the path towards the abbey. After a metal gate, turn left, signed Abbey and Water Garden. Go steeply downhill to a metalled path by the abbey ruins.

❷ After exploring the abbey ruins, return to this path. Pass Fountains Hall and leave the estate through the gate. Turn left up the road, bearing left at the junction. Just after the road bends right, go left over a signed stile beside a gate.

❸ Follow the path to a waymarked gate in a crossing wall. The track beyond curves right then left through two gates to a farmhouse. Turn right alongside the shed. Follow footpath signs, going left then right, to a metal gate and on to a track.

❹ Where the hedge ends, go ahead down the field to a gate into the wood. Follow the track to a ruined archway. Go through the kissing gate left of the arch and follow the track ahead, winding downhill and bending right to the valley.

❺ Just before reaching a weir, turn sharp right down the valley, and follow the track over three bridges to a kissing gate. Continue through woodland, passing a footbridge and winding left uphill. The track passes Plumpton Hall on your left, and continues to the Studley Royal Estate entrance.

❻ Turn left up the drive towards the church. At the crossroads turn left towards the lake and follow the road, with the lake on your right, to the entrance gate. Just

beyond the pay kiosk (show your membership card or entrance ticket to regain admission), turn left and cross the canal.

❼ Follow the canalside path almost to the Temple of Piety, turning sharp left uphill before it, signed High Ride. The path goes through a tunnel and then bends right, passing the Octagonal Temple and winding through woodland. By the Temple of Fame, the path bends left.

❽ Continue past Anne Boleyn's Seat to turn sharp right, downhill, to another lake. Turn left and continue. Follow the path beside the canal and then slightly uphill. Go right, into the abbey ruins, and retrace your steps back uphill to the visitor centre.

**• DON'T MISS •**

*Ripon is only 3 miles (5km) from Fountains Abbey. It is a cathedral city with a history that dates back to 886 when it was granted a charter by Alfred the Great. The cathedral has a crypt constructed by St Wilfrid in AD 672 – more than 450 years before the monks arrived at Fountains. In the handsome market square is England's oldest free-standing obelisk.*

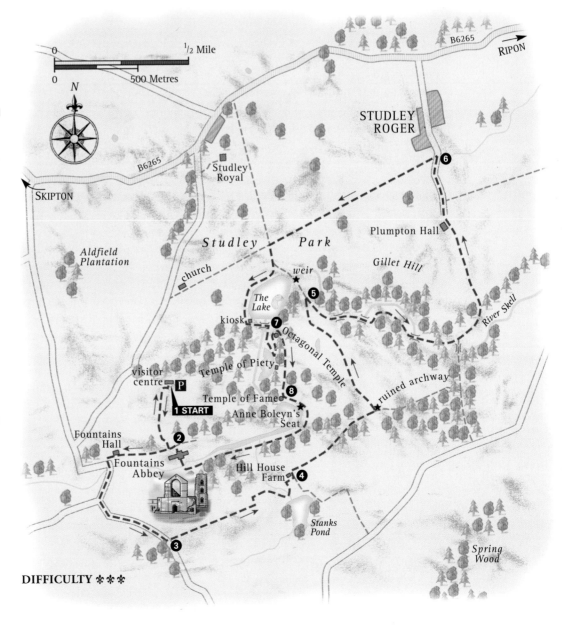

**DIFFICULTY ✳ ✳ ✳**

**1209**

**1209** Cambridge University is founded.

**1215** King John signs the Magna Carta, a charter of rights and privilege. It is the first step towards democracy, and a milestone in English constitutional history.

**1216**

**1216–72** John dies in 1216 leaving England in the hands of Henry III, a nine-year-old boy. Until 1227, when Henry takes over government himself, England is ruled wisely by two regents nominated by John in his will. Henry's rule is less wise.

**1236**

**1236** Henry marries Eleanor of Provence and provokes the anger of the English barons by bestowing favours on foreign rather than English noblemen. Civil war breaks out, led by Simon de Montfort, Earl of Leicester.

# Echoes of Dundrennan's Past Glories

*A pleasant stroll round a forgotten coastal backwater steeped in history*

**THE NORMANS**

**ERA OF CONQUEST**

Nestling in a tranquil valley in south-west Scotland, the bare, grey ruin of Dundrennan Abbey is all that remains of one of the finest Scottish examples of a once mighty religious order. The Order of the Cistercians, founded in 1098 at Cîteaux in Burgundy, wanted to lead a simple life of prayer and hard work, directed by the fundamentals of the Rule of St Benedict of poverty, chastity and obedience. The austere life of the Cistercians monks was reflected in the architecture of their abbeys, and none more so than Dundrennan, constructed of locally quarried freestone ashlar, giving it a stark grey appearance in contrast to the warm sandstone of nearby Sweetheart Abbey. Like Rievaulx it followed a strict design of church and domestic buildings built round a cloister, and the whole site was enclosed by a wall.

In the 12th century several reformed Benedictine orders were founded in France and monasticism underwent a considerable expansion throughout Europe. At the invitation of David I, white monks of the Cistercian order came north in 1136 from their mother house at Rievaulx, in Yorkshire, to found the abbey of Melrose, and six years later to Dundrennan in Galloway. By the end of David's reign in 1153 Scotland had four Cistercian abbeys. Dundrennan became in turn the mother house for two more abbeys in Galloway – Glenluce, near Stranraer, and Sweetheart, near Dumfries. By the time Lady Devorgilla dedicated Sweetheart Abbey to the memory of her husband, John Balliol, in 1273 there were 11 Cistercian monasteries in Scotland.

The influx of the religious orders transformed the economy of rural Scotland in the 12th century. They raised sheep on large areas of previously uncultivated land and continual contact with the mother house in France and with their own daughter houses enabled them to operate as an early trading group. The Cistercians were the largest single producers of wool in the country and at their peak the 11 abbeys had combined flocks of over 40,000, accounting for 5 per cent of Scottish wool production. They exported wool, imported grain and, as the major source of employment in the area, played a significant part in the development of towns and burghs. The now quiet and isolated village of Dundrennan was then a thriving community on a busy trade route, with the abbey as the economic hub. The abbey would have provided the community with employment, religious services, education and medical help. The pilgrims passing through on their way to St Ninian's shrine at Whithorn would stop for hospitality and bring news of the wider world.

The 16th-century Reformation brought an end to the monastic life of the white monks at Dundrennan. Perhaps the most famous event in Dundrennan's long history was on the eve of 15 May 1568 when Mary Queen of Scots, fleeing from defeat at the battle of Langside, spent her last night on Scottish soil here. Next day she set off for England to seek help from her cousin Queen Elizabeth. Like the monks and their way of life, she never returned.

ABOVE: *Dundrennan Abbey was also the mother house of Glenluce and Sweetheart abbeys.*

BELOW: *Many of the Gothic and Romanesque features have survived at Dundrennan Abbey, such as this statue of a saint.*

BELOW: *The abbey was founded by David I and Fergus, Lord of Galloway, in 1142, but fell into ruin after the monastery was closed in 1606 during the Dissolution.*

**ABOUT DUNDRENNAN ABBEY**

*Mary, Queen of Scots, spent her last night in Scotland in this abbey, founded in 1142 by a Cistercian order of monks from Rievaulx in North Yorkshire. No early written records of the abbey have survived but the remains suggest a wealthy past.*

## Dumfries & Galloway • SCOTLAND

**DISTANCE** • 6 miles (9.6km)

**TOTAL ASCENT** • 98ft (30m)

**PATHS** • good, but can be very muddy in wet weather

**TERRAIN** • country lanes, farm tracks, fields and a section of A-road

**GRADIENTS** • gentle

**REFRESHMENTS** • none on route. The Selkirk Arms, Kirkcudbright

**PARK** • car park, Dundrennan Abbey

**OS MAP** • Explorer 312 Kirkcudbright & Castle Douglas

# A simple life at Dundrennan Abbey

❶ From the car park in Dundrennan village return to the A711 and turn left. Take the first turning on the left, signed Port Mary, and continue along this road. At the next junction go left again avoiding the military road.

❷ Follow this road as it winds round the farm steading and past the entrance of Port Mary House. Stop for a moment and consider the fate of Mary Queen of Scots. She fled here after her disastrous defeat at Langside in 1568 and

**• DON'T MISS •**

*Kirkcudbright is one of the most colourful towns in Scotland, with streets of brightly painted Georgian houses. The town has a rich history which dates back to the 13th century when the fortress of Castlemains came into the possession of John Balliol, the Lord of Galloway, and Edward I is believed to have stayed here during this time. In the late 19th and 20th centuries, Kirkudbright prospered under a new trade – brought by the artists of the day – and quickly gained a reputation as an artists' haven for the quality of its light. A number of famous artists were attracted to the town, including EA Hornel, who donated his home at Broughton House to the town – the house is now a museum.*

**DIFFICULTY** ❁ ❁

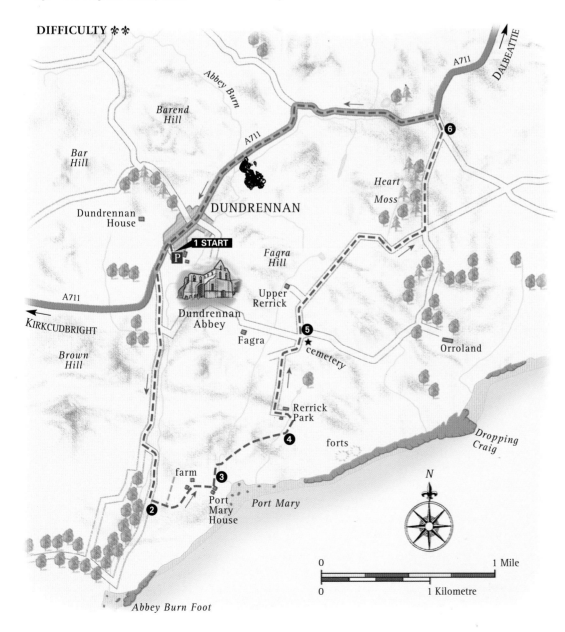

set sail from here for England, hoping to receive the protection of Elizabeth I, but she was never to return. Go through the gate at the end of the road, along a farm track and through a second gate.

❸ Walk ahead for approximately 100yds (91m), then turn right and cross a small burn. Head across the field parallel to the telegraph poles and look for the gate in the far side. Go through it.

❹ Turn left and follow the line of the burn then turn left again, cross the burn and enter the steading at Rerrick Park farm. Turn left on to the road, which runs up the side of the farm house and then turns sharp right.

❺ At the crossroads, beside a cemetery, go forward on the middle road. Pass the entrance to Upper Rerrick on the left and follow the road as it turns first right and then left to end at a T-junction.

❻ Turn left and at the junction with the A711 turn left again. Continue along this quiet road for about 2 miles (3.2km) to reach the village of Dundrennan (note that the stone from the ruined abbey was used in the construction of the village) and return to the abbey car park.

**1265**

**1265** Simon de Montfort captures the King and summons the first English Parliament at Lewes. However, some of his former supporters turn against de Montfort and he is killed at the Battle of Evesham, leaving King Henry III to resume control.

**1272**

**1272–1307** The reign of Edward I.

**1275** The Statute of Jewry obliges Jewish people to wear yellow stars for identification, and dictates the nature of their trades and their dwelling places.

**1282**

**1282** Edward I demands homage from the Welsh prince, Llywelyn ap Gruffadd. When Llywelyn refuses, Edward seizes Gwynedd and mid-Wales, securing his victories with a ring of fortresses.

ABOVE: *Two actors reconstruct the scene inside the remarkable remains of Restormel Castle, home to Edmund Earl of Cornwall.*

# Restormel Castle – Symbol of Wealth and Power

*A rewarding exploration of the splendid Norman castle and the hidden delights of Lostwithiel, former capital of the county of Cornwall*

You wouldn't think that the little town of Lostwithiel, situated at the highest tidal point of the River Fowey, played a highly significant role in Cornish history. This walk, however, will take you to the 13th-century seat of the feudal government of the Duchy of Cornwall and the evocative ruins of Restormel Castle (Castle Rostormolgh), just a few minutes' walk away from the town centre.

Lostwithiel is situated on an ancient crossing point of the Fowey, and the present bridge dates from the medieval era, when the town's prosperity, due to the lucrative tin trade, was at its height. In the 12th century Devon and Cornwall were the only sources of tin in the known world, and the industry centred on Bodmin. Lostwithiel, the nearest navigable point to the south, developed as Bodmin's seaport and was granted a charter in 1189. Evidence of former quayside activity can be seen by the river on the walk. This was one of the country's most important ports from the 12th to mid-14th centuries, after which, ironically, silting of the river by waste from tin-streaming works initiated its decline, and Fowey, further south, took

over much of its trade. Lostwithiel's former wealth is reflected in its fine 13th-century buildings, including the Church of St Bartholomew. During the same period the earls of Cornwall moved the county's administrative centre here from Launceston, and the Duchy Council and Stannary Court, the latter concerned with regulating the tin trade, sat here.

At the same time Edmund, Earl of Cornwall (1272–99), a cousin of Edward I, was refurbishing Restormel Castle in stone, and most of the present-day remains date from this period. There is evidence of an earlier wooden castle here, dating from about 1100, which took advantage of a high spur of land overlooking the Fowey a mile (1.6km) north of the town. But Edmund's rebuilding programme was not carried out for defensive purposes: it is likely that Restormel was his main residence and, situated in the heart of the largest deer park in the county, that it was developed as a forceful symbol of Norman power and prosperity, used largely for entertainment purposes. He and later owners (including the Black Prince) probably only visited occasionally, and the castle would have been managed by a steward. The extensive dry-moated ruins are wonderfully atmospheric – the oldest and best-preserved example of Norman motte and bailey construction in Cornwall.

As the importance of Lostwithiel declined, so did the fortunes of Restormel, and by the mid-14th century it had fallen into disrepair. Its only military encounter occurred during the Civil War (1642–9) when, having been slightly 'patched up', it was occupied briefly by Parliamentarian troops under the Earl of Essex, but recaptured by the Royalists on 21 August 1644. The Parliamentarians withdrew and were eventually defeated at Castle Dore, just north of Fowey, on 1 September 1644. By the 18th century the castle was in ruins and, still owned by the Duchy of Cornwall, was passed to English Heritage in 1984.

BELOW: *An aerial view of Restormel Castle shows the substantial remains including the keep. In its heyday the castle would have been considered to be a very modern building with its fireplaces and windows.*

THE NORMANS

WALK 35

**ABOUT • LOSTWITHIEL**

*In the 13th century, Bodmin was the centre of Devon and Cornwall's thriving tin industry and Lostwithiel, as a result, developed as an important seaport. Then, in the 13th century Restormel Castle became the seat of the feudal government of the area.*

**Cornwall • SW ENGLAND**

**DISTANCE** • 4½ miles (7.2km)

**TOTAL ASCENT** • 410ft (125m)

**PATHS** • woodland tracks and fields

**TERRAIN** • mixed woodland and farmland; short stretch of pavements through the town

**GRADIENTS** • gradual; one short steep ascent from Restormel Farm to Hillhead

**REFRESHMENTS** • café at Lanhydrock House; The River pub and Duchy Coffee Shop both in Fore Street, Lostwithiel

**PARK** • National Trust car park by Respryn Bridge (honesty box) for Lanhydrock House (signed off the A38 just east of Bodmin, and off the A390 west of Lostwithiel)

**OS MAP** • Explorer 107 St Austell & Liskeard

# The rise and fall of Lostwithiel

DIFFICULTY ✤✤

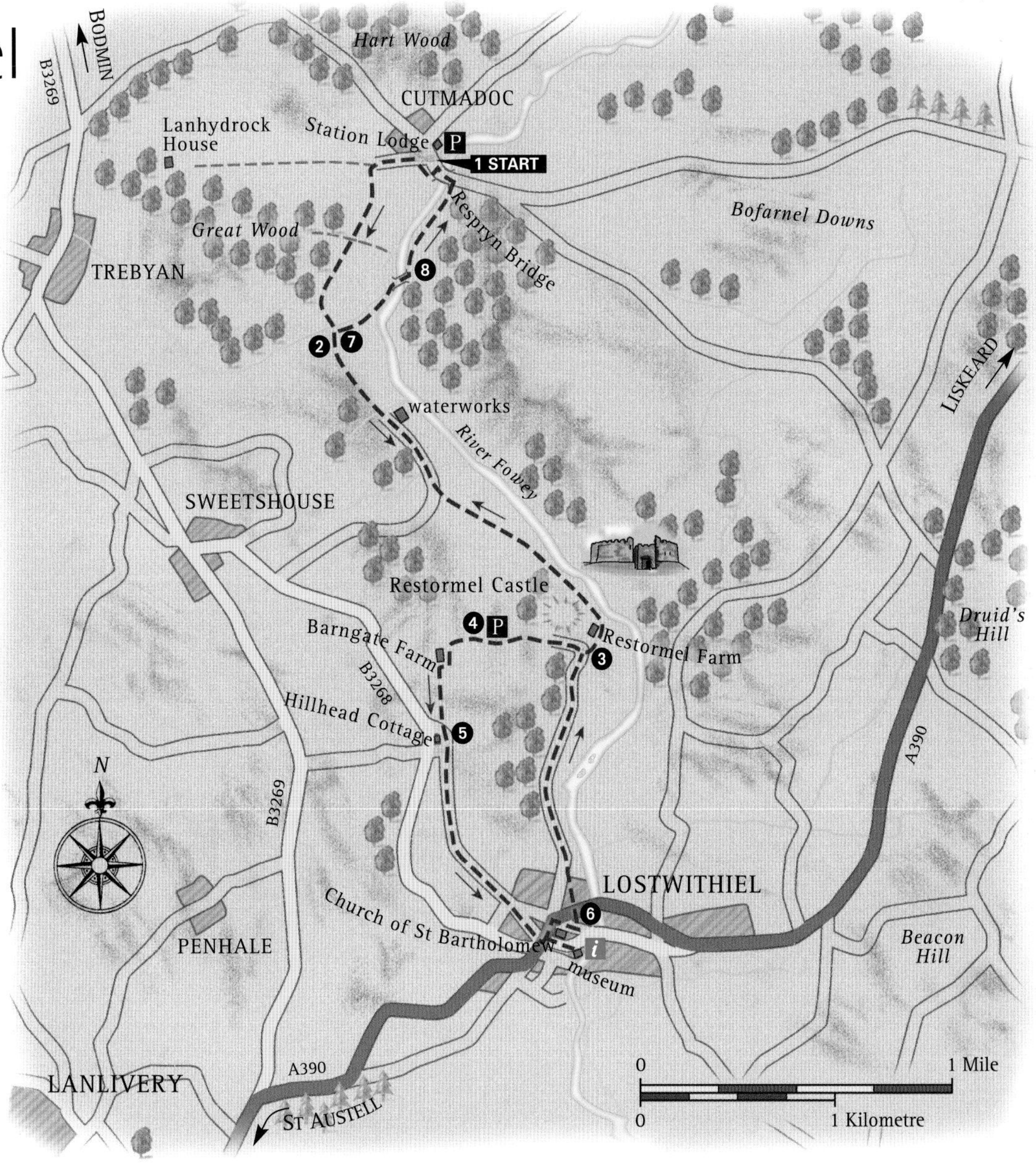


❶ Leave the car park via the exit and turn right. Take the first lane left by Station Lodge, signed Lanhydrock. At the Lodge and gates to The Avenue, turn left down Newton Lane, signed permitted footpath only. Continue to a wooded track which descends for ¾ mile (1.2km); veer left to meet two dark red gates, ahead and right.

❷ Turn right through the gate, signed footpath to Restormel Castle, and cross the field. Go through the next gate, and then another by the waterworks to join a lane then continue for 1¼ miles (2km). Where the lane bends right, keep straight on along the farm lane (dead end), with views to the castle ahead. The lane runs through Restormel Farm to meet another lane.

❸ Turn right uphill (in summer the gates are open; in winter climb over the stile) to reach the car park; turn right for the castle.

❹ On leaving the castle go through the car park, over a stile in the far left corner, and up the field, keeping the hedge on your left. Cross the wooden ladder stile and pass through a gap in the hedge. Continue uphill, keeping the hedge on your right. The path veers left, ignore the first stile on the right. At the top, turn right over a stile, then left at the footpath post near Barngate Farm. Cross the next ladder stile and pass through a gate to meet the road opposite Hillhead Cottage.

❺ Turn left; descend Bodmin Hill for ¾ mile (1.2km) to meet the A390 in the centre of Lostwithiel. Cross the road and continue down Fore Street to the museum, St Bartholomew's Church and the River Fowey. Retrace your steps to the A390 and turn right to pass the Royal Talbot, on your left, and Tourist Information Centre, on your right.

❻ Turn left along Restormel Road (unmarked), following the brown tourist signs to the castle. At the entrance to Restormel Farm keep straight on to retrace your steps past the waterworks and through the fields to reach the red gate at Point 2 of the walk.

❼ Go through the gate and turn right to pass almost immediately through another red gate. Follow the woodland path to meet the River Fowey; the path bends left to meet a wooden footbridge.

❽ Cross the footbridge and turn left to walk along the river bank. The path ends at a kissing gate; turn left to cross Respryn Bridge, then turn right into the car park.

**DON'T MISS**

*The 18th-century **Restormel House**, just below the castle, has superb battlements in the Gothic style.*

**1284**

**1284** Llywelyn is ambushed and killed: the Statue of Rhuddlan sweeps away Welsh laws and imposes English rule and an English Prince of Wales; the future King Edward II.

**1286** Alexander III of Scotland dies

**1286**

and the kingdom falls into dispute between John Balliol, John Coming and Robert the Bruce.

**1296** William Wallace of Scotland makes an alliance with France in the fight for Scottish independence.

**1298**

**1298** Edward I invades Scotland and successfully seizes the throne, triggering a series of vicious wars between the two nations.

ABOVE: *Edward I investing his son (later Edward II) as Prince of Wales in 1301.*

**THE NORMANS**

**ERA OF CONQUEST**

# Conwy: A Conqueror's Town

*The walled northern town, legacy of Edward I's subjugation of the Welsh*

Edward I became King of England in 1272 and was crowned two years later in Westminster Abbey. He was a natural military leader and tactician, and set his sights on ruling the whole of Britain by conquering Wales and Scotland.

During the reign of Edward's father, Henry III, a treaty had been made between Henry and Llywelyn ap Gruffydd, whom the king formally acknowledged as the Prince of Wales. However, Llywelyn deliberately antagonised Edward by not attending his coronation, and refusing to pay homage to the King.

In 1276 Edward decided to use force to subdue Llywelyn and declared war, flushing Llwelyn out of his strongholds in Snowdon and cutting off his supply routes to Anglesey. With Llywelyn almost defeated, and with the prospect of a cold winter and possible starvation ahead, the Treaty of Aberconwy was made, by which Edward seized all lands except Gwynedd, west of the River Conwy. But in 1282 Llywelyn's brother, David, led the Welsh in a revolt against Edward. Llywelyn died in battle and David was later betrayed and executed.

The final defeat of Gwynedd by Edward was little more than the culmination of a process – the Anglo-Norman conquest of Wales – that had started two centuries earlier. Edward's successes served to bring in greater English influence. No other English king had made such effort to rule the whole of Britain. Following his campaigns in Wales, Edward

ABOVE: *View of Conwy Castle across the bay with Conwy Mountain in the distance.*

reorganised Welsh law and government, created counties in the north of Wales very similar to those in England, notably in Flint, Anglesey, Merioneth and Caernarfon, and established boroughs for English settlers, which the native Welsh were forbidden to enter.

This was also Edward's great castle-building period, when Aberystwyth, Builth, Flint, and Rhuddlan were built, followed by Harlech, Caernarfon, and, of course, Conwy. Work started on his last castle, Beaumaris, in 1295, but neither this nor Caernarfon was ever completed. In 1301 he made his eldest son, Edward, Prince of Wales, a precedent followed by every subsequent English monarch who was able to do so.

The conquest of Wales had throughout been a piecemeal affair, with each conquering Norman lord allowed to obtain whatever land he could for himself. This had the effect of reproducing a continental style of feudalism in Wales, under which the barons were virtually independent – a system of feudalism that had been strenuously resisted by William the Conqueror in England.

In this manner, the Welsh Marches (borders) produced an intricate pattern of almost autonomous states. The power of the border barons grew, and succeeding English kings sought to control them. Ironically, Edward remained dependent on their support, and this led to the creation of new lordships out of the lands he had conquered.

LEFT: *Edward started work on Conwy Castle in 1283, soon after his conquest of the Welsh. This architectural feat took only four and half years to complete.*

### ABOUT · CONWY

*This walk starts at Conwy Castle, built by Edward I after his conquest of Wales. The route then wanders along the estuary and up on to Conwy Mountain, a vantage point from where the tactical positioning of the castle is most evident.*

## Conwy · WALES

**DISTANCE** • 7¼ miles (11.7km)

**TOTAL ASCENT** • 985ft (300m)

**PATHS** • minor roads, A-roads, rough tracks and paths

**TERRAIN** • remote farmland and hill country

**GRADIENTS** • road mostly flat; paths steep in places

**REFRESHMENTS** • Liverpool Arms in Conwy, many cafés and take-away food bars in town centre

**PARK** • Vicarage Gardens car park, inside the castle walls

**OS MAP** • Outdoor Leisure 17 Snowdonia – Snowdon & Conwy Valley

# In the shadow of the mighty Conwy Castle

❶ From the car park turn right to reach the Guild Hall. Cross the road, turn right, then left, following signs for the Quay. Pass through a small archway and walk along the harbour front. Continue through another archway and bear right on to the signed North Wales Path (NWP).

❷ Continue alongside the Conwy estuary, parallel with Bodlondeb Woods. At a T-junction, turn left and walk to a main road. Go into the road opposite, and cross the railway by a footbridge. Continue past the drive to Beechwood Court, soon bearing right at the T-junction (waymarked). Just past the last houses on the right, branch right again at the fork to follow the NWP, and climb to a wooden stile giving access to Conwy Mountain. Ascend through bracken and gorse, eventually to follow a more level course across the flanks of the mountain.

❸ Continue for just over a mile (1.6km) to a waymark. Leave the NWP and bear left, descending to a more pronounced path beside a wall. Further on, rejoin the NWP and continue to a lateral farm track. Cross this and go forward on to a broad track to the parking area at Sychnant Pass.

❹ Cross the road and go up to a gate. After a short distance, take an obvious track turning sharp right on to higher ground. Shortly, bear left on a green track following waymarked NWP. Further on, as you pass under power lines for the third time, the track forks directly under them. Branch left here and continue along the track to a ladder stile over a wall.

❺ Beyond the stile, descend a little across the western slopes of Maen Esgob, and when the main track bears right, turn left through a pronounced pass between low hills, now leaving the NWP. Follow a track past a small lake (Llyn y Wrach), and shortly turn left, roughly parallel with a wall. Follow the track (which doesn't always stay by the wall and finally leaves it), to reach a group of walled enclosures. Bear right. Shortly the path descends quite steeply, and meets a surfaced road. Turn right.

❻ Soon, just before Y Bwthyn (The Cottage) and 109yds (100m) before the cattle grid, turn left through a gate on to an enclosed path to a field. Bear left across the field towards a stile, then follow an obvious route across two fields. In the next field, the route is less obvious but aims for the right-hand corner of a fence. From here, walk alongside a stream, aiming to the right of a red-roofed house, near which you meet a road. Turn right and follow the road passing Oakwood Hall Park on the right. At a T-Junction turn right and soon turn left at a footpath sign. Continue through three fields, pass through a kissing gate then bear left along a field edge to meet another road. Turn right.

❼ Head towards Conwy and enter the town by passing through a pedestrian archway in the Town Walls. Turn right on to the main street to return to the start point of the walk.

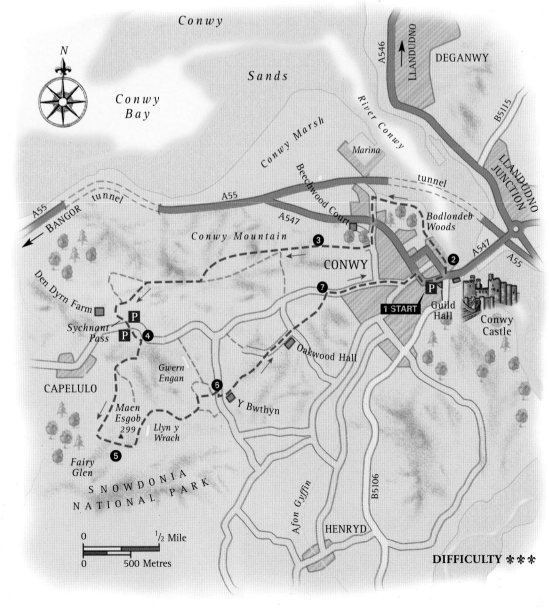

**DIFFICULTY** ❄ ❄ ❄

*For most people, life in medieval Britain was hard work but reasonably predictable, within a fairly rigid social order. But in the mid-14th century the old world was changed beyond recognition – by the bite of a flea.*

## MEDIEVAL

## 1300–1485

# Plague & Conflict

Britain in the first half of the 14th century was familiar enough with upheaval and war. The enmity between England and Scotland had rumbled on, exploding into battle at Bannockburn in 1314, where Edward II's troops were routed by Robert the Bruce. In 1337 the more warlike Edward III sent his knights across the Channel to enforce his claim to the French throne, setting in train the Hundred Years' War. Still, in most communities the daily routine was predictable, if tough – until, in 1348, an epidemic swept in from Europe that seemed to herald Judgement Day itself.

The Black Death was a form of bubonic plague, carried by fleas on the rats that infested ships and towns. The first signs of infection were swellings, or 'buboes', on armpits or groin, followed by coughing, chills and delirium. Victims were usually dead within days. By the time the epidemic had run its course Europe's population had been halved, Britain's reduced by a third. Estates and villages were left to rot, with no one to plant or harvest crops, tend or slaughter cattle, produce or sell goods. Those still capable of work found that the old feudal rules tying them to their lord's land no longer applied: they could move around, selling their labour to the highest bidder. When the crown tried to rein in this burgeoning wage economy, imposing a poll tax on everyone over the age of 14, the peasants revolted, only retreating from all-out confrontation with the young King Richard II when their leader, Wat Tyler, had been cut down by his bodyguard.

Faced with the uncertainty of earthly existence, people turned in their thousands to the comforting rituals of religion, and trekked to pilgrimage centres in the hope of sharing in the miraculous powers of holy relics.

With their stalls and souvenirs, inns and religious sites of interest, pilgrimage routes were as much a holiday as a journey of faith – as is clear in Geoffrey Chaucer's rumbustious *The Canterbury Tales*, started in 1387.

### POWER STRUGGLES

The ravages of plague and food shortages continued to have their repercussions. A minor Welsh noble, Owain Glyndwr, indignant at the loss of a legal dispute over land rights, attracted a huge following of disaffected countrymen when he took arms against the king, Henry IV. At its height the rebel movement was calling its own parliaments and signing international alliances, but in 1413 the English gained the upper hand and Glyndwr vanished into hiding.

Two years later, the English celebrated another victory – against the French in Agincourt; and in 1420 the Treaty of Troyes pronounced Henry V heir to the throne of France. But the English kingdom's future was far from settled. The tussle over the crown between major political players was about to spark off 30 years of intermittent fighting between the houses of Lancaster and York, while families, towns and castles across England and Wales declared and sometimes shifted their loyalties.

In 1485 the Lancastrian claimant, Henry Tudor – son of Margaret Beaufort, the great-granddaughter of John of Gaunt, Duke of Lancaster – returned from exile in Brittany and marched to Bosworth to face the Yorkist king, Richard III.

After a fierce and arduous battle, Richard was finally unhorsed and killed. Having chased Richard's demoralised soldiers across the marshes, the new king's followers performed an impromptu crowning ceremony in the field, and the Tudor era was under way.

### HISTORIC SITES

**Bosworth battlefield, Leicestershire:** site of the clash between Richard III and Henry Tudor.

**King's College, Cambridge:** founded by Henry VI.

**Bannockburn, near Stirling:** site of Robert the Bruce's famous victory.

**Caernarfon Castle, Gwynedd:** built by Edward I to be the seat of Welsh government in North Wales.

**Berkeley Castle, Gloucestershire:** Edward II abdicated at Kenilworth Castle, before being taken to Berkeley where he was imprisoned, tortured and finally murdered.

**1306**

**1306** Robert the Bruce sets out to oust the English, having killed his main Scottish rival, John Comyn. He is crowned Robert I at Scone before he flees into hiding from the English army. In retaliation, English troops massacre his followers..

**1307**

**1307** Edward I dies en route to Scotland and Edward II, his son, succeeds the throne.

**1314** Robert the Bruce routs the feckless Edward's army at Bannockburn.

**1315**

**1315–17** Floods, called 'the Little Ice Age', create food shortages and cause an economic crisis.

**1318** Scottish raiders reach York and ten years later Scottish accession is finally acknowledged.

# Clash of Nations at Glen Trool

*Walk in the footsteps of Robert the Bruce to the site of the Battle of Loch Trool*

ABOVE: *Robert the Bruce and his second wife, daughter of the Earl of Ulster. The Scots liked and welcomed Bruce as their new king despite his involvement with the murder of his rival and cousin, John Comyn.*

At Glen Trool, on 31 March 1307 a guerrilla force of 300 Scots, using their knowledge of the local terrain, drew the vastly superior English force of 1,500 men into an ambush. King Robert the Bruce lured part of the Earl of Pembroke's army, under the command of Lord Clifford and Aymer de Valence, along the southern shores of Loch Trool. With the English strung out over a mile (1.6km), the Scots turned, blocking the track, and at the same time the rest of Bruce's men hurled boulders from the steep slopes above. It was a total rout and Clifford only just managed to escape. This small victory was the turning point in Bruce's fortunes. From here he launched a series of guerrilla offensives, which would culminate in victory over the English at the Battle of Bannockburn in 1314.

Robert the Bruce was the grandson of another Robert Bruce, who had made a claim to the Scottish throne after the death of the Maid of Norway left the country without a monarch in 1290. Edward I of England, called in by the Guardians of Scotland to settle the disputed succession, rejected Bruce's claim in favour of his rival, John Balliol. Balliol's reign lasted only four years before he was deposed and ritually humiliated by Edward at Montrose Castle in July 1296.

The Wars of Scotland, which ensued, were more than a fight against the English for recognition of Scotland's independence. They were also a bitter civil war between the contenders for the throne, Robert the Bruce and John, the Red Comyn. The dispute was brutally curtailed on 11 February 1306 when Bruce murdered the Red Comyn in Greyfriars Church in Dumfries. Excommunicated for this sacrilegious murder, Bruce went on the rampage and was crowned King of Scots at Scone on 25 March. However, undermined by the excommunication and defeated in successive battles over the summer, Bruce fled, demoralised, to Rathlin Island off the Antrim coast.

Whether he was inspired by a spider spinning its web (as legend has it), or whether he spent his time planning and regrouping, by the spring of 1307 Bruce was back in Scotland. Having left Pembroke in disarray at Glen Trool, he harried the English, first in Ayrshire and then in the north-east, while his brother Edward continued the campaign in Galloway. After Edward I's death, Bruce successfully recaptured all the strategic castles, culminating with Stirling at Bannockburn.

Although Bannockburn is widely regarded as the decisive battle of the Wars of Scotland, the conflict did not end there. The Scots were fighting in direct contradiction of a papal prohibition, a powerful sanction at that time, and Edward II mounted a successful counter-offensive during 1317–19, recapturing Berwick. The pope's support for Scotland's independence was not granted until 1324, following an appeal from the Scottish nobles in the Declaration of Arbroath in 1320 and a Scots invasion of England in 1322. It was not until the Treaty of Edinburgh in 1328 that England recognised Scotland as an independent nation and Robert I as its king. Bruce himself died of leprosy the following year, and was buried at Dumfermline Abbey.

BELOW: *The Bruce Stone laid in memorial for one of Scotland's greatest warriors near the site of one of his most famous battles – Glen Trool.*

**ABOUT • GLEN TROOL**

*This walk takes you to southern shores of Loch Trool where Robert the Bruce and his 300 men routed the superior force of the English troops. Their victory marked the turning point in Scotland's fight for independence and their ultimate goal, the Crown.*

## Dumfries & Galloway • SCOTLAND

**DISTANCE** • 5 miles (8km)

**TOTAL ASCENT** • 150ft (46m)

**PATHS** • good; firm footing even in wet weather

**TERRAIN** • forest paths, gravel paths and single-track roads

**GRADIENTS** • moderate

**REFRESHMENTS** • House of Hill, Bargrennan, 4 miles (6km) southwest off the A714

**PARK** • car park at entrance to Caldons Campsite

# Robert the Bruce, ambitious patriot

**❶** From the car park at the entrance to the campsite, turn left following the waymarks for the Loch Trool Trail. Go over a bridge, enter Caldons Campsite and turn left on to the path which follows the river. Cross another bridge and pass between two toilet blocks.

**❷** Continue following the waymarks as the trail winds round a picnic area and crosses a green metal bridge. Continue on the path then veer right across the grass to join a trail which heads uphill into the forest.

**❸** Keep on this path as it goes uphill and crosses a bracken covered clearing. Go through a kissing gate, continue through the clearing, re-enter the wood and keep walking to the interpretation board marking the site of the battle. It is at this point you can imagine Robert the Bruce's men lying in wait to ambush the 1,500-strong English force. When the English were lured to the southern shores of Loch Trool, and unable to form a tight battalion, then Bruce's soldiers attacked, blocking their escape route and hurling boulders from the slopes above.

**❹** Continue on the path from the interpretation board as it emerges from the woods and go downhill towards the end of Loch Trool. Turn left, cross a stile and a footbridge on to the Southern Upland Way and turn left.

**❺** Go through two gates and cross a wooden bridge. Soon after the stone Buchan Bridge, look out for a track branching to the left and go uphill toward the Bruce Stone and one of the best views of the loch.

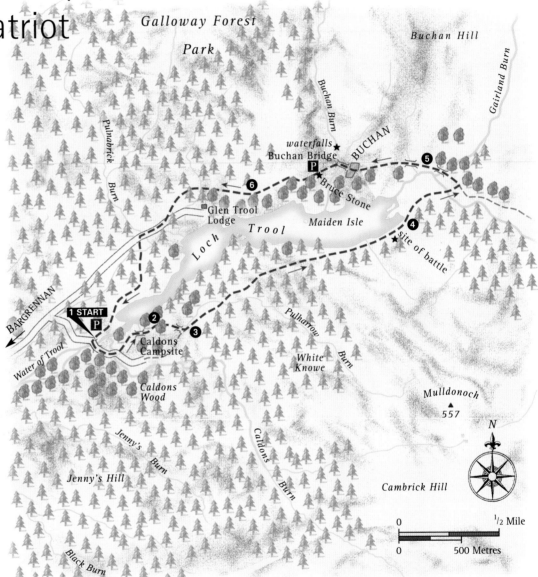

**DIFFICULTY ✲✲**

**❻** Continue on the track past the Bruce Stone – laid in memorial for one of Scotland's greatest warriors – and turn left on to the road through the car park. Keep going until you see a waymark on the left then turn left on to a forest trail to eventually return to the start of the walk and your car.

**• DON'T MISS •**

*St Ninian founded the first Christian church in Scotland in the 5th century at nearby* **Whithorn**, *which thus became known as the Cradle of Scottish Christianity. Archaeologists have recently uncovered his church and can be visited at the dig. There are also the remains of a 12th-century priory. The archaeological visitor centre offers guided tours and exhibitions, and the museum contains the 5th-century Latinus Stone, Scotland's oldest Christian artefact and memorial. St Ninian's cave lies to the south, with 8th-century carvings, once used as his retreat.*

**1327**

**1327** Owing to a poor choice of advisers, Edward II suffers rebellion and is deposed by Parliament. He is executed at Berkeley Castle and his son Edward succeeds the throne.

**1327–77** Edward III reigns.

**1328**

**1328** Scotland's independence is recognised. Bruce, now officially King of Scotland, dies in 1329 and is succeeded by his son, David II.

**1337** Edward III claims to be heir to the French throne and the Hundred Years' War with France begins.

**1346**

**1346** David II invades England but is defeated and imprisoned. He is released in return for a huge ransom, but after his death in 1371, the debt proves impossible to maintain and conflict between the two countries continues under the reign of Robert II.

MEDIEVAL

PLAGUE & CONFLICT

# The Battle of the Pass of Brander

*Six years before Bannockburn, Robert the Bruce proved his military genius in a wild Argyle glen*

Robert 'the Bruce' (1274–1329) is renowned largely for his victory at Bannockburn in 1314, when he decisively defeated Edward II and maintained Scotland's independence. There were however, years of civil war and internecine conflict prior to this famous battle, for Scotland was a bitterly divided nation and Bruce himself was far from being a straightforward patriot. Belonging to a wealthy Norman family with distant links to Scottish royalty, he pursued a ruthless rise to power. Six years before Bannockburn, he narrowly avoided ignominious defeat at the hands of a highland clan in the Battle of the Pass of Brander.

In 1308 Bruce was fighting for his throne and for his life. Two years earlier, he had been defeated by the English at Methven. Soon afterwards, he was routed by the Clan Macdougall at Dalreigh in vengeance for his murder of their relative, John Comyn, a rival claimant to the throne. Bruce had become a fugitive, hiding in the western islands, before launching a guerrilla war that regained him northern Scotland. Now, in August 1308, he was heading back into the

ABOVE: *Illustration of a statue of Robert I (the Bruce) wearing full armour.*

Macdougall heartlands of Argyle to settle his blood-feud with the clan and assert his rule over the nation.

His route lay through the Pass of Brander, a narrow defile between 3,000ft (914m)-high mountains and an arm of Loch Awe. It was here that the Macdougalls planned an ambush. As Bruce's force approached, they were waiting on the slopes above, ready to release an avalanche of scree and boulders down on to the path. Their chief watched from a galley on the loch, confident that he would see his adversary's aspirations crushed.

But Bruce was a guerrilla fighter who was familiar with the tricks of mountain warfare. He sent a lightly armed detachment even higher up the mountain, and as the Highlanders began to struggle with their heavy stones, they found themselves attacked from behind. The Macdougalls were completely routed, fleeing up the path in disarray. Their chief sailed down the loch to the safety of his castle at Inchchonnell. The clan paid dearly for their failure. Their lands were forfeited for two generations and in the longer run it was the Campbells who were to rule Argyle.

This walk provides fine views of the intimidating Pass of Brander and of Loch Awe with its archipelagos of wooded islands. The first half of the route is along a quiet lane that runs through grazing land and forestry plantations before entering an area of wild native woodland typical of the forests that still cloaked the Highlands in the 14th century. Then you take to the hills along an ancient path that passes ruins dating from the days of Bruce. At about 11 miles (18km), it is a fairly lengthy circuit that takes four hours to complete, but the effort is worthwhile. The landscape is every bit as beautiful and wild as it was 700 years ago. So awe-inspiring is the backdrop and so strong the sense of history that there may be moments when you feel an eerie sense of dislocation from the modern world.

LEFT: *Overlooking the Pass of Brander where Robert the Bruce and his troops routed the Clan Macdougall.*

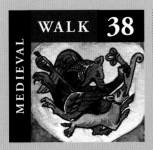

MEDIEVAL

WALK 38

**ABOUT • PASS OF BRANDER**

*Enjoy fine views over the Pass of Brander, as you follow the route taken by Robert the Bruce in 1308 into the territory of the Macdougall clan to settle a blood-feud. The successful ambush demonstrated Bruce's skills as a guerrilla fighter and as a tactician.*

**Argyll & Bute • SCOTLAND**

**DISTANCE •** 11 miles (17.7km)

**TOTAL ASCENT •** 320ft (98m)

**PATHS •** mainly firm, but some very muddy sections around Tervine

**TERRAIN •** woods and mountain moorland

**GRADIENTS •** gentle

**REFRESHMENTS •** Kilchrenan Inn (erratic winter opening )

**PARK •** pull-in on roadside below Kilchrenan church

**OS MAP •** Pathfinder 345 Loch Awe (North)

# Guerrilla warfare in the Scottish hills

❶ From Kilchrenan church, follow the road down to Kilchrenan Inn and turn left up the lane to Ardanaisaig. After passing modern forestry plantations, the road enters a wood (about 3 miles/ 4.8km from the start) where huge oaks tower above a lower canopy of hazel, silver birch and alder. Such forests covered almost all the Highlands at the time of Bruce.

❷ At the end of the public road, turn left in front of the gatehouse of Ardanaisaig Hotel to take the private road towards Tervine. Soon, you will see the Pass of Brander up ahead, with the steep, scree-covered slopes of Ben Cruachan plunging down into the loch.

❸ Just beyond the second white cottage on your left, turn left through a gate (faint marker for Fank's Cottage) over rough ground. Turn left through a gate towards a sheepfold, then immediately right through another gate on to a muddy track beside a drystone wall. At the end of the wall the track swings downhill to the right and fords a shallow burn.

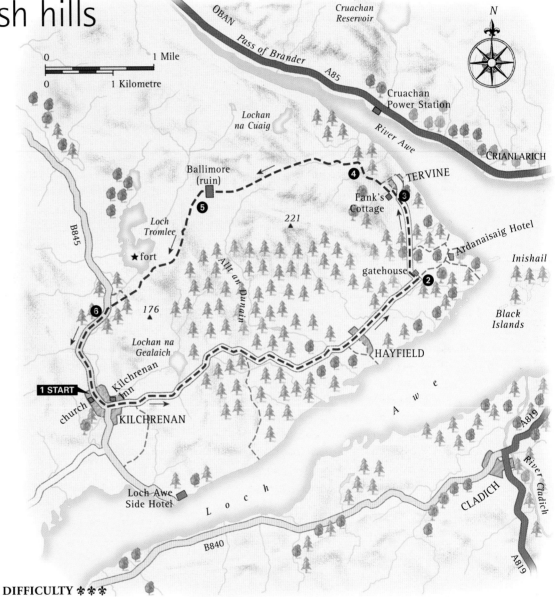

**DIFFICULTY** ❁ ❁ ❁

• DON'T MISS •

*Kilchrenan Church, an attractive building dating from the early 18th century, contains the grave-stone of Sir Colin Campbell, who was killed in a skirmish with the clan of the Macdougalls in 1294. His descendants were given vast tracts of their territory by Bruce and the Campbells eventually became the most powerful clan in Scotland.*

❹ Passing a small clump of fir trees, the track swings to the left. There are stepping stones across a burn, which the track then follows upstream. The path is very faint across the grassy hillside, but is marked by a slight embankment. Stay close to the burn. Beyond a gated fence the path rises to the watershed with dramatic views

towards the west, then swings round to the right below a craggy hill. Beyond another gate, it drops down to a ruined farmhouse.

❺ From the shell of Ballimore there is a firm, clear track to Loch Tromlee. On an island in the loch are the remains of a small medieval fortress, stronghold of the

MacCorquodales of Phantilands, sacked by the Macdonalds in 1646. The track continues through a forestry plantation before reaching the Kilchrenan road.

❻ Turn left down the road, which was once an important route to a ferry on Loch Awe, to return to the village of Kilchrenan.

**1348** A virulent disease, carried by flea-infested rats, sweeps through 14th-century Europe and Asia and wipes out over 50 million people. The Black Death, or Bubonic Plague, hits England, Scotland and Ireland in several waves, killing one-third of the population.

**1351** The king is given power over Church appointments in the Statute of Provisors.

**1362** *Piers Plowman* (William Langland) is written.

**1366** The Statute of Kilkenny forbids the speaking of Gaelic.

**1376** In England, the heir to the throne, the Black Prince, dies a year before his father, Edward III. The Black Prince's young son, Richard, becomes the new heir.

# Dunstanburgh – Castle of Legends

*A romantic castle dramatically set on the unspoiled Northumberland coast*

It is difficult to imagine a more romantic site for a ruined castle than Dunstanburgh. Set on a ridge of hard dolerite rock that juts menacingly into the North Sea, the jagged ruins of the castle's three main towers are the subject of legends and have provided material for many artists, including Joseph Turner.

Dunstanburgh is the largest of all Northumberland's castles – a massive 11 acres (4.5ha). So dramatic are the cliffs on its north side that it never needed walls. A moat dug around much of the rest provided extra protection, while to the south there was a harbour big enough to hold the Royal Fleet that called here in 1514. The castle was built to protect the harbour.

Begun in 1314 by Thomas, Earl of Lancaster, it was intended to form part of the English fortifications against the Scots after Robert the Bruce defeated King Edward II's army at Bannockburn. Thomas's great gatehouse, with its pair of semi-circular towers copied from Edward I's Welsh castles, was turned into a keep by John of Gaunt in the 1380s. He also built a new entrance to the west, to make Dunstanburgh less vulnerable.

A great curtain wall snaked away from the gatehouse, much of it now fallen. To the west is the Lilburn Tower, while in the southeast corner is the Egyncleugh Tower, named after the deep cleft in the rocks below it. It was from this tiny inlet that Queen Margaret of Anjou, wife of Henry VI, escaped in a rowing boat from imprisonment at the castle.

Dunstanburgh Castle, which was taken and recaptured several times in its history, and finally fell into ruin in the 16th century, is not the only fortification along the coast. Approaching from the north, you will pass two 20th-century concrete pillboxes, where troops waited for German invasion from across the sea. In Craster, near the start of the walk, is Craster Tower, an early 15th-century three-storey square construction, with a house, built in 1769, attached. The arch across the road near by was also built in the 18th century. The tower is the home of the Craster family, who constructed the harbour in the nearby village in the 1900s to ship road stone.

Just north of Dunstan (the name means 'the stone on the hill') is Dunstan Hall. Parts of the structure date from the 14th century, though the tower is a century or two later. It is said that the philosopher Duns Scotus was born here in about 1260. One of the most learned men of his time, he was Professor of Divinity at Oxford and died in 1308. Curiously, some of his later followers, who rejected new ideas, were known as Dunses – from which we get the word dunce, meaning a fool incapable of learning.

BELOW LEFT: *Illustration of Thomas Arundel, statesmen, prelate and a bitter opponent of the Lacastrians. He was banished by Richard II in 1397 but returned from exile with Henry IV and crowned him king in 1399.*

BELOW: *The ruins of Dunstanburgh Castle. Built in the 14th century the gatehouse, in the foreground, was originally six storeys. In the background is Lilburn Tower – strategically placed as a watch-tower.*

MEDIEVAL

**WALK 39**

**ABOUT • DUNSTANBURGH**

*This walk offers a wealth of history: from 14th-century Dunstanburgh Castle, part of the fortifications built to defend England against the attacks of Robert the Bruce, to 20th-century pillboxes, where troops awaited German invaders in World War II.*

**Northumbria • N ENGLAND**

**DISTANCE** • 5 ¼ miles (8.4km)

**TOTAL ASCENT** • 460ft (140m)

**PATHS** • field paths, roads and farm tracks

**TERRAIN** • undulating farmland and fine coastland with grassy dunes

**GRADIENTS** • moderate

**REFRESHMENTS** • Bark Potts café and Robson's fish restaurant, Craster; Cottage Inn, Dunstan

**PARK** • signed car park at entrance to Craster

**OS MAP** • Explorer 332 Alnwick & Amble, Craster & Whittingham

# Dunstanburgh Castle: a mighty fortress

**DIFFICULTY ❊ ❊**

❶ From the car park, take the path behind the tourist information centre signed Craster South Farm. Fork left near a bench and at a kissing gate bear half-right across the field and uphill. Go through another gate on to a lane.

❷ Turn right, then right again at a crossroads. Go through the archway across the road then turn left through a gate, signed to Dunstan (the nearby Dunstan Hall is believed to have been the birth place of Duns Scotus, a famous 13th-century philosopher). At the next gate go half-left, through another gate and past the row of houses to the road.

❸ Turn right and follow the road as it bends left. Go straight on at the next junction, towards Embleton. Take the next lane right, signed Dunstan Square. Pass the houses then bend left though the farmyard. Go straight on through a gate, signed Dunstan Steads.

❹ Follow the farm road for a mile (1.6km). As you approach the hamlet of Dunstan Steads, go

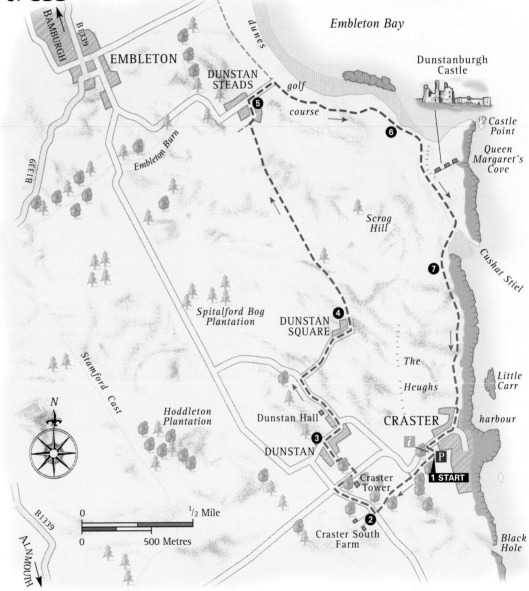

through a gateway and wind between farm buildings to a road. Turn right, and follow the road as it bends left to reach a lane.

❺ Turn right, following a sign to Dunstanburgh Castle. At the bottom of the lane, go through a gate and turn right beside the golf course. The path goes alongside a green to a kissing gate by a National Trust sign.

❻ Go through the gate and follow the path inland round the castle rock, to arrive at the gatehouse entrance. After visiting the castle, leave the gateway and continue

straight ahead along the ridge to reach a kissing gate.

❼ Continue ahead along the coast, through another kissing gate to enter Craster village by a gate on to a lane. Pass the houses to reach a T-junction above the harbour, and turn right, to the car park.

**1377**

**1377–1399** Richard II reigns.

**1381** The introduction of a poll tax to supplement government funds leads to the Peasants Revolt. The young king agrees to the peasants' demands, but withdraws his promises when the revolt is over.

**1390**

**1390** Robert III succeeds to the Scottish throne. He dies in 1406 but his son James I, imprisoned by the English, is prevented from returning to Scotland until 1424.

**1398** *The Canterbury Tales* (Geoffrey Chaucer) are completed.

**1399**

**1399** While Richard is in Ireland, his cousin, Henry Bolingbroke, lays claim to the throne. On his return, Richard is deposed by Bolingbroke and imprisoned in Pontefract Castle until his death in 1400.

**1399-1413** The reign of Henry IV.

# Abbotsbury and its Benedictine monks

*Hilly walking country around Abbotsbury offers superb views over its monastic complex, set against a backdrop of Chesil Beach*

**MEDIEVAL**

**PLAGUE & CONFLICT**

The exceptional size of Abbotsbury's tithe barn reflects the importance and wealth of the Bendictine monastery that was founded here in 1044. Imagine this buttressed stone building at twice its size, for what we see today is half the barn that was built in 1400. Lay people were required by medieval law to contribute a tenth of their income (a tithe) for the maintenance of religious foundations. These payments, which were normally made up of crops or farm stock, were stored in the tithe barn. Today, Abbotsbury tithe barn plays its part in the local economy by hosting a children's farm.

The monastery was dissolved by Henry VIII in 1539, and bought by the Strangways family on condition that it was demolished. You will see where the great St Peter's Abbey Church and ancillary buildings stood, between the tithe barn and the Church of St Nicholas, begun in 1320. Virtually nothing remains but a solitary gable wall, known as Pynion End, with a fireplace in it. Half the tithe barn was retained for agricultural purposes, while stone from the abbey buildings was used to build houses in the village.

St Catherine's Chapel is the next stop on your walk, on top of a steep little knoll. Built as part of the monastic complex at about the same time as the barn, the chapel was dedicated to St Catherine, patron saint of spinsters. The walls are heavily buttressed to support the barrel-vaulted stone roof and to withstand gales blowing straight off the sea. After the Dissolution, the chapel was retained as a sea-mark. Inside, it is completely bare, except for a copy of the prayer made by women in search of a husband. On the side of St Catherine's Hill, and elsewhere on the walk, notice the medieval strip lynchets. These terraces were cut in monastic times to form strip fields for cultivation.

From the hill there's a good view of the Fleet, the largest tidal lagoon in the country. It stretches from Abbotsbury to Portland Harbour, 8 miles (12.8km) away. Here, in its western corner, you can visit the Swannery (closed in winter). Records go back to 1393, and it may have been in existence before the monks began to breed swans here for their table; today, 100 pairs of semi-domesticated mute swans, joined by up to 900 overwintering birds, enjoy a more secure life.

Protecting the Fleet from the sea is the high bank of the stony Chesil Beach, created by the action of storm waters after the last Ice Age. From the hilly vantage points on this walk, you will see it stretching eastwards to Portland. In the opposite direction, it extends to West Bay, a total of 17 miles (27km). Over thousands of years, waves have graded the stones from tiny pieces of shingle in West Bay to large pebbles in Portland. Your walk takes you alongside Chesil, then up to the ridge of hills behind Abbotsbury. An Iron Age hill fort and Wears Hill offer some spectacular views. Finally, drop down to the village along Blind Lane, a medieval track known to generations of monks.

ABOVE: *The large and well-preserved tithe barn at Abbotsbury. Abbeys depended on agriculture to raise money for the monastic order. The tithes (taxes) were gathered in the form of crops – generally the tithe payable was a tenth of the farmer's yield.*

LEFT: *View of the tithe barn, with the stone-built village of Abbotsbury and Wears Hill beyond.*

### ABOUT • ABBOTSBURY

*The Benedictine monastery at Abbotsbury was founded in 1044 and demolished during the Dissolution of Monasteries, ordered by Henry VIII. The tithe barn is all that remains but it is a powerful reminder of this gentle order of monks.*

### Dorset • SW ENGLAND

**DISTANCE** • 6½ miles (10.4km)

**TOTAL ASCENT** • 650ft (198m)

**PATHS** • well-marked throughout; ascent to Abbotsbury hill fort and some paths can be muddy and difficult after prolonged rain; otherwise firm; road-walking in village

**TERRAIN** • village roads, grassland, short stretch of shingle, tarmac track and fields

**GRADIENTS** • gradual climb to St Catherine's Chapel, short steep climb to Abbotsbury hill fort

**REFRESHMENTS** • choice in Abbotsbury

**PARK** • village car park

**OS MAP** • Outdoor Leisure 15 Purbeck & South Dorset

# The monastic complex at Abbotsbury

❶ With your back to the entrance to the village car park, take the path in the far right corner of the car park. Turn left at a ruined gable wall, part of an abbey outbuilding, turn right at the pond, and then left on to the lane. The tithe barn is ahead of you. Continue to a fork. Take the right-hand road, signed Swannery Pedestrians.

❷ At a low stone waymarker, turn right on to a track to St Catherine's Chapel. Keep ahead over a footbridge and skirt the hill. Join the track that climbs 437yds (400m) to the chapel.

❸ From the stile behind the chapel, walk to the brow of the hill and then go downhill, aiming right and following the line of a copse. At the foot of the slope, reach a stone waymarker. To visit the Swannery (Mar–Oct), keep straight ahead for just over ½ mile (800m). Retrace your steps to this point.

❹ From the waymarker, follow signs for the Sub-Tropical Gardens, skirting the hill with the sea on your left. Turn left along the coast path (may be muddy), signed Chesil Beach, for ½ a mile (800m).

A short stretch (800ft/250m) on shingle brings you back to the beach car park.

❺ Continue on the tarmac path, with Chesil Bank on your left. Pass the drive to Lawrence's Cottage, and at a low stone waymarker turn right uphill, for the hill fort. Go round the back of East Bexington Farm and diagonally right uphill towards a cottage in trees. Over a stile turn immediately right, with the hedge on your right. Enter an area of scrub and trees and follow the sign to the hill fort. The path is steep and can be muddy and slippery. At the top, follow the stone wall to the right. Reach the road and, across it, the double-bank Iron Age hill fort.

❻ Walk along the southern rampart with superb views over the Fleet, Chesil Beach and Portland. Past the trig point, drop down to a stile and cross a lane. Continue along Wears Hill.

❼ Just beyond a gate, reach a signpost. Following directions for Abbotsbury village, walk diagonally right downhill for 328yds (300m), through old stone quarries, and continue for 875yds (800m) to join Blind Lane. Turn right into Back Street and left on to the main road through the village for village car park. If you used beach car park, continue from Point ❶.

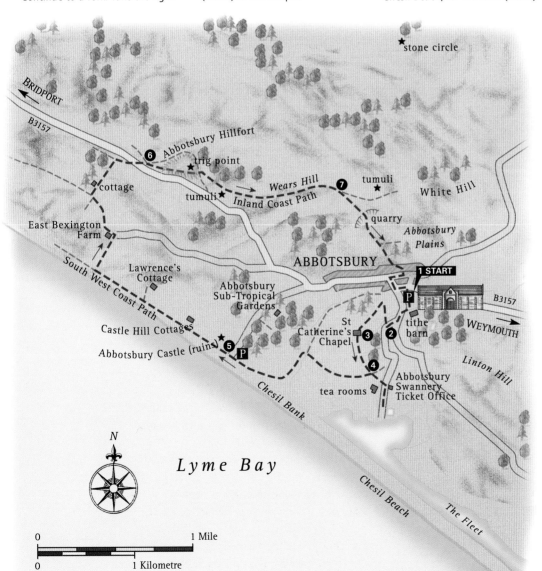

stone circle

BRIDPORT

B3157

Abbotsbury Hillfort

❻ trig point

cottage

Wears Hill

tumuli  Inland Coast Path

tumuli

❼

tumuli

White Hill

quarry

East Bexington Farm

Abbotsbury Plains

South West Coast Path

Lawrence's Cottage

ABBOTSBURY

❶ START

Abbotsbury Sub-Tropical Gardens

B3157

Castle Hill Cottages

St Catherine's Chapel

❸ ❷

tithe barn

WEYMOUTH

Abbotsbury Castle (ruins)

❺ P

❹

Linton Hill

Chesil Bank

tea rooms

Abbotsbury Swannery Ticket Office

*N*

*Lyme Bay*

Chesil Beach

The Fleet

0 ———————— 1 Mile

0 ———————— 1 Kilometre

### • DON'T MISS •

*The walk passes close to the **Abbotsbury Sub-Tropical Gardens**. The collections of tender plants and exotic birds here were founded by the Strangways family in the grounds of Abbotsbury Castle, which burnt down in the early 1900s. Open daily all year except two weeks at Christmas.*

**DIFFICULTY** ✲✲

# Warwick's Medieval Castle

*When not at war, England's 14th-century knights were stars of the country's favourite spectator sport: the tournament*

## An Impregnable Stronghold

After the 17th century, Warwick Castle evolved into a stately home, whose lavish house parties often included the monarch among the guests. Earlier, it had served more utilitarian purposes and, well before the Normans arrived, there had been a Saxon fort to defend against Viking raiders. Henry de Beaumont, one of William the Conqueror's vassals, built the first stone castle, but that was largely destroyed during the Barons Revolt in 1264. Today's castle dates mostly from

14th- and 15th-century rebuilding and was designed to be both imposing and impregnable. Seemingly both objectives were achieved, for the only assault on its formidable defences was an unsuccessful attack by Royalist forces during the Civil War.

## Entertainment Medieval Style

Despite the disturbances of the 14th century, there was some comfort within the castle's Spartan exterior and, for the nobility at least, life

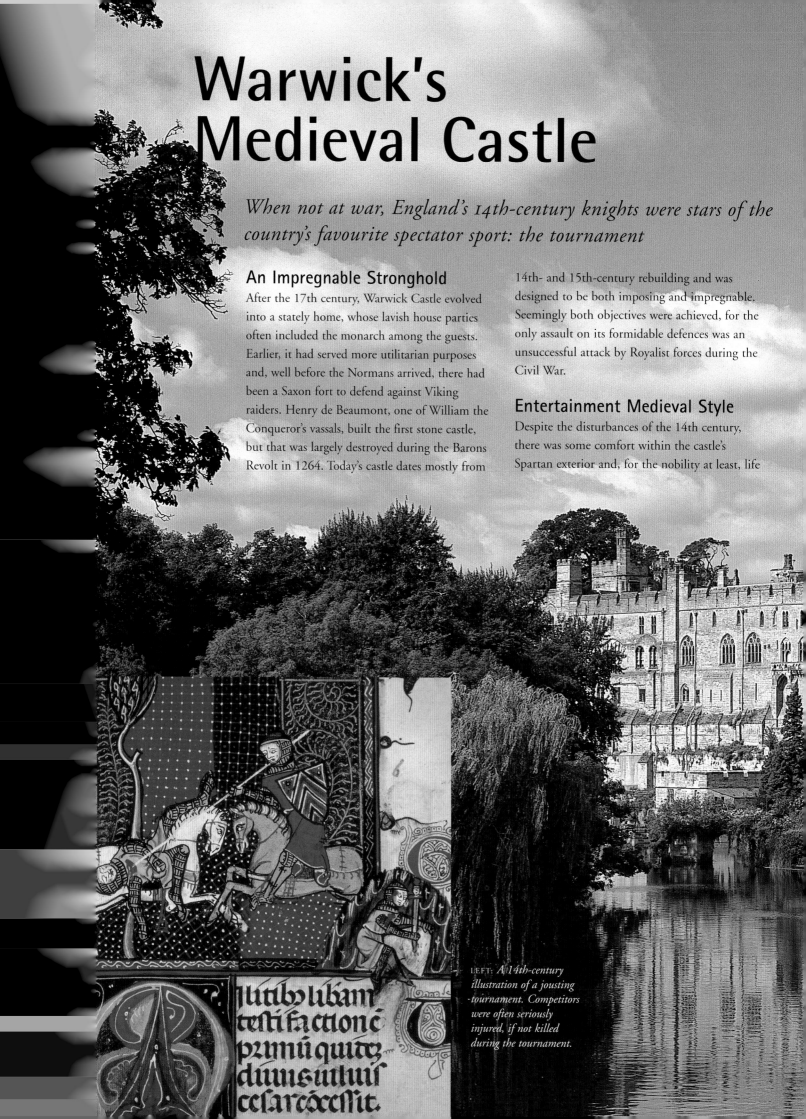

LEFT: *A 14th-century illustration of a jousting -tournament. Competitors were often seriously injured, if not killed during the tournament.*

had many pleasurable diversions. Knights were the superstars of the day and, when not seeking honour on the battlefield, spent their time practising combat or competing in tournaments. These were great spectacles, the champions and their horses clad in shining armour and colourful liveries, which, besides adding glamour to the occasion they served a practical purpose on the battlefield by identifying the combatants. Jousting and single combat contests were popular, with prizes for the victor, the possible bonus of the loser's forfeited armour and horse, and favours from lady admirers. More unruly was the mêlée, a mock battle between opposing teams. Although the objective was victory through surrender, by unseating, knocking down or disarming opponents, things often got well out of hand.

Hunting parties, led by the lord, were more civilised. These, too, gave an opportunity to demonstrate skills with horse, bow and sword, and to display favourite hunting birds and dogs. Many castles had menageries, with collections of hawks and dogs, but there were also more exotic animals, such as bears and lions. It is said that Richard the Lionheart had a crocodile, before it escaped into the Thames.

Little excuse was needed for a feast, and while the poor were lucky to have coarse bread, pottage and weak beer, the tables of the rich were a gastronomic delight. Beef, mutton, venison and boar were served, together with fish and game birds and such delicacies as peacock and heron. Rich and spicy sauces often flavoured the dishes, probably to disguise the taints of over-ripe food. Pastries, sweets and puddings were also popular, all washed down with imported wine. Jesters, jugglers and acrobats provided a floor show to a musical background from the minstrel gallery and, once the tables had been cleared, it was time to dance.

BELOW: *The age of chivalry revived at Warwick Castle.*

BELOW LEFT: *Warwick Castle set on the wooded banks of the River Avon.*

## WALK **41**  A WANDER AROUND WARWICK

❶ Walk through St Nicholas' Park to the river and turn left. Past a footbridge beyond the park, continue along a wooded riverside path. After a railway bridge and then the Grand Union Canal, carried high above on a three-arched aqueduct, turn left and climb steps to the canal's towpath. Instead of crossing the bridge, turn right and follow the canal around the town's northern edge, passing old warehouses and workshops that exploited the canal's cheap and relatively swift transport. After some 2 miles (3km), immediately before bridge number 51, leave the canal and climb on to the road above. Turn left over the bridge and then go right into Budbrooke Road. Walk through a small car park on the left and carry on, following a short length of canal, the Saltisford Arm.

❷ Forced back to the road beyond its far end, pass beneath a railway bridge and immediately go right, crossing a redundant canal bridge. Over a gate/stile on the right, climb left up a tree-planted bank on to Warwick Racecourse and keep going between a driving range and golf course. Where the range ends, turn left past the club house and continue off the course.

❸ Carry on ahead up Linen Street and then turn right, down to the main road. At the main road, go left through West Gate, past the Lord Leycester Hospital and along the High Street. At Castle Street, turn right and then fork right beside Oken House. Cross the road at the bottom and enter a gate to the Warwick Castle. Its entrance is to the left.

❹ When you have visited the castle, leave the courtyard by the opposite gate and turn right down a flight of steps. Go left at the bottom and walk out to the main road. The car park is down to the right.

**Distance:** 5¼ miles (8.5km)

**Total ascent:** minimal

**Paths:** riverside and canal paths may be muddy; otherwise well surfaced-paths and tracks

**Terrain:** river and canalside; pavements

**Refreshments:** plenty within Warwick and at the castle

**Parking:** car park off A41, by St Nicholas' Park and the River Avon

**OS Map:** Explorer 221 Coventry & Warwick, Royal Leamington Spa

**Difficulty:** ✱

1300–1485

| 1400 | 1404 | 1414 |
|------|------|------|

**1400** Development of the modern English language begins.

**1401–15** Owain Glyndŵr, a descendant of the last independent Prince of Wales, leads the campaign for a return to Welsh autonomy.

**1404** The first Welsh parliament meets at Machynlleth and the second parliament meets a year later at Harlech Castle, where Owain is crowned Prince of Wales.

**1413–22** Henry V accedes the throne in England.

**1414** In Italy the Medici family become bankers to the papacy. Under the Medici influence, Florence becomes the cultural centre of the Renaissance by 1450.

**1415** The French armies are defeated at the Battle of Agincourt.

106

# Canterbury – Centre of Christianity and Pilgrimage

*Follow in the footsteps of Chaucer's pilgrims through the city of Canterbury, birthplace of English Christianity and one of Europe's most celebrated places of pilgrimage*

ABOVE: *St Augustine's Priory in Canterbury has been a monastic site for nearly 1000 years.*

Canterbury has played an important part in England's history since its early beginnings as the Roman town of *Durovernum*. After the Romans left, Canterbury emerged as the capital of the kingdom of Kent, and it was here that St Augustine journeyed in AD 597 to re-establish Christianity. With the construction of the cathedral and an abbey, the town quickly rose in importance to become the centre of the Church in England.

It was in 1170, following the brutal murder of Archbishop Thomas Becket in the cathedral and his subsequent martyrdom, that Canterbury's future as a religious centre was assured. Becket's shrine became the most popular place of pilgrimage in Christendom and brought immense wealth to the archbishopric and to Canterbury.

Money pouring in from pilgrims helped fund the building of the present cathedral (1275–1400), the fifth largest in England, and vast lodging houses were built to accommodate the growing number of pilgrims. The recorded annual numbers of pilgrims to Canterbury during the heyday of pilgrimage in the 14th century exceeded 200,000, out of a total population estimated at around four million on the outbreak of the Black Death in 1348. Most wanted to pray at Becket's shrine and appeal directly to the saint for a cure to an illness or disability, or for success in a business venture.

Canterbury's other great promoter was Geoffrey Chaucer. The 'Father of English Poetry' was born in 1343 and spent much of his life as a king's messenger and minor ambassador before losing his influence at the court of Richard II in 1386. His name is inextricably linked to Canterbury through *The Canterbury Tales*, which he started writing in 1387. In a wry, humorous style, it tells of 29 worldly pilgrims, who enliven their four-day journey from the Tabard Inn in Southwark, London, to Canterbury by recounting tales, spurred on by the offer of a free dinner at the Tabard Inn for the best story told. The tales show a cross-section of English society, and a robust irreverence for monastic life and the cult of relics.

This walk follows the path of Chaucer's pilgrims through the city, starting at the Westgate, where they would have entered the city, and finishing at the cathedral. Having called in at the 12th-century Eastbridge Hospital, a medieval pilgrim's hospital, with undercroft and two chapels, you can visit the Canterbury Tales Visitor Attraction and step back in time to the 14th century, joining the pilgrims on the walk. Chaucer's tales are recited through headphones and dramatisations are enhanced by the sights, sounds and smells of the period. Pass the Canterbury Heritage Museum, which outlines the city's 2,000-year history, and the ruins of the Norman castle keep; then, following a stroll along the city walls, you have the opportunity to view the ruins of St Augustine's Abbey. A monastic site for almost a thousand years, it has an excellent museum and visitor centre. Back within the city walls, allow plenty of time to explore the city's crowning glory and the destination of countless pilgrims, the cathedral.

BACKGROUND: *The Latin gospels presented by King Athelstane to the Church of Canterbury.*

BELOW: *Pilgrims leaving Canterbury. The city has been a shrine for pilgrims since the murder of Thomas Becket in 1170.*

**ABOUT • CANTERBURY**

*Birthplace of Christianity and mecca for pilgrims, Canterbury is famous for its association with the poet Geoffrey Chaucer, author of* The Canterbury Tales. *After your walk, step back in time with a visit to the Canterbury Tales Visitor Attraction.*

## Kent • SE ENGLAND

| | |
|---|---|
| **DISTANCE •** 3 miles (4.8km) | **REFRESHMENTS •** cafés, pubs and restaurants in the city centre |
| **TOTAL ASCENT •** 66ft (20m) | |
| **PATHS •** surfaced roads | **PARK •** long and short stay car parks (fee) around the city walls |
| **TERRAIN •** city streets | |
| **GRADIENTS •** level; short ascent to city walls | **OS MAP •** Explorer 150 Canterbury & the Isle of Thanet |

# The tale of Canterbury

**DIFFICULTY ✱**

❶ With your back to Westgate Archway and Museum, walk along the pedestrianised St Peter's Street towards the town centre. Cross the River Stour and pass Eastbridge Hospital (Pilgrims Hospital) on your right. Continue past the library and Guildhall Street, turn right along St Margaret's Street.

❷ Pass the Canterbury Tales visitor attraction and the Tourist Information Office, then turn right down Hawks Lane, signed to Canterbury Heritage. At Stour Street, turn left, pass the Canterbury Heritage Museum and at the end of the street, keep ahead along Church Lane to pass St Mildred's Church.

❸ Before the ring road, turn left between metal bollards and walk past the Norman castle. At Castle Street, turn right then left along the pavement by the ring road. In a few paces, bear left along Castle Row, then right by the toilets into Dane John Gardens. Keep right, climb on to the city walls.

❹ Climb the path to the monument on top of Dane John

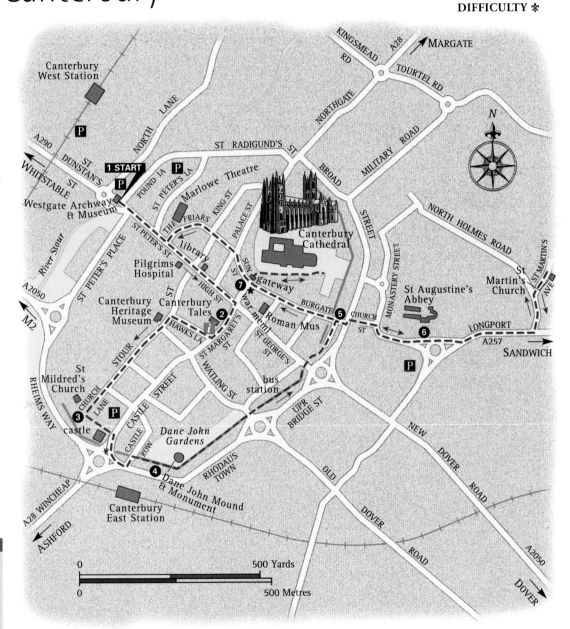

Mound for the fine city view. Continue along the walls above the bus station and descend to cross St George's Street. Continue to Burgate.

❺ Turn right, cross the pedestrian crossing over the ring road and walk along Church Street to the junction with Monastery Street.

Cross over to the fine gatehouse, turn right and follow Longport left to reach St Augustine's Abbey.

❻ To visit St Martin's Church, keep left at the roundabout, turn first left, then right into St Martin's Avenue. Retrace your steps back to the pedestrian crossing over the ring road and walk ahead along

Burgate to the war memorial and the cathedral gateway.

❼ Turn right through the gate to visit the cathedral. Go ahead along Sun Street, then over a junction into Orange Street. Continue along The Friars to pass the Marlowe Theatre. At St Peter's Street, turn right back to Westgate Archway.

**1420**

**1420** Henry's marriage to Catherine of France forces Charles VI of France to accept him as heir to the French throne.

**1422–1471** Henry VI inherits both the English and French thrones when he is only one year old.

**1429**

**1429** Joan of Arc begins to put into action her vision of ridding France of the English.

**1431** Joan of Arc is condemned as a witch and burnt at the stake in Rouen.

**1437**

**1437** The Scottish king, James I, whose zeal for reform makes him many enemies among the Highland lords, is assassinated. His son, James II, succeeds to the throne.

**1450** Glasgow University is established.

# The Desertion of Wharram Percy

*An abandoned village provides a window into medieval society*

ABOVE: *This engraving shows the devastating effects of the plague. Victims suffered disfiguring and contagious boils before almost certain death.*

A photograph taken from the air in 1948 alerted the archaeological community to the deserted village of Wharram Percy. Since then, it has been the most studied and perhaps the best known of deserted medieval villages in England.

The Yorkshire Wolds have been settled and farmed for thousands of years. In the neolithic period, trees were cleared to allow crops to be grown; early cultivation terraces are visible near North Grimston. Bronze Age settlers kept animals on the hills,

ABOVE: *Little remains of the medieval village of Wharram Percy, as the whole area was infected with the plague during the 14th century, forcing the residents to flee.*

and in the Iron Age permanent farms were established. The Romans, too, used this landscape; Wharram le Street is on a Roman road, and villas have been excavated near by.

Wharram le Street, like Wharram Percy, has an ancient church, partly Norman and with an Anglo-Saxon tower. But Wharram Percy's church stands ruined and isolated amid fields, not surrounded by a living village. So how did Wharram Percy die?

The Black Death, which ravaged England between 1348 and 1379, is often blamed for the death of villages, but it was not the only factor. Wharram Percy's farmland was not productive,

and the inhabitants would always have struggled to make a living. Nevertheless, even as late as 1368 there were still 30 houses here. Ninety years later there were only 16, as the landowners converted the arable land to sheep runs. The last homes were demolished in 1500.

Approaching the site from the north along the sunken lane – once the village street – to your right are the raised earthworks on which the wooden houses stood. Built on chalk foundations, they were of cruck construction – curved tree trunks were split lengthways to produce arches that formed walls and supported the thatched roof. Each house had an open hearth, and housed both humans and animals.

From the 12th century Wharram Percy had two manor houses. The North Manor was owned by the Percy family, who gave their name to the village – Wharram means 'the enclosure in the cauldron-shaped valley'. South Manor originally belonged to the Chamberlains. The North Manor was a complex building, which included private apartments for the lord of the manor, a chapel, bakehouse and brewery. All this was dismantled in the 13th century, when the Percy Family took over the South Manor House.

Wharram's church, started in the 10th century, achieved its present form over the next 400 years. As the population increased and then declined, the church followed. Aisles were built and then demolished – notice the arches now built into the nave walls. After the village was abandoned, the church decayed. Part of the tower fell in 1959, and the roof was removed.

The brick cottages near by are from the 19th century – the Wharram sign came from the railway station. The walk follows part of the track. South of the church is the mill pond, a valuable resource in this dry region. The beck here has been dammed since at least the 9th century, and in medieval times a watermill stood at the north end of the pond. It is here, perhaps, that today's visitors can best conjure up a vision of medieval life in this remote valley.

WALK 43

MEDIEVAL

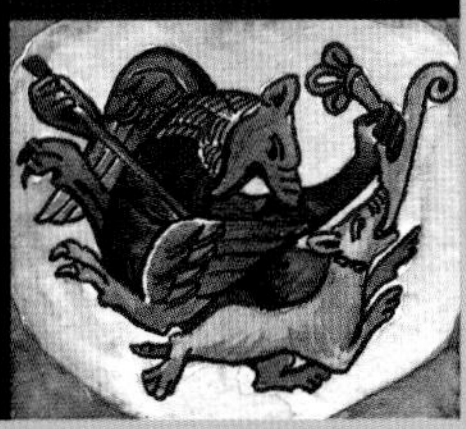

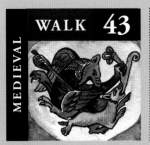

ABOUT • WHARRAM PERCY

*The discovery of Wharram Percy in 1948 led to extensive excavations revealing a 5000-year-old community. The village was deserted during the 15th century due to the Black Death which ravaged many settlements in England between 1338–79*

## North Yorkshire • N ENGLAND

**DISTANCE** • 8 miles (13km)

**TOTAL ASCENT** • 1,640ft (500m)

**PATHS** • field paths and track, some roads

**TERRAIN** • undulating chalk landscape

**GRADIENTS** • one steep climb through fields, one on road

**REFRESHMENTS** • Middleton Arms, North Grimston

**PARK** • roadside parking in North Grimston, near the church, or in the Wharram Percy car park near Bella Farm

**OS MAP** • Explorer 300 Howardian Hills & Malton

# Plague and pestilence in the Yorkshire Wolds

❶ Follow the main road south, past the Middleton Arms pub. Just beyond the speed derestriction sign take a track left over a cattle grid, towards Wood House Farm. Cross two more cattle grids. On the rise beyond, turn right at the Wolds Way sign.

❷ Go downhill and cross a bridge between two stiles. Bear slightly left and ascend the valley to a signpost. Turn left, going over a stile at another signpost. Then continue along the side of the field. At the next signpost go right, then go through the hedge on to a track.

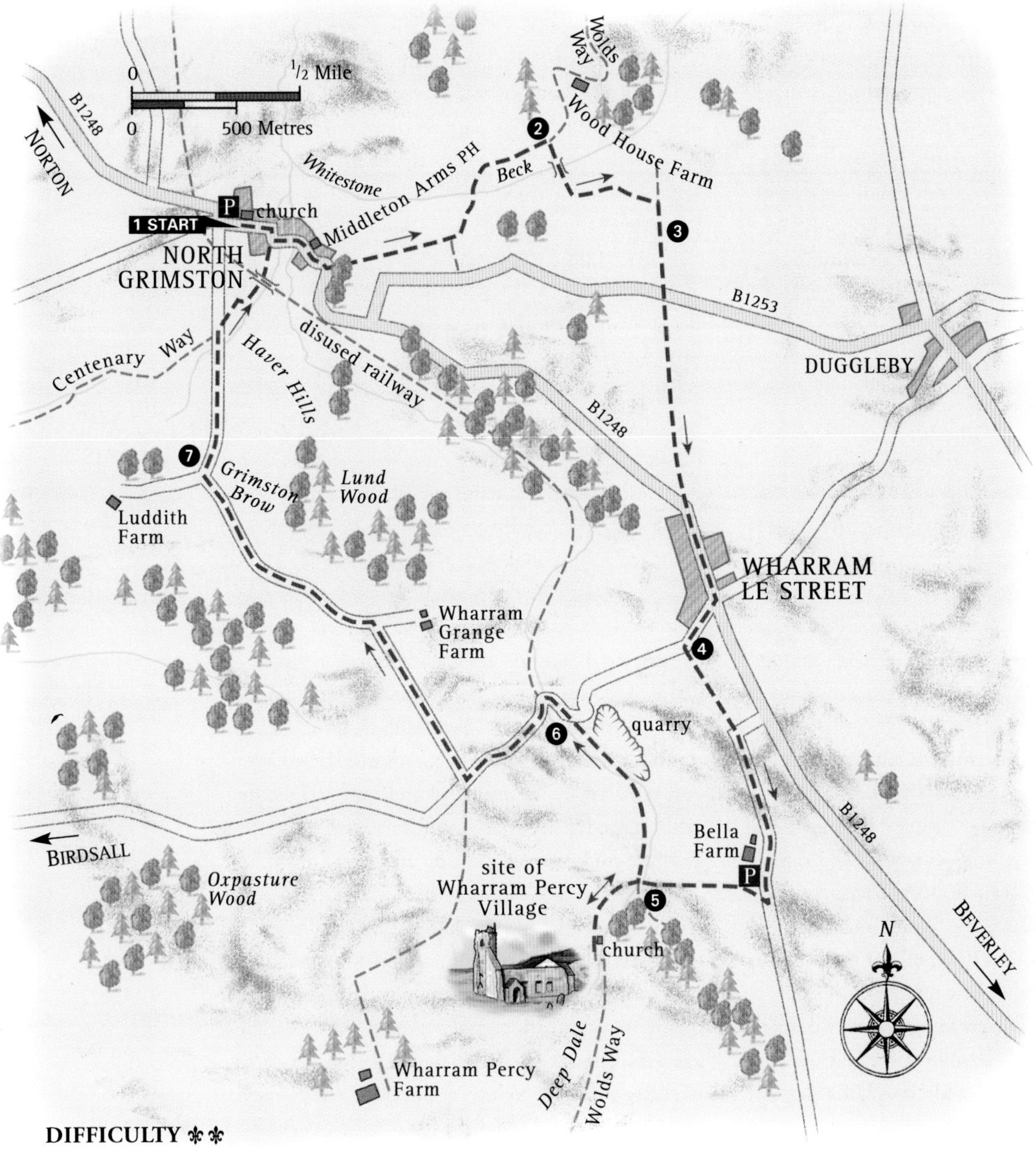


DIFFICULTY ⚜⚜

• DON'T MISS •

*In Wharram Percy's church there are a number of slabs that once covered the graves of important villagers. Some of them are decorated with crosses and other symbols. Excavations have revealed more than 1000 skeletons – almost half of them children.*

❸ Follow the track across a road and downhill. At the next road turn left and walk uphill through Wharram le Street. At the crossroads turn right, towards Birdsall. Just beyond the houses on your left, go over a stile, signed Wolds Way.

❹ Follow the field edge to a road, then go straight ahead, passing Bella Farm. Beyond the farm, follow the sign for Medieval Deserted Village. Go through the car park and down the track. After the second kissing gate veer right to another gate.

❺ Go through the gate and down the steps on to the former railway line. To visit Wharram Percy, cross and follow the lane opposite. Return to the same point and turn left (not under the bridge). Follow the disused line to a road.

❻ Go straight ahead, and follow the road to a crossroads. Turn right, signed North Grimston. Follow the road, turning left at a T-junction by the entrance to Wharram Grange Farm. Go over a cattle grid, and right at a T-junction near Luddith Farm.

❼ After the next cattle grid turn right, signed CW. Follow the field edge then go through a gate and ahead, left of the stream. After another gate, pass under the railway bridge. Follow the path on to the road. Turn left to return to the start point.

**1449**

**1449** The French recapture Normandy and four years later the Hundred Year War ends leaving the French victorious. England has lost all her French lands except Calais.

**1452–1519** Leonardo da Vinci is born. During his lifetime he is

**1452**

celebrated as an artist, inventor, enineer, architect and mathematician. The Mona Lisa, his most famous painting, is completed in 1503.

**1455** Outbreak of the War of the Roses as the Regent, Duke of York,

**1455**

is dismissed and the King takes over rule of the government.

**1461** Edward, Duke of York, deposes Henry and is crowned King of England, he is deposed briefly in 1470 but restored in 1471 and reigns until his death in 1483.

# Harlech and the Wars of the Roses

*Around the castle made famous in song, and along the sands of Cardigan Bay*

ABOVE: *The royal seal of Henry IV (1399–1413), showing the King riding into battle.*

During the second half of the 15th century, the Royal Houses of Lancaster and York battled and conspired against each other, both claiming a right to the English throne. As the balance of power shifted to and fro between the symbolic red rose of the Lancastrians and the white rose of the Yorkists, Harlech Castle became inextricably caught up in their vicious tug-of-war.

The walk starts at the castle's entrance, and it is immediately clear why Edward I chose this towering site for his fortress in the 13th century, for the castle rises out of a sheer rock promontory, and there are superb views of both the sea and the mountains of Snowdonia. It provided a formidable place of safety for Margaret of Anjou, wife of Henry VI, when he was defeated by his Yorkist rivals in 1460. Having fled here, she conferred with her great ally Jasper Tudor, and was soon on her way to Scotland to summon reinforcements.

Today you can cross the plains that stretch 200ft (61m) below the castle walls, to reach the sand dunes and beach. But during those turbulent times the sea washed up against the castle's watergate, presenting yet another obstacle for would-be attackers. Harlech's reputation as an impenetrable stronghold was enhanced during the 1460s, and celebrated in the stirring anthem 'Men of Harlech'.

ABOVE: *Engraving of Edward IV, King of England from 1461–1483.*

When the Lancastrian cause crumbled in 1461, Henry VI was ousted and his vanquisher proclaimed the new king, Edward IV; but Harlech continued to hold out, harbouring Lancastrian ministers and refugees, defying calls from parliament to yield, and withstanding a seven-year Yorkist siege.

One of the leading figures of the continuing rebellion against the king was Jasper Tudor, whose nephew, Henry, had a claim to the throne through his mother, the Lady Margaret Beaufort. Dodging in and out of various secret hiding places in

Wales and abroad, Jasper kept the Lancastrian momentum going, and eventually landed near Harlech to rally support. He then managed to reach the castle and recruit the help of its still undefeated garrison. At this point, Edward IV realised that Harlech was more than an isolated trouble-spot. Determined to subdue the castle once and for all, he sent troops thundering across North Wales. As you

walk along the beach and turn back towards the castle rock, you take in a wide view of the coast where the King's men plundered and razed Snowdonia's communities en route to Harlech. Some towns were so devastated that they were still recovering a century later. Edward's army approached in a pincer movement, from north and south, overwhelming the rebels, and Harlech surrendered on 14 August 1468. Fifty of the castle's garrison were imprisoned in the Tower of London; two were executed, before Edward issued a general pardon.

Meanwhile, Jasper Tudor slipped away. After one brief reappearance in 1471, he finally burst back on to the scene in 1485, helping his nephew, Henry, to the throne as the first of the Tudor monarchs.

ABOVE: *Harlech Castle in Cardigan Bay, with the mountains of Snowdonia in the distance.*

### ABOUT • HARLECH

*Built of local grey sandstone by Edward I in 1283–90, Harlech Castle has served as both a fortress and a refuge. In the Wars of the Roses it was besieged by Yorkists for nearly eight years, and the struggle is remembered in the song 'Men of Harlech'.*

## Gwynedd • WALES

**DISTANCE** • 5 miles (8km)

**TOTAL ASCENT** • 200ft (61m)

**PATHS** • rocky track through woods – can be muddy; sandy track through dunes

**TERRAIN** • surfaced roads, steps, gravel track, sand dunes and beach, woodland track. **Make sure you complete the walk during low tide.**

**GRADIENTS** • steep steps to sea level; steep climb (rocky track and steps) to castle rock

**REFRESHMENTS** • cafés and pub in Harlech

**PARK** • castle forecourt; Upper Bron y Graig car park in town

**OS MAP** • Outdoor Leisure 18 Snowdonia – Harlech, Porthmadog & Bala

# Song of the 'Men of Harlech'

❶ Start at the top castle entrance. With your back to the castle, turn right. Following the sign towards Harlech raliway station, take the road that snakes downhill. Part way down, take the public footpath, left, down a flight of slate steps.

❷ Cross the road and follow the public footpath opposite. Cross the railway line with care and go through the metal gate. Follow the path, keeping the wire fence to your right. As you leave the golf course, ignore the track which forks right and take the sandy path between the dunes to the beach.

❸ Turn right and walk along the beach for about a mile (1.6km). From here you can enjoy magnificient sweeping views of the castle and bay. Then turn back and retrace your steps as far as the red-and-white striped pole (lifebelt point H7).

❹ Turn left along the marked sand path, which soon becomes a surfaced path. Go through the metal kissing gate and continue ahead to the main road.

❺ Cross the road. Turn left, then right (just past the Queen's Hotel) towards the railway station. Cross by the level crossing and turn left. Pass the turning to Woodlands Caravan Park and continue beyond the fire station to the public footpath sign.

❻ Turn right to go through the woods. Continue ahead, presently climbing quite steeply. Climb the gap in the stone wall and continue up a rocky slope to the more

clearly marked path. Turn right, uphill, and climb the steep steps.

❼ At the top of the steps climb over the metal bar. Turn right, and

follow the road back into town. At the crossroads, turn right, following the sign to return to the castle where it is worth leaving plenty of time to explore.

### • DON'T MISS •

*Barmouth, a popular beach resort about 12 miles (19km) south of Harlech, was the port used by Jasper Tudor and the other Lancastrian rebels. Jasper and his ally, Griffith Vaughan, plotted their assault on the throne in a house on the harbour, Ty Gwyn, now largely rebuilt.*

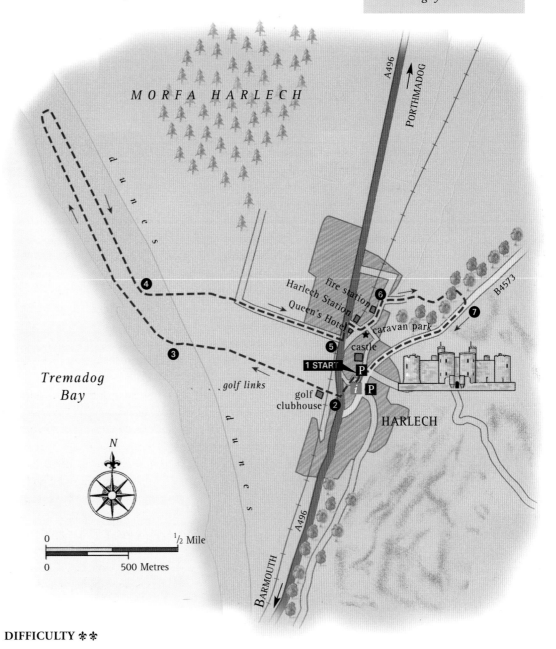

**DIFFICULTY** ✳ ✳

**1469**

**1469** Spain is unified following the marriage of Ferdinand and Isabella.

**1471** Henry VI is murdered.

**1472** Scotland acquires Orkney and the Shetland Islands from the Norwegians.

**1474**

**1474–5** William Caxton prints the first book in English, *The Recuyell of the Historyes of Troy.*

**1483** Edward V succeeds to the throne but is declared illegitimate. He and his brother vanish without trace and Richard claims the throne.

**1483**

**1483** Martin Luther is born in Germany. He becomes founder of the Reformation, and dedicates his life to establishing a religious doctrine that is not based on corruption and dogma.

**1483–85** Richard III reigns.

# The Marcher Lords of Ludlow

*Almost 1,000 years old, the castle at Ludlow was a royal base for 350 years, and before that the home of the Marcher Lords*

Today Ludlow is a small Shropshire market town with a reputation for culinary excellence, but in its heyday it was the centre of power for the untamed border-lands, or marches, between England and Wales.

Ludlow Castle was one of a series built by the Normans to control the countryside and to guard against incursions by the Welsh. It overlooks the River Teme and across towards the Welsh Marches, an area ruled by the powerful Marcher Lords, noblemen who were originally awarded large border estates by the King, in order to guard the frontier and provide a springboard for Norman forays into Wales. Ludlow became by far the strongest of these lordships as the town expanded in the 12th and 13th centuries.

By the 14th century the town and its castle were the base of Roger Mortimer, England's wealthiest lord, who embellished the castle with grand buildings including the Great Hall and the Solar palace. Mortimer led a rebellion against the king, Edward II, but was forced to surrender in 1321. After a daring escape from the Tower of London, he fled to France, where he took up with Edward's wife, Isabella. Together, the lovers invaded and deposed the King in 1327. Mortimer and Isabella ruled for three years, before a coup by her son (the future Edward III), which ended in Mortimer's execution.

At the far end of the market square stands St Laurence's church, the largest parish church in Shropshire, much of which was built in the prosperous 14th and 15th centuries. The misericords in the choir stalls, which date from 1447, show imagery relating to both Yorkist and Lancastrian factions of the Wars of the Roses. The Lancastrian symbols are a dutiful recognition of allegiance to the King, Henry VI; the Yorkist examples reflect the loyalties of Ludlow's manorial lord – Richard Duke of York. In this way, town and church hedged their bets at a time of unpredictable power-shifts.

The marches had, by this time, become a more or less autonomous region, embracing a Welsh, English, French and home-grown population and its own customs and laws, beyond the reach of the king. To remedy this situation, Edward IV sent his eldest son to Ludlow in 1473 to make the castle the headquarters of a 'Council of the March', taking responsibility for the Welsh principality, the marches and the border English shires. This marked the beginning of a centralising policy that culminated in the Act of Union of 1536, bringing Wales and the Marches under the English legal and administrative system.

From the church you walk along Broad Street, one of the finest wide streets in the country, and down to the River Teme; from here you start to see the marches. After visiting some Forestry Commission land, the path winds back to the river and past Whitcliffe Common, used for grazing livestock in medieval times, before returning to the town.

ABOVE: *The keep at Ludlow Castle which in the 15th century became the headquarters of the 'Council of March'.*

BELOW: *Ludlow Castle was built in the 12th century as part of the Norman castle-building programme to guard against Welsh attacks.*

WALK 45

MEDIEVAL

**ABOUT • LUDLOW**

*Ludlow found fame in A E Housman's* A Shropshire Lad, *but in the 15th century it was better known as a seat of power. In 1473 Edward IV sent his son to take control of the feudal marches and it marked the beginning of the end of Welsh independence.*

## Shropshire • C ENGLAND

**DISTANCE** • 5 miles (8km)

**TOTAL ASCENT** • 330ft (100m)

**PATHS** • mostly defined tracks; can be very muddy in wet weather. A little safe road walking

**TERRAIN** • some cultivated fields and forestry tracks

**GRADIENTS** • very gentle

**REFRESHMENTS** • numerous in Ludlow, but none on walk

**PARK** • car park off Castle Square, Ludlow. Larger car park behind Feathers hotel on Corve Street (follow signs to railway station)

**OS MAP** • Explorer 203 Ludlow, Tenbury Wells & Cleobury Mortimer

# The seat of power in Ludlow

DIFFICULTY ✤✤

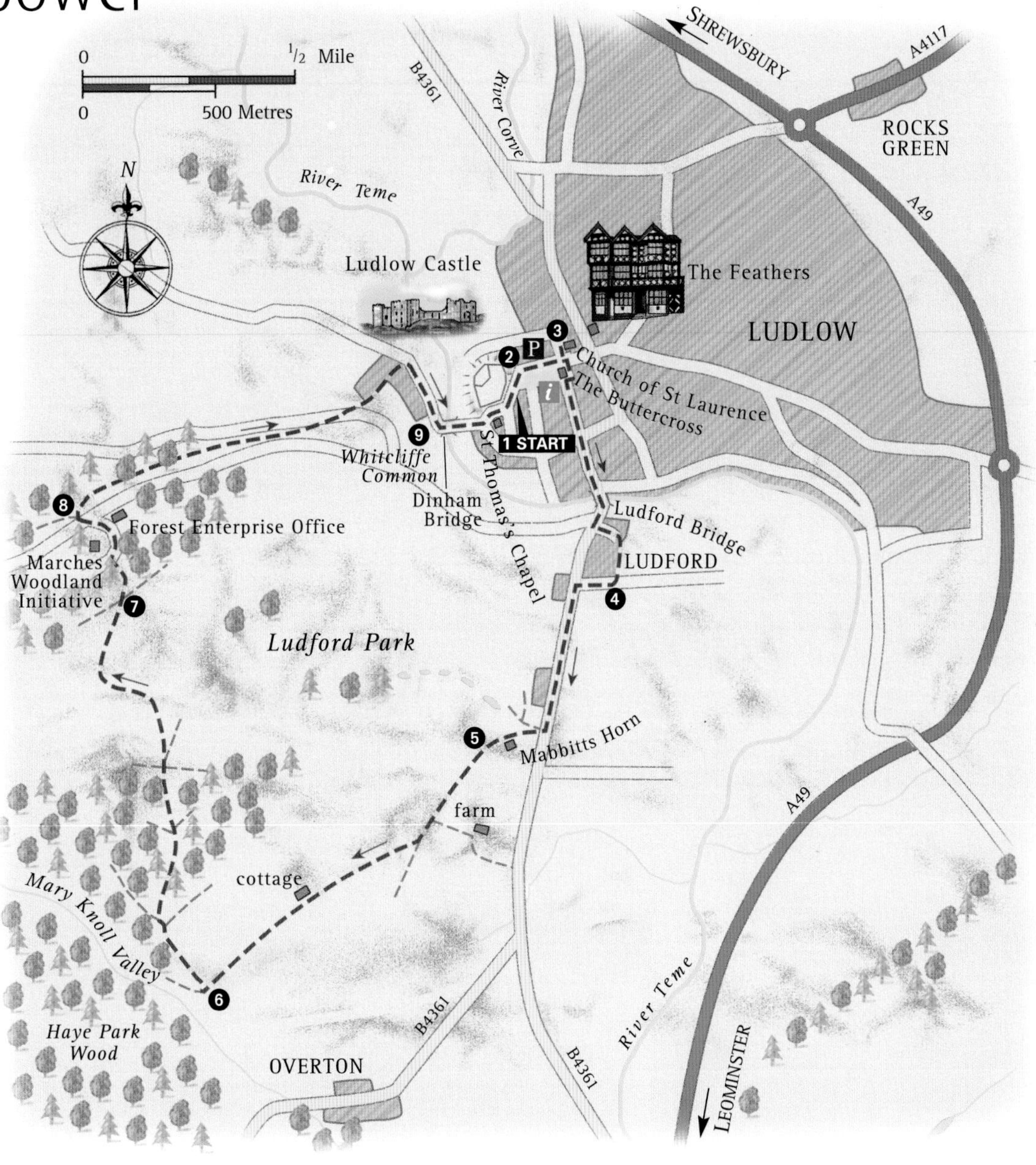


❶ Start at the Tourist Information Centre and museum, opposite the car park in Castle Square. Turn left out of the TIC and walk to Ludlow Castle at the end of the square. A full tour of the castle can take an hour

❷ From the castle walk back past the car park exit and down a cobbled arcade. Turn left when you see narrow College Street, then turn right to explore St Laurence's parish church, the largest in the county. The west window shows several of the Marcher Lords.

❸ Walk back down College Street, turn left and in 5yds (4.5m) turn right through the arches of The Buttercross (now Ludlow Town Council offices) and down Broad Street to Ludford Bridge. Beyond the bridge turn left into Park Road and follow it to the end. Cross the stile and walk ahead, keeping the wall/hedge on your right.

❹ At a driveway turn right, pass through a gate, and continue down to the main road (B4361). At the road turn left, continue for 383yds (350m) and, beyond three houses, take the driveway to Mabbitts Horn. Just beyond this house reach a stile.

❺ Cross the stile. After 219yds (200m) the path becomes a track with hedgerows on both sides. After a track marked 'Private', which leads to a farm on the left, take the right fork (waymarkers). Continue between hedges along this sunken lane for 437yds (400m). Pass through a gate into a field and in 109yds (100m) go through another gate in front of a cottage on to a track.

❻ After 383yds (350m) go through a tall gate before a hairpin bend on a gravel forestry road; turn right here, uphill, signed Mortimer Trail, permissive route. In 219yds (200m), at a bench, take a footpath at marker post 106. Follow these sequentially numbered marker posts carefully, later through a felled area, until, when in trees again, reach a rutted junction and post 119.

❼ Follow marker post 120, with a dense coniferous plantation on your left. At the main track turn right, pass the Forest Enterprise Office on your right, and reach the main road.

❽ Cross the road and take footpath signed Ludlow, which goes left then turns back to the right. This track has Mortimer Trail waymarks on it, follow these to a road. Turn right, then soon left, downhill, at a hairpin bend on the main road. Eventually continue round a right-hand bend to Dinham Bridge.

❾ Just before the bridge is Whitcliffe Common, on the right. Cross the bridge and walk uphill back to the castle, bearing left in front of St Thomas's Chapel, the oldest building in Ludlow.

groote koopstadt de voor **LONDEN** appelle Londonia une grande ville mar **LONDEN** ver diesem genahmste Londonia ein gro...
gelegen aen de Rivier chande et la plus celebre en grand bretagne une Siege du Rey est vernahmiste in gros Britanien ein palleys des Konincks is
groote hoofse met sitie sur la riviere du Thoms edifie par Brit: Constantin te Riviere de Thoms gefondiert durch Britis Constan...
Paulis is de hoofst grand l'at fortifie de murailles orne de 12e eschifes s' Paul est la cathe sticht oder gefortificieret met mauren rontom verciert
ost Arcenael en andere drale et une trescelebre boürse et un Tower en Arcenal et autres basti Paulis is die haupt kirche vndt hadt een kostelichen b...
t alle gerüineert nevens ments estant par le dernier grand in ceud presque toit riine avecq la plus gaderinge vndt Tour oder Arcenael vndt andere gebau...
des inwonders herbeüt grande partie de la ville mais asteur par la grande richesse des Citoyens rebasti brant by na alle verbrant neffens die grootste deyl der s...
omme durch den grosen reichdom der inwonders gebau...

*The Tudors reigned for only 118 years, but their
dynasty has captured the British imagination more than
any other. From the accession of Henry VII until the death
of the Virgin Queen, Elizabeth, theirs was an era of
unforgettable characters and profound social change.*

# THE TUDORS
## 1485–1603

# Building a Dynasty

With Henry VII's marriage to Elizabeth of York, the Wars of the Roses were effectively brought to a close. When the King died, his young heir – the sporty, musical, dashing Prince Henry – was welcomed as a bright new star. Henry VIII made an impact on the European stage, too: his mentor, Cardinal Wolsey, arranged the magnificent peace summit with France at the Field of the Cloth of Gold, near Calais; and the King's anti-Lutheran pamphlet earned him the Pope's gratitude and the title 'Defender of the Faith'.

Domestic matters soon cast their shadow over Henry's reign – specifically the absence of a male heir. Henry had married Catherine of Aragon in 1509, but by 1527, with only a daughter, Mary, surviving, he was seeking a way out. Having failed to gain a Papal annulment, Henry took direct action, declaring himself Supreme Head of the Church of England and pronouncing his own marriage invalid. Within a year of marrying the vivacious Anne Boleyn in 1533, who bore him another child: Elizabeth. Three years later Anne was dead, executed on trumped-up treason charges. Henry's third wife, Jane Seymour, died giving birth to his longed-for son, Edward. There followed three more wives, but no more children.

Henry took full advantage of his new role as head of the reformed Church, dissolving and looting hundreds of monasteries. By the end of the 1530s the countryside was littered with the disintegrating shells of religious buildings, and the previously Catholic population found itself abruptly converted to the Protestant cause.

### AFTER THE HENRIES

Edward VI was a sickly child of nine when he became king, and reigned for only six years, guided by staunchly Protestant courtiers. The crown then passed to the devoutly Catholic Mary, who, to her subjects' alarm, married the Spanish king, Philip II. The 'pregnancy' that she celebrated in the same year turned out to be early symptoms of the dropsy that would eventually kill her. Taking this as divine retribution for heresy, Mary became a ruthless persecutor of Protestants, instigating the infamous 'turn or burn' policy.

When Elizabeth succeeded Mary she was already an old hand at the political game, having survived in spite of her half-sister's jealousies. As queen, she aimed for a middle course, avoiding religious extremes. She also resisted Parliament's pressure to marry her off and secure the dynasty's future. The succession was a particularly thorny issue, as Mary, Queen of Scots, herself claimed the English throne as granddaughter of Henry VII. After her Scottish opponents had forced her to abdicate, Mary fled to England, where, for nearly 20 years, she was moved from place to place, a potentially dangerous figurehead for Elizabeth's enemies. Eventually, a plot was uncovered to snatch the crown for Mary, and she was executed – sparking the wrath of Catholic Spain. When the Spanish Armada, sent to wreak vengeance, was battered by the English and foundered in rough seas, Elizabeth's popularity hit an all-time high.

Elizabeth's long reign was a golden age in many ways: music flourished, with composers such as Byrd and Tallis making their names; Shakespeare was a leading light of English drama; Francis Drake and Walter Raleigh typified the spirit of adventure and exploration; and in the absence of civil war, the building and woollen trades boomed. Gloriana, the Virgin Queen, would long remain a charismatic symbol of the Tudor age at its best.

## HISTORIC SITES

**Little Moreton Hall, Staffs:** half-timbered manor house built 1440–1589.

**Burghley House, Lincs:** exotic home of Elizabeth I's adviser.

**Mary Rose, Portsmouth Historic Ships, Hants:** glimpse of the Tudor sailor's life, and the remains of Henry VIII's flagship.

**Hampton Court, Surrey:** Tudor palace complete with Henry VIII's real tennis court.

**Shrewsbury:** wool-trade centre with many surviving half-timbered houses.

**Stratford-upon-Avon:** site of Shakespeare's birthplace.

**1485**

**1485–1509** Henry VII is crowned King and his marriage in 1486 to Elizabeth of York, Edward IV's daughter, unites the houses of Lancaster and York.

**1492** Christopher Columbus discovers America.

**1508**

**1508** Michaelangelo begins work on the Sistine Chapel ceiling. The painting takes only six years to complete.

**1509-1547** Henry VIII accedes the throne and the Tudor dynasty appears assured. Henry marries

**1509**

Catherine of Aragon, a daughter of Ferdinand and Isabella of Spain.

**1513** James IV of Scotland invades England in support of his French allies, but he and many of the Scottish court are killed at the battle of Flodden Field.

# Lavenham: a Tudor Wool Town

*A walk through the picturesque historic streets of a medieval Suffolk wool town and the surrounding countryside*

THE TUDORS

BUILDING A DYNASTY

Lavenham grew up as a commercial and industrial wool town, at its peak during the reign of Henry VIII (1509–47). For centuries, wool, yarn and the manufacture of cloth were the mainstay of local wealth and employment. Lavenham continued to be a manufacturing centre until the early 20th century, but today its crazy, beautiful, timbered old houses draw a steady stream of tourists, summer and winter.

Lavenham didn't always look like this. Exposed timbering on this scale is largely a 20th-century fashion. When the houses were built – mostly between the 15th and 17th centuries – their wooden frames were almost certainly hidden away behind a protective layer of plaster. This was often a decorative feature in itself, with bold raised ornamentation called 'pargetting', as seen on some of the shops and houses in the High Street. The Priory on Water Street is also a good example. The plasterwork was painted with limewash, traditionally in the dark reddish brown colour known as 'Suffolk pink'. Today, many of the houses in the town are painted in harmonious shades of red, pink, gold and orange. Two of the finest buildings eschew such colour, however – the magnificent Guildhall of the Guild of Corpus Christi (c.1529) in the market square and the wonderful, rambling Swan Inn both remain defiantly white, showing off their weathered, silvery oak beams to great effect.

There were originally four guildhalls in the town, indicating its prosperity and importance. One was demolished to make space for a much-needed car park. Another – the 15th-century Wool Hall, on the corner of Lady Street and Water Lane – was dismantled in the early 20th century but rebuilt after local outcry, and incorporated into the back of the Swan.

Not all the houses in Lavenham are what they seem. Georgian façades, for example, often hide much older buildings. The impressive De Vere House, with its decorative brick infill, is a little too good to be true – it was largely reconstructed in the 1920s. Laneham House, near the car park on

Church Street, is a new house built with old timbers. A detailed guide to the town's architectural highlights, published by the Suffolk Preservation Society, is available from the Tourist Information office.

The parish church, dedicated to St Peter and St Paul, is one of the finest of the Suffolk wool churches. Building started in the early 14th century and was completed around 1525, funded primarily by the Lord of the Manor, John de Vere, 13th Earl of Oxford, and the family of clothier Thomas Spring. Its tall square tower is covered in dark, knapped flint, and the long, airy nave was built of limestone, probably brought from the Midlands at great cost.

Lavenham's fortunes waned, along with the wool trade, in the 18th century. Small factories dotted around the town indicate a determined revival in the 19th century, with the introduction of horsehair weaving. The first factory opened on Hall Road in the 1850s and another, on Water Street, dates from 1891. The railway has also long since disappeared, but you can follow its route most of the way to Long Melford.

ABOVE: *Lavenham's timbered façade. Although generally associated with Tudor style, exposed timbering is largley a 20th-century fashion.*

BACKGROUND: *A charming 16th-century illustration of sheepshearing in June.*

**THE TUDORS**

**WALK 46**

*ABOUT • LAVENHAM*

The timbered façade of Lavenham offers the perfect image of a Tudor wool town, at its peak during the reign of Henry VIII. Lavenham offers some superb 16th-century architecture including the Guildhall of Corpus Christi and the Swan Inn.

**Suffolk • SE ENGLAND**

**DISTANCE •** 5 miles (8km)

**PATHS •** mostly firm, but sections can be muddy; keep dogs under strict control in the town and through farmyard and fields

**Terrain •** town, former railway, open farmland, quiet lanes

**GRADIENTS •** some gentle slopes, but mostly fairly level

**REFRESHMENTS •** Swan Inn, Lavenham; National Trust tea rooms in Guildhall, Market Square

**PARK •** in the car park, Lavenham, signed near the church; other parking available in the town

**OS MAP •** Explorer 196 Sudbury, Hadleigh & Dedham Vale

# Lavenham – a timbered treasure

❶ Turn right out of the car park and head down hill into the town centre. Turn right just before the timbered Swan Inn into Water Street. Turn into the bottom of Lady Street to admire the old guildhall, now part of the inn but once one of four guildhalls around the town. Continue down Water Street. Pass the bottom of Barn Street, pause to admire its houses.

❷ Turn left up Shilling Street, passing Shilling Grange and other splendid timbered and plastered houses. Nos 22-24 are particularly fine. Turn left at the top into Bolton Street, and bear right into Market Square, passing a memorial to US airmen of World War II.

❸ After exploring the square, with its magnificent timbered Guildhall, little houses, butter cross and Angel Hotel, leave via Market Lane and turn right on the High Street. Continue over the brow of the hill, admiring the lovely old row of houses, Nos 61-63.

❹ At the bottom, just before the railway bridge, take the muddy path down to the left, signed Lavenham Walk. This bends left to join the route of the old railway line (which can be followed all the way to Long Melford), a lovely walk with occasional benches. Continue along this for about a mile (1.6km), with the big square tower of Lavenham church looming to your left, and trees forming a natural arch overhead.

❺ Cross the road via two metal gates and continue along the railway path for about a mile (1.6km). Go through the banks of a cutting, and through a squeeze gate under a brick road bridge. Stay on the line, to pass a Site of Special Scientific Interest with

unusual chalk downland vegetation. After another area of woodland the path deteriorates, emerging on to an open field. Keep straight ahead along the lower edge of the field to meet a junction of tracks.

❻ Turn left up the farm track, back over the hill. Stay on this track and follow the yellow waymarkers as it bends right, towards the farm, then left

between two old black barns. Follow the road round to the right, and at the junction with the track, keep left down the main drive towards Lavenham.

❼ At the end, turn right along the road for a short distance. A fingerpost indicates the path left. Follow it straight across the field towards the barred wooden gate. Cross the stile and keep straight on, with the hedge on your right.

Cross another stile, and go straight on to meet the lane.

❽ Turn right here towards the church, and turn left up the stone steps below the tower. Walk round three sides of the church, keeping it on your left, and take the little path in the bottom corner through the old wooden kissing gate.

❾ Head down the grassy path towards the pond. Go through the gate and over the bridge, and at the end of the lane turn right into Hall Road. Where this meets High Street, turn right to return to the car park.

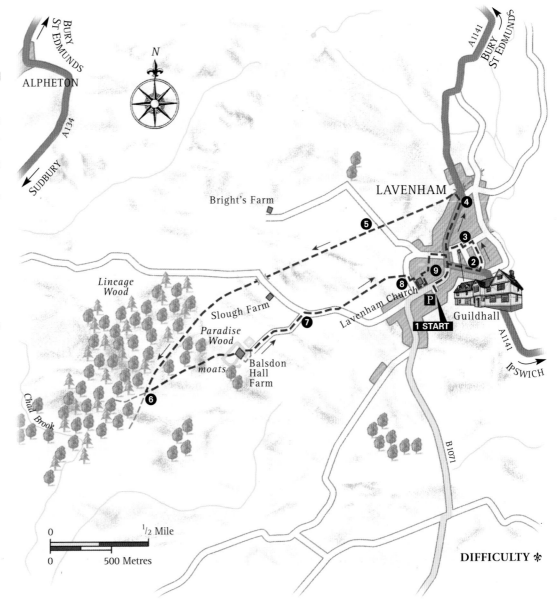

**DIFFICULTY ❋**

**1514**

**1514** Hampton Court is built for Cardinal Wolsley but later, hoping to regain the King's favour, he gives it to Henry.

**1516** Mary is born to Henry and Catherine, but the lack of a male heir causes the King to turn his attentions to Anne Boleyn.

**1517**

**1517** Martin Luther publishes his 95 attacks against the Roman Catholic Church.

**1519–1550** The Spanish Conquistadors invade the lands of the Inca; the Inca Empire is destroyed by 1535.

**1529**

**1529** Despite the solicitous attentions of Cardinal Wolsey, the Pope refuses to grant Henry a divorce from Catherine, and in 1534 Henry splits from Rome and declares himself the Supreme Head of the English Church.

# St Catherine's Castle and the Saints' Way

*A lovely clifftop walk to Henry VIII's picturesque coastal fort, overlooking the Fowey estuary in southern Cornwall*

**THE TUDORS**

ABOVE: *St Catherine's is not the only point of interest in Fowey as the town itself is densely packed with attractive buildings dating from the 16th century.*

S t Catherine's Castle, 143ft (44m) above sea level on St Catherine's Point, at the mouth of the Fowey estuary, is a real gem. There was a small church here in the Middle Ages, dedicated to St Catherine of Alexandria, home of the Pharos lighthouse. Such headland churches often had beacon fires, which acted as navigation aids; hence the link. The views upriver and over Readymoney Cove to the little town of Fowey, with picturesque Polruan opposite, are stunning at all times of year, and if you look carefully at the opposite headland to the castle you can see the craggy remains of St Saviour's Chapel. It's hard to imagine that this peaceful scene has ever been anything but that.

St Catherine's Castle, a small, two-storey artillery fort, was built into the cliff face by the citizens of Fowey around 1510, when Henry VIII was set on invading France, and the locals feared reprisal raids. The castle then became part of Henry's south-coast defence system, begun in 1539 when England became increasingly isolated from the continent as a result of his repudiation of the Pope's authority. This chain of fortifications includes Pendennis

Castle at Falmouth, and St Mawes Castle on the opposite side of the Fal estuary, one of the finest natural harbours in the British Isles. During Tudor times Falmouth was the busiest port on the south coast. Fowey, which had been a thriving seaport throughout the Middle Ages and had taken over almost all of Lostwithiel's seaborne trade in the late 14th century only to lose out to Truro by the 15th, was still sufficiently significant to feature in Henry VIII's scheme.

Although few of Henry's coastal castles saw active service, they have been adapted over the years according to the political climate of the times. Pendennis was strengthened during the reign of Elizabeth I, and again before the Civil War (1642–6); it was the penultimate Royalist stronghold to surrender on the mainland, and saw action in World War II. St Mawes, the most perfectly preserved of Henry's coastal fortresses, fell to Parliamentarian forces in 1646 and was not properly refortified until the late 19th and 20th centuries.

St Catherine's Castle has two rows of gunports, resembling those at the fort at Bayard's Cove at Dartmouth in Devon. There are no domestic quarters, and probably no permanent garrison, making it a fort rather than a true castle. It was manned during the Civil War, in ruins by 1684, and refortified in the mid-19th century under threat of attack from France, hence the construction of the two-gun battery below the D-shaped tower in 1855. Anti-aircraft guns were placed there during World War II to protect D-Day invasion craft gathering in the estuary.

The castle is managed by English Heritage, and is open all year round. An additional feature of this walk is that the return route is along the Saints' Way, which runs for 30 miles (48km) from Padstow to Fowey.

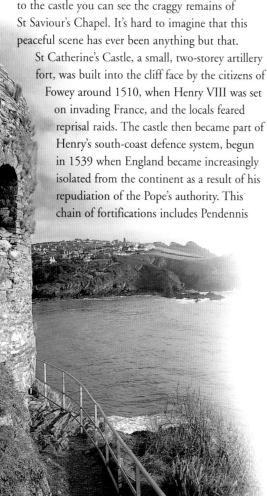

LEFT: *St Catherine's Castle, looking across the mouth of the River Fowey to Polruan. The castle was carefully sited to be a watch-tower on the lookout for possible attacks from England's disgruntled French neighbours.*

**ABOUT • ST CATHERINE'S CASTLE**

*This walk starts from the old pilchard-fishing hamlet of Polkerris and leads you along the cliffs to the lovely St Catherine's Castle, which is actually more of a fort. It was built by the town's residents in 1510 to protect them from attacks from France.*

**Cornwall • SW ENGLAND**

**DISTANCE** • 6 miles (9.6km)

**TOTAL ASCENT** • 246ft (75m)

**PATHS** • coast path, woodland and field tracks (some muddy after wet weather), and country lanes

**TERRAIN** • cliffs, farmland, wooded valleys

**GRADIENTS** • some short, steep ascents/ descents on coast path and inland valleys

**REFRESHMENTS** • Rashleigh Arms, Polkerris; café at Readymoney Cove; pubs, cafés and restaurants in Fowey

**PARK** • free parking in Polkerris; unsurfaced, unmarked car park on right, before village, descending lane signed off the A3082 Fowey to St Austell road just east of Polmear

**OS MAP** • Explorer 107 St Austell & Liskeard

# Henry VIII's coastal fort of St Catherine's

❶ From the car park entrance turn right and head for the Rashleigh Arms by the beach. Turn left (signed public toilets), and follow the coast path signs up concrete steps, and zigzag steeply up through woodland. At the T-junction turn left away from the sea to reach a coast path post at the field edge.

❷ Turn right; follow the coast path along the field and through a gate. Pass through another gate, then climb for 2 miles (3.2km) up to a gate/stile. Just past the National Trust sign for The Gribbin the path divides; keep right to reach the daymark.

❸ Follow the coast path downhill for ¾ mile (1.2km) to reach Polridmouth. Ignore the footpath left (to Menabilly); follow the path behind the beach past the house and lake, to cross the weir on stepping-stones.

❹ Continue up steep steps on to Lankelly Cliff (NT). Pass through the next gate, go round the field edge, and drop down steeply to a stile. Walk up the next field. Descend through a gate to Coombe Haven. Continue over a stile to enter Alldays Fields, then through a small gate into Covington Wood.

❺ Turn sharp right to reach St Catherine's Point; take the next path, right, to the castle. Retrace your steps and turn right to rejoin the coast path, descending to a T-junction behind Readymoney Cove.

❻ Turn left, uphill, for ½ mile (800m) following the deeply banked Saints' Way (signed with a cross), to meet a lane. Turn left to reach Coombe Lane. Turn right to to lead into Prickly Post Lane.

❼ Follow signs left through a drive and down a narrow footpath. Go through a gate and downhill over a stream, under a bridge and uphill over a stone stile. Continue downhill, over a stile, to reach Trenant; cross the drive and the stone stile. Go through the next gate, then downhill and over a stream on a railed footbridge. The path continues over a stile by a ruined cottage, then uphill through a gate into Tregaminion farmyard. Walk through the farmyard, turn right, then left at the farmhouse to reach a T-junction.

❽ Turn right along the lane; after 200yds (183m) turn left on a footpath to rejoin the coast path post at Point 1. Go ahead and retrace your steps downhill to Polkerris.

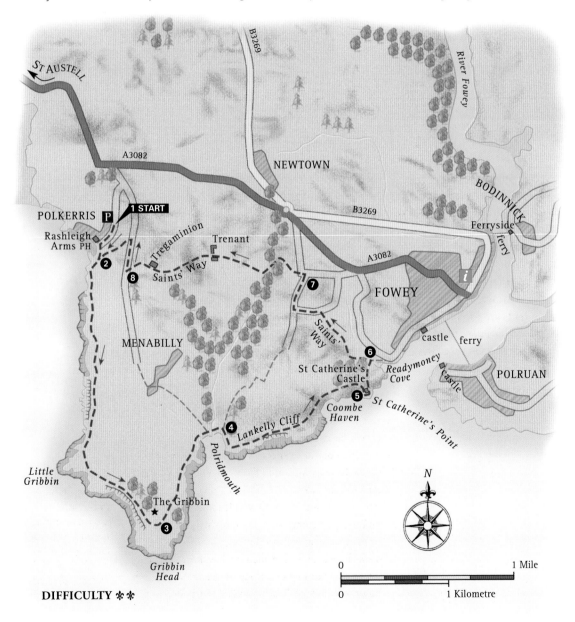

**DIFFICULTY ✸✸**

**• DON'T MISS •**

*Daphne du Maurier fell in love with Cornwall while on holiday in Fowey in her early 20s. She lived for several years at Ferryside, next to the Bodinnick Ferry, and based many of her best-known novels on the area. Every May the town hosts the du Maurier Festival of Arts and Literature.*

**1532**

**1532** John Calvin starts the Protestant movement in France.

**1532-6** St James's Palace is built.

**1533** Sir Thomas Cranmer grants Henry a divorce and he marries Anne Boleyn.

**1533**

**1533** Elizabeth I is born the year before the separation between England and the Catholic Church. Throughout her lifetime, Elizabeth was to remain a stalwart defender of the Church of England.

**1535**

**1535** Sir Thomas More is executed for his refusal to accept the King as head of the Church.

**1536** Ann Boleyn is executed on the grounds of high treason, and Henry marries Jane Seymour.

THE TUDORS

BUILDING A DYNASTY

# Llyn Brianne and the Welsh Robin Hood

*The secret haunts of a 16th-century outlaw in the lovely Tywi Valley*

Today the countryside around Llyn Brianne – the reservoir that provides drinking water and electricity for thousands of homes in South Wales – is a place of tranquillity and beauty, home of the red kite. But in the 16th century this was the hunting-ground of notorious thief, highway robber and master of disguise, Twm Sion Catti.

Born in 1530, son of Catherine Jones of Ffynnon Llidiad, near Tregaron, Twm – or Thomas, to use his real name – was widely believed to be the illegitimate child of Sir John Wynne, lord of the noble North Wales Gwydir family. His nickname simply means 'Cathy's Tommy John'. As an adult Twm quickly gained a reputation for his illegal activities, close escapes from the authorities and practical jokes. One of his favourite tricks was to steal a horse or a cow, give it a quick makeover with some dye and an artificial tail, and sell it back to the original owner. Another story is told by George Borrow, who described his 19th-century journeys through Wales in *Wild Wales*. According to this tale, Twm Sion Catti entered an ironmonger's shop, announcing that he wanted to buy a porridge-pot. Having been handed a large pot, he complained that there was a hole in it. When the ironmonger stepped

ABOVE: *An 18th-century illustration of a drover.*

forward to examine it, Twm jammed the pot over his head, gathered up the rest of the shop's stock and remarked, as he left, that if there hadn't been a hole in the pot, the ironmonger's head wouldn't have gone into it.

Twm was a popular figure, who was often protected from the king's officers by locals in return for an evening's songs and anecdotes; and he was famous for targeting the rich and donating half the proceeds of his crimes to the poor. Twm made much of his aristocratic blood, putting on the airs and graces of a gentleman and promising that one day he would take his due place among the nobility. That day must have seemed far off when he was sheltering from the forces of law in his secret cave, a few miles south of Llyn Brianne. This walk passes it, but doesn't go directly to the entrance. Even at close range, however, the low and narrow entrance, surrounded with trees and boulders, is hard to spot. The gentleman thief would have had to crawl in on his hands and knees.

Twm made an abrupt career change after holding up a coach on the Llandovery highway. In it was the widow of the High Sheriff of Carmarthenshire, the heiress of Ystradffin, and the two took an immediate fancy to each other. While the young woman's father summoned all the forces at his disposal to hunt the miscreant down, Twm hid in his cave and sent a stream of marriage proposals to her home. Eventually she accepted, and managed to obtain him a royal pardon on 1 January 1560. Within two years Twm Sion Catti was a justice of peace – a pillar of respectable society and a member of the local gentry, just as he had always promised.

LEFT: *The picturesque winding reservoir of Llyn Brianne in the Upper Twm Valley.*

BELOW: *The reservoir and the dam were built at Llyn Brianne in 1972 to provide the growing town of Swansea with a new water supply.*

**ABOUT • LLYN BRIANNE**

*This walk takes you along a drovers' road before visiting the cave of the 16th-century outlaw Twm Sion Catti, thief, highwayman and master of disguise. He was a popular figure of the day and often protected from the king's officers in return for an evening's entertainment.*

**Carmarthenshire • WALES**

**DISTANCE •** 6 miles (9.6km)

**TOTAL ASCENT •** 300ft (91m)

**PATHS •** minor roads and forest trails. Paths very muddy and slippery in wet weather

**TERRAIN •** woodland, farmland

**GRADIENTS •** undulating roads. Tarmac tracks mostly flat or slightly uphill. Paths can be steep in places

**REFRESHMENTS •** Rhadirmwyn Bridge and Rhandirmwyn (nearest villages to the walk)

**PARK •** ample car parking spaces at start point by the dam

**OS MAP •** Explorer 166 Rhondda & Merthyr Tydfil

# Along a drovers' road to the cave of Twm

**❶** Facing Llyn Brianne, bear left down a road, and at a T-junction turn right. Further on where the road forks branch left and after about 1/2 mile (800m) turn right into a car park serving the RSPB Dinas Reserve just entered.

**❷** Head for a wooden kissing gate at the left-hand side of the car park. Follow a raised wooden pathway leading through woodland. When the boardwalk forks, branch right and follow a nature trail which runs parallel to the river.

**❸** Taking care, follow the path through an ancient oak woodland and pass the cave and sometime home of Twm Sion Catti. (A path does lead from the nature trail to the cave, but it is not obvious and may be dangerous in wet weather.)

**• DON'T MISS •**

*The **drovers' roads** which you walk along this route have played an important part in history. Welsh drovers were the cowboys of their day, driving vast herds of cattle, sheep, pigs and flocks of geese to English markets in the hope of a good sale. They also acted as bankers, delivering and returning the locals' investments, and as an unofficial postal service. Their regular routes through Wales were punctuated with resting places and inns; one of the most remote and spectacular is the road over the hills from Tregaron to Llandovery.*

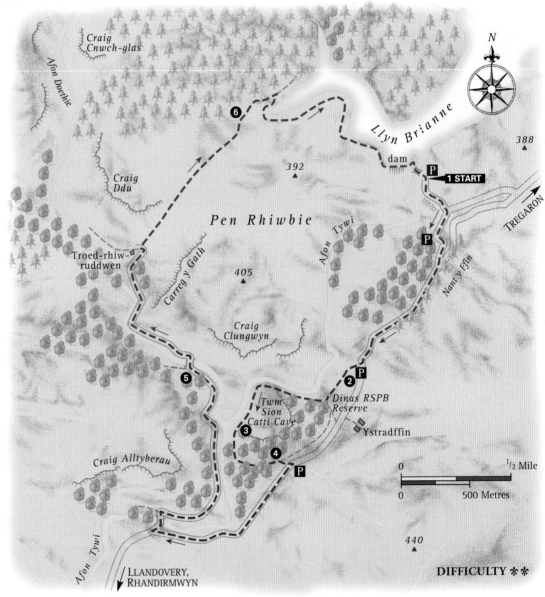

**❹** Branch right when the woodland path forks and pass through a large wooden gate. Turn right on to a tarmac road and follow this for about a mile (1.6km). Then turn right on to a single-track road heading for Troedyrhiw and, passing over a bridge, press on, climbing gently.

**❺** Cross a metal bridge and then continue until the surfaced road ends in front of a farm and bears sharply right, gently climbing a rough-surfaced vehicle track leading up a narrowing valley.

**❻** Near the top of the valley, the path runs through a forest and, beyond its high point, emerges on the other side, bearing sharp right. A short way on, climb gently to the left on a broad track parallel with the shore of Llyn Brianne, and eventually return to the dam. Cross and walk back to the car park and your car.

**DIFFICULTY ✲✲**

**1536**

**1536** The Act of Union between England and Wales is passed. The dissolution of the smaller monasteries takes place in England, and in 1539 the remaining monasteries are suppressed. Henry makes gifts or sells the land at enormous profit.

**1537**

**1537** The queen, Jane, Henry's most favoured wife, gives birth to a son, but dies shortly afterwards.

**1540** Henry's marriage to Anne of Cleeves ends in divorce within a year. Thomas Cromwell is accused of treason and executed.

**1542**

**1542** Henry marries Catherine Howard, but has her executed for treason two years later.

**1542** In Scotland, Mary Queen of Scots accedes the throne a week after her birth.

# Furness Abbey and the Dissolution of the Monasteries

*A walk around the fields of Furness to see an abbey, a castle and an ancient packhorse bridge*

**THE TUDORS**

**BUILDING A DYNASTY**

It was 1536. Trouble was brewing for Abbot Roger Pele and the monks of Furness Abbey. King Henry VIII had broken away from the Roman Catholic Church, and two of his advisors, Thomas Cromwell and Thomas Cranmer, were leading a fervent religious revolution in his name. The Act of Supremacy had declared the King to be 'Supreme Head on Earth of the Church of England'; the Treason Act had been expanded to condemn those who denied the Supremacy; and the Act Concerning First Fruits and Tenths had been drawn up to divert funds that were previously sent to Rome into the King's coffers. The two men now turned their attentions to the monasteries. An Act of Parliament had already wound up the smaller 'corrupt' monasteries worth less than £200 per year, and Furness had received one visitation. The monks, encouraged by the locals, rose up in defiance. It was just one more protest in the anti-reformation movement known as the Pilgrimage of Grace, but it brought Furness to the attention of those it feared.

The abbot fled for his life, and on 9 April 1537 the inevitable happened: the King's men arrived with revenge in their hearts. They forced the monks to surrender. Two of the monks were imprisoned. The abbey was systematically looted and destroyed; its roof was robbed of the lead; the walls were cannibalised for buildings elsewhere. Here was an end to 400 years of civilised monastic rule, and, for the locals, a return to poverty.

The abbey was founded in 1127, when monks of the Savignac Order, led by Abbot Ewan d'Avranches, moved here from their base at Tulketh. In 1147 the monks merged with the Cistercian Order, under the mother abbey in Cîteaux, France. The new order rapidly expanded and soon controlled most of the Furness Peninsula — its forests, its pastures and the harbour at Piel Island. In wealth and grandeur Furness became second only to Fountains Abbey in Yorkshire, establishing daughter abbeys as far away as Ireland and the Isle of Man.

The abbey was the major employer and landlord of the area. Together with their tenants, the monks tended sheep, grew crops on the rich, fertile soil, quarried stone and mined iron-ore. The tenants would pay a 'fine' of 1d, known as God's Penny, and a rent that might include corn, geese and hens. They would take an oath of allegiance to the abbot, and, collectively, they would have to supply armed men to defend the harbour at Piel. In return the monks would distribute iron for repairing the ploughs, and supplies of bread and ale. They would also offer places for the children at the monastery school.

Though the days of monastic rule are long gone, the relics of those bygone years are scattered across the whole of the walk: the 14th-century Bow Bridge; the mounds and shafts of the iron mines east of Newton; the old grange farms; the keep of Dalton Castle on the hill; and the lichen-mottled red sandstone ruins of the abbey, which hide quietly from the world in the wooded Vale of Nightshade.

ABOVE: *17th-century illustration depicting Henry VIII supressing the Pope Clement VII.*

LEFT: *The ruins of Furness Abbey, one of the many victims of the Dissolution of Monasteries in 1537 by Henry VIII.*

### ABOUT • FURNESS ABBEY

*Like so many other monasteries in England, Furness was a victim of Henry VIII's split with the Catholic Church. Abbot Roger Pele and his monks rose up against the king but were quickly forced into submission and the abbey looted and destroyed.*

## Cumbria • N ENGLAND

**DISTANCE** • 6 miles (9.6km)

**TOTAL ASCENT** • 260ft (79m)

**PATHS** • field paths, lanes and tracks

**TERRAIN** • rolling farmland, can be muddy in winter

**GRADIENTS** • easy

**REFRESHMENTS** • cafés and inns at Dalton and the Farmers Arms at Newton

**PARK** • Goose Green car park at the bottom of Church Street opposite Furness Park Garage

**OS MAP** • Outdoor Leisure 6 The English Lakes – South Western area

# The Abbot of Furness

**❶** Turn left out of the car park, signed Public Footpath, Mill Wood, and pass through a gate at the end of the lane, signed Public Footpath to Broughton Road. Take the raised path beyond, following a beck and passing under a railway bridge before continuing through three tall gates into another field. At the far side, turn left across a footbridge, go under another railway bridge, and follow an enclosed path to the road.

**❷** Cross the road before turning right along a field-edge path through the Vale of Nightshade. Pass under another railway bridge and left along the road to abbey.

**❸** Swing left at the junction beyond the abbey. Pass the car park and just beyond a left-hand bend, follow a clear but unsigned path on the right. Cross the railway with care and turn right by the cottage to follow a Mill Beck. Cross the beck on a slab bridge, before recrossing it at Bow Bridge.

**❹** Turn left along the lane. After 300yds (274m) a footpath sign points the way uphill over two fields to Newton. Turn half-right past The Village Inn, then left, passing the Farmers Arms and out of the village.

**❺** Go left at the T-junction. After 200yds (183m) take the path on the right, which cuts diagonally northeast across fields, crossing primitive stiles before coming out on to another lane. Continue along an enclosed muddy track, which is staggered slightly right across the road, to pass Malkin Hall. Turn right along the next lane for 50yds (46m), then left up a gravel track.

**❻** Beyond some outbuildings, climb a raised bank on the left of the track and head north on an old mine railway trackbed. Continue through a bush-lined cutting past a water-filled mining hollow, then descend beside a hedge towards Standing Tarn.

**❼** Turn left though a squeeze stile above the tarn and head diagonally away from the tarn at the top right-hand corner of a large field. Staggered to the right, across a rough farm track, the next path begins at a squeeze stile and continues by a field edge. Turn left beyond the next stile and descend on a winding lane past some cottages, then pass beneath the railway to reach the main street in Dalton.

**❽** Turn left up the main street, past the shops and the castle. Turn left along Church Street, descending past the Brown Cow Inn back to the car park.

**DIFFICULTY ✤✤**

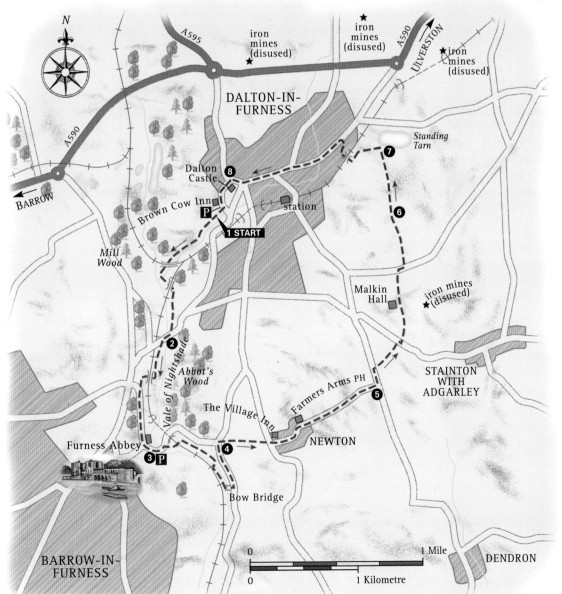

### • DON'T MISS •

*Dalton Castle where you can view a display of restored armour from the Civil War. Built by the monks of Furness Abbey, following 14th-century raids on their territories by the Scots (including one by Robert the Bruce), the castle has been both a courthouse and a prison. Today, it is in the care of the National Trust.*

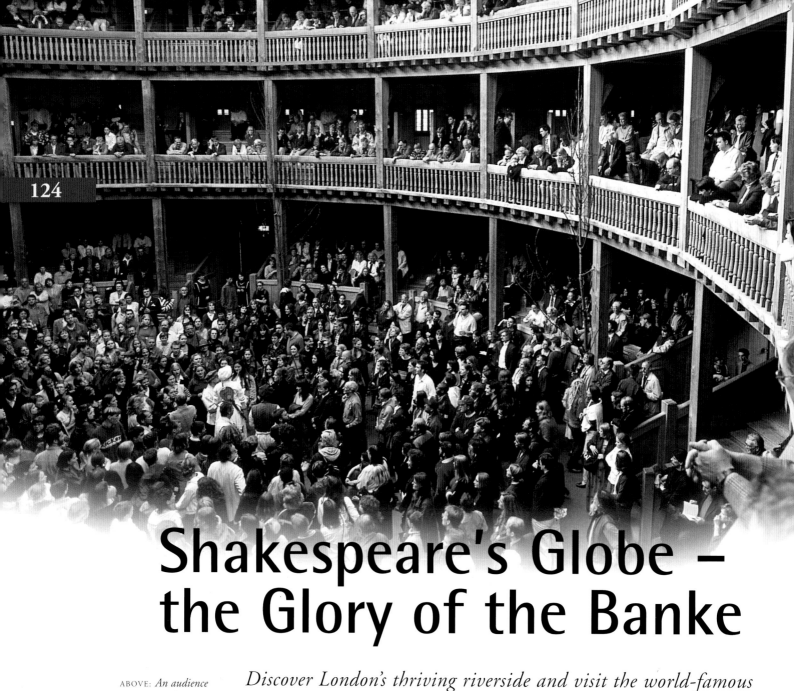

# Shakespeare's Globe – the Glory of the Banke

ABOVE: *An audience enjoys a 16th-century style production at The New Globe Theatre on the South Bank.*

BELOW: *An illustration of the original Globe Theatre, which burned to the ground in 1616.*

*Discover London's thriving riverside and visit the world-famous Globe theatre on this fascinating walk along the South Bank*

## Elizabethan London

Extending from Vauxhall Bridge downstream to Tower Bridge, this riverside walk shows how much the South Bank has changed since William Shakespeare came to London, joined a theatre company as an actor and performed many of his plays on the stage of the historic Globe. It was on this stretch of the Thames, at the Hope, Swan, Rose and Globe open-air playhouses, that the world's finest drama was staged.

During the latter part of the 16th century, Southwark was a rowdy place littered with taverns and brothels and renowned for bawdy entertainment. The Globe overlooked a river and a city teeming with life. River wherries ferried passengers from one bank of the Thames to the

other, all heavy goods were transported by water and the only way to cross the river on foot was via London Bridge.

The scene today is very different, but one landmark, the Globe, remains. It may be a replica but it serves as a lasting memorial to the genius of one man – William Shakespeare (1564–1616).

## A Sumptuous Stage

In 1576 actor-manager James Burbage established the first purpose-built playhouse, near the Lord Mayor's Reach. He called it The Theatre, and it prospered for the next 20 years. As the 16th century drew to a close, Burbage's lease expired and he was forced to look for new premises. He found a suitable venue in the Blackfriars below

St Paul's but the local inhabitants opposed the project.

Burbage died in 1597 and his sons, Cuthbert and Richard, leased a plot of land across the river in Southwark, using the materials from the old Blackfriars theatre to construct the new building on Bankside in 1599.

For the next 14 years the Globe, 'the glory of the Banke', gained an enviable reputation for its drama and for the skill of William Shakespeare, its most talented actor and playwright. But in 1613, during a performance of Henry VIII, a cannon spark set fire to the roof and the building quickly burned to the ground. The only casualty was a man whose breeches caught fire. Undeterred, the company rebuilt the Globe, this time with a tiled roof.

More than 370 years later, in 1989, archaeologists discovered the remains of the Globe's foundations, confirming that part of it is buried under Southwark Bridge Road and part of it under nearby Anchor Terrace. One engraving survives, indicating that the second Globe was built on the foundations of the first.

Arriving in London in 1949, American actor Sam Wanamaker was appalled to find that the only reference to the Globe's existence was a blackened bronze plaque on a brewery wall. Wanamaker rebuilt the Globe, completing the project in 1994, close to its original site and using authentic materials and building methods.

*BELOW: The New Globe Theatre was the brainchild of American actor, Sam Wanamaker, who sadly died before the building was finished.*

*BELOW INSET: William Shakespeare remains England's most-beloved and revered playwright.*

## WALK 50 — ALONG THE RIVERSIDE PROMENADE

❶ Approach Vauxhall Bridge from the underground station, keeping the MI6 building on your right. Bear right and follow the Thames Path along Albert Embankment towards Lambeth Bridge. Pass under it and see Big Ben and the Gothic façade of the Palace. Pass St Thomas's Hospital and take the subway under the road at Westminster Bridge.

❷ Keep the old County Hall building on your right and walk beneath the London Eye. Make for Hungerford Bridge, pass the Royal Festival Hall and approach Waterloo Bridge, with the National Film Theatre on the right. Beyond it lies the National Theatre with Blackfriars Bridge and St Paul's Cathedral ahead. Walk along to the Oxo Tower, with its design shops, cafés and coffee bars, and pass through the subway at Blackfriars Bridge.

❸ Walk alongside Tate Modern to reach the Millennium Bridge. Just beyond it lies the Globe Theatre. Turn the corner by the Anchor Inn and follow Clink Street, passing the museum and the remains of Winchester Palace remains, once part of the medieval town house of the Bishops of Winchester. Continue along Pickfords Wharf to the reconstruction of the Golden Hinde and keep right here for Southwark Cathedral.

❹ Pass to the left of the cathedral and look for the Mudlark pub. Walk to a sign on the left for London Bridge, City Pier and Thames Path East. Return to the river and turn right. Pass HMS *Belfast* and head for Tower Bridge. Cross over and make for Tower Hill tube station or Fenchurch Street station.

**Distance:** 3 miles (5km)

**Terrain:** riverside promenade and pavements

**Refreshments:** plenty of cafés and bars on or near the route

**Park:** South Bank car parks or use the train and underground

**OS Map:** Explorer 173 London North, the City, West End, Enfield

**Difficulty:** ✽

| **1542** | **1547** | **1553** |
|---|---|---|

**1542** The Mongols invade China.

**1543** Henry marries Catherine of Parr and enjoys her quiet companionship until his death.

**1547** Henry dies, riddled with disease.

**1547–53** Edward VI reigns with the help of two Protectors, but only outlives his father by six short years before he dies of tuberculosis.

**1549** Thomas Cranmer's *The Book of Common Prayer* is introduced.

**1553–58** During Mary Tudor's short reign, she earns herself a lasting reputation as the zealous persecutor of the Protestant faith. Despite her gentle personality, she is obsessed throughout her reign with her mission of returning the English Church to Rome.

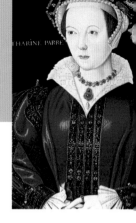

# The Barons of Kendal

*From relatively humble beginnings the Parrs became a most powerful dynasty, ruling Westmorland from their hilltop castle*

**THE TUDORS**

**BUILDING A DYNASTY**

ABOVE: *Catherine Parr (1491–1547) the sixth wife of Henry VIII and the only one fortunate enough to survive her husband.*

From the high hilltop position of Kendal Scar, you descend the limestone slopes to confront Kendal, as the Scottish armies may have done in times past. Life in medieval and Tudor Kendal would have been hard and uncertain. To find a more comfortable life you had to climb to the top of Castle Hill. Kendal's castle was built here in the 1200s and was enlarged over the next three centuries as the power of its occupants, the barons of Kendal, increased. The most celebrated of these families was the Parrs. Their rise to high places began in most unlikely fashion, when in 1371 William del Parre was convicted of murder. However, by joining John of Gaunt's army to fight in Europe, this young man from Prescot in Lancashire secured a pardon. William served his master well, and was given permission to marry Elizabeth, heiress of the de Roos family of Kendal Castle. He achieved the title Sir William Parr, and by the time he died in 1404 had served as king's councillor to both John of Gaunt, Duke of Lancaster, and Henry IV.

However, it was William's grandson, Thomas, who really advanced the family's influence. A ruthless landowner and politician, Sir Thomas forged alliances with the powerful Neville family. Together they ruled Westmorland. With the help of his influential friends, Sir Thomas connived his way to becoming the county's Member of Parliament and a Justice of the Peace. But in 1459 his Yorkist alliances almost proved his undoing. Siding with Richard Neville, the Earl of Salisbury, Parr went into battle against the royal troops at Ludlow Hill. They were routed. Parr fled the country and Kendal Castle

was confiscated. Luckily for Sir Thomas, the Yorkist pretender, Edward IV, came to the throne in 1461, and his titles and deeds were reinstated.

So the foundations were laid to enable the Parr dynasty to have a voice in court circles. Sir Thomas's eldest son, William, was made a Knight of the Garter — you can see reference to this on his tomb in Kendal's parish church – and the grandson, another Sir Thomas, became controller to Henry VIII. When the monarch was looking for a sixth wife he turned to Sir Thomas's daughter, Catherine. She would forever be known as the queen who survived King Henry VIII. But the last of the Parrs, William, died childless, and by 1572 the castle was in ruins, scavenged by the locals from the bottom of the hill. The Crown assessor said it was worth no more than 'four score pounds'.

The crumbling walls of the three towers and the manor hall that remains paints quite a different picture from the wealth and grandeur of the original building, but as you walk through the narrow streets of Kendal's 'auld grey town' you can feel for the humble townsfolk whose destiny lay in the hands of those men in the castle.

BELOW: *Kendal Castle's dominant hilltop position above the small town of Kendal.*

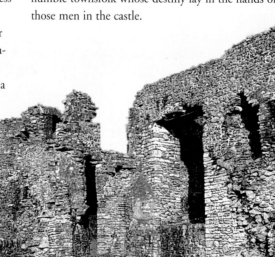

**ABOUT • KENDAL CASTLE**

*Climbing Castle Hill leads to Kendal Castle, home of the ruling barons of Kendal from the 13th century. The Parr family lived here and their long and intriguing history only became known when Catherine Parr became the only wife to outlive Henry VIII.*

## Cumbria • SW N ENGLAND

**DISTANCE •** 7½ miles (12km)

**TOTAL ASCENT •** 650ft (198m)

**PATHS •** well-defined, firm paths

**TERRAIN •** limestone hills and town streets

**GRADIENTS •** steady climb from the town back to Kendal Scar

**REFRESHMENTS •** Castle Inn, Castle Street; the 1657 Chocolate Shop, off Finkle Street

**PARK •** Scout Scar car park, Underbarrow Road

**OS MAP •** Outdoor Leisure 7 The English Lakes South Eastern area

# Kendal Castle

**DIFFICULTY ❋ ❋**

❶ Go through the kissing gate across the road from the signed car park and climb through scrub hawthorns towards Scout Scar. Follow the edge path south.

❷ Turn left at a large cairn and follow the limestone path across the plateau. Beyond the second access (a kissing gate) through crosswalls, the path traverses a field to reach a country lane.

❸ Turn left along the lane over the by-pass down towards Kendal. Take the right fork on the edge of town, then turn right down Gillinggate. Go straight across the main road at the bottom, into Dowker's Lane, and through the arched stone gate into the recreation ground. Take the left-hand path through the recreation ground and cross the footbridge spanning the River Kent.

❹ Cross the road, turn right then go left up Parr Street (which becomes Sunnyside) before climbing the path to the castle.

❺ Head north along the grassy ridge back into Kendal. Turn left along Castle Road, then left again along the A684. Where this bends right go straight ahead to cross the river at Stramongate Bridge.

❻ Continue along Stramongate and Finkle Street, then turn left along Stricklandgate. Turn right by the Tourist Information Centre to climb up Allhallows Lane and Beast Banks. Turn right by the triangular green in to Mount Pleasant (leading to Serpentine Road). At the main road turn right, then take the left fork into Queens Road.

❼ Go left up a narrow tarmac lane, signed footpath to Helsfell

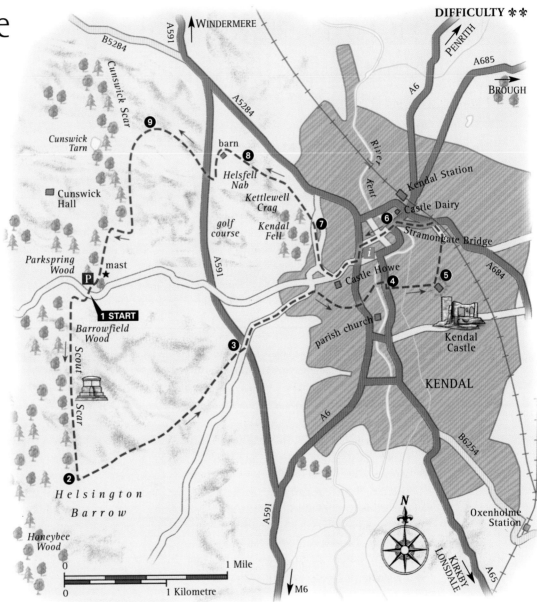

Nab. Half-way up the hillside this becomes a gritty track heading northwest on the slopes of Kendal Fell.

❽ Beneath Kettlewell Crag the path turns right over a stile (look for a small yellow arrrow) and follows the right-hand field edge beneath Helsfell Nab. Beyond an old barn swing left on a path parallel to the by-pass. Cross two ladder stiles before reaching a third to cross the footbridge over

the by-pass. Cross another ladder stile to leave the footbridge and then cross one more over the wall to the right. Continue on the faint footpath across the field, aiming for the grassy hilltop ahead.

❾ Beyond the stile in the left corner of the field, swing half left to the edge of Cunswick Scar. Head south along it, crossing a stile, then turn right, following the permissive route signed to Scout Scar. Go over the stile into the

woods and take the right fork back to the car park.

**• DON'T MISS •**

*The 14th-century **Castle Dairy** on Wildman Street is Kendal's oldest building. It was probably part of a dowry given by Sir Thomas Parr to his daughter Agnes on her wedding to Sir Thomas Strickland in 1455.*

**1554**

**1554** Mary marries Philip of Spain, but the union is unpopular. In the same year Mary returns England to Papal authority, and thousands of Protestants are given the option to 'turn or burn'. Among those who choose to burn is Thomas Cranmer, who dies in 1556.

**1558**

**1558–1603** Following the death of 'Bloody Mary', the accession of Elizabeth I to the throne is welcomed with relief.

**1558** Mary, Queen of Scots, daughter of James V of Scotland, marries the French Dauphin.

**1560**

**1560** The Scottish parliament proclaims the nation Protestant, ending their alliance with France.

**1562** Sir Francis Drake voyages to America for the first of many slave-trading expeditions.

# Sherborne Castle:
# Sir Walter Raleigh's refuge

*Discover historic Sherborne and the fascinating life of Sir Walter Raleigh, the great Elizabethan courtier and explorer, in the magnificent parkland surrounding his former homes*

**THE TUDORS**

**BUILDING A DYNASTY**

Sir Walter Raleigh was born at Hayes Barton Farm in East Budleigh, Devon, in 1552 and educated at Oxford. He first saw military service in the Huguenot army in France in 1569 and in 1578 engaged in the first of his expeditions against the Spaniards. Following a successful spell of service in Ireland, where his actions attracted the attention of Queen Elizabeth, Raleigh entered the English court and rapidly fashioned himself as the perfect Elizabethan courtier. Through famous incidents – such as gallantly throwing his cloak over a puddle so that the Queen wouldn't get her feet dirty – Raleigh delighted the Queen, and by 1582 had become her favourite. He received a knighthood in 1584, and would remain at her side for ten years.

Raleigh first saw Sherborne Castle in 1591, while riding to his fleet at Plymouth, and was so enchanted by the view that he tumbled from his horse. Aware that the land was owned by the Bishop of Salisbury, Raleigh presented the Queen with a gift of jewellery with the words 'to make the Bishop'. Under royal pressure, the lease for Sherborne Castle was transferred to Raleigh in 1592, just after he had secretly married Bess Throckmorton, one of the Queen's ladies-in-waiting. A few months later, their secret discovered, the couple were imprisoned in the Tower of London by the furious Queen. After five weeks they were freed but Raleigh was exiled from the court for five years.

During this time he set about making Sherborne a home for his family. However, he quickly found the 12th-century fortress impractical for his needs and decided to build a new castle across the River Yeo. This had four elaborate storeys, with tall chimneys and mullioned windows; in the grounds he laid out water gardens and a bowling green, and planted exotic trees from the New World. The building you see today was extended by the Digby family in the

17th century and its magnificent parkland was land-scaped by 'Capability' Brown in the 18th century.

Bored with his semi-enforced lifestyle as a country squire Raleigh became a writer, philosopher and poet but his 'greed, arrogance and religious scepticism' soon made him unpopular. In 1602 he was sent to the Tower, accused of conspiring against James VI of Scotland. James's accession as James I of England in 1603 sealed Raleigh's fate, and he remained in the Tower for 13 years, during which time he wrote his *History of the World*. Liberated in 1616, he set sail for yet another disastrous expedition to Venezuela in search of gold, returning just in time to be executed on the old charge of treason in 1618.

ABOVE LEFT: *Sir Walter Raleigh (1552–1618) was Elizabeth's favourite courtier but he quickly fell out of favour when he married one of her ladies-in-waiting.*

BELOW: *Aerial view of Sherborne shows both of Sir Walter Raleigh's homes in Sherborne – the New Castle in the foreground and the Old Castle is behind.*

ABOVE: *Sir Walter fell in love with Sherborne Castle the first time he saw it. He went to great pains to get the lease transferred to him and before he was executed he asked to be buried here.*

**ABOUT • SHERBORNE**

*Founded by the Saxons and set amid green valleys and wooded hills, Sherborne is a lovely, mellow-stoned town. It was also home to one of the most famous figures of the Elizabethan court, Sir Walter Raleigh, who lived here from 1592 until his death in 1618.*

**Dorset • SW ENGLAND**

**DISTANCE** • 5½ miles (8.8km)

**TOTAL ASCENT** • 400ft (121m)

**PATHS** • good, but field paths can be waterlogged after heavy rain

**TERRAIN** • parkland, farmland, town streets

**GRADIENTS** • gradual; one steep ascent

**REFRESHMENTS** • choice of pubs and cafés in Sherborne; tea room in Sherborne Castle

**PARKING** • main long-stay car park accessed off Long Street or Ludbourne Road (close to Sainsbury's). Alternative parking at station

**OS MAP** • Explorer 129 Yeovil & Sherborne

# Sir Walter Raleigh

**DIFFICULTY ✻✻**

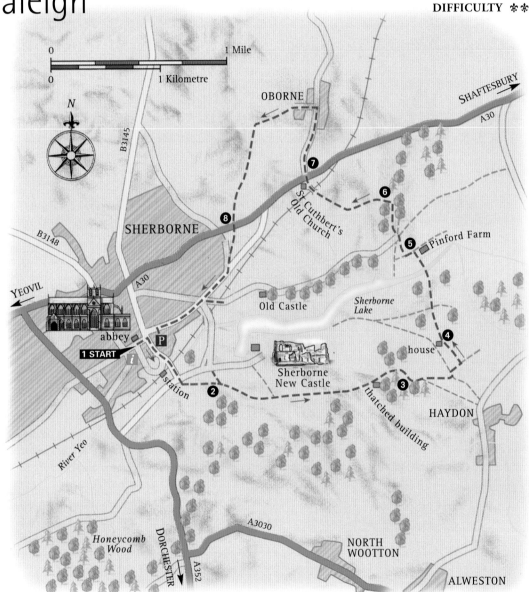

❶ With your back to the abbey, turn left along Half Moon Street, then right down South Street. Fork left past Sainsbury's and cross the railway to a T-junction. Cross over and take the waymarked path left, diagonally uphill. Bear left beside railings down to a turnstile gate and right along the drive to visit Sherborne New Castle.

❷ Return along the drive to the turnstile gate and go uphill. Bear left and beyond the gate take the grassy path between fields to a gate. Bear right on a track to a gate and go uphill towards a thatched building in trees. Go through a gate and go steeply uphill into the deer park. Bear right at the top to a gate into woodland.

❸ Shortly, follow the path left, and disregarding the concrete path right, keep ahead to farm buildings. Turn right along the access road to a drive. Turn left, then right with a yellow marker down a track along the field edge. At a junction of paths, cross the stile on your left and walk beside woodland to a gate (house left).

❹ Enter the deer park and proceed straight ahead, downhill along the line of telegraph poles, towards a farmhouse. Keep ahead beyond a gate to cross a bridge over the River Yeo. Continue along the right-hand field edge to a gate beside Pinford Farm.

❺ Turn left along the drive, then just beyond a gate, turn right through a gate into a field. Head uphill towards an ornate drive entrance and a gate. Turn right through the gateway and take the second path left. In a few paces, bear right following yellow markers along a path through a copse, eventually reaching a stile.

❻ Head straight across the field to a gate, then bear half-left to double stiles in the hedge. Proceed diagonally right to a gate and pass beneath the railway bridge. Just beyond, bear off right to a stone stile and walk to the A30, beside St Cuthbert's Old Church.

❼ Cross and follow the lane to Oborne. Cross the small bridge on your left, pass the church and keep ahead, uphill along a cobbled path. Remain on the path to the A30.

❽ Follow the bridleway opposite, beside Four Acres, to a stile and descend to a gate. Keep ahead to a gate and go through the farmyard to a lane. Turn left, then right at the T-junction into Sherborne. For the Old Castle take the first road left; otherwise, keep ahead along Long Street into the town.

**• DON'T MISS •**

*St Cuthbert's Old Church in Sherborne, is an enchanting small stone building between the A30 and the railway station. Only the chancel survives of the 1553 church. Note the 14th-century slip-tiles, the rustic, 17th-century communion rails, and the medieval pillar piscina.*

**1568**

**1568** Mary Queen of Scots flees from Scotland to England, but is imprisoned by Elizabeth.

**1586** Sir Walter Raleigh introduces tobacco and potatoes into England from the Americas.

**1587**

**1587** Elizabeth I signs a death warrant for Mary Queen of Scots for alleged plots against the English monarch. Her execution triggers a reaction from Philip of Spain, who disapproves of Elizabeth's refusal to return to Catholicism.

**1588**

**1588** Determined to depose Elizabeth, Philip gathers 130 ships off the south-west coast of England, but most of the fleet is destroyed by English gunfire, and the survivors fall prey to bad weather as they retreat. It was to be Elizabeth's greatest triumph.

# The Royal Palace of Falkland

*A Renaissance masterpiece in Fife that was the favourite home of Mary, Queen of Scots*

Although scarcely larger than a village, Falkland is a town with a long and regal history that is still reflected in its streets. Aside from its magnificent Renaissance palace there are quaint old

ABOVE: *An aerial view of Falkland Palace and the town set in the Lomond Hills in Fife.*

cottages, public buildings, mansions and townhouses, all of which contributed to Falkland being chosen in 1970 as Scotland's first Conservation Area.

The settlement grew around a castle built by the MacDuff Earls of Fife in the 12th century, but it was only when the lands reverted to the Crown in 1424 that Falkland rose to prominence. The countryside for miles around was then a hunting forest, with woods and moors that provided some of the best sport in Scotland. For the Stuart monarchs, Falkland was the most desirable and loved of all the royal properties: an escape from affairs of state in Edinburgh or Stirling and, at times, a refuge. James I created it a Royal Burgh in 1458 and in 1495 James IV entertained Perkin Warbeck, pretender to

the English throne, in the hunting lodge that he was then starting to transform into a palace. The King, along with most of Scotland's aristocracy, died on Flodden Field in 1513, but his infant son, James V, grew up to acquire his father's passion for fine architecture. His work at Falkland Palace is extraordinary. At a time when English architecture still remained rooted in the medieval Gothic style, he looked to new châteaux in France and celebrated the rebirth of classicism with a building based on symmetry and Grecian order, the first of its kind in Britain.

James V's daughter, Mary, Queen of Scots, loved the palace, escaping here as often as she could from the political manoeuvrings and sexual intrigues that marked her tragic life. Her days there were spent in falconry and hunting, with music and dancing in the evenings. She became Queen of Scotland aged just six and married the King of France's eldest son when she was 16 years. When she returned to England, after her husband's death, in 1561 she made two fatal mistakes – she declared that she would take the English throne from the 'illegitimate' Elizabeth, and she married her cousin Lord Darnley. He arranged the murder of her chief adviser, David Rizzio, and a year later she was implicated in her husband's murder and was forced to abdicate. Mary raised an army but to no avail, she was forced to flee to England where she was imprisoned by Elizabeth I for 19 years before she was finally executed in 1587 for treason.

Following her flight to England in 1568, the palace lost its importance, and its fate was sealed when the Scottish court moved to London in 1603. Occupied and vandalised by Cromwell, who also cut down what remained of Falkland Forest's woodland, the palace gradually became a ruin, while the splendid town that it supported declined into a quiet village. These long years of neglect effectively froze Falkland in a time-warp until 1887, when the 3rd Marquess of Bute acquired the title of hereditary keeper and, driven by his passion for romantic architecture, undertook a massive restoration programme that saved the palace and preserved the centre of the town.

ABOVE: *Mary, Queen of Scots (1542–1587) was Elizabeth's greatest adversary swearing to take the throne from the 'illegitimate' Elizabeth I.*

BELOW: *Built in the mid 16th century in the Renaissance style, Falkland Palace is now owned by the National Trust for Scotland*

WALK 53

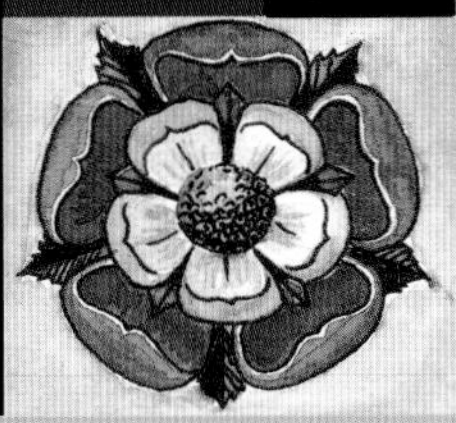

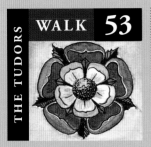

**ABOUT • FALKLAND PALACE**

*A steep, demanding climb is rewarded with panoramic views over Fife, with the Highland mountains on the far horizon. The moor is a wild place and not so very different from when Mary, Queen of Scots, rode the hillside with a falcon on her wrist.*

**Fife • SCOTLAND**

**DISTANCE** • 5 miles (8km)

**TOTAL ASCENT** • 1,148ft (350m)

**PATHS** • mostly good, but some stretches muddy in wet weather

**TERRAIN** • woods and open moorland

**GRADIENTS** • steep on East Lomond Hill

**REFRESHMENTS** • tea rooms, restaurants and pubs in Falkland

**PARK** • near the town hall

**OS MAP** • Explorer 370 Glenrothes North, Falkland & Lomond Hills

# Favourite home of Mary, Queen of Scots

❶ Follow the lane out of the car park and turn left up Back Wynd. Bear right at the factory entrance gates, then turn left at the crossroads into East Loan. Continue uphill where the road turns into a track with the factory entrance on the left.

❷ After 60yds (55m) fork right on to the signed track. Soon take the signed footpath left to climb a long flight of steps, with a handrail, cut into the hillside through trees.

❸ Continue up the steps to an attractive area of beech wood. The route, now a path, levels off slightly. As you gain height the path becomes steeper entering coniferous pines. The woodland clears to reveal an expanse of moorland and heather. The path is well-defined until near the summit where it becomes steep and demanding. Look back for views of Falkland and its palace almost directly below.

❹ The only evidence of the Pictish hill fort is the ramparts which encirle the site. Ben Lomond can be seen to the west, the Grampian Highlands to the north, the North Sea and the East Neuk of Fife to the east and the Firth of Forth and Edinburgh to the south. From the far side of the summit follow a faint path downhill to the left to join the straight clear track that can be seen further down the slope, cutting across the moorland.

❺ Pass through a kissing gate, bear right along the clear track, an old limestone-burners' road enclosed by drystone dykes. In August and September the heather moorland is a purple blaze of colour. The track (take care in wet conditions as the track can be muddy and boggy) leads down to a minor road.

❻ At the junction with the road turn right. Here there are toilets, a picnic area and car park. Continue on the road downhill, with woodland on your left, for 2 miles (3km) into Falkland. Enter the town and pass a number of well-restored cottages dating back to the 17th and 18th centuries. One, the Old Room, opposite Mill Wynd, is now a cunningly disguised electricity sub-station. Many cottages have 'marriage lintels', engraved with initials, hearts and dates above their doors.

❼ Having visited the palace, then turn right into Beck Wynd to return to the car park.

**• DON'T MISS •**

*Just after reaching the main track at Point ❺, a signed path to the left leads to a large, early **19th-century lime-kiln**. In the days before artificial fertilisers, lime was essential for improving acid soils. The flooded quarry pits around the kiln are now an attractive nature reserve.*

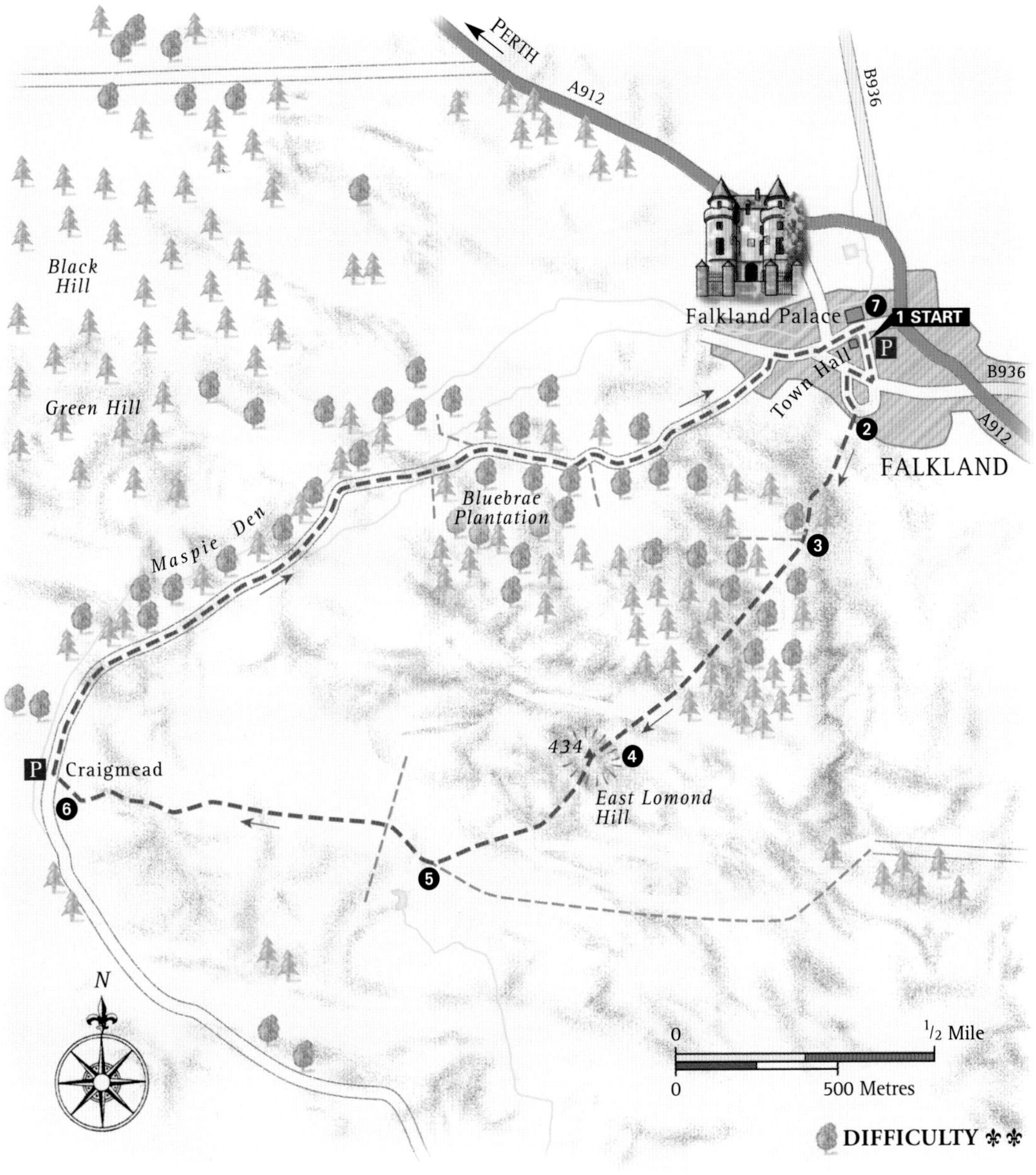

**1589** Sir John Harrington invents the first WC, but it does not come into use for another 300 years, when a national sewerage system is introduced.

**1595** William Shakespeare writes *Romeo and Juliet.*

**1599** The Globe Theatre, near Southwark Cathedral, is completed.

**1601** The Earl of Essex, stepson of the Queen's 'favourite', the Earl of Leicester, leads a revolt against Elizabeth's government and is punished by execution.

**1603** Elizabeth dies a childless spinster. The throne passes to James VI of Scotland and thereby unites the two crowns.

# Around the Majesty of Hardwick Hall

*Through the back garden of one of Britain's most imposing Tudor mansions, high on a hill in north-east Derbyshire*

ABOVE: *Elizabeth, Countess of Shrewsbury (1518–1608) was one of the most memorable figures of the Elizabethan period.*

Hardwick Hall towers on a limestone ridge, as it has done for the past four centuries. Boasting tall glass windows and honey-coloured stone, rising to six towers and battlements carved with the initials 'ES', the mansion was built to be noticed by a woman who lived to be noticed.

Born in 1527 into minor gentry, Elizabeth rose from humble beginnings to wed four wealthy men in succession, outliving them all to become 'Bess of Hardwick', one of the richest women in the kingdom, second only to Queen Elizabeth I. Her last husband was George Talbot, 6th Earl of Shrewsbury, regarded as the wealthiest nobleman in England, and the man appointed by the Queen as guardian of Mary, Queen of Scots.

After Talbot died in 1590 Bess, although in her 70s, began building Hardwick Hall while still living in the Old Hall, the ruins of which stand near by. Her chosen archictect was Robert Smythson, considered one of the greatest archictects of the time. His design for Hardwick Hall was lavish and combined an elegant suite of state rooms and large windows – which would have dramatically increased the building cost. Started in 1591 the structure of the building was completed in just three years and by 1597 the house was decorated and furnished.

Bess was given her dream – a house fit for a queen, furnished with richly coloured carpets, silk damask curtains, satins and taffetas trimmed with tassels. Hardwick today is famous as being a quintessential Elizabethan house with its rich collection of paintings, furniture, tapestries and many beautiful 16th-century ornaments and objects. The formal gardens, which consist of carefully clipped yew hedges and borders, create the perfect backdrop.

Bess died in 1608 and is buried at Derby Cathedral. After her death, Hardwick Hall became the home of the Cavendish family, who added sympathetic changes, but it is still Bess's extravagant presence that fills the lofty chambers.

This walk concentrates on the 300-acre (121ha) Hardwick Park, a dense woodland that widens to agricultural plains edged by former mining villages. The only public right of way is the bridleway, all other paths are 'permitted paths'. And though Hardwick Hall has seasonal opening times, from March to October, the park is always open.

Look out for the Ice House, a store for ice from the pond for use in the kitchens, and historic Row Ponds, now numbering five, where once there were seven. Stainsby Mill stands on the site of a 13th-century mill, used to grind flour for the Hardwick estate, and atmospheric Hardwick Inn was built by Bess in 1608 to replace an earlier inn.

However, it's unlikely that you'll be following in Bess's footsteps: the grand old lady hardly ventured outdoors. Instead, she had a long exercise gallery built in the house, and ordered her workers to sort out the grounds. After all, she was the boss.

ABOVE: *The grandeur of Hardwick Hall, now owned by the National Trust.*

BELOW: *Looking south over the formal gardens at Hardwick Hall.*

**ABOUT • HARDWICK HALL**

*Discover one of the most fascinating women in British history in this walk around Hardwick Hall. Born in 1527, Bess wed four wealthy men, outlived them all and inherited their estates to become one of the richest women in England, only outdone by Elizabeth I.*

## Derbyshire • C ENGLAND

**DISTANCE** • 6 miles (9.6km)

**TOTAL ASCENT** • 584ft (178m)

**PATHS** • mostly wooded, or surfaced; open fields can be muddy in wet weather

**TERRAIN** • dense woodland opening out on to agricultural pastures. **Note: keep dogs on the lead whilst in the park**

**GRADIENT** • gradual and comfortable

**REFRESHMENTS** • Hardwick Inn, café in the Old Hall

**PARK** • Hardwick Information Centre (signed)

**OS MAP** • Explorer 273 Lincolnshire Wolds South, Horncastle

# Bess of Hardwick

**DIFFICULTY** ✤ ✤

❶ In the car park at the Tourist Information Centre, face the lake and take the wooded track to the left alongside Miller's Pond. Cross the bridge and at the end of the pond, bear left after passing through a kissing gate. Follow the grassy track to another kissing gate, and continue to Blingsby Gate on the left.

❷ Turn left, passing through Blingsby Gate and follow the firm gravel road. Pass a farm on the right and a blue sentry box on the left. Very soon pass through blue gates (entrance to Hardwick Park) to meet the road. Turn left, on the right is Stainsby Mill.

❸ Retrace your route back through Blingsby Gate, continue on the road and pass through the next gate. Immediately turn left and climb up over the meadow following the wire fence on the left which leads to another blue gate.

❹ Pass through the blue gate and take the right fork which leads to the village of Ault Hucknall. Emerge from the track immediately opposite the Church of St John the Baptist. Turn right along the road until a bend reveals a bridlepath, signed Rowthorne Trail, on your right. Cross cultivated fields to a stile and a road.

❺ Turn right, then right again to the entrance gates of Hardwick Park. Walk towards Hardwick Hall. At the main entrance to the house, and just before the Old Hall, turn right down a wide grass track. Pass through the kissing gate and immediately turn right, hugging the fence downhill.

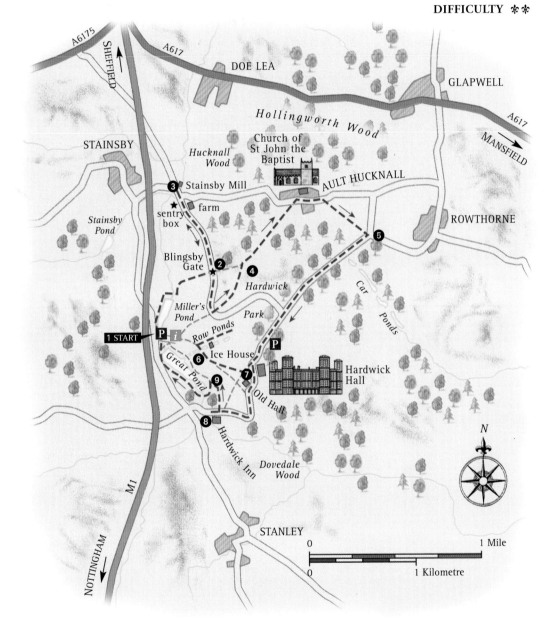

❻ Pass through another gate to the five historic Row Ponds. The Ice House can be seen between the third and fourth pond. Retrace your steps back to the Old Hall.

❼ Return to the road in front of Hardwick Hall, turn right and follow the road down through trees to another gate. This is another entrance/exit to the Park. On the left is Hardwick Inn.

❽ At the Park gate bear sharp left and walk across the field, hugging the fence as it circles round woodland. Eventually pass through a gate in the fence.

❾ Follow the path through the woodland, leading to the Great Pond on your right. Continue to the road and turn right to return to the car park and the start of the walk.

*During the 17th century Britain endured a roller-coaster ride through religious and political controversy, and was nearly torn apart by civil war. By the dawn of the 18th century, the foundations of a modern nation state had been laid.*

## THE STUARTS

### 1603–1714

# Gunpowder to Wig Powder

James VI of Scotland, son of Mary, Queen of Scots, became James I of England when Elizabeth died without an heir. He left Calvinist Edinburgh to take up his throne in London, where Puritans were pushing to get rid of all remnants of Catholic ritual in the Church. Their bid to abolish bishops went too far for the new King, but when, in 1605, Guy Fawkes and his Catholic conspirators tried to blow up the Houses of Parliament, James hardened his stance and reimposed anti-Catholic penalties.

James was a big spender and patron of the arts. Shakespeare's *Measure for Measure* was written in his honour; during his and his son's reigns drama and poetry flourished under Webster, Jonson, Donne, Milton and many others; royal funds were splashed out on the construction of the Banqueting House in Whitehall Palace, designed by Inigo Jones. Asked to vote him money to cover these costs and to pay for war with Spain, Parliament presented its 'grievances'.

Charles I found himself in similar difficulties, seeking funds for wars with Spain and France, and alienating Parliament with his 'High Church' views. In 1629 the Commons passed resolutions condemning the King, while the Speaker was held down in his chair. For the next 11 years Charles ruled without calling a Parliament. The interlude ended with the King's defeat by Scottish Presbyterians resisting the English-style religious practices. Parliament returned, in defiant mood, and the wrangle continued.

In 1642 Charles entered the House of Commons with troops to arrest the ringleaders, only to find that 'his birds had flown'. Neither side was prepared to yield, so both prepared for war.

The Civil War is still a vivid popular memory, as are the long-haired, droopy-hatted Royalists, or Cavaliers, and the helmeted Roundheads who took prominence under Puritan general Oliver Cromwell. Seven years of bitter fighting devastated the country, dividing families and destroying crops, buildings and lives. After Charles' execution in 1649 the nation was left in a state of exhaustion and shock. In 1651 the political philosopher Thomas Hobbes called for a 'Leviathan' – a strong sovereign – and reflected the general post-war despair. Enter Oliver Cromwell as Lord Protector. His vicious campaigns in Ireland and his Puritanical domestic policies made him a hate-figure to many, and after his death Charles II was restored to the throne to widespread acclamation.

### AFTER THE RESTORATION

Theatres reopened in 1660 for the first time since 1642, but religious conflicts continued, and a split between the King's supporters and opponents – Tories and Whigs – marked the beginnings of a political party system. In the mid-1660s two disasters hit – the Plague and the Great Fire of London. But despite all this, plus a series of poor harvests and wars against the Dutch, parts of Britain, at least, were prospering. American and West Indian colonies supplied tobacco, cotton, rice and sugar in a closed trade system that excluded Scotland altogether. Fortunes were made; money opened doors to power and influence. Even the Great Fire had benefits, providing Christopher Wren with the opportunity to make his architectural mark.

In 1688 the Glorious Revolution took place. The Catholic king, James II was deposed in favour of William of Orange, and Parliament established a constitutional, Protestant succession. Everywhere, the old certainties of religion, power and knowledge were being challenged. Two years before the Glorious Revolution, Isaac Newton had put forward his laws of physics, changing man's view of the universe for ever.

---

### HISTORIC SITES

**Hatfield House, Herts:** superb Jacobean mansion.

**Parliament House, Edinburgh:** built for the Scottish Parliament in the 1630s.

**Queen's House, Greenwich:** Inigo Jones's masterpiece.

**Eyam, Derbyshire:** village struck by the plague in 1665 and put into voluntary quarantine.

**Lancaster Castle, Lancs:** ten witches were tried and sentenced here in 1612, and executed on Gallows Hill near by.

**Audley End, Essex:** built for the Lord Treasurer in 1614; at the time, England's largest house.

**1603** When James I took over the English throne, having ruled for 36 years in Scotland, religion was a burning issue. The King was caught between the Puritans who were pressing for reform and the Catholic influences of his court.

**1605** James gives way to his Puritan advisers and introduces penal laws against Catholics.

**1605** Alarmed by his religious policies, a group of Catholic conspirators plan to blow up the King, his family and the Houses of

Parliament. Guy Fawkes is discovered and caught before he is able to light the fuse of several barrels of gunpowder.

**1606–16** The Blue Mosque in Istanbul, Turkey, is completed.

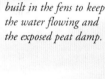

# Nordelph: at the Heart of the Fens

*Endless skies and long, straight waterways dominate the reclaimed landscape surrounding the fenland village of Nordelph*

The Fens of East Anglia are famous for their huge skies and fertile, featureless land. Once they were thought of as mysterious, a vast and sinister area of watery peat and bog, where the inhabitants lived on isolated little islands amid the unwholesome marsh, on a muddy diet of eels and waterfowl. Even today it's whispered that those who live in the Fens have webbed feet. In the early 17th century, speculators sought to drain the land, and were called 'Adventurers'; the local people who fiercely fought off this threat to their traditional way of life became known as 'Fen Tigers'.

The Fens are essentially a man-made landscape. The Romans and the Saxons sought to reclaim this vast area south of the Wash for agriculture, but it was Charles I who made it happen, granting permission for the 4th Duke of Bedford to bring in engineers from Holland. The most famous of these was Cornelius Vermuyden (c.1595–c.1683). He first came to Britain in 1621 to stem a breach of the River Thames, and from 1634 to 1652 he worked on draining the 301,000 acres of the Bedford Level, building a system of banks and channels to allow water to collect and be drained away. Massive locks controlled the flow of tidal rivers and allowed shipping to pass through. Denver Sluice, a few miles south of Nordelph, was the main lock between the South Level River System and the Great Ouse, a tidal river that led on to the Middle Level and finally the sea. First built in 1651, it was effectively a gate, allowing through-navigation only four times a day when the water levels were equal on both sides. There is still a lock on the site, with vast steel lift-gates.

The drains became a significant communication network between isolated farming settlements – Nordelph grew up where Popham's Eau (pronounced 'ee') meets Well Creek. An important channel with a packet service to the inland port of Wisbech, this is still used by pleasure boats today.

A side effect of drainage was that drying land shrank down below the level of the rivers, calling for windmills – and later steam pumps – to keep everything flowing. The fertile exposed peat, above a layer of soft clay, is ideal for growing crops such as potatoes, cabbages, hops, pumpkins and other vegetables and fruit, but is unsuitable for building on. Many of the older houses of yellow fenland brick, cheaply built, now tilt at uncomfortable angles. Nordelph's undistinguished 19th-century church is cracked and has been condemned, its foundations undermined by dried-out peat.

With its bridges and waterside houses, Nordelph has the appealing air of a Dutch village, though its houses are mostly Victorian. The walk leads from the village along the straight-cut, high bank of the Old Bedford River, which runs parallel with the River Delph, and eventually the tidal New Bedford River (also known as the Hundred Foot Drain). Man-made, the Old and New Bedford Rivers stretch for 21 miles (34km). In winter, the area between the channels becomes a flood-plain, popular with swans and ducks from nearby Welney; in summer, it provides rich pastureland and a haven for wading birds.

ABOVE: *Windmills were built in the fens to keep the water flowing and the exposed peat damp.*

BACKGROUND: *The huge skies and level landscape of the Norfolk Fens.*

BELOW: *View along the Old Bedford River, in Welney.*

**ABOUT • NORDELPH**

*From the village of Nordelph, you explore the man-made landscape of the Fens, which caused deep controversy in the 17th century. With the permission of Charles I, Dutch engineers drained huge tracts of bog land to create a fertile landscape.*

## Norfolk • SE ENGLAND

**DISTANCE** • 5 miles (8km)

**PATHS** • mostly good, but field path can be very muddy; some road walking

**TERRAIN** • village, fields, river bank

**GRADIENTS** • mostly level walking; a climb up the bank, and two awkward stiles and bridges to negotiate

**REFRESHMENTS** • Chequers Inn, Nordelph

**PARK** • car park by phone box, just over bridge off A1122, signed Welney.

**OS MAP** • Explorer 228 March & Ely, Chatteris & Littleport

# The wide skies of a man-made landscape

❶ From the car park and picnic area by the landing stage opposite the Chequers Inn, turn away from the bridge and walk down the High Street, parallel with Well Creek, which is on your left. Pass a row of terraced cottages, and the church (due for demolition at time of writing). Pass the village hall and war memorial on your right. Continue past a squat pepper-pot house, and a row of modern housing.

❷ Follow the main road as it bends sharp right and continues as Birchfield Road, away from Well Creek. A ditch, or lode, on your right separates you from the expansive fields.

❸ Where the road bends left, follow the footpath sign straight ahead along a grassy path by the lode. Stay along the field edge, following the course of the lode, heading for a lone poplar tree. At the tree, where the lode disappears underground, keep straight on, following the line of concrete fence posts.

❹ At the end of the field, cross the reedy drain via a footbridge. Cross the stile, climb up the river bank and turn right. Walk along the grassy river path of the Old Bedford River for about a mile (1.6km), with excellent views over the flat fen landscape. Note the flood meadow between the river and the parallel line of the New Bedford River.

❺ Descend near the oblong artificial fish pond on to the lower path, continuing through a gate. Shortly after passing under the pylons, look for a stile and

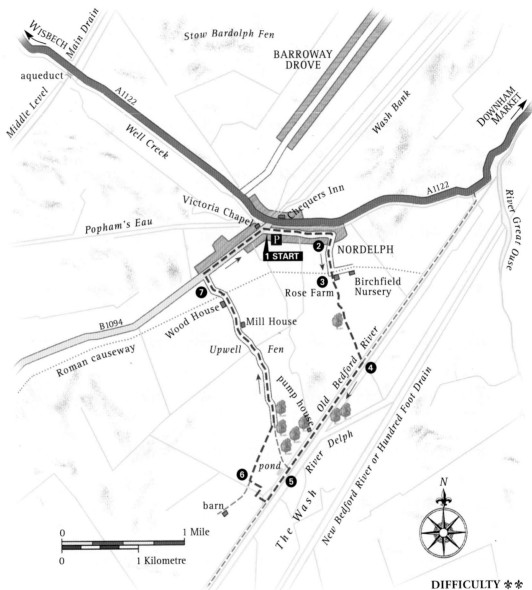

footbridge with a handrail down to your right – stepped access may be slippery. Cross over, and turn right on the opposite bank, bearing left with the field edge along the lode.

❻ At the concrete bridge, turn right on to the farm track. This becomes a tarmac road, passing through farm buildings and scattered houses. Just past Wood House farmhouse, look out for the

track off to the right (private) – this is the line of an old Roman causeway. Stay on the road, to reach a junction.

❼ At the junction, turn right and walk on the verge back towards the village. Where Coronation Avenue opens up on the left, cross over and continue into the village on the footpath. Turn right by the Victoria Chapel to the car park.

**DIFFICULTY ✳✳**

**• DON'T MISS •**

*For a rare glimpse of what the Fens were like before they were drained, visit the nature reserve at* **Wicken Fen.** *Also worth a visit is* **The Wildfowl & Wetlands Trust,** *at Welney, which attracts thousands of whooper and Bewick swans in winter.*

**1611**

**1611** King James commissions a new translation of the Bible.

**1620** The *Mayflower* sets sails to America, carrying the Pilgrim Fathers. During the following two decades, 20,000 emigrants travelled from England to join the colony.

**1625**

**1625** Charles I accedes the throne, but within a year causes controversy by dissolving the powers of Parliament.

**1642–49** The English Civil War breaks out when Charles I attempts to arrest five MPs for treason. The

**1642**

Court moves to Nottingham as outrage grows in the capital.

**1642** The Royalists suffer a defeat at Edgehill. It is the first of a string of victories for Oliver Cromwell in the Civil War.

# Proud Northern Lady

*Appleby-in-Westmorland owes much to a great benevolent aristocrat, who spent the last 40 years of her life rebuilding and restoring her northern estate*

ABOVE: *The rolling hills of Appleby.*

In 1649 Lady Anne Clifford, Countess of Dorset, Pembroke and Montgomery, rode into Appleby to reclaim the estates denied to her on her father's death in 1605. She had spent the previous 40 years trying to overturn a will, which left the 90,000 acres (81,396ha) and six castles to her uncle, the 4th Earl of Cumberland. As the eldest child of the 3rd Earl, she felt they were hers by right. But she was also a 15-year-old girl, and her father had trusted his brother to look after her interests. He neglected to do so, and it was not until the death of his own son in 1643, and the resulting extinction of the earldom, that Anne received her rightful inheritance.

When Anne arrived in Appleby Charles I had just been executed and there was a Commonwealth garrison in the castle. Despite this, she embarked on a comprehensive re-building programme. Appleby Castle had not been habitable since the 'Rising in the North' in 1569. Of the other castles she inherited, Pendragon was a heap of rubble, Brough (pronounced Bruff) and Brougham (pronounced Broom) were equally dilapidated and Skipton bore the scars of its siege in the war. But her record in the first few years at Appleby is impressive.

In 1653 she laid the foundations for the Hospital of St Anne in Boroughgate. In 1654 she paid for a family vault in the Parish Church of St Lawrence's, celebrating her lineage back to the Vipont family at the time of King John. She had St Lawrence's renovated in 1655 and St Michael's, Bongate in 1659. All the while she kept up a show of public contempt for the new regime and for Cromwell in particular. Nevertheless, she was allowed to restore her castles, when others were being deliberately demolished.

Appleby was occupied by troops led by Robert Atkinson, a Clifford tenant from Mallerstang and a particular target for Anne's venom. After the Restoration, in 1664, he was found to have taken part in a plot against the new monarch. He was hung, drawn and quartered in the castle grounds and Anne declared herself well rid of her 'great enemie'. But she let his widow and family stay on at their house for a nominal rent.

Anne died in March 1676 at the age of 86. The Bishop of Carlisle, who led her funeral service, announced that the 'monuments she had built … shall speak loud in the ears of a profligate generation'. Lord Thanet inherited the estate and in 1680 gave permission for stone to be taken from both Brougham and Brough castles to modernise Appleby and make it more befitting of a lord in the age of enlightenment.

This walk passes Appleby Castle, the two churches and a number of large farms, which were once part of the huge Clifford estates. St Michael's is now a private house. The Hospital of St Anne (almshouses) has tenants still, but you are allowed to peek through the courtyard arch. The best monument is St Leonard's, where the remains of Anne and her mother lie in the crypt.

ABOVE: *Portrait of Lady Anne Clifford (1609–75).*

LEFT: *The courtyard at Appleby Castle. Anne was responsible for a comprehensive rebuilding programme at Appleby Castle but is best remembered for her numerous good works in the local community.*

**ABOUT • APPLEBY CASTLE**

*This walk visits Appleby Castle, restored in 1651 by the extraordinary Lady Anne Clifford. She won fame as a great adversary of Cromwell and for her prolific building and restoration work, including St Anne's Hospital and St Michael's in Bongate.*

**Cumbria • N ENGLAND**

**DISTANCE •** 6½ miles (10.4km)

**TOTAL ASCENT •** 375ft (114m)

**PATHS •** field tracks and farm lanes

**TERRAIN •** pastureland and town

**GRADIENTS •** no steep ascents

**REFRESHMENTS •** several pubs and tea shops in Appleby. The Royal Oak on Bongate is next to the start of the walk

**PARK •** roadside parking by the war memorial and St Michael's Church at the top of Mill Hill on Bongate

**OS MAP •** Outdoor Leisure 19 Howgill Fells & Upper Eden Valley

# The indomitable spirit of Lady Anne Clifford

❶ Walk down Mill Hill to cross Jubilee Bridge over the River Eden by Bongate Mill. Walk up the hill and turn right at the top for 200yds (183m). Cross the road to the shop opposite, go along Colby Lane for 15yds (14m) to a footpath on the left signed Bandley Bridge.

❷ Cross the stile and go along the left-hand edge of the field to another stile. Turn right down a green lane for 10yds (9m) and turn left at a metal stile. Go over the rise in the field, cross the stile and turn right on to a green lane. As the track turns right, turn left over a stile along the edge of a field. Soon turn right over next stile.

❸ Continue through the middle of the next field, aiming for a gate just below the horizon. Cross the stile by the gate and continue through the middle of the field. Over the brow of the hill, descend to the right-hand corner to cross a beck at the bottom. Turn right through a gate in a wall then left to cross Bandley Bridge. Cross a stile by a gate, turn right through a grassy field and a gate. After a ruined wall, bear left up the bank towards a marker pole. At the top, bear left through a gate, then right on to a track to Nether Hoff.

❹ Go through the farmyard, then along the lane over a bridge and past some modern houses. At the junction with a road, cross to a footpath through a garden diagonally opposite, signed Village Green and Colby Hall. Go through a gate and across a field to a footbridge then, bearing right, cross over two stiles. Bear left, round the base of the bank on your left and at the end of the field go through a gate on to an access road. In 30yds (27m) turn right over a bridge to follow a concrete track over the hill. As Colby Laithes comes into view turn right up a footpath signed Appleby.

❺ Follow this track as it turns sharp right, then left, and becomes indistinct. Go through several fields and join a track coming in from the left. As the track bends right through a gate, cross a stile and turn left. By bungalows at the field corner join a path behind gardens. Pass a playground and turn left on a snicket (alley) into Appleby. Turn left on Holme Street, pass the fire station and cross Holme Bridge. Turn right through a metal gate signed Sands. Another gate leads to a woodland path, which eventually drops down to join a metalled road. Continue to the Sands (the road by the river) and turn right over the Eden.

❻ Walk along Bridge Street into Boroughgate, turn right through the Cloisters to St Lawrence's Church. After visiting the church return to walk up the left-hand side of Boroughgate. Pass the Hospital of St Anne, left, to the castle gates then follow Shaws Wiend, descending to Scattergate. Pass the rear entrance to the castle, retrace your steps down to Jubilee Bridge and Mill Hill.

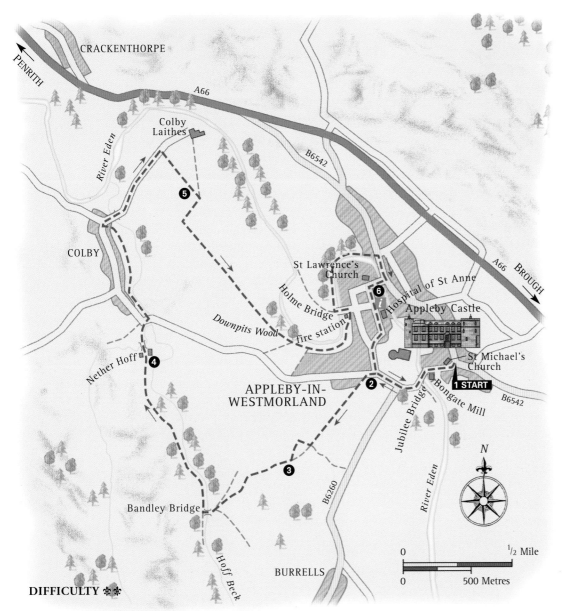

**DIFFICULTY** ❀❀

**1645**

**1645** Royalist hopes of victory are dashed when Cromwell introduces his New Model Army at Naseby.

**1647** Charles is captured and imprisoned at Carisbrooke Castle, Isle of Wight, despite rallying support from the Scots.

**1648**

**1648** Cromwell routs the Scots.

**1649** Cromwell orders the execution of Charles I and announces a commonwealth.

**1649–60** Cromwell is appointed as Chairman, but his puritanical and

**1649**

brutal rule, and that of his New Model Army, is relieved only by his death in 1648.

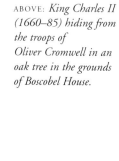

# Royal Refuge at Boscobel

*Follow in the footsteps of the future king, Charles II, as he travelled through Shropshire pursued by Cromwell's troops*

Boscobel House and the Royal Oak, which stands in its grounds, have a unique and colourful place in the history of Britain, for it was here that the future king, Charles II, hid from Cromwell's troops while fleeing to France after the Battle of Worcester. This walk passes a number of the landmarks associated with his journey.

The events took place in 1651, following the Civil War, the execution of Charles I and Oliver Cromwell's declaration of a commonwealth. The young Prince Charles, having fled abroad in 1646, had now returned to reclaim the throne. He landed in Scotland, which was loyal to his cause, and with his troops made his way south virtually unopposed as far as Worcester. His welcome was short-lived: Cromwell's highly trained troops arrived some days later and a battle took place on 3 September 1651. By the end of the day Charles and his forces were thoroughly defeated and he needed to find a way to escape back to France.

The party was forced to head north, guided by one Charles Giffard, who was related to the owners of Boscobel House – which he suggested as a place to hide. The Giffards are still the owners of Chillington Hall and Estate, which is seen from the early stages of the walk. In order to throw their pursuers off the scent, the royal party made first for White Ladies Priory, dissolved during the Reformation and by then a private house, where the Penderel family sheltered the King and helped disguise him as an ordinary traveller. White Ladies itself is now a ruin, which can be visited towards the end of the walk. From there the King and his companion Richard Penderel spent a rainy day hiding in a wood called Spring Coppice, seen to the right as you return to Boscobel from White Ladies. They then headed south, but

Cromwell's troops had reached the Severn before them, and they were forced to turn back, reaching Boscobel House on 6 September.

Boscobel was known to Cromwell's troops as a possible hiding place, so on arrival Charles and his officer Major William Careless were advised to hide in the grounds. They spent 14 miserable hours in the rain in the leafy branches of an oak tree, while, it is said, Cromwell's men hunted for them below, even discussing their terrible fate should they be caught! A descendant of the Royal Oak, as it is known, still stands in the grounds of Boscobel House, although now ravaged by time and the weather. At nightfall the King moved to the scarcely less miserable, but safe confines of a priest hole, which can still be seen today in the attic in Boscobel House.

Charles left Boscobel House on 7 September 1651 with the four Penderel brothers, and successfully reached France, where he remained in exile until the Restoration in 1660. It is said that Charles II always harboured a soft spot for this part of Shropshire. When he reclaimed the throne, he certainly remembered the people who had helped him in his hour of need, and rewarded them well.

ABOVE: *After a cold, damp night in the grounds of the house, Charles fled back to France, where he remained until the Restoration in 1660.*

RIGHT: *The Royal Oak in the grounds of Boscobel House.*

ABOVE: *King Charles II (1660–85) hiding from the troops of Oliver Cromwell in an oak tree in the grounds of Boscobel House.*

**ABOUT · BOSCOBEL HOUSE**

*After defeat at the Battle of Worcester Charles II fled to Boscobel House. To avoid Cromwell's troops, who were searching the grounds, the King hid in an oak tree for 14 hours before fleeing to France where he stayed until the Restoration in 1660.*

**Staffordshire · C ENGLAND**

**DISTANCE** · 8 miles (13km)

**TOTAL ASCENT** · 135ft (41m)

**PATHS** · minor roads (one fairly busy but with wide verges), tracks and paths, some wet and muddy at times

**TERRAIN** · rolling countryside, arable fields, woodland

**GRADIENTS** · very gradual; mainly flat

**REFRESHMENTS** · two pubs passed on the route: The New Inns (sic) at Kiddemore Green and The Royal Oak at Bishop's Wood

**PARK** · at Boscobel House (English Heritage), open daily Apr–Oct 10–6, Nov 10–4; Dec Sat, Sun 10–4

**OS MAP** · Explorer 242 Telford, Ironbridge & The Wrekin

# The Royal Oak at Boscobel House

❶ Turn right out of the car park and right again at the T-junction. Ignore the left turn and follow the road for 1¼ miles (2km), keeping to the grass verge. About 250yds (229m) after a large, red-brick farmhouse, take the track signed bridle path, to the left.

❷ Continue, soon following a wall, and at the end turn right on to the lane. Take the track to the left to Chillington Farm. Follow the blue arrow waymarks through the yard, between two farm buildings. Follow the distinct path along the edge of a field, with a hedge on your left, then across another field.

❸ Turn right at a T-junction. Ignore drive to house with ponds on left, pass through the gate, leave the main track, taking the path to the left round the edge of the garden then across the field to a copse. Bear right to the wooden footbridge, follow the edge of the field, then a tree-lined path.

❹ At the end, turn left and follow the lane for ¾ mile (1.2km), passing Villa Farm, to reach a road, to the right, signed Black Ladies and Top Barn Farm. Follow track, curving left between The Black Ladies

(period house) and stables, bearing sharp left after the farm. Where the track forks, keep left.

❺ After Invicta Farm, follow the track to the left, ignoring bridleway signs to the right. Turn right on to the road; at the staggered crossroads go ahead into Old Weston Road. Keep left into Royal Oak Drive and follow this to the right, then left, then left again at the T-junction.

❻ Take the signed footpath to the right, between fences, in front of the school at the end. Cross the stile, cross the field diagonally up to the left (or skirt round the field to the right if the field is in crop) to a stile, which becomes visible near the corner. Cross stile, turn right on to the road. Continue, and after about ½ mile (800m), beyond the woods, take the road, left.

❼ Bear left, then right to the farm. In front of the house, follow the faded arrows through the black gate to the left, round two sides of the stable yard, through another gate, round a shed, then through another gate into open country.

❽ Follow the path along the edge of a field (hedge/fence on left), down to a gate in the corner and on to a tree-lined path (can be muddy in places). Pass the ruins of White Ladies Priory; turn left on to a lane to return to the car park at Boscobel House.

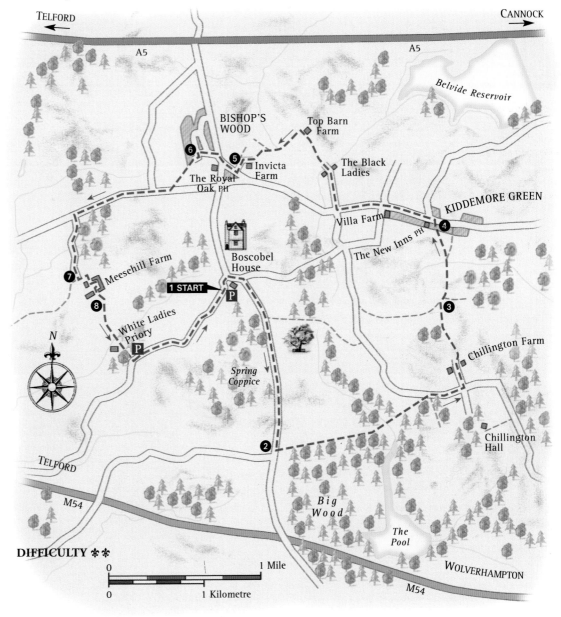

DIFFICULTY ✱✱

0 — 1 Mile

0 — 1 Kilometre

**1660**

**1660–1685** Charles II is restored to the throne by a new Parliament. The Restoration brings with it a shrewd King, and religious tolerance presides over a new era, which sees a blossoming of literature, drama, scientific discovery and architecture.

**1665**

**1665** The outbreak of the great plague in London kills 14,000 people a week, resisting preventive measures such as scented posies and 'purifying bonfires'. The plague claims 80,000 lives before slowing its course.

**1666**

**1666** The Great Fire breaks out in a baker's shop in Pudding Lane, London, and burns for three days, destroying 13,000 houses and 80 churches. Only a few people die in the blaze and the fire destroys the last vestiges of the plague, but medieval London is all but lost.

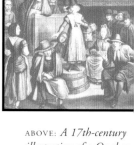

# Dolgellau's Quaker Trail

*A walk in the beautiful Snowdonia countryside, where many Quakers suffered for their faith before finding new homes in America*

In 1657 two men arrived in the small town of Dolgellau on a mission that would change many hundreds of lives. George Fox and his companion John ap John were touring Wales to spread the message that God spoke to people not through priests or kings, but directly. They called themselves Friends; others called them Quakers, and their teachings certainly had an electrifying effect on the townspeople, hill-farmers and country gentry of this remote area.

This was a troubled time, when religion and politics formed an unstable and sometimes explosive mix – the Civil War was still a very recent memory. When Charles II was restored to the throne in 1660, Quakers refused to swear allegiance to him, rejecting all authority except Christ's. Condemned as traitors, many were imprisoned or dispossessed of their lands. One local convert, Robert Owen of Dolserau, paid for his beliefs by languishing for five and a half years in a dank Dolgellau prison on the banks of the River Aran.

As you cross the River Aran to leave the town, look out for Bwthyn Pont yr Arran (Cottage of the Arran Bridge) – a grey-stone cottage built as Quakerism made its first impact. A steep climb soon takes you away from Dolgellau and up into the hills. Here, it is easier to appreciate the power of a movement that could forge links between the scattered mountain communities, bringing faith out of the churches and into homes. The Friends would trudge across these high fields to gather at their meeting houses, one of which, Tabor (now a private house), is tucked into the roadside at the top of the rise.

Quakers were forbidden from burying their dead in churchyards, and established burial grounds of their own. Tyddyn Carreg, the next stop on the route, is one of few to survive – a single small field, ranked with simple headstones, looking out across the lonely Meirionnydd mountains.

The walk continues across wild countryside in the shadow of Cader Idris, before swinging round for a bird's-eye view of Dolgellau in the valley far below. Standing out clearly among the dark-stone buildings is St Mary's Church, whose vicar was a central figure in the persecution of Quakers.

Eventually the constant harassment and evictions took their toll, and in the 1680s hundreds of Friends sailed to America, where they had bought a 'Welsh Tract' of land from William Penn, founder of Pennsylvania. Here, they were promised the freedom to speak their own language and follow their own laws – a promise that came to nothing when new boundaries split the tract in two. Meanwhile, whole districts of Meirionnydd county had been left depopulated, and the severely depleted Quaker cause faced an even tougher future.

As you emerge from a conifer wood to return to Dolgellau, you'll catch a glimpse of Bryn Mawr, the former home of an early emigrant, Rowland Ellis. It gave its name to Ellis's new home in Philadelphia, and later to the prestigious US women's college.

ABOVE: *A 17th-century illustration of a Quaker meeting in a Tabor (Quaker meeting house).*

BELOW: *Brenin Forest in the Snowdonia National Park.*

ABOVE: *The stone bridge crossing the River Aran leading to Dolgellau.*

**ABOUT • DOLGELLAU**

*This walk celebrates the Quakers or Friends who journeyed from this small Welsh town to Pennsylvania, USA, in the 1680s to escape persecution and give voice to their faith in a new land. Don't miss the Quakers' Heritage Centre, in Eldon Square.*

**Gwynedd • WALES**

**DISTANCE** • 6 miles (9.6km)

**TOTAL ASCENT** • 590ft (180m)

**PATHS** • some rocky and muddy tracks; can be slippery

**TERRAIN** • surfaced roads, tracks, fields

**GRADIENTS** • some steep ascents and descents

**REFRESHMENTS** • several pubs and cafés in Dolgellau; Fronoleu Country Hotel near top of first ascent

**PARK** • Marian car park, Dolgellau

**OS MAP** • Outdoor Leisure 18 Snowdonia – Harlech, Porthmadog & Bala

# A mission of faith

**DIFFICULTY ✿ ✿ ✿**

**❶** From the Tourist Information Centre in Eldon Square, cross the square and take the left-hand road to Pont yr Aran/Aran Road. Cross the river and continue ahead, past the ambulance depot. Turn right, signed Tabor, to climb Fron Serth. Where the road forks, keep left.

**❷** As the route descends, turn left in front of Tabor Cottage cottage. Shortly, turn left following public footpath sign. At the next junction pass Tyddyn Carreg farmhouse and through the metal bar gate, left. Follow the boundary wall across the field to the burial ground.

**❸** Retrace your steps, pass the farmhouse and take the track to the right. Beyond Tŷ Newydd, go through the wooden gate keeping on the track ahead through *coed* (mixed woodland). Emerging from the wood, follow the track left and go through the gate.

**❹** Cross the road and follow the public footpath opposite, up the drive past a house, through a farmyard and two further gates. At the top take the gate, right, and cross the field ahead. Go through the gap in the stone wall, a gate, and the next gap ahead. Bear right towards the ruined farm building.

**❺** Turn right just before the cottage and follow the field boundary. Bear left to the metal gate and climb the wooden stile to its right. Follow the path between ferns, downhill.

**❻** The route descends through woods bearing left at a wall above a farm. Cross two stiles, and follow the arrow to the left. Go through the metal gate (arrowed) and jump across the small brook. Continue ahead, with two houses on your right. Join the part-gravel track and cross the cattle grid; continue for 164yds (150m) to the lane.

**❼** Follow the tarmac road left. Beyond the stream, take the footpath, right. At the wooden gate, follow the arrowed track, left, across a footbridge over the river. Go through the kissing gate and climb the track. Cross a stream via stepping stones, then climb the stile into woods.

**❽** Where the trail forks, take the left, ascending, path. At the T-junction, turn left and climb the steep, arrowed track. At the top, go through the wooden gate. Shortly, turn left along the stony track. Continue to the tarmac road.

**❾** Turn right along the road, continuing through the gate across the road and past Esgeiriau farmhouse after about ¼ mile (400m). Ignore footpath signed right. In ½ mile (800m) follow a bridleway sign, right. Take the main track round the hillside and downhill. Go through the metal gate just after a gap in the wall, left, to descend into town. At the first house, turn right. Continue ahead at the road, go straight across at the crossroads, then turn left for Eldon Square.

# Carisbrooke's Royal Prisoner

*Combine an invigorating downland walk with a visit to a magnificent castle and discover more about King Charles I, Carisbrooke's famous prisoner*

ABOVE: *King Charles I (1600–1649).*

## Carisbrooke's Medieval Castle

Set on a sweeping ridge of chalk downland, 46m (150ft) above the village on the site of a Roman fort, the majestic medieval ruins of Carisbrooke Castle are regarded as one of the Isle of Wight's finest treasures. Originally a fortified camp built by the Saxons as defence against the Vikings, and later strengthened by the Normans, who built the impenetrable stone walls, magnificent gatehouse and fine keep, it overlooks the Bowcombe Valley and the approaches to the central downs and the heart of the island. But the castle only experienced military action twice, in 1136 and in 1377. In the late 16th century the outer bastions were built to guard against the threat of Spanish invasion. The most important episode in the castle's long history was the imprisonment there of Charles I in 1647. You can walk the lofty battlements in the footsteps of Charles I, view the bowling green created for his amusement in the outer bailey, and see the window from which he tried to escape.

BELOW: *Carisbrooke Castle set on the chalk downlands of the Isle of Wight in Hampshire.*

## The Rise and Fall of Charles I

There had been an uneasy relationship between Crown and Parliament during the reign of James I, and after the accession of his son, Charles I, to the throne in 1625 things went from bad to worse. Charles's High Church views and demands for war funds provoked a series of crises and disputes, and in 1630 he dispensed with Parliament altogether and embarked on a period of personal rule.

There was nearly a decade of relative political calm and stability between his three kingdoms before Charles's lack of empathy, stubbornness and high-minded approach to statecraft led to the collapse of royal authority in the late 1630s and the descent into rebellion and civil war by 1642. Bitter battles between the Royalist and Parliamentarian armies raged across the country for four years, until major strategic errors by Charles led to crushing defeats at Naseby, Langport, Bristol and, finally, at Oxford in May

1646. A virtual prisoner of his rebellious Scottish army, Charles still considered it his divine right to rule the country as an autocrat, and he refused to negotiate a political settlement with the Parliamentarians.

Rumours spread of a plot to murder him, and Charles escaped from Hampton Court Palace in 1647 and sought refuge at Carisbrooke Castle. Governor Robert Hammond was torn between his loyalty to the King and his duty to Parliament, but promised to do what he could for Charles. He was treated with respect, had the best rooms in the castle and was allowed freedom to move around the island. On hearing that Charles had signed a secret treaty with the Scots in December 1647, by which they undertook to invade England and restore him to the throne, Hammond imprisoned Charles in the castle. During his ten-month incarceration Charles made two unsuccessful attempts to escape before being taken to taken to London for trial and execution in 1648.

ABOVE BACKGROUND: *The execution of Charles I at Whitehall, London, on 30 January 1649. His head is held aloft to the pleasure and sorrow of the crowd.*

INSET ABOVE: *A vivid reconstruction of Parliamentarian soldiers at Carisbrooke Castle.*

---

## WALK 59 — EXPLORING CARISBROOKE CASTLE'S DOWNLAND VISTA

❶ Facing Carisbrooke Priory, turn left along the road and take the footpath, opposite Quarr Business Park, to Carisbrooke Castle – built on a Roman site Carisbrooke once marked the capital of the island. At the castle walls, follow the grassy rampart right around the walls, keeping ahead at the lane to pass the castle entrance. Take the footpath, signed Millers Lane, to the right of the car park entrance and descend to a lane. Turn left, cross a ford, then at a T-junction, turn right to Froglands Farm. Pass the farm, then bear right at gates to follow a bridleway through Bowcombe Valley.

❷ After a sharp right bend, gently descend and cross the stile on your left. Keep straight on, following the grassy path to a track. Turn left and keep right at a fork. At the field boundary on the left, follow the field edge to a gate. Ascend through a copse to a gate, then keep to the left-hand field edge, steadily uphill to a gate. Maintain direction to a further gate. Keep to the wide track beside a coniferous plantation and take the footpath left, signed Gatcombe. Go through a gate and keep ahead, passing a dew pond, to a further gate. On reaching a stile on the left, bear

right downhill to a T-junction of paths and turn left, signed Garstons.

❸ Descend off the down. Go through a gate and shortly bear right beside Newbarn Farm. Turn right along the metalled access lane into the hamlet. Keep right on merging with Snowdrop Lane and turn left along the Shepherds Trail, signed Carisbrooke.

❹ Ascend a concrete drive and pass a house. Then, at the top, keep to the main path (Shepherds Trail) across fields via gates. Disregard the path merging from the left and shortly

follow the sunken path gently downhill to Whitcombe Road. Keep ahead back to the car park.

**Distance:** 5½ miles (8.8km)

**Total ascent:** 600ft (183m)

**Paths:** generally firm but can be muddy in wet weather

**Terrain:** farmland and open downland

**Gradients:** undulating; one steep ascent and one long steady climb

**Refreshments:** Coach House tea room at Carisbrooke Castle

**OS Map:** Outdoor Leisure 29 Isle of Wight

**Difficulty:** ✳✳

**1675** The Royal Observatory is founded at Greenwich by Charles II for the discovery of 'the longitude of places for perfecting navigation and astronomy'.

**1675–1710** St Paul's Cathedral, London, is completed. The cathedral

is remarkable for its fine dome and the impact it makes on London's skyline.

**1684** Sir Isaac Newton (1642–1727), mathematician and scientist, publishes his revolutionary *Theory of Gravity*.

**1685** James II accedes the throne, but because he is a Catholic he is regarded with suspicion, and is described as being 'as very papist as the Pope himself'.

**THE STUARTS**

**GUNPOWDER TO WIG POWDER**

# Wren's London – a City of Churches

*Follow this trail to the heart of the City of London and discover how it rose, phoenix-like, from the ashes of the Great Fire*

To walk through the City of London is to walk through 2,000 years of history. Only by exploring it on foot can you appreciate its unique spirit, fascinating character and sense of tradition. Much of the city of the history books has long vanished, and today towering office buildings and financial institutions crowd in from every direction. But there is still a great deal of the old city to see; the clues are there if you are prepared to look. Avoid weekdays, when the pavements throng with traders and bankers. Weekends are best, when the city assumes a calmer, more sedate air.

By the Stuart period, London was a prosperous capital, with a splendid bridge, numerous churches and some dreadful housing conditions. However, on two separate occasions during the 1660s, the city found itself fighting for survival. First, there was the Great Plague of 1665. A year later came a second disaster, which in the space of four days changed the face of London beyond recognition. On 2 September 1666, a fire broke out in a timbered baker's shop in Pudding Lane. The blaze, caused by an overheated baking oven, swept through the city with breathtaking speed and ferocity. More than 13,000 buildings were destroyed and 84 churches razed to the ground, although miraculously only a few people perished. Four days later the silent, charred ruins confirmed the true scale of the disaster.

London was devastated – two thirds destroyed by the fire. Yet within a week, so it is claimed, Sir Christopher Wren drew up and

submitted a plan for rebuilding the ruined capital. Others followed suit but, like Wren, to no avail. Not one of the applications was taken up. However, Wren did build over 50 churches in the city. He also spent much of his life attempting to realise his dream of building a magnificent new cathedral – St Paul's. Thwarted by planners at first, Wren's designs were eventually accepted in 1675 and his masterpiece was finally completed in 1708. The dome of St Paul's, as seen from the Thames, remains one of the world's most instantly recognisable landmarks and, mercifully, was not damaged on the night of 29 December 1940 when a German air raid produced an inferno twice as destructive as the Great Fire of London. Many fine buildings and Wren churches burned that night and by the morning the city lay in ruins once again.

This fascinating walk visits many of the landmarks associated with Wren, beginning at the 202ft (61m)-high Monument, which he designed to commemorate the Great Fire. Its height signifies the distance from its location to the spot where the blaze started. The trail heads east, then north to Fenchurch Street and the London Wall. From here, it's an easy stroll to the Guildhall and on to St Paul's Cathedral. The final leg of the walk takes you through the secret alleyways and quaint old passages of the Bank of England and the Royal Exchange.

Along the way, several of Wren's historic churches are visited, including the famous St Mary at Hill, Billingsgate's parish church. Appropriately, the walk finishes by turning into Pudding Lane, where a routine fire became a raging inferno, a defining moment in the history of London.

RIGHT: *The Monument, built 1671–77 by Christopher Wren which stands 62m (202ft) high and marks the place where the Great Fire began in 1666, which destroyed most of medieval London.*

BELOW: *Elevation, section and plan of the Church of St Bride, designed by Sir Christopher Wren.*

**ABOUT • LONDON**

*Discover 17th-century London – the plague, the Great Fire and the beginning of banking and commerce. At this time, London was undergoing enormous changes, and mostly at the hands of one man, architect Sir Christopher Wren (1623–1723).*

## Greater London • SE ENGLAND

**DISTANCE •** 3 miles (4.8km)

**TOTAL ASCENT •** nil

**PATHS •** city streets

**TERRAIN •** pavements, cobbles, streets and alleyways

**GRADIENTS •** level

**REFRESHMENTS •** numerous inns and coffee shops along the way

**PARK •** plenty of car parks in London, though it can be expensive and the streets are often congested. Nearest underground station – Monument

**OS MAP •** Explorer 173 London North, The City, West End, Enfield

# London: churches and commerce

❶ From The Monument walk along Monument Street. Approach the junction with Lower Thames Street, bear left into cobbled Lovat Lane. Pass The Walrus and Carpenter pub and look for Church of St Mary at Hill. Visit the church, leave by a different door and turn left to the junction with Eastcheap.

❷ Turn right and follow it into Great Tower Street. Pass St Dunstan's Hill, approach All Hallows-by-the-Tower, cross over into Mark Lane and turn right into Hart Street. Pass Seething Lane and continue into Crutched Friars. Pass under the railway and turn left into Lloyds Avenue. Bear right along Fenchurch Street towards St Botolph's Church.

❸ Keep left, go to the rear of the church, and take the subway to Houndsditch. Soon turn left into St Mary Axe. The Baltic Exchange is ahead. Turn right along Camomile Street, cross Bishopsgate and Old Broad Street to pass All Hallows London Wall Church. Pass Great Winchester Street, Blomfield Street and Finsbury Circus, and turn left into Copthall Avenue.

❹ When the road bends left, veer right down an alley to Telegraph Street. Turn left at Moorgate and walk along to the back of the Bank of England. Turn right and follow Lothbury to Gresham Street and continue to Guildhall Yard. See St Lawrence Jewry, and cross to turn left into Milk Street.

❺ Bear right at Cheapside and walk to St Paul's Cathedral. Retrace your steps briefly along Cheapside and look for flower beds and an arch on the right between

two banks. Through the arch turn immediately left to reach steps (gardens and fountains to the right), and cross Bread Street to a alley leading to St Mary-le-Bow.

❻ Keep to the right of the church, bear right at the junction and walk along the narrow pedestrianised street for a few paces, turning left into Well Court. Follow it round to the right. Cross Queen Street into Pancras Lane, then cross Queen Victoria Street to Bucklersby. Keep to the left of the Saxon church of St Stephen Walbrook and take the alley, St Stephen's Row, next to it.

❼ Look for the little churchyard, hemmed in by buildings, and turn right at the next junction. Bear right into St Swithins Lane. At Cannon Street, turn left and left again into Abchurch Lane. Pass St Mary Abchurch and, at King

William Street, bear left and walk to the Bank of England and the Royal Exchange.

❽ Keep right and follow Cornhill. Pass St Michael's Church, then turn right into Gracechurch Street. Swing left into Leadenhall Market and take the first right turning. Keep right at Lime Street and cross Fenchurch Street into Philpot Lane. Turn right at the next road junction, then left into Pudding Lane. Return to Monument. Monument Underground Station is on the right.

**DIFFICULTY ✳**

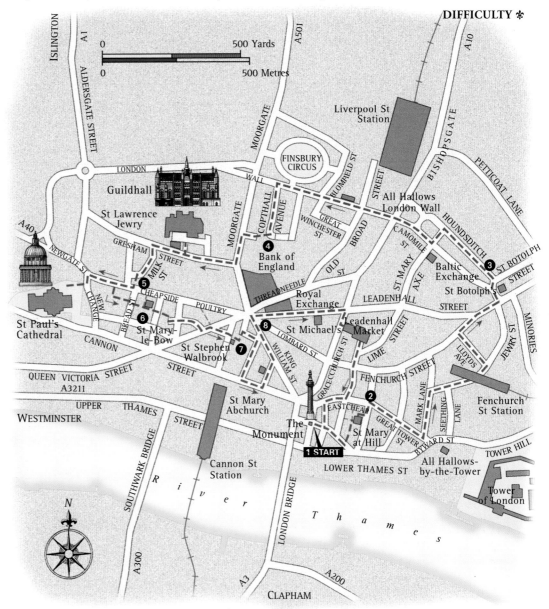

**1688**

**1688** James II attempts to gain toleration for the Catholic Church but sparks rebellion and earns hostility in the House of Commons. They invite the King's Protestant Dutch son-in-law, William of Orange, to invade. James flees to Ireland, a deposed king.

**1689**

**1689** William III and Mary II begin their rule as joint monarchs.

**1690** William confronts James in Ireland. James is defeated at the Battle of Boyne and is forced into exile in France, without his crown.

**1692**

**1692** After sharing their hospitality, troops commanded by Campbell of Glenlyon massacre men, women and children of the Clan MacDonald at Glencoe in Scotland, under the orders of William III.

# Bloodshed in the Pentland Hills

*In the wake of the Civil War, the Battle of Rullion Green was fought over Charles II's determination to control the Scottish Church*

On the morning of 28 November 1666, a small, bedraggled army of about 1,000 men drew to a halt in the shadow of the Pentland Hills, some 7 miles (11km) from Edinburgh. The men were Covenanters, Presbyterian dissenters who refused to accept the authority of kings or bishops over church affairs. Implacable in their beliefs, they belonged to a movement that had fallen foul of Cromwell under the Protectorate and was now being persecuted by the government of Charles II. A minor incident in Galloway involving brutal soldiers, a suspect and an angry crowd had sparked their insurrection, which was more a protest march than a rebellion. Ill-equipped and sickening with hunger, the ragged little army had been marching for two weeks through freezing rain, finding few who were prepared to risk their lives on such a desperate venture. Turned away from Edinburgh, they were now retreating back towards their homes with Sir Tam Dalyell, commander of the Scottish army, in hot pursuit with 3,000 well-trained troops. As the men threw down their packs and collapsed, exhausted, on the sodden heather, they saw a line of horsemen on the skyline. Before they had a chance to rest, they faced the prospect of battle.

This walk begins alongside Glencorse Burn, which, back on that November morning in 1666, would have been a raging torrent after days of heavy rain. Most probably Dalyell crossed close by the

modern footbridge and caught his first view of the Covenanters from the hillock up above. They were half a mile (800m) away, scrambling to their feet as they were ordered into line along the flank of Turnhouse Hill. Their commander, James Wallace, had been a colonel in Cromwell's army and many of his men had served on one side or the other in the Civil War, but they cannot have appeared a particularly impressive force. The battle that ensued was fought out like a chess-game. It began soon after noon with a skirmish between cavalry detachments that was won convincingly by Wallace. Wallace then advanced his infantry along the steep side of the hill, where Dalyell's horsemen were unable to manoeuvre. It was only in the late afternoon, as dusk was falling, that Dalyell was able to gain the advantage by attacking across the lower, level ground and overwhelming opposition by sheer weight of numbers.

By nightfall the Covenanters had been routed, with 50 dead and 80 taken prisoner. Thirty-six were subsequently hanged and many more perished as they attempted to escape across the wild country you will see further along the walk. But the battle settled nothing, for it was fought over principles that could not be resolved by military means. In the course of 30 years some 18,000 people died in the dispute. Even in the present century, Rullion Green remains a thought-provoking place.

ABOVE: *The majestic Pentland Hills, site of the bloody Battle of Rullion Green.*

BELOW: *A crowd queues to sign the National Covenant in front of Greyfriar's churchyard in Edinburgh, 1638.*

**ABOUT • RULLION GREEN**

*The Covenanters, having refused to accept the authority of bishops or kings over church matters, were pursued here and routed by Scottish troops. The Battle at Rullion Green was part of a 30-year-long dispute, which caused the death of 18,000 men.*

## Midlothian • SCOTLAND

**DISTANCE •** 5 miles (8km)

**TOTAL ASCENT •** 1,300ft (396m)

**PATHS •** mostly well-maintained and dry, but rough descent from Turnhouse Hill

**TERRAIN •** mostly mountain moorland and wooded waterside. Dogs must be kept on leads. The Pentland Hills Regional Park is grazed by sheep and a habitat for ground nesting-birds

**GRADIENTS •** steep on Turnhouse Hill

**REFRESHMENTS •** Flotterstone Inn

**PARK •** car park at Flotterstone Information Centre

**OS MAP •** Explorer 344 Pentland Hills, Penicuik & West Lothian

# Church matters versus military men

❶ From the car park, follow the footpath up the glen beside the metalled drive. Glencorse Burn, which has now been tamed by dams and reservoirs further up the valley, would have been a broad, ferocious torrent at the time of the battle.

❷ At the end of the footpath cross the road and bear left through a gate on to a track signed Glencorse. At the end of the stone wall on your left, turn left and follow the path across a footbridge. This is probably the point where Dalyell crossed the burn, when he brought his army through the hills on the north side of the valley.

❸ Following the burn upstream, the path fords a shallow rivulet and then climbs to the top of the ridge. Only at this point would Dalyell's army have been spotted by the Covenanters, camped half a mile (800m) away beneath the southern slope of Turnhouse Hill. The path continues down into the valley beside a ruined drystone wall before starting on the long ascent of Turnhouse Hill.

❹ From the summit, you will have a grandstand view of the battlefield below. The Covenanters occupied the higher ground, ranged along a spur, now crowned with trees over to the right. Dalyell was attacking from the left and failed to outflank his enemy owing to the steepness of the hill. When he lost every skirmish, he quickly abandoned subtle tactics and used his great superiority in numbers to launch a sustained frontal assault across open ground.

❺ Continue along the path, to the bottom of a deep cleft in the hills. Cross a stile and turn immediately right to follow a faint path downhill beside a drystone wall. Crossing a small stream, the path drops down into the valley, where there is a footbridge, which crosses Logan Burn.

❻ Once over the bridge, turn right along the metalled drive, which runs along the shore of Glencorse Reservoir. This did not exist at the time of the battle and on his march to Rullion Green Dalyell would have passed the ruins of St Catherine's Chapel, which now lie beneath the water.

❼ Just beyond Glen Cottage, at the end of the reservoir, turn right through a gate to follow a path through pine woods and past the 19th-century filter beds. The path continues beside Glencorse Burn

**• DON'T MISS •**

*The 19th-century filter beds used to clean the reservoir's water can now be seen as works of art, with their strange iron ventilation shafts thrusting from the roots of trees. The beds themselves have been transformed into attractive water-gardens and tree-nurseries.*

to rejoin the metalled drive back to the car park.

**DIFFICULTY ✽ ✽ ✽**

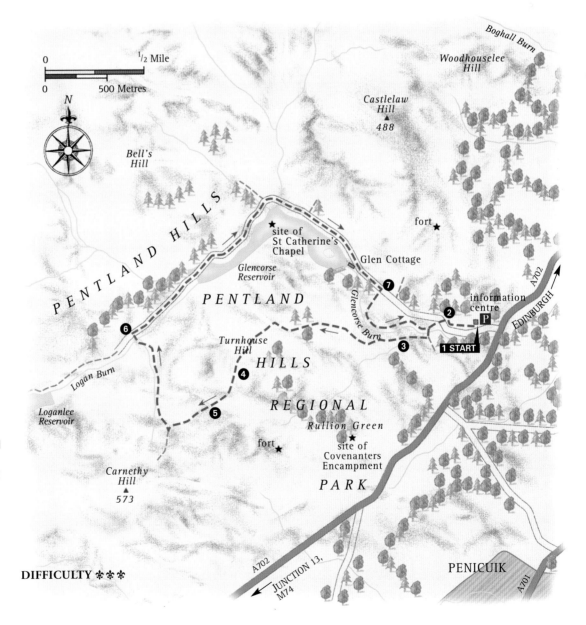

**1694**

**1694** The Bank of England is established by the government, on the advice of a group of businessmen who raise £1,500,000 to lend to the government in return for a regular interest payment into the bank. The enterprise was to be a roaring success.

**1695**

**1695** A new coinage is introduced, funded by a tax on windows.

**1700–1789** The Age of Reason begins with the greater thinkers, such as Kant, Locke, Rousseau and Thomas Paine.

**1701**

**1701** Jethro Tull invents the seed drill, revolutionising farming.

**1702** After the death of King William (Mary having died in 1694), Queen Anne accedes the throne, and within a year England declares war on France.

# Monmouth's Rebellion and the Bloody Assize

*The historic city of Wells, and the Mendips which rise above it, witnessed the bloody aftermath of the 'Pitchfork Rebellion'*

**THE STUARTS**

In July 1685 the country you see from the high point of this walk was torn by civil strife. A rebel army led by James Croft, Duke of Monmouth and illegitimate eldest son of Charles II, was on the march, raising recruits from West Country towns and villages.

Five years earlier, the Duke had toured the region and the streets and taverns had rung to the chorus 'A-Monmouth, A-Monmouth'. Now the charismatic peer was back and trying to overthrow the King, his uncle James II, under the guise of defending the Protestant religion from Papist tyranny.

Monmouth landed with barely a handful of supporters at Lyme Regis in Dorset on 11 June 1685, and many of those expected to join the rebellion stayed at home. By the end of the month his rag-tag alliance of farmers, cloth-workers and petty gentry was in retreat. A heavily armed government force had been despatched to destroy the revolt, and the rebels' march north had been halted at Keynsham. Marching through Bath, Frome and Shepton Mallet, they arrived in Wells on 1 July. They were dispirited and expressed their despair by ransacking the town as punishment for its failing support. In the cathedral

they smashed the organ, stabled horses in the nave and pulled down statues from the west front. The next day they moved on through Glastonbury to Bridgwater. The King's army was camped near by, across the marsh of Sedgemoor at Westonzoyland. Monmouth, with 8,000 or so supporters, mostly drawn from Somerset, Devon and Dorset, gambled on a night attack on 6 July. His plans went awry and, by dawn, artillery had reduced his flagging army to tatters. Cavalry charges put the rest to flight and over 1,000 rebels were killed or captured. Monmouth himself was taken to London where, on 15 July, he was executed on Tower Hill.

The King despatched his loyal advocate, the Lord Chief Justice Jeffreys, to dispense retribution in the west. Jeffreys' travelling assize came to an end in Wells on 23 September, by which time he had hanged over 300 rebels and condemned another 600 to transportation in a slaughter which became known as the 'Bloody Assize'.

In Wells the Tythe Barn, seen on Silver Street at the start of the walk, was used to hold prisoners in squalid conditions. Jeffreys held court at the assize building that stood in the centre of the market place. In his distinctively brutal style, nine local men were sentenced to be hanged, the first two, there and then, in the market place. The rest died later in the Gallows Close on the southern edge of town, where the houses of Bishoplea Close now stand. The prisoners bound for transportation to the West Indies were marched to Bristol like cattle. They left by the Old Bristol Road, crossed at this walk's halfway point. Much of the city dates from after this period of strife but there are still many buildings which would have witnessed the bloodshed. The north and east side of the market square is largely unchanged, as are many precincts around the cathedral. Several pubs, notably the Swan and the City Arms, can also trace their foundation to before 1600.

LEFT: *Bishop's Palace in Wells. The rebels ransacked the town on 1 July, 1685.*

BELOW: *Several rebels hanged from a tree; a playing card from a set commemorating the Monmouth Rebellion in 1865.*

THE STUARTS

WALK 62

ABOUT • WELLS

*In 1685, Wells was the centre of strife as a rebel army arrived looking for new recruits to overthrow the papist King. After the Battle of Sedgemoor, Lord Chief Justice Jeffreys arrived in Wells and condemned hundreds of rebels to death or transportation.*

**Somerset • SW ENGLAND**

**DISTANCE** • 9½ miles (15.3km)

**TOTAL ASCENT** • 1,000ft (305m)

**PATHS** • streets then field tracks and farm lanes, a little road walking

**TERRAIN** • town, pastureland and woodland

**GRADIENTS** • a steep ascent up the Mendip escarpment out of Wookey Hole

**REFRESHMENTS** • several pubs and tea shops in Wells and Wookey Hole, none on rest of route

**PARK** • by the old Tythe Barn in Silver Street

**OS MAP** • Explorer 141 Cheddar Gorge & Mendip Hills West

# Wells and the 'Pitchfork Rebellion'

DIFFICULTY ✣✣✣

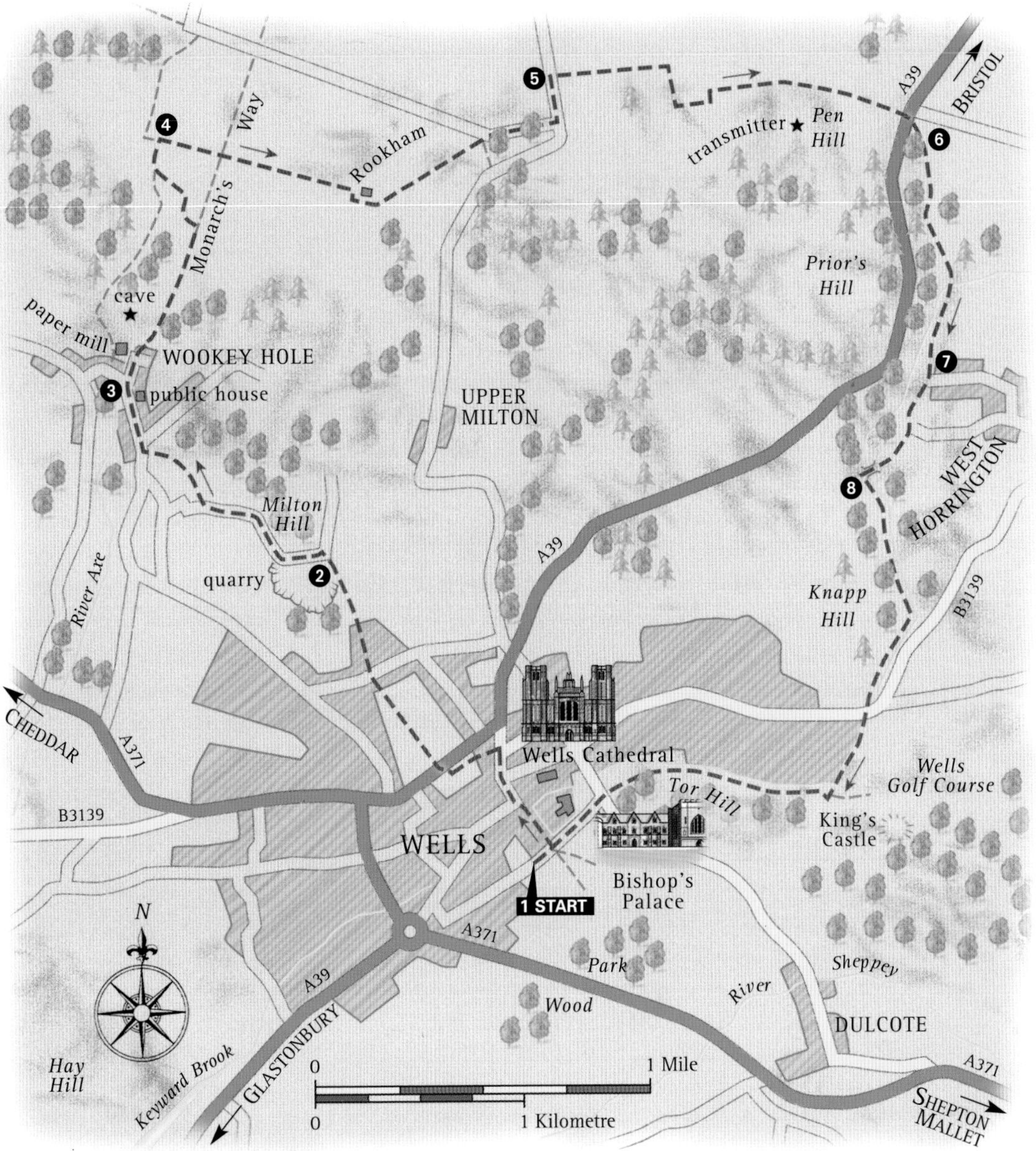


❶ Walk up Silver Street to the Bishop's Palace. Turn left by the moat, go under arch into Market Square. Turn right at the far right corner up Sadler Street. Go right on to New Street and follow it round to the left. Turn left, signed West Mendip Way, and follow the alley around to a left turn, down Lover's Walk. At the back of the sports' pitches fork right, and right over the footbridge. Go through the school grounds to a gate on the far side. Continue up the hill towards houses. Cross the road and at the top of the footpath opposite, cross to another footpath. Go through a gate to emerge on a track.

❷ In 50yds (46m) turn left on a road, uphill past a quarry. Turn left (workings on your left). Bear right through the woods at a stile just before the road bends right. By lime kilns, turn left down a lane. In 400yds (366m), as lane veers left, go through gate, right, to a fenced path, left. Go down the left edge of a field, turn right on the road into Wookey Hole, pass the pub, bear left in front of the paper mill. Turn right towards the caves.

❸ Walk up the lane until it bends round right. Cross the fields, following signs for Monarch's Way. Go half right up the field, aiming for a fence into some woods. Continue up the hill to a junction of hedges. Beyond this, turn left to meet the top of Green Lane, coming up from the other side of the Coomb. Turn right and continue up the hill.

❹ At top go right, in front of wall. Cross three fields; in fourth, aim for hedge in front of buildings. Turn right down to a gate on left. Go through and follow hedge, carry on half-left to a track. Over cattle grid go left past a bungalow and right at junction with Durston Drove. At T-junction, go left along Old Bristol Road for 200yds/183m.

❺ Turn right, signed Pen Hill, cross two fields, a stile and tuen right. Follow field edge to stile on far side. Turn right, to transmitter support. Through gate to follow a track round to the right, emerging on road in front of a white house.

❻ Go through a gate opposite to join a bridleway to the right of a field. Go through a gate in the corner and descend to the stream. Continue down through the woods then through a gate and stile on the left. Bear right with the stream and stay with the rising track.

❼ In a clearing by a white house turn right and follow the track left to a stile. Cross and follow the left-hand field edge to a stile in the next field. Immediately beyond, turn right down to a stile. Descend steps to cross a bridge, turn left.

❽ Follow the path to Wells Golf Club. Cross the road, go through the gate to the path between the golf course and houses. Continue on this streamside path to a road. Cross, go through gate opposite and return to Silver Street.

**1704**

**1704** The Royal estate of Woodstock is given to the Duke of Marlborough in gratitude for his victory over the French at the Battle of Blenheim. The building of Blenheim Palace starts in 1705, and is completed in 1722, two years after the Duke's death.

**1707**

**1707** The Act of Union between England and Scotland combines the two parliaments into a single governing body.

**1711** Horse racing is held at Ascot for the first time.

**1713**

**1713** The war with France ends.

**1714** The death of Queen Anne also marks the end of the Stuart monarchy, making way for a new order, the Hanoverians.

THE BURIAL MARCH OF DUNDEE.

O'er the broken ground and heath,
Wound the long battalion slowly,
Till they gained the plain beneath;
Then we bounded from our covert.—
Judge how looked the Saxons then.

# The Jacobites' Highland Charge

*Government troops faced the full fury of Stuart supporters at the Pass of Killiecrankie*

The battle of Killiecrankie, often relived in song and story, was the first battle of the Jacobite Rebellion. Although famous in Scottish history, its origins lie in England. In 1688 the Protestant nobility deposed James II (James VII of Scotland) for his adherence to the Church of Rome, and offered the crown to his nephew and son-in-law, William of Orange. James fled to France but his supporters refused to accept that he was no longer King.

The Scottish Jacobites were the staunchest and longest supporters of the House of Stuart. Chief among them was John Graham of Claverhouse, Viscount Dundee – Bonnie Dundee to his followers, Bloody Clavers to the lowland Presbyterians, whom he brutally oppressed and massacred. Dundee led the first Highland Jacobite revolt when he raised the King's standard at Dundee Law in April 1689 with the intention of marching on Stirling Castle. But mustering the fighting men of the clans was a notoriously slow process, with many chiefs impartial and awaiting the outcome before deciding which side to back. These delays allowed William's government troops to muster and head north to intercept the Jacobites.

Some 4,000 men under the command of Major-General Hugh MacKay of Scourie marched from Stirling towards Blair Castle, which Claverhouse had under siege. MacKay rested his troops for the night of 26 July at the town of Dunkeld, knowing that Dundee was advancing on the Pass of Killiecrankie. The following morning they marched to Killiecrankie and, ignoring advice to send his baggage train first, MacKay proceeded through the pass. By late afternoon Dundee's smaller force of 2,000 Highlanders had appeared on the high ground of the pass above them. MacKay's order to his troops to spread out to avoid being surrounded left them lethally exposed when the attack came, just before sunset. The Highland clans rushed headlong upon them, broadswords raised, howling battle cries. In the confines of the Pass of Killiecrankie, the full Highland Charge overwhelmed the government troops. The battle was over in ten minutes and MacKay's army turned tail and fled, pursued and slaughtered by the Highland horde. One government soldier escaped with his life and entered folklore with an almost supernatural leap across the River Garry to the opposite bank.

The Jacobites won the battle but Dundee, their charismatic leader, was fatally wounded. Deprived of his driving force, they were defeated a month later at the Battle of Dunkeld on 21 August and at Cromdale on 1 May 1690. But the Jacobites continued to plot and rebel for another 55 years until the famous Jacobite Rising of 1745, when Bonnie Prince Charlie raised his father's standard at Glenfinnan. After a successful incursion into England as far as Derby, Jacobite hopes finally perished on 16 April 1746 at Culloden. The famous Highland Charge, so successful on the steep rocky braes of Killiecrankie, foundered on the sodden moor of Culloden, where the exhausted Jacobite troops, bogged down in the mire, were slaughtered by the government artillery.

ABOVE: *Dundee leads a charge against the Royalists at Killiecrankie. The Jacobites won the day but Dundee was killed in the process, which caused a loss of morale among Jacobite supporters.*

BELOW: *Soldier's Leap, named after a desperate Royalist soldier jumped the gorge in an attempt to escape from the charging Jacobite troops.*

BELOW: *Ben Agloe rises in the distance whilst the River Garry winds it way through the Pass of Killiecrankie.*

**ABOUT** • **KILLIECRANKIE**

*The first victory of the Jacobite Rebellion by followers of James VII took place in 1689 in Killiecrankie. The terrifying Highland Charge overwhelmed the government troops and their leader, General Hugh MacKay, in just ten minutes.*

**Perth & Kinross** • **SCOTLAND**

**DISTANCE** • 6½ miles (10.4km)

**TOTAL ASCENT** • 500ft (152m)

**PATHS** • good trails, metalled roads

**TERRAIN** • forest trails and country roads

**GRADIENTS** • moderate

**REFRESHMENTS** • Killiecrankie Visitor Centre and Boating Station

**PARK** • forest car park at Faskally Boating Station

**OS MAP** • Explorer 21 Pitlochry & Loch Tummel

# Killiecrankie: the first of the Jacobite battles

❶ From the car park walk past the boating station and continue uphill following the lochside path for Killiecrankie which leads underneath both the A9 flyover and Clunie footbridge.

❷ Follow the loch, past the viewing point where the Old Bridge of Clunie stood before it was demolished for the hydro-electric scheme in 1950. Loch Faskally is a man-made feature following the deep, natural river valley.

❸ Keep left on the single-track metalled road towards Killiecrankie. Just before the entrance to Faskally House, turn left on to the signed footpath following the lochside. Pass the point where the rivers Tummel and Garry meet.

❹ Pass under the Garry Bridge and a short distance further on turn left and cross the river on a metal footbridge. Turn left up the steep slope to Garry Bridge car park. Immediately after the car park, turn right on to an unclassified metalled single-track road that climbs up past Tenandry Parish Kirk. Soon after there are views of the valley and east towards the mountains.

❺ After 1½ miles (2.4km), turn sharp right and then bear right and cross the River Garry on a stone bridge. Cross the rail bridge and turn right on to the B8079 and follow the footpath past the primary school. The path peters out and after a very short distance bear right on to a track leading downhill following the riverside, but still to the east of the railway.

❻ Continue to the Killiecrankie visitor centre (where you will find refreshments and toilets). From here continue on the path downhill, passing Soldier's Leap and the railway viaduct. You are

• **DON'T MISS** •

*The picturesque town of **Dunkeld** owes its present appearance to the victorious Highland army that descended on its defending Covenanting forces after Killiecrankie and all but destroyed it. The partially ruined Gothic cathedral is all that remains of that time.*

now on the east bank of the River Garry. Continue southwards, passing Balfour's Stone, to the metal footbridge.

❼ Take the path on the left here, uphill and over the railway bridge to exit on to the B8079. Turn right and follow the B-road, continuing straight ahead as it becomes the B8019 at Garry Bridge, eventually returning to the car park.

**DIFFICULTY** ✳✳

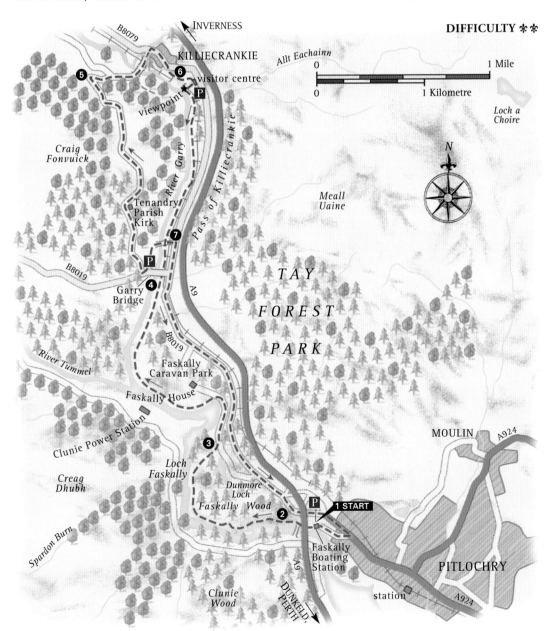

# GEORGIAN

## 1714–1837

# Birth of Industry

George was not universally welcomed. The 'Old Pretender', son of James II, pressed his own claim to the throne, but fled to France after the ill-fated Jacobite uprising of 1715. A few years later came a different crisis, the South Sea Bubble – an 18th-century version of the Wall Street Crash. The South Sea Company went under in 1720, and hordes of its investors, from government ministers to household servants, faced ruin. Norfolk squire Robert Walpole, who had consistently condemned the Company's fund-raising schemes, was one beneficiary, becoming the first British Prime Minister in 1721.

Britain spent much of the 18th century at war, and along the way gathered lands and gained the naval prowess celebrated in the 1740 ditty 'Rule Britannia'. At home, agriculture and industry were progressing rapidly and new inventions popped up by the hundred. Successful experiments in stock-breeding prompted landowners to turf out their tenants to make way for more sheep and cattle. In 1730 Charles 'Turnip' Townshend revolutionised farming methods with crop rotation. The textile industry was mechanised – and many spinners were put out of work – by James Hargreaves' Spinning Jenny; Richard Arkwright devised a hydraulic spinning frame in 1769, and in the same year James Watt patented his steam-engine. Improved smelting techniques increased iron production, and a network of canals carried the industrial materials from source to market.

### REFORM AND REVOLUTION

London was now the financial and social hub of a growing empire. People gathered in the city's coffee-houses to read newspapers and discuss the day's issues, and satire found an eager audience. William Hogarth's prints provided graphic social comments on greed, decadence and ambition. Political corruption became a target for radicals such as John Wilkes, whose popular support foreshadowed the campaign for parliamentary reform and the 1832 Reform Act, which extended the vote to all 40-shilling freeholders.

The Jacobite threat resurfaced briefly in 1745, now led by the Young Pretender, 'Bonnie Prince Charlie'. After the terrible massacre of his followers on Culloden Moor the following year, Charles escaped to Skye, disguised in women's clothes. Both Jacobite and Hanoverian supporters had taken up a popular anthem, albeit with variations in the lyrics; today it is known as 'God Save the Queen'.

In 1763 Britain emerged from the Seven Years' War with France and the government set about replenishing its funds with heavy taxes. When a stamp duty was imposed on the American colonies, it met with an angry response, which presently escalated into war. By 1783 the former colonies had won their independence from the 'mother country'. Revolutionary ideas carried home by America's French allies contributed to the French Revolution, at first welcomed by romantic British radicals such as William Wordsworth and political philosophers such as Tom Paine. But soon revolution turned to terror, and before the end of the century Napoleon Bonaparte was leading his armies through Europe. British patriots found their heroes in Admiral Lord Nelson, who died fending off the French at the Battle of Trafalgar in 1805, and the Duke of Wellington, victor at Waterloo ten years later.

Meanwhile, the future George IV, acting as Prince Regent during one of his father's bouts of madness, commissioned John Nash to create Brighton Pavilion at the fashionable sea-bathing resort of Brighton. Thus ended the Georgian era with a fitting foretaste of the 19th century's imperial swagger.

### HISTORIC SITES

**Brighton Pavilion, Sussex:** inimitable Regency frivolity.

**Edinburgh:** Georgian elegance in the New Town.

**Cheltenham, Gloucestershire:** spa town favoured by King George III.

**10 Downing Street, London:** home of Robert Walpole and his successors.

**Syon Park, Surrey:** mansion and gardens remodelled by Robert Adam and Capability Brown.

**Ironbridge Gorge, Shropshire:** preserved site of early advances in the iron industry.

**1714**

**1714–27** George, Elector of Hanover of Germany, reigns as George I, but his inability to speak English combined with his reliance on Germany for advice leads to the appointment of the first Prime Minister, Robert Walpole, in 1721.

**1715**

**1715** The first Jacobite rebellion in Scotland is easily crushed. The cause passes to Bonnie Prince Charlie, the 'Young Pretender'.

**1718** The Transportation Act authorises the deportation of convicts to new territories.

**1719**

**1719** *Robinson Crusoe* is published (Daniel Defoe).

**1720** Thousands of investors lose their savings in the 'South Sea Bubble', the share collapse of the South Seas Trading Company that took the government down with it.

# Arkengarthdale's Mining Legacy

*The bleak slopes of this northern dale once resounded with the noise of lead-mining*

**GEORGIAN**

**BIRTH OF INDUSTRY**

Langthwaite and its neighbour, Arkle Town, are grey clusters of houses set amid the bleak splendour of Arkengarthdale, a valley that runs north from Swaledale into hostile moorland. Today they are quiet villages, with only farm machinery and the sound of grouse-shooting to disturb them. But for almost 300 years, until the start of the 20th century, the hills around were mined for lead, giving the villages, inhabited by miners and their paraphernalia, the feel and appearance of frontier towns.

The great lead veins that lie beneath these hills have been mined since prehistoric times, but it was in the 17th century that the initial impetus for industrial-scale mining began. There was a smelt mill beside the Slei Gill, passed on the walk, as early as 1628, and the landscape around it reflects the earlier methods of lead extraction. Mining techniques continued to develop, and by the 18th century the hamlet of Booze was a thriving mining community with more than 40 houses. Despite the appropriateness of its name to hard-drinking miners, its name is Norse and means 'the house on the curved hillside'.

Between Booze and Slei Gill, you will pass the arched entrance to a level – the tunnel used by the miners – and, behind it, a desolate valley full of tumbled rock. These are the remains of Tanner Rake Hush. Hushes were an early method of reaching the ore; at the top of a steep slope a stream was dammed with turf. The dam was breached and the collected water rushed downhill, gouging a trench in the slope to expose the lead veins.

Beyond, you pass the spoil heaps of the Windegg Mines, then descend back into the valley near Scar House, a shooting lodge owned by the Dukes of Norfolk. Near the road by Eskeleth Bridge is a small octagonal building set alone in a field. This is the powder house, built in about 1804 to serve the nearby Octagonal Smelt Mill, whose remains can be traced near by. Nearer the road junction are the ruins of Langthwaite Smelt Mill. The nearby C B Inn is a reminder that the mining rights in this area were for many years held by the 18th-century lord of the manor, Charles Bathurst.

The mining area on the west slopes of Arkengarthdale were known in the 19th century as the Hungry Hushes, suggesting that the lead mined there was scarce and hard-won. The miners' tracks ascend the hill, and eventually pass the junction of two of the enormously long chimney flues that are a feature of Dales lead mines. Long flues were an advance in mining technology that allowed smelt mills to use high temperatures to separate the lead from the slag. Because lead vapourises at high heat, much was lost into the atmosphere. The long flues solved the problem by cooling the gases as they went towards the chimney on the hillside. The lead solidified in the walls of the flues and men could be sent in to recover the deposited lead when the furnaces had been extinguished.

BELOW: *Nestling in the woods in Arkengarthdale is Scar House, a shooting lodge owned by the Dukes of Norfolk.*

BELOW: *The valley of Arkengarthdale; the tall chimney stacks and rows of terraced houses serve as a reminder of its past as an industrial giant.*

**ABOUT • ARKENGARTHDALE**

*Lead has been mined here for thousands of years but it wasn't until the 17th century that intensive mining began and small 'frontier' towns began springing up. This walk has plenty of history to offer as it wends its way through the Yorkshire Dales.*

**North Yorkshire • N ENGLAND**

**DISTANCE** • 8 miles (13km)

**TOTAL ASCENT** • 1,213ft (370m)

**PATHS** • mostly clear tracks; a little walking on heather moor

**TERRAIN** • steep, mined valleys and moorland

**GRADIENTS** • two stiff climbs, but generally gradual slopes

**REFRESHMENTS** • Red Lion in Langthwaite and the CB Inn in Arkengarthdale

**PARK** • car park at southern end of Langthwaite village

**OS MAP** • Outdoor Leisure 30 Yorkshire Dales – Northern & Central areas

# Arkengarthdale's ancient lead-mining industry

❶ From the car park, turn right, then right again. Cross the bridge, continue ahead between cottages and climb the hill. Follow the lane to the hamlet of Booze (note that hamlets in Arkengarthdale are early Norse settlements). Pass the farmhouse and a stone barn and follow the track to a gate.

❷ Beyond the gate, where the track bends left, go ahead, beside a tumbled wall. Bear right to pass a ruined cottage and follow the path to the stream. Walk upstream, pass through a gate, and cross the stream on stepping stones.

❸ Follow the course of the steam through moorland to a wooden hut. Turn left along the track beyond. Go straight ahead at a crossing, then turn left at a T-junction. Where the wall on your right ends, take the path, right, down to a gate.

❹ Follow the gill downhill to go through another gate. Turn right along the track beyond it. Continue through a gateway and on to another track by a barn. Follow the track, which bends left by a stone wall and passes farm buildings, through two gates to a white gate.

❺ Go through the gate into Scar House grounds. Bear right down the drive, over a bridge and cattle grid and turn right on to a track. Continue to a road. Turn left, then right at a T-junction. After a cattle grid, turn left on a signed track.

❻ Bear right at a gravelled area and continue uphill on the track. Where it divides, go left beside slag heaps and pass the junction of two flues. The track bends right then left, uphill, to a T-junction. Turn left here. Follow the track downhill to a road.

❼ Turn left. Beyond the farmhouse turn right at a bridleway sign towards the house, and turn left before reaching it. Follow the signed track though a gate. Continue downhill and turn left before a small barn. Go over four stiles to the road. Turn left back to the car park.

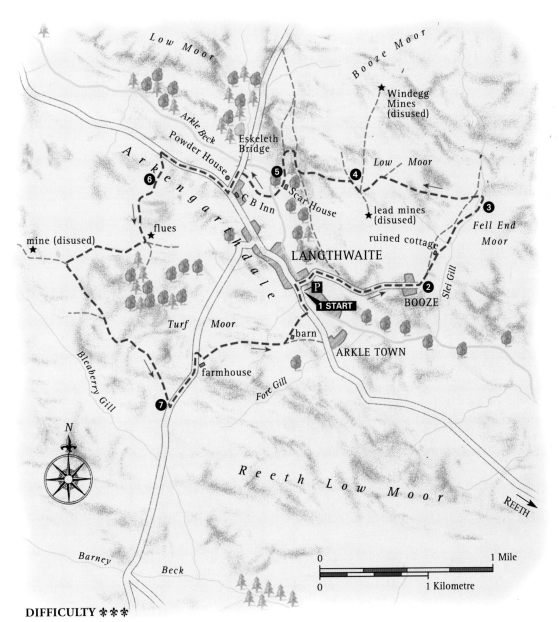

**• DON'T MISS •**

*The attractive village of **Reeth**, set around a wide, sloping green, has been a market town since 1695 and still holds sheep sales. It formerly had an important knitting industry.*

**DIFFICULTY ✾ ✾ ✾**

**1721**

**1721** Sir Robert Walpole is elected First Lord of the Treasury, making him effectively Prime Minister and the most powerful man in Britain.

**1726** The publication of *Gulliver's Travels* (Jonathan Swift).

**1727**

**1727–60** The reign of George II.

**1736** Witchcraft is abolished as a punishable crime.

**1739** John Wesley founds the first Methodist Chapel in Bristol.

**1740**

**1740–48** War breaks out with Austria over the Austrian Succession.

**1742** The *Messiah*, probably Friedrich Handel's most popular choral work, is performed in Dublin.

# The Prince in the Heather

*Bonnie Prince Charlie's escape took him on a perilous journey through the Highlands and Islands*

The defeat of the Jacobite forces on the battlefield of Culloden on 16 April 1746 ended the dream of restoring the Royal House of Stuart to the British throne, but it was not the end of Prince Charles Edward Stuart. The prince had landed at Loch nan Uamh, near Arisaig, on 25 July 1745. Following Culloden he would sail again from Loch nan Uamh, to France and a life of exile, but before that he was the subject of the greatest manhunt the Highlands has ever seen.

For five months he travelled on foot across the Highlands and Islands of Scotland, living rough or with supporters, narrowly evading the thousands of government troops that were scouring the countryside hoping to capture him. Despite a price of £30,000 on his head, an enormous fortune then, nobody betrayed him.

Before the battle was over the prince was spirited away by supporters to the house of Lord Lovat. He crossed some of the roughest and most inhospitable countryside in Scotland to Loch nan Uamh to take ship for France. When no vessel appeared the prince dared not wait, and planned to cross the Minch to Lewis. Blown off course by a storm, he ended up on Benbecula, instead. From there he sailed north to Scalpay, sending his guide ahead to Stornoway. The townspeople there got wind of the prince impending arrival and said they would refuse him admittance.

The government, by now aware that the fugitive was in the Outer Hebrides, poured troops and warships into the pursuit. On 10 May the Prince sailed south, just ahead of his pursuers, first to Carradale and then to Loch Boisdale on South Uist. With help from Hugh MacDonald of Armadale, he crossed South Uist by night to meet Flora MacDonald near her home at Milton. From here he made his famous escape to Skye dressed as her Irish maid, Betty Burke. After landing near Vatternish Point, he walked slowly south to Portree and crossed to the island of Raasay, where he sheltered overnight in a small hut at Glam on the west shore of the island.

Raasay had suffered terribly in the aftermath of Culloden. Government troops had razed most of the islanders' dwellings, including the Laird's house, taken their clothes and killed their cattle. Devastated Raasay could offer no shelter and the prince took to the water again, first to Portree, then to Elgol on the south of Skye and finally to the mainland at Mallaig. After a further two months as a fugitive, including eight days living in the cave of Cluny MacPherson on Ben Alder, the prince boarded the French ship *L'Heureux* on 20 September, and sailed from Scotland forever.

He died in Rome, aged 68, on 30 January 1788, after a lifetime of drunkenness and cruelty to women. Despite this, and despite his reputation for arrogance and cowardice, he remains one of the most romantic characters in the history of Scotland. There is no doubt that he endured many hardships during his flight, displaying unsuspected reserves of stamina and strength of character. It was probably his finest hour.

ABOVE: *Charles Edward Stuart (1720–88) advanced within 130 miles of London before being beaten back to Culloden and forced into hiding to avoid capture by government troops.*

BELOW: *Dusk over Raasay, from Skye.*

**ABOUT · RAASAY**

*The defeat of the Jacobites at Culloden in 1746 ended all hopes to return a Stuart to the throne and led to a relentless manhunt for Bonnie Prince Charlie. This walk takes you to Raasay, one of his final hiding places in Scotland, before he fled into exile.*

## Highland · SCOTLAND

**DISTANCE ·** 6 miles (9.6km)

**TOTAL ASCENT ·** 540ft (165m)

**PATHS ·** mostly good but can be muddy after heavy rain

**TERRAIN ·** green lanes, moorland, hillside and tarmac road

**GRADIENTS ·** mostly gentle

**REFRESHMENTS ·** Raasay Hotel

**PARK ·** parking area before the last house on the road to North Fearns

**OS MAP ·** Pathfinder 187 Narrows of Raasay

# Bonnie Prince Charlie's escape to Raasay

**❶** From the car park at the end of the road continue along the green lane. The sea is on your right and you will have a superb view across to the islands of Scalpay, Longay and Pabay.

**❷** After a mile (1.6km) look up to the left as you pass the impressive cliffs of Beinn na' Leac. Continue on past the headland of Rudha na' Leac, beyond which you will see a memorial cairn on the path.

**❸** Stop at the cairn to read the inscription to the gaelic poet Sorley McLean, who was from Raasay, and also to those who were cleared from the land to make way for sheep. McLean's poem Hallaig is reproduced here. From here the path narrows, entering woodland and passing a ruined building. Follow the path out of the wood and where it forks, keep left. Re-enter woodland, go downhill and cross the Hallaig Burn where it meets the path.

**❹** Climb uphill from the burn and veer right towards the top corner of a drystone wall. At the corner

*Loch a Chadha Chàrnaich*

*Loch na Mna*

waterfall ★

**❺** ★ ruined buildings

HALLAIG

**❹**

Rudha na' Leac

ruined building

**❸** ★ memorial cairn

RAASAY

**❻**

Hallaig Burn

*Inverarish Burn*

**❷**

Inner Sound

310
Beinn na' Leac

**❼**

INVERARISH ←

NORTH FEARNS Ⓟ

**1 START**

N

0 ½ Mile

0 500 Metres

**DIFFICULTY** ✤ ✤

you can see the best preserved of the houses of Hallaig township which was cleared of people in the 18th and 19th centuries to make way for sheep.

**❺** Continue by following the track round the rest of the ruins, heading towards a rocky crag in the north, then turn left and head

uphill. Turn left again and with the crag behind you head south towards another crag on the distant hills.

**❻** When you intersect the Hallaig Burn, turn right and follow its course uphill until it disappears. Then pick up the rough track, heading round the back of Beann

na' Leac. Eventually the track will disappear but by then you will see the road below.

**❼** Descend the hill heading towards the road. When you reach the burn turn left and walk along it until it flows under the road. Turn left and return to your car.

**1745**

**1745** Bonnie Prince Charlie captures Edinburgh and defeats the English at Falkirk.

**1746** The Jacobites' luck runs out at Culloden Moor, ending their bid to regain the throne. Bonnie Prince Charlie is forced to return to France.

**1748**

**1748–9** *Clarissa* is published (Samuel Richardson).

**1749** The publication of *Tom Jones* (Henry Fielding). The book causes scandal in polite society, and is blamed for the two earthquakes that hit London that year.

**1752**

**1752** Benjamin Franklin discovers electricity.

**1756–63** The Seven Years' War with France breaks out.

**1769** Josiah Wedgwood's first pottery opens in Staffordshire.

# Shipwrecks and Smugglers at Hartland Quay

*A short but demanding walk along the spectacular cliffs and combes in the far northwest corner of Devon*

ABOVE: *The charming 13th-century Docton Mill at Lymebridge.*

Hartland is one of the most rugged and unforgiving stretches of coastline to be found anywhere in the country. This is a stunning area: south of Hartland Point the jagged rocks run in parallel lines along the seabed, like enormous sharks' teeth, towards the massive cliffs. There is nothing kind or inviting about the landscape here; there are no natural inlets or safe havens. It's hard to imagine that any kind of seaborne trade could ever have been possible, and you can understand why this part of the coastline, commonly known as 'the sailors' grave', is peppered with shipwrecks.

From Warren Cliff there is a wonderful view of Hartland Quay, built on a natural ledge of rock and dating back to 1586, when its construction by one William Abbott was authorised by Act of Parliament. Determined to increase the prosperity of the area, and hindered by the appalling state of inland communications, Abbott had to turn to the sea as the key to Hartland's future fortunes. Trade was particularly active here during the 17th and 18th centuries, with cargoes of coal, lime and timber coming in, and corn being exported. During the Georgian era, when Britannia ruled the waves and shipping was a vital part of the economy and international strategy, this was an active place. The buildings, including the stables for the donkeys that carried goods up the cliff when the quay was operating, have now been converted into the Hartland Quay Hotel, museum and shop, but it's still possible to get a sense of how tough life must have been here for the harbour master and his staff, particularly in wild, stormy weather when the huge Atlantic seas pound against the rocks.

The quay continued to be active until 1893; once abandoned it was soon destroyed by the sea. Today is is hard to see any traces of the old harbour, which ran out from the limekiln across Warren Beach to the north of the quay buildings. Many other victims were claimed by the waves, too: British sea power was great, but shipping was a dangerous business. The great rock in the cove, known as Life Rock, provided a watery refuge for many shipwrecked mariners. Records were patchy until the 18th century, when the first named wreck was the *Anne* in 1753. Other losses during the Georgian period included an unidentified sailing ship in 1784; the *Triton* in 1800; a sailing smack in 1806; and the *Edward and Ann*, a smack, in 1809. The last was significant, since the vessel was owned by Edward Hockin, owner of the quay from 1789 until his death in 1835, and caused the deaths of the ship's master and boy. A cutter, *Maria*, foundered just to the south of the quay in 1826; and the notorious 'Cruel Coppinger', a rogue and smuggler who terrorised the local population, lost a ship just off Speke's Mill Mouth in 1792. But despite the obvious dangers of this coast the lighthouse at Hartland Point was not completed until 1874.

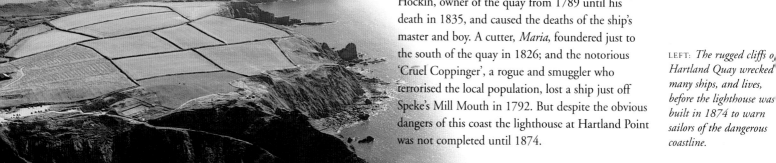

LEFT: *The rugged cliffs of Hartland Quay wrecked many ships, and lives, before the lighthouse was built in 1874 to warn sailors of the dangerous coastline.*

### ABOUT • HARTLAND

*The coastal scenery off Hartland Point may seem spectacular but to the sailors of the 18th century it must have offered a cruel welcome. The jagged cliffs were responsible for a number of shipwrecks and, inevitably, the lives of many sailors.*

## Devon • SW ENGLAND

**DISTANCE** • 3½ miles (5.6km)

**TOTAL ASCENT** • 360ft (110m)

**PATHS** • fields, grassy coast path, quiet country lanes and farm tracks

**TERRAIN** • dramatic and rugged coastal scenery, rolling farmland

**GRADIENTS** • some short but steep climbs on the coast path

**REFRESHMENTS** • Wreckers' Retreat pub at Hartland Quay; cream teas available in Stoke in the summer; The Hart Inn, The Anchor and the King's Arms pubs in Hartland village

**PARK** • west of St Nectan's Church in Stoke, signed from Hartland

**OS MAP** • Explorer 126 Clovelly & Hartland

# The unforgiving coastline of Hartland

**❶** With the church on your right, follow the wall round to meet a footpath sign pointing left. Follow the path between the cottages and the lane, over a stile, through a kissing gate and over a stile into a field. Turn right, downhill, with views of the sea at Blackpool Mill. Walk along the lower edge of the field to enter the woods above the Abbey River, right, to reach the coast path.

**❷** Turn left through a gate; follow the path uphill to Dyer's Lookout, and across Warren Cliff past the ruined tower, left. Leave the field by a stile by the Rocket House.

**❸** Turn right; follow coast path posts along the cliff edge and down steps to join the lane leading to Hartland Quay.

**❹** From the car park follow coast path signs on and up steps to pass along the cliff edge round the back of Well Beach. Go through a kissing gate and follow the coast path to the right passing through a five-bar gate to avoid mighty

St Catherine's Tor. Cross the stream, cross the next field and pass through a gate. The path now continues uphill, towards the coast, and over a stile before dropping down to Speke's Mill Mouth. Pause for a moment to enjoy its impressive run of waterfalls, totalling 160ft (49m).

**❺** Turn left up the track, following coast path signs inland, then turn right at the next post to cross the stream on a footbridge. Turn left at the next post, signed coast path valley route. Keep straight on at the next two signposts, signed Milford. Leave the heathland over a stile into a field; walk straight to the top and out through a gate, to join a farm track that meets the lane at Milford.

**❻** Turn left downhill, pass Docton Mill to reach the crossroads at Lymebridge.

**❼** Turn left and continue uphill through Lymebride to reach Kernstone Cross. At the crossroads continue straight ahead along the green lane, signed unsuitable for motors. At the entrance to Wargery Farm turn left downhill and follow the track to the edge of Stoke, where it veers right. Go straight on to reach the village centre.

**❽** Turn left and walk through the churchyard, turning left at the church door to return to the start of the walk.

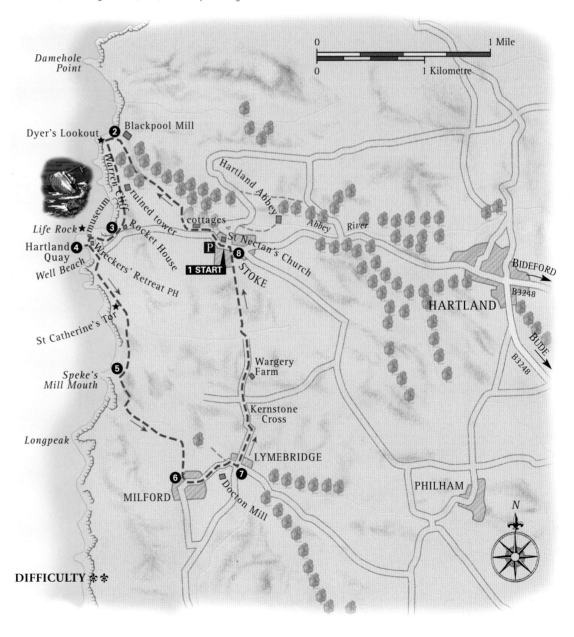

**DIFFICULTY** ✿✿

**1760**

**1760–1820** George III reigns.

**1760** The clearances begin in the Scottish Highlands and Islands and by the end of the century three-quarters of the land is in the hands of a few wealthy landowners.

**1761**

**1761** The Bridgewater Canal opens, running from Manchester to Runcorn to transport coal.

**1769** James Watt patents his invention of the steam engine.

**1773** Bostonians show their fury at

**1773**

trade controls and taxes imposed by Britain by dumping a shipload of tea into the harbour.

**1775** The American War of Independence begins.

# Bristol and the Slaving Triangle

*A fascinating tour from Bristol's regenerated waterfront up to the 18th-century suburb of Clifton and back on the Slave Trade Trail*

**GEORGIAN**

**BIRTH OF INDUSTRY**

Bristol's quayside has been transformed in recent years. Executive apartments now occupy the warehouses, once full of sugar and tobacco; bars and exhibitions crowd the wharves. But this latest boom is just one in a series of upturns experienced by a city whose wealth has often come upstream on the River Avon. Back in the 18th century a very different form of prosperity came to shape the urban landscape of the historic port.

In 1698 the monopoly on trade with Africa was relinquished by the London-based Royal Africa Company. Bristol merchants, members of the Society of Merchant Venturers, were eager to cash in on potential new markets and began a form of triangular trading which was to have far-reaching consequences, even up to the present day. Ships from Bristol set sail for the coast of West Africa, loaded with iron and copper goods from local manufacturers. Once there they traded in their cargoes and set sail again, across the stormy Atlantic, for the West Indies. In their holds they carried thousands of people, Africans sold by local slave traders to work in the plantations of the new colonies. The final leg of the journey back to Bristol brought the cocoa, sugar and tobacco that were to fill the quays and warehouses of the booming port.

In the years between 1698 and 1807, when Britain abolished slavery, over 2,000 ships left Bristol to ply their trade on the Atlantic waters. They accounted for the transportation of half a million Africans, or one fifth of all the slaves carried by British ships. Merchants such as Henry Bright, Edward Colston, Mark Davies and the Farr, Codrington and Pope families amassed huge fortunes, not just from the slave ships themselves but also from the plantations which they quickly came to control.

As the money rolled in, the old city was reshaped. Up Constitution Hill into the new suburb of Clifton, you can see the results: grand terraces, striking town houses and opulent new streets laid out to house the beneficiaries of this new-found wealth. In the fashionable coffee houses of Broad Street and Corn Street, merchants gathered to deal and find effective ways of investing their takings. Entrepreneurs were also quick to realise that here was a source of ready capital for their nascent industrial ventures. Insurance companies and banks began to develop. There were canals and ironworks to invest in, coal mines and glassworks, brickworks, potteries and a host of other outlets. The Industrial Revolution was taking off and the capital came from the slaving triangle.

The walk starts on the quayside, by the industrial museum, and then crosses St Augustine's Reach by Pero's Bridge. The name commemorates one of the few slaves actually to be brought to Bristol. Pero came from Nevis with the merchant John Pinney in 1783. Later, on Park Street, you join part of the city's official Slave Trade Trail.

ABOVE: *A poster advertising the 'sale' and 'let' of 'slaves of good character'. As well as human merchandise, rice, muslin and needles and other luxury and household goods are offered for sale.*

BACKGROUND: *The elegant York Crescent in Clifton.*

BELOW: *The regenerated waterfront at Bristol on the River Avon.*

**ABOUT • BRISTOL**

*A walk around Bristol will reveal the city's role in the 18th-century slaving triangle. It is worth picking up a booklet on the Slave Trade Trail, from the Tourist Information Centre, as it makes a valuable companion as you tour the city.*

**Bristol • SW ENGLAND**

**DISTANCE** • 4½ miles (7.2km)

**TOTAL ASCENT** • 215ft (66m)

**PATHS** • pavements throughout

**TERRAIN** • city centre, parkland, quayside and residential streets

**GRADIENTS** • very steep ascent of Constitution Hill

**REFRESHMENTS** • a huge range throughout route

**PARK** • Bristol Industrial Museum pay-and-display (maximum three hours)

**OS MAP** • Explorer 155 Bristol & Bath

# On the Slave Trade Trail

❶ From the museum turn left over Wapping Bridge. Turn left on the quayside and walk around the Arnolfini Gallery, to cross Pero's Bridge. Go ahead towards the TIC then veer right by Explore@Bristol. Turn right in front of the museum and cross the road to go up some steps. Pass the cathedral on your left to emerge on College Green and turn left.

❷ Continue to Deanery Road and take the second right up York Place, opposite the Three Tuns. Cross into Brandon Hill Park up some steps and take the left-hand path. Walk through the park and emerge on Jacob's Well Road by the Wildlife Trust. Cross and walk up Constitution Hill.

❸ At the top cross Lower Clifton Hill and Clifton Road. Bear left, on the level, to Regent Street and turn right up Merchant's Road. Turn left and walk round Victoria Square. At the end of the second side, turn right in front of Lansdown Place, then left down Queen's Road. Take the first left down Richmond Park Road to Pembroke Road.

❹ Turn right and cross Queen's Road down Richmond Hill. At the bottom, turn left down Queen's Road and cross the Triangle. Turn left down Park Street and second left on Great George Street to see the Georgian House. From here the walk follows the Slave Trade Trail.

❺ Return to Park Street and turn right. Cross and take next left along Unity Street then right down Denmark Street . At the bottom, turn left on St Augustine's Parade. Go along Colston Avenue under the Centregate arch to the Three Loaves of Sugar. Continue under the arches of modern buildings to Lewin's Mead Sugar House on the left.

❻ Turn right and cross through the arch opposite to Broad Street. Take the third alley on the left to see Taylor's Court, then return to Broad Street, past the Guildhall and turn right to look at Corn Street. Turn round at the Commercial Rooms and return towards Broad Street but turn right in front of No 56, down All Saint's Lane by All Saint's Church.

Go straight ahead through the covered market and across two roads. Descend steps by St Nicholas's Church and cross to the waterfront along Welsh Back.

❼ Take the second right up King Street, past the Llandoger Trow and the Theatre Royal. At the bottom, turn left and follow the pavement round into Queen Square. From the Custom House, cross the park, turn left to the Hole in the Wall, cross the road and then the bridge on Redcliffe Way.

❽ Go right, round roundabout past the Quaker Burial Ground (left) and St Mary Redcliffe (right) on to Redcliffe Hill. Take the second right on Guinea Street, and right down Alfred and Jubilee Places. Turn right on to Redcliffe Parade East, and cross to descend a ramp to the quayside by Redcliffe Caves.

❾ Follow the quayside round to the left and cross the footbridge in front of the Ostrich. Turn right to Merchant's Wharf, Wapping Bridge and the Industrial Museum.

**DIFFICULTY** ⚜

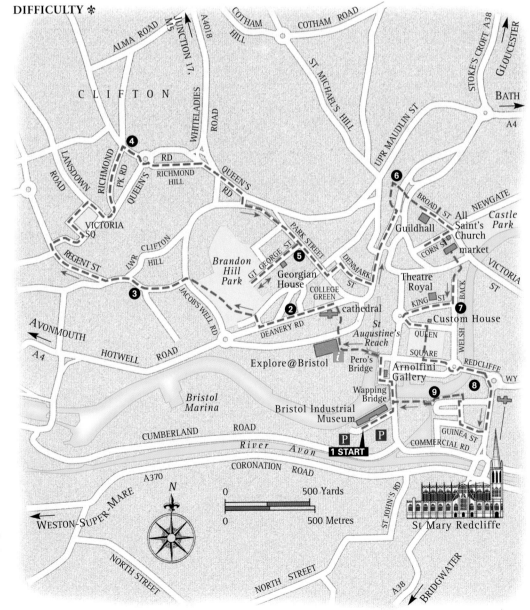

# The Age of Canals

*The motorway interchange of its day, Braunston's canal junction and marina are still busy with the passage of barges*

ABOVE: *Navvies start work cutting the first sods of the canal.*

BELOW: *The junction at a canal crossroads in Birmingham.*

### Pre-industrial Britain

Before the railways, the only effective bulk transport was by boat. After the Romans left Britain, roads fell into decline and overland trade relied largely on packhorses. Although 18th-century turnpike roads greatly improved mail and passenger services, the movement of heavy loads remained a slow and laborious process, and only towns on the coast or a navigable river grew to any significance. Early improvements using weirs and flash locks helped, but by the 17th century, only 700 miles (1,126km) of navigable waterway existed. Although the next 150 years added a further 600 miles (966km), there was still little effective access for inland coalfields and new factories. The emerging industrial revolution was seriously threatened. Although already existing in Europe, it was not until around 1760 that the first 'dead-water' canals appeared in Britain. The Sankey and Worsley canals, constructed to transport coal from the mines, were an overnight success, instantly halving the price of coal in Manchester and Liverpool.

### The Early Waterways

The impact of the canals was spectacular, prompting a massive investment, and in less than 25 years all the major navigable rivers had been linked. Development was rapid, with cuttings, aqueducts and improved locks being employed to create more direct routes and allow changes in level. Indeed, many of the first canals were later straightened, as at Wolfhampcote, where an aqueduct now carries the waterway across the River Leam, saving over 2 miles (3km) against its former route. Tunnels were also excavated, and

WATERBUS
SHERBORNE WHARF
0121 455 6163

THE UNITY WATERBUS ARIEL

ABOVE: *Gas Street Basin in Birmingham.*

the one near Braunston, carrying the Grand Junction, is around 1¼ miles (2km) long. Engineers also faced problems in providing a reliable water supply to elevated sections, since a lock uses around 25,000 gallons (113,650l) of water each time a boat passes. Rivers and streams were one source, but because mill-owners complained about the loss of their water, reservoirs were built and, sometimes, pumping stations employed to lift water back. The walk passes a former pumping station beyond Braunston Marina. Another strategy employed in the Midlands was the construction of narrow canals, with 7ft-(2m)-wide locks rather than the standard 14ft (4m). But as their use was restricted to narrow boats, cargoes on boats from other parts of the country had to be reloaded and many canals were later widened to improve their competitiveness.

Living in barges, the boatmen and their families became a race apart, inhabiting a world perhaps 100 miles (160km) long, but only 50 yards (46m) wide. Undertaken whatever the weather, the work was often hard; the hours were long and the living conditions frequently poor, though later legislation brought some improvement.

By the 1860s the canals' heyday had passed and competition from the railways heralded their inexorable decline. Despite an attempt at revival during the 1930s, the end was inevitable and, with the last cargoes in the 1960s, a way of life disappeared.

*Colourful canal boats moored at Birmingham Street Basin. Although the canals are no longer used by industry they remain one of the most popular and best-used leisure resources in Britain.*

# WALK 68

## EXPLORING THE OXFORD AND GRAND UNION CANALS

**❶** Join the Oxford Canal towpath where it passes beneath the A45 and walk south from the bridge towards a canal junction, which comes into view ahead. Ignore the bridges carrying the path over the fork on to the Grand Union Canal and instead turn right to pass beneath. The two canals run together for the next 5 miles (8km), before the Grand Union branches north at Napton. However, in three quarters of a mile (3km), beyond a dismantled railway bridge and immediately after passing beneath bridge number 98, climb up the embankment to a stile. Turn right across the bridge and carry on along a track towards a farm at Wolfhampcote. There, join another track coming from the right and go on, crossing the original line of the canal. Bear right at the farm entrance and on past a cottage and Wolfhampcote church. In the fields beyond, humps, hollows and ditches are all that is left of the abandoned medieval villages of Wolfhampcote and Braunstonbury.

**❷** At the far end, the track rises past cottages to the main road; instead, go left after the last cottage to return to the towpath. Now on the Grand Union, turn right and walk beneath the road, passing Stop House, where there is an exhibition about the canals, to reach Braunston Marina.

**❸** Beyond the marina, the canal climbs 35½ feet (11m) through six successive locks and then enters a cutting leading to the eastern portal of the Braunston Tunnel. There, the towpath ends; while the boatmen 'legged' their boats through, the horses were led over the hill to the other end, 1¼ miles (2km) away. You can still follow their track, which rises beside the tunnel entrance. However, the return route lies back along the canal, past the marina and junction and on to the bridge where you started.

**Distance:** 5½ miles (9km)

**Total ascent:** none

**Paths:** short sections of the towpath can be muddy, otherwise well-surfaced paths and tracks

**Terrain:** open, rolling countryside

**Refreshments:** the walk passes two canalside pubs

**Park:** layby beside the A45, just beyond the canal, ¼ mile (0.4km) east of Braunston

**OS Map:** Explorer 15 (234) Rutland Water

**Difficulty:** ✳

1714–1837

**1783**
**1783** American independence is recognised by the British.

**1778** The Australian Penal Colony is established. Thousands of convicts are offloaded at Port Jackson, later to become Sydney Harbour.

**1779**
**1779** Abraham Darby III casts the world's first iron bridge to span the river Severn, near Coalbrookdale.

**1789** The French Revolution starts.

**1789** George Washington becomes the first American president.

**1793**
**1793–1802** War between Britain and France breaks out.

166

# The Utopian Village of New Lanark

*A brave experiment in social engineering on the banks of the River Clyde*

The colossal wealth generated by the Industrial Revolution in the late 18th century improved the living standards of the rich enormously, but was seldom used to benefit ordinary workers and their families. Squalid housing, violent crime and brutish ignorance blighted the existence of all who were forced to live in the appalling slums that sprawled around Britain's booming factories. A rare exception to this rule was the village of New Lanark on the River Clyde. In its day this was the largest industrial enterprise in Scotland and a world-renowned centre of the cotton industry, but it also shone out as a beacon of enlightenment in a world of dark, satanic mills.

The village was established in 1785 by David Dale, a Glaswegian banker and industrialist who combined shrewd business sense with missionary zeal for moral education and reform. The isolated site, in a deep wooded valley, allowed him dictatorial control over his employees, while the mighty waters flowing through the gorge provided power for his mills. Within ten years, New Lanark was employing more than 1,500 people, all of whom lived on site. More than half the work force consisted of young children and, by modern standards, life was hard, but Dale at least ensured that his employees were well fed and housed from the cradle to the grave. In contrast to the fetid slums of Manchester or Glasgow, New Lanark was Utopia.

Dale was the creator of New Lanark, but its spirit owes more to his son-in-law, Robert Owen, who took over ownership in 1800. It was Owen, a far more radical reformer than his predecessor, who gradually phased out child labour and improved the housing. He established a new school and the world's first adult education centre, the Institute for the Formation of Character. He turned the shop into a co-operative venture owned by the community. He provided land for cultivation and ornamental walks for recreation. Although opinionated and arrogant, he made New

Lanark an example that would inspire idealists until the creation of the welfare state.

Today New Lanark's only industry is tourism, although some 200 people still live in its Georgian tenements and cottages. Just the first part of the walk, through the perfectly restored centre of the village, could easily occupy a morning, since several of the mills and other buildings are open to the public and provide a fascinating insight into Owen's vision. The remainder of the route is in breathtaking, unexpected contrast, following a wild, wooded gorge past waterfalls and rapids that inspired painters such as Turner and the Romantic poets. Owen was a firm believer in the moral benefits of exercise, but it is unlikely that many of his workers had sufficient leisure-time or energy to indulge in a hike for pleasure. The fact that we can do so, two centuries on and a social revolution later, is due, in no small part, to the example that he set at New Lanark.

ABOVE: *An aerial view of New Lanark. It was a model industrial town which inspired idealists and social reformers.*

LEFT: *Schoolgirls dancing a Quadrille. Robert Owen sought not only to create an ideal working community but also to provide education and a healthier lifestyle for his employees.*

ABOVE: *Robert Dale Owen (1807–77). He was born in Glasgow and devoted his life to social reform and improvement.*

**ABOUT • NEW LANARK**

*David Dale, a Glaswegian banker and industrialist, was the visionary behind New Lanark's town planning. In an age where the chasm between the rich and poor was largely ignored, he provided social housing and 'cradle to the grave' care of its townsfolk.*

## South Lanarkshire • SCOTLAND

**DISTANCE** • 8 miles (13km)

**TOTAL ASCENT** • 200ft (61m)

**PATHS** • mostly firm but some muddy stretches

**TERRAIN** • woodland and riverside gorges

**GRADIENTS** • steep in some sections, but with steps to ease ascents

**REFRESHMENTS** • Mill Hotel in New Lanark

**PARK** • car park above New Lanark

**OS MAP** • Explorer 335 Lanark & Tinto Hills, Lesmahagow & Douglas

# The social reformers who built New Lanark

❶ From the car park take the path down to New Lanark, where there are a number of buildings open to the public and exhibitions of the community's history.

❷ Beside Robert Owen's School, bear left off the road along a path that continues through a gate into Scottish Wildlife Trust's nature reserve. Follow the path up steps and along the river, past the thundering Dundaff Linn and weirs that once powered the cotton mills.

❸ Turn right at the approach drive to Bonnington Power Station, which in 1927 was Britain's first hydro-electric scheme. At the power station, fork right off the drive to follow a footpath signed to Falls of Clyde. The waterfalls, Corra Linn and Bonnington Linn, are most dramatic after prolonged heavy rain, when there is more water than the power station needs, and the excess flows freely through the gorge.

❹ Keeping to the path, cross the river over Bonnington Weir, then turn right down a woodland track into the Corehouse Estate. After 200yds (183m), turn right on to a footpath down towards the river. From here there are spectacular views of the falls.

❺ Keep to the riverside path, ignoring other paths up to the left. Beyond the ruins of Corra Castle, there are views of New Lanark on the opposite bank. At a junction with a track, turn right and continue until you reach some houses on your left. Just beyond their gardens, climb the bank to your left and follow a faint path through the trees to a gap in the

wall along Kirkfield Road. Turn right and then right again at the bottom of the hill into St Patrick's Lane and follow signs for Clyde Walkway.

❻ Cross the river on Clydesholm Bridge, then turn right through the gate of Old Brigend (private property). Follow the Clyde Walkway up to the treatment works, then climb steeply, with several steps, and bear right to follow a lane to Castlebank Park. Just beyond a sign to Jookers' Johnnie, turn right down the drive to Castlebank House. Follow the path signed Clyde Walkway down from Castlebank Park to river level and on to New Lanark and your car.

**• DON'T MISS •**

*Near by you'll find the **Falls of Clyde**, part of a Scottish Wildlife Trust reserve, which offers a full ranger service including badger watching and bat walks (between May–September). Plus, an open hide, manned 24 hours a day, offering unrivalled views of breeding peregrine falcons (telephone 01555 665262).*

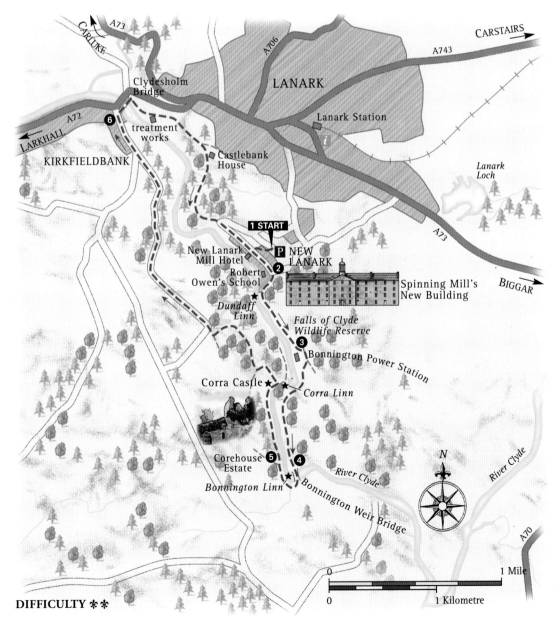

**DIFFICULTY ✷✷**

**1794**

**1794** The Cardiff Coal dock opens, and within 50 years Cardiff has become the world's biggest coal-shipping port.

**1796** Napoleon Bonaparte is made commander of the French armies and takes power in 1799.

**1801**

**1801** The Act of Union with Ireland achieves its first aim, to unite the Irish and Westminster parliaments; but George III refuses to give Catholics their freedom, and Pitt, Prime Minister, resigns as a result.

**1803–15** The Napoleonic Wars.

**1807**

**1807** The Slave Trade Reform Bill is passed and by 1833 the trade is abolished throughout the empire.

**1811–16** The mechanised processes of the Industrial Revolution cause unrest, and factory machinery is destroyed in riots led by Ned Ludd.

# One Man went to Mow

*An 18th-century folly tops the hill on the Staffordshire–Cheshire border – the birthplace of Primitive Methodism*

On a cold May Sunday in 1807, a Stoke-on-Trent wheelwright named Hugh Bourne climbed to the windswept 1,100ft (335m) summit of Mow Cop, on the borders of Staffordshire and Cheshire, to launch the Primitive Methodist movement.

Bourne, his brother and his friend William Clowes of Burslem were anxious to return to a far simpler form of religious observance, and they invited a number of like-minded friends to that first 'camp meeting' of the new order. The meeting is said to have lasted between 12 and 14 hours, and was the precursor of many similar mass gatherings on this well-known viewpoint.

While he was still working as a wheelwright, Bourne found time to conduct similar meetings all over Britain and even in the United States. Before

his death, at the age of 80, he had seen over 5,000 chapels established, including the large building in the village of Mow Cop in 1860, and a total congregation of Primitive Methodists of over 100,000 souls. Over 70,000 of Bourne's disciples gathered to worship here in 1907 at what had become their 'Holy Mount', and in 1932 the movement merged with the parent church by an act of union. Five years later, over 10,000 Methodists attended a service at Mow Cop, when the summit was handed over to its present owners, The National Trust.

Mow Cop, with its extensive westward views over the broad Cheshire Plain as far as the Berwyn Mountains of North Wales, north-east to the hills of the Peak and southwards as far as the dark conifers of Cannock Chase and the dim outlines of the Shropshire Hills, is certainly an inspiring place. Nearer at hand the huge, upturned white saucer of the Jodrell Bank Radio Telescope is prominent in the broad green plain below, with the tower blocks of Stockport and Manchester in the north, beyond wooded Alderley Edge, and the airliners coming in and out of Manchester's International Airport.

The strange, mock-Gothic folly castle which tops the hill was built in 1754 by the local squire, Randle Wilbraham, to adorn the eastern skyline as seen from his home 3 miles (5km) to the west, at Rode Hall. The folly takes the form of a two-storeyed circular tower alongside a Gothic-arched curtain wall which steps down the hillside. Wilbraham used the tower when it was roofed as a summerhouse, gazebo or prospect tower for guests visiting his home in the plain below.

Before that, the hilltop of Mow Cop had been used as the site for a beacon which was lit to warn the armed forces of the coming of the Spanish Armada in 1588, linking The Wrekin in Shropshire with Alderley Edge. The nearby quarries to the north of the tower contain an isolated, leaning splinter of rock left by the quarrymen and known as the Old Man of Mow.

LEFT: *Mow Cop in Cheshire which Hugh Bourne and William Clowes of Burslem climbed to preach the first sermon of the Pimitive Methodist movement.*

**ABOUT • MOW COP**

*Starting near the summit, you descend through woodland to the Ackers Wood railway, crossing the plain below, and following the Macclesfield Canal before climbing up to Mow Cop, where Hugh Bourne launched the Primitive Methodist movement.*

## Cheshire • C ENGLAND

**DISTANCE •** 5½ miles (8.8km)

**TOTAL ASCENT •** 600ft (183m)

**PATHS •** field and woodland paths, lanes and canal towpaths

**TERRAIN •** paths, especially descending to the canal, can be boggy

**GRADIENTS •** a gradual descent, level

towpath and then a steepish ascent to Mow Cop

**REFRESHMENTS •** The Rising Sun, Kent Green, near Scholar Green

**PARK •** National Trust car park at Mow Cop

**OS MAP •** Explorer 258 Stoke-on-Trent & Newcastle-under-Lyme

# Mow Cop and the birth of a new faith

**DIFFICULTY ✲✲**

❶ From the car park, head north, following the Gritstone Way and Mow Cop Trail signs, bearing left after 22yds (20m) on the broad track towards residential Wood Street. Turn right after crossing the road and then immediately left, signed Old Man of Mow.

❷ Take this track, passing the strange pinnacle of the Old Man of Mow on the right. Just before a prominent radio mast, follow a yellow waymark downhill to the left for 656yds (600m), across muddy fields (keep to the left-hand wall), and then steeply down through Roe Park Wood.

❸ Emerge from the woodland at a stile, follow the track through the field past a farm and through a gate to join a wide lane. In 109yds (100m) bear right around Wood Farm to eventually reach a metalled lane, which leads left to the Ackers railway crossing.

❹ Take care crossing the high speed line and enter Yew Tree Lane, turning right in 219yds (200m) at the junction into New Road to reach the canal bridge. Descend to the towpath on the far side of the bridge (No 85) via the steps on the right-hand side, hard against the bridge.

❺ Turn left and follow the canal towpath south for about 1½ miles (2.4km), with the tower of Mow Cop to the left and passing the fine, red-brick Georgian façade of Ramsdell Hall on the other bank.

❻ Just past the Heritage Narrow Boats marina at Kent Green, take the stile on the right before bridge No 87 and turn left on the road.

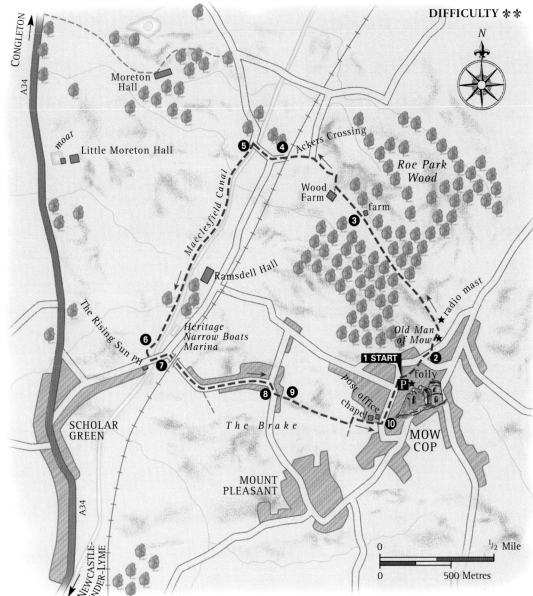

❼ Continue under the railway line and up the hill towards the village of Mount Pleasant.

❽ In 875yds (800m), at the top of the hill, Mount Pleasant Road turns sharp right. After 100yds (91m) take the track on the left (The Brake), signed Brake village.

❾ This soon becomes a footpath which goes straight and steeply up

the hill on an embankment for 547yds (500m), towards Mow Cop village. Emerge on to a rough track and turn left. In 164yds (150m) go right up steps pass the Primitive Methodist Memorial Chapel.

❿ Cross Woodcock Lane, pass the village Post Office and Stores on the left. Turn left into the High Street and return to the car park at Mow Cop in 400yds (366m).

**• DON'T MISS •**

*The **Macclesfield Canal**, part of the famous Cheshire Ring of canals, was begun in 1826, and took only five years to complete. The 28-mile (45km)-long waterway linked the Peak Forest Canal in Marple to the Trent and Mersey Canal at the Hardings Wood Junction.*

1714–1837

**1813** *Pride and Prejudice* (Jane Austen) is published.

**1815** At the Battle of Waterloo, the Duke of Wellington defeats Napoleon Bonaparte, marking the end of the Napoleonic Wars.

**1815** The Corn Laws are passed to regulate prices and imports, causing public outrage as a few landowners profit while the poor starve.

**1820–30** George IV's reign.

**1824** The National Gallery opens.

**1825** The first railway line opens, the Stockton and Darlington.

**1828** Arthur Wellesley, Duke of Wellington, is made Prime Minster.

**1830–37** William IV accedes to the throne, aged 64.

170

# The Dispossessed of Strathnaver

*A walk that recalls the trauma and controversy of the 18th- and 19th-century Highland Clearances*

Between 1785 and 1850 tens of thousands of people were compelled to leave their Highland homelands by a combination of poverty, famine and greedy landlords. It is a period burned into the folk memory of Scotland, and still sparks passionate debate. Highlanders and emigrant communities abroad retain, to this day, ill-feeling against the landlords responsible for the evictions.

However, the greatest contumely is reserved for Elizabeth, Countess of Sutherland and her notorious factor, Patrick Sellar. He ordered countless evictions and personally attended some of the most harrowing, pitilessly ordering the firing of houses still containing old and bedridden people. Sellar rented large tracts of land, continually striving to increase his holdings.

He was a workaholic who studied and practised the latest innovations in agriculture, becoming the largest sheep-farmer in Scotland. Although educated and intelligent, he was, according to the Countess herself, exceedingly greedy and harsh and constantly in dispute with his neighbours, scorning the indigenous population as savages and sheep-stealers. Sellar personally supervised the evictions at Rosal village. As a result he found himself on trial in Inverness early in 1816 for the murder of two people, including an old woman who had died in the Rosal evictions. However, after 15 hours of evidence, a jury of 15 gentlemen found him not guilty. The verdict of Highlanders – then and now – was different. Universally hated in his own lifetime and vilified by history, Patrick Sellar died a wealthy man at the age of 70 in 1851.

The origins of the Clearances were varied and complex. The defeat of the Jacobites at Culloden, the government's determination to prevent future risings by destroying the clan system, and general demographic changes caused by agrarian reform all contributed. The tenant population of the Highland estates was not capable of producing the income required for the increasingly expensive lifestyles of landlords who spent most of the year in London. During this period of the great agricultural improvers

were introducing new crops, new methods of farming and machinery. Wool prices were high and Highland landlords saw sheep-farming as a way of maximising income from their estates. The rough ground of the straths was ideal for huge sheep runs, but incompatible with the subsistence farming of the scattered population.

Between 1807 and 1821 some 10,000 people were removed from Strathnaver and elsewhere on the Sutherland estate. They were relocated on marginal land by the coast, where the crofts were kept deliberately small so that people were obliged to gather kelp for low wages to sustain their families. When the lucrative kelp industry collapsed, the coastal crofting communities were destitute. Many emigrated to the New World. With failures of the potato crop in 1836 and 1846, even greater numbers left. Today the straths are empty and there is no longer money to be made from sheep. Looking at this forbidding and abandoned land it is difficult to imagine the thriving communities who once lived here.

ABOVE: *Many of the dispossessed tenants were relocated to marginal land by the coast.*

BELOW: *Piles of stones are the only evidence that remains of the tenants who once lived in Strathnaver.*

**ABOUT • STRATHNAVER**

*This walk is a reminder of the brutal clearances of Strathnaver (1785–1850). Ten thousand tenants were evicted from Strathnaver by Elizabeth, Countess of Sutherland and her ruthless factor, Patrick Sellar, to make way for intensive sheep-farming.*

**Highland • SCOTLAND**

**DISTANCE •** 5 miles (8km)

**TOTAL ASCENT •** 50ft (15m)

**PATHS •** mostly good but can be a little muddy in wet weather

**TERRAIN •** metalled road, forest roads, moorland and forest trails

**GRADIENTS •** mainly flat with a few slight gradients

**REFRESHMENTS •** none on the route; seasonal coffee shop near the Strathnaver museum at Bettyhill

**PARK •** off the road at the corner of the junction of the B873 and the B871 at Syre

**OS MAP •** Pathfinder 64 Mid Strathnaver

# The Higland Clearances at Strathnaver

❶ From Syre church head south along the B873. Look out for the memorial to Donald MacLeod on the right-hand side of the road. Rosal village is across the river from here but hidden by the forest.

❷ Continue along the road for a mile (1.6km), then cross the river via two anglers' bridges. Take great care when crossing, particularly in wet weather conditions. A forest road runs parallel to the River Naver but access is prevented by a deer fence.

❸ Turn left and continue to follow the track beside the deer fence for about ¾ mile (1.2km) until you reach a stile. Cross the fence and walk up the fire break to reach the forest road.

❹ Turn left on to the road and continue until a large, green waymarker indicates the entrance to Rosal village. Leave the road and turn right on a track through the trees leading to a gated enclosure. Through the gate is the Rosal village.

**• DON'T MISS •**

*Strathnaver Museum in the former St Columba's Parish Church at Bettyhill, some 12 miles (19km) north of Syre, tells the story of the Sutherland clearances in graphic detail, featuring models and artefacts from the period. While you are at the museum look out for the intricately sculptured Pictish Cross, located in the church graveyard, which dates from about AD 800.*

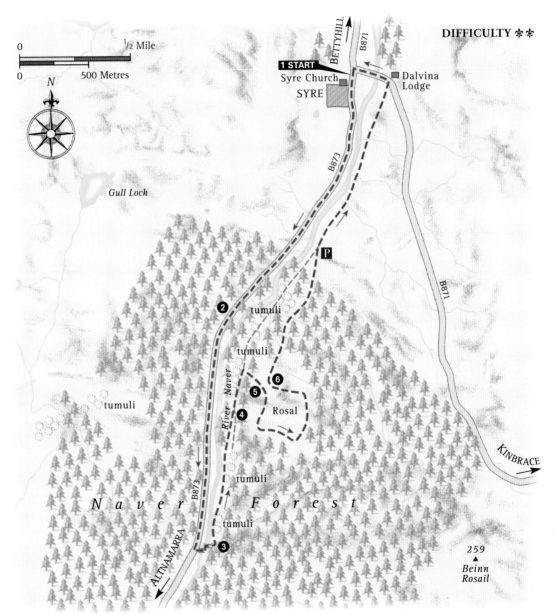

**DIFFICULTY ✱ ✱**

❺ Walk clockwise round the village following the numbered interpretation boards, which tell the story of the clearances. (At the top cairn turn around and shout in the direction of Beinn Rosail and listen to the echo.) Continue on the trail, then leave through the enclosure gate and retrace the path for 20 yds (18m) to the right.

❻ Follow a very faint track uphill and into the forest, where it becomes a well waymarked trail.

When it rejoins the forest road turn right and go through a gate. Continue to the junction with the B871, turn left and return to the start and your car.

**1832**

**1832** The Great Reform Bill raises the electorate from 478,000 to 814,000 men. The reforms are moderate but it is the first of a series of political reforms which culminate in a one-man (and eventually also one-woman) one-vote democracy.

**1834**

**1834** In Tolpuddle, Dorset, six agricultural labourers form a 'friendly society' but are promptly arrested and sentenced to transportation. The action provokes an outcry and the 'martyrs' are pardoned two years later.

**1834**

**1834** The Houses of Parliament are destroyed by fire.

**1835** The Municipal Reform Act brings in local government.

**1837** Charles Dickens publishes *Oliver Twist*.

# Anglesey's Masterpiece of Engineering

*Thomas Telford's impressive Menai Suspension Bridge, spanning the notorious waters of the Menai Straits*

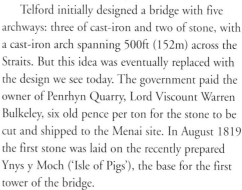

**GEORGIAN**

**BIRTH OF INDUSTRY**

Situated on the southerly shores of Anglesey, the town of Menai Bridge was once a busy port with many ships regularly passing through the Straits. Being on the road from Holyhead to London, its importance steadily grew. But unscrupulous ferrymen, who charged excessively to carry passengers across this stretch of water, finally prompted a decision to span the Straits with a bridge: a very difficult task in itself, as spring tides and whirlpools were to prove dangerous obstacles.

A proposal in 1776 of an embankment on each side and a bridge in the middle, and a suggestion of a wooden viaduct nine years later, were dismissed because of high costs. Later, in 1810, a committee was established to inquire into the condition of the roads from Shrewsbury to Holyhead and the difficult task of spanning the Straits. Thomas Telford's impressive engineering feats led to his being asked to report on the most effective solution and he was duly appointed principal engineer for the Menai Bridge.

Born in Westerkirk, Scotland in 1757, Thomas Telford was a qualified stonemason and self-taught engineer, whose construction works in Shropshire and on the Ellesmere canal earned him a high-profile reputation. He was responsible for many outstanding engineering exploits, including the Pontcysyllte Aqueduct in the Dee Valley, Conwy Suspension Bridge, the Gota Canal in Sweden, St Katherine Docks in London, and almost 1,000 miles (1,600km) of roadway (including the main road between London and Holyhead).

Telford initially designed a bridge with five archways: three of cast-iron and two of stone, with a cast-iron arch spanning 500ft (152m) across the Straits. But this idea was eventually replaced with the design we see today. The government paid the owner of Penrhyn Quarry, Lord Viscount Warren Bulkeley, six old pence per ton for the stone to be cut and shipped to the Menai site. In August 1819 the first stone was laid on the recently prepared Ynys y Moch ('Isle of Pigs'), the base for the first tower of the bridge.

The seven archways were completed in the autumn of 1824 and ready to house the massive chains that would support the roadway. A raft was built, 6ft (2m) wide and 400ft (122m) long, to carry the first chain from its mooring at Treborth Mill to the main towers of the bridge. Once the raft was in place, blocks were fitted to the chain, and 32 men lifted it up and over the Anglesey tower, allowing the raft to float away. This was an immense achievement, for the first time connecting Anglesey to the mainland of Wales. Over the next ten weeks, all 15 chains were put into place, and on 9 July 1825 a huge ceremony took place to celebrate.

The opening ceremony was held on Monday 30 January 1826, and at 1.35am the Royal London and Holyhead Mail Coach, pulled by elegant grey horses, and carrying mail bags from Dublin, crossed the Menai Suspension Bridge for the first time.

ABOVE: *Ships passing under the Menai Bridge and Tubular Bridge.*

BELOW: *The elegant simplicity of the seven-arched Menai Bridge, designed by Thomas Telford, which opened in 1826.*

**ABOUT • MENAI BRIDGE**

*The Menai Suspension Bridge (1826) was considered a feat of modern engineering. Started in 1819, Thomas Telford's design consisted of seven archways which supported the massive roadway, linking Anglesey to mainland Wales for the first time.*

### Isle of Anglesey • WALES

**DISTANCE •** 5 miles (8km)

**TOTAL ASCENT •** 104ft (32m)

**PATHS •** some minor roads; paths can become muddy and slippery in wet weather

**TERRAIN •** minor roads through village and farmland

**GRADIENTS •** roads mostly flat or slightly uphill; paths can be steep in places

**REFRESHMENTS •** Liverpool Arms Hotel and The Mostyn Arms public houses; tea rooms on Cadnant Road towards town centre

**PARK •** Coed Cyrnol car park, behind the Jade Cantonese restaurant in Menai Bridge; ample car parking

**OS MAP •** Outdoor Leisure 17 Snowdonia – Snowden & Conwy Valley

# Crossing the Menai Bridge

**❶** Leave the car park down a small flight of steps and turn right on to a tarmac path. Gently descending, this soon forks. Straight ahead is Church Island; to the left a broad promenade now runs parallel with the Straits. Continue along what is now a road through the arches of the Menai Suspension Bridge. Turn right immediately before the Liverpool Arms Hotel and walk on, bearing left into St George's Road. Pass The Mostyn Arms, go through the no entry signs and veer left.

**❷** At the T-junction, turn right on Cadnant Road and, after 273yds (250m), cross to pass through a kissing gate. Ascend a waymarked path between the houses, cross the roadway part way up and follow the footpath sign carefully. An uneven path eventually leads to a stone stile. Turn left.

**❸** After 22yds (20m) turn right on to a tarmac road, which later becomes a grassy, waymarked track. Go through a gate and continue along the right-hand field edge and through the hand gate. Go straight ahead towards the single tree and through the hand gate in the right-hand corner ahead. Follow the right-hand hedge, going through two more hand gates, then go down steps.

**❹** Turn right along the roadside verge and take the next turning on the right (signed Llandegfan and Beaumaris). Follow a surfaced road and in ¹⁄₂ mile (800m) turn right on to a waymarked track.

**❺** At the end of the track, just before the house, go through the gate on the left (waymark arrow on fence). After passing through

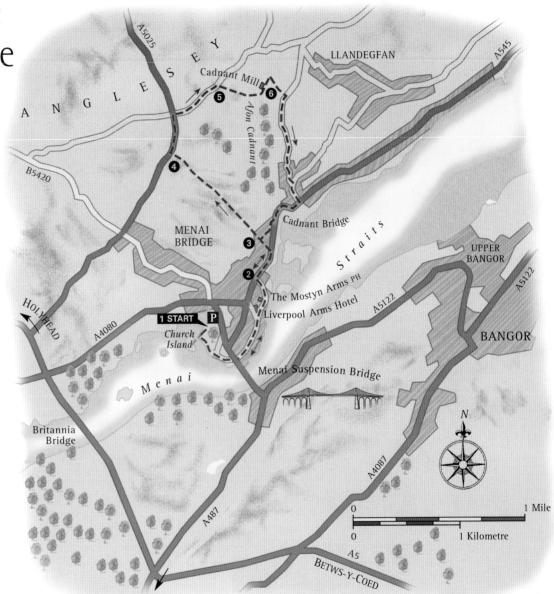

**DIFFICULTY ❀❀**

three small paddocks, head for a wooden stile on the left-hand side of the field. In the next field cross another stile half-way down the right-hand field edge. Descend a narrow path towards the left, cross a stream by a rock bridge and turn left through a wooden gate ahead.

**❻** Pass Cadnant Mill on the left and, bearing right at the waymark sign, continue through the

farmyard to a T-junction. Bear right and continue for ¹⁄₂ mile (800m). At another T-junction, bear right to join the main road after 328yds (300m). Turn right, cross Cadnant Bridge, immediately turn right and 11yds (10m) along on the left, head along a waymarked path. The path gently rises, passing a large house on the right. Bear left here through a break in the hedge. Continue along

the path then, as the it veers right, turn left on to a narrower path. Go down to Cadnant Road again at the kissing gate and retrace your steps to the car park.

### • DON'T MISS •

*Near Menai Bridge is **Church Island**, the 6th-century home and refuge of Prince Tysilio, the son of Brochfael Ysgythrog.*

PIMPERNEL. MORRIS & Cº

THE IRONM
UNIVERSAL ENGINEER &
METAL TRADES ADVERTISER
SEPTEMBER 30TH 1911
Nº 1976    VOL CXXXVI

Charles Dickens

Power Looms.

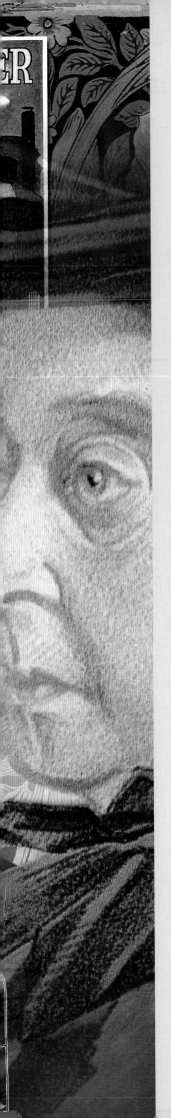

*Queen Victoria's reign saw the British Empire at the peak of its influence and confidence, extending so far around the globe that 'the sun never set' over its territories. This was also the era when Britain emerged as the world's leading industrial power.*

# VICTORIAN

## 1837–1901

# Age of Optimism

The Machine Age gathered speed in the 19th century; factories and mills became the focus for new communities, formed higgledy-piggledy wherever there was the promise of work. Cheap housing was thrown up and families at the bottom of the industrial heap lived in terrible squalor. In his novel *Sybil,* or 'The Two Nations', future prime minister Benjamin Disraeli described a society divided into 'haves' and 'have-nots'. The misery and poverty of the rapidly expanding industrial cities was also vividly documented by Charles Dickens and Elizabeth Gaskell. Throughout the century, the ballooning urban centres were worlds of extremes. Pompous civic buildings and monuments, neo-Gothic libraries, schools, churches and railway stations typi-fied the self-assurance of the age, while back-to-back houses and belching chimney stacks characterised the working-class areas. A pronounced prudery and outward piety in the middle-class drawing rooms contrasted with the increasingly popular and raucous music halls and a thriving trade in prostitution.

In the face of glaring inequalities the Chartist movement called for a 'people's charter' guaranteeing a number of democratic rights: universal male suffrage; a secret ballot, and salaries for MPs, to make parliament accessible to those without private incomes. The road to reform, however, was to be long, slow and piecemeal.

### GREAT EXPECTATIONS

Despite the problems of working and living condi-tions, poor sanitation (leading to several bouts of cholera) and some-times violent unrest, Victorian Britain was proud of its achievements and of the progress made in industry and science.

In 1851 the Great Exhibition opened at Crystal Palace, in London's Hyde Park. The brain-child of Victoria's beloved prince consort, Albert, this was a showcase of international crafts, inventions and cultures, dominated by 7,000 British exhibits. It attracted over a million visitors a month, and with the funds generated, Albert oversaw the establishment of the Victoria and Albert Museum.

In 1861 Prince Albert died of typhoid fever and Victoria entered a period of profound and protracted grief, closeting herself away from all public appearance and ceremony. Her prolonged absence from the public stage provoked mockery and complaint from the press and public, especially when her manservant John Brown was deemed to be too close to the Queen – or 'Mrs Brown' – for comfort. Some of the anti-monar-chy sentiments of the time took a more extreme form and there was more than one suspected anarchist plot; other threats to the establishment were perceived in the Fenian Movement, calling for Irish independence.

Meanwhile the Liberal government of William Ewart Gladstone ushered in a stream of reforms to cope with the changing face of Britain. A secret ballot was introduced; schooling was extended; and attempts were made to address the 'Irish Question', though attempts to introduce Home Rule in Ireland fell flat.

As the 20th century loomed, new discoveries encouraged the development of a consumer society. The electric telegraph made communi-cations faster and wider. Photography, cinema and gramophones heralded a new kind of mass enter-tainment. Motor cars and bicycles began to appear on the roads, and at the turn of the century powered flight became a serious possibility.

Victoria celebrated her Gold and then Diamond Jubilee – to huge popular acclaim. By the time she died, in 1901, her reign had seen Britain transformed beyond all recognition.

### HISTORIC SITES

**Palace of Westminster, London:** Pugin's neo-Gothic home for the 'Mother of Parliaments'.

**Osborne House, Hampshire:** the superb home of Queen Victoria and Prince Albert in the Isle of Wight.

**Saltaire, West Yorks:** purpose-built mill town created by Sir Titus Salt.

**Forth Rail Bridge, Lothian:** world's first major steel bridge (1890).

**Blackpool Tower, Lancs:** opened in 1894 at the height of the seaside holiday craze.

ABOVE: *Thomas Telford*
*(1757–1834).*

**1837** Victoria is crowned Queen of England at the age of 18. Her reign lasts for almost 64 years.

**1838** The first camera is developed, called a daguerreotype; George Eastman develops the first photographic film five years later.

**1840** The penny post is introduced; along with the telegraph, it revolutionises communication.

**1845–8** The Irish potato crop is wiped out by blight, and hundreds of thousands die of starvation. Landlords evict families unable to

pay their rent, and masses emigrate to America and England in search of work.

**1846** The Corn Laws are repealed, allowing imported food to compete with British crops.

VICTORIAN

AGE OF OPTIMISM

# Climbing Neptune's Staircase

*The engineering wonders and dramatic scenery of the Caledonian Canal*

Canals revolutionised Britain's transport system in the early 19th century. By the time of Queen Victoria's accession, more than 2,000 miles (3,219km) of inland waterways had been constructed, and even after the arrival of the railways this extraordinary network, which connected coal mines, factories and ports, remained the most efficient means of moving heavy goods such as timber, coal and stone. Most canals were designed for the use of horse-drawn 'narrow-boats', but some, designated ship-canals, were wide enough for ocean-going vessels. Of these, the most ambitious and spectacular was the Caledonian Canal.

Unusually, the canal was funded by the government and built for rather special reasons. Although not finally completed until 1847, the project had been started more than 40 years before, during the Napoleonic Wars. French privateers were a constant threat off Scotland's north coast, and the inland waterway through the Great Glen was intended as a safe short-cut between the North Sea and the Atlantic. Furthermore, the project would provide young Highlanders with work and teach them skills much needed in the empire's far-flung colonies. Lastly, like a Roman road, the canal would be a symbol, representing modern commerce and the power of central government in a region where the Jacobite Uprising was still a living memory.

The waterway runs 60 miles (97km) from Banavie to Inverness, although two-thirds of this distance is through a series of existing lochs: Loch Lochy, Loch Oich and Loch Ness. The 22 miles (35km) of true canal, including in particular the stretch this walk explores, are, however, an unparalleled example of Georgian civil engineering. When work began in 1803 the architect and engineer Thomas Telford faced problems that had never been encountered on canals in lowland Britain. Just

within the first 12 miles (19km), from Banavie to Loch Lochy, he had to carry the canal along a steep hillside above torrential burns and raise substantial ships from sea level to a height of 93ft (28m). The canal was, supposedly, to be finished within seven years at a cost of £474,000. In fact it took 19 years to open and was not finally completed until 1847 at a total cost of over £1.3 million. By then Napoleon was history, the Highlands were depopulated and railways had made the canals redundant.

The walk takes in the canal's most impressive feature: a flight of eight locks known as Neptune's Staircase. Each lock is large enough to take a 150ft (49m) ship, or, as is more usual nowadays, a flotilla of small pleasure cruisers. Until the relatively recent boom in the popularity of boating, the canal was largely used for local transport of heavy goods such as grain or timber and, most of all, by fishing boats. It is said that on occasions the entire Oban fleet would sail 500-strong up the canal, forming an unbroken line from Banavie to Inverness. You will certainly not see such activity today as you walk along the towpath. The great canal is now a quiet backwater and although on rare occasions you may be overtaken by some palatial private yacht or glamourous tallship, your reveries are more likely to be disturbed only by the putter of a passing dinghy. But while listening to the birdsong and enjoying the inspiring views, bear in mind that, just 200 years ago, this amazing feat of engineering was a wonder of the modern world.

*Left: Neptune's Staircase which consists of eight locks.*

BELOW: *Telford's Caledonian Canal with Ben Nevis in the backdrop; it was to the masterpiece of his engineering career.*

**ABOUT • CALEDONIAN CANAL**

*Of all the canals built during this era the Caledonian Canal, designed by Thomas Telford and completed in 1847, is undoubtedly the most impressive. Its 60 miles (97km) length includes an impressive flight of eight locks known as Neptune's Staircase.*

## Highland • SCOTLAND

**DISTANCE •** 5 miles (8km)

**TOTAL ASCENT •** 64ft (19m)

**PATHS •** firm, dry path

**TERRAIN •** waterside and woodland

**GRADIENTS •** level, apart from one short descent

**REFRESHMENTS •** hotels in Banavie, Corpach and Fort William

**PARK •** Banavie Station or at Neptune's Staircase and cross canal by lock gate

**OS MAP •** Outdoor Leisure 38 Ben Nevis & Glen Coe

# Telford's Caledonian Canal

**❶** From the car park at Banavie Station, cross the main road (A830) and go through a metal gate on to the canal towpath. On your left is Neptune's Staircase, a flight of eight locks that raises the canal 64ft (19m) in height. Above the locks, yachts lie moored in a sheltered basin.

**❷** Follow the towpath, with the canal on your left, for approximately 2½ miles (4km). The ground drops steeply to the right and through gaps in the woodland there are fine views of the Ben Nevis range and of Inverlochy Castle Hotel, a Gothic mansion that is now one of Scotland's most exclusive hotels.

**❸** The canal and towpath bridge a stream, with some houses visible below. Continue for 20yds (18m), then turn right down a path between the trees. Beyond the gate at the bottom, turn sharp right to follow the stream through the tunnel under the canal and past a weir. Reaching an

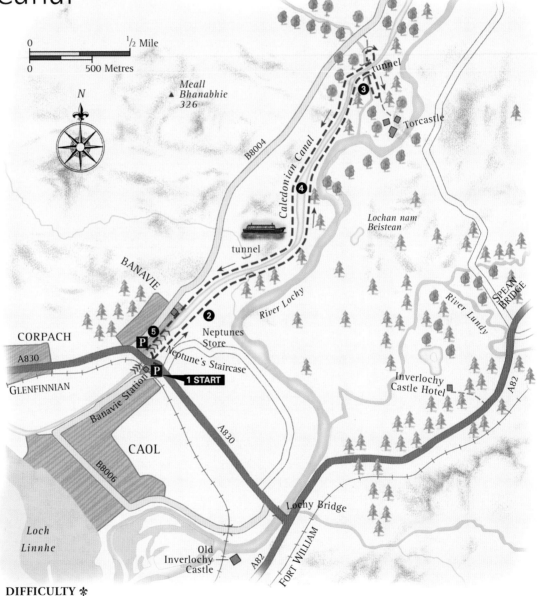

**DIFFICULTY ✤**

intersection, turn sharp right to return to the canal and right again along the towpath.

**❹** On the return walk there are fine views along Loch Linnhe to the Corran Narrows and of the 4,406ft (1,343m) summit of Ben

Nevis, Britain's highest mountain. The town of Fort William, on the east shore of the loch, was still a military garrison at the time of the canal's construction.

**❺** Pass Neptune's Store, a small post office and shop, offering

tourist information, toilets and facilities for yachtsmen (limited winter opening). The bow-windowed cottages overlooking Neptune's Staircase date from the early 1800s. Cross the canal by the lock gates to return to the car park.

**1848**

**1848** Unrest by the Chartists who demand votes for all men.

**1851** The Great Exhibition in Hyde Park, housed in a huge cast-iron and glass crystal palace, is a resounding success attracting six million visitors. The profits are used

**1851**

to establish the Science, Natural History and Geology Museums and the Victoria and Albert Museum.

**1854–6** Britain and France join forces against Russia in the Crimean War over the Tsar's bid to control Turkey and the Black Sea.

**1854**

**1854** Florence Nightingale and 38 nurses travel to Crimea to care for the wounded.

**1855** Photographs showing the graphic reality of the Crimean War are taken by Roger Fenton, founder of the Royal Photographic Society.

# The Wool Mills of Marsden

*A visit to the hill town of Marsden to discover the effects of the Industrial Revolution on the North*

**VICTORIAN**

**AGE OF OPTIMISM**

Grim gritstone moors, lanced by deep-sided valleys that house dark streams and rivers, are the bedrock of West Yorkshire's textile world. It was a sombre scene in the 18th and 19th centuries, and focused on one general pursuit – textiles – but with considerable variety of application. Here, the weaving of cloth began in the 14th century, using wool brought in on packhorses to the weavers' houses, which were part living quarters, part factory.

This walk begins in the old hill town of Marsden, tours the valley and crosses many of the ancient highways used by the packhorse trains and the hardy men who guided them across the often inhospitable moors. The elevated nature of the walk provides a superb view of the valley, the town and its terraced rows of mill houses and multi-storeyed mills.

In the early part of the 18th century, England's woollen industry looked destined to be shared between Yorkshire and Lancashire. However the entry of cotton imports into Lancashire ports coincided with the advent of the Industrial Revolution in the form of power machinery, better able to work cotton than wool. Cotton, as a result, became the dominant industry in Lancashire, and wool the prevailing force to the east of the Pennines.

By the start of the 19th century, Marsden was heading for a period of prosperity it could never have imagined. Textile mills, many of which can still be seen in and around the town, sprang up everywhere. Demand for labour is said to have been so great that orphaned children were transported to Marsden from London to spend 13 hours a day working in the mills. During World War I, one of the Marsden mills had a thousand looms operating almost non-stop to produce blankets for British troops.

Not everyone saw the new machinery as a distinct improvement, however, and during the early 19th century organised bands of handicraftsmen rioted, calling for the destruction of the textile machinery that was displacing them. The movement began in Nottinghamshire and soon spread to Yorkshire, Lancashire, Derbyshire, and Leicestershire. Known as the 'Ludds', or 'Luddites', their leader, real or imaginary, was known as King (or General) Ludd, after a probably mythical Ned Ludd. They eschewed violence against persons and often enjoyed local support, but in 1812 a band of Luddites was shot down under the orders of a threatened employer named Horsfall (who was afterwards murdered in reprisal). The government instituted harsh repressive measures which culminated in a mass trial at York in 1813, and a large number of hangings and transportations of the gang members.

Back on track, the prosperity of Yorkshire and its mill towns grew, and so too did the living standards of many of the local people. Donations of land and money from philanthropic mill owners provided Marsden with a fire service, an ambulance, a fine park, sportsfields, its own church, dedicated to St Bartholomew, and many town improvements. When the depression of the 1930s led to short-time working and hardship, one of Marsden's most benevolent mill-owners shot himself. On the day of his funeral, the whole town mourned.

ABOVE: *Marsden Canal Museum on the Huddersfield Narrow Canal. The canal played a vital part in the logistics of the wool industry.*

LEFT: *Luddites attacking machinery that they believe will take their jobs in a textile factory.*

**ABOUT • MARSDEN**

*The rise of the textile industry brought great prosperity to a number of towns during the 19th century, including Marsden. The effect this had on the landscape is evident as you walk from the town and view its rows of terraced houses and mills.*

## West Yorkshire • N ENGLAND

**DISTANCE** • 6 miles (9.6km)

**TOTAL ASCENT** • 920ft (280m)

**PATHS** • tracks, moorland paths and country lanes

**TERRAIN** • rough moorland, pastures and farmland

**GRADIENTS** • variable, steep in places

**REFRESHMENTS** • pubs and cafés in Marsden

**PARK** • parking places in Argyle Street, also plenty of roadside parking

**OS MAP** • Outdoor Leisure 21 South Pennines

# Marsden: a West Yorkshire wool town

❶ From Argyle Street turn into Station Road. Climb to the station, turn right into Reddisher Road, and left into Spring Head Lane, a steep track rising to Inglenook. Turn right along a vehicle track to a radio mast. Turn left up a narrow, enclosed path, climbing steeply to a horizontal track at a top gate.

**DIFFICULTY** ✤ ✤

❷ Turn left and follow the track behind a farmhouse. A short way on, when the track forks, go left, descending. The track shortly turns right. Keep following the main track, which later becomes surfaced for a while, descending steeply. When the track next forks, just past Hey Cottage, bear right.

The route is obvious, enclosed by fences or walls. Go past farm buildings on the left and keep on the track until the next junction (waymarked). Turn right, soon leaving the lane for a walled path that breaks out on to the hillside.

❸ Keep forward on an obvious grassy path to a gate, beyond which it continues as a waymarked route across rough pasture, passing a derelict farmhouse to descend into a stream gully. Cross the stream, turn left, and climb beside a wall, go through a gate on to a

narrow lane. Turn left, continue to a bridge opposite the entrance to Hey Green Hotel. Cross the bridge and take a rising lane to the A62.

❹ Cross the A-road to a step stile, beyond which a rough path rises, right, on to Marsden Moor Estate. At an estate signpost, bear left, climbing across the hillside, below rock outcrops and through low, hummocky terrain.

❺ The route continues, always parallel with overhead power lines, and on to the Pule Hill part of Marsden Moor. Aim for the lower of two prominent ventilation shafts, beyond which an improving path strikes across the moor, finally, as it approaches the Carriage House pub, moving away from the power lines.

❻ When the path reaches a moorland road, turn left until, 80yds (73m) before a cattle grid, where you turn left into Old Mount Road. Almost immediately branch left on to an access track signed Hades Farm.

❼ Follow the farm track for 547yds (500m), past two paths to the right and branch right on to a grassy track beside the wall. Descend to a gate, beyond which the track, overgrown with rushes, continues between dilapidated walls. The distinct track continues towards a farm. Just before the farm, bear left, descending steeply beside a wall to a step stile below.

❽ Cross the stile and bear left across a hill slope, soon walking beside a wall until you meet a step-stile in a corner of a wall. Cross the stile, turn right and descend to meet the A62 again. Turn right and, near the church, turn left into Towngate. Take the first turning on the right, cross a bridge and turn left into Argyle Street to return to the start point of the walk.

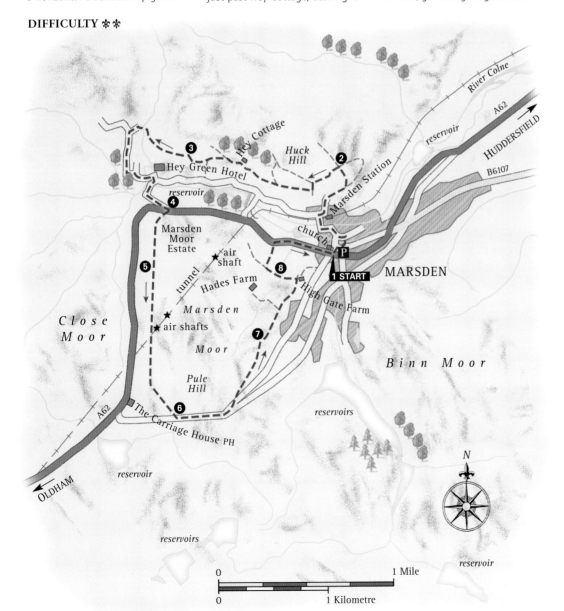

0    1 Mile

0    1 Kilometre

**1857**

**1857–8** The Indian Mutiny breaks out against British rule in India after there is widespread famine in the country. The mutiny is aggressively suppressed by British troops, who massacre thousands of Indian men, women and children in retaliation.

**1859**

**1859** Charles Darwin's thought-provoking publication *On The Origin of Species by Means of Natural Selection* causes outrage among traditionalists. Science and religion seem finally to have reached a parting of the ways.

**1861**

**1861** The death of Victoria's consort, Prince Albert, leaves her inconsolably grief-stricken and she withdraws from public life.

**1869** John Sainsbury opens his first dairy shop.

# The Darker Side of Cornwall

*An exploration of the rise and fall of the 19th- and 20th-century tin-mining industry of West Penwith*

**VICTORIAN**

**AGE OF OPTIMISM**

The popular tourist image of Cornwall is one of brightly painted cottages overlooking harbours filled with fishing boats, of window-boxes and ice-creams, of sandy beaches and long, sunny days. The real story of Cornish life throughout the centuries, particularly in the far western extremities of the county, couldn't be more different. This fascinatingly varied walk through the stark, rugged, 'no frills' coastal landscape of West Penwith, taking in the abandoned mineworkings of Geevor, Levant and Botallack, brings you face to face with reality. This is a bleak yet beautiful place: villages here are grey and utilitarian, fields small and divided by stone 'hedges', and the environment is harsh: all testimony to an area where life has been – and still is – tough.

Cornish miners were renowned throughout the world, and over the years many hundreds have emigrated to work abroad due to the fluctuating fortunes of the tin industry at home. Geevor Tin Mine was the last surviving metal mine in this area, and was worked for around 2,000 years until it finally closed in 1990. The main underground area of the mine is now flooded to sea level. Today the Geevor Heritage Centre forms the largest preserved mine site in the UK, and is run by the Trevithick Trust. The walk passes through the main area of Victorian and earlier workings above Trewellard Zawn, where you can see the remains of old settling tanks, chimneys and buildings, and where you can still pick up little pieces of tin. There's an extraordinary feeling of drama here, as you wander through the remnants of powerful Victorian industrial architecture, stamped on a natural and magnificent Cornish coastline. In the 19th century the mine was known as East Levant; it closed in 1840 and re-opened in 1951 under the name of North Levant, and continued with only minor interruptions until

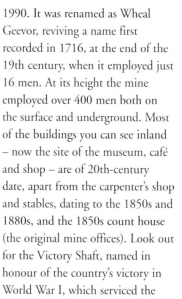

ABOVE: *Botallack tin mine on the rough and windy West Penwith Cornish coast.*

ABOVE: *Miners sinking a shaft in a tin mine.*

1990. It was renamed as Wheal Geevor, reviving a name first recorded in 1716, at the end of the 19th century, when it employed just 16 men. At its height the mine employed over 400 men both on the surface and underground. Most of the buildings you can see inland – now the site of the museum, café and shop – are of 20th-century date, apart from the carpenter's shop and stables, dating to the 1850s and 1880s, and the 1850s count house (the original mine offices). Look out for the Victory Shaft, named in honour of the country's victory in World War I, which serviced the underground workings stretching far out to sea.

Further along the coast is the Levant mine, closed in 1930. The beam engine, restored by the Trevithick Society, is now operating again, and is the oldest surviving engine in Cornwall. Owned by the National Trust, there are regular steaming days throughout the year, barring November to March. You can experience the sights, sounds and smells of working life here when the engine is running, and the Levant mining disaster exhibition also offers a dramatic insight into the dangers of life underground.

BELOW: *The austere architecture of the Levant mine buildings near Cape Cornwall.*

**ABOUT • GEEVOR**

In this walk you will discover another side of scenic Cornwall — its 2000-year-old history as a tin mining area, which was at its peak during the Victorian era. While you're there visit the Geevor Heritage Centre, the largest preserved mine site in Britain.

**Cornwall • SW ENGLAND**

**DISTANCE** • 5 miles (8km)

**TOTAL ASCENT** • 246ft (75m)

**PATHS** • undulating coast path, gritty tracks and field paths

**TERRAIN** • coastal cliffs and farmland

**GRADIENTS** • some non-strenuous ascents and descents on coast path; inland paths fairly level

**REFRESHMENTS** • Queen's Arms, Botallack; The North Inn and The Radjel Inn in Pendeen; café at Geevor Tin Mine

**PARK** • free parking at Pendeen lighthouse, signed off the B3306 at Pendeen (St Just to St Ives road)

**OS MAP** • Explorer 102 Land's End, Penzance & St Ives

# The tin mines of Cornwall

❶ Walk inland up the lane for ¼ mile (400m). Opposite Enys, No 6 of the row of whitewashed cottages, turn right signed Cape Cornwall. Follow the marked path downhill, descend stone steps to cross a stream, then up and over two stiles to a wooden bench at the top of a steep slope (views of the tin workings ahead). Follow coast path signs through the workings, ignoring signs to Geevor.

❷ Continue along the coast path to pass Levant Beam Engine, right. Walk straight through the car park and along a gritty track, following a coast path sign, to meet and walk by a wall, left.

❸ Keep on the coast path for ¾ mile (1.2km), ignoring tracks leading inland, to reach Roscommon Cottage and then the remains of Botallack mine, marked by two big chimney stacks (left and right), and a huge metal headworks gantry, left. Just before the gantry, at a coast path sign, bear right on the narrow path and descend. In 50yds (46m) reach a flat area with views down to the restored engine houses of the Crowns mine. Return to the track.

❹ Continue ahead on the main route and in a few yards pass Botallack Count House Workshop. Continue to Botallack Manor Farm, left. Just beyond the farmhouse, where the lane bends right, turn left (right of way, not signed) along a grassy path to the right of the entrance to farmyard. Continue for a few yards by a stone hedge on the right, then join a track. In 300yds (274m) emerge between stone hedges, bear left and descend gently. A solitary granite

chimney stack lies ahead. Ignoring side tracks, keep on the main track for 400yds (366m) to reach the entrance to a field.

❺ Go through the entrance, turn right, go up stone steps and over a stile. Walk along the top of the next field, which you leave between two walls. Walk round the top edge of the next field (houses and buildings, right); keep on to cross the stone bank (right) and cross the next field, keeping the wall on your right. Cross a wooden stile, a track and a stone stile, to join a narrow path.

❻ Turn left. The path joins a track. Turn right then keep right at a junction to meet Levant Road and turn right. Just past the 30mph sign at Hillside, turn left by

Pentrew and follow the lane straight on past Merivale House, left. Keep straight on through the farm. The lane becomes a track, then a narrow path, which you follow to pass Geevor Tin Mine. The path ends at a T-junction with a huge boulder, left. Go up and over the bank ahead and walk downhill (wire fence, right) to rejoin the coast path at the Levant/Geevor signpost (Point ❷).

❼ Turn right, retrace your steps along the coast path to your car.

**DIFFICULTY** ❋❋

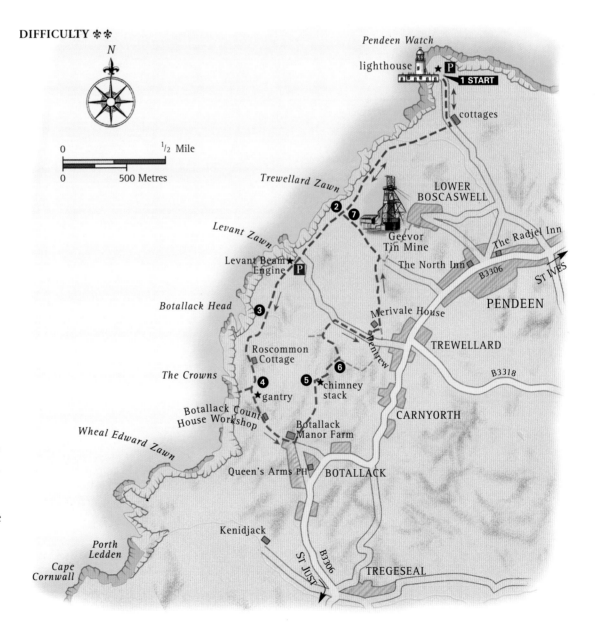

**1861**

**1861–65** American civil war breaks out between the abolitionists of the northern states and the slave masters of the southern states.

**1863** The mass production of cars by Henry Ford begins in America.

**1867**

**1867** Doctor Barnardo opens his first children's home in Stepney.

**1868–74** Gladstone is elected Prime Minster.

**1870** Primary education is made compulsory.

**1872**

**1872** The first Welsh University opens at Aberystwyth.

**1874** Disraeli begins his second term as Prime Minster.

**VICTORIAN**

**AGE OF OPTIMISM**

# A Poet's Lincolnshire Garden

*From the flat plains to the gentle pastures around Somersby, birthplace of one of the greatest poets of the Victorian age*

ABOVE: *Poet Laureate, Alfred, Lord Tennyson (1809–92).*

Lincolnshire has the reputation of being flat and uninspiring, yet from the ploughed fields that seem to stretch to infinity rise the chalk uplands known as the Lincolnshire Wolds. The Meridian line of 0 degrees longitude passes through these gently rolling hills before it strikes south. Aside from the odd car on minor roads, and the rumbling of a tractor, little has changed since the birth of Alfred Lord Tennyson in 1809, at Somersby, a village with a few houses, set at the southern end of the Wolds.

Tennyson was one of 11 children born to George and Elizabeth. He began writing poetry at the age of eight and in 1827 entered Cambridge University. There he became close friends with Arthur Hallam, another brilliant Victorian scholar, who died aged just 22. Arthur's death had a profound effect on Tennyson, prompting him to write *In Memoriam*, regarded as one of his greatest poems.

In 1842, on publication of his works, *Poems*, Tennyson gained popularity and by 1850 he was was

made Poet Laureate, counting Queen Victoria and William Gladstone among his admirers. His reputation as a poet was assured but Tennyson, a shy man, did not enjoy the fame. In 1853, Tennyson and his wife, Emily Sellwood, moved to the Isle of Wight and despite being hounded by admirers, his lyrical poetry continued to flow. Some of his best known poems today are: *Idylls of the King* (dedicated to Prince Albert); *The Lady of Shallott*, and *Ulysses*. After a short illness, Tennyson died in 1892; he is buried in Westminster Abbey.

This walk leads you through the countryside captured in *In Memoriam*:

> *Calm and deep peace on this high wold,*
> *And on these dews that drench the furze…*

Following in Tennyson's footsteps, the route takes you through the village of Somersby, with its Dutch gabled houses, to Tennyson's birthplace, a rambling old rectory fronted by a row of rounded yews, now a private house. However, the walk passes close enough for a view of the windows where the poet sat as he worked. Opposite is the church, with a simple tribute to Somersby's famous son and a bronze bust before the altar. Nothing is overdone: the poet's varied and imaginative work speaks volumes. From the church you can, if you wish, detour a mile (1.6km) to Bag Enderby, where Tennyson's father moved to become rector.

Depending on which season you choose to do this walk, you may find that parts of the route are across ploughed fields that churn into mud in wet weather. The latter section, en route to 14th-century Tetford church, crosses stiles and filters through meadows. The walk begins and ends at The White Hart Inn, parts of which date back to 1520. By the fire is a fine settle where Tennyson is said to have rested, enjoyed his drink and contemplated. Today, the pub meals are hearty and welcoming after a hike in the great outdoors.

ABOVE: *Church of St Margaret where Tennyson was baptised.*

BELOW: *The lovely rambling rectory in Somersby where Tennyson was born.*

**ABOUT • SOMERSBY**

*Follow in the footsteps of the poet Alfred Lord Tennyson (1809–92). The walk begins at The White Hart Inn, frequented by Tennyson who is reputed to have enjoyed a drink by the fire, and takes you to his birthplace, a rambling, yew-fronted rectory.*

## Lincolnshire • C ENGLAND

**DISTANCE •** 5 miles (8km)

**TOTAL ASCENT •** 65ft (20m)

**PATHS •** good

**TERRAIN •** surface roads, grassy fields, cultivated fields

**GRADIENTS •** slight

**REFRESHMENTS •** White Hart Inn and Cross Keys

**PARK •** White Hart Inn (ask permission beforehand)

**OS MAP •** Explorer 273 Lincolnshire Wolds South, Horncastle

# Tennyson's home in Somersby

❶ Turn left out of The White Hart Inn and follow the road round to the left through the village. Continue until you reach a fork in the road, take the right fork past the attractive stableyard on the right.

❷ At the next junction, with Wood Farm on the right, turn left and continue past the old school building on the right.

❸ Follow the road as it bends left past the new doctor's surgery and continue to the junction overlooked by a war memorial. Turn right at the memorial and continue towards the Cross Keys pub. Turn left on to the public bridleway just before the pub.

❹ Stroll along this pretty, grassy track through the corridors of brambles before entering more open countryside. When the bridleway meets a public footpath ensure that you follow the bridleway, keeping the open fields to your left and the hedge and earth bank to your right. When the path meets a minor road, turn left and walk along the road alongside a shallow wood.

### • DON'T MISS •

*Harrington Hall (further along from Bag Enderby) is a 17th-century manor, once the home of Rosa Baring, who would come down from the steps to the terrace garden to walk with Tennyson. His famous line 'Come into the garden, Maud' was probably about Rosa. (The Hall is not open to the public, but the gardens are on occasions.)*

❺ As you walk along this road note the small carved face in the rocky outcrop set back to the left-hand side of the road. Pass the junction signed Ashby Puerorum and Horncastle and carry on into Somersby village. Look for Grange Cottage on the right with its white fence, and then next door, the birthplace of Tennyson. Opposite is the church where Tennyson's father was rector.

❻ Walk through the churchyard and around to a gate diagonally opposite the entrance. Turn left along the road until you come to Somersby House Farm. Turn right up the birdleway opposite the farm. Continue to Warden Hill Cottage. Turn left through the outbuildings, following the footpath signposts.

❼ At the edge of Warden Woods turn left down a limestone path with the wood on your right.

As the path rises again at the end of the wood, turn right and follow the path along the bottom edge of the wood. At the T-junction turn left and follow the bridleway up and over the hill.

❽ As you go down the hill note the no right of way over the stile. Follow the track down to the road, turn left then right on to a footpath over a footbridge. Trek across a lovely chain of fields to St Mary's Church in Tetford. Pass through the graveyard to the road, turn left and return to the White Hart Inn.

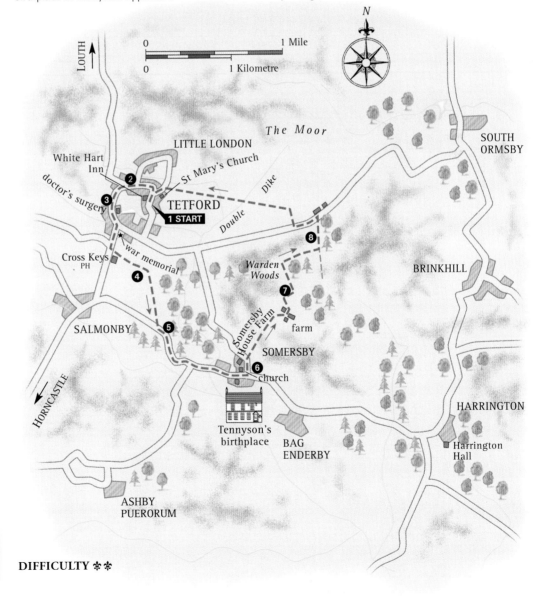

**DIFFICULTY ✳✳**

VICTORIAN

AGE OF OPTIMISM

ABOVE: *Cyclists enjoying a ride along the Taff Trail Bike Path. Many of the disused railway tracks now provide a valuable leisure resource.*

LEFT: *A steam engine at Duffryn Yard, Taff Railway.*

# The Tracks of Industry

*Following the course of a railway through the former industrial heartland of Wales*

RIGHT: *The locomotive was probably the most valuable and enduring invention of the Victorian era and quickly replaced other transport methods, such as the canals.*

## Transforming a Landscape

The mineral-rich valleys that run from the Brecon Beacons to the major urban centres of Cardiff and Swansea have teemed with industrial activity for centuries. This walk traces a route that, until relatively recently, was a major artery for the transportation of goods and people. Since the decline of the coal industry, the South Wales slagheaps have changed from black to grassy green, railways have become country tracks, and – ironically – as mining communities struggle to maintain their existence, the scenery has regained some of its pre-industrial beauty.

The Taff Trail runs, in its entirety, from Brecon to Cardiff; this section of the trail leads along part of the former Barry and Rhymney railway lines, skirting the hillside above the River Taff, the original means of moving cargoes from the Rhondda Valley mines (north of the route) to the southern shipping ports, and from there to destinations all over the world.

## Mines and Railways

South Wales was already a target for industrial speculators by the late 18th century. At first, iron was the main resource, but coal was needed to smelt it, and soon furnaces and pits were mushrooming all along the river valleys south of the Brecon mountains. Canals, river barges and horse-drawn trams shifted the produce at first, but the quicker, cheaper steam engine came hot on the heels of the industrial boom. It was in Merthyr, further up the Taff, that steam-driven transport had an early breakthrough, when Richard Trevithick's locomotive train made its first brief trip on an old tramroad in 1804. This was the first steam-powered journey along iron rails. From then on, the 19th century was destined to be the age of the train. Railways appeared all over Britain, providing fast links between centres of industry and ports, improving business communications and sparking off a craze for seaside holidays, as quick jaunts to the coast became a possibility even for people of modest means.

In South Wales the emphasis was on King Coal, as mines churned out millions of tons of the 'black gold', to fuel the engines and furnaces of the world. Around each pit, a mining town appeared, with rows of terraced houses clinging to the hillsides. People poured in to this once rural area; farm labourers abandoned the land, and workers arrived from abroad looking for employment. Mining families lived and worked in appalling conditions, while the industrial barons reaped huge profits. The Valleys became hotbeds of radicalism, and the whole shape of Welsh political, cultural and social life changed beyond recognition. Having passed the estates and factories of the Taff Vale towns, this route shows the sharp contrast between Victorian masters and workers, ending up at the extravaganza of Castell Coch, a folly built for the coal magnate Lord Bute in the 1870s.

RIGHT: *The lovely woodland section of the Taff Trail, once a disused railway line.*

## WALK 77 — DOWN THE VALLEY LINE

**❶** Start at the Treforest Park and Ride, at the railway station, and near the University of Glamorgan, originally founded as the South Wales and Monmouthshire School of Mines. To reach the old railway bed, cross the footbridge and go down the slope. Cross into Castle Street; at the end of the street, cross Forest Road and the pedestrian bridge over the Taff. Bear left to go under the road bridge and follow the pavement under the motorway bridge. Cross the road with care. Go round to the left and into Cemetery Road.

**❷** Turn right and pass the cemetery and crematorium. Cremation was made legal in 1884, after local man Dr William Price had been prosecuted for cremating his baby son Iesu. Follow the Taff Trail sign to the right. The track passes between the houses of Ryhdyfelin, whose name probably derives from *rhyd felen*, 'yellow ford': iron in the clay turned the water here a distinct yellow.

**❸** Presently the trail moves into oak woodland and passes the remains of an old colliery on the hill to the left. Above the trees, glimpses of sheep grazing on the mountain recall the pre-steam, pre-industrial era, when travellers admired the natural drama of the 'Glamorgan Alps'. At Nantgarw the trail twists down into another estate and across the road on the valley floor, before climbing to the top of the opposite ridge.

**❹** As the trail approaches the beech woods of Fforest Fawr, it passes Tŷ Rhiw Farm, built before the railways and the coal boom. It's possible to leave the trail here, following the sign left past the farm, to descend to Taff's Well railway station for the train back to Treforest. But it's worth continuing to Castell Coch, the fairytale 'red castle' designed by William Burges. It's a mile and a half (2.4km) on foot or by local bus from nearby Tongwynlais to Taff's Well station.

**Distance:** 6 miles (9.6km) to Taff's Well; another mile (1.6km) to Castell Coch

**Total ascent:** 250ft (76m)

**Paths:** surfaced paths, tracks: can be muddy and waterlogged in poor weather

**Terrain:** streets, paths, tracks

**Gradients:** one steep stretch

**Refreshments:** cafés, pubs in Treforest, café in superstore at Upper Boat (access from trail)

**Park:** Treforest Park and Ride

**OS Map:** Explorer 151 Cardiff & Brigend

**Difficulty:** ✳✳

**1876**

**1876** Queen Victoria is proclaimed Empress of India.

**1876** Alexander Graham Bell patents his invention of the telephone.

**1879** Joseph Swan demonstrates the first electric light bulb.

**1884**

**1884** The Greenwich meridian is given official approval, and Greenwich Mean Time becomes the worldwide standard.

**1884** The Fabian Society is founded, the forerunner to the Labour Party.

**1884**

**1884** The Statue of Liberty is presented to the USA as a gift from France in recognition of a hundred years of Independence.

**1886** The first Crufts Dog Show is held by Charles Cruft.

# On Darwin at Down House

*The rural home where Charles Darwin wrote his revolutionary book about evolution*

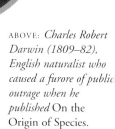

ABOVE: *Charles Robert Darwin (1809–82), English naturalist who caused a furore of public outrage when he published* On the Origin of Species.

At Charles Darwin's home at Down [sic] House, it looks as if the great man has only just stepped out of his study, his books, papers and specimen jars at the ready. Here Darwin spent 40 years and penned his seminal work *On the Origin of Species by Means of Natural Selection*. The downstairs rooms have been meticulously recreated, complete with much of the original furniture, while upstairs exhibitions chronicle his life.

ABOVE: *View of the rear and grounds of Down House, now a museum evoking Darwin's life and work.*

Darwin was a keen walker, though often unwell, and must have known many of the paths on this walk – so you are in good company. He observed: 'The charm of the place to me is that almost every field is intersected by one or more footpaths. I never saw so many walks in any other county … It is really surprising to think London is only 16 miles off.'

As a Cambridge graduate, at the age of 22, Darwin joined a five-year surveying voyage round the world via South America as ship's naturalist and gentleman companion to Captain FitzRoy. Darwin filled his cramped, shared cabin with his study materials, and the *Beagle* set sail in December 1831. He became a much-liked member of the crew, known as Philos, the ship's philosopher. His detailed notes on animal behaviour, their geographical distribution, and the relationship between living and extinct species laid the foundations for his life's work.

Darwin married his cousin Emma in 1839. They shared as grandfather Josiah Wedgwood, the great potter: Wedgwood and Charles's paternal grandfather, the inventor and scientist Erasmus Darwin, held each other in high respect and greatly approved of the marriage. Accordingly there were both brains and money in the family, so Charles could live like a country gentleman, with as much time as he needed for his scientific research.

Down House provided the Darwins with a rural home that was nevertheless convenient for London, though when they moved there in 1842 they thought it ugly. Darwin settled into a life of strict routine, working six hours a day, generally in the morning. He took three walks daily, and did much of his thinking on the Sandwalk path within the gardens.

The publication of *On the Origin of Species* in 1859 was a sensation. The revolutionary element of Darwin's species theory, on which he worked for 20 years, was the way he combined ideas into a coherent argument in which mankind was treated on the same level as other animals. The notion that man had descended from ape-like creatures over millions of years was deeply shocking to a Christian public that had been taught the literal truth of Genesis: that God made Adam and Eve in his own image on the sixth day of creation. Even now, Darwinism is controversial amongst some fundamentalists. His theory profoundly influences the way we think, promoting greater respect for the diversity of plant and animal life on earth. By the end of his life in 1882, Charles Darwin's name was known throughout the kingdom: he was honoured with a state funeral at Westminster Abbey.

BELOW: *Darwin's study at Down House where he did much of his research and writing. He encouraged his children to help him with his experiments.*

**ABOUT • DOWN HOUSE**

*Down House, Charles Darwin's home for 40 years, has been carefully recreated by English Heritage. This walk explores the countryside he knew, and passes the former estate of High Elms House, where his friend the naturalist, Sir John Lubbock, lived.*

**Greater London • SE ENGLAND**

**DISTANCE •** 6½ miles (10.4km)

**TOTAL ASCENT •** 500ft (152m)

**PATHS •** clearly waymarked and defined tracks; mud; some roads

**TERRAIN •** woodland and downland

**GRADIENTS •** one fairly steep woodland descent; otherwise well-graded

**REFRESHMENTS •** bar, café, toilets at High Elms golf club house; pubs, tea room and shop in Downe; tea room at Down House

**PARK •** public car park for High Elms Golf Course between Downe and Farnborough; roadside parking in Downe.

**OS MAP •** Explorer 162 Greenwich & Gravesend

# Evolution at Down House

❶ Turn left out of the car park, on to the road. Opposite the Clock House, turn right on a path by a post-box, signed Cudham Circular Walk, follow this to Downe. Turn left on the road, then right on to a track, Bogey Lane. Soon ascend the steps on your left and go along the field edge.

❷ Avoid the London Loop which bears right, and continue to the far field corner by a pylon. Cross a stile and left on a track. Go ahead at the junction of tracks, signed Downe, across the fields (yellow waymarks). Continue to the road.

❸ Turn left on to the road. At Downe village centre, go forward along Luxted Road, past the Baptist church. Turn left before railings (signed Cudham with a red and white English Heritage sign denoting route to Down House), between the houses and along a field edge. In the second field keep right at a junction of paths and go forward into the next field to cross a stile on the right on to the road opposite Down House.

❹ After visiting Down House return to the field by the same stile opposite Down House. Turn right along the field edge, turn left in the field corner to a stile and go forward to take a waymarked path on the right (Leaves Green Circular Walk). Pass Downe Court Farmhouse, go over a concrete drive and left along the field edge.

❺ Go left at the path crossing midway through the field; go along the next field edge, and down through the woods. Turn right on to the road, then left on a signed bridleway by Cudham

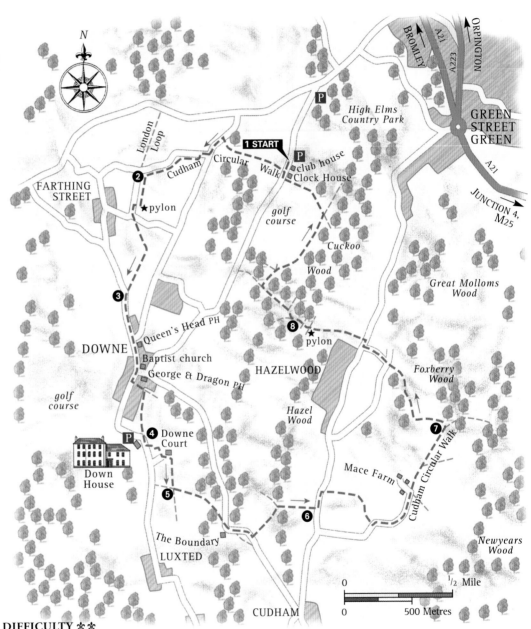

**DIFFICULTY** ✸✸

village sign. Ascend steps, ignore a left turning, and go forward by buildings to a road junction.

❻ Go left along the road. After 70yds (64m) turn right on a field path (Cudham Circular Walk, continues to the car park), which bends right at the end of the third field. Go left along a lane. Continue forward at a junction by some houses, on a track signed

Green Street Green. Later, ignore the path to your right.

❼ In woodland, turn left at the junction, to go out of the woods. Go forward at the next junction, along the road. At the main road, turn right and immediately left through a gate, along a field and into Cuckoo Wood near a pylon. Go uphill on the path and forward at two junctions.

❽ Ignore the path into the field but keep right, inside woods, and continue up to the track corner. Keep left uphill. Turn right at Cudham Circular Walk sign, then take the next right fork (near the edge of a golf course), along a broad path. Go left by a barrier and signpost, on to a fenced path which leads down through the golf course to the road. The car park is on the right.

**1886**

**1886** The workers at the Royal Arsenal in Woolwich found Arsenal football club, later to be known as the 'Gunners' by their supporters.

**1887** St John Ambulance is founded.

**1887**

**1887** The first tyre is developed by John Boyd Dunlop.

**1888** Jack the Ripper commits a series of horrific murders in Whitechapel. The police fail to trace the Ripper, and after eight weeks the murders simply stop.

**1889**

**1889** The Eiffel Tower is completed in Paris.

**1890** Queen Victoria opens the Forth Bridge.

**1893** Keir Hardie founds the Independent Labour Party.

# A Victorian Spa Town

*Taking the waters and enjoying the fresh air – see what made Llandrindod Wells so attractive to the Victorians*

VICTORIAN

AGE OF OPTIMISM

The presence of mineral springs has been known in the Llandrindod Wells area since Roman times. However, no Roman remains have been found in the town and it was not until the 19th century, and the Victorian craze for 'taking the waters', that their potential was fully developed.

The healing benefits of the chalybeate spring had always been known, but the first to rediscover the saline and sulphur springs was a Mrs Jenkins, tenant of the former Lower Bach-y-Graig farm, in the 1730s. She used to sell the waters to travellers, and their fame soon spread. However, despite the reputation of the waters it was some time before the spa of Llandrindod Wells achieved its full potential. The springs were located on bleak heathland, not to the tastes of visitors at the time, and the town was quite remote in the pre-railway era. Llandrindod's fortunes turned with the enclosure of the common in 1862, making land available for building and the development of appropriate facilities, and the opening of the Central Wales railway between 1865 and 1868, giving easy access to the populous industrial towns and cities of northern and central England. With the improved ease of transport, visitors began to flock to the spa and numerous hotels, shops and other facilities were developed.

The Pump House Hotel was rebuilt in 1885 on the site of Mrs Jenkins' original farm. It has now, in turn, been replaced by the County Council offices, which can be seen from the edge of the lake where this walk starts, although the only original building which remains today is the restored Pump House itself. From the lake with its Victorian boat house, the walk takes you through the town, with the streets of shops and guest houses, built to serve the 19th-century visitors, and on to the open space of Temple

LLANDRINDOD WELLS. PUMP HOTEL & OLD PUMP ROOM. 5936.

Gardens at its heart. Passing the former Gwalia Hotel, also now council offices, you come to Rock Park and the arboretum, developed around the location of the most important springs. The Pump House, restored in 1982–3, today houses a restaurant and tea rooms, along with an interesting exhibition on the history of the town. The adjacent former bath house is now a centre for complementary medicine, continuing the healing tradition on which the town's reputation is founded. As you pass, you can also sample the waters of the chalybeate spring, as they issue from a marble fountain in the wall by the bridge in the park.

The open country section of the walk was also popular in Victorian times, when the fresh air complemented the waters as part of the overall cure. The climb out of the town is rewarded with magnificent views over the surrounding countryside to the picturesque Castle Bank, topped by the scant remains of Cefnllys Castle, with the 13th-century church of St Michael's, Cefnllys nestling beneath. Returning through the Happy Valley, a sea of bluebells in the spring, you again climb to a vantage point from where you obtain a panoramic view of the town.

ABOVE: *Guests relaxing in the grounds of the Wells Pump Hotel and old Pump Room.*

LEFT: *The Spa Building in Rock Park, Llandrindod Wells. In its heyday the town drew thousands of Victorian visitors in search of the health-giving waters.*

**ABOUT · LLANDRINDOD WELLS**

*The promise of health-giving waters at Llandrindod Wells brought Victorians here in their thousands. The walk takes you past the Pump Room and Temple Gardens before heading out of the town to the open countryside and views of the town.*

## Powys · WALES

**DISTANCE ·** 7 miles (11km)

**TOTAL ASCENT ·** 443ft (135m)

**PATHS ·** good; can be muddy in places

**TERRAIN ·** town streets, woodland, heathland

**GRADIENTS ·** gradual; one short steep descent

**REFRESHMENTS ·** selection of cafés in Llandrindod Wells

**PARK ·** lakeside picnic area, at the top of Princes Avenue

**OS MAP ·** Explorer 200 Llandrindod Wells & Elan Valley, Rhayader

# Llandrindod Wells

**❶** Follow Princes Avenue towards town, turn left at the end and cross the road on to Spa Road. Follow this, bearing left before and after the railway bridge, to a roundabout. Go through Rock Park Spa gate and descend the main path. Cross the wooden footbridge towards the pump house.

**❷** Turn sharp left to the stone bridge and chalybeate spring in the wall. Over the bridge, take the steep path (left, right) up the hill ahead. Continue under the railway arch and keep to the main path, lined with street lights.

**❸** At the main road, cross, turning left and immediately right into a side street leading to a path through the park, back up Princes Avenue. In 109yds (100m) beyond the picnic area is Lake Cottage; go 82yds (75m) beyond this and turn left through a signposted gate.

**❹** Follow the tarmac path for 55yds (50m); when the route swings left go ahead on the main path through the woods, for about 328yds (300m), to a clearing. On returning to the trees bear left (keep the boundary fence on your right). Cross the stile and go down towards a sign at the bottom of the field. Through the gate here, by the new houses, turn right, then immediately left between gardens, following the waymark arrow.

**❺** Turn right on to the street; after 273yds (250m) take waymarked footpath to the right between numbers 9 and 10. Cross the stile and follow the path up through the woods, for 273yds (250m).

**❻** Through the gate, follow the path between the gorse bushes to an open field; bear right towards a stile bisecting a conifer plantation.

Cross a stile and immediately take the small path, left, cross another stile to leave the plantation.

**❼** Bear right, with waymarker. In 164yds (150m) cross a farm track; recross it 55yds (50m) further on. Continue for 219yds (200m), skirting a small hill. When this green track curves left, cross a stile ahead. Go through the gateway, right, in 11yds (10m), then cross the stile, left, following path with

further stiles and gates down to Bailey Einon farm and the minor road.

**❽** Turn right, then right again after 219yds (200m). Descend for 273yds (250m), cross stile, left, heading diagonally, and steeply, down the field to a stile at the bottom. Cross this, turn right to tarmac road, then left to a picnic area.

**❾** Take the path opposite, ascending through the woods, emerging from conifers after 109yds (100m). At a lane, turn

right and continue to a stile on the right opposite a plantation at the brow of the hill.

**❿** Cross the stile and follow the path to the trig point. Bear slightly left to a stile and cross two fields. Bear down, right towards gorse bushes, behind which is a signpost and a stile. Cross the stile and head towards the woods, keeping right where the path forks near a pond. Continue for 328yds (300m) to another stile. Cross and turn left, to another stile in 44yds (40m). Cross to rejoin the outward route.

**DIFFICULTY** ❀❀

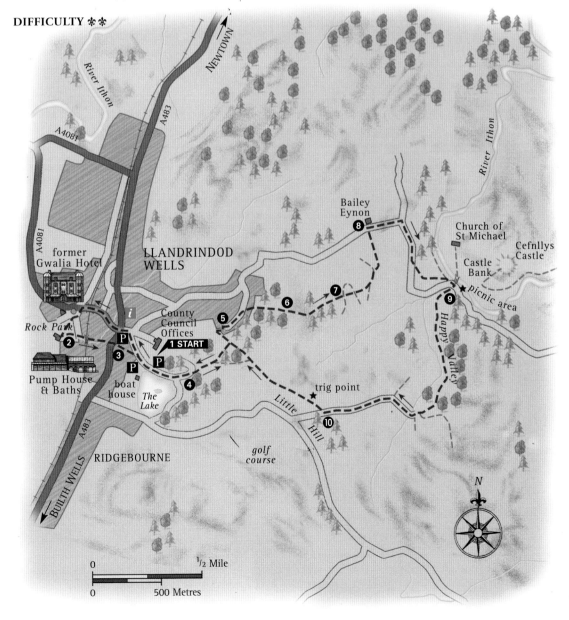

**1894** The Manchester Ship Canal opens and Manchester becomes the first inland port.

**1894** Japan attacks China.

**1895** The radio is invented by an Italian, Marconi.

**1895** *The Importance of being Earnest* (Oscar Wilde) opens to huge acclaim. Wilde was later shunned by 'polite society' after being found guilty of homosexual practices and imprisoned.

**1895** The National Trust is founded.

**1897** Queen Victoria's Diamond Jubilee is celebrated in style by her subjects on 22 June. Her reign is recognised as being one of unprecedented achievement.

# The Peaceful Waters of Lake Vyrnwy

*Built to provide water for Liverpool, Lake Vyrnwy and the surrounding countryside are a haven of tranquillity for visitors and wildlife*

**VICTORIAN**

**AGE OF OPTIMISM**

The impressive Lake Vyrnwy is a reservoir, built between 1880 and 1889 and now a renowned beauty spot. It's hard to believe that the lake and its surrounding landscapes were created little more than a century ago.

In 1877 the area was surveyed with a view to finding a new water supply for the ever-growing city of Liverpool. The bedrock was found to provide a safe foundation for a dam which would hold back 10,000 million gallons (45,460 million litres) of water. The first part of this walk takes you across the dam and down past its base, enabling you to marvel at this feat of Victorian engineering. It was built using local stone from a quarry about a mile (1.6km) away, and over 1,000 stonemasons were employed in the construction of what, at the time, was the largest masonry dam in Europe. Local legend tells of an evil spirit, Ysbryd Cynon, imprisoned years before in a rock by one Dic Spot. This rock needed to be moved during construction, but none of the local men would touch it. After it was blasted by English and Irish workers, a sleepy toad was found in a muddy pool and deemed to be the spirit. For days afterwards the sound of dragging chains was said to have been heard, and years of poor harvests followed.

The work meant drowning the village of Llanwddyn and building new houses and a church below the dam. It is interesting to contrast the relative ease with which the project was approved by the Victorian authorities with the controversy surrounding the construction of Llyn Celyn in the 1950s and 60s (see Walk 101). The valves were closed on 28 November 1888, and the reservoir was full by the following November.

Water leaves the reservoir through the straining tower, a beautiful example of fairy-tale Victorian Gothic architecture, which can be seen as you cross the dam. From here, a 2-mile (3km) tunnel forms the start of an aqueduct which leads via a holding reservoir at Oswestry to Liverpool.

In addition to the land needed for the dam and reservoir, the corporation also bought up over 23,000 acres (9,308ha) of the surrounding estates and, in conjunction with the Forestry Commission, planted almost 5,000 acres (2,023ha) of woodland in the decades which followed. The moorlands above were managed for grouse-shooting, and the magnificently located Lake Vyrnwy Hotel was built, mainly for sporting parties, around the turn of the century.

Forestry and estate management brought the twin benefits of employment (although, as in many rural areas, the numbers employed have dropped drastically in recent years) and nature conservation. Large areas of the catchment now form an RSPB reserve, with hides at various points around the lake and forest trails.

ABOVE: *The Gothic design of the dam at Lake Vyrnwy is typical of Victorian design.*

LEFT: *Liverpool in the late 19th century. The city required a new source of water in order to cope with its rapid expansion.*

BELOW: *Lake Vyrnwy is a renowned beauty spot and a testimony to the skills of the 19th-century engineers.*

**ABOUT • LAKE VYRNWY**

*Lake Vyrnwy, a reservoir built in the 1880s, was created to give the expanding city of Liverpool a new water supply. It is now a renowned beauty spot and panoramic views of the dam and lake can be enjoyed just before the end of the walk.*

## Powys • WALES

| | |
|---|---|
| **DISTANCE** • 4½ miles (7km) | **REFRESHMENTS** • two cafés in Llanwddyn |
| **TOTAL ASCENT** • 400ft (122m) | **PARK** • village car park, entrance opposite |
| **PATHS** • good; can be muddy in places | workshops and Tourist Information Centre |
| **TERRAIN** • dam road, lanes, forestry tracks | **OS MAP** • Explorer 239 Lake Vyrnwy & |
| **GRADIENTS** • two moderate climbs | Llanfyllin, Tanat Valley |

# Lake Vyrnwy: giving water to Liverpool

❶ Leave the village car park at the end nearer the village. Follow the path and steps up the side of the woods. On reaching the road follow the footpath past the visitor centre car park on the right. Turn right on to the dam and cross.

❷ At the far end of the dam turn right immediately down the steps. Follow the path to a footbridge, cross and keep along the side of the fence. On reaching the track follow it to the left, through the gate and along the river bank.

❸ Shortly go over a footbridge, cross the stile you see ahead, left. At the top of the path, cross another stile and turn left on to the lane. In 109yds (100m) take the right fork, (not Grwn Oer). In 219yds (200m) continue ahead, following a blue waymarker, and later round a right bend.

❹ When the tarmac lane bears down and left to a farm track, keep straight on, following the unmade track (blue marker). Enter forestry 328yds (300m) beyond. Follow the track, which later descends pleasantly, for 766yds (700m).

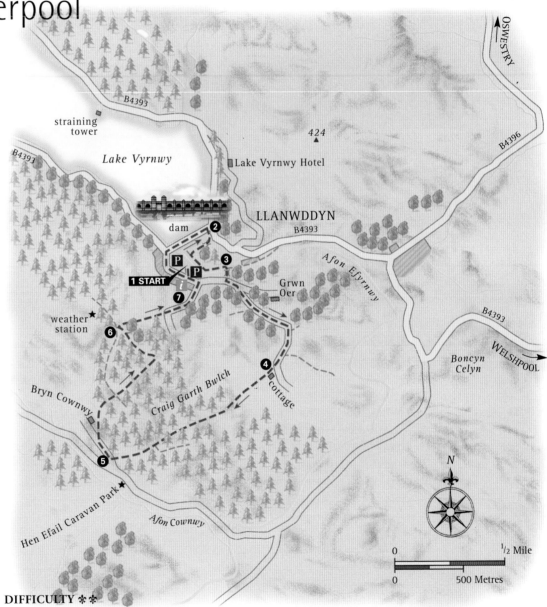

**DIFFICULTY** ❋ ❋

At the left hairpin bend, keep ahead, soon descending again.

❺ On meeting a T-junction with a lane, turn right. Just before Bryn Cownwy farmhouse, fork right and follow the forestry track steeply and steadily uphill. At a crossroads of forestry tracks keep straight on.

Keep on the main track, later following it round to the left.

❻ At a junction of tracks as you leave the trees, look for the waymarked gate straight ahead of you. Go through this and follow the waymarked path steeply descending by the side of the

fence to a stile in the far right-hand corner.

❼ Cross, turn right and go through stile and gate in 55yds (50m). Join a lane and follow it back down to the village. Cross the road, head left then right, and follow the access road back to the car park.

**1898**

**1898** After the Opium Wars (1830–64), the Chinese government signs a 99-year lease giving Britain power over new territories.

**1898** Publication of *The War of the Worlds* (HG Wells). An adaptation, written and read by Orson Wells, is

**1898**

broadcast on radio in 1938, causing mass panic in America as residents believe they are being invaded.

**1898** Marie and Pierre Curie discover radium, bringing a huge advance to the medical world.

**1899**

**1899–1902** The Boer War.

**1901** Queen Victoria's death on 22 January is mourned by the nation. Victoria's 64-year reign had been one of imperial expansion, massive industrial growth and profound social change.

# Scarborough, Queen of Watering Places

*One of the earliest resorts, Scarborough boasts a proud tradition of welcoming visitors*

ABOVE: *View over Scarborough which, to a Victorian tourist, had everything – spa waters, sea water and promenade entertainment.*

A guide for visitors to Scarborough in 1890 spoke of the view of the South Bay as 'the chief glory of Scarborough; and those upon whom this bright vision bursts … will not soon forget the pleasure of the sight.'

The first known picture of a bathing machine was drawn by local artist John Setterington in a panorama of the South Bay in 1735, and by 1777 Scarborough even turned up in the title of a play by Sheridan – *A Trip to Scarborough*. But it was the Victorians who really developed the town as a resort. Early visitors were accommodated in modest houses around the harbour, and entertainment was provided at the spa. The present spa buildings date from 1877; you can reach them by the South Cliff Lift, Britain's first funicular railway, built two years earlier.

Lodging houses gradually spread around the bay and along the cliff tops – developments given a huge boost in 1845 when the railway arrived from York.

Thousands of visitors came – among them the Brontë sisters; Anne died in Scarborough in 1849. Her grave is near the castle. The site of the house where she died is now occupied by Scarborough's most impressive hotel, the gargantuan Grand. Designed by Cuthbert Brodrick in 1863, it dominates the bay with its bulbous domes and balconies.

Scarborough's great headland, more than 250ft (76m) high, on which the 800-year-old castle stands, separates the South Bay from the North. Until the Marine Drive was built in the 1890s, development to the north, started in 1844, consisted mainly of lodging houses and hotels – though a pier, built in 1866 and destroyed by storm in 1905, and the Clarence Gardens, laid out in the 1880s, provided some genteel entertainment. Once access was improved, great efforts were made to develop North Bay. Peasholm Park was laid out in 1912, complete with a boating lake and Red Indian gateways.

Near the castle entrance are reminders of the old town, with narrow streets and flights of steps linking different levels, while the Crescent, with its fine houses facing the valley, was laid out in 1830. This part of Scarborough is linked to the smart South Cliff area by the delicate Cliff Bridge of 1826 and the more substantial Valley Bridge of 1865. Behind the railway station, the Westbourne estate was laid out in 1862.

To serve the new estates, Scarborough's best church, St Martin-on-the-Hill, was designed by Bodley in 1862. A symbol of the wealth and vitality of Victorian Scarborough, it is a treasure-chest of stained glass and decorative art by William Morris and his friends – a fitting climax for a walk through the queen of watering places.

BELOW: *Children paddling on the beach at Scarborough in Yorkshire – the beginning of the British seaside resort tradition and widespread tourism.*

VICTORIAN

**WALK 81**

**ABOUT • SCARBOROUGH**

*By the end of the 18th century Scarborough was a magnet for people of good fashion – ever since Elizabeth Farrer discovered medicinal waters springing beside the beach. The waters, no longer thought fit to drink, still flow from a niche near the spa.*

**North Yorkshire • N ENGLAND**

**DISTANCE •** 6¾ miles (10.8km)

**TOTAL ASCENT •** 590ft (180m)

**PATHS •** town pavements and beach, tides permitting

**TERRAIN •** two wide bays set either side of headland

**GRADIENTS •** one gradual climb form North Bay; ascent to castle entrance quite steep

**REFRESHMENTS •** plenty of hotels, pubs, restaurants, cafés and tea rooms throughout Scarborough

**PARK •** Albion Road car park on the South Cliff, off A165 Bridlington road

**OS MAP •** Explorer 301 Scarborough, Bridlington & Flamborough Head

# Medicinal waters at the seaside

**❶** From the car park, follow Albion Road towards the sea. Turn right and by Esplanade Gardens take the cliff lift (tramway) down, or the winding path beside it, to the spa buildings. At the seashore, turn left, along the beach or the road.

**❷** Walk towards the harbour. Pass the lifeboat station and follow the road past the harbour, bending left through an archway on to Marine Drive (closed in bad weather). Follow Marine Drive for 1½ miles (2.4km) to a roundabout.

**❸** Turn left, and left again at the next roundabout, then take the next left. Turn left again, along Queen's Parade. Follow the road along the cliff top. Go left of the Boston and Norbreck hotels, to descend along Mulgrave Place to a crossroads.

**❹** Turn left to visit the castle. Return from the castle to the crossroads, and turn left. Anne Brontë's grave is behind the wall to your left. Follow the lane downhill, going left along Paradise, then bending right. Take the second turning right, Longwestgate.

**❺** Go left down St Mary's Street. Continue downhill by the Leeds Hotel, bending right down a cobbled path for 22yds (20m) to join a main road. Turn right, uphill. At the traffic lights turn left along St Nicholas Street, bending right by the Royal Hotel. The Grand Hotel is to your left.

**❻** Continue along Falconers Road. At the roundabout, take the second exit (the Crescent Hotel is now on your right) and walk round

the Crescent. Turn left by the Chessington Hotel, cross the next road and go straight on. At the top, turn left and then left again at the traffic-lights.

**❼** At the next traffic-lights go right towards Tesco. Follow the

road as far as Falsgrave signal box and turn left. At the bottom turn left, then left again after 33yds (30m) down Valley Road. Cross at the roundabout beyond Valley Bridge, then bear left to pass the Rotunda Museum.

**❽** Continue up the slope and steps and over Cliff Bridge. At the end bear right up steps beside the Spa Chalet. Follow the road past the Crown Hotel, and go right at the Villa Esplanade along Albion Road to the car park.

**DIFFICULTY ✿✿**

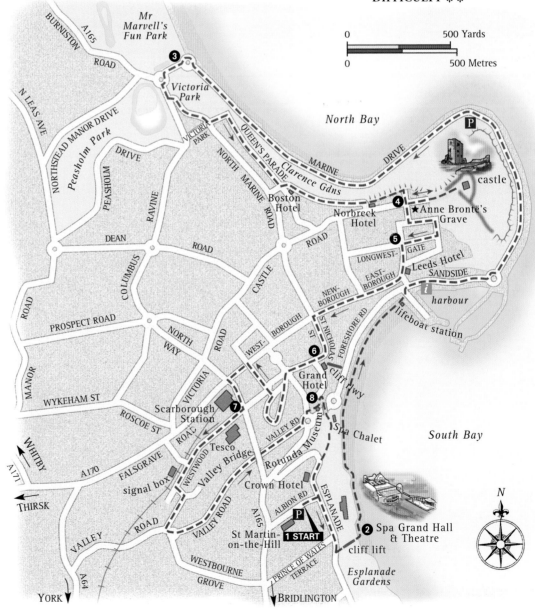

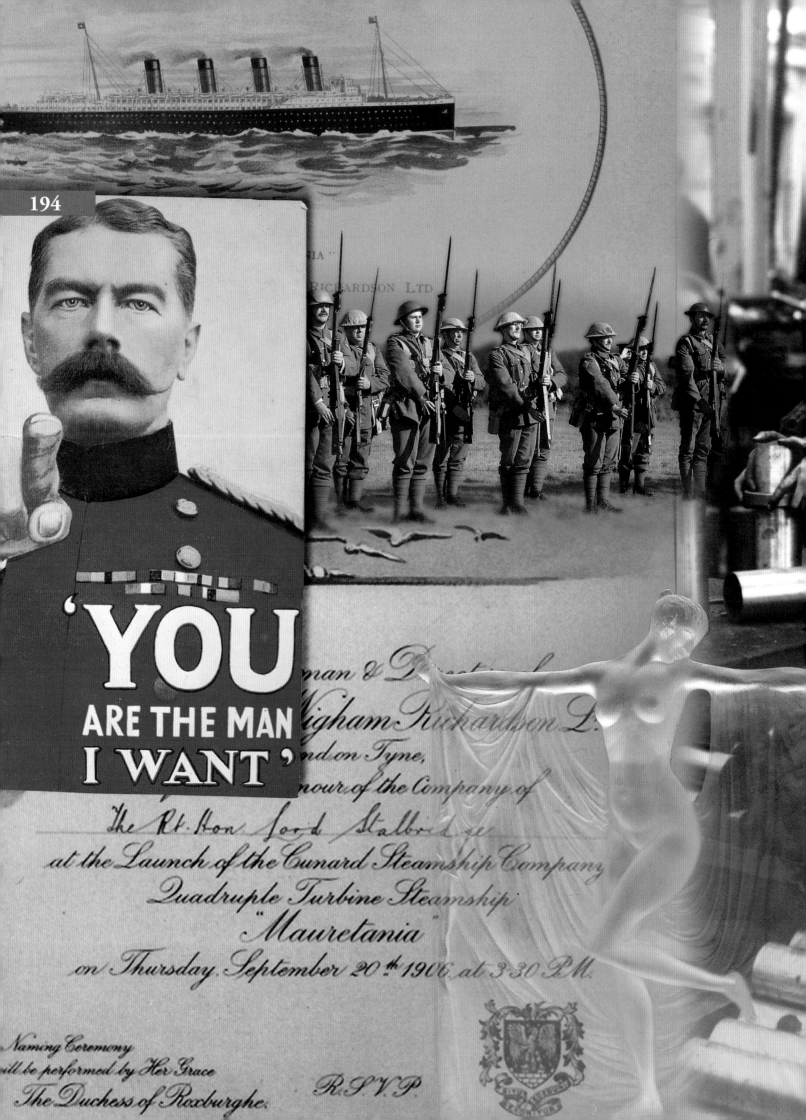

'YOU
ARE THE MAN
I WANT'

man & Pemton L

igham Richardson L

nd on Tyne,

nour of the Company of

The Rt Hon Lord Stalbridge

at the Launch of the Cunard Steamship Company

Quadruple Turbine Steamship

"Mauretania"

on Thursday, September 20th 1906, at 3.30 P.M.

Naming Ceremony
ill be performed by Her Grace
The Duchess of Roxburghe.

R.S.V.P.

*As the 20th century opened, the world was shrinking. Aeroplanes, cars, the telephone and the cinema were extending global communications and seemed to promise increased understanding and even peace. But within two decades such hopes had been buried in the trenches of World War I.*

# EDWARDIAN

## 1901–1918

# A New Century

Edwardian Britain was the hub of a rich empire, and still a society divided into sharply defined classes: 'upstairs' and 'downstairs' had precious little overlap. Women were starting to make inroads into education and professions, but only in individual, exceptional cases. On the whole, women played a decidedly backstage role in public life, and in the early years of the century there was a growing call for change. Many men and women pressed for further electoral reform – demanding the vote not only for all men, but for some women as well.

Frustrated at their lack of progress, a section of the suffrage movement began to employ headline-grabbing tactics. Known as the Suffragettes, women such as Emmeline Pankhurst chained themselves to railings, broke windows and led public demonstrations to bring attention to their cause; some who were gaoled went on hunger strike, and endured the horrors of force-feeding.

The need for reform was, in fact, acknowledged in a series of policies that sought to tackle industrial Britain's problems of poverty and inequality. While the new Labour Party brought the working-class voice into the political forum, Chancellor of the Exchequer Lloyd George laid the foundations of a welfare state, taxing luxury items such as motor cars to pay for old age pensions. Nevertheless women had to wait until 1918 for even a limited right to vote, as the normal business of government (which also included Home Rule for Ireland) was suspended during four years of devastating warfare.

Meanwhile technology was progressing quickly at the turn of the 20th century, with important advances in medicine, communications and entertainment. In 1903 the Wright brothers made the first successful man-powered flight in North Carolina; the next goal was to travel long distances by air. A prize of £1000 was offered by *The Daily Mail* for the first flight across the English Channel. The winner was Frenchman Loius Blériot who made the 43-minute journey from Calais to Dover Castle on 25 July 1909. Within five years Britain and the rest of the world was at war and the air force brought a new dimension to international conflict.

### THE GREAT WAR

In 1914 a Serb terrorist assassinated the Hapsburg Archduke Ferdinand, and plunged the world into chaos. A complex network of alliances and enmities brought nation after nation on to the stage of war, and hundreds of thousands of men suffered in rat-infested, waterlogged trenches as battles raged on to gain a few feet of muddy field on the European front. The effects of relentless, deafening shelling and appalling mustard-gas attacks were characteristics of war on a previously unknown scale, recorded by a generation of young poets such as Siegfried Sassoon and Wilfred Owen. Nevertheless it took a long time for the full magnitude of events to filter back to those at home, who had, on the whole, greeted the outbreak of hostilities with patriotic fervour.

By the time the war ground to a close, a generation of young men had virtually been wiped out. The survivors were promised homes fit for heroes, but too many came back to unemployment and despair. Meanwhile, women had proved their ability to do 'men's work', stepping into the breach in factories and on public transport; and at the same time the common experiences of officers and the lower ranks had at least begun to break down some class barriers. In just four years, lives and attitudes had been shattered. The only generally held certainty was that this had been the war to end all wars.

---

### HISTORIC SITES

**Civic Centre, Cardiff, South Glamorgan:** outstanding Beaux-Arts architecture.

**Glasgow School of Art, Glasgow, Strathclyde:** designed by Charles Rennie Mackintosh and displaying his unique style and its art nouveau influences.

**Alhambra Theatre, Bradford, West Yorks:** restored Edwardian splendour from the age of music hall.

**The Cenotaph Memorial, London:** memorial to the dead of World War I, designed by Sir Edwin Lutyens.

**Dartmouth, Devon:** an important naval base was established here in 1905.

| 1901 | 1903 | 1903 |
|---|---|---|
| **1901** The coronation of Edward VII. | **1903** Plans for Letchworth Garden City in Hertfordshire are proposed by Ebenezer Howard to merge country and town life. | **1903** The Wright brothers make the first powered flight in North Carolina, America. |
| **1902** *Heart of Darkness* (Joseph Conrad) is published and the modern novel is born. | | **1904** *Peter Pan* is published (JM Barrie). It is later granted copyright in perpetuity, with proceeds to Great Ormond Street Children's Hospital. |
| **1902** The Boer War ends with the signing of the terms of surrender. | **1903** The Women's Social and Political Union is formed by Emmeline Pankhurst. | |

# Beatrix Potter's Sawrey

*Inspired by the beauty of the Lake District, authoress and artist Beatrix Potter left London to settle in Far Sawrey, between the shores of Windermere and Esthwaite Water*

Sawrey is small – just a church, a pub, a village shop and a scattering of cottages tucked into the folds of green pastures. It's a peaceful scene so typical of South Lakeland, a pastoral idyll that enticed children's author Beatrix Potter away from her parents' South Kensington home.

Beatrix had been introduced to the Lake District as a teenager, when her mother and father took her on holiday to Wray Castle. There she met Canon Rawnsley, then Vicar of Wray, for the first time. He was to be a major influence on her life, explaining to her his theories on the countryside and its conservation, and encouraging her talent for drawing. The Potters were to take their holidays in Cumbria for the next 21 years.

Back in London, Beatrix made greetings cards from her sketches and started to write books for children. In 1902 her first book, *The Tale of Peter Rabbit*, was published by Frederick Warne and Son. Norman Warne, youngest son of the publisher's founder, formed a close friendship with the authoress, and in 1905 proposed to her by letter. She accepted, but her acceptance was greeted with scorn by her parents. To them, this marriage was beneath her. Warne died that same year of pernicious pneumonia. Heartbroken, Beatrix, now 39, immersed herself in her work and produced many of her best-known books. At this time she would visit her Lake District home, Hill Top, whenever she could, sketching the house, the garden and the surrounding countryside for her books. *The Tale of Tom Kitten* takes place in the house and garden, *The Tale of Ginger and Pickles* in the village shop, and the nearby Tower Bank Arms featured in *The Tale of Jemima Puddle-Duck*.

Beatrix Potter made many land and property purchases around the Lakes, based on tip-offs given to her by Hawkshead solicitor, William Heelis, known locally as Hawkshead Willie, to distinguish him from his cousin and partner, also called William. Willie proposed. Again the Potter elders were against their daughter's marriage. Her father had become unwell, and was expecting his spinster daughter to look after her mother. But this time Beatrix married her suitor and they moved into Castle Cottage, a short way from Hill Top.

This was to be the end of Beatrix Potter's career as a writer and the start of Mrs Heelis, the farmer. She became an expert on Herdwick sheep, winning many prizes at local fairs. On her death in 1943 she left 15 farms and 4,000 acres (1,619ha) of land to the National Trust, including Hill Top, now maintained as a Beatrix Potter museum, and Tarn Hows.

For anyone who's read the books and seen the lovely illustrations, this walk will be a case of déjà vu.

ABOVE: *Beatrix Potter's home, Sawrey, where she wrote her characterful tales of Peter Rabbit, Jemima Puddle-Duck and Mrs Tiggie-Winkle.*

BELOW: *Wise Een Tarn at Claife Heights – part of the Lake District National Park. While on a holiday in the lakes with her family, Beatrix Potter fell in love with the place and eventually chose to settle here.*

ABOVE: *A portrait of Beatrix Potter (1866–1943) aged 26.*

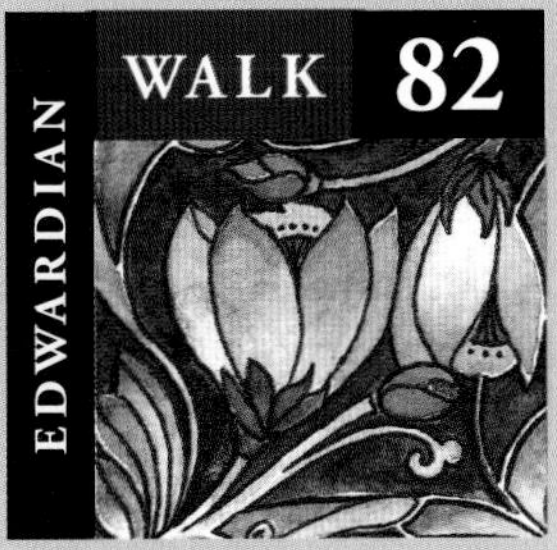


ABOUT • WINDERMERE

*This walk follows in the footsteps of Beatrix Potter. It passes Far Sawrey and climbs the rolling hills to Moss Eccles Tarn. Passing through the forests of Claife Heights, you will catch glimpses of Bowness and Windermere through the tree boughs.*

**Cumbria • N ENGLAND**

**DISTANCE** • 6 miles (9.6km)

**TOTAL ASCENT** • 850ft (259m)

**PATHS** • field paths can be muddy in winter

**TERRAIN** • rolling hills and woodland

**GRADIENTS** • Steady but gentle climbs. The descent back to the car park can be slippery after rain

**REFRESHMENTS** • Tower Bank Arms in Near Sawrey

**PARK** • National Trust car park above Windermere Ferry landing stage

**OS MAP** • Outdoor Leisure 7 The English Lakes – South Eastern Area

# The world of Beatrix Potter

❶ From the south of the car park follow the footpath signed to Far Sawrey, Near Sawrey and Hill Top. After a short way it crosses the road, eventually to emerge on the High Cunsey Lane (not named), close to its junction with the B-road.

❷ Turn right, then left, up the B-road. At a sharp left-hand corner turn right, along a track marked to Far Sawrey, Near Sawrey and Hill Top. Follow it northwest through woodland and past a few cottages.

❸ Rejoin the B-road, turn right, then first left, descending along the lane towards St Peter's Church. Go right through a kissing gate by a whitewashed cottage, then follow the clear cross-field path towards Near Sawrey. The path returns to the road just short of Hill Top Farm.

❹ Through the village turn right along the lane opposite a post-box. This becomes a stony track that climbs past Moss Eccles and Wise Een tarns before entering the Claife Heights conifer plantations.

❺ Ignore the footpath on the left, and instead stay with the forestry road. Turn right along a path signed to the ferry and Far Sawrey. White waymark posts (look out for these as path may be unclear after major tree felling) highlight the route from here back to the car park. The winding path climbs to the Claife Heights viewpoint, where you can look down the length of Windermere.

❻ The continuing path crosses a wide forestry track. Turn right to reach High Blind How (the viewpoint is off the path). Just south of the viewpoint the path rounds some huge rocky outcrops. Beyond the outcrops follow the path to the left back into thick woodland.

❼ Turn right at a junction of paths and head south, signed Far Sawrey. The path becomes a wide track on entering an open area of pasture and crag with a wall on the left. Turn left at the T-junction of tracks, following the signed route to Windermere ferry and the lakeshore. At the next signpost turn right through a kissing gate, signed to ferry.

❽ After traversing high fields with a view to Bowness the path re-enters the woods and zigzags down steep slopes to the ruins of the old viewing station. Beyond these, descend the stepped path back to the car park.

**• DON'T MISS •**

*Explore the places in **Windermere** that were home to Beatrix Potter – where Peter Rabbit, Tom Kitten and others came to life on the pages of her books.*

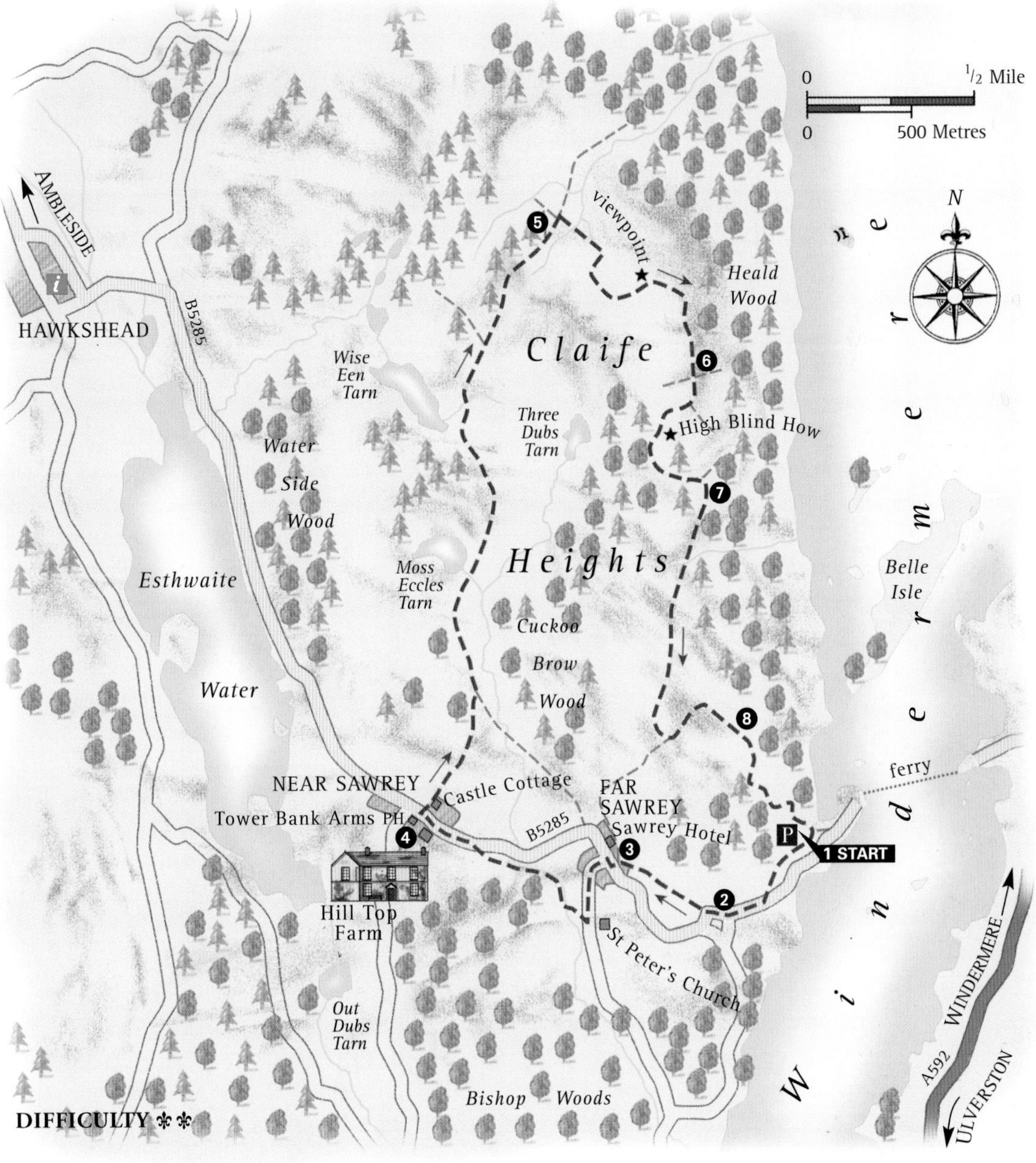

1901–1918

**1904**

**1904** Lhasa is captured by the British, forcing the Dalai Lama to flee from Tibet to India.

**1905** The 'Bloody Sunday' massacre in St Petersburg sows the seeds of the Russian Revolution and the downfall of Tsar Nicholas II.

**1905**

**1905** The Automobile Association is formed by a small group of automobile owners.

**1906** San Francisco is hit by a massive earthquake, devastating the city and killing 2,500 people.

**1907**

**1907** Major General Sir Robert Baden Powell, hero of the Boer War, organises a camp for 20 boys on Brownsea Island in Dorset. The event marks the foundation of the worldwide organisation known as the Boy Scouts, and leads later to the formation of the Girl Guides.

198

# The First Garden City

*A walk around Letchworth, the planner's vision of an ideal town*

EDWARDIAN

A NEW CENTURY

Modern town planning and suburban development owes a great deal to Letchworth. The town was the first of the so-called Garden Cities, meticulously laid out at the beginning of the 20th century as an idealised space where people would live well and work happily.

Conscious town planning was a response to the sprawling city slum dwellings and overcrowded terraces of Victorian England, and was inspired by Ebenezer Howard's famous pamphlet, *Tomorrow: a Peaceful Path to Real Reform*, published in 1898. Howard, a self-educated clerk, wrote of an ideal city that would function as a balanced, self-sufficient, economic, social and political whole, combining the very best of town and country, and with low-density housing. It was an ideal supported with enthusiasm by social reformers, enlightened politicians and industrialists, including William Lever in Merseyside and George Cadbury in Birmingham.

In 1903 a pioneer company was set up to realise the vision at Letchworth, in Hertfordshire. The chosen site already had a railway running through the centre and some major roads in place, notably Hitchin Road, Norton Way and Icknield Way. Architects Barry Parker and Raymond Unwin won the competition to make Letchworth a reality, and building started in 1904, interrupted by a shortage of funds and eventually a world war.

The town radiates from the large, leafy central Town Square, surrounded by what were supposed to be important neo-Georgian buildings, but which are in reality a disappointing collection reflecting a mish-mash of styles. This lies just south of the cosy little station (built 1912), with the main shopping area to the east, and the open parkland of Norton Common to the north. Light-industrial units stretch out along the railway, and schools and colleges for adult education lie dotted around.

ABOVE: *Ebenezer Howard (1850–1928) – reformer and originator of the concept of the Garden City.*

The 19th-century Arts and Crafts movement had a great influence on the style of building. Houses were given picturesque leaded windows, porches and tall gables, set in short rows around open green spaces, and given decorative front gardens and extensive back gardens that seem luxurious by today's planning standards. Embracing the spirit of experiment, many houses were built of cheap new materials such as prefabricated concrete (see Nevells Road), often concealed by the rough-casting which unifies the town.

While it is the cheaper housing that dominates and characterises Letchworth, there were different scales of housing, from the workers' cottages up to individual mansions. Some of the most characterful of these are seen along Wilbury Road and Norton Way, and the most exclusive are set privately to the west of Sollershott Hall (itself an experiment in communal living). With its tower and open turrets, The Cloisters, on Barrington Road, is surely the most eccentric, built by a wealthy spinster as a progressive School of Psychology for just 20 students.

Letchworth was followed three years later by Hampstead Garden Suburb, and 17 years later by Welwyn Garden City. While the Garden City ideal is sometimes mocked as whimsical, the heart of Letchworth retains considerable charm, and its more modern housing – for example, on Cloisters Way – seems rather disappointingly monotonous and cramped by comparison.

ABOVE: *An aerial view of Letchworth which shows conscientious town planning at work. The town radiates outwards from the central town square.*

BACKGROUND: *The leafy suburban Broadway, Letchworth. Each house was carefully designed and set in its own garden.*

**ABOUT • LETCHWORTH**

*The Garden City of Letchworth pioneered the idea of conscious town planning. Inspired by a pamphlet written by Ebenezer Howard in 1908, Letchworth aimed to resolve the problem of unhealthy slum dwellings and overcrowded terraces.*

# Hertfordshire • SE ENGLAND

**DISTANCE** • 6 miles (9.6km)

**TOTAL ASCENT** • negligible

**PATHS** • pavements, with a short stretch through a park

**TERRAIN** • town, parkland

**GRADIENTS** • some gentle ascents

**REFRESHMENTS** • plenty of choice in the town

**PARK** • Station Place West long stay car park next to the station; multi-storey car park behind the cinema

**OS MAP** • Explorer 193 Luton & Stevenage, Hitchin & Ampthill

# Letchworth: new town

❶ In Station Place, with the war memorial on the right, head west out of the square, noting leafy Broadway down to the left, and the Broadway Hotel. Turn right over the railway bridge. Admire the Spirella underwear factory, left.

❷ Turn right into Nevells Road. Pass houses dated 1914 to more individual, small houses, built as experimental low-cost homes in 1950, with different building materials, such as the rock-like tin cladding at No 212. The Settlement, built as a temperance pub, is now a community centre. Retrace your steps and turn right up Cross Street.

❸ Turn left at the end on to Icknield Way, and near the unusual brown timber-clad house at the entrance to The Quadrant, cross the main road and take the tarmac path straight across the park of Norton Common.

❹ Where the path emerges on Willbury Road, cross over and turn right. Pass the crescent of Westholm, on the left, the epitome of Garden City design, with its white rendered and gable houses grouped around a tree-filled green. Eastholm is a corresponding arc on the next corner. Cross Willbury Road again, and descend, right, into Norton Way North. Note the bigger houses, set back from the road with trees and hedges.

❺ At the modern St George's Church, turn left into Common View. The further you walk up here, the more interesting the little terraced groups become, with each distinctive row of four proclaiming its designers. Keep right along here to the end, then retrace your steps to Cromwell Green, a lower-scale contrast to Westholm.

❻ Turn down here between the houses, and right on to Glebe Road, back towards the town centre. The factories are only a row away, but this is still very pleasant. At the junction, go left down Norton Way North and pass under the railway bridge.

❼ Bear left, cross at the bollards, and enter Rushby Mead, a long and delightful breath of country in the town. Stay on this road across two junctions, and at the end, turn right and cross at the crossing.

❽ Continue to the next traffic-lights, turning left into Willian Way, a beautiful avenue of bigger individual houses. Turn right into Barrington Road to pass the extraordinary Cloisters (private), and turn right again into Cloisters Road, past modern, much less individual housing. Cross the main road and the little green (note the thatched kiosk, right) and bear left into Sollershott East. Pass Sollershott Hall, left, and turn right up the main avenue of Broadway.

❾ At Souberie Avenue, turn right and follow this curve to its junction with Meadow Way. Turn left here, and right into the big Broadway square. Pass the museum on your right, turn right, and bear immediately left at the cinema into the main shopping area of East Cheap. Follow this back down to Station Place.

**DIFFICULTY** ❋

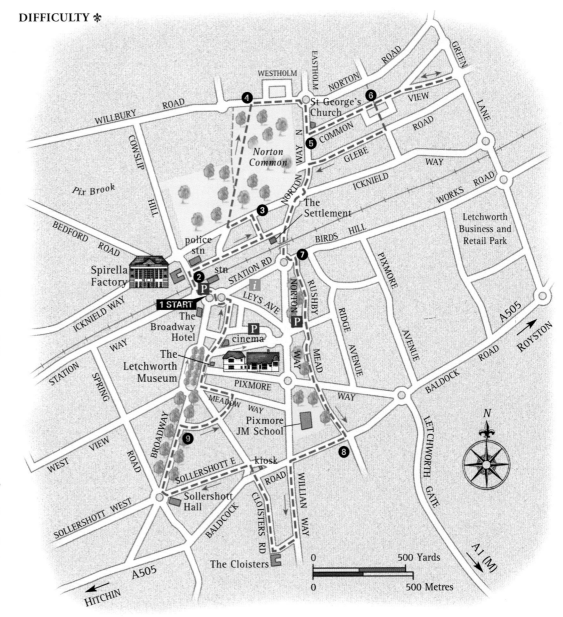

**1908**

**1908** The first state pensions are created.

**1908** The *Daily Mail* sponsors the first Ideal Home Exhibition.

**1908** *The Wind in the Willows* (Kenneth Grahame) is published.

**1909**

**1909** Release of the first Hollywood movie, *In Old California*.

**1909** Commander Peary reaches the North Pole on 6 April.

**1909** A Frenchman, Louis Blériot, makes the first successful flight

**1909**

across the English Channel, landing near Dover Castle on 25 July.

**1909** Leo Baekelite invents Bakelite, an early form of plastic.

**1910** Death of Edward VII.

ABOVE: *King Edward VII mounted on his favourite pony at Sandringham.*

**EDWARDIAN**

**A NEW CENTURY**

# Sandringham: a Stretch of Royal Estate in Norfolk

*A walk around the Sandringham estate, the much-loved country retreat of the Queen and her family*

The Sandringham branch of the Women's Institute boasts the Queen and the Queen Mother among its members, something that could probably happen nowhere else in Britain. There's a relaxed air to this lovely corner of Norfolk, which Edward VII (1841–1910), at that time a youthful Prince of Wales, spotted back in 1862, when he purchased the modest Sandringham Estate. The estate now covers some 20,000 acres, including neat carrstone villages and farms, and carefully managed heath and woodland that attracts and supports a wide variety of wildlife.

Edward and his glamorous young Danish wife, Alexandra, were popular society figures, known for their lavish balls and entertainments, and for their love of horseracing and theatre. They proved great fodder for the tabloid press of the day – and a much more appealing face of monarchy than the grief-stricken, reclusive Queen Victoria, who continued to deny her eldest son a political role in the affairs of State. The gay young couple suffered their fair share of scandal, of course – notoriously, the Prince was cited in a divorce case in 1870 – but this was mostly linked to public life in London and abroad.

Sandringham offered the Prince a more private retreat, where he could relax and play the prosperous country gentleman, entertaining friends and neighbours, farming, pursuing country sports, and looking after his tenants. It was a role that he relished, and that he fulfilled admirably. While it is familiar to us from the similar role adopted by the present Prince of Wales, in its own time it was perceived as unusual, and a welcome shift from the excesses of Edward's predecessor, the Prince Regent, at Brighton.

The house at Sandringham is neither beautiful nor imposing, and has been unkindly described as having the appearance of a rather up-market hotel. The original house was extensively rebuilt in 1869 by designer A J Humbert, with a splendid ballroom added in 1885, and much more work and enlargement after a major fire in 1891. Today it is a pleasantly mellow red-brick mansion with a forest of neo-Tudor chimneys, gables and cupolas. It was first opened to the public by the Queen in the year of her Silver Jubilee, 1977, but this is no museum piece or chilly showpiece palace. The house was designed for comfortable, informal entertaining on a large scale, and the rooms are full of photos, portraits and mementoes that give it a more personal touch than you might expect, for successive members of the Royal Family have loved the place.

Exploring the grounds, it is not difficult to understand why. The gardens, first opened to the public in 1968, are full of interesting plants and colour whatever the time of year, and offer tantalizing views through to the private areas of the park.

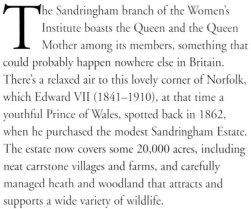

LEFT: *The architecture and interior design of Sandringham saw a departure from the formality of the archetypal royal palace. Instead it was designed as an extensive but comfortable family home suitable for entertaining large numbers of guests.*

**ABOUT • SANDRINGHAM**

*Sandringham offers the epitome of an Edwardian royal country house. It was designed to be a large, comfortable home, suitable for entertaining large parties. Opened in 1968 as a country park, this part of the estate offers free access for walkers.*

**DISTANCE •** gardens 1½ miles (2.4km); country park 3½ miles (5.6km)

**TERRAIN •** landscaped, formal gardens with wheelchair access throughout; woodland

**PATHS •** gardens: mainly firm, gravel paths; country park: mostly firm, but sections in woods can be muddy

**GRADIENTS •** gardens: level, easy walking;

## Norfolk • SE ENGLAND

country park: some slopes and steps

**REFRESHMENTS •** tea room and restaurant at visitor centre; tea room by museum

**PARK •** car park by the visitor centre

**CONTACT •** the Estate Office (01553) 772675 for details of opening times

**OS MAP •** n/a

# A very royal estate

❶ From the visitor centre, cross the main road, pass the war memorial on your right, and bear left, via the ticket office, into the gardens. Turn left on a gravel path, and follow it through the woods.

❷ Leave the path to see a wall, with memorials to Sandringham's working dogs. Keep along the main path and through an area of rhododendrons. Go under the arch and turn left to see Norwich Gates.

❸ Retrace your steps and turn left through another rhododendron arch, following the main path. Note the *Wellingtonia gigantica*, right, before you bear left on to the main drive. Follow this round to the yew hedges in front of the house, turning right to the main entrance.

❹ Leaving the house via the ballroom, turn left and right through the hedge, and take the path diagonally right to rejoin the main drive. Keep straight here, and take the small path, left, to visit the museum and tea room (and toilets) in the old stable block.

❺ Walk out of the courtyard, turn left on the drive and right at a grass triangle, downhill. Leave the path and turn right along the stream, with York Cottage up to the left. Turn right on the path,

and keep left, passing the lake on your right. At the gates, follow the path right for views of the house.

❻ At the intersection of paths, turn right and go up to the house, exploring the terrace. Bear left through the formal North Garden, and at the Old Father Time statue turn left and join the path, passing memorials to the Queen's corgis.

❼ Turn right and pass through the turnstile to the church (or exit via the entrance). Leave the church and go left to the car park.

❽ With the visitor centre behind you, face the adventure playground and take the woodland path to the left, following yellow spots on the trees. At the sign turn right, following the yellow trail, and pass through a squeeze gate. Cross the estate road, follow the path across the grass and go through the wooden arch.

❾ Descend shallow steps, passing a pond and hide on the right, and through another squeeze gate. Continue through the woods and follow the yellow marks left. After about ¼ mile (400m), ignore the path on the left and keep straight on. Follow the yellow arrow up the steep path and steps to the left, to emerge on heathland.

❿ Turn right on the estate road and follow it to meet the main road. Cross over and descend the sandy track through woods.

⓫ At the bottom, follow the yellow arrow left up a straight grassy sward through trees, parallel with the road (right). Continue past the Donkey Pond, follow the yellow spots into the trees at the top, and turn right on to a broad grassy ride. At the triangular junction, cross the road to the left and pick up the yellow arrow, right, into the trees. Follow this path back to the visitor centre.

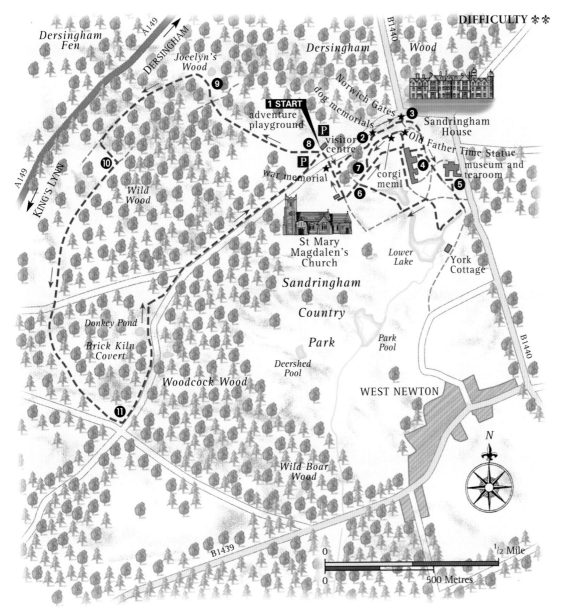

**DIFFICULTY ✿ ✿**

**1911**

**1911** The coronation of George V.

**1911** A Norwegian, Roald Amundsen, beats the British expedition to the South Pole in December. Captain Robert Scott's party reaches the South Pole on 12 January 1912, but none of the

**1912**

team survives the return journey; tragically the party die just a few miles from their main depot.

**1912** The invasion of Greece, Bulgaria, Serbia and Montenegro by the Turkish Army sparks the start of the Balkan Wars (1912–13).

**1912**

**1912** *Titanic*, the 'unsinkable' flagship of the White Star Cruise Line, sets sails for New York. *Titanic* hit an iceberg off Newfoundland and within hours disappears under the Atlantic. Over 15,000 crew and passengers are lost.

# A Walk Through Elgar Country

*Discovering the haunts of Edward Elgar, the landscape composer and self-made Edwardian gentleman*

ABOVE: *Edward Elgar (1857–1934) was Britain's most popular composer until his patriotic music fell out of favour with disillusioned post-war British audiences*

Rising abruptly between the lowlands of Herefordshire and the Vale of Evesham is a short spine of land. Take this route up through woodland on to the commonland which nowadays tops these Malvern Hills and your modest effort will be disproportionately rewarded with panoramic views, among which Edward Elgar found both relaxation and inspiration.

Elgar's Victorian childhood was unexceptional. Born in 1857, he was one of five survivors in a clutch of seven: Harry, aged 15, died from scarlet fever, and Jo, aged seven, succumbed to tuberculosis. Their father, William Elgar, was a piano-tuner, with a music shop in Worcester High Street. Unsurprisingly, all the children were musically competent, but it was little Jo, not Edward, who had come closest to being a child prodigy. Edward did, however, want to be a musician from an early age, and his parents let him abandon a law office job after just a year. Thus began his long, hard graft to success. From his late teens he earned money through teaching, but he later resented the composition time it 'stole' from him. Edward's compositional gifts did not mature – or at least bear fruit in the musical community – until he was well into his 30s. It was his *Coronation Ode* that greeted the new king, Edward VII.

As befitted a self-made Edwardian gentleman, Elgar sought wealth and social prominence and had many diverse hobbies. He collected vast numbers of second-hand books; he enjoyed oils and watercolours; he loved to walk and cycle; he learnt to play golf, and he played billiards (badly). In later years he drove a motor car for pleasure. (He also had a slightly eccentric enthusiasm for amateur chemistry, which once led him to accidentally blow up his water butt with a phosphoric compound.) In 1912 the Elgars bought a house in Hampstead Heath – all their previous homes had been rented – but in truth they had overextended themselves.

During World War I Elgar remained busy composing, but his work reflected the immeasurable disaster going on around him – marches and grand symphonies gave way to melancholic pieces. His earlier music, so warmly embraced by pre-war German audiences, had fallen out of favour, and Britain's post-war mood was not of patriotism but of disillusionment. Worse followed: his wife, Alice, died in 1920. Thereafter, up until his own death from a malignant tumour in 1934, he failed to finish any more major pieces, although he assured the survival of his works by making many recordings using the new technology of the gramophone.

For a man capable of writing such grand music, his grave lies modestly, beside his wife's, in the corner of St Wulstan's churchyard, tucked beneath his beloved Malverns. He was moved to write: 'The place she chose long years ago is too sweet. The blossoms are white all round and the illimitable plain with all the hills and churches in the distance which were hers from childhood looks just the same – inscrutable and unchanging.'

The highest point on this route is the Herefordshire Beacon, also known as the British Camp. This Iron Age site was built by the Celts in about 200 BC. It embraces over 30 acres (12ha) of ground, and at one time might have accommodated a community of several thousand people.

ABOVE: *The Elgar Window at Worcester Cathedral.*

BELOW: *The grandeur of the Malverns were a great inspiration to Elgar who loved to walk in the hills near his home.*

EDWARDIAN

**WALK** 85

ABOUT • GREAT MALVERN

*Edward Elgar (1857–1934) is best remembered for his music, inspired by the dramatic backdrop of the Malvern Hills. It was here that he composed some of his greatest pieces and chose it to be the final resting place for himself and his beloved wife, Alice.*

## Worcestershire • C ENGLAND

**DISTANCE** • 6 miles (9.6km)

**TOTAL ASCENT** • 750ft (228m)

**PATHS** • good; slippery in places

**TERRAIN** • tracks, field paths, stiles and tarmac roads

**GRADIENTS** • some quite steep but not long

**REFRESHMENTS** • kiosk (hot and cold drinks) and hotel near the end of route

**PARK** • Blackhill car park 328yds (300m) past Malvern Hills Hotel on B4232

**OS MAP** • Explorer 190 Malvern Hills & Bredon Hill, Tewkesbury

# Music in the Malverns

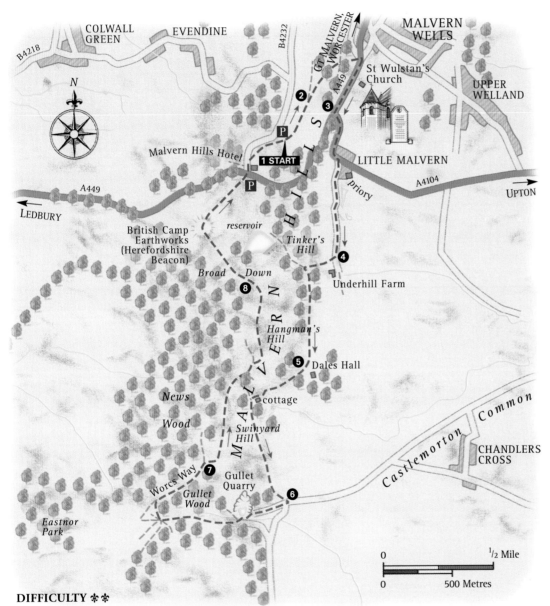

**DIFFICULTY** ✿ ✿

❶ Take a gently rising footpath from the far left-hand corner of Blackhill car park. Walk slightly to the left of the crest to a wooden seat dedicated to Florence Stuart and Harold Woodyatt Harvey.

❷ Take the right fork, soon descending steadily through woodland (ignore crossing path) to reach a tarmac road. Turn right, then right again at the main road,

to view St Wulstan's Church and Elgar's grave. Afterwards, continue to the road junction.

❸ Follow the road signed Upton A4104. At a sharp bend cross carefully to take a bridleway marked Little Malvern Estate Trust. Pass behind Little Malvern Priory, a former monastery, to admire the topiary in an extensive yew hedge. Reach a large solitary yew tree,

just as farm buildings become visible ahead.

❹ Turn right across a stile into a field. Walk diagonally left across the field to a rusty gate, well to the left of a modern grey gate. Continue to follow the path into dense woodland. At a T-junction turn sharply left. Come out of the woodland and continue until telephone wires supported on

double (not single) wooden poles are almost overhead.

❺ Turn two-thirds right, uphill through bracken. Ascend moderately, then later steeply, to eventually pass to the right of a faded-pink cottage. Here a farm track soon joins another. Descend steadily on this stony track to reach a road junction.

❻ At the road turn sharply back right along it to soon skirt Gullet Quarry and pool. Go straight ahead up a stony path to where seven tracks meet. Turn right, signed Worcs Way North, and continue for several hundred yards.

❼ At a clearing go up, right, to the ridge. Turn left. Look out for a low pointer (not obviously an arrow), marked Hangman's Hill, Broad Down, set in cement and stones at a junction. Take the right path to the indistinct top of Broad Down, continuing left along the ridge.

❽ Aim for a partly flagged stone path visible ahead to the left, to reach British Camp Earthworks (Herefordshire Beacon). Continue ahead, descend steps and gravel path, and, bearing right, take any of the clear paths leading down to a large car park opposite the Malvern Hills Hotel (kiosk and toilets nearby). Cross to take the B-road opposite (brief pavement then cross to a path) to return to the Blackhill car park.

• DON'T MISS •

*Elgar's Birthplace Museum, in Broadheath, 3 miles (5km) west of Worcester, was established by his only child, Carice. Worcester Cathedral is a magnificent specimen in itself, and also pays homage to Elgar with a stained-glass window showing scenes from his* Dream of Gerontius.

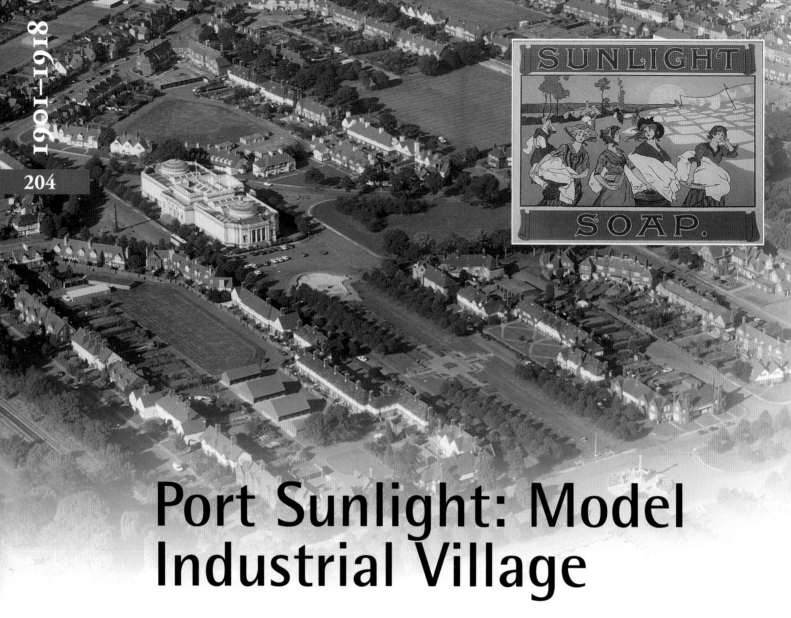

# Port Sunlight: Model Industrial Village

*The garden village of Port Sunlight, purpose-built in the late 19th and early 20th centuries*

ABOVE: *An aerial view of Port Sunlight.*

INSET ABOVE: *Advertisement for Sunlight soap – girls bring in their washing from a field.*

BELOW: *Baron Lever (1851–1925).*

## Enlightened Employment

William Hesketh Lever was an enlightened employer, all too rare in the industrial north of England. He believed that the workers at his Port Sunlight soap factory should have decent housing, which was both of good quality and attractive, and with plenty of recreational space around. To provide this he employed 30 architects, who designed a range of houses, each different, lining spacious streets.

Lever also provided his employees with their own hospital, two schools, two village halls, a church, an inn, social clubs and – very advanced for the time – both a swimming pool and a gymnasium. Workers also received an allowance of Port Sunlight soap, an allowance which continues to this day for the houses, which are mostly still in private hands.

Port Sunlight today is a Conservation Area, and is unique among such model villages not only for its architecture but because it retains its original boundaries and remains much as it was when first built.

## The Workers' World

There are several examples of towns or villages in the north of England that were purpose-built to house factory workers. Saltaire in Bradford is one such, but perhaps the finest example is Port Sunlight on the Wirral. Just across the Mersey is Liverpool, where more typical examples of packed back-to-back terraced housing can be found. Lord Lever wanted better for the people who would be working in his soap factory, however. He felt not only that it was his moral duty but also that a happy work force was a productive work force.

Today's visitor is not merely seeing a worthy project, but also fine examples of late 19th- and early 20th-century architecture. Gladstone Hall, for example, was built in 1891 and was a men's dining hall, but today serves as the village's Gladstone Theatre. The modern Post Office dates from the same period, and was Port Sunlight's general store.

Hulme Hall was built in 1900–1 as a women's dining room, and is now used for social functions as well as computer and antique fairs. For a while it was home to Lord and Lady Lever's art collection, still one of the village's prime attractions, the Lady Lever Art Gallery, was begun in 1913 and finally opened in 1922 by Princess Beatrice, the daughter of Queen Victoria. No visit should miss this excellent collection of fine art objects, especially noted for its Pre-Raphaelite paintings by Millais, Rossetti and others.

The Heritage Centre is another building that must be seen, providing as it does the background to the whole project, with old photographs and even movie footage, as well as a scale model of Port Sunlight, to help plan a walk around its streets. During the summer there are also guided walking tours on Sundays and Bank Holiday Mondays.

BELOW: *William Lever employed 30 architects to ensure that each street was different and the town offered a range of house styles.*

## WALK 86
## AROUND THE MODEL VILLAGE

❶ Begin at the Heritage Centre on Greendale Road, close to Port Sunlight railway station, which provides residents with rail links to Liverpool and to Chester. After emerging from the Centre, note the Gladstone Theatre opposite. Turn left and left again into Wood Street, which runs alongside the factory where all Port Sunlight's residents worked. Many still do.

❷ At Poet's Corner turn left and left again to double back down Park Road, built in 1892, towards the Heritage Centre; at the junction with Greendale Road is the Post Office. Walk past the Post Office along Greendale Road and turn right into Bolton Road.

❸ Take the second on the left, Church Drive, which naturally leads to Christ Church, the parish church that was built in 1902–4. It is quite a modest church, whose roof blends in with the domestic architecture and which has some fine stained glass windows. Behind the church take Walker Street, turn left down Pool Bank, left into Circular Drive and Primrose Hill, and left on Lower Road to the Lady Lever Art Gallery.

❹ On leaving the gallery walk left down Queen Mary's Drive, which leads to the war memorial. This imposing village focal point was begun in 1916 and not finished until 1921. Touching bronze sculptures depict soldiers guarding women and children, and civilians protecting each other from the horrors of war. Turn right down the Causeway then left into Greendale Road to the start.

**Distance:** 3 miles (4.8km)

**Total ascent:** none

**Paths:** pavements

**Terrain:** town

**Gradients:** very slight

**Refreshments:** Lady Lever Art Gallery

**Park:** Heritage Centre. Note that traffic is not permitted on some streets in Port Sunlight

**OS Map:** Explorer 266 Wirral & Chester

**Difficulty:** ✳

**1913** Suffragettes gain their first martyr when Emily Dickinson throws herself in front of the King's horse at the Derby and is trampled to death. Captured on film, the incident becomes a symbol for the desperate struggle and frustration of the women's movement.

**1913** The Royal Horticultural Society organises the first Chelsea Flower Show.

**1913** The Panama Canal is opened, creating a shorter shipping route between the Atlantic and Pacific oceans.

**1914** *Pygmalion* (George Bernard Shaw) opens in London.

**1914** The heir to the Austro-Hungarian throne is assassinated by a Serbian terrorist. Austria declares war on Serbia and Russia mobilises its troops to defend Serbia.

# Casualties of War

*Craiglockhart, where officers traumatised by war were given treatment unavailable to the ranks*

EDWARDIAN

A NEW CENTURY

Scotland suffered the highest percentage of casualties in 'the war to end all wars'. Proportionally greater numbers of volunteers responded to the call to arms and, of the 557,000 who signed up, over 26 per cent were killed, compared with an average death rate of 11 per cent for the rest of Britain. Three hundred and seven British soldiers, 39 of whom were Scots, were executed for 'cowardice' during the course of World War I. In fact, far from being cowards, they were suffering from what is now known as shell shock. Officers exhibiting the same symptoms were shipped off quietly to special hospitals for treatment. Craiglockhart House, in the countryside outside Edinburgh, was one such establishment.

Siegfried Sassoon, already a well established poet, had been sent there to avoid a court martial after his *Declaration against the War* was read out in the House of Commons. Wilfrid Owen was there, too, recovering from shell shock. The months they spent together at Craiglockhart were productive for both. Owen edited six issues of the hospital magazine, *Hydra*, which published several of Sassoon's poems, written here. It also contained the first two published poems of Wilfrid Owen.

Elsewhere in Scotland the class divide of the war effort was replicated. Landlords in Glasgow sought to exploit the influx of workers, needed for the production of munitions, by raising rents. Glasgow was already badly overcrowded, and the extra workers made things worse; in addition, rents rose by an average of 23 per cent between 1914 and October of 1915. A rent strike was organised and 20,000 people refused to pay. When a handful of defaulting tenants were taken to court in November, the workers in the shipyards and munitions factories walked out and threatened an indefinite strike. The protesters included men, women and children and political activists from the Independent Labour Party, the Socialist Labour Party, the suffragettes and Glasgow Trades Council. They joined the tenants in demonstrations against the court case.

By 1917 the protests were supporting the revolution in Russia and on 1 May 100,000 went on strike against the war. The establishment had come to fear that the Russian Revolution would be repeated in 'Red Clydeside'. The culmination came after the war in 1919, when the government, fearing that the Scots were about to revolt, imported troops from England, kept the Scottish troops inside Maryhill Barracks and had George Square, the traditional gathering ground for marchers, surrounded by tanks. Several of the leaders, including Emmanuel, later Lord Shinwell, ended up in jail and the veteran Socialist agitator Harry McShane would later tell how he had been beaten over the head by police batons: 'They thought that we were there to start a revolution when all we wanted was fair wages and rents.' In 1922 the Independent Labour Party returned 29 MPs to Westminster, ten of them from Glasgow, including several, like Shinwell and James Maxton, who had been involved in the campaign against unfair rents.

ABOVE: *Siegfried Sassoon (1886–1967) – poet and author – was a patient at Craiglockhart after he was sent back from the front suffering from shell shock.*

RIGHT: *The lovely countryside surrounding Craiglockhart Hospital, must have seemed like paradise after the blood and dirt of the trenches in France.*

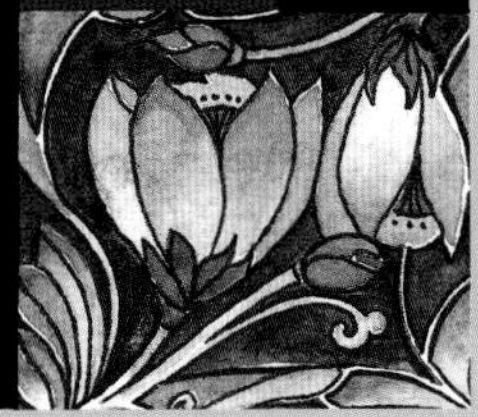

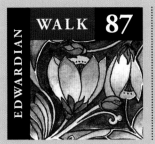

ABOUT • CRAIGLOCKHART HOUSE

*World War I, called 'the war to end all wars' suffered more casualties than any other. Thousands more suffered from shell shock, including war poets, Siegfried Sassoon and Wilfred Owen. Being officers they were lucky and sent to Craiglockhart to recover.*

**City of Edinburgh • SCOTLAND**

**DISTANCE** • 7 miles (11.3km)

**TOTAL ASCENT** • 275ft (84m)

**PATHS** • mostly good but can get boggy in wet weather

**TERRAIN** • pavements and woodland paths

**GRADIENTS** • moderate to steep

**REFRESHMENTS** • none on route

**PARK** • Hermitage Drive

**OS MAP** • Explorer 350 Edinburgh, Mussellburgh & Queensferry

# Craiglockhart House: a World War I hospital

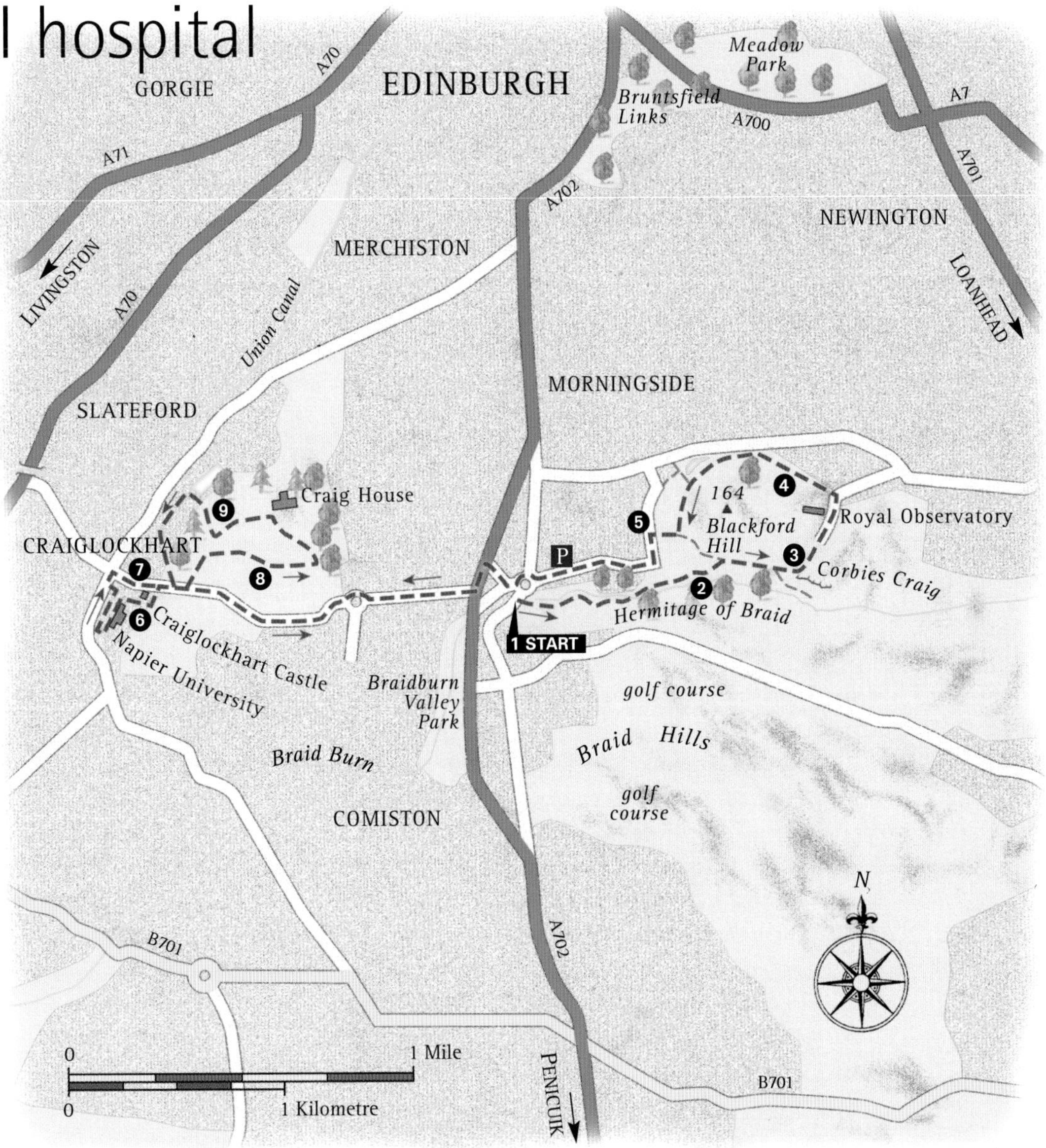


❶ Enter Hermitage of Braid park, turn left through a kissing gate and head along the river path. At the toilets re-join the driveway and at the visitor centre take the left fork and head uphill.

❷ Fork left and keep heading uphill untill you reach a stone wall. Continue along the wall, go through the gap and turn right on to a path. Take a left fork and head up hill keeping Corbies Craig on your right.

❸ At a grassy area turn left and at the top of the hill cross over to the Royal Observatory, keeping the buildings on your left. Follow the footpath to Observatory Road North then turn left at the end of the buildings.

❹ Take the right-hand track, cross another track and fork right and head downhill. Continue on a rutted track, go down steps on to a path, turn left, continue past allotments, then turn right through a metal gate and cross a field.

❺ Exit through a car park and head along Hermitage Drive. Cross Braid Road, turn right into Greenbank Place, turn left at Comiston Road and right into Greenbank Drive. At the roundabout keep right along Glenlockhart Road, then turn left to Napier University.

❻ Follow the road to a large sandstone building and turn right. Turn right again in front of the clock, go down steps and turn right on to a path. Exit through the gate, turn right, then right again at the traffic-lights.

❼ Cross the road and turn left along a path by the white house. Turn right at the end of the wall, go uphill and turn right again through a gap in the wall. Go uphill and pass stone marker 5.

❽ Go through a gate, turn right, then left, following the woodland path behind some buildings. Go right towards the large sandstone building, turn left on to the path. Continue, turning left through some gorse bushes then right at stone marker 9.

❾ Go downhill and leave the woods through a gate. Follow the path round some houses then turn left on to a path past a pond. Climb the steps, to return to the white house, turn left on to the road and return to the start and the car park.

**DIFFICULTY** ✽✽

**• DON'T MISS •**

***Roslin Chapel**, near Penicuik, was built by the Knights Templar. Like a great French cathedral in miniature, Roslin has a haunting atmosphere and some unique stone carvings, including the death mask of Robert the Bruce.*

**1914**

**1914** Germany declares war on Russia and France on 1 August, and invades Belgium two days later.

**1914** On 4 August Britain declares war on Germany, and by early September the Battle of Marne stops the German advance at the

**1914**

Marne River. German and British troops dig themselves into the ground, and four years of bloody trench warfare ensues.

**1914** The Irish Home Rule Bill is passed by the Liberal government, despite the opposition of the

**1914**

Conservatives and the Ulster Unionists. Because of the war, however, little attention is paid to the growing political unrest in Ireland.

# Castle Drogo – Lutyens' Masterpiece

*Through the wooded gorge of the sparkling upper River Teign to the youngest castle in Britain*

Situated 1,000ft (305m) above sea level, high above the gorge of the upper Teign river, the solid granite mass of Castle Drogo is a magnificent sight. This walk, which follows the pretty Teign to Fingle Bridge, provides the chance to enjoy the castle from every angle. The return route runs along the edge of the gorge, with fantastic views over Dartmoor. Apart from the steep (but brief) ascent from Fingle Bridge, the walk is an easy one.

Castle Drogo, built of massive blocks of local granite, is the result of a successful collaboration between the renowned architect Sir Edwin Lutyens and self-made millionaire and founder of the Home and Colonial Stores, Julius Drewe. The latter, who retired at the age of 33, was keen to establish his family seat here because of a romantic notion that his ancestors had connections with the nearby village of Drewsteignton. The castle, built between 1910 and 1930, is a reduced version of Lutyens' original plan, which was curtailed due to various practical considerations and the onset of World War I. Drewe died in 1931, soon after the castle's completion, and in fact

Lutyens' original plan for a gateway was never executed – Drewe lost heart in the idea after his eldest son Adrian died in the war.

Lutyens was one of the foremost architects of his time, and his reputation continues to grow today. He was responsible for designing both country houses and public buildings, and his later work reflected the principles of classical baroque architecture. He designed the Cenotaph in Whitehall and Liverpool's Roman Catholic cathedral, as well as the British Embassy in Washington DC, and was also responsible for one of the most prestigious projects in the world: the building of New Delhi.

His design for Castle Drogo combines the qualities and grandeur of a medieval castle with those of a comfortable 20th-century home, and displays all the elements that made his work so popular: his designs are always of the highest quality and use local materials, so are sympathetic with their surroundings, and the interior décor reflects his belief in grand yet simple architectural effects. He was knighted in 1918 and made president of the Royal Academy in 1938, and a collection of his letters and designs for the castle can be seen in the Gun Room.

The garden, designed in 1915, is a delight at all times of the year. It comprises a series of three terraces with granite steps and walls, glorious herbaceous borders, a beautiful woodland spring garden and an impressive circular, yew-hedged croquet lawn. Following their meeting in 1889, Lutyens frequently collaborated with the celebrated garden designer Gertrude Jekyll (1843–1932), who had an enormous influence on the British attitude to gardens. At the time of Castle Drogo's construction she was in her 70s and so unable to travel to Devon from London and become involved with the project. The results of their partnership can, however, be seen at sites such as Lindisfarne Castle in Northumberland and Hestercombe in Somerset.

FAR LEFT: *A cartoon portrait of Sir Edwin Lutyens (1869–1944).*

ABOVE: *Inside Drogo Castle the hand of Edwin Lutyens is evident – in his use of natural materials and an interior design that combines the grandeur of a medieval castle with the comforts of a modern home.*

RIGHT: *The austere, dark granite entrance tower of Castle Drogo.*

**ABOUT • CASTLE DROGO**

*Castle Drogo, built in 1930, is now owned by the National Trust. Built of local granite, it was the result of a partnership between the architect Sir Edwin Lutyens, one of the foremost architects of the Edwardian era, and millionaire, Julius Drewe.*

**Devon • SW ENGLAND**

**DISTANCE** • 4½ miles (7.2km)

**TOTAL ASCENT** • 395ft (120m)

**PATHS** • good field and woodland tracks; some muddy after wet weather

**TERRAIN** • steep-sided river gorge, mixed deciduous woodland and open moorland

**GRADIENTS** • one long, steep climb from Fingle Bridge

**REFRESHMENTS** • The Angler's Rest at Fingle Bridge; the Sandy Park Inn, Sandy Park

**PARK** • Roadside parking at Dogmarsh Bridge, just south of Sandy Park on the A382 Whiddon Down to Moretonhampstead road

**OS MAP** • Outdoor Leisure 28 Dartmoor

# Castle Drogo, a famous partnership

**DIFFICULTY ✿✿**

❶ Walk from your car towards the bridge. Turn left through the kissing gate, following the footpath signed Two Moors Way, to enter the Castle Drogo Estate. Walk along the river, passing through two kissing gates. Go over a footbridge to enter oak woodland then negotiate a stile/small gate.

❷ Turn right to cross the river on a suspension bridge*, ascend steps to cross the big granite wall. Turn left along the track, which leads through a five-bar gate. Continue along this undulating track, soon passing a pumping station on your left, part of the castle's hydro-electric scheme. Continue along the track through Hannicombe Wood to reach Fingle Bridge.

❸ Turn left to cross the old packhorse bridge and take a break at The Angler's Rest. To continue the walk turn right from the pub and up the lane through the parking area.

❹ After 100yds (91m) turn left, following a footpath signed Hunter's path. This narrow wooded path climbs steeply up to reach open moorland above the gorge and joins the Hunter's path (which comes in from the right); keep left and pass through granite gateposts towards the castle, which can be seen ahead.

❺ At the next signpost (Drewsteignton) turn right up wooden steps; do not cross the stile ahead, but almost immediately turn left across Piddledown Common following the signs for Castle Drogo. The next sign directs you along the Gorse Blossom Walk to reach the castle drive.

❻ Turn left; at the car park sign turn right to reach the entrance to the castle and gardens. After your visit, retrace your steps out of the car park and turn left down the drive to continue the walk.

❼ Almost immediately turn right, signed Hunter's Path. Keep straight on downhill, and descend wooden steps, to meet the path along the edge of the gorge. Turn right and follow the path below the castle, veering right to meet a lane through two wooden gates.

❽ Turn left downhill, signed Fisherman's Path. Cross the cattle grid and follow footpath signs to pass to the left of the thatched Gibhouse and down the wooded path to the river. Turn right over the footbridge and stile, and retrace your steps across the meadows to your car.

* At the time of going to press the suspension bridge was closed due to flood damage. If it has not reopened, continue on Fisherman's Path close to the north bank, to Fingle Bridge and pick up the directions part way through Point ❸.

**Map labels:** DREWSTEIGNTON · D A R T M O O R · Castle Drogo · Drewston Wood · Prestonbury Castle · P *i* · ❻ · ❼ · ❽ · Piddledown Common · Hunter's path · Fingle Bridge · The Angler's Rest PH · ❹ · ❺ · Sharp Tor · River Teign · ❸ · Hunter's Tor · Sandy Park Inn · SANDY PARK · ❷ · pumping station · suspension bridge · Hannicombe Wood · Hore Wood · 1 START · Mill End Hotel · A382 · N A T I O N A L · Cranbrook Castle · B3206 · EASTON · P A R K · CHAGFORD · MORETONHAMPSTEAD · A382 · 0 ½ Mile · 0 500 Metres

**1915** The *Lusitania*, a ship carrying munitions and civilian passengers, is torpedoed and sunk by a German U-boat. The attack provokes moral outrage and soldiers are dispatched to quell anti-German riots. In the United States feelings also run high as many passengers were American.

**1916** Nicholas II, Tsar of Russia, is executed together with his family as the Russian Revolution gets under way.

**1916** A German zeppelin crashes on British soil at Potters Bar.

**1916** Frustrated over the lack of progress of the Irish Home Rule Bill, members of the Sinn Fein Party capture several buildings in Dublin and proclaim a provisional government (known as the Easter Uprising). The leaders are captured within a week and shot.

# Criccieth: the Road to Power

*A Llŷn Peninsula walk, following the footsteps of the area's most famous son and statesman*

*Above: David Lloyd George (1863–1945) – Welsh statesmen and social and government reformer.*

Raised first in the little village of Llanystumdwy and then in the seaside town of Criccieth, David Lloyd George – the 'Welsh Wizard' – went on to become one of the most charismatic politicians of the 20th century. With his shock of snow-white hair and fervent rhetoric, 'Ll G' cut a

ABOVE: *Aerial view of the town of Criccieth and the castle.*

flamboyant figure among the sober-suited Edwardians of the day. Controversy was always at his heels – a lack of private means prompted some questionable profit-making schemes, and while his wife stayed in Criccieth, Lloyd George's secretary, Frances Stevenson, became his London companion from 1911 (they married in 1943).

When he laid the foundation stone of Criccieth's Memorial Hall (Neuadd Goffa) in 1922, Lloyd George's career had already passed its peak. As Chancellor of the Exchequer, he had set the scene for a welfare state, introducing pensions and unemployment insurance. Taking over as Prime Minister in 1916, he created new ministries, such as Food and Labour, to tackle the problems of a nation at war; and the post-war years saw the vote extended to over

8 million women, and the establishment of limited home rule in Ireland. But scandal dogged him throughout, and after a row over the sale of knighthoods and baronetcies, he resigned – in the same year that work began on the Memorial Hall.

As you turn away from the town and the sea, the route takes you back to Lloyd George's early life in Criccieth, passing the former Particular Baptist Chapel, where he was baptised from steps leading to the stream that flows alongside the road. The chapel is now a private residence, but you can still glimpse the headstones in the old graveyard.

Houses soon give way to fields and misty views of the sea and Llŷn mountains, and the walk leads past a nursing home, Bryn Awelon ('hill of breezes'). Lloyd George lived here before World War I, and it later became the home of his daughter, Lady Megan.

The path continues into lush coastal countryside and towards Llanystumdwy, his first home. Presently you hear the rushing Dwyfor river, below the road to the right: it comes into view as you reach Lloyd George's grave and memorial, set on the riverbank at a spot where he loved to sit. Opposite is the entrance to the Lloyd George Museum and access to Highgate, the stone cottage where he spent his early years.

From here the walk heads gradually back to Criccieth, passing, on its final leg, the former solicitor's office (at 14 Tan-y-Grisiau Terrace) where Lloyd George embarked on his first job, as a lawyer. The return journey meanders through stunning Llŷn landscapes, following the Dwyfor to the sea and swinging round with glorious views of Criccieth and its 13th-century castle, and the coastline beyond. Little wonder that after his long Westminster career, the Welsh Wizard asked to be laid to rest among the beautiful haunts of his youth.

BELOW: *Lloyd George's grave at Llanystumdwy.*

**ABOUT • CRICCIETH**

*Born in the small town of Llanystumdwy, David Lloyd George, the 'Welsh Wizard', was one of the most charismatic politicians of the 20th century. He was elected Prime Minister in 1916 and was responsible for great social and political reforms.*

**Gwynedd • WALES**

**DISTANCE** • 5 miles (8km)

**TOTAL ASCENT** • 131ft (40m)

**PATHS** • some rough tracks; fields may be muddy

**TERRAIN** • surfaced roads, fields, stony tracks, pebble beach. **Make sure you complete the walk during low tide**

**GRADIENTS** • gradual

**REFRESHMENTS** • several pubs and cafés in Criccieth

**PARK** • Criccieth car park off Y Maes

**OS MAP** • Explorer 13 (previously 254) Lleyn Peninsula East

# In the steps of the 'Welsh Wizard'

❶ Start at the Memorial Hall, at the bottom end of Y Maes, the green at the centre of Criccieth. With your back to the hall, turn right, then right again, following the Caernarfon (B4411) sign. Climb the hill away from town.

❷ At the Bron Eifion sign just beyond the former Baptist Chapel, now called Pen-y-Maes, turn left. Follow the single-track road past Bryn Awelon and bear right, into the countryside, where the road forks. Continue past the entrance to the Bron Eifion Fishery, right.

❸ After visiting Lloyd George's memorial, right, turn back and retrace your steps as far as the entrance to Tŷ Newydd, now on your right. Take this turning, following the public footpath sign.

❹ Continue past Tŷ Newydd and follow the public footpath arrow ahead, past a row of cottages. Go through the kissing gate and continue alongside the hedge.

• DON'T MISS •

*It's worth breaking your journey to visit the Lloyd George Museum and Highgate, two minutes' walk away, where the statesman's Victorian childhood home has been recreated, along with a 19th-century schoolroom, his uncle's shoe-making workshop and an immaculate cottage garden. You also pass Tŷ Newydd, the house which Lloyd George bought in 1943 and where he lived until his death in 1945.*

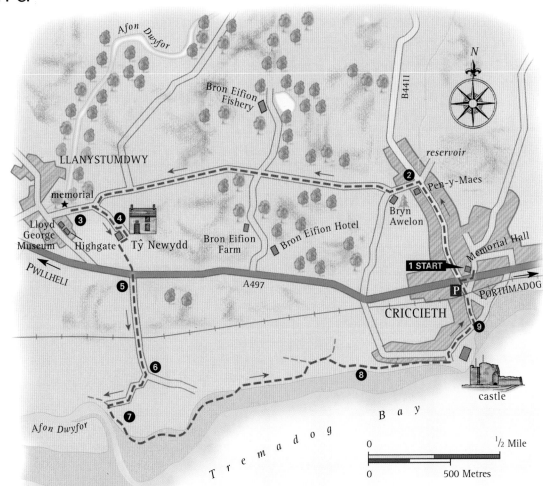

**DIFFICULTY** ✤ ✤

Climb the stone stile and cross the field towards the road.

❺ Cross the road and continue along the public footpath ahead. After crossing the railway bridge the track swings round to the left; fork right to the gate, signed footpath only, and climb the wooden stile.

❻ Follow the path round to the right. Go through the wooden picket gate (alongside a wooden five-bar gate) and continue to

meet the river. Turn left to follow the river's course to the sea.

❼ Continue on the track, which swings left and peters out into pebble beach: take care here and make sure the tide is out. Follow the beach round the headland. Climb to the path above and parallel to the beach, passing a National Trust marker on a boulder where the coast has eroded.

❽ At the end of the track turn right towards Criccieth. Where the

track bends to the left, take the path along the cliff straight ahead, leading back into the town. Go through the kissing gate and continue ahead following the esplanade.

❾ After passing the castle hill, just before the road begins to descend and with the pillar box on the corner, turn left up Tan-y-Grisiau Terrace. Continue to the end and cross the railway line. The Memorial Hall is diagonally ahead, to the right.

1901–1918

**1916**

**1916** Tanks are used for the first time against German troops at the Battle of the Somme, which ends in stalemate.

**1917** Mata Hari, an exotic dancer turned German spy, is executed in France.

**1917**

**1917** America declares war on Germany on 6 April, restoring hope to the allied forces.

**1918** Germany signs the armistice agreement on 11 November, marking the end of the war.

**1918**

**1918** Political reforms give women over 30 the right to vote in a General Election for the first time, in recognition and appreciation of their tremendous efforts during the war. The emancipation of women had at last taken an enormous step forward.

212

# Steep: in the Steps of Edward Thomas

*The spectacular beech hangers and dramatic downland of east Hampshire, hardly changed since a famous Edwardian poet was moved to write about this delightful area in his work*

The simple hilltop monument to Edward Thomas not only commemorates the life of a famous Edwardian poet, but also symbolises the futility of war, evoking disturbing images of bitter conflict, bloodshed and brutality. Thomas died 18 months before World War I ended. At not yet 40 years of age, he was killed at the Battle of Arras in France in the spring of 1917.

Edward Thomas was born at Lambeth in 1878 and published his first book at the age of 19. In the early years, he gained something of a reputation as a literary critic and nature writer; it wasn't until 1913, with the outbreak of war looming, that he began writing poetry.

Although Thomas is regarded as a war poet, essentially his work concentrates on the English landscape. Characterised by a lyrical clarity, his poetry and prose reflect the beauty and magical quality of nature. His love of the countryside is unmistakable, its changing character and variety of scenery providing an endless source of inspiration.

Thomas's writing shows that he loved walking, and he was known to hike up to 30 miles (48km) a day, between dawn and dusk. After moving to the village of Steep, near Petersfield, in 1906, Thomas spent many happy hours roaming this corner of East Hampshire, savouring the glorious beech hangers, the distant downland glimpses and the sheer beauty of the landscape.

With its rolling hills and spectacular scenery, it is not surprising that this area is sometimes known as Little Switzerland. Thomas knew every inch of it and one of his most cherished haunts was Shoulder of Mutton Hill, which looms spectacularly above Steep. From the top, the views to the south are breathtaking, perfectly described by Thomas as 'sixty miles of South Downs at one glance'.

During his last leave from France, Thomas walked hereabouts with a friend. When asked if he knew what he was fighting for, Thomas paused for a moment and then stooped to run a few particles of earth between his fingers. 'I think, literally, this,' he replied. It was that unique and tangible sense of British peace and beauty that he and his compatriots had been fighting to defend. Thomas returned to battle and died five weeks after his 39th birthday.

Twenty years later, in 1937, the then Poet Laureate Walter de la Mare unveiled a sarsen memorial stone to Edward Thomas on the summit of Shoulder of Mutton Hill. De la Mare paid the poet a glowing tribute, claiming that 'when he was killed in Flanders, a mirror of England was shattered'.

This superb country walk captures the spirit and essence of Edward Thomas. Following in his footsteps, it visits the Red House, where he lived for four years, and Berryfield Cottage, his first home in the area. But it is the stunning beauty of Shoulder of Mutton Hill which is most closely associated with the man. Here, you can picture Steep's most famous resident facing an uncertain future and yet at peace with himself, strolling the tree-shaded hilltop.

ABOVE: *View from the top of Shoulder of Mutton Hill, home and inspiration of Edward Thomas.*

LEFT: *Edward Thomas (1878-1917).*

BACKGROUND: *Ashford Hangers Nature Reserve in Steep, Hampshire.*

**ABOUT • STEEP**

*This hilly walk in Steep introduces the landscape that inspired the poetry of Edward Thomas. The walks visits his two homes and Shoulder of Mutton Hill, his poetic inspiration, and the Sarsen Stone, laid in his memory by Walter de la Mare.*

**Hampshire • SE ENGLAND**

**DISTANCE** • 5 miles (8km)

**TOTAL ASCENT** • 545ft (166m)

**PATHS** • field, woodland paths and tracks

**TERRAIN** • rolling countryside at western end of the South Downs. Some tracks and paths are suitable for dogs off the lead

**GRADIENTS** • hilly on the outward leg; steep ascent to Shoulder of Mutton Hill

**REFRESHMENTS** • the Harrow Inn and the Cricketers Inn at Steep

**PARK** • roadside parking in the vicinity of All Saints' Church, Steep

**OS MAP** • Explorer 133 Haslemere & Petersfield

# The poet of Steep

❶ With All Saints' Church on your right, follow Church Road for 50yds (46m) to a sharp right-hand bend. Bear left into woodland and swing immediately right. Follow the clear path between trees and down to a galvanised kissing gate. Cross a stream and head towards Steep Farm, to cross two stiles.

❷ Pass the farm and veer right at the end of the buildings. Keep left after a few paces and follow the track down to a stream. As the track curves right, go towards a stile at the foot of a steep bank. Don't cross it; instead turn left and follow the woodland path. Cross a stream and make for a cottage in trees. Cross over the drive and continue on a clearly defined path.

❸ Keep to the left of silos and outbuildings and look for a finger post here. Swing left to a stile and gateway and follow the field edge to the corner. Head for a gap in the trees and take the path uphill, along the woodland edge. Make for a stile in the right-hand boundary and cross the field, parallel to power lines. Look for a stile by a metal gate and join a path which runs up above some woodland. Continue on the enclosed path to the lane.

❹ Turn right and keep left after 400yds (366m) when the lane forks. Bear left after a few paces to a stile and follow the path between lines of trees, up the hillside to a stile in the woodland boundary. Turn left and follow the green lane as it climbs steeply through the trees. Ignore paths left and right, and eventually pass a green sign for Ashford Hangers, followed in 200yds (183m) by a barrier. Further on, the walk coincides with a section of the 21-mile (34km) Hangers Way.

❺ To visit the Poet Stone, follow Hangers Way, left, 100yds (91m) after it joins the main path from the right. After a few paces it goes right, go straight on, steeply descending to the stone. Return to main track, turn left and follow lane until it leads between houses. Look for The Red House, before The Edward Barnsley Workshop, and continue to the road junction.

❻ Bear left, then immediately left again on a sunken bridleway. Descend steeply for 500yds (457m), to a fork. Keep right and rejoin the Hangers Way. Follow it over a stream and between trees. After 600yds (549m), at the road by a barrier, turn left and pass Old Ashford Manor.

❼ Walk along 200yds (183m) to Berryfield Cottage, right, followed by Ashford Chace. Continue for 50yds (46m), and turn right signed Hangers Way. Follow the track and as it bends right by a private sign, veer left to a woodland path. After a right and left bend, continue for 400yds (366m) then turn right down some steps to a waterfall.

❽ At the road beyond, keep right and continue for 200yds (183m) to a right-hand turning. Bear left here, through a kissing gate. Turn right and skirt the field to a plank bridge and stile in the corner. Cross into woodland, follow the path to a playing field. Cross and emerge opposite All Saints' Church.

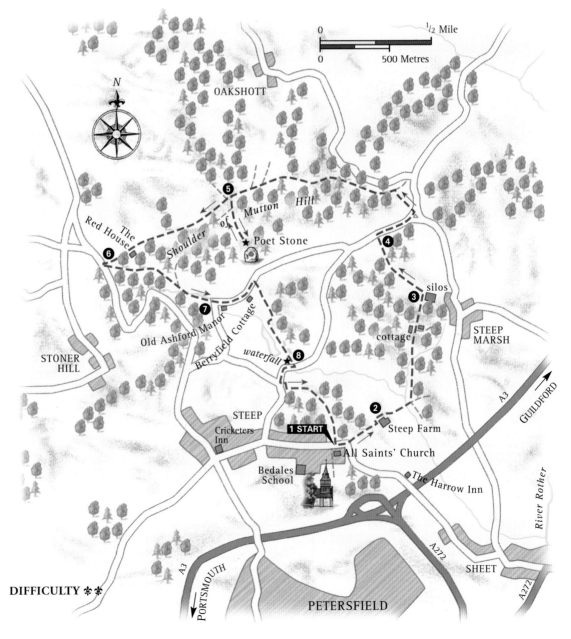

**DIFFICULTY** ✽ ✽

SUL M
R-100
FOR GALLANTRY
DEL GRUPPO ARMATORIALE
ICH · LLOYD TRIESTINO

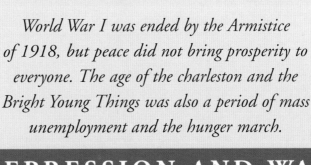

*World War I was ended by the Armistice of 1918, but peace did not bring prosperity to everyone. The age of the charleston and the Bright Young Things was also a period of mass unemployment and the hunger march.*

# DEPRESSION AND WAR

## 1918–1945

# Jazz Age to Atomic Age

Old conventions were thrown aside and taboos broken in the 1920s. Skirts grew shorter and parties wilder; literature became more explicit, as writers such as D H Lawrence dealt with sex and working-class culture. But the Jazz Age was the experience of a privileged minority. For many more people, life in post-war Britain was a struggle to make ends meet. A dispute between coal miners and mine-owners threatening to cut already meagre wages drew in workers from other industries, and in 1926 a General Strike seemed about to bring the country to a standstill. Three years later the New York stock market crashed, and the repercussions were felt across the Western world. Personal fortunes were lost and whole sectors of industry floundered: the Jarrow 'hunger march' to London of 1936 highlighted the plight of ship-builders unable to make a living.

There could be no greater contrast than the world presented in the increasingly popular movies, all-singing and all-dancing since the introduction of sound in 1929. They provided a regular dose of escapism and brought a taste of Hollywood glamour into the most ordinary lives. In the 1920s another form of entertainment had been brought even closer to home, as the radio began to appear in households across the country. Under the sole guardianship of the BBC, established in 1922, it promised to 'inform, educate and entertain'. In 1936 television made its début, but only to a very limited audience.

With the increased use of the car came the spread of suburbs, as families flocked from cities to live in new housing estates that were springing up on their rural edges. Streamlined architecture, using the stylised curves and corners of Art Deco, took its place alongside the ornate finery and terraced brick of the Victorian age. Some of the most notable buildings met the needs of modern electrical industries – consumer goods factories such as the Hoover Building in Perivale, for instance, and massive power stations such as Battersea.

### BACK TO THE FRAY

Across Europe, the opposing forces of Fascism and Communism were drawing up their battle-lines during the 1920s and '30s. About 2,000 volunteers joined the Republican forces of Spain against General Franco in 1936, while at home British Fascists looked to former Labour politician Oswald Moseley, figurehead of the so-called blackshirts. But the main concern of the British press was the abdication of Edward VIII, who gave up the throne in 1936 in order to marry American divorcée Wallis Simpson.

As Hitler's Germany set about annexing and occupying territories and persecuting the Jewish population, Britain pursued a policy of appeasement, until the German army invaded Poland in 1939 and made war inevitable. Winston Churchill took the helm as Prime Minister in 1940, the year of Britain's 'darkest hour', as France fell and many British cities suffered devastating 'blitz' bombing. In the following year America entered the war and those who were billeted 'over here' made a deep impression with their easy-going informality.

On 6 June 1944 British, Commonwealth and American forces landed on the Normandy beaches to begin the final thrust that would end in Germany's surrender. The war with Japan dragged on, however, until August 1945, when the first atomic bombs were dropped on Hiroshima and Nagasaki, and the world faced up to the realities of the nuclear age.

## HISTORIC SITES

**Eltham Palace, Greater London:** Art Deco extravaganza.

**Tyne Bridge, Newcastle:** built in the 1920s as Britain's biggest single-span steel bridge.

**Mr Straw's House, Worksop, Notts:** time capsule of a middle-class 1930s house.

**Delaware Pavilion, Bexhill-on-Sea:** modernist architecture.

**Cabinet War Rooms, London:** Churchill's underground operations centre.

**Bletchley Park, Beds:** the secret wartime code-breakers' HQ.

**1919**

**1919** Ernest Rutherford splits the atom and leads the way to nuclear power and weapons.

**1919** Aviators John Alcock and Arthur Brown make the first non-stop transatlantic flight, landing in Ireland 16½ hours later.

**1919**

**1919** In a last act of defiance, the Germans scupper their own fleet, which is interned at Scapa Flow, Orkney.

**1919** The Treaty of Versailles is signed, and the terms burden Germany with huge reparations.

**1919**

The formidable German navy is handed over to Britain and Germany is forbidden from rebuilding her armed forces.

**1919** Nancy Astor is elected Britain's first female MP.

# Wigan Pier: Testament of Poverty

*Trace the famous journey taken by George Orwell to illustrate working-class hardship in Lancashire*

**DEPRESSION AND WAR**

**JAZZ AGE TO ATOMIC AGE**

Before World War I, Lancashire had prospered on the strength of cotton and coal, two of Britain's foremost industries. The demands of war, however, stretched the coal industry to capacity, while cotton, by contrast, saw a decline in manpower and shipping space. The inter-war years, although peaceful, exposed underlying problems, including loss of markets in the textile trade as pre-war markets, such as India, became self sufficient, and new producers in Japan and Italy proved more economically efficient by using newer machines and paying lower wages. Coal deposits, too, were steadily running out, and the industry was beset by over-manning and poor output.

In 1929 came the Wall Street Crash and a world slump that pushed unemployment in Britain to 21 per cent by 1931. The greatest impact was on the mining and industrial areas of the North. For Wigan, the 1930s saw unemployment rise to an incredible 35 per cent, and even higher in more localised areas.

Against the subsequent background of hopelessness among miners and their families, Victor Gollancz commissioned George Orwell (Eric Blair) to report on working-class life in the industrial heartlands of the North. His book *The Road to Wigan Pier* (1936) provided an unappetising insight to many who had never experienced the physical and social devastation wrought by lack of work. The experience profoundly changed Orwell, and his book is an outstanding polemic – bitter and brilliant.

This walk begins from Wigan Pier, which today is the focal point of a modest leisure enterprise. It stands on the Leeds and Liverpool Canal, along which coal and other goods were transported in

*RIGHT: Wigan Pier, Wigan, on the Leeds and Liverpool Canal.*

barges. Much of the walk stays close by the canal and its many locks, a fascinating engineering masterpiece in its own right, but halfway round it wanders about the grounds of Haigh Hall Country Park.

In the 1930s, Orwell estimated, the income of an unemployed family was a mere 30 shillings (£1.50) a week, of which 25 per cent went on rent. Yet to receive even this pittance, a family would be subjected to the means test, by which the income of the entire family was investigated to determine the measure of relief due. Any so-called 'luxury' items had to be sold, and the whole degrading experience induced a climate of 'tale-telling' about unsold possessions or other sources of income, and gave rise to a heavy atmosphere of mistrust, ill feeling and, occasionally, violence.

Demoralisation was arguably the most potent consequence of unemployment. Those out of work went picking coal from slag heaps, or hung about on street corners, in the public library reading room, the billiards halls and cinemas. It was a sorry time, and one that finds echoes even today in the way Wigan features in television dramas old and new, and visitors flock to Wigan Pier to see The Way We Were.

ABOVE: *George Orwell (1903–50) is best remembered for* Animal Farm *(1945) and for his frightening prophecy novel* 1984 *(1949).*

**ABOUT • WIGAN**

The Road to Wigan Pier *(1936) by George Orwell is a moving testament to the poverty-stricken lives of those living in northern parts of Britain during the 1930s depression. Our walk begins at Wigan Pier which is, ironically, now a centre of enterprise.*

## Lancashire • N ENGLAND

**DISTANCE •** 9 miles (14.5km)

**TOTAL ASCENT •** 390ft (119m)

**PATHS •** mainly towpaths and surfaced pathways

**TERRAIN •** canalside pastures and country park woodland

**GRADIENTS •** gentle

**REFRESHMENTS •** Wigan Pier; the canalside Commercial Inn and the Kirkless Hall pub; Stables Café, Haigh Hall

**PARK •** car park at Trencherfield Mill, near the Mill at the Pier

**OS MAP •** Explorer 276 Bolton, Wigan & Warrington

# George Orwell on the road to Wigan

**❶** From the car park near the Mill at the Pier, go past the barge *Roland* and through the Pier Gardens to reach the towpath of the Leeds and Liverpool Canal. Turn left and follow the towpath to Top Lock, the last in a long series of locks. On the way cross three busy roads, by pedestrian crossings.

**❷** Beyond Top Lock the canal changes direction. Continue on the towpath to reach Bridge 60. Leave the canal and turn right over the bridge. Follow a surfaced driveway to eventually reach Haigh Hall.

**❸** Pass to the right of Haigh Hall, and continue ahead until, directly opposite Haigh Golf and Visitor Centre, you turn left into a car park. Walk across the car park to the far right-hand corner, and turn left along a lane. Soon take the first turning on the left, a rough track descending to the Leeds and Liverpool Canal. Cross a bridge and go down to walk along the towpath.

**❹** When you reach Bridge 60 again (this time from the opposite direction), climb steps to the right of the bridge, to regain the estate driveway. Turn right, ignore an early turning right, and continue descending gently through mixed woodland until, just as the

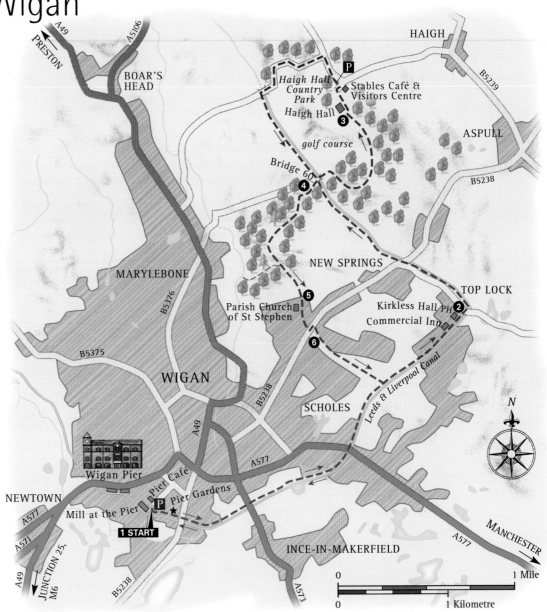

*Haigh Hall stands at the centre of Haigh Hall Country Park. This is the former home of the Earls of Balcarres, an influential family in the history of Wigan and once owners of the massive estate.*

**DIFFICULTY** ✿ ✿

driveway makes a wide sweep to the right, you branch left on to a rough track alongside a stream.

**❺** The track continues to the edge of a built-up area. Go forward to a road junction near the Parish Church of St Stephen. Turn left

and walk to the main road a short distance away. Cross the road with care, moving left to a nearby path signed the Leeds and Liverpool Canal. The path initially descends wooden steps, which can be slippery when wet, and joins the trackbed of a disused railway.

**❻** Turn right along the trackbed and, always continuing to keep ahead, follow the on-going path to reach the towpath of the canal once more. Here, turn right and retrace your outward route to Wigan Pier and the car park near the Mill, at the Pier.

**1920**

**1920–1933** Prohibition on alcohol is declared in America.

**1920** A spate of killings carried out by the Irish Republican Army forces Britain to declare martial law in Ireland.

**1922**

**1922** After three years of vicious warfare between Irish nationalist and British forces, Prime Minister Lloyd George introduces the Government of Ireland Act, which establishes two parliaments in Ireland. The Irish free state comes into being and civil war ensues.

**1922**

**1922** Italy has a new leader, a fascist dictator in the form of Benito Mussolini. His 'trademark' is his black shirt, and his fascist followers are known as 'Blackshirts'.

**1922** The British Broadcasting Corporation is established

# The Artists of St Ives

*Discovering the landscapes that inspired artists such as Alfred Wallis, whose work was said to have 'grown out of the Cornish earth and sea' (Ben Nicholson)*

ABOVE: *Barbara Hepworth (1903–75), English sculptor, known for her abstract works in stone, metal and wood.*

The picturesque old fishing town of St Ives is renowned for its narrow, cobbled streets, cottage-lined courtyards and superb sandy beaches and coastline. These and its equable climate attract thousands of visitors to this part of west Cornwall. But another group of enthusiasts was drawn here by the natural scenery and incredible qualities of light and space. This was the famous St Ives colony of artists, founded in the great 'plein air' movement of the 19th century, and which has, ever since, attracted hundreds of artists from all over the world.

The painter Ben Nicholson (1894–1982) once remarked that he found drawing a pencil line as exhilarating as a coastal walk from St Ives to Zennor. That sentiment was probably shared by many other artists, such as Peter Lanyon (1918–64), whose memorial is passed at the top of Trevalgan Hill. Cornish-born Lanyon, who was killed in a gliding accident, produced an important series of paintings depicting the area between St Ives and St Just. No 3 Back Road West was the home of local mariner and artist Alfred Wallis (1855–1942) who, after his wife's death, took up painting in 1925 at the age of 70 and revealed himself as a natural genius, yet never regarded himself as a 'proper artist'. His primitive, beautiful paintings inspired the work of Ben Nicholson and fellow artist Christopher Wood (1901–30), after they had 'discovered' Wallis during

a holiday visit to St Ives in 1928. Wood died tragically young two years later, but Nicholson went on to become one of Britain's major abstract artists. In 1939 he returned to live in Cornwall with his wife, the sculptor Barbara Hepworth (1903–75), first at Carbis Bay and then in St Ives. Over the next two decades they turned St Ives into one of the leading centres of British art, attracting gifted younger artists such as Lanyon, Patrick Heron (1920–99) and others.

In the 1950s, following their divorce, Nicholson moved to Switzerland, but Hepworth, an immensely innovative non-figurative sculptor and powerful artist, remained in the town until her death in 1975. The Barbara Hepworth Museum and Sculpture Garden, a permanent exhibition of her work at her former home, is passed during the walk. Bernard Leach (1887–1979), one of the foremost potters of the 20th century, also made his mark here when he established a pottery in St Ives in 1920 on his return from studying the art in Japan.

On his departure for Switzerland, Ben Nicholson left his studio to Patrick Heron, whose magnificent stained-glass window can be seen at the Tate St Ives. This impressive building, designed and built by Eldred Evans and David Shalev and opened in June 1993, houses exhibitions of works produced by St Ives' artists from the late 1880s to the present day.

LEFT: *Looking over the town of St Ives to the sea. The quality of light in this part of Cornwall has attracted artists to paint here since the late 19th century.*

BACKGROUND: *The Tate St Ives.*

**ABOUT • ST IVES**

*This walk starts at the coast to the west of the town and reveals the aspects of light and landscape that has inspired artists to visit and paint here since the early 1920s. While you're in St Ives visit the Tate Gallery St Ives and the Barbara Hepworth Museum.*

## Cornwall • SW ENGLAND

**DISTANCE •** 7 miles (11.3km)

**TOTAL ASCENT •** 607ft (185m)

**PATHS •** rocky coast path, lanes, farm tracks and fields

**TERRAIN •** undulating coast path, narrow town lanes and farmland

**GRADIENTS •** some fairly steep, short ascents on coast path and in St Ives;

**REFRESHMENTS •** pubs, restaurants, and cafés in St Ives; coffee shop and restaurant at Tate St Ives; the Tinner's Arms at Zennor

**PARK •** small car park by the National Trust sign for Rosewall Hill on the B3306 St Ives to St Just road, ½ mile (800m) past the sign to Trevalgan Farm (right)

**OS MAP •** Explorer 102 Land's End, Penzance & St Ives

# Aspects of light at St Ives

❶ Cross the road and follow the path across Little Trevalgan Hill (NT) past a huge boulder and memorial to artist Peter Lanyon. Continue downhill to a field; turn right to the bottom corner, and cross the wall into the lane.

❷ Turn left and in ½ mile (800m) reach Trevega Wartha Farm; 100yds (91m) beyond turn right down a signed bridleway between hedges. Cross a grassy track and follow footpath signs straight on, to walk downhill through a metal gate and over a stream to Trevail Mill. Walk up the drive.

❸ Past the cattle grid turn right, signed River Cove. Follow the path through a wood to meet the coast path. Turn right and continue for 2 miles (3.2km) where it branches. Go left past a sign for Hellesveor Cliff and continue to Clodgy Point.

❹ Continue right along the coast path for ¾ mile (1.2km) to reach a car park above Porthmeor Beach (toilets). At the road keep straight on to pass the Tate St Ives (right).

❺ Follow the road round right, then left at a junction, passing

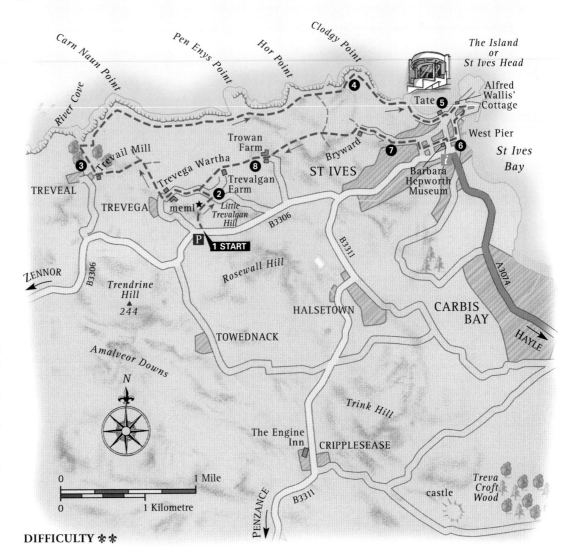

**DIFFICULTY ❊ ❊**

Harry's Court and Alfred Wallis' cottage. Continue for 250yds (229m) then turn sharp right down Fish Street to the harbour. Turn right along Wharf Road to reach West Pier and the lifeboat house.

❻ Turn right up Lifeboat Hill; take the second lane right (Back Street) to the entrance to the Barbara Hepworth Museum. Turn left up Ayr Lane and across a junction to a T-junction (Kenwyn Place sign). Turn right, and left at the top of the hill. Keep on this road for

¼ mile (400m) until you reach Burthallan Lane.

❼ Right along Burthallan Lane for ¼ mile (400m), then just past the house named Bryward follow signs for Zennor, left, over a stone stile and along a narrow hedged path, to a stone stile into a field. Keep ahead, then cross the wall right. Reach a grassy area, go right to a hidden stile next to two metal gates. Follow right-hand field edge for ¾ mile (1.2km) through fields and over stiles to Trowan Farm.

❽ Cross a stile into the lane; turn left, then right, through a farmyard. Go left over a stile at the next cottage, and right over another stile. Follow the field path to pass behind Trevalgan Farm. Go over a stile alongside a gate beside the final buildings. Go straight across the field to a stile and continue through small fields and over stiles to a surfaced lane. Turn left and reach the end of Point ❶ in 200yds (183m). Retrace your steps across Little Trevalgan Hill to the car park.

**1922** The publication of the poem *The Wasteland* causes a public sensation as T.S Eliot uses the work to describe the darkness of post-war Britain and the frailty of the human condition.

**1923** Adolf Hitler addresses the first Nazi Party Rally in Munich on 27 January. He is later sentenced to five years in prison, where he writes *Mein Kampf*.

**1923** German inflation spirals and bartering replaces paper currency.

**1923** The *Flying Scotsman* is built by Nigel Gresley.

**1924** Wembley Stadium opens and remains in use until 2000.

**1925** The *Exposition des Arts Décoratifs* is launched in Paris.

# Dover: World War II Frontline Town

*An exhilarating ramble along the White Cliffs with a visit to Dover's magnificent castle and the secret wartime tunnels that served as a wartime command centre*

ABOVE: *Below the cliffs of Dover, the 'ack ack' guns (anti-aircraft guns) are ready for action as warni is given of approaching enemy planes (1942).*

**DEPRESSION AND WAR**

**JAZZ AGE TO ATOMIC AGE**

Cradled between formidable white cliffs and standing at the narrowest crossing point to France, the seaside town of Dover has borne the brunt of invading forces ever since Caesar sailed up the Dour in 55 BC and created the Roman walled city of *Dubris*. Although besieged on several occasions during medieval times, its greatest moment was undoubtedly during World War II.

Towering above the town and commanding Britain's busiest ferry port and the English Channel is Dover's magnificently preserved castle, a giant fortress that has protected this stretch of English coast since the Iron Age. The castle is best visited after the walk, when you can stroll the battlements and join a tour that takes you deep into the network of tunnels beneath the castle. Nicknamed 'Hellfire Corner' due to the constant artillery bombardment from above, the tunnels became an underground wartime nerve centre, complete with coding and cipher centre, operations rooms, a hospital and accommodation for headquarters staff. It was here, in 1940, that Admiral Ramsay and Winston Churchill masterminded the evacuation of 338,000 troops from Dunkirk in 'Operation Dynamo'. Authentic smells and sounds, including the terrifying drone of bombers overhead, help create the wartime atmosphere of Dover at war.

At the White Cliffs Experience Museum in the town you can learn more about Dover's wartime

history, notably in the 'Our Finest Hours' gallery, which includes a full-size reconstruction of a 1940s Dover street. The citizens of Dover suffered constant artillery attack until 1944, from huge German guns around Cap Gris-Nez in France. With some 2,226 shells the Germans killed 148 civilians and 69 servicemen in the area, and seriously injured 403 civilians and 100 members of the armed forces.

The walk begins on Langdon Cliff, one of the white cliffs that are famous throughout the world. The clifftops at Langdon, Fan Bay, Wanstone Farm and South Foreland housed artillery batteries with railway-mounted guns that could fire 2,500lb (1,136kg) shells up to 62 miles (99km) into German-occupied France. If you venture to the bottom of Langdon Steps you will see the fighting lights in the cliff. Built in 1909 to assist shipping entering Dover Harbour. Their wartime intention was to illuminate enemy ships entering the harbour displaying incorrect signal lights, thus enabling the battery above to open fire. Visible at low tide are the twisted metal remains of *The Summity*, wrecked here in July 1940 following heavy bombing by German planes. The cliffs also played an emotional role during the war. Among soldiers departing to war and returning to English shores, they were a symbol of home, most famously celebrated in the popular wartime song *There'll be Bluebirds over the White Cliffs of Dover*, sung by 'the forces' sweetheart, Vera Lynn.

BELOW: *View over the English Channel towards Dover, a fortress town since the Iron Age, and the battle-scarred face of the White Cliffs of Dover.*

**ABOUT • DOVER**

*Since the first Roman invasion in 55 BC, Dover has borne the brunt of invading forces. This walk takes you along a historic stretch of the White Cliffs to Dover Castle, which was used as an underground nerve centre during World War II.*

**Kent • SE ENGLAND**

**DISTANCE •** 7 miles (11.3km)

**TOTAL ASCENT •** 498ft (152m)

**PATHS •** generally good, some field paths can be muddy

**TERRAIN •** clifftop, farmland and some pavements through the town

**GRADIENTS •** gentle climbing along cliff; otherwise fairly level

**REFRESHMENTS •** café at visitor centre; pub and tea room at St Margaret's Bay; pubs and a tea room in St Margaret's at Cliffe

**PARK •** NT car park (fee) at Gateway to the White Cliffs visitor centre on Langdon Cliff, follow signs to Dover Castle

**OS MAP •** Explorer 138 Dover, Folkestone & Hythe

# Along the White Cliffs of Dover

**DIFFICULTY ❀❀**

❶ From the Gateway to the White Cliffs visitor centre walk away from Dover. Take the path at the end of the last parking area and fork right, signed Saxon Shore Way (SSW). Gently ascend to the top of the cliff to a stile. Follow concrete markers and descend beside fence to a track. Cross over with SSW marker and climb out of Langdon Hole (NT), passing the steep steps down to Langdon Bay, to a stile.

❷ Soon turn right with SSW marker and stay on the clifftop path towards South Foreland Lighthouse (NT). At the boundary by properties below the lighthouse, follow the path inland. Pass the gates to the lighthouse and turn right at a junction of paths (SSW). Keep right at a crossing of routes. Follow the track past the windmill to a gate on your right leading on to Lighthouse Down (NT).

❸ Follow the clifftop path to a gate by a house. Rejoin the track, descend to a crossing of tracks and turn right. Pass St Margaret's Museum and Pines Garden and bear right at a junction to reach the road at a sharp bend. Turn right to visit St Margaret's Bay.

❹ Climb the steps on your left by the footpath post. At the top, keep ahead on the pavement for ½ mile (800m) into St Margaret's at Cliffe. Walk through the village and take the road on the left, signed Dover.

❺ Keep to the left-hand verge and soon bear left to a waymarked stile. Walk through a narrow paddock to a stile, then proceed alongside the right-hand fence to a stile. Bear half-right along the defined field path to a stile and maintain

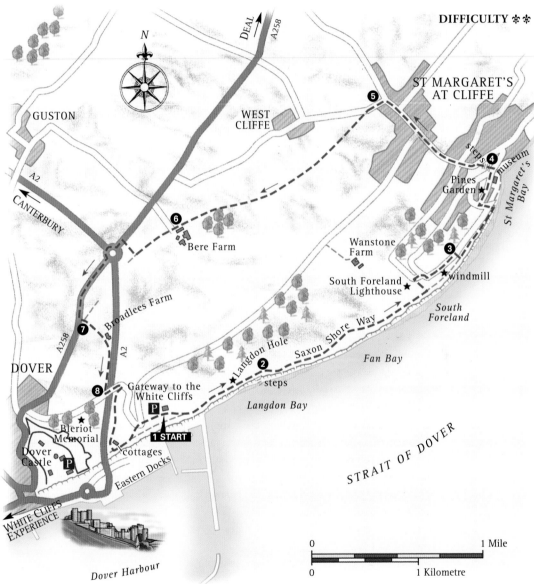

direction. Briefly walk by a copse, then follow the path half-right to reach a stile by trees.

❻ Pass to the right of a farm, cross the drive and a stile and walk along the left-hand field edge to a stile. Turn right to the A258. Turn left to the roundabout, cross Jubilee Way and keep to the pavement beside the road for Dover Castle.

❼ In ¼ mile (400m), cross the stile on your left and pass through Broadlees Farm. Descend the track to a gate and turn immediately right through another gate. Walk parallel with the A2 to a stile and ascend steps to a road.

❽ Turn left across the bridge, bear right with the road and shortly take the path right (unmarked). Follow the path left across scrubland,

parallel with the A2, and eventually pass in front of cottages to join the SSW. Turn left and climb to the road, turning immediately right back to the visitor centre.

**• DON'T MISS •**

*The great views of Dover at **South Foreland Lighthouse**, built in 1843 and used for early radio experiments.*

**1926**

**1926** John Logie Baird demonstrates the first television.

**1926** Fuelled by salary cuts, Britain experiences its first General Strike.

**1926** *Winnie-the-Pooh* (AA Milne) is published.

**1927**

**1927** Al Jonson stars in the first 'Talkie', *The Jazz Singer*.

**1927** The first television pictures are sent across the Atlantic.

**1928**

**1928** The discovery of penicillin by Alexander Fleming is announced.

**1928** All women over the age of 21 are given the vote.

# The Dambusters' Dry Run

*The quiet waters of the Derwent and Howden reservoirs in the Upper Derwent Valley in Derbyshire were the scene of practice runs by the wartime Dambusters*

**DEPRESSION AND WAR**

**JAZZ AGE TO ATOMIC AGE**

Local farmers complained that the ear-shattering roar of the Merlin engines of low-flying Lancaster bombers over the Upper Derwent Valley in early 1943 were creating havoc and upsetting their livestock. Little did they know that these flights were in preparation for one of the most daring air raids of World War II – the legendary 'bouncing bomb' attack on the Ruhr dams by the ace 'Dambuster' squadron.

Indeed, such was the security clampdown on the raid when the practice runs were taking place over the Derwent and Howden reservoirs that even the young pilots and crew of the specially formed 617 Squadron didn't know what their targets were to be until the day before.

The twin reservoirs in the Upper Derwent – the Howden and the Derwent – had been built between 1901 and 1916 to provide water for the fast-expanding cities of Derby, Nottingham, Leicester and Sheffield. A temporary corrugated iron village known as Tin Town was built on the western side of the valley at Birchinlee, which housed about a thousand of the navvies and their families for 15 years while the construction took place. The larger Ladybower Dam, lower down the valley, was still under construction at the time of the practice runs. The Howden and Derwent dams were chosen as the mock targets for 617 Squadron because of their remarkable resemblance to the Moehne, Eder and Sorpe dams in the hills of western Germany, which fed water and power to the vital armament factories of Nazi Germany in the Ruhr.

It was here, in addition to a number of other similarly sited reservoirs in the Pennines and Wales, that the brave young crews tested their ability to fly at extremely low levels – as low as 50ft (15m) – which was what was required to drop accurately Barnes Wallis's revolutionary 'bouncing bomb' (which was actually a mine). The surrounding moors of Derwent, Howden and Ronksley, dropping steeply down to the reservoirs, proved a perfect match for the hills in which the Ruhr dams had been built. Even the twin castellated towers of the Howden and Derwent dams, on which the bomb-aimers lined up their targets, were very similar to those on the German dams.

The connection between the Derwent Valley and 617 Squadron has never been forgotten. All new pilots in the squadron, which now flies Tornado jets, are required to fly over the Derwent dams as one of their first flights, in tribute to their brave predecessors. Anniversary celebrations of the raid have been held on several occasions in the valley, attended by crowds of up to 24,000 people. They were entertained by displays by the Red Arrows and flypasts by the last remaining flying Lancaster bomber, *The City of Lincoln*, from the RAF's Battle of Britain Memorial Flight.

Displays in the West Tower of the Derwent Dam (open summer weekends and Bank Holidays, 10–5 and winter weekends, 10–4) tell the story of the Dambusters. A memorial in the gateway of the tower pays tribute to the 53 gallant men of 617 Squadron who did not return, with the simple message: 'They paid for our freedom'.

ABOVE: *View towards th Howden and Derwent reservoirs where flight crews tested their ability to fly at very low altitudes and drop the revolutionary Barnes Wallis bouncing bomb.*

FAR LEFT: *Barnes Wallis (1887–1979), designer of the 'bouncing bomb' a his desk in his secret 'den'. Behind him on the wall are photographs of the Mohne Dam in Germany before and after it was breached.*

BELOW: *Derwent reservoir dam in the Peak District National Park, chosen as a mock target for 617 Squadron due to its similarity to the intended target in Germany.*

**ABOUT · DERWENT DAM**

*Derwent Dam will forever be linked with 617 Squadron or 'the Dambusters'. In 1943, the squadron used this area as a practice ground prior to their successful air assault on dams in Germany, which fed vital Nazi armament factories.*

## Derbyshire · C ENGLAND

**DISTANCE ·** 6 miles (9.6km)

**TOTAL ASCENT ·** 564ft (172m)

**PATHS ·** lanes and moorland paths

**TERRAIN ·** rough moorland paths, requiring boots and waterproofs

**GRADIENTS ·** a gradual climb to Pike Low and steep descent down Abbey Bank

**REFRESHMENTS ·** refreshment kiosk at Fairholmes

**PARK ·** Fairholmes Visitor Centre, Upper Derwent Valley

**OS MAP ·** Outdoor Leisure 1 The Peak District – Dark Peak Area

# The Dambusters' of Derbyshire

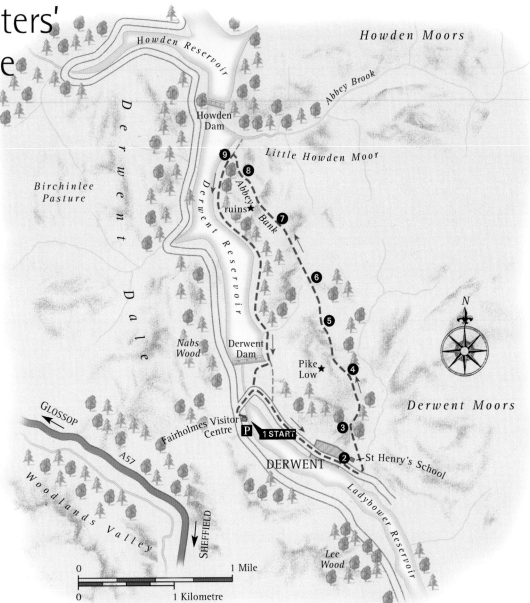

❶ From the Fairholmes Visitor Centre, take the signed path to the road which passes under Derwent Dam. Follow the road to the right, passing through Derwent hamlet.

❷ After about a mile (1.6km) St Henry's schoolhouse can be seen on the left-hand side. Three hundred yards (274m) further on there is a track off to the left with a gate and stile set slightly back off the road. Cross the stile and follow the path as it passes a ruined barn, left, and a private National Trust barn, right.

❸ Continue along the path to the left of the barn, cross the stile and ascend the steep tree-lined hollow way crossing several more stiles before reaching a farmhouse on the left. Here the path divides; follow the left-hand course as it ascends in zigzag fashion out on to Briery Side. Keep to the marked footpath to reach a wall and stile marking 'Open Country'. Here look back and admire the view down across Ladybower reservoir towards Bamford in the distance.

❹ Follow the path as it bears left for 200yds (183m) before turning right on to a broad track with a ruined wall on the right. Follow this for about ½ mile (800m) climbing past Pike Low, a Bronze Age burial mound (no access) at 1329ft (405m) on the left. This is the highest point of the walk.

❺ Continue on this track with the wall on the right. As the route nears a linear group of trees on the right the path bears left and crosses a ruined wall. Follow the path across the open moorland for about 250yds (229m) to another

**DIFFICULTY ✤ ✤ ✤**

ruined wall. Follow route signed Abbey and Howden Dam.

❻ With the ruined wall on the left, walk up the gradual slope and at a gate cross a stile. Here the path gradually descends. Continue to another signpost.

❼ Continue on the path that bears slightly left and downhill with the ruins of Bamford House Farm on

the left. Follow this path (ruined wall on left) down Abbey Bank; Howden Dam comes into view. The path bears left and descends steeply for about 50yds (46m) to a sign marking the way to the now submerged Abbey Grange. Follow this path as it drops steeply towards the reservoir.

❽ Go through the gap in the wall, leaving Abbey Bank behind, and

follow the path through the trees down to the reservoir service road.

❾ Turn left and follow the road for 2 miles (3.2km) along the eastern shore of the reservoir. At the dam turn right over a stile and follow the hedge-lined path down to steps which drop to the foot of the dam wall. At the bottom cut left across the grassed area to the road back to Fairholmes Visitor Centre.

ABOVE: *An aerial view of the lovely Italianate village of Portmeirion.*

# Portmeirion: One Man's Fantasy

*A walk around the bizarre Italianate village on a quiet North Wales headland*

ABOVE: *British architect Clough Williams-Ellis (1883–1978).*

## Creating Portmeirion

In 1925, Clough Williams-Ellis bought an overgrown finger of land at the base of the Llŷn Peninsula. In its day, this had been occupied by two castles – Deudraeth and Aber Iau – as well as a foundry, a shipyard and some cottages. But it had since been abandoned, and the neglected site provided Clough, already a distinguished architect, with the perfect opportunity to realise a cherished dream.

Clough Williams-Ellis was one of those who, in the early 20th century, became preoccupied with the need to combine functional building with aesthetic beauty. Portmeirion was a chance to put his own theories into practice. Here, he would prove that a new development need not ruin its surroundings; he would reconstruct 'fallen buildings' rescued from demolition, and give his

own architectural imagination free rein. Between 1925 and 1976 the project evolved, staying true to Clough's motto: 'Cherish the past, adorn the present, construct for the future.'

## A 1920s Oddity

Portmeirion is the embodiment of one man's ideas and, in many ways, the embodiment of an age. It was begun in the inter-war years, when Britain was caught between economic difficulty and post-war euphoria. Thousands of soldiers had returned from the trenches in 1918 to find themselves out of work; no new homes had been built during the hostilities, and there was an acute shortage of housing. At the same time, in the face of urban expansion, many began to fear for the survival of the countryside, which seemed all the more precious and vulnerable after four years of

BELOW: *Portmeirion brings together a wide range of architectural styles and features from Arts and Crafts to Eastern mystic.*

global warfare. These concerns all played a part in Clough Williams-Ellis's career. He became involved with the housing movement, taking up a challenge, issued by the editor (his future father-in-law) of *The Spectator*, to design affordable rural accommodation. He was also a tireless campaigner for conservation, helping to found the Council for the Protection of Rural England in 1926 and the Campaign for the Protection of Rural Wales in 1928. The natural landscape was an essential part of his plans for Portmeirion, and for all its eccentricity, the village still sits in perfect harmony with the surrounding wooded hills and coastal scenery.

As well as being an experiment in town development, Portmeirion was a splash of colour in a world made bleak by war and its after-effects. Clough's intention was always to give everyone 'a taste of lavishness, gaiety and cultivated design'. Its strange and wonderful mixture of styles brings together Arts and Crafts, Palladian, baroque, Eastern mystic and downright fantastic. A year after its completion in 1965, television cameras moved in to film the cult fantasy-mystery series *The Prisoner*.

BELOW: *Portmeirion, Gwynedd, built in the 1920s by Clough Williams-Ellis.*

# WALK 95

## AROUND THE VILLAGE AND ITS ENCHANTED GARDENS

❶ The walk begins with a circuit around the village itself, reached past two pink Palladian tollbooths, where you pay your admission fee (which funds the upkeep of the village and grounds). Follow the path under the arch of the Gatehouse, with its painted ceiling, and then of the Classical Bridge House, and pass Toll House, a weatherboarded building decorated with bells, signs and a painted statue of St Peter. To the left is the Battery, and behind that the Italian-style bell tower, partly built with stones from Deudraeth Castle. On the right is the Pantheon, or Dome; beneath it, a painted loggia houses a gilt Buddha. The path continues to the central Piazza, with its fabulous arrangement of pool, fountain, gloriette, Gothic pavilion and columns bearing Burmese dancers.

❷ Throughout the walk, as it leads round the village and out to the headland gardens, there are unexpected touches and embellishments – a painted mermaid; intertwined dolphins; a bust of

Shakespeare; a stone lion. Walking through this Snowdonia landscape is like stepping into the elaborate escapism of a Hollywood set.

❸ Having left the village itself past Fountain, the house where Noël Coward wrote *Blithe Spirit* in 1941, and the Portmeirion Hotel, the route leads round the headland, passing the Observatory Tower with its figure of Nelson, on the way to the Lighthouse, at Portmeirion's southernmost point. You soon reach a left-hand track to a viewpoint above White Sands Bay; after enjoying the sea view, return to the main route and continue to the Ghost Garden, named after the whispering of the wind through the

eucalyptus leaves. You now turn back towards the village, passing the June-flowering rhododendrons before re-entering the site past Salutation, originally a stable block and now housing a shop selling Portmeirion pottery, designed by Clough's daughter, Susan.

**Distance:** 3 miles (4.8km)

**Total ascent:** 150ft (46m)

**Paths:** surfaced paths, woodland tracks: can be muddy and slippery

**Terrain:** village streets, cliff path, woods, stone steps

**Gradients:** some steep climbs in the gardens

**Refreshments:** Cadwallader's ice-cream parlour; Town Hall restaurant; hotel restaurant

**Park:** car park near entrance to village

**OS Map:** Outdoor Leisure 18 Snowdonia – Harlech, Porthmadog & Baal

**Difficulty:** ✿✿

**1928**

**1928** The Scottish National Party is founded.

**1929** On 24 October the Wall Street crash in America costs thousands of investors their livelihoods and, for some, their lives also. The world economy is in crisis.

**1929**

**1929** Women receive the same voting rights as men.

**1930** The first Soccer World Cup is won by Uruguay.

**1932** Mass trespass on Kinder Scout by the Ramblers' Association.

**1932**

**1932** Publication of *Brave New World* (Alduous Huxley).

**1933** Adolf Hitler is appointed Chancellor of Germany, and by 1934 is made president of Germany.

**1934** The driving test is introduced.

# The Secrets of Slapton Sands

*Civilian evacuation and military tragedy are revealed during this pleasant stroll through the South Hams coastal countryside*

ABOVE: *The long stretch of beach at Slapton Sands.*

When you walk along the shingle beach at Slapton on a sunny day, gazing along the glorious South Devon coast towards the lighthouse at Start Point, it is hard to imagine much ever happening here. The calm waters of Slapton Ley, a Site of Scientific Interest (SSSI), is the largest freshwater lake in the south-west and an important wetland habitat, home to a myriad of species of birdlife and plants.

But back in1943 the people who lived and farmed in this quiet corner of Devon experienced a huge and almost unbelievable shock. Due to the similarity of Slapton Sands to the beaches of Normandy in northern France, an area of 30,000 acres (12,141ha) was completely cleared and handed over to the US army to provide a training ground in preparation for the D-Day invasion of France in 1944. This amazing operation was completed in six short weeks towards the end of 1943, when 3,500 people were forcibly evacuated from eight villages and 180 farms and moved to temporary accommodation. They wouldn't go home again for at least six

months. The simple granite obelisk near the memorial car park, presented by the US army authorities in 1954, forms a fitting tribute to the generosity and co-operation of the local population. The car park itself lies on the site of the Royal Slapton Sands Hotel, another casualty of the war years, which was so badly damaged during the practice exercises that it had to be demolished. The original narrow bridge over the ley to Slapton was also destroyed at the same time. As you pass the church at Stokenham, imagine how it must have felt on 12 November 1943, when local people gathered there to listen to the Lord Lieutenant of Devon, Lord Fortescue, pronouncing that they would have to pack up their possessions and leave their homes by 20 December. As you stroll past ancient farms and cottages along the narrow lanes round the back of the Lower Ley towards Slapton village, the whole story seems quite fantastic.

But there's more. There's an American Sherman tank in the car park at Torcross, which was lost during the D-Day landing practices in 1944, and recovered from the sea in 1984. It now stands alongside other memorials as a tribute to those American servicemen lost during Operation Tiger, a training exercise.

The second extraordinary event in the history of this area occurred in the early hours of 28 April 1944, when nine German torpedo boats intercepted a 3-mile (5km)-long convoy of US vessels moving from Portland to Slapton Sands during a landing rehearsal. Two landing craft were destroyed, and two more damaged, leading to the loss of almost 1,000 lives.

The lessons learned in this tragedy contributed significantly to the success of the allied forces in the D-Day landings, but it was a high price to pay – and the full story of what really happened on that dreadful day did not come to light until over 40 years later.

BELOW: *Soldiers training at Slapton for D-Day..*

### ABOUT · SLAPTON SANDS

*Slapton Sands serves as a reminder of the lives that were both lost and saved in World War II. In 1943, the US army trained here for the D-Day landings but during a rehearsal a convoy of vessels was torpedoed by German craft, killing 1,000 soldiers.*

### Devon · SW ENGLAND

**DISTANCE** · 5 miles (8km)

**TOTAL ASCENT** · 328ft (100m)

**PATHS** · narrow, quiet country lanes and paths; some muddy after wet weather

**TERRAIN** · shingle beach, rolling farmland and freshwater ley

**GRADIENTS** · level on beach and round ley; some short steep ascents/descents inland

**REFRESHMENTS** · the Start Bay Inn at Torcross, also cafés and fish and chips; pubs at Stokenham and Slapton

**PARK** · memorial car park on Slapton Sands off A379, just below Slapton Bridge

**OS MAP** · Outdoor Leisure 20 South Devon – Brixham to Newton Ferrers

# Victory and tragedy at Slapton Sands

**❶** Walk along the back of the beach, keeping the toilets and road on your right, and the sea on your left, to reach the edge of Torcross. The Sherman tank memorial is across the road in the car park.

**❷** Follow the concrete walkway between the houses and sea. At the end, turn right before the old Tor Cross Hotel (holiday apartments), then left before the post office up a steep narrow lane (toilets, right). Pass Torcross viewpoint, a butterfly garden. Continue up the lane to pass through the hamlet of Widewell.

**❸** After 400yds (366m) turn right down a narrow unsigned lane, opposite a footpath to Beeson and a post-box. Walk steeply downhill past Widewell Plantation to reach the A379 opposite the Church House Inn at Stokenham.

**❹** Cross the road and go up the lane between the pub and the Church of St Michael and All Angels. The lane veers left; when you can see the Tradesman's Arms ahead turn right by Sunnyside up a narrow lane to meet Kiln Lane. Turn right.

**❺** Almost immediately, turn left up another quiet lane. Leave the houses and descend to ancient Frittiscombe. Pass the farmhouse on your right and an old barn on your left. When the lane veers left and uphill, turn right along the track signed Scrubs Lane to Deer Bridge Lane. Follow this as it veers left uphill to meet the lane.

**❻** Turn right and proceed downhill, with views of the ley to your right, to cross Deer Bridge.

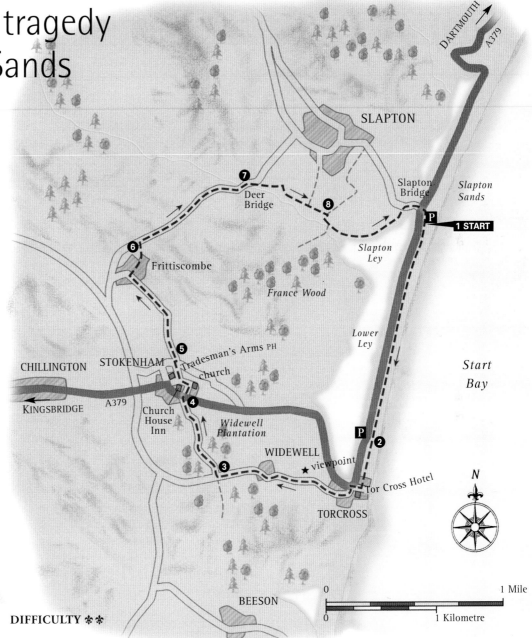

**DIFFICULTY** ❈ ❈

**❼** Turn right along a small wooded path signed Marsh Lane. The route follows the marsh edge to reach a junction of paths; Slapton village is signed to the left. Walk straight ahead along the boardwalk, signed permissive route to nature reserve, passing through an area of willows. Ascend wooden steps to a T-junction and follow another footpath, left, which leads to the village.

**❽** Turn right, signed Slapton Sands via nature trail, and follow the narrow, undulating path as it weaves along the ley edge. There are four dog-friendly stiles and occasional wooden steps along this section, but nothing difficult. As the road comes into view note the pillbox below the path, right. The path meets the road via a gate; turn right towards the sea, then right to reach your car.

### · DON'T MISS ·

*The remains of **Hallsands**, just to the south of Torcross, provides another example of how this part of the coast has suffered over the years. This small fishing village was almost completely destroyed during a huge storm on the night of 16 January 1917.*

**1935**

**1935** The introduction of the FT Ordinary Share index.

**1936** King George V dies.

**1936** On 7 March, in defiance of the Treaty of Versailles, German troops occupy the Rhineland.

**1936**

**1936** The Crystal Palace, which housed the Great Exhibition, goes up in flames.

**1936–1939** Civil war breaks out in Spain as a result of conflict between Republican and Nationalist factions.

**1936**

**1936** Mass unemployment sparks the Jarrow March towards London.

**1936** Fred Perry wins Wimbledon for the third consecutive year. To date, he is the last British player to have won the coveted trophy in the Men's Singles.

# Scotland's Wartime Legacy

*Discovering Eisenhower and the Scottish role in World War II at Culzean Castle Country Park*

**DEPRESSION AND WAR**

**JAZZ AGE TO ATOMIC AGE**

During World War II Scotland was a major producer of arms and munitions, bringing prosperity to its traditional heavy industries. The Rolls Royce factory at Hillington, near Glasgow, produced hundreds of Merlin engines for the new Spitfires being built to replace those lost in action. One of the first attacks of the war was an attempt on the Forth rail bridge, which was thwarted by Spitfires from Glasgow and Edinburgh. Ernest Stevens, the leader of the Edinburgh Squadron, shot down the first German bomber.

The shipyards on the Clyde, at the peak of their production, launched five new ships each week to replace those sunk by German U-Boats. The Clyde was also the supply port for Russia, and ships for North America gathered there prior to sailing the treacherous Atlantic, where German U-boats lay in wait. So lethal were the U-boats that, in 1939, one penetrated to the heart of the home fleet deep-water base at Scapa Flow in Orkney, sinking the battleship HMS *Royal Oak* with the loss of 786 men. The following year saw the first civilian casualty of the war in Orkney.

Although Scotland didn't suffer to the same extent as England from the German Blitzkrieg, the town of Clydebank was all but razed during two nights of continual bombing on 13 and 14 March, 1941. Wave upon wave of aircraft pounded the small town with a carpet of high explosive and incendiary bombs. Their aim was to cripple the shipyards, but what they achieved was the almost total destruction of the town. Only seven houses remained undamaged, a thousand people lost their lives and nearly three quarters of the population was made homeless.

When America entered the war after the bombing of Pearl Harbour, Prestwick airport became the busiest in the world, with continual streams of aircraft carrying American troops to Scotland. Many were stationed here, mixing with the local population, their popularity guaranteed by easy access to scarcities such as nylon stockings and chocolate.

American resources were predominant in Europe and on 24 December 1943, US General Dwight D Eisenhower was appointed Supreme Commander of the Allied Expeditionary Force with orders to 'enter the continent of Europe and, in conjunction with the other Allied nations, undertake operations aimed at the heart of Germany and the destruction of her armed forces'. Sensitive to British feelings, Eisenhower selected British principal commanders, but he alone bore the responsibility for the D-Day landings in Normandy on 6 June 1944 and thereafter stayed in Europe for the remainder of the war, accepting the unconditional surrender of the German Army at Rheims. Eisenhower was a saviour, and after the war he was gifted with the lifetime use of an apartment in Culzean Castle on behalf of the people of Scotland. He visited four times and being a keen golfer played a few games at nearby Turnberry. When he became President of the United States of America, Culzean was for one short visit his 'Scottish White House.' An Exhibition at the castle tells of his connection there and of his role as Supreme Commander. As well as photographs and memorabilia, there is one of his uniforms and the desk he used to coordinate the Normandy landings.

ABOVE: *Portrait of General Dwight D Eisenhower (1890–1969) in uniform wearing a Legion of Merit and Distinguished Service Emblem.*

BELOW: *Culzean Castle, which commands this part of the Ayrshire coast.*

**ABOUT • CULZEAN CASTLE**

*General Eisenhower was presented with the gift of an apartment in Culzean Castle in recognition for his contribution during World War II. An exhibition at Culzean tells about his role as Supreme Commander of the Allied Expeditionary Force.*

## South Ayrshire • SCOTLAND

**DISTANCE** • 5½ miles (8.8km)

**TOTAL ASCENT** • 150ft (46m)

**PATHS** • very good, although some stretches can be boggy in wet weather

**TERRAIN** • estate roads, farm tracks, forest paths, beach, old railway line and roads

**GRADIENTS** • moderate

**REFRESHMENTS** • restaurant at visitor centre

**PARK** • visitor centre car park

**OS MAP** • Explorer 326 Ayr, Troon, Girvan and Maybole

# Eisenhower: Supreme Commander

**❶** Go diagonally through the visitor centre courtyard and turn left on to a path. Turn right at the junction, then second left, through an arch and into the castle forecourt. Keep left, go through a gate and at the next gate turn left.

**❷** Go down some steps, about turn and follow the path to the sign for the Battery, Cliff Walk and Swan Pond. Turn right, go through the trees, through a gate, across a grassed area and down some steps into the Battery.

**❸** Turn left, exit at the other end and turn right on to a forest path. Follow this until you reach a path signed Cliff Walk and turn right. Go right at the T-junction by the Swan Pond.

**❹** Turn right again at the sign for Barwhin Hill and Port Carrick. In 200yds (183m) turn right and go down some steep steps to Port Carrick beach. Turn left and head back uphill by the next steps. Turn right.

**❺** Follow the cliff path until it descends by some wooden steps to Maidenhead Bay. Turn left and walk along the beach until the pavement beside it turns left.

**• DON'T MISS •**

*The **Robert Burns National Park** in Alloway, which has a superb audio-visual version of his poem Tam O' Shanter. Follow the trail of the hapless Tam as he was pursued by witches from the auld haunted kirk to the Brig O' Doon.*

Cross the grassed area diagonally towards a white cottage with a red roof.

**❻** Turn left into Kirkoswald Road and then first right into Shanter Road. Continue to follow the road as it turns into a farm road and then turn left at a derelict World War II building and head for Shanter Farm. Turn left and enter the farm steading.

**❼** Cross the farm yard diagonally and exit at the other side. Then continue to follow the farm road round the side of a cottage then turn left, go through a gate and follow the line of the fence until you can cross it and continue along the old railway.

**❽** Continue through a caravan park, fork left, turn right on to the A719 and follow it for just over a mile (1.6km) to pass Morriston Farm. Just past the sign for Souter Johnnie's Cottage is a farm track.

**❾** Turn left along here, right and down some steps at a railway bridge and follow the line of the old railway to the next bridge. Exit right, via the steps, turn right, then left on to the estate road and follow it to the car park.

**DIFFICULTY ❀ ❀**

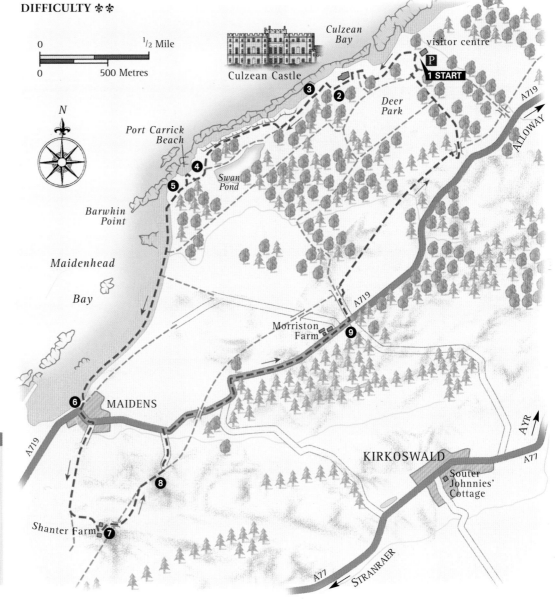

**1936**

**1936** In December, Edward VIII is presented with an ultimatum – the throne or American divorcee Mrs Simpson. He chooses Mrs Simpson, and signs the Instrument of Abdication passing the throne to his brother, George VI. The couple are married on 3 June 1937 in France.

**1937**

**1937** Coronation of George VI.

**1937** The celebrated Hindenberg airship explodes over New Jersey.

**1938** Neville Chamberlain announces 'Peace in our time' after signing the Munich Agreement.

**1939**

**1939** During World War II a code-breaking operation is established at Bletchley Park in Milton Keynes. The famous 'Enigma' code is deciphered here and the efforts of the code-breakers shorten the war by at least a year.

# The War Cemeteries of Cannock Chase

*Forest and natural heath concealing remnants of military camps are a tranquil setting for memorials to the dead of two world wars*

ABOVE: *The care of wounded soldiers from the front fell mainly to female nurses, who enthusiastically volunteered their skills to the war effort.*

In 1914 Britain was drawn into a European war, and early optimism that it would be 'over by Christmas' rapidly dissipated as a stalemate developed. Confronting each other from heavily defended slit trenches across the horribly bleak and battered landscape of the western front, neither side could gain any advantage, and British initiatives invariably ended in cataclysmic failure and an almost incomprehensible loss of life. But the populace perceived the cause – to defeat Germany's aggressive expansionism – as just, and there was no lack of volunteers for the army. With such an influx of men, billeting, training and transit facilities were urgently needed.

The 17th-century deforestation that fuelled the local iron industry had left the former hunting forest of Cannock Chase bare and inhospitable, which perhaps reflected the desolation of the front and influenced the decision to build two camps here: Brocton and Rugeley. The surrounding heath formed a training ground, where British and New Zealand infantrymen were instructed in the disciplines of trench warfare. Many of the support functions were, for the first time in history, undertaken by women, volunteers of Queen Mary's Auxiliary Army Corps, and others served as nurses in a thousand-bed military hospital. As the war progressed, German POWs were brought here and held in a camp at Brocton.

Post-war demobilisation and repatriation left the camps empty and what wasn't dismantled soon became overgrown. The hospital continued until 1924, after which the site served as a small mining village before being cleared in the 1950s. Forestation began in the 1920s, as part of a countrywide policy to lessen the nation's dependency on imported timber, one of the weaknesses revealed by the German blockade on British shipping. The plantings are now mature, and felling and imaginative replanting are creating more varied habitats for plants and wildlife.

The Great War was proclaimed as 'the war to end all wars', but peace was short-lived, and 20 years later Europe was again torn apart by war. Once more

Cannock was chosen for a military training camp, and RAF Hednesford was built near today's visitor centre. The surrounding area was used for Home Guard training, tank-testing and bombing practice.

Little visible evidence remains of the occupations, and the area, now designated an Area of Outstanding Natural Beauty, is a popular haunt for naturalists, walkers and cyclists. It is also a place of remembrance, with several monuments honouring those who lost their lives during the terrible years of strife. Allied and German servicemen of World War I, who died while in Cannock's camps or hospital, lie side by side in the Commonwealth War Cemetery, many of them victims of a devastating influenza epidemic in 1918. In 1967, the German Cemetery was opened and almost 5,000 Germans who lost their lives on British soil during both wars were brought together for reinterment. Nearby, the Katyn Memorial remembers 14,000 Polish prisoners of war massacred by the Russians in 1940 and, by the visitor centre, a small woodland copse commemorates those killed during the Burma Campaign.

BELOW: *The heath and woodland at Cannock Chase are popular with cyclists and walkers but remain a special place of remembrance for those who died during the two world wars.*

BACKGROUND: *The Commonwealth War Cemetery at Cannock Chase.*

**ABOUT • CANNOCK CHASE**

*POW camps, a military hospital and training camps, Cannock Chase is rich in 20th-century history. Now designated an Area of Outstanding Natural Beauty, it is a place of remembrance to those who lost their lives in World Wars I and II.*

## Staffordshire • C ENGLAND

**DISTANCE** • 7¼ miles (11.6km)

**TOTAL ASCENT** • 492ft (150m)

**PATHS** • generally good forest paths and tracks

**TERRAIN** • undulating commercial forest at various stages of maturity, broken by views across areas of natural heathland

**REFRESHMENTS** • café at Cannock Chase visitor centre

**PARK** • pay-and-display car park adjacent to visitor centre

**OS MAP** • OS Explorer 244 Cannock Chase & Chasewater, Stafford

# Cannock Chase and the price of war

**DIFFICULTY ✿ ✿**

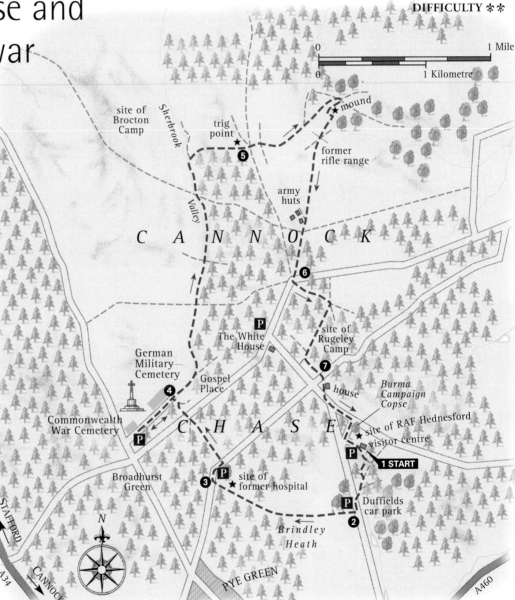

❶ From the visitor centre walk past the toilet block and on along a woodland track. As the trees clear, take the second path on the right and then bear left at a fork. When you reach a tarmac drive, turn right to a main road.

❷ A hundred yards (91m) to the left, a bridleway leaves on the right through Druffields car park. Rising gradually along a shallow valley, the way crosses Brindley Heath towards forest. After ¾ mile (1.2km), you will emerge through another car park onto a road. The site of the former hospital lies amongst the trees on the right.

❸ Go right for 250 yards (230m), then left along another forest bridleway. After half a mile (1km) that, too, ends at a road, but continue along a path directly opposite. Emerging on to a re-planted area at the second junction, bear left to a broad track by the German War Cemetery. Its entrance lies to the left and the Commonwealth Cemetery at Broadhurst Green, 500 yards (460m) beyond.

❹ After dropping through forest to the right, bear left at a junction marked Gospel Place. Beyond there, ignoring crossing tracks, follow the boundary between heath and forest for 1 mile (1.6km) into Sherbrook Valley. Eventually, where the track rises around a right-hand bend to a fork, bear right to climb the valley side, past a trig point to a main junction. Brocton Camp occupied the high ground to the west of the valley.

❺ Continue ahead, descending a quarter of a mile (0.4km) to a fork

above a valley and bear right, rising to a six-way junction a quarter of a mile (0.4km) beyond. Turn sharp right on to a narrower bridleway which, after bending below a high mound, rises beside a former rifle range. Part-way up, bear left along the main track and, after passing a group of huts, keep going to a road. The next section of the walk passes through the former Rugeley Camp.

❻ Go over to a bridleway opposite and follow it 300 yards (275m) to a crossing. Go sharp right along a grass track beside a forest camp site, and after ½ mile (1km), turn left along 'Heart of England Way'.

❼ At a road junction, walk ahead along Marquis Drive towards continue along a wide track to a barrier; the visitor centre is on the right.

**1939**

**1939** On 15 March Prague is taken as German forces march into Czechoslovakia.

**1939** On 1 September Adolf Hitler invades Poland. Britain declares war on Germany on 3 September and Chamberlain appoints Winston

**1940**

Churchill as First Lord of the Admiralty. The following year Churchill is elected Prime Minster, and holds the post for the duration of World War II.

**1940** Denmark and Norway are invaded by German troops.

**1940**

**1940** Allied troops, caught on beaches in Dunkirk, are evacuated.

**1940** German troops take control of the Channel Islands.

# Dylan Thomas: Master of Words, Slave to Drink

*Savour the sights and sea air of this famous little town, last resting place of Wales's most famous poet*

Laugharne (pronounced 'Larne') was, and mostly still is, an unpretentious and unremarkable small town hugging one of the many estuaries dotted along the coast of South Wales. It has retained much of the appeal that led Dylan Thomas to live here for the last years of his tragically but perhaps inevitably foreshortened life. Here he enjoyed a life of much-needed routine, which included writing steadily every day from 2pm to 7pm, and chatting (and drinking) at Brown's afterwards. Since Thomas's death, in 1953, Laugharne has been a magnet for the academic and the curious. A few allowances have been made for its unsolicited fame – it has a museum dedicated to its legendary former resident, a generous number of coffee shops, and parking space for visitors – but the town appears otherwise unscathed.

The locality is also a Mecca of a different sort: for birdwatchers, who flock to see the many bird species on the estuarine habitat. In reality Laugharne may not possess the uniqueness Thomas attached to it; nevertheless, a whole day can be spent effortlessly in and around the town, and many visitors stay for several. (If you do stop overnight, be sure to stroll down to the castle after dark: its illumination is as effective as it is simple, rising almost ghost-like from the tidal plain.)

The technical excellence of Thomas's poems is undisputed. His prose too, has been highly acclaimed, and benefits from being accessible to a wide audience. Outside academic literary circles Thomas's best-known work is, ironically, not a poem at all, but *Under Milk Wood*, a largely plotless radio play portraying a day in the life of a small Welsh community – a thinly veiled Laugharne – called Llareggub ('bugger all' spelt backwards).

Through acting for the Swansea Little Theatre,

the young Dylan Thomas honed his skills of voice projection. He breathed not just life but fire and passion into everything he read. Even when well-established, Thomas read not just his own work at his poetry readings and on his American tours but that of other poets, and he was immeasurably better than any of them at reading aloud.

Many poets have failed to achieve recognition in their own lifetimes, but Dylan Thomas had become a household name by the time he died, because he was writing in the heyday of radio. He was much in demand at the BBC, where he enjoyed a high profile, making frequent broadcasts as narrator, actor, writer, critic and poetry-reader. (Television was still in its infancy and Thomas made only one appearance, in 1953, when he read his own prose comedy, *A Story*.)

Thomas's prose writing, which included film scripts, gained him his steadiest earnings. Sadly, his money rarely made its way back to his wife, Caitlin, and their three children. Many do not like to read that Dylan Thomas was a slave to drink, but it was through drink that he lost control of his life, running heavily into debt. Besides, his wife was an alcoholic – drink often made her violent towards him. According to her autobiographical writings, he and she were, in the end, copiously unfaithful to one another. By the time Dylan died she was a wretched and embittered woman and their marriage was effectively over. It took Caitlin 20 years to dry out after Dylan's death, and she lived for a further 20 years.

ABOVE LEFT: *The Boat House at Laugharne where the Dylan family lived between 1949–53 and now a museum.*

BELOW LEFT: *The poet and playwright Dylan Thomas (1914–53).*

BELOW: *Laugharne Castle on the River Taf.*

**ABOUT • LAUGHARNE**

*The Boat House Museum at Laugharne was home to Dylan Thomas and where he wrote much of his poetry. Perfect for Dylan fans, this walk will also appeal to birdwatchers, and the 12th-century Laugharne Castle is definitely worth a visit.*

## Carmarthenshire • WALES

**DISTANCE •** 6 miles (9.6km)

**TOTAL ASCENT •** 490ft (149m)

**PATHS •** good; slippery in places

**TERRAIN •** tracks, field paths, stiles, tarmac roads; **take care on the short stretch of road just after the caravan park, it can be busy**

**GRADIENTS •** mostly gradual

**REFRESHMENTS •** abundant in Laugharne

**PARK •** in Laugharne, just past the town square on the left-hand side. This is a tidal area, so check that it won't flood in your absence!

**OS MAP •** Explorer 177 Carmarthen & Kidwelly

# Home of Dylan Thomas

❶ Turn along the shore, away from the castle. Shortly after a modern kissing gate ascend a signed footpath into woodland, emerging on ciffs overlooking the Taf estuary. Take the left, descending fork at information board. After steps, follow a track for 328yds (300m), past Salt House Kennels. Continue to the quarry road (Causeway Cottage).

❷ Turn right, up to the A-road. Turn right, following the road for 191yds (175m); take care here. Just after a caravan park, go left. Soon a set-back finger-post points to a stile at the back of a lay-by. Cross stile, go right and cross a field with telegraph poles, parallel to stream.

❸ On the other side of the field find a sunken track on the right, just around the left corner of a hedge which juts out. After 109yds (100m) pass a rusty gate. Further along pass a white house to join a dirt track to a tarmac road.

❹ Turn right and continue for 109yds (100m). Just after the 30mph sign take the left fork. The Lacques Water Pump is next to the fork on the right-hand side. Where the road bends sharply right and down, go straight ahead along Holloway Road (dead end sign). Beyond a row of cottages take a sunken lane and cross two fields to a minor road.

❺ Turn right, over the bridge and soon turn right on to the A-road. Continue for 22yds (20m) then turn left (dead end sign) and right through gates into the churchyard. Pass in front of the church, to cross a footbridge into a second churchyard. Dylan and Caitlin share a simple wooden cross, on the left. Leave through a kissing gate at the top of the churchyard. Turn right to a T-junction.

❻ Turn left up a waymarked sunken lane; if wet take care over slabby rocks. Continue for 328yds (300m). When in pasture, near a farm, move right, over stiles by an ash tree. In the field take a vague green track, right. Descend to a small wooded area. The path, later a sunken lane, emerges near a farmhouse.

❼ Turn right, away from the house, following waymarkers into a field above a vegetable garden. Cross the field and go over a stile by a large tree. The pasture deteriorates into a field of gorse, thistle and scrub, then rises gently to a good waymarked path through woodland to a hairpin bend on a tarmac road.

❽ Cross and follow a small lane. Soon steps on the left descend to Dylan Thomas's house, the Boat House, now a museum. Further along this path (Dylan's Walk), is Dylan's writing shed (a small garage with a blue door). Soon there is a choice of routes.

❾ Either take steps down to the shore, and follow a flagged causeway skirting the castle, or continue on Dylan's Walk. Turn left, then follow the road round to King Street. Near by is Brown's, and, opposite, the Pelican (where Dylan's parents lived). Turn left, passing Castle House, where Dylan and Caitlin often stayed, and pass the castle entrance down to the car park.

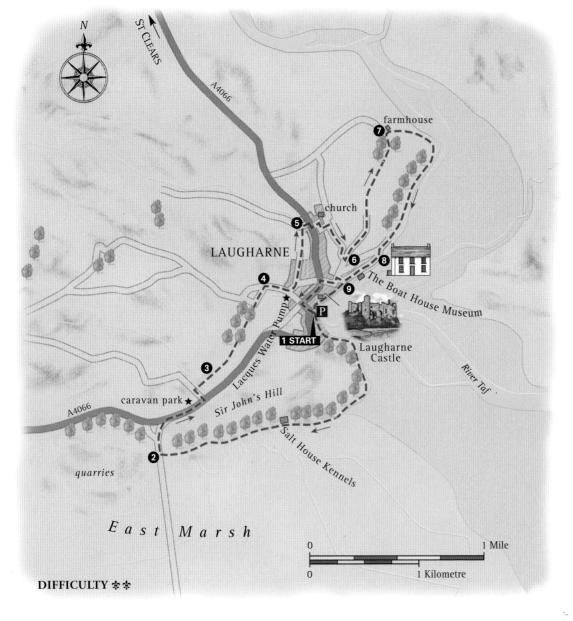

**DIFFICULTY ✳✳**

234

1950

AN AND HOME
AND GOOD NEEDLEWORK MAGAZINE

Knitting Instructions Inside

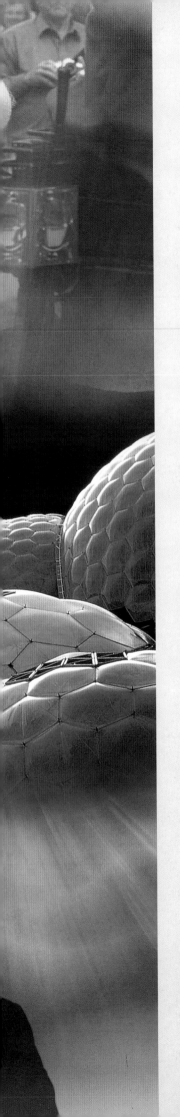

*During the last 50 years of the second millennium, Britain grappled with its identity – as a declining empire, as a European power, and as a multiracial and multinational society.*

## MODERN BRITAIN

## 1945 – Present

# To the Next Millennium

In the post-war years the last vestiges of empire fell away. Mahatma Gandhi's long campaign of peaceful resistance to British rule in India culminated in independence in 1947, and in the ensuing decades a series of former colonies followed suit.

Britain entered the 1950s a war-weary and austere place, though the Festival of Britain in 1951 made a concerted, and successful, effort to lift public spirits. The economy did pick up and by the late 1950s jobs were plentiful, and immigrants were encouraged, especially from the Commonwealth countries, to swell Britain's work-force.

A new generation, with disposable income and a liberal outlook, exploded into the 1960s and created the permissive age. London and Liverpool were the unofficial capitals of pop, and Mary Quant revolutionised street fashion with mini skirts, high boots and a futuristic look that celebrated the Space Age. Motorways began to criss-cross the country just as railways and canals had before them, and cars became accessible to more and more families – as did luxury goods such as the television, complete with a new commercial channel to promote new products.

Throughout the 1960s Britain had been negotiating to enter the European Common Market, and in 1973 Conservative prime minister, Edward Heath, finally oversaw its accession. Britons had already had to come to terms with a new currency, replacing pounds, shillings and pence with a simpler decimal system.

But no amount of modernisation could prevent the crisis that hit Britain and the rest of the Western world in the mid-1970s, when Arab-Israeli war provoked a dramatic rise in oil prices. Fuel tanks ran empty; petrol was rationed; and prices rapidly increased. Demands for higher wages to meet the rising

cost of living stoked industrial conflict, and strikes and picket lines became an enduring image of the 1970s. The emergence of punk music and fashion seemed to epitomise an angry and disillusioned decade.

### CROSSING THE MILLENNIA

The 1980s saw a another shift in the industrial landscape, as computing and service industries flourished and older industries suffered, with the closure of coal mines and steel plants and the decline of ship-building. As whole communities faced the bleak prospect of long-term unemployment, yuppies – young, upwardly mobile professionals – enjoyed the benefits of conspicuous consumption. The Filofax-wielding, mobile-phone-toting city slicker was an icon of late-1980s prosperity.

It also brought the revival of a proposal that had been on the political agenda since the 1880s – an underwater tunnel between Britain and France. The idea was rejected in 1930 and new proposals after World War II were greeted with horror and talk of invasion, smuggling and rabies. However in 1986 a Channel Tunnel agreement was signed between the British and French governments and in 1994 two passenger tunnels and one service tunnel were opened.

In the approach to the 21st century, Britain began to take stock of itself and its place in the world. Devolution of power from Westminster to Scotland and Wales, and continuing the search for a solution to the troubled relationship with Northern Ireland; issues of immigration, multi-ethnicity and an increasingly pluralistic society; and the love-hate association with Europe – all these issues have played a part in shaping the 3rd-millennium nation. Britain now faces the 21st century as fascinated with its future as it is with the past.

### HISTORIC SITES

**Royal Festival Hall, South Bank, London:** legacy of the Festival of Britain.

**Milton Keynes:** purpose-built 1960s city, tailored to accommodate the car.

**Longleat House, Wilts:** lots of visitor entertainment and a safari park shows the changing face of the stately home.

**Angel of the North:** modern testimony to regional pride.

**London Eye:** a millennial view of the capital.

**1947**

**1947** The marriage of HRH Princess Elizabeth and Lieutenant Philip Mountbatten takes place.

**1947** British rule in India comes to an end, starting a trend for other imperial colonies to break away and become independent.

**1948**

**1948** The annual Aldeburgh Festival in Suffolk is founded by the composer Benjamin Britten and tenor Peter Pears.

**1948** On 30 January Mahatma Ghandi is assassinated in New Delhi.

**1948**

**1948** The Welfare State is born in response to the 1942 Beveridge report of Aneurin Bevan, a Welsh ex-miner, who recommended state care from 'the cradle to the grave'.

**1949** NATO is formed and signed by 12 nations.

MODERN BRITAIN

TO THE NEXT MILLENNIUM

# Trespassers in the Peak

*This moorland walk follows the route of the famous Mass Trespass on Kinder Scout – an important catalyst in the fight for National Parks*

In 1951 the creation of the Peak District National Park in Derbyshire – the first in Britain – heralded a new approach to providing public access to the country's mountains and moorlands. An important step towards this post-war policy had been taken 19 years earlier, on Sunday 24 April 1932, when around 400 ramblers gathered on the cricket field in the small town of Hayfield, ready to walk on Kinder Scout.

Kinder Scout, at 2,088ft (636m) the highest point in the Peak District, was then a 'forbidden mountain', with only one right of way crossing a shoulder of its wild, peaty summit. The ramble had been organised by the British Workers' Sport Federation, a youth organisation which had recently been turned off Bleaklow, another of the Peak's jealously preserved grouse moors, by a band of aggressive gamekeepers.

After a brief meeting at the Bowden Bridge quarry on the Kinder road, east of the town, the walkers set off arm-in-arm and singing, around the Kinder Reservoir and up into William Clough on the only undisputed right of way crossing Kinder Scout, on the route we will follow. At a pre-arranged signal, the ramblers left the path and set off up the open moorland of Sandy Heys, climbing towards the forbidden summit plateau, which was guarded by a band of stick-wielding gamekeepers.

There were some scuffles when the two groups met, during which one gamekeeper fell and injured his ankle. However, after a brief victory meeting on the summit plateau with other trespassers from Sheffield, the ramblers headed back to Hayfield, where the police were waiting for them. Six ramblers, supposedly the ring-leaders, were arrested and taken to New Mills police station. At their later trial, they were charged with riotous assembly and incitement to violence, and five received prison sentences of between two and six months.

The harsh treatment inflicted on the protesters united the rambling movement, and up to 10,000 people later attended open-air rallies held in the Winnats Pass, near Castleton, in support of the need for National Parks and access to these moors.

The action of the Kinder trespassers, together with that of others who had campaigned peacefully for many years for the right to roam on open moorland, is now acknowledged as a catalyst in the creation of the 555-square-mile (1,438sq km) Peak District National Park, which celebrated its 50th anniversary in 2001. One of the first things the newly created National Park authority did was to negotiate access agreements with landowners to allow walkers the freedom to roam on those once forbidden moors. The new Countryside and Rights of Way Act recently passed by Parliament will allow the right to roam on all uncultivated open country – something of which those trespassers of 70 years ago could only dream.

ABOVE: *The Mass Trespass, organised by the British Workers' Sport Federation. The protest led the way in obtaining access to the forbidden moors of the Peak District and establishing the need for National Parks.*

FAR LEFT: *Kinder Downfall, just below the summit of Kinder Scout.*

BELOW: *The dramatic landscape of the Peak District National Park.*

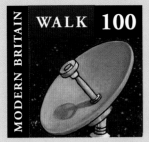
**ABOUT • KINDER SCOUT**

*The Mass Trespass on Kinder Scout in 1932 led to prison sentences for five of the ramblers. However their brave action, combined with many years of peaceful campaigning, eventually led to the opening of the first National Park in the Peak District in 1951.*

# Derbyshire • C ENGLAND

**DISTANCE** • 6 miles (9.6km)

**TOTAL ASCENT** • 1,475ft (450m)

**PATHS** • lanes, moorland paths and tracks

**TERRAIN** • high moorland, requiring boots, waterproofs, map and compass. **This route is for experienced hillwalkers only. It should not be attempted in poor weather conditions**

**GRADIENTS** • stiff climb to the Kinder plateau, followed by a steep, boggy descent

**REFRESHMENTS** • Royal Hotel, Twenty Trees café in Hayfield

**PARK** • Bowden Bridge National Park car park (fee), Hayfield; or in the village

**OS MAP** • Outdoor Leisure 1 The Peak District – Dark Peak area

# The first National Park

❶ Start from the National Park car park at Bowden Bridge, turn left and follow the minor road beside the River Kinder. Branch right after ½ mile (800m) by a footpath sign near the waterworks gates. Cross the river, turn almost immediately left, through a gate on to a broad path by the side of the river. Eventually cross the river by a footbridge below the grassy dam of the Kinder Reservoir.

❷ Go through a gate on the right, signed White Brow, and follow the paved path which climbs, with a wall to your right, up the slopes of White Brow.

❸ The path levels and degenerates to a rocky and sometimes boggy footpath. Follow this through a gate and then around Nab Brow, with fine views across the Kinder Reservoir to your right towards the distant cleft of Kinder Downfall – the highest waterfall in the Peak.

❹ The path eventually descends into William Clough by a cascade. Turn left before a footbridge to follow the signed Snake Path up beside the clough (steep valley) into its narrowing confines.

❺ The rough, rocky path rises steeply, frequently crossing the stream or winding high on its banks, passing the point where the trespass took place. Eventually, after climbing a rocky reconstructed staircase of stones, it emerges beneath Ashop Head.

❻ About 20yds (18m) from the top of the stone staircase, a flagged path leads off to the right towards the prominent headland of Ashop Head. Climb the steep, award-winning reconstructed stairway, now on the Pennine Way

(south), which leads to the top of Ashop Head.

❼ Turn right at the top near a large cairn and go over a stile, marked by a sign stating that you are entering an Environmentally Sensitive Area. Follow the edge path up and below Mill Hill Rocks towards the next prominent headland of Sandy Heys, about ½ mile (800m) of rough walking ahead. This is where the victory meeting was held in 1932.

❽ When you reach the prominent rocks of Sandy Heys, which form the southwestern buttress of Kinder Scout, take the path leading off right (southwest) steeply down the crest of the ridge. Cross rocky

steps and boggy ground, then cross a stream in a dip, and head down towards the foot of William Clough.

❾ On reaching William Clough, cross the footbridge passed on your outward journey and retrace your steps around Nab Brow and White Brow above the reservoir, and down the Kinder Road back to the Bowden Bridge car park and the start of the walk.

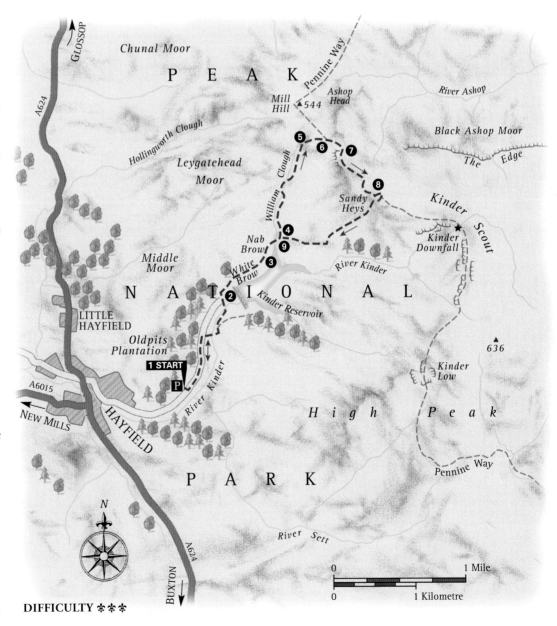

**DIFFICULTY** ✤ ✤ ✤

**1950**

**1950** *The Archers* is broadcast for the first time on radio in June.

**1950** North Korea invades South Korea and civil war breaks out.

**1951** The Festival of Britain, designed to boost morale,

**1951**

transforms the bombed-out South Bank into an exhibition complex.

**1951** The first National Park is opened in the craggy Peak District of central England.

**1952** The death of George VI.

**1953**

**1953** Edmund Hillary and Sherpa Tenzing conquer Everest.

**1953** On 2 June, thousands watch the first televised coronation, of Queen Elizabeth II.

**1954** War-time food rationing ends.

# Still Waters Run Deep

*The campaign to save the valley of Cwm Tryweryn and village of Capel Celyn from drowning beneath Llyn Celyn Reservoir became a focus of the Welsh nationalist movement*

MODERN BRITAIN

TO THE NEXT MILLENNIUM

Looking at the peaceful waters of Llyn Celyn Reservoir from various vantage points on this walk, it is hard to believe that the lake was at the heart of a fierce controversy in the 1950s and '60s. Beneath the reservoir towards the western end of the lake is the site of the former village of Capel Celyn. Some 12 houses, a school, a chapel and over 800 acres (324ha) of valley-bottom farmland forming part of a dozen or so farms were submerged when the dam was built. A sad enough event in itself, but the campaign by the inhabitants to save their community and their valley, Cwm Tryweryn, also united the people of Wales behind them, providing a significant boost to the growing feelings of Welsh national identity and the desire for increased independence.

The reservoir and dam across the Tryweryn River were planned and built by Liverpool City Council. In the mid-1950s, the council claimed that the increase in the number of households and the growing needs of industry in Liverpool and surrounding authorities meant that the amount of water needed would grow significantly in the near future. Despite the existing supply from Lake Vyrnwy (see Walk 80), the situation could reach crisis point if an additional source was not found.

The Welsh argued that the figures were exaggerated and the scheme was substantially in excess of what was required. But it was the nature of the community under threat that made this issue so significant. The village of Capel Celyn was an embodiment of all that was good about local culture and tradition, against a background of ongoing rural depopulation and the threat of the disappearance of the Welsh language and culture. With widespread unemployment across North Wales, the people would be scattered, as the scheme would mean losing the best valley-bottom agricultural land, affecting even those farms which were not actually to be drowned. There was also strong reaction against a valuable Welsh resource being taken by an English authority, to a large extent not even to serve the needs of the city, but sold on to other authorities for profit.

In 1956 around 70 villagers marched through Liverpool to draw attention to their plight. As the measure passed though parliament, most of Wales, and many people from beyond, united behind them, and the issue was seen as a classic case of English dominance. Starting with the non-violent protest at the opening ceremony by the dam in 1965, 'Cofiwch Dryweryn', 'Remember Tryweryn', became a rallying cry of the Welsh nationalist movement.

From the River Tryweryn just above Llyn Celyn itself, the walk climbs to the remote lake of Llyn Arenig Fawr, the source of drinking water for Bala. Then the walk follows the course of the former railway which once linked Bala and Blaenau Ffestiniog. The closure of rural railways represents a loss experienced throughout Britain; this one has added poignancy as it was a further result of the drowning of the valley.

LEFT: *A peaceful protest by the villagers of Capel Celyn in Liverpool attempts to draw attention to their cause.*

INSET: *Graves were transplanted from Capel Celyn to this site near Bala. The chapel, 12 houses, a school and extensive farmland were flooded to create the new reservoir.*

BELOW: *The peaceful expanse of water of Llyn Celyn Reservoir now covers the former village of Capel Celyn.*

## MODERN BRITAIN

# WALK 101

**ABOUT • CWM TRYWERYN**

*Beneath the tranquil waters of Llyn Celyn lies the small village of Capel Celyn. Despite the peaceful protests of villagers to save their town and their rural way of life it was flooded in the 1960s to provide Liverpool with a new water supply.*

## Gwynedd • WALES

**DISTANCE •** 6 miles (9.6km)

**TOTAL ASCENT •** 300ft (91m)

**PATHS •** mainly clear tracks, paths and lanes; moorland can be marshy at times

**TERRAIN •** wild, open moorland

**GRADIENTS •** mainly gradual, one steeper ascent

**REFRESHMENTS •** none on route; picnic area by Llyn Celyn

**PARK •** lay-by on A4212, beyond the picnic area on the western edge of the lake

**OS MAP •** Outdoor Leisure 18 Snowdonia – Harlech, Porthmadog & Bala

# The drowned village of Capel Celyn

**❶** From the large lay-by turn right on to the road. (If starting from the picnic area, turn left on to the road – this involves a longer walk on the verge of the main road.)

**❷** Turn off the road at a small gate with public footpath sign on the right. Follow the path, crossing first the small bridge in the field, then the larger bridge over the Afon Tryweryn. Bear left, and soon see a waymark arrow on the telegraph pole before the hill.

**❸** Head up the hill; at the post with the waymark arrow bear right and head towards the gate. Go through and follow the path downhill to the old railway.

**❹** Turn left on to the old railway. Where the courtesy/permissive bridleway meets some houses and diverts on to the road, do not return to the railway, but stay on the road for about ¼ mile (400m).

**❺** Reach a stile and clear track to the right. Follow this up to Llyn Arenig Fawr, climbing steeply in places. By the dam and the refuge hut, ignore the gate, continuing on the footpath towards the left over the shoulder of the hill.

*(Map showing the walking route around Llyn Celyn Reservoir in Snowdonia National Park, Wales, with labelled features including Afon Gelyn, Foel-Boeth, Afon Hesgyn, Llyn Arenig Fach, Arenig Fach, chapel, picnic area, Snowdonia, A4212, Bala, dam, Porthmadog, Haulfryn, Isfryn, Bryn Ifan, National Park, Mynydd Nodol, Nant Aber-Derfel, Llidiardau, Nant Aber-Bleiddyn, Llyn Arenig Fawr, hut, dam, Arenig Fawr, with numbered points 1 START through 8 and compass rose)*

**DIFFICULTY ✳ ✳**

**❻** In the valley, on reaching the stream, divert to the right to cross the footbridge then return to the path straight on up the hill. At the top of the hill, take the small indistinct path to the left which leads across to the far side of the hill to your left.

**❼** Head for the right-hand corner of the stone wall, following the path along the side of this to the road. Turn left on to the road, pass the farmhouse Bryn Ifan and cross a bridge. Take the track to the right (signed) on to the courtesy path along the old railway.

**❽** Follow the waymarks, keeping to the course of the old railway. Where the path meets a private garden and diverts on to the road, return to the path through the gate just after the house called Haulfryn, and retrace the route from Point ❹ back to the start.

**1955**

**1955** Ruth Ellis is the last woman to be sentenced to death in Britain.

**1955** Mary Quant opens her first shop on the King's Road in Chelsea.

**1957** The first space satellite is launched by the Soviet Union.

**1958**

**1958** An 8-mile stretch of motorway is opened on the Preston Bypass.

**1959** The first Hovercraft crosses the Channel.

**1960** The first episode of the 'soap' *Coronation Street* is broadcast.

**1963**

**1963** On 22 November President John F Kennedy is assassinated. His death sends shockwaves across the world.

**1964** *Charlie and the Chocolate Factory* is published (Roald Dahl).

**MODERN BRITAIN**

**TO THE NEXT MILLENNIUM**

# Spanning the Severn, Gateway to Wales

*A fascinating walk which combines glimpses of a pastoral landscape with fine views of the Severn Estuary and its renowned box-girder suspension bridge*

The Severn Bridge is one of the great engineering success stories of the late 20th century. Opened in the mid-1960s, it is somehow synonymous with that exciting decade when so much seemed to be happening – the era of the mini, the motorway, Carnaby Street and the Beatles.

Before the bridge opened, motorists travelling between southern England and Wales were required to cross the Severn at Gloucester and the Wye at Chepstow. For those who didn't possess their own transport, a small ferry service enabled foot passengers to cross the estuary at the point where the bridge now stands. A railway tunnel under the Severn was completed in 1886.

The idea of a river crossing was first mooted in 1914, though it wasn't until 1960 that a decision was finally taken, putting the Severn Bridge in the context of Britain's initial 1,000-mile (1,609km) motorway network. The world's first box-girder suspension bridge was completed six years later in September 1966, with the project funded by the British government. Tolls were introduced to recover the investment and help pay for maintenance; they are still in force today.

When it opened, the Severn Bridge was deemed a huge success. Never before had it been possible to drive directly between South Wales and the west of England. The swiftness with which people could reach their destination boosted industry and tourism, which in turn helped the local economy.

Not only was the bridge seen as a major improvement in accessibility between the two banks of the Severn, but its simple, unfussy design was visually stunning. In the 1960s this remarkable landmark was one of the world's longest single-span arches; at first glance it is reminiscent of the famous Golden Gate Bridge in San Francisco. There are even echoes of the

bridges which span the Hudson and the East rivers in New York.

Strictly speaking, the Severn Bridge is two structures. A slender isthmus of land, part of England, divides the Severn from the Wye and here the two bridges are joined by a viaduct. The bridge crosses the Wye before it enters Wales.

Fast and easy though the crossing was in those early years, traffic congestion on the M4 gradually slowed the motorist down to a predictable crawl and by the mid-1990s a second, longer bridge had appeared further downstream. This modern structure cost £330,000,000 to build and is the longest bridge in Britain, stretching for 3.2 miles (5.1km) into South Wales. The new bridge carries the M4 across it, while the old Severn Bridge conveys the M48. The new bridge may be breathtaking to look at, but the original, unchanged bridge further up the river remains an unforgettable part of the landscape.

This walk begins in the village of Aust, known in the area as the last settlement on the route to the old Severn ferry crossing. Crossing pleasant farmland, the walk makes for the village of Littleton-upon-Severn, before reaching the banks of the broad estuary and the Severn Way long-distance trail.

The views of the Severn Estuary are impressive, although, with the exception of the Severn Bridge, few landmarks or signs of civilisation stand out on this remote, featureless riverbank. However, seeing the bridge in the context of the landscape creates a fascinating blend of the natural and man-made. Take care by the water's edge, as the Severn has the second largest tidal range in the world, with extremely strong currents.

ABOVE: *View of the Severn beach – the land between the new and old Severn Bridges.*

BACKGROUND: *Motorists paying the toll to cross the newly opened Severn Bridge in 1966.*

LEFT: *When the Severn Bridge was opened in 1966 it was one of the longest spanning bridges in the world.*

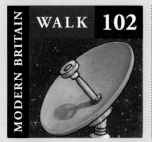
### ABOUT · SEVERN BRIDGE

*The opening of the Severn Bridge in 1966 was a remarkable event. It was then one of the world's longest spanning bridges and still remains a remarkable landmark. During your walk it is worth pausing at the viewing platform to enjoy the views.*

## Gloucestershire · SW ENGLAND

**DISTANCE** · 5½ miles (8.8km)

**TOTAL ASCENT** · 262ft (80m)

**PATHS** · field and riverside paths and tracks

**TERRAIN** · gentle farmland on the eastern shore of the Severn

**GRADIENTS** · one steep climb near the end of the walk

**REFRESHMENTS** · Boars Head, Aust; White Hart, Littleton-upon-Severn

**PARK** · roadside parking in Aust

**OS MAP** · Explorer 167 Thornbury, Dursley & Yate

# Views of the Severn Estuary

**❶** With Aust church behind you, walk through the village and turn left just before the Boars Head into Sandy Lane. Bear right by cottages and modern houses and pass beneath the motorway. Go straight over at the next junction towards Manor Farm offices and keep to the left of the farmhouse.

**❷** When the track swings right to a house, continue ahead through a galvanised gate. Head up the right-hand boundary of the field to a waymark by the hedge corner. Veer diagonally right across the field and make for a gate in the bottom corner. Follow the field edge for a few paces to reach a galvanised gate and stile. Turn left here and follow the track to Cote Farm. Just beyond the farm buildings, veer off to the right to a gate and stile.

**❸** Pass under power lines and make for a stile in the field corner. Keep ahead, following the field boundary round to the left and right. Head for a gate, cross a stream and then join a clear track which runs all the way to the village of Littleton-upon-Severn. Turn left at Salmon Lodge and follow the road to the White Hart

Inn. Head out of the village to a green and turn left at the junction.

**❹** Follow the lane through countryside, passing cottages on the left. Oldbury Nuclear Power Station is in the distance, over to the right. Pass a footpath on the left and a bridleway on the right and follow the lane to the entrance to a cottage on the right. Bear left over a stile and join the Severn Way, following the path up the embankment.

**❺** Walk along the old sea wall towards the Severn Bridge. When you reach an electricity substation on the left, look for a gate and stile. Cross over and head up the steep hillside to the remains of an old look-out. Keep right and cross two stiles into the grounds of the

Severn View service station. Walk along to the Severn Bridge viewing area and follow the path to a sign for Aust.

**❻** Go down the steps and across the top of the motorway toll booth. Bear left on the far side and walk down to the next junction. Keep right and pass the Severn River Crossing maintenance unit before reaching the next junction. Turn left and cross the A403, following the road back to Aust and the start of the walk.

### · DON'T MISS ·

*The **Severn Bridge** was officially opened by Queen Elizabeth II on 8 September 1966. Note the plaque, which records the names of all those involved in the building of the bridge, including Barbara Castle, the then Labour Transport Minister.*

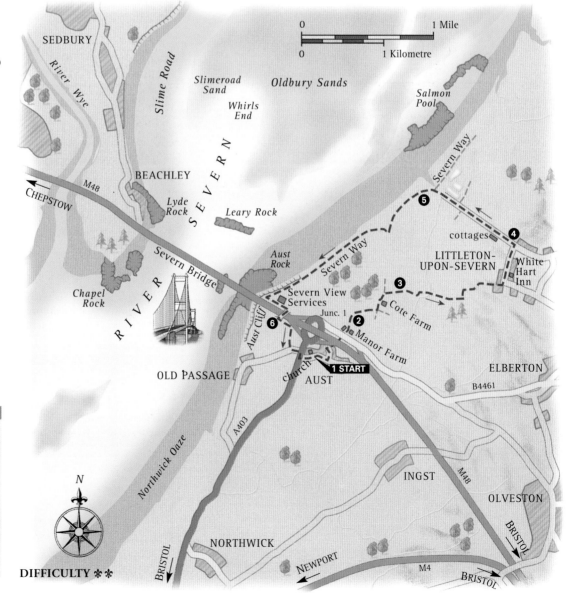

SEDBURY

River Wye

Slime Road

Slimeroad Sand

Oldbury Sands

Whirls End

Salmon Pool

Severn Way

0 — 1 Mile

0 — 1 Kilometre

BEACHLEY

CHEPSTOW M48

Lyde Rock

Leary Rock

SEVERN

RIVER

Chapel Rock

Severn Bridge

Aust Rock

Severn Way

Severn Way

cottages ❹

LITTLETON-UPON-SEVERN

White Hart Inn

❺

❸

Cote Farm

Severn View Services

Junc. 1

❷

Aust Cliff

❻

Manor Farm

ELBERTON

church

AUST **1 START**

B4461

OLD PASSAGE

Northwick Oaze

A403

INGST

M48

OLVESTON

N

NORTHWICK

NEWPORT

M4

BRISTOL

BRISTOL

BRISTOL

**DIFFICULTY** ❋ ❋

**1964**

**1964** Nelson Mandela is sentenced to life imprisonment for treason.

**1964** An audience of 73 million Americans tune in to watch the Beatles on the Ed Sullivan Show. When The Beatles split up in 1970 it marked the end of a heady era.

**1966**

**1966** England wins the World Cup against West Germany.

**1968** Civil liberties leader Martin Luther King is assassinated.

**1969** Neil Armstrong, American astronaut, lands on the moon,

**1971**

**1971** British currency is decimalised in line with the rest of Europe.

**1972** A Catholic march ends in bloodshed in Londonderry, Ireland, when British paratroopers kill 13 civilians. The IRA retaliates with a renewed terror campaign.

# The Beatles' Liverpool

**MODERN BRITAIN**

*Once the second city in the British Empire, Liverpool owes much of its present fame to four local boys who formed a band*

Liverpool received its town charter in 1207, during the reign of King John, but remained undistinguished until the 18th century. Then it became the second biggest port in Britain through trade in sugar, spices, tobacco and slaves. This sorry aspect of its past is depicted in the Maritime Museum at the Albert Dock, where this walk begins.

The walk takes you along the waterfront by the river, across which travels the ferry made famous in song (*Ferry Across the Mersey*) by Gerry and the Pacemakers, another Liverpool group. The same ferry took the Beatles – Paul McCartney, John Lennon, Ringo Starr and George Harrison – to ballrooms in New Brighton and Wallasey, where they played in their early days. Ringo Starr worked for a short while as a barman on these ferries. Little could he have known that by 1964 the city would be honouring the Beatles at a civic reception at the Town Hall, for the northern première of their first film, *A Hard Day's Night*.

From here it is a short walk to Mathew Street, site of the famous Cavern Club, where the Beatles made 275 appearances. Note the statue high on the wall opposite the reconstructed Cavern, by Liverpool sculptor Arthur Dooley. Hessy's music shop in Stanley Street is where John's Aunt Mimi bought him his first guitar, and the Ann Summers shop used to be the NEMS music shop, where a fan brought the Beatles to the attention of Brian Epstein by asking for a copy of a recording they had made in Hamburg.

Other city sights include St George's Hall, where 10,000 people paid tribute to John Lennon after he was murdered. Across from here is the Empire Theatre, where the band made its last live appearance in Liverpool, on 5 December 1965. Lime Street Station was a familiar sight to the Beatles, as was the Adelphi Hotel, where they would stay when playing concerts in the city, after they had moved to London.

At 64 Mount Pleasant you will find the Registry Office where John married his first wife, Cynthia, and nearby is the Philharmonic Pub, where he played snooker while a student at the Art College in Hope Street. The early Beatles, known as the Quarry Men, played lunchtime sessions to the students in the Art College canteen.

At the end of Hope Street is the grand Anglican Cathedral, where Paul failed the audition as a choirboy in 1953, and where later he saw the performance of one of his classical pieces. Paul and George went to school at the Liverpool Institute on Mount Street, and later Paul McCartney was prominent in turning this into the Liverpool Institute for the Performing Arts.

On the way back to the city centre the walk passes their more humble beginnings. At the Blue Angel, John, Paul and George auditioned Pete Best, who was the band's drummer before Ringo Starr. In the Jacaranda, the Beatles also performed a few times and the club's basement still has murals painted by John Lennon and another early band member, Stuart Sutcliffe. The Beatles may have left Liverpool a long time ago, but their presence is still felt everywhere.

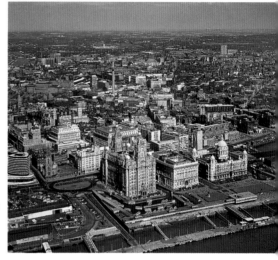

ABOVE: *Aerial view of Liverpool with the Liver Building and the Mersey in the foreground.*

LEFT: *The Beatles on the Ken Dodd Show in 1963. Beatlemania gripped Britain and the United States but their most loyal fan remains the city of Liverpool.*

**ABOUT · LIVERPOOL**

*Liverpool is the celebrated home town of the Beatles. This walk through the city takes you to all the famous Beatle landmarks from the Cavern Club on Mathew Street to the Empire Theatre, where the band made its last live appearance in 1965.*

## Merseyside · N BRITAIN

**DISTANCE** • 5 miles (8km)

**TOTAL ASCENT** • 110ft (33m)

**PATHS** • footpaths

**TERRAIN** • city streets

**GRADIENTS** • very gentle

**REFRESHMENTS** • Tate Gallery Café at Albert Dock; the Philharmonic Pub

**PARK** • Plenty of free parking at Albert Dock

**OS MAP** • Explorer 275 Liverpool, St Helens, Widnes & Runcorn

# Liverpool: city of the 'Fab Four'

❶ Visit the Beatles Experience on Albert Dock. On leaving, turn right to the waterfront and right again for 700yds (640m) to the Mersey Ferry Terminal. Turn right into Water Street on the near side of the Royal Liver Building – with the unmistakable Liver Birds on top.

❷ Pass the Town Hall on your left, turn right into North John Street, continue for 200yds (183m) and turn left into Mathew Street and the Cavern Quarter. On the right is the reconstructed Cavern Club, next to the Cavern Walks shopping development.

❸ In 30yds (27m), on the left, is The Grapes pub, popular with the Beatles; the Beatles Shop is further along. At the end of Mathew Street turn left into Stanley Street to see the Eleanor Rigby statue in 20yds (18m) on the right.

❹ Walk back down Stanley Street, passing the site of Hessy's music shop on the right (currently unoccupied, next to Wade Smith). At the end, look to your right along Whitechapel, where the Ann Summers shop now occupies the NEMS shop, once owned by Brian Epstein's family.

❺ Turn left along Whitechapel, past the bus station, for 500yds (457m), and turn right along St John's Lane, passing St George's

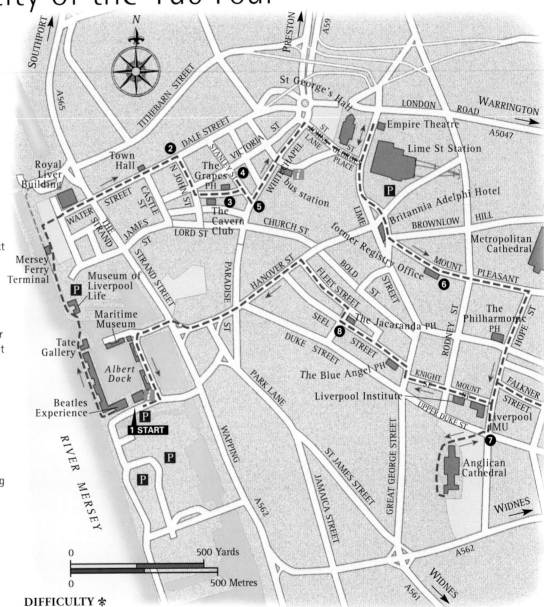

0 — 500 Yards

0 — 500 Metres

**DIFFICULTY** ❋

Hall, left. Cross to Lime Street Station and turn left to the Empire Theatre. Retrace your steps past the station and continue for 200yds (183m) past the Britannia Adelphi Hotel. Turn left, up the hill, on to Mount Pleasant. Note the former Registry Office on the right, now a cancer resource centre.

❻ Continue and turn right into Hope Street, opposite the Roman

Catholic Metropolitan Cathedral, down to the Philharmonic pub. Continue for 100yds (91m) and turn left into Falkner Street to No 36, John and Cynthia's first home together. Return to Hope Street and turn left. At the end, visit the Anglican Cathedral, which has several Beatles connections.

❼ Turn back along Hope Street and left into Mount Street just past

Liverpool John Moores University Hope Street Campus. Continue down the hill for 300yds (274m), turn right into Berry Street and left into Seel Street. The Blue Angel is on the left at No 108.

❽ Turn right into Slater Street, the Jacaranda is on the right at No 23. Left into Fleet Street for 500yds (457m) then left into Hanover Street to return to Albert Dock.

# The Millennium Forest

*Renewal of the ancient Caledonian Forest*

ABOVE: *Caledonian pine in Glen Affric with Sgurr Na Lapaich in the background.*

RIGHT: *Planting native Caledonian pine is regenerating the woodland at Glen Affric.*

## Scotland's Native Trees

Once, most of Scotland was covered in a dense forest. Huge, majestic pine trees, birch and rowans covered the land. The bears, wolves and wild boar that roamed free, using the forest as a source of food and shelter and feeding on a host of smaller creatures, were hunted in turn by the greatest predator of all, *Homo sapiens*. As well as hunting, early humans gathered nuts, berries and roots, and in time they acquired the skills of husbandry, abandoning their nomadic lifestyle and becoming farmers. They cleared vast areas of the forest to provide land on which to grow crops, and harvested the timber to build their houses and barns, and stockades to contain their domesticated animals. As the pace of development increased, so too did the amount of timber required. Eventually, whole areas were cleared to the extent that today only one per cent of Scotland's original native woodland survives.

## Restoration of the Native Pine Forests

What remains of the native forests represents specimens that descended from the trees that grew here at the end of the last ice age – over eight thousand years ago. Scots pine is renowned for its long life and many of the specimens that grow around Loch Affric are extremely old and knotted. (The same trees provided shelter for Bonnie Prince Charlie when he fled from Government forces after the Battle of Culloden in 1746.) It is quite possible that many of the trees were mere seedlings back when wolves, bears and lynx still lived here. However, as these natural predators became extinct the forest came under serious threat from increased numbers of red deer, browsing the forests for food.

By the end of World War II, most of the remaining trees were reaching the end of their lives. Continual grazing of deer and sheep meant that none of the young seedlings were surviving to replace them, and the forest faced extinction.

Fortunately, in 1951, the Forestry Commission acquired control of the woodland. In response to the failing forest, they erected fences and started controlling the numbers of deer within the enclosures. They also started a planting programme of young trees, raised from seeds gathered in the Glen, in an attempt to kick-start the regeneration process of the forest. Eventually, as the numbers of deer reduced, so the seedlings began to survive and it was no longer necessary to continue planting.

On this walk, you will enter a new enclosure funded by the Millennium Forest for Scotland Project. This is part of a nationwide scheme to increase the area of native woodland that is being managed for conservation.

LEFT: *River Affric with Caledonian pine trees on its banks.*

BELOW: *Autumnal colour in Glen Affric.*

## WALK 104 — AROUND LOCH AFFRIC THROUGH THE MILLENNIUM FOREST PROJECT

❶ From the car park, head back to the road and turn left. At the fork in the forestry road keep left, go over a bridge and then through a gate in the deer fence. Continue on the forest road. Pass a cottage on your right, cross another bridge; go uphill and across a cattle grid. The area on either side of the track is now part of the pinewood regeneration. Follow the road as it winds round the side of Loch Affric. After a couple of miles you will reach the houses at Athnamulloch. Cross the river by the bridge and follow the track uphill.

❷ This path leads to the youth hostel at Altbeith just over three miles away, but keep a sharp lookout for the narrower track that branches to the right in approximately quarter of a mile. Turn right and follow the track uphill. Although it can be muddy at times of high rainfall, the going is generally easy. Pass through another gate in the deer fence and re-enter the regeneration area.

❸ Continue along the track and enjoy the grand view over Loch Affric – but be sure to apply a powerful insect repellent, particularly on this section, to ward off the horse-flies. Exit the regeneration area through another gate and continue ahead on the path past Affric Lodge and back to the fork in the road, and from there return to the car park.

**Distance:** 8 miles (13km)

**Total ascent:** 328 feet (100m)

**Paths:** good, except in wet weather when can become boggy

**Terrain:** forest roads; hill tracks

**Gradients:** mainly gentle

**Refreshments:** none available

**Park:** car park at the end of the road at Loch Beinn a Mheadhoin.

**OS Mao:** Landranger 25 Glan Carron & Glen Affric

**Difficulty:** ✿✿✿

| 1972 | 1976 | 1980 |
|------|------|------|
| **1972** Britain enters the Common Market under Edward Heath. | **1976** *Concorde* makes her maiden flight, breaking the speed of sound. | **1980** The Humber Bridge is completed, stretching 1440m (4624ft). |
| **1973** A ceasefire is declared in the Vietnam war. | **1979** Margaret Thatcher is elected to serve as the first female Prime Minister. Her policies and imposing personality inspire both fervent devotion and fierce hostility. | **1980** John Lennon's death in New York causes huge public mourning. |
| **1975** North Sea oil is discovered, and the first supplies piped ashore. | | **1981** The first London Marathon takes place. |

# The Black Gold of the North Sea

*Oil has brought prosperity and tragedy to the old fishing port of Aberdeen*

ABOVE: *While many ports have suffered decline Aberdeen remains busy and prosperous due to oil drilling and a good fishing trade in the North Sea.*

Aberdeen had been a major maritime centre throughout the 19th century, when a group of local entrepreneurs purchased an ageing paddle tug and launched it as the first steam-powered trawler. From small beginnings the steam trawling industry expanded and by 1933 Aberdeen was Scotland's top fishing port, employing nearly 3,000 men with 300 vessels sailing from its harbour. By the time oil was coming on stream, much of the massive trawling fleet had relocated to Peterhead. Although an early morning visit to the fish market will verify that Aberdeen still brings in substantial catches, the tugs, safety vessels and supply ships for the huge offshore rigs which pack the harbour far outnumber the trawlers.

Geologists had speculated about the existence of oil and gas in the North Sea since the middle of the 20th century, and although the technology to extract oil from beneath the sea had existed since the late 19th century, when the Gulf of Mexico had first

been tapped, the deep and inhospitable waters of the North Sea were another story. However, with the oil sheiks of the Middle East becoming more aware of the political and economic power of their reserves, the industry began to consider the North Sea as a viable source of oil. Exploration commenced in the 1960s and the first major find in the British sector was in November 1970 in the Forties field, 110 miles (177km) east of Aberdeen.

By late 1975, after years of intense construction, the hundreds of miles of pipes, massive offshore rigs, supply ships, helicopters and an army of oil workers were finally in place. In Aberdeen, at BP's (British Petroleum) headquarters, the Queen pressed the button that would set the whole thing moving. Oil flowed from the rig directly to the refinery at faraway Grangemouth, and brought a new prosperity to Aberdeen, as well as an influx of people connected with the industry, and a rise in property prices.

The human costs of oil prosperity were brutally brought home on the night of 6 July 1988. A huge fire lit the sky as the Piper Alpha oil platform, 120 miles (193km) offshore, exploded, and helicopters flew all night bringing the dead and injured to Aberdeen. In all, 167 died; the survivors lived with the horrific memories of escaping from the burning rig to the chill black depths of the North Sea. A memorial to the dead stands in Hazlehead Park. The subsequent inquiry revealed that safety regulations had been ignored. The industry learned a bitter lesson, and the rigs are now safer places.

Aberdeen has become an important international oil centre, with considerable expertise, which can now be exported to other areas of the world. The industry supports about 47,000 jobs locally and known reserves are such that oil will continue to flow well into the 21st century.

ABOVE: *An oil rig in the North Sea. Although the industry has brought wealth to Aberdeen, life on an oil rig remains a dangerous business.*

### ABOUT · ABERDEEN

*Oil caused havoc in the 1970s as rising prices led to government cuts and threats of petrol rationing but in 1975 oil was stuck in the North Sea. This walk around the old fishing port celebrates the prosperity and tragedy that oil has brought to Aberdeen.*

### Aberdeen City · SCOTLAND

**DISTANCE** • 6 miles (9.6km)

**TOTAL ASCENT** • negligible

**PATHS** • excellent in all weather

**TERRAIN** • mainly roads and pavements with a short section of beach (underwater at high tide)

**GRADIENTS** • fairly level throughout

**REFRESHMENTS** • Aberdeen Maritime Museum or Harry Ramsden's

**PARK** • outside Harry Ramsden's on the Esplanade or Queen's Link Leisure Park

**OS MAP** • Pathfinder 246 Aberdeen

# Striking oil in the North Sea

**DIFFICULTY** ✿ ✿

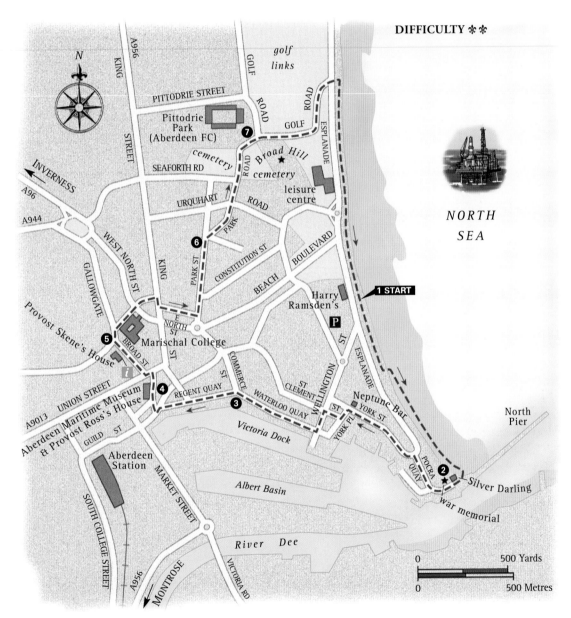

and John Ross's House, Provost of Aberdeen between 1710–1711.

❹ From here head along Exchequer Row, turn left into Union Street, continue and turn right into Broad Street, where you will find Provost Skene's House and the Tourist Information Office on the left, behind the offices.

❺ Continue past Marischal College (which houses the Marischal Museum), turn right into Littlejohn Street, cross North Street. At the end of Meal Market Street turn right into King Street and then left into Frederick Street. At the junction with Park Street turn left and keep walking until the road crosses the railway.

❻ Shortly after this is a roundabout. Head along Park Road, almost straight ahead. Follow it through the cemetery and towards Pittodrie Park, home of Aberdeen Football Club, and its junction with Golf Road.

❼ Turn right into Golf Road and walk through the golf links. Detour to the top of Broad Hill, the mound behind the cemetery, for magnificent views to the north and out to sea. The road turns sharply left towards its junction with the Esplanade. Cross the Esplanade and turn right on to the promenade which you can follow back to the start of the walk.

❶ Head southwards on the promenade beside the shore with the sea on your right. Go down the slipway on to the beach and continue for a short distance. Step over the rocks to reach the wooden steps on the right and leave the beach into a children's play area.

❷ Walk past the Silver Darling restaurant and into the harbour area. Continue past the war memorial, keeping the blue storage tanks on your left, and along Pocra Quay. Turn left into York Street and at the Neptune bar, turn left into York Place. Then, take the first right, the first left

and first right again to emerge on Waterloo Quay.

❸ Where Waterloo Quay becomes Commerce Street, turn left into Regent Quay and at the T-junction cross the road at the pedestrian lights. Turn left, then first right to reach Aberdeen Maritime Museum

**1981**

**1981** Prince Charles marries Lady Diana Spencer at St Paul's in July.

**1982** Henry VIII's ship *Mary Rose* is salvaged and restored.

**1982** The Falklands War breaks out between Britain and Argentina.

**1982**

Argentine troops surrender on 14 June, but 255 British and 652 Argentinean lives are lost.

**1984** A huge fund-raising drive is launched by the pop-singer Bob Geldof to provide aid to starving Ethiopians.

**1984**

**1984–5** Pit closures brings about the miners' strike.

**1987** In October gale force winds hit southern Britain, causing chaos.

**1988** *A Brief History of Time* is published (Stephen Hawkings).

# Past meets Present in the Heart of Wales

*Explore the effects of Celtic heritage and the legacy of a national hero in Machynlleth*

In the geographical centre of Wales, Machynlleth has always been of historical significance. Lying at the western end of the pass between the mountains from England and the lands of the marcher lords of Montgomeryshire and Shropshire, it is also where the north, south and central Welsh regions, as represented by the modern counties of Gwynedd, Dyfed and Powys respectively, meet.

It is now the home of an interesting centre for the exploration of the Celtic origins of Wales and the relevance of this historical and legendary past to the present-day Welsh identity. The Celtica Centre was founded in 1995. Housed in Plas Machynlleth, the former home of the Marquis of Londonderry, it houses a range of exhibitions placing the 3,000 years of Celtic culture and history in context and providing the ideal background for an exploration of Wales as a nation today. The main audio-visual exhibition brings to life the Celts of the Bronze Age, depicting a variety of aspects of their history, culture and mythology. The interpretive centre provides a more traditional exhibition of Welsh history in a wider Celtic and European context. One of the most popular exhibits is a tape with examples of the six Celtic languages; the Welsh language being one of the key factors that defines the national identity. As you walk round Machynlleth you will hear the language in everyday use, and of course it is most evident in road signs and on public buildings wherever you look.

When Wales was given decentralised status in 1998 and the Welsh Assembly was formed, Machynlleth was one of the places put forward for its location. Cardiff's recognition as the official capital in 1955 was relatively recent in the context of Wales's long history. The significance of the town to political history dates back to Owain Glyndŵr, the last native Prince of Wales and leader of the last main rebellion against the English and King Henry IV. The uprising began in 1400 and lasted for about a decade. In 1404 Glyndŵr founded the first Welsh Parliament in Machynlleth and was crowned Prince

of Wales here. This Parliament was of sufficient status for it to be recognised by France and further afield in Europe. The Parliament Centre on the main street, Heol Maengwyn, gives an interesting and informative history of this period, and can be visited by taking a detour to the right as you return to Machynlleth after the riverside walk,. Although the rebellion was relatively short-lived, the English soon gained the upper hand and Owain became an outlaw – the location of his grave is still unknown – he is a national hero still remembered with great affection, and a powerful symbol of Welsh independence. Celebrations were held on 16 September 2000 to mark the 600th anniversary of the start of the uprising, and a monument of Owain was erected in the grounds outside the Celtica Centre.

ABOVE TOP: *Mural of Owain Glyndŵr (c.1305–1416).*

ABOVE: *The Clock Tower in the centre of Machynlleth.*

RIGHT: *From the rolling hills outside Machynlleth you will also catch a glimpse of another part of the town's history – the windmills of CAT (Centre for Alternative Technology).*

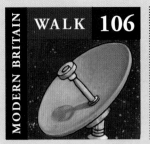
**ABOUT • MACHYNLLETH**

*This walk around Machnylleth celebrates the town's long history: from the foundation of the first Welsh Parliament by Owain Glyndŵr in 1404 to the Celtica Centre founded in 1995 which offers a superb exhibition of Welsh culture and language.*

### Powys • WALES

**DISTANCE •** 5 miles (8km)

**TOTAL ASCENT •** 675ft (206m)

**PATHS •** pavements, tracks and paths

**TERRAIN •** town, river meadows, moorland

**GRADIENTS •** one fairly steep climb; one moderate descent

**REFRESHMENTS •** various pubs and cafés in Machynlleth

**PARK •** main car park, off Heol Maengwyn, Machynlleth

**OS MAP •** Outdoor Leisure 23 Snowdonia – Cadair Idris & Bala Lake

# Machynlleth's long history

❶ From the clock tower at the end of the main street, Heol Maengwyn, take the road to the north for 328yds (300m), towards the station. Pass the station and Dyfi Eco Park, and just before the Dyfi Bridge, take the surfaced footpath to the right along the river bank.

❷ Keep ahead, leaving the surfaced path where it goes over the new footbridge, and carry on along the river bank, crossing a low barbed wire fence. Follow the river through the meadows for 547yds (500m), crossing a stile.

❸ As the route nears the railway and the river swings left, climb the stile to the right and cross the railway with care. Bear left up the hill. On leaving the trees, bear right across the field towards a stile uphill from the gate; cross and turn right on to the track.

❹ Where the houses start, join the road and continue straight on for 656yds (600m), past Maes-y-Garth; at the T-junction by the cemetery, turn right. After the side turning, (Maes Dyfi, on the left, before the 'no entry' signs), turn left down the one-way street. At the end turn left on to the main

street then right, up the road signed Llyn Clywedog/Llanidloes.

❺ Past Treowain Enterprise Park, opposite where the houses finish, take the signed footpath to the right. Follow the waymarkers, and after 219yds (200m) follow the wall for 328yds (300m), then bear right at the corner of the wall before zigzagging up a fairly steep hill. At the top of the hill, bear right to the corner of the forest.

❻ On reaching the trees, take the path to the right, away from the trees, passing between boulders 22yds (20m) ahead. In 328yds (300m), go through a gate and follow the track downhill for 109yds (100m). Go through the gate at a T-junction with a track, continue downhill, past the shale track on the left, through the woods, and past the farm Brynglas.

❼ In 437yds (400m) at the road, turn right. After 219yds (200m) turn right on to the path signed Glyndŵr's Way, cross the drive to the cottages and follow the path to the road. At the bottom, turn right into the grounds of the Celtica Centre.

❽ Cross the car park; go round to the front of the Plas (mansion) and entrance to the Celtica Centre. Follow the drive round to the left in front of the leisure centre, turning right at the roundabout to return to the clock tower.

**DIFFICULTY ✽✽**

**• DON'T MISS •**

*From the hills above Machynlleth you will see one of the windmills belonging to the **Centre for Alternative Technology (CAT)**, about 2 miles (3.2km) to the north of the town. This innovative centre, researches and practices sustainable forms of energy.*

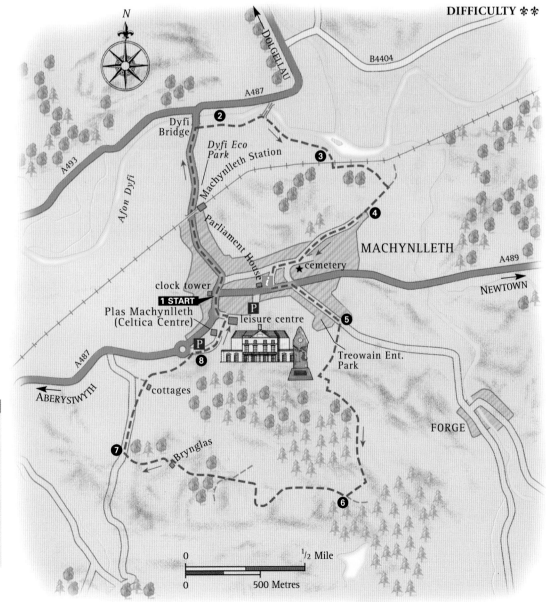

**1988**

**1988** A Pam Am flight explodes killing more than 300 passengers and residents of the quiet Scottish town of Lockerbie.

**1989** The Berlin Wall between East and West Germany comes down, 40 years after its construction.

**1990**

**1990** Nelson Mandela, leader of the African National Congress, is released from prison.

**1991** On 16 January Allied forces launch Operation Desert Storm against Iraq. A ceasefire is called by President Bush on 27 February.

**1991**

**1991** The USSR is replaced by the Commonwealth Independent States.

**1991** The Channel Tunnel opens.

**1996** The Scottish Stone of Scone, seized by Edward I in 1296, is returned to Scotland.

**MODERN BRITAIN**

# The Cuckoo Trail of Sussex

*A homage to the bicycle and to the development of sustainable transport along the former railway line at Horam*

The peaceful former railway line forming the Cuckoo Trail doesn't seem initially like the site of a revolution. Yet in its way it is part of one of the most radical transport schemes of the post-war years – the National Cycle Network, established by the charitable organisation Sustrans, whose name is a contraction of 'sustainable transport'.

The closure in 1965 of the Eridge to Polegate 'Cuckoo Line' – named after a Sussex tradition that the first cuckoo of spring was released at Heathfield Fair – eventually gave the local council and Sustrans the opportunity to open up the section of trackbed from Polegate to Heathfield to cyclists, horse-riders, pedestrians and wheelchair-users. In 1990 the Cuckoo Trail was born.

Sustrans aims to promote sustainable transport – cycling and walking in particular – and to get more of us cycling or walking to work and school and during our leisure time. Britain lags behind many other European countries in this respect: although many of us own bikes, we rarely use them. The charity gained a huge cash boost from the Millennium Commission to establish a National Cycle Network. The network signposts cyclists along quiet roads and specially constructed cycle paths, soon to pass within 2 miles (3km) of half the UK population.

The bicycle, the most efficient human-powered form of transport ever devised, was enthusiastically taken up in Sussex. In 1868 William Martin from Ringmer, near Lewes, made what is said to have been the first true bicycle in England. In 1873–4 H J Lawson built the first safety bicycle, with two wheels of equal diameter – much more stable than the previous penny-farthing variety – and a rear wheel driven by a chain. Lawson frequently rode around Brighton and through the Sussex countryside.

The invention of the pneumatic tyre in the 1880s by a Scotsman, John Dunlop, spelt the end of the solid tyre 'bone-shakers', and with this safety development, a mass market opened up. Suddenly the bicycle factories of the Midlands were busy and people could travel further than ever before.

Cycling proved a milestone in the emancipation of women. Victorian fears for the health and morals of female cyclists gradually gave way: bicycle design was adapted for female riders, and bloomers became accepted wear. In 1895 cycling became the rage of society women for a season, and the barriers of convention crumbled. Cycling clubs sprang up; huge groups of riders going out on weekend tours dominated the routes out of cities, with couples on tandems and bicycles with side-cars for babies. Time trial racing also became popular. It was illegal in the early days, so racers avoided the police by competing at first light, dressed all in black.

With the advent of the motor car came talk, in the inter-war years, of the government building special off-road lanes and paths for cyclists. The Cyclists' Touring Club (CTC) opposed such schemes vehemently, fearing that cyclists would lose their freedom of the road. The CTC's success in getting what it wanted was perhaps, with hindsight, unfortunate: few at that time could have conceived the massive increase in private car-ownership and the dramatic decline in cycling in post-war years.

ABOVE: *Cyclists enjoying themselves in 1900; cycling was only allowed in Hyde Park from 1895 onwards.*

LEFT: *The Sustrans Cycle Network offers traffic-free routes for cyclists, walkers and horse-riders.*

BACKGROUND: *On the Cuckoo Trail, south of Heathfield.*

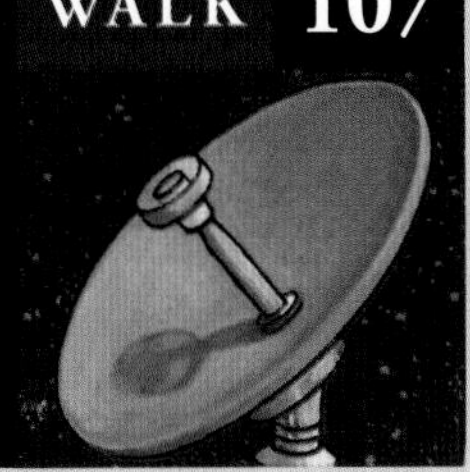

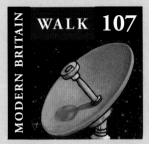

**ABOUT • THE CUCKOO TRAIL**

*The Cuckoo Trail, opened in 1990, runs along the track of a former railway and is part of the 9,000-mile (15,000km) Sustrans Cycle Network due to be completed in 2005, which aims to promote a traffic-free 'sustainable transport' network.*

**East Sussex • SE ENGLAND**

**DISTANCE** • 6 miles (9.6km)

**TOTAL ASCENT** • 300ft (91m)

**PATHS** • clearly waymarked tracks and field paths, mostly along Cuckoo Trail and Wealdway; lanes; some muddy sections

**TERRAIN** • disused railway track, quiet lanes, gently rolling farmland. Many stiles

**GRADIENTS** • gentle

**REFRESHMENTS** • pub, café, chip shop and food shops at Horam; Gun Inn, Gun Hill; picnic benches along trail

**PARK** • Cuckoo Trail car park at Horam: turn off A267 at village centre by Horam Inn on to B2203; first turn on right, Hillside Drive, signed car park and toilets

**OS MAP** • Explorer 123 South Downs Way – Newhaven to Eastbourne

# Along the Cuckoo Trail

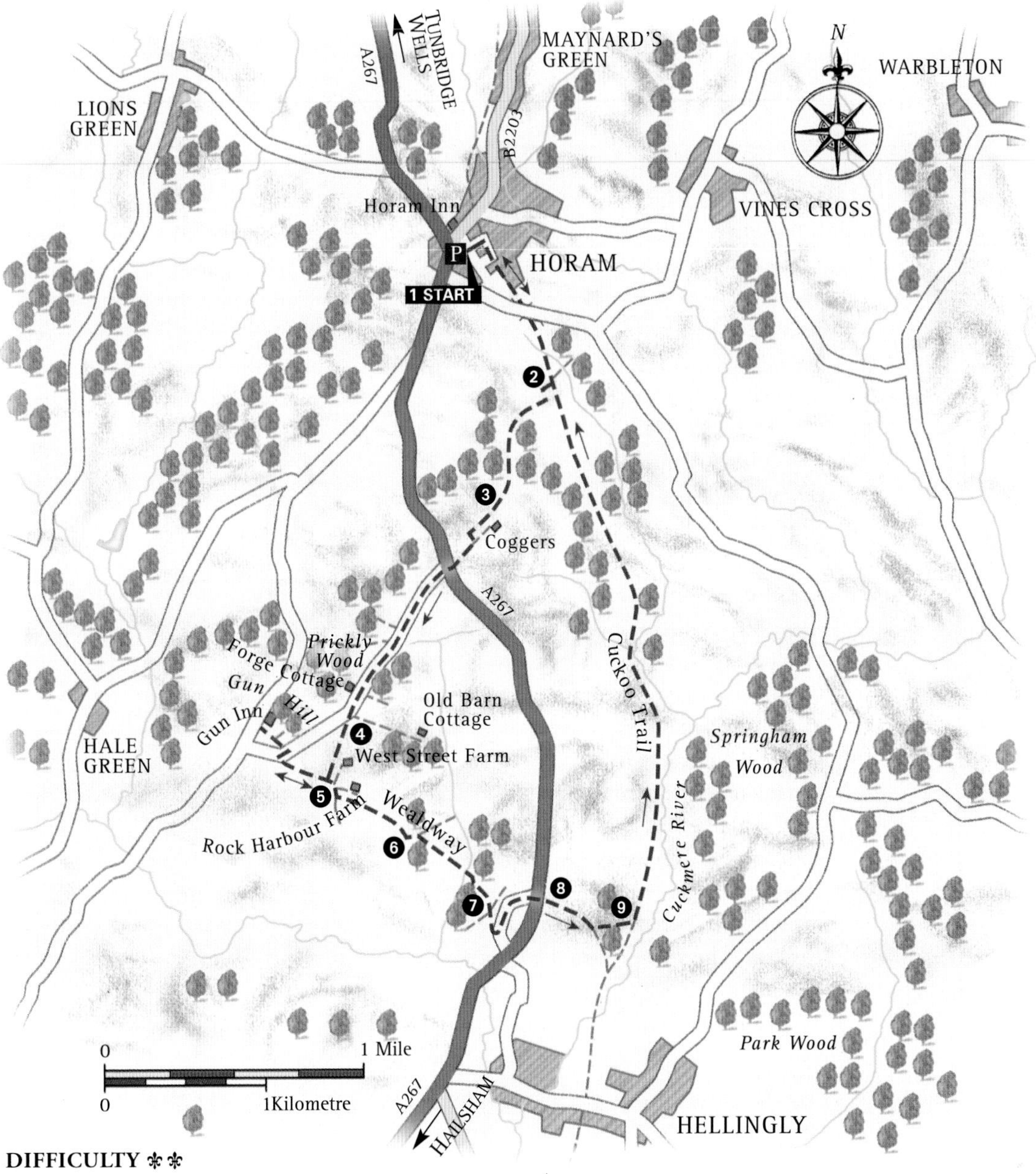


**DIFFICULTY** ✽✽

❶ Turn right out of the car park, then immediately left at a Cuckoo Trail sign, into a housing estate, bearing right as signed. Ignore the next right, signed Cuckoo Trail with horse-rider symbol, but keep ahead on the Cuckoo Trail (a former railway track), signed Hailsham/Polegate.

❷ After passing under a brick bridge and 130yds (119m) after a wedge-shaped bench on your left, turn right down steps to a stile and follow yellow arrows, first turning left along a field. The route continues along the left edge of three larger fields, then down through woodland and crosses over a footbridge.

❸ Emerge from woodland, continue forward to the top left corner of field, over a stile, then along the left edge of the next two fields (cross by stile). Cross another stile on the left. Turn right along the driveway, cross the A267 and take Swansbrook Lane opposite. Continue for 547yds (500m) to Forge Cottage on your right.

❹ In ¼ mile (400m) past the cottage take the right-hand path of two signed paths on your left (the left-hand path follows a driveway to Old Barn Cottage). Follow the left edges of three fields. At a farm track, turn left (or to detour to the Gun Inn, turn right, right at a T-junction, then left over a stile after 100yds (91m), and follow the field edge to the pub; return the same way).

❺ Keep right at the first junction (left goes to West Street Farm) and follow WW (Wealdway) waymarkers, almost immediately turning left as signed just after the entrance to Rock Harbour Farm. Follow the left edge of the field and continue forward across the middle of the next two fields.

❻ Beyond the third field go through a small wooded area, then turn right along field edges (avoiding a path branching to the left). Near the end of the second field take a stile on your right then turn left inside the edge of the wood, then go over a footbridge.

❼ Leave the wood and go up into the field, soon joining the left edge, then cross a stile to the right of houses. Continue in the next field, cross a driveway 15yds (14m) right of a cattle grid, and down to a stile. Turn left on the road (leaving the Wealdway), which bends right to the A267.

❽ Cross the A267 and cross the stile opposite, go down a bank and follow the left edges of two fields. Beyond the second field take a stile on your left and cross two fields diagonally to take a stile into trees – avoid a gate to the left of this.

❾ Turn left along the Cuckoo Trail for 2½ miles (4km) to Horam and the start of the walk.

**1997**
**1997** After 18 years of Tory rule, Tony Blair, leader of New Labour, is elected Prime Minister.

**1997** The Princess of Wales dies in a tragic car accident with Dodie Fayed in Paris, and Britain enters a period of intense mourning.

**1998**
**1998** The Lost Gardens of Heligan open in Cornwall.

**1998–2001** The Eden Project is built in a disused China pit in Cornwall.

**1999** Devolution of the Scottish and Welsh Parliaments takes place.

**2000**
**2000** The Millennium Dome and the London Eye open; part of the huge celebrations for the millennium.

**2000** The Queen Mother celebrates her 100th birthday.

# A Visit to Eden

*Spend a day exploring this inspirational site just east of St Austell – and do your bit for the environment by getting there on foot*

The Eden Project is the last thing you would expect to find buried in the strange, almost lunar landscape of central Cornwall, sandwiched between the busy A390 holiday route to the south, and the A30 and the 'Cornish Alps' – the mountainous heaps of waste generated by centuries of china clay working – to the north. This traditionally strongly Methodist area feels run-down and forgotten, but nothing could be further from the truth. It's an overwhelming experience to gaze down into the old Bodelva china clay quarry, now completely transformed by the construction of massive conservatories, or biomes. The largest – the humid tropics biome, at 180ft (55m) high – will house fully mature rainforest trees and is the biggest structure of its kind in the world, capable of containing the Tower of London.

The brainchild of Tim Smit, who was originally better known for unearthing the Lost Gardens of Heligan, the Eden Project has taken the world by storm since work began in 1998 in the quarry, almost exhausted after 150 years of working. It took a year to find a suitable site, one that faced south, with a good water supply, and that was far enough away from working pits to avoid the associated problems of dust pollution. The aim of its creators was 'to create a spectacular theatre in which to tell the story of human dependence on plants; to build a series of giant conservatories … [and] to create an international symbol – the 8th wonder of the world, and place all this in a landscape bold enough to cope'. The scale of the place is incredible: the crater holding the project is 200ft (60m) deep, and covers an area equivalent to 35 football pitches. As well as the humid tropics biome there is the smaller but no less impressive warm temperate biome, housing plants from the Mediterranean areas of the world and

three times the size of the Palm House at London's Kew Gardens. There is also the 'roofless' or temperate biome: the mild Cornish climate enables a huge range of temperate plants, gleaned from all over the world, to grow in the open air. The biomes are linked by a grass-roofed building holding a restaurant and visitor centre – 'the building at the centre of the

earth' – and an amphitheatre and lake are planned, as well as an arid or desert biome at the south end of the site. The scale of interest in the project is proven by the fact that half a million people visited the site during its construction period, and the enormous pride of the Cornish people is evidenced by the glowing comments that were written in the visitors' book during that time.

So what better way to approach the Eden Project than on foot? Walkers and cyclists pay a reduced entrance fee, and this easy walk, which takes you to the entrance to Eden and then offers you a choice of return routes to your car, should help you to feel that you've done your bit to support the ethics of conservation and sustainability that lie behind this inspirational place.

ABOVE: *The brainchild of Tim Smit, the Eden Project is home to huge conservatories and covers an area equivalent to 35 football pitches.*

BACKGROUND: *One of the massive biomes at the Eden Project.*

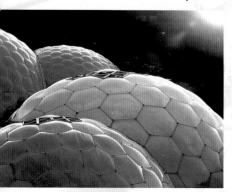

LEFT: *The biomes offer a range of climates; from the temperate weather of Cornwall to the humid tropics of the Brazilian rainforest.*

**ABOUT • THE EDEN PROJECT**

*The Eden Project, completed in 2001, is a spectacular theatre which tells the story of human dependence on plants. The huge biomes are able to produce a range of world climates and house a wide variety of plants from arid desert cactii to mature rainforest trees.*

**Cornwall • SW ENGLAND**

**DISTANCE** • 3 miles (4.8km)

**TOTAL ASCENT** • 361ft (110m)

**PATHS** • country lanes and well-maintained bridlepaths (some muddy after wet weather)

**TERRAIN** • undulating farmland, wooded valleys and old china clay workings

**GRADIENTS** • one short steep ascent near the start; a long downhill run at the end

**REFRESHMENTS** • café and restaurant at the Eden Project; The Britannia Arms on the A390 opposite Tregehan Gardens; Cornish Arms at St Blazey Gate

**PARK** • by the roadside near the Methodist Church in Tregehan village, signposted off the A390 St Blazey Gate to St Austell

**OS MAP** • Explorer 107 St Austell & Liskeard

# Eden: eighth wonder of the world

**❶** Walk up the lane from your car, leaving the church on the left and the metal-railed stream on the right. Keep on uphill through a wooded area, with evidence of old mine workings.

**❷** After ½ mile (800m), where the lane bends sharp left, turn right up the track signed bridlepath/ footpath/cycle route 3 to pass Restineas Cottage, left.

**❸** About 200yds (182m) further on you pass a signed path, right, that enters the project. Just beyond this, turn left along a new signed bridlepath created by the building of Eden, which has removed the original path that ran a little to the south. The path runs steeply uphill then veers left to reach a small wooden gate. (For a picnic spot with good views of the coast to the south, turn right just before the gate, walk through the grassy area, then turn right through the shelter belt to reach a second field.) To

continue on the main route walk through the gate; the path runs into a large level area, part of the old china clay workings.

**❹** Turn right, unsigned, and continue for 766yds (700m); the broad path runs slightly uphill, then downhill along a field edge, before ascending again to reach one of the entrance roads into Eden. Turn right and within 400yds (364m) you will be able to see the biomes.

**❺** If you don't want to visit the Eden Project at this point of this walk cross the road and follow the bridlepath, which runs along a green lane to reach the road at Quarry Park.

**❻** Turn right down the busy road to pass another way into the Eden Project on the right; you can see the site through the hedge here.

**❼** At the next staggered crossroads turn right down a quiet country lane, signed Tregrehan and St Austell. This lane runs steeply downhill to meet a crossroads in Tregrehan; turn right here and walk past the children's playground and the church to the start of the walk.

## • DON'T MISS •

*If you want a clearer picture of what working life was like in a Cornish china clay quarry, visit the **Wheal Martyn China Clay Heritage Centre** (open Easter–end October), 3 miles (5km) to the northwest at Carthew. This, the nearest working quarry to Bodelva, will give you a good insight into the industrial history of this unique area. There are woodland walks as well as a visitor centre with exhibitions, gift shop and café.*

**DIFFICULTY ❋ ❋**

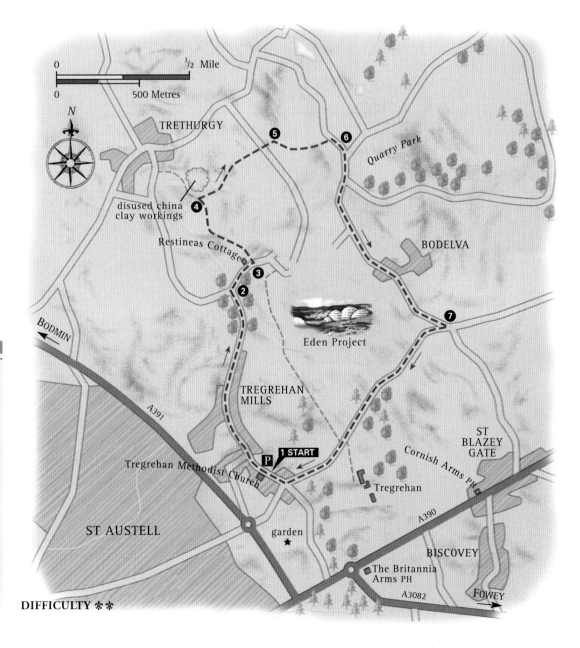

TRETHURGY

Quarry Park

disused china clay workings

Restineas Cottage

BODELVA

BODMIN

Eden Project

TREGREHAN MILLS

ST BLAZEY GATE

A391

Cornish Arms PH

Tregrehan

Tregrehan Methodist Church

**P** **1 START**

ST AUSTELL

garden

A390

BISCOVEY

The Britannia Arms PH

A3082

FOWEY

# Index

## A

Abbotsbury Sub-Tropical
  Gardens                         103
Abbotsbury Swannery        102, 103
**Abbotsbury tithe barn        102-3**
**Aberdeen                      246-7**
air travel    195, 196, 200, 216, 246
Alfred the Great    55, 62, 66, 70, 72
Angel of the North              235
Anne, Queen                150, 152
**Antonine Wall              42, 44-5**
**Appleby-in-Westmorland        138-9**
Ardoch Old Bridge                43
**Ardoch Roman Fort            42-3**
**Arkengarthdale               156-7**
Arthur, King                 55, 56
Arundel                          72
Audley End                      135
Ault Hucknall                   133
**Avebury                      22-3**

## B

Bank of England                 150
Bannockburn, Battle of    95, 97, 98
Barbara Hepworth Museum 218, 219
Barmouth                        111
barrows and cairns    15, 20, 21, 22,
                          23, 26
Bath                        35, 40
Beatles                         242
Becket, Thomas          75, 82, 106
Bess of Hardwick                132
Bexhill-on-Sea                  215
**Bignor Roman Villa           52-3**
Black Death          95, 100, 108
Blackpool Tower                 175
Blenheim Palace                 152
Bletchley Park            215, 230
**Boscobel House               140-1**
Botallack                       181
Boudicca                     35, 38
Bradford                        195
Bradford-upon-Avon               55
Brecknock Museum             68, 69
Bridgewater Canal               162
Brighton Pavilion               155
**Bristol                      162-3**
Broadheath                      203
brochs                        32-3
Brockenhurst                 80, 81
Bronze Age                       15
Bryn-Celli-Ddu                   15
Burghley House                  115
Burnsall                         55
**Burpham                      72-3**

## C

Cabinet War Rooms               215
Caerleon                         35
Caernarfon                       75
**Caledonian Canal             176-7**
**Caledonian Forest            244-5**
Cambridge University         75, 88

canals        164-5, 169, 176-7, 190
**Cannock Chase                230-1**
**Canterbury                   106-7**
**Capel Celyn                  238, 239**
Cardiff                         195
**Carisbrooke Castle           144-5**
Carn Alw                     20, 21
Castell Coch                    185
castle building          75, 78, 92
**Castle Drogo                 208-9**
**Castlerigg Stone Circle      18-19**
Celts                            15
Cenotaph                        195
Centre for Alternative
  Technology (CAT)              249
chalk hill figures           26, 27
Chanctonbury Ring                17
Channel Tunnel            235, 250
Charles I    135, 138, 140, 144, 145
Charles II         135, 140, 142
Chartists                 175, 178
Chaucer, Geoffrey               106
Chedworth Roman Villa            48
Cheltenham                      155
Chesil Beach                    102
**Chester                      46-7**
Chester Zoo                      47
Chillington Hall                141
Christianity       46, 50, 55, 56, 66
Church Island                   173
Cirencester                  35, 42
**Cissbury                     16-17**
Civil War     90, 135, 138, 140, 145
Clifford, Lady Anne             138
Clydebank                       228
coal mining                     185
Colchester                       36
Common Market             235, 246
Commonwealth War Cemetery   230
Compton Beauchamp                27
**Conwy                        92-3**
Conwy Castle                 92, 93
Cotswold Way                     49
Covenanters               148, 149
**Craiglockhart House          206, 207**
crannogs                         68
Craster                    100, 101
Creswell Crags                   18
**Criccieth                    210-11**
Crimean War                     178
Croes Fihangel                   20
Cromwell, Oliver      130, 135, 140
Crusades                     75, 86
**Cuckoo Trail                 250-1**
Culloden             152, 155, 158
**Culzean Castle Country Park 228-9**
Cwm Tryweryn                    238

## D

Dale, David                166, 167
Dalton Castle                   123
Dambusters                      222
Dark Ages                        55
**Dartmoor                     24-5**
Dartmouth                       195
Darwin, Charles                 186
Dissolution of the
  Monasteries         102, 120, 122
**Dolaucothi gold mines        36-7**
**Dolgellau                    142-3**

Domesday Book                78, 82
**Dover                        220-1**
**Down House                   186-7**
Downing Street                  155
drovers' roads                  121
Du Maurier, Daphne              119
Dun Telve                    32, 33
Dun Troddan                      33
**Dundrennan Abbey             88-9**
Dunfermline                      75
Dunkeld                         153
**Dunstanburgh Castle          100-1**
**Durham                       76-7**

## E

**Earls Barton                 66-7**
Ecton                            67
**Eden Project                 252-3**
Edinburgh                       155
Edward 'the Confessor'       72, 75
Edward I        75, 90, 92, 96, 110
Edward II         95, 96, 98, 112
Edward III            95, 98, 112
Edward IV                110, 112
Edward VI                115, 122
Edward VII               196, 200
Edward VIII              215, 230
Edwardian Britain             194-212
Eilean Donan Castle              33
Eisenhower, Dwight D            228
Elgar, Edward                   202
Elizabeth I     115, 118, 126, 128,
                       130, 132
Elizabeth II             236, 238
Eltham Palace                   215
Ewe Close and Ewe Locks          61
Eyam                            135

## F

Fal estuary                     118
**Falkland                     130-1**
Falklands War                   248
Falls of Clyde                  167
**Far Sawrey                   196-7**
**Fens                         136-7**
Festival of Britain       235, 238
Fishbourne Palace            35, 40
The Fleet                       102
flint mines                  16, 17
Foel Feddau                      20
Foel Trigarn                 20, 21
Forth Rail Bridge         175, 228
**Fosse Way                    36, 40-1**
**Fountains Abbey              86-7**
Fowey                           118
**Furness Abbey                122-3**

## G

Garden City movement      196, 198
Geevor                     180, 181
George I                   155, 156
George II                       158
George III                      162
George IV                  155, 170
George V                   202, 228
George VI                  230, 238
Georgian Britain              154-73
Glasgow School of Art           195

Glastonbury                      55
**Glen Trool                   96-7**
Glencoe                         148
**Glenelg                      32-3**
Globe Theatre            124-5, 132
Glorious Revolution       135, 148
Glyndwr, Owain       95, 106, 248
gold mines                    36-7
**Grand Union Canal           165**
Great Depression          215, 216
Great Exhibition          175, 178
Great Fire of London  135, 142, 146
Great Plague                    142
**Great Witcombe              48-9**
Grime's Graves                   15
Grimspound                   24, 25
Gunpowder Plot                  136

## H

Hadrian's Wall               35, 42
Haigh Hall                      217
Hallsands                       227
Hampton Court            115, 116
**Hardknott Roman Fort        50-1**
**Hardwick Hall               132-3**
**Harlech Castle              110-11**
Harold Godwineson            75, 76
Harrington Hall                 183
**Hartland                    160-1**
Hartland Abbey                  161
Hartland Quay                   160
Hatfield House                  135
Henry I                          80
Henry II                     75, 82
Henry III                        88
Henry IV                         95
Henry V                      95, 106
Henry VI                   108, 110
Henry VII                   95, 115
Henry VIII    115, 116, 118, 120,
                       122, 126
Hepworth, Barbara               218
Herefordshire Beacon            202
Heron, Patrick                  218
Highland Clearances  159, 162, 170
hill forts  16, 20, 28, 30, 31, 84, 102
Howard, Ebenezer                198
Hundred Year Stone               19
Hundred Years' War           95, 98
Hyde Abbey Church                71

## I

Ice Ages                     15, 16
Independent Labour Party        206
Industrial Revolution     155, 166,
                       168, 178
**Iona                        56, 58-9**
Ironbridge Gorge                155

## J

Jacobites        152, 153, 155, 156,
                       158, 160
James I of England    128, 135, 136
James I of Scotland       108, 130
James II of England   135, 146, 148,
                       150, 152
Jekyll, Gertrude                208
Jodrell Bank                    168

John, King 75, 88

**K**

Kendal 126
**Kendal Castle** **126-7**
Kilchrenan Church 99
Kinder Scout 236
Kirkcudbright 89

**L**

**Lake Vyrnwy** **190-1**
Lancaster Castle 135
Lanyon, Peter 218
**Laugharne** **232-3**
**Lavenham** **116-17**
**Laxton** **82-3**
Leach, Bernard 218
lead-mining 156-7
**Letchworth** **196, 198-9**
Levant 180, 181
Lever, William Hesketh 204
**Lewes** **78-9**
Lincoln 75
Lindisfarne 55
Little Moreton Hall 115
**Liverpool** **242-3**
**Llandrindod Wells** **188-9**
Llangasty Nature Reserve 68
Llangasty-Tal-y-llyn 68, 69
**Llangorse** **68-9**
Llanymynech Hills 30
Lloyd George, David 210, 211
**Llyn Brianne** **120-1**
Llyn Celyn Reservoir 238
Llynclys Common 62
Llywelyn ap Gruffydd 90, 92
Loch Affric 245
Loch Awe 98, 99
**London** **146-7**
London Eye 235
Longleat House 235
**Lostwithiel** **90-1**
Luddites 178
**Ludlow Castle** **112-13**
Lutyens, Sir Edwin 208
**Lyvennet Valley** **60-1**

**M**

Macclesfield Canal 169
**Machynlleth** **248-9**
Magna Carta 75, 88
Maiden Castle 15, 28
**Malvern Hills** **202-3**
**Marsden** **178-9**
Mary Tudor (Mary I) 115, 122, 126
Mary Queen of Scots 88, 115, 120, 126, 128, 130
*Mary Rose* **115, 248**
Mass Trespass 236
medieval Britain 94-113
**Menai Suspension Bridge** **172-3**
Mersey Ferry 242
Methodism 158, 168
Millennium 235, 252
Millennium Forest Project 245
Milton Keynes 235
modern Britain 234-53
monasticism 58, 86, 88, 102, 122

Monmouth, James, Duke of 150
Monument 146, 147
moon landing 242
motte and bailey castles 82
Mount Caburn 78
Mousa Broch 32
**Mow Cop** **168-9**

**N**

Napoleonic Wars 168, 170
National Cycle Network 250
Neptune's Staircase 176, 177
**New Forest** **80-1**
**New Lanark** **166-7**
Nicholson, Ben 218
Nodens Roman Temple 48
Nordelph 136, 137
Norman Britain 74-93
North Sea oil 246

**O**

**Offa's Dyke** **55, 60, 62-3**
**Old Oswestry** **30-1**
**Old Sarum** **84-5**
open-field farming system 82
Orwell, George 216
Osborne House 175
Owen, Robert 166
**Oxford Canal** **165**
Oxford University 75

**P**

Palace of Westminster 175
Parliament House, Edinburgh 135
Parrs of Kendal 126
**Pass of Brander** **98-9**
**Pass of Killiecrankie** **152-3**
**Peak District National Park** **236-7**
Peasants Revolt 102
Pendennis Castle 118
Pentland Hills 148
Pentre Ifan 21
Pilgrimage of Grace 122
**Pilsdon Pen** **28-9**
**Port Sunlight** **204-5**
**Portmeirion** **224-5**
Potter, Beatrix 196
prehistoric Britain 15-33
**Preseli Hills** **20-1**
prince-bishops 76

**Q**

Quakers 142
Queen's House, Greenwich 135

**R**

Raasay 158, 159
railway age 170, 184-5
Raleigh, Sir Walter 128
Ravenglass and Eskdale railway 51
Reeth 157
Reformation 88, 110, 116
Restoration 135, 142
Restormel Castle 90
Richard I 'the Lionheart' 75, 86, 105
Richard II 95, 102

Richard III 95, 110
Ridgeway 22, 23, 26, 27
Ripon 55, 87
Robert the Bruce 95, 96, 98, 123, 207
Robert Burns National Park 229
Rollright Stones 15
Roman Britain 34-53
Roman roads 40, 48, 50, 52
Roslin Chapel 207
**Rough Castle** **45**
**Rullion Green** **148-9**

**S**

St Albans 35
**St Catherine's Castle** **118-19**
St Columba 55, 56, 58
**St Ives** **218-19**
St Materiana's Church 56
St Mawes Castle 118
St Pancras Priory 78
St Paul's Cathedral 146
Saints' Way 118
Saltaire 175, 204
Sandaig 33
**Sandringham** **200-1**
Sassoon, Siegfried 206
Saxon church architecture 66
Saxon and Viking Britain 54-73
Scar House 156
**Scarborough** **192-3**
Severn Bridge 240, 241
**Severn Estuary** **240-1**
Shakespeare, William 124, 125, 132, 135
**Sherborne Castle** **128-9**
Shoulder of Mutton Hill 212
Shrewsbury 115
Silbury Hill 22, 23
**Silchester** **38-9**
Sion Catti, Twm 120
Skara Brae 15
**Slapton Sands** **226-7**
slave trade 162, 168
**Somersby** **182-3**
**South Bank** **125, 235**
South Downs Way 52, 53
South Foreland Lighthouse 221
South Sea Bubble 155, 156
Southover Grange 78
spa towns 188-9
Staffa 59
Stane Street 52
**Steep** **212-13**
stone circles 18-19, 22, 23
Stonehenge 15, 20, 26
Stratford-upon-Avon 115
**Strathnaver** **170-1**
Stuart, Prince Charles Edward ('Bonnie Prince Charlie') 152, 155, 156, 158, 160
Stuart period 134-53
Studley Royal 86, 87
Suffragettes 195, 206
Sweetheart Abbey 88
Syon Park 155

**T**

**Taff Trail** **184, 185**
Tate Gallery, St Ives 218, 219

television 222
Telford, Thomas 172, 176
Tennyson, Alfred, Lord 182, 183
textile industry 155, 178, 179
Thatcher, Margaret 246
Thomas, Dylan 232
Thomas, Edward 212
tin-mining 180-1
**Tintagel** **56-7**
Tolpuddle Martyrs 172
Tudor Britain 114-33
Tyne Bridge 215

**U**

**Uffington** **26-7**
**Upper Derwent Valley** **222-3**
Urien 60, 61

**V**

Victoria, Queen 175, 176, 186, 190, 192, 200
Victorian Britain 174-93
voting rights 155 172, 195, 212, 226

**W**

Wallis, Alfred 218
Wars of the Roses 110, 112, 115
Wars of Scotland 96
**Warwick Castle** **104-5**
Wayland's Smithy 26, 27
Wayside Folk Museum 219
welfare state 195, 210, 236
**Wells** **150-1**
Welney Wildfowl & Wetlands Trust 137
Welsh Marches 92, 112
West Kennet Long Barrow 22, 23
**West Penwith** **180-1**
Wharram Percy 108-9
Wheal Martyn China Clay Heritage Centre 253
Whitby Abbey 55
White Ladies Priory 140, 141
Whithorn 97
Wicken Fen 137
**Wigan Pier** **216-17**
William the Conqueror 75, 76, 78, 80
William of Orange 135, 148, 150, 152
William IV 170
Williams-Ellis, Clough 224, 225
Wimborne Minster 55
**Winchester** **70-1**
Windermere 197
Windmill Hill 22, 23
Windsor Castle 75
wool trade 116
Woolstone 27
Worcester Cathedral 202, 203
World War I 195, 202, 206, 208, 210, 212, 216, 230
World War II 118, 146, 215, 220, 222, 226, 228, 230, 232
Wren, Sir Christopher 135, 146

**Y**

Y Gaer 69
**York** **64-5**

# Acknowledgements

Walks written and compiled by: Chris Bagshaw, Nick Channer, Mike Gerrard, John Gillham, Sue Gordon, David Hancock, Martin Husband, Lee Karen Stow, Dennis Kelsall, Alison Layland, Timothy Locke, Moira McCrossan, Terry Marsh, Nick Reynolds, Hamish Scott, Roly Smith, Ann Stonehouse, Hugh Taylor, Sue Viccars, Nia Williams, David Winpenny
Introduction written by Jenni Davis
Historical openers written by Nia Williams
Picture Research: Deborah Pownall

With thanks to Jenni Davis, Pam Stagg and Nia Willams for their editorial input, and Jennifer Gill of Skelley Cartographic Services, Surrey, for co-ordinating the maps.

Bringing history alive! English Heritage organises an exciting and varied programme of events at historic properties across the country.
For a free copy of the EH events brochure, please call 0870 333 1181.

The Automobile Association would like to thank the following establishments, libraries and photographers for their assistance in the compilation of this book:

ADVERTISING ARCHIVES 234br; AKG LONDON 34cl, 36c Erich Lessing; 100bl British Library; ART ARCHIVE 3 British Museum (Eileen Tweedy); 38bl Lincoln Museum (Eileen Tweedy); 42bl National Museum Bucharest (Daghi Orti); 46tr British Museum (Eileen Tweedy); 58 Jarrold Publising,, 214 cr Lloyd Triestino Gallery Trieste (Dagli Orti); MARVIN and JOSEPH BARBERICH 2; BRIDGEMAN ART LIBRARY 3 & 94tr Edward IV of England landing in Calais, school of Rouen, 16th century (manuscript) Memoirs of Philippe of Commines (1445-1509) Musee Thomas Dobree-Musee Archeologique, Nantes, France/ Giraudon, 10 & 50 Daily Life in a Roman Camp, from Trajan's Column, 2nd century AD (carved stone) (detail) Rome, Italy/ Merilyn Thorold, 14tl Bronze shield ornament (detail), River Witham British Museum, London, UK, 16tr Pottery, axes and arrowheads, from a Neolithic Camp in Abingdon, Berkshire, probably 6000-4000 BC (pottery and stone) Ashmolean Museum, Oxford, UK, 22br Cauldron, from Shipton on Cherwell, Oxfordshire, 7th century BC (sheet bronze) Ashmolean Museum, Oxford, UK, 22tr Beaker pot and flint knife found accompanying a burial at Barnwood, Glos;, c;2000 BC Cheltenham Art Gallery & Museums, Gloucestershire, UK, 34ct Sestertius of Hadrian from Newcastle Upon Tyne, 132 A;D; Shows bust of Hadrian as a victorious commander Museum of Antiquities, Newcastle upon Tyne, UK, 34 Barbarian fighting a Roman legionary, Roman relief panel, 2nd century AD (stone) Louvre, Paris, France/ Lauros-Giraudon, 42bl Portrait bust of Emperor Antoninus Pius (86-161) from the Baths of Caracalla, Rome, c;140 (marble) Museo Archeologico Nazionale, Naples, Italy, 44bc Solidus (obverse) of Honorius (393-432) drapes, cuirassed, wearing a diadem; Inscription: D N HONORIVS P F AVG (gold) by Roman (5th century AD) Private Collection, 54tr Kingston Brooch, 6/7th century AD City of Liverpool Museum, Merseyside, UK, 54c A Dragon Ship from a manuscript (vellum) by Anglo-Saxon (10th century) British Museum, London, UK, 54br St; John's Crucifixion Plaque, Celtic, late 7th Century (gilt bronze) National Museum of Ireland, Dublin, Eire, 56 King Arthur and his Knights around the Table, by Robert de Boron, French (vellum) L'Histoire de Graal, (c;1290) Bibliotheque Nationale, Paris, France, 66cl St; Guthlac is Ordained Priest by Bishop Hedda Roll of St; Guthlac, (13th century)British Library, London, UK, 72tr "Comes Litoris Saxon Per Britaniam", Anglo-Saxon map, c;950 AD Bibliotheque Municipale, Rouen, France, 74cr St; Cuthbert and two of the brethren returning from the land of the Picts, by Bede, Latin (Durham) Life and Miracles of St Cuthbert, (12th century) British Library, London, UK, 76cr St; Cuthbert, by Bede, Latin (Durham) Life and Miracles of St Cuthbert, (12th century)British Library, London, UK, 80tr William I The Conqueror (1027-87) King of England, Duke of Normandy: penny coin British Museum, London, UK, 82tr Harvesting, from a Calendar (for detail see 61654) Anglo-Saxon Miscellany, (c;1030) British Library, London, UK, 92tr Edward I (1239-1307) of England investing his son Edward (1284-1327) as Prince of Wales (later Edward II) in February 1301 Commendatio Lamentabilis in transitu Edward IV British Library, London, UK, 94b Tournament , Froissart's Chronicle, (late 15th century) British Library, London, UK, 96tl Robert the Bruce, and his second wife, the daughter of the Earl of Ulster Seton's Armorial Crests National Library of Scotland, Edinburgh, Scotland, 98c Statue of King Robert the Bruce (1274-1329) at Stirling (engraving) (b/w photo) by English School (19th century) Private Collection, 104br A Tournament (vellum) by Spanish School (14th century) Biblioteca Monasterio del Escorial, Madrid, Spain, 106br Lydgate and the Canterbury Pilgrims Leaving Canterbury from the 'Troy Book and the Siege of Thebes', 1412-22 (vellum) John Lydgate Poetry, (15th century) British Library, London, UK, 108tr The Black Death, 1348 (engraving) (b&w photo) by English School (14th century) Private Collection, 114br Elizabeth I, Armada Portrait, c;1588 (oil on panel) by George Gower (1540-96) (attr; to) Woburn Abbey, Bedfordshire, UK, 116 June: shearing sheep Book of Hours, c;1540, by Simon Bening (1483-1561) British Library, London, UK, 120bl Smithfield Drover from 'Costume of Great Britain' (coloured aquatint) by William Henry Pyne (1769-1843) Museum of London, UK, 122tr Illustration from a history book showing Henry VIII suppressing Pope Clement VII (engraving) (b&w photo) by English School (17th century) Private Collection, 126tr Portrait of Catherine Parr (1512-48) sixth wife of Henry VIII (1491-1547) (panel) by English School (16th century) National Portrait Gallery, London, UK/ Roger-Viollet, Paris, 130tr Portrait of Mary Queen of Scots (1542-87) from 'Memoirs of the Court of Queen Elizabeth', published in 1825 (w/c and gouache on paper) by Sarah Countess of Essex (d;1838) Private Collection/ The Stapleton Collection, 134l Violin, bearing arms of the House of Stuart, possibly belonged to either Charles II or James II, English, 17th century Victoria & Albert Museum, London, UK, 134tl Illustration of Cannon Fire in 'The Art of Gunnery' by Thomas Smith (fl;1600-27) 1628 (woodcut) by English School (17th century) Private Collection, 134 Jacobean style textile design, c;1920s (block-printed linen) by French School (20th century) The Design Library, New York, USA, 134tr A Custody Warrant for Robert Tichborne (d;1682), Written by King Charles II to the Governor of Holy Island where Tichborne was to be Imprisoned, 25th July 1662 (ink on paper) City of Westminster Archive Centre, London, UK, 138c Lady Ann Clifford, Countess of Dorset and Pembroke (d;1675) (oil on canvas) by John Bracken (17th century) Abbot Hall Art Gallery, Kendal, Cumbria, UK, 142tr The Quakers' Meeting (engraving) (b&w photo) by English School (17th century)Private Collection, 144lt King Charles I (1600-49) in Garter Robes (oil on canvas) by Sir Anthony van Dyck (1599-1641) (after) Wallace Collection, London, UK, 145tr Execution of Charles I (1600-49) at Whitehall, January 30th 1649 (engraving) (b&w photo) by German School (17th century) Private Collection, 148b A Crowd Queues to Sign the National Covenant in front of Grey Friar's Churchyard, Edinburgh in 1638 (litho) (b/w photo) by English School (18th century) Private Collection, 150br Several Rebels Hanged from a Tree, five of hearts playing card from a set commemorating Monmouth's Rebellion in 1685 (engraving) (b&w photo) by English School (17th century) Private Collection, 154bl George I (1714-27) by Anonymous Bristol City Museum and Art Gallery, UK, 158tr Bonnie Prince Charlie by G; Dupre (1689-1770) Private Collection, 162tr Poster advertising an auction of slaves to be sold and let, 18th May 1829 Wilberforce House, Hull City Museums and Art Galleries, UK, 174t "Pimpernel" wallpaper by William Morris, 1876 Victoria & Albert Museum, London, UK, 194br "Suzanna Bathing", opalescent glass statuette by Lalique Bonhams, London, UK, 214bl The George Cross, awarded for gallantry, 1940 Imperial War Museum, London, UK; 216tr George Orwell (1903-50) (b&w photo) Private Collection; BRITAIN ON VIEW 66bl, 110cr, 138tr, 148tr, 168bl, 180br, 210br, 226br, 252cr; BRITISH MOTOR INDUSTRY HERITAGE TRUST 234cl; BRITISH MUSEUM 62tr; CAMERA PRESS 234;CORBIS 234; NICK COTTON 250, 250bl; JAMES DAVIES 70tr; COLLECTIONS John D;Beldom 105t; Gena Davies 140br 188bl, Paul Felix 38, Michael George 78b, Fay Godwin 36bl, Robert Hallmann 180t, 200bl; Nigel Hawkins 198, David M; Hughes 156cr, Mike Kipling 108bl, 156b, Iain McGowan 52cr, Archie Miles 30bl, John Miller 146c, Julian Nieman 92bl, Robert Pilgrim 212, 225b; Roger Scruton 64bl, Clive Shenton 230, Brian Shuel 82cl, 240bl, Liz Stares 102bl, 128bl, 182cr, 182bl, Roy Stedall-Humphryes 78, Peter Thomas 28b 28bl, John Vere Brown 208cr, Paul Watts 118bl, Robin Weaver 22c, 68b, 236br; Bill Wells 136, 136br; Jeffery Whitelaw 96br, Robin Williams18tr, EDEN PROJECT 234, 252, 252bl, EDINBURGH PHOTOGRAPHIC LIBRARY 98bl, 206br, ENGLISH HERITAGE20b, 24- 25t, 38cl, 140cl, 186br,186bl, ENGLISH HERITAGE SPECIAL EVENTS 44bl, 84bl, Dick Clark 94cl, 145tr, 145cr, Neil Holmes 45bl, Paul Lewis 74tr, 90tr, 194c, MARY EVANS PICTURE LIBRARY 110bl, 124bl, 125bl, 140tr, 152tr, 164t, 166cl, 166br, 172tr, 174tr, 174cr, 176tr, 178bl, 180cl, 182tr, 186tr, 194cl, 198bl, 202tr, 204bl, 204tr, 208tl, 210tr, 212bl, 214tr, 218tr, 230cl,250tr;EYE UBIQUITOUS 32cr, 86b, 120br, 142bl, 176br, 222tr, 225tl; 226cl, FFOTOGRAFF 248tr, FORESTRY COMMISSION 244tr, 244cl, 244b, 245b; FORTEAN PICTURE LIBRARY 40cl; J. GILLHAM 126b; MICHAEL HOLFORD 14c, 40bl, 74c; HULTON ARCHIVE 11br, 188tr, 192b, 194tr, 196bl, 200tr, 206tr, 194cr, 220tr, 222tl, 224bl, 226b, 228tr, 232bl, 240, 242bl; ILLUSTRATED LONDON NEWS 214tl; MILEPOST 92 1/2 12bl, 184tr, 184t, 184bl, 185; MUSEUM OF LONDON 25br, 28tr, 30tr; NATURAL HISTORY MUSEUM 14b; NATIONAL LIBRARY OF WALES 238 tl; NATIONAL TRUST PHOTOGRAPHIC LIBRARY 132tl; Chris Gascoigne 208bl, Anthony Marshall 132b, Geoff Morgan 132cr, Stephen Robson196 tr; PEAK DISTRICT NATIONAL PARK AUTHORITY Mike Williams 236tr; PICTOR INTERNATIONAL 46bl; RHEGED DISCOVERY CENTRE 60tr; SCRAN 170bl; REX FEATURES LTD;234b, 246br; ROBERT HARDING PICTURE LIBRARY Rob Cousins 162, David Hughes 196b, David Hunter 162br, Michael Jenner 32, 42cr , David Lomax 14tr, Mark Mawson 116cr, Duncan Maxwell 142br, John Miller 154 cl , Roy Rainford 56cr, 56tr, 86tr, 222br, Geoff Renner 164b, Andy Williams 24b; SKYSCAN PHOTOLIBRARY 10-11, 20tr, 20bl, 26tr, 26bl, 56bl, 64-65, 70bl,84-85, 90bl, 100br, 106cl, 122bl, 144b, 150bl, 224t, 240tr; Ian Bracegirdle 82b; Colour Library Books 128 br, 130cl, 202br; William Cross 204t; Bob Evans 118tr, 160bl; 228b; Brian Lea 40bl; Edmund Nägele 242tr; Pitkin Unichrome 62bl, 210cl; Skyscan/© AIR IMAGES 88cr, 166cr, 170tr; Skyscan/© JASON HAWKES PHOTO LIBRARY 16b; Skyscan/© LONDON AERIAL PHOTO LIBRARY 198t; SONIA HALLIDAY PHOTOGRAPHS 66tr, 74cb, 202cl; WALES PHOTO LIBRARY 238b, 238bl, 248cr, 248br; WORLD PICTURES, 58b, 76bl, 104-105, 216b, 218b, 220b, 246cl.

The remaining pictures are held in the Association's own library (AA PHOTO LIBRARY) with contributions from the following photographers:
PETER BAKER 80cr; 102tr, 160tr, 230 bl; JEFF BEAZLEY 88bl; ASH BENNETT 60bl; M. BIRKITT 236bl; E.A. BOWNESS 138bl; JIM CARNIE 130br; 130br; DEREK CROUCHER 212cr; STEVE DAY 50b, 152bl, 154tr, 176tl; RICHARD ELLIOT 158b; JIM HENDERSON 6-7, RICHARD IRELAND 48bl, 48br; CAROLINE JONES 92cr, 112b 172b, PAUL KENWOOD 125b; ERIC MEACHER 18bl; C. MELLOR 120tr, 190tr, COLIN & ANDREW MOLYNEUX 68tr; ROGER MOSS 25tr, 218; KEN PATERSON 44t, 45cl; TONY SOUTER 34tl, 52tr, 52bl; MARTIN TRELAWNY 178tr; RICHARD TURPIN 124t; WYN VOYSEY 54bl, 72bl, 72b, 112tr; RONNIE WEIR152b; JONATHON WELSH 165tl, 165br; LINDA WHITMAN 205b;1 PETER WILSON 192tr.